Effective
Public
Relations

Third Edition

EFFECTIVE

PUBLIC

RELATIONS

SCOTT M. CUTLIP

Professor of Journalism
The University of Wisconsin

ALLEN H. CENTER

Vice President for Public Relations
Motorola, Inc.: Lecturer in Public Relations
Northwestern University

Prentice-Hall, Inc., *Englewood Cliffs, New Jersey*

Library of Congress Catalog Card No.: 64-24066

Printed in the United States of America   C-24499

Current printing (last digit):

13   12   11   10   9   8   7   6

PRENTICE-HALL INTERNATIONAL, INC., *London*
PRENTICE-HALL OF AUSTRALIA, PTY., LTD., *Sydney*
PRENTICE-HALL OF CANADA, LTD., *Toronto*
PRENTICE-HALL OF INDIA (PRIVATE) LTD., *New Delhi*
PRENTICE-HALL OF JAPAN, INC., *Tokyo*

To

Erna and Nancy

PREFACE

This launches the third edition of a book first published in 1952 and first revised in 1958. In twelve years this book has become widely used as a textbook. There is reason to believe it has had a constructive effect on the professional practice of public relations, both in the United States and abroad. For its wide acceptance, the authors are most grateful. When the first edition appeared, the field of public relations was mushrooming, its function was not clearly defined, and its essentiality not fully accepted. Today, by contrast, the growth is slower but steady, the function is more clearly defined and more widely understood, and the essentiality is seldom questioned. The practitioners of public relations, individually and collectively, have made progress in improving their competence and in raising the ethical level of their work. The growing number of college and university teachers in public relations have had a major role in these advances. These dozen years have brought much progress in public relations; there is need for more. The authors hope that their efforts continue to contribute to this progress.

Our objective has remained constant. As stated in the first edition:

We have endeavored to be comprehensive in our approach, yet not to be trapped into an "umbrella" concept of the public relations function. The content focuses on the role of the practitioner as a specialist in communications, an analyst of public opinion, and as a counselor to administrators in these areas. Behavioristic study of the function will demonstrate that these tasks comprise the responsibilities delegated to most practitioners. There is need to concentrate more on the matters in which the practitioner may lay justified claim as a specialist. There is ample challenge within this area for the best talent we can muster without ranging far afield for worlds to conquer. We have tried to point this up by dealing with two aspects generally neglected—the *ecology* and the *evolution* of this specialized administrative staff function.

The book has been thoroughly revised for this edition. We have tried to make it more readable and to include the fruits of the experience and research accumulated in this field. The Case Problems, which were introduced in the second edition, have been retained on the advice of teachers who find these a basis of many spirited class discussions. The supplementary readings, based on Scott Cutlip's bibliographic research, have been updated. Fresh examples of public relations practice have been woven into the text where they best serve to illustrate principles and procedures. The rapid growth of public relations around the world in the past decade is recorded in a wholly new chapter on public relations abroad. The increased public scrutiny of the impact of public relations on our society and the redoubled efforts of practitioners to police their ranks are given more adequate attention in this edition; new developments, new tools, and new problems in the practice are also covered more thoroughly. Nonetheless, the basic organization and philosophic approach which characterized the first two editions have been retained because of widespread endorsement by our fellow teachers and practitioners.

The authors have incurred a heavy debt to many people for friendly encouragement, wise counsel, and for information generously provided over these dozen years. Some have been acknowledged in earlier editions, and only a few new debts contracted in preparing this edition can be acknowledged here.

In preparing this revision, Scott Cutlip both enlarged and extended his indebtedness to many colleagues, former students, and friends. He is particularly grateful to these persons for help on this edition: Professor Percy Tannenbaum of the University of Wisconsin; Anand Akerkar of Bombay, India; Erwin Böll of Bonn, Germany; Robert Lindsay of the University of Minnesota; Miss Clara Meyers of the European Common Market staff; Philip C. Minter of Sydney, Australia; Allan W. Ostar, Washington, D.C.; Lt. Col. William R. Stroud and Maj. Gen. George V. Underwood, Jr., of the U.S. Army; Joaquin Maestre of Barcelona, Spain; and Miss Elma Williams and Roy K. Wilson of the National Education Association.

In editing the second edition preparatory for this one, Allen Center was reminded of the values in practical experience gained through the years at the Parker Pen Company, Motorola, Inc., and the Leo Burnett Co., and from the exchange of professional views with colleagues in the Public Relations Society of America. In the course of this revision he is particularly indebted to his secretary, Mrs. Perry Frangos, for her invaluable assistance.

The authors believe that no textbook can be more effective than those who translate it for students. We believe that those who teach public relations should be singled out, applauded, and encouraged. For these reasons we wish to salute the teachers who have used this book the past decade or so and who have gone beyond normal call of duty to offer us thoughtful suggestions for its improvement. Specifically, we salute Professors Ernest F. Andrews, State University of Iowa; Marion K. Browne, Youngstown University; Raymond W. Derr, Bowling Green State University; Edwin Emery, University of Minnesota; Wayne Hodges, Cornell University; Paul V. Peterson, University of Omaha; Frazier Moore, University of Georgia; Walter Seifert, Ohio State University; Raymond Simon, Utica College of Syracuse University; William Taylor, Kent State University; R. H. Wherry, Pennsylvania State University; and James R. Young, West Virginia University; also to Professors Stewart Harral of the University of Oklahoma and Fred E. Merwin of Rutgers University, who read the manuscript for the first edition, and to Professor John V. Hinkel of George Washington University, who read the manuscript for the second edition.

Scott M. Cutlip
Allen H. Center

CONTENTS

xvi · *Contents*

Chapter One

CONTEMPORARY

PUBLIC

RELATIONS—

AN

INTRODUCTION

The public relations function is the planned effort to influence opinion through acceptable performance based upon two-way communication.

Public relations, as a management concept and as a staff function in organizations, has grown rapidly over the past three decades. This rapid development comes as a result of the increasing complexity of modern society and the growing insights into what motivates individuals and groups. Gaining the support and cooperation of others through persuasion is part of the day-by-day business of every organization—government agencies, business firms, labor unions, universities, and welfare agencies. Public relations has become a commonplace term in the language and thought of twentieth-century America. It is a part of our daily conversation, a standard topic on convention programs, and an important factor in contemporary decision making. The essentiality of public relations is seldom debated today. Even so, the term is not always understood. This reflects the fact that public relations is still in the fluid state of defining itself. The function embraces whatever it is assigned to do, and this varies widely.

A wide variety of activities parades under the banner. There is still some difference between the function as defined in textbooks and the function as practiced. The literature and shoptalk of the craft are filled with an abundance of definitions. Some lack universality; others are too broad. Many define PR as it ought to be, not as it sometimes is. As a term and as a vocation, it means different things to different people. Nonetheless, the clear outlines of a mature, accepted concept are emerging.

The practice is frequently held out as a cure-all for the ills and problems which confront organizations and individuals. Tavern owners are warned to "avoid mistakes in public relations or be voted out of business." Industrial executives are advised that "sound public relations is the only salvation of free enterprise." Union members are exhorted to improve their public relations if they are to stave off antiunion legislation. Conservationists are counseled that "wildlife management cannot function in America without public support achieved through public relations."

On the other hand, public relations continues to be scorned as pressagentry and worse. An editor tells his readers, "if you want to get plausible disguises for unworthy causes, hire a public relations expert." A high public official once described public relations practitioners as "pitch men, complete with Harvard accent and trick polls." A newspaper columnist once wrote, wryly, that "public relations is only an aristocratic term for publicity or pressagentry." A major United States newspaper calls public relations "a parasite on the press." Such sweeping charges are generally outmoded and unfounded. However, the activities of an unscrupulous few on the fringes of the practice tend to give such accusations validity in the public mind.

Public relations thinking has served to deepen the sense of social responsibility in our public enterprises. It has contributed to public welfare. It has improved the communications required in our society. Public relations thinking is a requirement for every successful administrator. Discussing the requirements of the Presidency, Peter Drucker asserts: "All our effective Presidents were expert at public relations, untiring propagandists for themselves and their ideas."

The calling, like most professions, suffers from the fact that its misdeeds are more widely heralded than are its accomplishments. Practitioners are, from time to time, identified with unworthy causes. Some of the practices labeled "public relations" are dishonest. Some are manipulative. Some are merely inept. But, on balance, the constructive far outweigh the harmful. All the publicity inevitably given to malpractice should not blind the professionals or the public to the essentially valuable contributions. The specialized knowledge and skills of the calling are available to fools, knaves, and saints alike.

Even among those who view public relations as a useful function in the direction of today's large enterprises, a few misconceptions persist. A common understanding of public relations would put an end to the belief that public relations is a black magic which will make people think favorably of an organization whether such opinions are deserved or not. That it consists mainly of getting favorable press reports about an organization and of suppressing the unfavorable is another misconception. No one can become an expert merely by having the tag pinned on him. There is need for a wider understanding of the basic fact that public relations does not constitute a handy umbrella to protect an institution against a storm of unfavorable public opinion.

A PROBLEM OF
SEMANTICS

That the term *public relations* is used in at least three different senses adds to the confusion. These are: (1) relationships with individuals and groups which compose the general public; (2) the ways and means used to achieve favorable relationships; (3) the quality or status of an institution's relationships. This one term, *public relations,* cannot be used to label both *means* and *ends* without creating confusion.

Clarity will replace confusion, in part, if the term is restricted to describing the *planned effort to influence opinion through acceptable performance and two-way communication.* Other needs for the term will be met if an institution's relations with various publics are labeled *public relationships.* Little is to be gained by creating artificial terms to serve these needs. This text will use the term *public relations* to encompass the performance and communications used to build profitable *relationships with the public.* Incidentally, although the term *public relations* is plural, it is used in the singular.

CURRENT DEFINITIONS

What, then, are the current definitions? *Webster's New International Dictionary,* Third Edition, defines public relations thus: [1]

1. The promotion of rapport and goodwill between a person, firm, or institution and other persons, special publics, or the community at large through the distribution of interpretative material, the development of neighborly interchange, and the assessment of public reaction. . . .
2. (a) the degree of understanding and goodwill achieved between an individual, organization, or institution and the public. (b) the application of the techniques for achieving this relationship.
3. (a) the art or science of developing reciprocal understanding and goodwill. (b) the professional staff entrusted with this task.

Public relations is often confused with and used as a handy synonym for some of its functional parts, such as publicity, press-agentry, propaganda, and institutional advertising. These may be parts of the whole of public relations, but the sum of the parts does not equal the whole. Reflection on these definitions will make it clear that, thus defined, publicity, press-agentry, propaganda, and advertising become tools of public relations, not its equivalent. For example, when someone in Indian headdress sends up the smoke signal "Give" on Michigan Avenue during a Red Cross fund campaign, this

---

[1] By permission. From *Webster's New International Dictionary,* Third Edition. Copyright 1961 by G. & C. Merriam Company.

is not public relations. It is an act of press-agentry, although it may be part of a PR program.

Author Robert Heilbroner has commented on the difficulty of definition. "In a word, public relations covers a lot of acreage—blurring out into advertising, slopping over into selling, dipping down into publicity, and touching—or at least aspiring to—the 'making' of public opinion itself."

One of the frequently quoted definitions is one fashioned by *Public Relations News: Public relations is the management function which evaluates public attitudes, identifies the policies and procedures of an individual or an organization with the public interest, and executes a program of action to earn public understanding and acceptance.* Implicit in this definition is the threefold function of the professional practitioner (1) to ascertain and evaluate public opinion, (2) to counsel management in ways of dealing with public opinion as it exists, and (3) to use communication to influence public opinion. The practitioner is essentially a specialist in communications. More ambitious claims are often made for him. His work has been variously described as "human engineering," "social engineering," or "the engineering of consent." Use of such terms is akin to fencing in the moon.

Professor Byron Christian defines PR as the "conscious effort to motivate or influence people, primarily through communication, to think well of an organization, to respect it, to support it, and to stick with it through trial and trouble." There are shorter ones. "Doing the right thing and getting credit for it." "Good conduct coupled with good reporting." "Earned recognition." There are platitudinous ones. "Human decency which flows from a good heart." Most definitions embrace the compound principle of good performance made widely and favorably known. PR, a short-cut term to refer to professional practice, is often defined thus:

P for PERFORMANCE plus R for RECOGNITION equals PR.

Another way to define PR is to put it as a formula:

X (the deed) plus Y (the interpretations of the deed)
equals Public Attitudes.

This is grounded in the elemental fact that we often are more influenced by the way an event is interpreted than we are by the event itself. The act of a steel company in raising its prices can be interpreted as a necessary move to insure adequate profits, or it can be interpreted as a harmful act inducing inflation. Much of the public relations practitioner's effort goes into putting the best possible interpretation on the acts of those identified with his institution—acts which these persons take in pursuit of the organization's mission.

Fundamentally, it is the performance of those identified with an organization as they carry out the organization's objectives that eventually cumulates in public attitudes toward the organization. This is shown in the chart on page 5.

Such definitions offer sound approaches. But they also serve to confuse

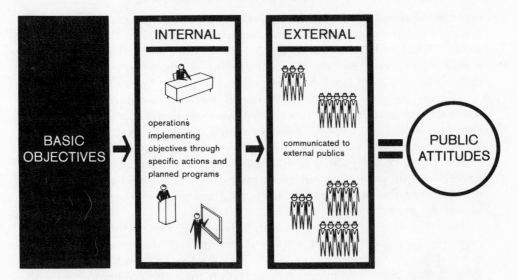

and blur what the function embraces, where it fits in the administrative scheme, and who is responsible for it. This confusion will be cleared away if we understand the distinction between public relations as an *operating concept of management* and public relations as a *specialized staff function in management*.

The first is a static, general operating principle which guides administrators to a greater or lesser degree and is the responsibility of every person identified with an enterprise. The President's "People to People" program for international understanding is a dramatic example.

The second is a dynamic, specialized function for which managers hire skilled practitioners. An illustration is the training of tourists to carry out the "People to People" idea of making every American a good ambassador abroad. The administrators of an organization must be responsible for its *public relationships*. But these administrators need and use the skills of PR practitioners.

THE MANAGEMENT CONCEPT

In today's interdependent society, all institutions are invested with public responsibilities. They must accept accountability for all of their actions that affect others. Full acceptance by public enterprises—profit and nonprofit alike —of their public obligations to those whom they serve or affect is far from realized. But the trend in this direction is clear. As one of the nation's business leaders put it: "We know perfectly well that business does not function by Divine Right, but, like any other part of our society, exists with the sanction of the community as a whole. The interests of the community are in turn expressed through governments. . . . Today's public opinion, though it may appear as light as air, may become tomorrow's legislation—for better or for worse. Therefore, a wise firm makes public relations a function not simply of a staff department, but of top management—so that every major business decision is considered from the standpoint of its public impact."

For the progress toward an increased sense of social responsibility in contemporary management, practitioners deserve much credit. This enlightened management concept has emerged slowly, unevenly, over the past several decades in response to the ability of our citizens to express themselves in the market place, in the polling booth, and through countervailing power blocs. Recognition of public as well as corporate or institutional responsibility is manifested in the adoption of a public relations point of view. This can best be termed *public relations thinking*.

Such thinking finds expression in this typical remark of a corporation executive: "At least half our time is taken up with discussing the repercussions of what we propose to do." Once embraced, the concept gathers strength as it goes. The more an organization woos the public, the more the public expects to be courted. And what one organization does, its competitors must match if they are to be successful in the spirited struggle for public favor. *Responsible performance on the part of a corporation, governmental agency, or nonprofit organization is the foundation of sound public relationships.* Public relationships, in these broad terms, are the responsibility of an organization's directing executives, not of its staff or line specialists. Practitioners must not be deluded into thinking that they "should rightfully be responsible for all the relations between a corporation and all of its publics." This would mean, in practice, "arrogation of most of the principal functions of administration." *PR specialists are not hired as managers.*

THE FUNCTIONAL CONCEPT

In the trend to big, farflung, impersonal organizations, American public enterprises have outgrown the directive capacities of any one man or small group of men. The United States Government, for instance, has nearly three million employees.

Today's administrator requires the assistance and counsel of a host of skilled specialists if he is to manage at all. The public relations specialist is one of these. He is hired by top management:

1. To facilitate and insure an inflow of representative opinions from an organization's several publics in order that its policies and operations may be kept compatible with the diverse needs and views of these publics.
2. To counsel management on ways and means of shaping its policies and operations to gain maximum public acceptance for what it deems essential in the best interests of all concerned.
3. To interpret widely and favorably an organization's policies and operations.

America's growing need for the specialist to perform these tasks is being met in one or a combination of three ways. We have (1) the full-time staff official on the organization's payroll who, with the aid of assistants, serves the employer exclusively; (2) the independent counselor who maintains his own offices and staff to serve a number of clients with nonconflicting interests; (3) the advertising agency which provides counseling and service either through a subsection in the agency or through a subsidiary firm.

The internal staff department represents the dominant pattern. However, whether the service is supplied by staff specialists on the organization's payroll, by outside counselors, or by a combination, the function is much the same.

IMPLICATIONS
OF THE DEFINITION

The common purpose of all that is labeled public relations is to influence public opinion. There can be no escape in today's world from the grinding wheels of public attitudes. The increased power of public opinion and recognition of that power constitute one of the mainsprings propelling the function. This is the era of "The Public Be Pleased." More than ever, "the genius of the people must be consulted." No individual, no institution, can long prosper without public support or, at the least, without public sufferance. Faith in the good sense of the people is the foundation of intelligent contemporary thinking and practice.

The practice of public relations is predicated on the belief that *only an informed public can be a wise public.* One of the basic precepts is: "People are essentially rational by nature; they respond to facts and want the truth; and they will ultimately find it and act upon it." There is abundant evidence in American history to sustain this faith.[2] Yet this precept is open to question. Satisfying the public interest to the mutual advantage of all parties in conflict is a prerequisite to profitable public relationships. Arriving at mutual interests requires public-minded performance and satisfactory two-way communication. The basic problem is to adjust the institution to the climate of social change in a way that will serve both the public and private interests insofar as this is possible. The specialist, in his role of communicator and interpreter, makes a vital contribution to this process. The practitioner is expected to counsel his institution on the social changes now coming with breath-taking rapidity and to help it find ways and means of adapting to these changes. For example, ponder the problems posed for the nationwide store chain in adapting an integrated way of life in the South, or the problems created by the scientific explosion. Or consider the problems posed

---

[2] For this point of view, see William Lydgate, *What America Thinks* (New York: Thomas Y. Crowell Company, 1944). For the opposite view, see Nicholas Samstag, *Persuasion for Profit* (Norman, Okla.: University of Oklahoma Press, 1957).

for state governmental agencies by the ballooning needs of education, public welfare, highways, and recreation.

A sure, sensitive reading of the changing environment can be the practitioner's most valuable service to his organization. To discharge this responsibility, the practitioner must be equipped with a fund of broad knowledge that keeps pace with the swift march of events. In the words of Counselor Earl Newsom, it is the hope of today's practitioner that "through the modern avenues of communication he may contribute to the elimination of prejudice and help to form bridges to understanding so that a highly complex and enterprising nation can keep steadily on toward the dreams of free men."

THE DAY-BY-DAY
PRACTICE

PR practice consists of a multitude of little things and a few big things. It is the daily application of common sense, common courtesy, and common decency. It can be doing favors for others. It can be pleading a cause in the arena of public opinion. It can be entertaining a visitor. It can be the preparation of a speech, or giving one. It can be a press conference, or the dedication of a new building. It can be as important as providing counsel that leads management out of a tight strike situation. It can be the creation of a winter resort in an abandoned Colorado mining camp. It can be the formulation of a program that turns disinterested stockholders into enthusiastic supporters. It can be helping a newsman get his story from a press-shy executive. It can be writing a letter to a hurt, irate parent whose son has been expelled from college. It is a multitude of things. To show the immense variety of activities conducted in the name of public relations, here are some actual examples.

To remind the nation of the progress made in commercial aviation, Trans World Airlines marked the thirtieth anniversary of its pioneering all-air transcontinental passenger service by once again flying a Ford tri-motor airplane over the initial route. The ancient Ford plane lumbered along at 110 miles an hour, taking 36 hours to complete a trip made by today's jet in some five hours. T.W.A. told the public that the Ford planes cost some $50,000 whereas today's jet airliner costs more than $6,000,000. The staged event was used to emphasize the advances in travel speed and in airline operating costs.

The Porsgrund Porselaensfabrik, a Norwegian manufacturer of porcelain, used its seventy-fifth anniversary year to dramatize an important innovation in the manufacture of dinnerware and to extend its market beyond Norway's borders. The highlight of the firm's anniversary celebration was the opening of a display and sales center, "Designs of Scandinavia," in London's main shopping center, with appropriate fanfare. In Norway, Porsgrund carried out an extensive public relations and sales promotion program for a full year under the direction of its public relations counselor.

To dramatize the spirit of our American Thanksgiving celebration, the

United States Ambassador to Ecuador invited 250 workers and their families to share in a Thanksgiving dinner given at a Y.M.C.A. in a worker's district of Quito, the capital. An estimated 600 persons, mostly children of the workers, were served the Thanksgiving dinner by American Girl Scouts, Brownies, and Boy Scouts. The Ambassador read the President's proclamation and explained the meaning of Thanksgiving in the United States and America's desire to share its abundance with all peoples. The event, planned by the Ambassador's information officer, was recorded for rebroadcast over Ecuador's radio stations, the main channel of communication in a nation where illiteracy is common.

Allis-Chalmers, a manufacturer of heavy industrial and farming equipment, dealt with problem drinkers among employees by trying to rehabilitate them rather than weed them out. Communication was established in two ways. The company hired a psychologist, himself a rehabilitated alcoholic, to counsel with those who sought help. Supervisors were taught to treat alcoholism as an illness, and to coax victims toward the counselor for medical care.

As part of its fortieth anniversary observance, Boeing Airplane Company wanted to get the company's history before the general public and into educational and personal libraries. Boeing gave its public relations director a year's leave to write the history. The book, *Vision: A Saga of the Sky,* was published by a nationally known publisher and hit the best-seller list.

Columbia University for its Bicentennial sought to develop participation of alumni, world scholars, faculty, press, and the New York community. Some $150,000 was spent on various meetings and other communications projects, all tied to the theme "Man's Right to Knowledge and the Free Use Thereof."

The United States Navy sponsored a combat art exhibit on tour to population centers. The exhibit was called "Operation Palette." It contained 100 original paintings of battle scenes by professional artists. This is only one of the many ways that the Navy communicates with potential recruits, reservists, and the general public.

The Illinois Central Railroad moved its offices from New York to Chicago, replaced eastern directors with businessmen who lived along the lines, and had directors ride the route regularly to meet employees and civic leaders. One motive was to dissipate criticism that the railroad was dominated by "Wall Street." Another was to humanize management.

Reflecting America's belief in the open society, the United States National Aeronautics and Space Administration (NASA) provides the world's news media with facts, pictures, and facilities to enable newsmen to report fully and at first hand America's manned space flights. For a space launch, NASA formulates a detailed information plan, accredits and provides facilities for some 600 newsmen, and operates a News Center. In this center newsmen are registered, given voluminous press kits containing background information, queries are answered, a fast reproduction and still-photo file operation is maintained, and telephone and telegraphic communications outlets are provided. Reporting a space launch requires elaborate and expensive public relations facilities. As of 1963, NASA had a public relations staff of 173 persons and an annual PR budget of $14.7 million.

THE ORGANIZED PRACTICE

1. PRESS-AGENTRY. There are no firm, fixed lines separating what is popularly termed press-agentry, product promotion, and product publicity. The emphasis, the objective, and the approach used largely determine how a particular publicity activity is classified. Press-agentry was born in the entertainment and political worlds of the nineteenth century. It still flourishes, though perhaps with less outright fakery than formerly. One of its commonest forms is in arranging for a product or person to be seen in association with celebrities—for example, being photographed with a motion-picture star, or giving away a product as a prize on a television program. In the orchestra of public relations, press-agentry represents the brass section. Mae Lyons, press agent for Ringling Bros. & Barnum & Bailey Combined Shows, Inc., says, however, "The circus drumbeater now plays all instruments in the public relations band," adding: ". . . there is more to circus public relations than exaggerated fibbing. There is far more to it than a story and picture in the newspapers." [3] She agrees with the clever Jim Moran—who, among other feats, has sold iceboxes to Eskimos—that "It is the fun part of the business."

The term and practice have become tainted. *The aim of the press agent is more to attract attention than to gain understanding.* Press-agentry is a necessary activity in the box-office worlds of circuses, theaters, movies, night clubs, resorts, hotels, and commercial sports. It has little stature and little value in the ultimate public relations aims. That many press agents, to achieve respectability, assume the title of "counselor" does not alter this fact. In the candid words of a Hollywood press agent: "We stoop to anything but our stuff gets printed." [4] Elizabeth Taylor's earning power may be more a tribute to the skill of her press agents than to her ability to act.

Press-agentry can best illustrated by the success of the late Steve Hannagan. He built monuments to his skill and the power of press-agentry in making the Memorial Day auto races at Indianapolis a national event and in making Miami Beach and Sun Valley internationally known resorts.[5] Another example

---

[3] Miss Lyons is the first woman public relations director in Ringling annals. Her views are recorded in an interview article, "Ringling's Public Relations Director 'Speaks' to Children of All Ages," *Public Relations Journal*, Vol. 19, April, 1963.

[4] For a candid look at work of Broadway press-agentry, see Richard Maney, *Fanfare* (New York: Harper & Row, Publishers, 1957).

[5] For the background on Hannagan, see "Steve Hannagan is Dead in Africa," *New York Times*, February 6, 1953, p. 19; "Steve Hannagan," *Current Biography*, Vol. 5, August 1944, pp. 29-31; and "Prince of Press Agents," *Collier's*, Vol. 120, November 22, 1947, pp. 75ff.

of the press agent build-up is told by *Fortune* in "The Case of Charles Luck-man." [6] Current examples of press-agentry are to be found in your daily news-paper under the datelines of Hollywood, Las Vegas, Miami Beach, Monte Carlo, and such places. The many beauty "Queens" are tools of press-agentry. For instance, Miss Drum Majorette, Miss Tuna Fish, Miss National Press Photog, Miss Rheingold, Miss Drum Stick, Miss Canner, Miss Junior Prom, and Miss Swim For Health.

2. PRODUCT PROMOTION. Product promotion has been developed in the business world as a supplementary tool to advertising in the marketing of mass-produced consumer goods and services. Product publicity is an important aspect of today's product promotion. Because of the skills and the knowledge of news media required in this task, this work is usually assigned to the public relations department. The work of many counseling firms and advertising agency PR departments is mainly product promotion—getting a free ride for the products in the news media. This is a service which business PR staffs provide to the marketing-sales staffs in the same way that they provide em-ployee communications counsel to the industrial relations department, or community relations counsel to plant management.

Today's practice in industry defines product publicity as a going part of the job. In some cases it becomes almost the whole job. Some persons in business will argue that the product-publicity task might be more properly assigned to sales and marketing. The basic public relations function is to build confidence in the maker of the products. This will indirectly contribute to the sale of goods. Yet the proper publicizing of a product can contribute as helpfully to building a corporate image as can other public relations methods.

Product promotion is most heavily used in the field of fashions, foods, furnishings, home design, cars, and appliances. One of the outstanding product promotions of this generation has been making "The Coffee Break" an American institution. Many examples can be found in daily newspapers in articles promoting wall-to-wall carpeting in homes or the opposite—open, waxed hardwood floors; articles suggesting a return to overhead lighting fixtures in the home; articles promoting the use of new synthetic fabrics in clothing, or a revival of cotton, and the like.[7]

3. PUBLICITY. Corporate institutional publicity and all the information output of governmental agencies, schools, nonprofit welfare agencies, and similar organizations are generally lumped under the elastic term *publicity*. Publicity to build a favorable image and understanding of a concern or agency

6 *Fortune*, Vol. 41, April, 1950. For a close-up view of the flamboyant Ben Sonnenberg, Luckman's press agent, read the lively profile by Geoffrey T. Hellman, "A House on Gramercy Park," *New Yorker*, April 8, 1950, pp. 40ff.

7 For elaboration on product publicity, see Philip Lesly, "How to Get more Sales Power from Public Relations When Business Is Off," *Sales Management*, Vol. 80, June 6, 1958; James E. Burke, "A Look at Product Public Relations," *Public Relations Journal*, Vol. 17, May, 1961.

is one of several PR tools. *It is not the whole*. The two are not synonymous. Publicity takes the form of reporting an institution's or industry's day-by-day activities which are deemed newsworthy. This would include the earnings reports of a corporation, the size of a new freshman dorm at a university, the progress of a Girl Scout fund drive, scientific findings from the nation's latest space flight by the National Aeronautics and Space Administration, and the return to duty of an ailing Congressman. Publicity also results from the staging of newsworthy events, such as ground-breakings, dedications, anniversary celebrations, seminars, and other special events.

The confusion of the publicity tool with the broader practice of public relations is understandable. The practice, in part, has evolved from publicity. Much of contemporary PR is still concerned with publicity. Many practitioners do little else. They are more accurately titled "information men" or "publicity men." There is a legitimate need for the publicist or information practitioner. This practitioner is most often found working in governmental agencies, the military forces, social agencies, and fund-raising campaigns.

4. LOBBYING. This has become an ugly word and is often used to connote the manipulation of government for selfish interests. Yet the right freely to petition our government is a basic constitutional right of every citizen, every organization. Public relations, by definition and practice, often embraces lobbying. Washington, D.C., and the state capitals are centers of such activities. This phase may include: (1) getting information from government officials; (2) persuasively informing government officials; (3) promoting legislative or administrative action for an organization or against an adverse interest; (4) obtaining governmental cooperation or sponsorship, such as a governor's proclamation of Fire Prevention Week.

Every firm and organization today has a host of relationships with the proliferating number of governmental agencies and activities. These relationships require the skills of opinion analysis, mediation, and communication. The specialist possesses such skills. Hence, he is used for such tasks. Relationships with government once were almost wholly the work of lawyers. Today this task is being shared. The registered list of lobbyists in the nation's capital and in state capitals where such registration is required carries many names of well-known practitioners. When the PR specialist is engaged exclusively in government relations, he will continue to be called "lobbyist" by popular usage, however distasteful the term.

Trade associations are major employers of public relations specialists. Much of the work for these interest groups involves lobbying. The railroads, airlines, and buslines all lobby to persuade lawmakers and voters that their mode of transportation deserves preferential consideration. Each will say, with logic and eloquence, that it serves the public interest first.

Beyond the direct representation to government lawmakers and law enforcers on behalf of a client or cause, there is the increasingly important task of building public support for issues and institutions in the voting precincts. This "telling your story to the people"—the most effective kind of lobbying—is primarily the task of practitioners trained for such work.[8]

Another phase of public relations-lobbying work that has grown rapidly in the postwar era is representation of foreign governments by American public relations firms. From 1944 to 1964, the number of nations having diplomatic relations with the United States doubled from 54 to 108. This and other postwar developments have brought a sharp increase in the utilization of public relations by foreign governments. Large industrial nations, each with clearly established United States public relations requirements, have, for the most part, established their own government information offices in this country. The British Information Service is an example. This need of foreign governments for United States public relations counsel simply reflects the fact that the United States today, by virtue of its size and the diversity of its economy, has a tremendous impact on the economic well-being of other nations in the world.

5. PUBLIC RELATIONS. The core of full-blown practice is *empathetic listening* and *persuasive communication*. To accomplish these functions, a wide variety of tasks are discharged. No two public relations programs have precisely the same objectives, or aim at the same publics, or embrace identical tasks. Nor should they. *A program, to be effective, must be tailored to the industry or institution it serves.* For example, there is little need for a formal, shareholder-relations program in a family business. And the program of a mental health association will differ markedly from that used by a trade association of florists. The principles of earning and getting public goodwill are constant, but the publics, tools, and emphases must vary considerably.

The content and emphasis in programs may be seen in this illustrative cataloging of publics for—

INDUSTRY	or a	UNIVERSITY
Employee relations		Student relations
Community relations		Faculty relations
Stockholder relations		Staff relations
Customer relations		Community relations
Governmental relations		Alumni relations
Educational relations		Donor relations
Dealer relations		Government relations
Press relations		Foundation relations
Public relations		Trustee relations
		Press relations

---

[8] For discussion of this aspect of PR, see Bert Goss, "PR Is Not Lobbying," *PR*, Vol. 1, July, 1956: Robert L. L. McCormick, "The Anatomy of Public Relations in Washington," *PR*, Vol. 2, January 2, 1957: Paul H. Becker, "Are You Reaching Your Man on the Hill?," *Public Relations Journal*, Vol. 18, May, 1962. For a discussion of lobbying, see Karl Schriftgiesser, *The Lobbyists* (Boston: Little, Brown & Co., 1951). For examples, see Stanley Kelley, Jr., *Professional Public Relations and Political Power* (Baltimore: Johns Hopkins Press, 1956). For the best-documented case detailing the use of public relations to influence legislation, study the *Eastern Railroads vs. Pennsylvania Truckers* case, which may be found in these court records: *Noerr Motor Freight, Inc., et al. v. Eastern Railroad Presidents Conference, et al.*, in *Federal Supplement*, Vol. 155, Dec. 23, 1957, pp. 768-841; 273 F. 2d 218 (1959); 81 *Supreme Court Reporter*, 523, February 20, 1961. There are also several articles discussing this celebrated case.

and in these media:

Formal public opinion polls	Employee letters
Informal opinion surveys	Shareholder letters
Questionnaires	Shareholder magazines
Personal contacts	Speeches
Correspondence	Art shows
Company newspapers, magazines	Booklets, brochures
News releases	Open house, plant tours
Radio and TV programs	Materials for schools
Exhibits, displays	Essay contests
Special events	Photographs
Bulletin boards	Suggestion systems
Employee awards	Visitors' parking
Annual reports	Recreational programs
Motion and slide films	Dividend inserts
Payroll inserts	Advertising

PATHWAYS TO PUBLIC FAVOR

By now, the destination toward which the practice and programs travel, whatever their nature, should be clear: *to gain and hold the favorable opinions of the publics of an institution or industry*. Agreement on this destination is general. Disagreement and divergence set in when the choice of route to this favorable environment is to be made. Practitioners are known by the routes they take, not the ones they pretend to travel.

There are, in the main, four possible pathways. Two are deceptive detours, full of bumps and chuckholes. Another is an old, almost abandoned, cow path, grown over with thorny underbrush. Only one, the fourth, is a cleared, graded, and open pathway, broad enough to carry two-way traffic. Even it is not paved. There is no easy road to public favor.

One detour has been beaten out by those who think publicity alone is the sure-fire answer to an organization's public relations problems. This is the pathway that leads simply to "getting publicity" without regard to its purpose or effectiveness. It is also taken by those who think that pretty words and pretty pictures can beautify the ugliest of institutions or situations. This detour has a road marker that reads: *The Fallacy of Publicity*.

The other detour, on the opposite side of the main-traveled path, is taken by those who assume that good works and good motives, even though unheralded, will produce a favorable public-opinion environment. This idea has considerable merit but fails to reckon with the babble and bedlam of today's arena of public opinion. This one is posted: *Virtue Earns Its Own Reward*.

The third, the old, overgrown cow path, is still taken by those who hold public opinion in contempt. This is the path originally cleared by the Robber Barons. This old path, also a detour, is marked by the sign, *"The Public Be Damned."* Those who take this route with the philosophy, "To hell with the public interest; let's get ours," may get to their destination. And then, they may not. Detours are usually the long way around. It's easy to get lost on them.

The fourth pathway, modern and in process of construction, is built to carry an increasing load of traffic. This pathway is chosen by those who recognize that sound public relationships are built of good works and sound communication practices. More and more are taking this pathway because people are learning that it is the safest, smoothest way. The road was cleared and graded by those who saw the importance of doing a good job and letting everybody know about it. More persons will probably take this route in the future. This signpost reads: *Good Performance Publicly Appreciated.*

Additional Reading

Anonymous, "Management's Self-Conscious Spokesmen," *Fortune,* Vol. 52, November, 1955.

Anonymous, "The New Model Press Agent," *Newsweek,* Vol. 53, March 2, 1959.

Anonymous, "Public Relations Today," *Business Week,* July 2, 1960. A *Business Week* Special Report.

Paul Garrett, "The Four Dimensions of Public Relations," *Printers' Ink,* Vol. 203, June 11, 1943.

————, "A New Dimension in Public Relations," *Public Relations Journal,* Vol. 12, October, 1956.

Robert L. Heilbroner, "Public Relations—The Invisible Sell," *Harper's Magazine,* Vol. 215, June, 1957. (Also available in Christenson and McWilliams, *Voice of the People,* pp. 426-37.)

Philip Lesly, ed., *Public Relations Handbook,* 2nd ed. Englewood Cliffs, N.J.: Prentice-Hall, Inc., 1962. See Chap. One, "Exactly What Is Public Relations?"

John Marston, *The Nature of Public Relations.* New York: McGraw-Hill, Inc., 1963

Irwin Ross, *The Image Merchants.* Garden City: Doubleday & Company, Inc., 1959. A candid look at "the fabulous world of public relations."

Howard Stephenson, ed., *Handbook of Public Relations.* New York: McGraw-Hill, Inc., 1960. See his chapter, "Public Relations Practice."

Chapter Two

HOW

IT

ALL

BEGAN—

THE

FORERUNNERS

The way to get at the nature of an institution, as of anything else that is alive, is to see how it has grown.
—A. G. Keller

Study of the origins of public relations provides a helpful insight into its functions and techniques. The history is a fascinating story, but an adequate, documented history remains to be written. Published histories have been telescoped and oversimplified. There has been an overemphasis on novelty and on a few of the many colorful personalities. Even a slight probing of history will quickly dull the sheen of novelty often given to public relations. The effort to deal with the force of opinion and to communicate with others goes back to antiquity. Only the tools, degree of specialization, and intensity of effort required today are relatively new. Increased specialization and current emphasis give the delusion of newness.

The growth has extended over many decades. The factors inducing its origin and development are many and complex. The turbulent stream of history rushes along in a manner that defies neat cataloging. The history of public relations cannot be told by simply saying that it grew out of press-agentry. Nor can it be fully told in terms of the influential career of an Ivy Lee.

The power of public opinion to control human affairs has been recognized down through the centuries. Although the term *public opinion* was not coined until the eighteenth century, the force of people's opinions was demonstrated and recognized in ancient times. Public relations perhaps began when Neolithic man traded a flint for the hindquarters of a sheep. With recognition of the power of people's opinions, there came in response practices we now call public relations. They were of

16

a most rudimentary sort, to be sure. Public opinion played a part in shaping events among the early Greeks and Romans, even though the publics were small in size and number, the channels of expression limited, and the communications crude.

The Greek theorists studied the importance of the public will, even though they did not specifically use the term *public opinion*. The urban culture of the later Roman Empire gave scope to the opinion process. Certain phrases and ideas in the political vocabulary of the Romans and in the writings of the medieval period are related to modern concepts of public opinion. The Romans inscribed upon their walls the slogan, "S.P.Q.R.—the Senate and the Roman People." Later, the Romans coined the expression *vox populi, vox Dei*—"the voice of the people is the voice of God." Machiavelli wrote, in his *Discoursi,* "Not without reason is the voice of the people compared to the voice of God." Machiavelli held that the people must be either annihilated or caressed.

Efforts to communicate information to influence actions likewise can be traced from the earliest civilizations. Archeologists found a farm bulletin in Iraq which told the farmers of 1800 B.C. how to sow their crops, how to irrigate, how to deal with field mice, and how to harvest their crops. This effort was not unlike today's distribution of farm bulletins by our United States Department of Agriculture. Much of what is known of ancient Egypt, Assyria, and Persia was recorded in efforts to publicize and glorify the rulers of that day. Much of the literature and art of antiquity was designed to build support for kings, priests, and other leaders. Vergil's *Georgics* represented a persuasive effort to get urban dwellers to move to the farms to produce food for the growing city. Demosthenes used publicity to oppose the imperialist schemes of Philip of Macedon. The walls of Pompeii were inscribed with election appeals. Caesar carefully prepared the Romans for his crossing of the Rubicon in 50 B.C. by sending reports to Rome on his epic achievements as governor of Gaul. Historians believe *The Commentaries* were written by Caesar as propaganda for Caesar.

Rudimentary elements of public relations can be found in the history of ancient India. In writings of the earliest times there is mention of the king's spies who did more than carry on espionage. Their functions included keeping the king in touch with public opinion. They also championed the king in public and spread rumors favorable to the government.[1] Public relations was heralded many centuries ago in England, where the kings maintained Lords Chancellor as "Keepers of the King's Conscience." These functionaries surely offer a historical counterpart. Long before the complexities of communication, there was acknowledged need for a third party to facilitate communication and adjustment between the government and the people. So it was with the church, tradesmen, and craftsmen. The word *propaganda* was born in the seventeenth century, when the Catholic Church set up its College of Propa-

---

[1] A. L. Basham, *The Wonder That Was India* (London: Sidgwick & Jackson, 1954), p. 122.

ganda to propagate the faith. The knight of old had his press agent in his *avant courier*. In a still later day, Catherine the Great, able autocrat of all Russia, displayed a "genius for publicity." "She looked on publicity as an essential instrument in the art of government. Always she drafted her *ukazi* and manifestoes in the way to make the fullest appeal to her people, and often this was their main, if not their only, purpose. Likewise on every public occasion she was conscious of the impression she must make." [2] Today's practitioner has had many counterparts in history.

Close examination of history reveals the direct relationship between the growth of the practice and the periods of intense struggle for power among the competitive elements of society. Public relations, as a prime agent in public-opinion formation, has been developed to meet the needs of power groups for public support. The American beginnings of PR are to be found in the American Revolution, which brought the struggle for power between the patrician-led patriots and the commercial, propertied Tories. It is evident in the conflict between the trade and property interests led by Hamilton against the planter-and-farmer bloc led by Jefferson; in the struggle between Jackson's agrarian frontiersmen and the financial forces of Nicholas Biddle; and in the nation's greatest internal conflict of all—the Civil War.

The later stages of development are directly tied to the power struggles evoked by the political reform movements of Theodore Roosevelt, Robert M. LaFollette, Woodrow Wilson, Franklin D. Roosevelt, Harry S. Truman, and John F. Kennedy. Their party programs, reflecting strong tides of protest against entrenched power groups, provided the catalytic agents for much of the growth. Contemporary practice has emerged from the political economy of the United States in the continuing struggle of political and economic groups for dominance and from the increasing necessity for each group to "have the public on its side."

The history is meaningful only when it is related to these power conflicts. For example, it is not mere coincidence that large business interests in the past have taken public relations most seriously when their position of power was challenged or threatened by the forces of labor, the farmer, and the small shopkeeper. Nor is it a coincidence that labor's programs have been intensified when an adverse public reaction to labor was crystallizing in regulatory legislation. Similarly, the most intense developments within government have come in periods of crisis: World War I, the Depression, World War II, the Korean War, and the uneasy years with Russia and China since World War II.

The origins need to be examined in their natural social and historical setting. The threads that form the tapestry, when pulled out of the fabric and examined singly, leave a confused, raveled impression. It is the old story of the blind men and the elephant.

---

[2] Ian Grey, *Catherine the Great, Autocrat and Empress of All Russia* (Philadelphia: J. B. Lippincott Co., 1962), pp. 143-44.

THE AMERICAN
BEGINNINGS

The origins of American public relations practice can be traced back to early colonial days. Today the persuasive promotional campaigns required to raise the some ten billions of dollars given annually to charitable causes in the United States represent a substantial part of public relations work. Probably the first systematic effort to raise funds on this continent was that sponsored by Harvard College in 1641 when that infant institution sent a trio of preachers to England on a "begging mission." Once in England, these fund raisers found that they needed a fund-raising brochure—today a standard item in a fund drive—and relayed this need back to Harvard. In response to this request came *New England's First Fruits,* largely written in Massachusetts but printed in London in 1643, the first of countless billions of public relations pamphlets and brochures.[3] And perhaps it was Columbia University that first used the press release as a means of gaining public notice. News announcements of the first commencement at King's College, as Columbia was then called, June 21, 1758, ran in all of the New York City journals and all accounts were identical. Someone, his name lost to oblivion, sent the copy to the publishers with a June 26 release date. The handouts quaintly said: "Mr. Printer. Please to insert the following in your next paper." This first college commencement itself was perhaps the first in a long series of events publicly staged to gain public attention.

The tools and techniques of public relations have long been an important part of the weaponry in political warfare. The origins of sustained efforts to move and manipulate public opinion lead back to the Revolutionary War and the work of men like Samuel Adams and Benjamin Franklin. "Sam Adams owned no superior as a propagandist. No one in the colonies realized more fully than he the primary necessity of arousing public opinion, no one set about it more assiduously." [4] Although the common people gave the Revolution its strength, it was a small group of men who organized and promoted the revolt. These men—among them Adams, Thomas Paine, Alexander Hamilton, Benjamin Franklin, John Dickinson, and Thomas Jefferson —brought about the birth of our nation.

They knew, intuitively, how to mold and manipulate opinion. They knew its importance. The Declaration of Independence was written "out of a decent respect to the opinions of mankind." These pioneers used staged events, oratory, pen, and organization. They circulated pamphlets by the thousands, filled the few colonial newspapers with articles, usually unsigned,

---

[3] Samuel Eliot Morison, *The Founding of Harvard College* (Cambridge, Mass.: Harvard University Press, 1935), p. 303.

[4] Philip Davidson, *Propaganda and the American Revolution, 1763-1783* (Chapel Hill: University of North Carolina Press, 1941), p. 3.

and spread their ideas of revolt through public meetings, correspondence, and word of mouth. Their methods can be found in use today. Davidson asserts: "Without their work independence would not have been declared in 1776 nor recognized in 1783."

Commager and Nevins hold that the American Revolution was not a popular uprising. "The revolt against the British government was not a vast spontaneous movement. Instead, it was carefully planned by shrewd men and laboriously and sagaciously executed by some of the most active spirits on the continent. It could never have succeeded if it had been left unorganized. It was because the patriots were well organized, and because the Tories or loyalists were not, the former won the day." [5] There was far from unanimity of opinion as to breaking away from England. In later years John Adams would reflect that the rupture with the Mother Country did not come about suddenly in 1775. "The Revolution was indeed effected in the period from 1761 to 1775. I mean a complete revolution in the minds of the people. . . . All this was done and the principles all established and the system matured before the year 1775." [6] Then, as today, public opinion could be moved, but the task took skill, time, and persistence.

In staging the Boston Tea Party, Sam Adams demonstrated the value of created events to dramatize a point of view or a situation. Adams pioneered in many ways in his effort to inflame the colonists against the British. He set ablaze the smoldering conflict that was created, in part at least, by the lack of adequate communications between the mother country and the new colony. These men knew, too, the importance of getting a story to the public first. The patriots got their account of the opening battle at Lexington and Concord to England first, where Benjamin Franklin disseminated it throughout the land.[7] Franklin's consummate skill in public relations has seldom been matched. Advertising and public relations, especially self-promotion, were as natural to Franklin as his curiosity, his restless mind, and his love of the gay life. He wrote: "Modesty is a virtue that can never thrive in public. . . . A man must be his own trumpeter, he must write or dictate paragraphs of praise in the newspapers, he must dress, have a retinue, and equipage, he must ostentatiously publish to the world his own writings with his name, and must write even some panegyrics upon them . . . and must perpetuate his fame." This Franklin did.

"Press-agentry took on more of its modern form in the years leading up to and during the first war with England," states Alfred McClung Lee, a student of both history and public relations. "Samuel Adams and his associates between 1748 and the Revolution centered a propaganda exchange about

---

5 Allan Nevins and Henry Steele Commager, *Pocket History of the United States* (New York: Pocket Books, Inc., 1951), p. 75.

6 Page Smith, *John Adams* (New York: Doubleday & Company, Inc., 1962). 2 vols. P. 1097.

7 Edwin Emery, *The Press and America* (Englewood Cliffs, N.J.: Prentice-Hall, Inc., 1962, p. 118). An excellent history of America's press and its impact on American society.

Rogers and Fowle's *The Independent Advertiser* (Boston) until 1750 and Edes & Gill's *The Boston Gazette* from 1775; that bureau had all the fundamentals of George Creel's organization of World War fame. . . . Adams supplemented this work by building up committees of correspondence in more than eighty towns; moreover, no town went without a copy of the *Gazette*. The manner in which Adams, the press agent, publicized the Boston Massacre of March 5, 1770, and the Boston Tea Party of December 16, 1773, characterizes his potent work. In both cases Adams hustled his eye-witness account—carefully biased—throughout the colonies." [8] Miller believes that Adams' Boston Tea Party marked "the crossing of the Rubicon," and "was a headlong plunge toward revolt which set free the forces, long gathering in America, that led to war. . . ." Little wonder that an overjoyed Sam Adams exulted, when he heard the rattle of musketry on the Lexington green April 18, 1775, "Oh, what a glorious morning is this!" He had done his work well. The shot that was heard round the world was heard because the news was systematically disseminated by partisan publicists.[9]

The initial skirmishes in the continuing struggle for power in this new land took place during the Revolutionary period. Later they were evident in the conflict of those brilliant protagonists, Hamilton and Jefferson. Without stretching the point, the *Federalist* papers can be called public relations documents. David Truman says, "The entire effort of which *The Federalist* was a part was one of the most skillful and important examples of pressure group activity in American history." Morrison and Commager hold that "unless the Federalists had been shrewd in manipulation as they were sound in theory, their arguments could not have prevailed."

Historian Allan Nevins describes the propaganda efforts of Alexander Hamilton, James Madison, and John Jay as "history's finest public relations job." He believes, "Obtaining national acceptance of the Constitution was essentially a public relations exercise, and Hamilton, with his keen instinct for public relations, took thought not only to the product but to the ready acquiescence of thoughtful people; and he imparted his views to others. . . . Once the Constitution came before the country, the rapidity with which Hamilton moved was a striking exemplification of good public relations. He knew that if a vacuum develops in popular opinion, ignorant and foolish views will fill it. No time must be lost in providing accurate facts and sound ideas." [10]

Professor William Crosskey strongly dissents from the Nevins' view, arguing that "the Federalist Papers were not widely read or copied hardly at all." "This fable," asserts Crosskey, "is repeated by writer after writer, with no ap-

---

[8] Alfred McClung Lee, *The Daily Newspaper in America* (New York: The Macmillan Company, 1937), p. 40. Another useful book.

[9] To learn how news was spread in this era, see Frank Luther Mott, "The Newspaper Coverage of Lexington and Concord," *New England Quarterly*, Vol. 17, December, 1944, pp. 489-505.

[10] Allan Nevins, *The Constitution Makers and the Public, 1785-1790* (New York: Foundation for Public Relations Research and Education, 1962), p. 10.

parent notion of the truth." [11] A more balanced view is expressed by Douglass Adair, who says, "The Federalist's propaganda value, as first published in the newspapers, should not be overrated; the essays probably influenced few votes among the general electorate." [12] Then, as now, it was hard to measure the impact of propaganda tracts. For certain, Hamilton never "neglected the cultivation of popular favor by fair and justifiable expedients."

Another crucial large-scale battle came with the Jacksonian Era. This power struggle produced another unsung pioneer in public relations, Amos Kendall. As the key member of President Jackson's "Kitchen Cabinet," Kendall, a former Kentucky newspaper editor, served Jackson as a pollster, counselor, ghost writer, and publicist. The "Kitchen Cabinet" was almost supreme in creating events to mold opinion. On all vital issues that arose, Jackson consulted these key advisers. Most of them were former newspapermen.

Jackson, an unlettered man inarticulate in political or social philosophy, could not get his ideas across with ease. He, like many a modern executive, needed Kendall, the specialist, to convey his ideas to Congress and the country. Jackson's political campaigns and his governmental policies clearly reveal the influence of Kendall's strategy, sense of public opinion, and skill as a communicator.

Although Samuel Adams had used the press, committees of correspondence, staged events, and other devices, his lasting influence on public relations is negligible. Once the Revolution was won, Adams turned to other things. Kendall, in contrast, more closely approached today's counselor in his concepts and practices. He closed out his life as a lobbyist. The role played by Kendall in Jackson's administration is quite comparable to that of James Hagerty in President Eisenhower's administration. Kendall worked at the top policy-making level and was always closely consulted on major issues while they were being shaped. He devised much of Jackson's strategy.

Amos Kendall wrote most of Jackson's speeches, many of his letters, reports, and so forth. He organized and developed the administration's official mouthpiece, *The Globe,* which set a new pattern for the party press of that day. He wrote and sent out countless press releases on a wide basis. By the time Jackson was elected President, the United States had more newspapers and more readers than any other country in the world. Kendall sensed the increased impact of the press on opinion. He possessed a sure sense of mass psychology and an ability to communicate complex ideas in the plain language of the frontier.

He also shrewdly polled public opinion. Kendall carefully analyzed newspaper comment and content and sensitively gauged the public temper. Jackson drew much of his strength from the people by offering ideas congenial to

11 William Crosskey, *Politics and the Constitution* (Chicago: University of Chicago Press, 1953). 2 vols. P. 9.

12 Douglass Adair, "The Authorship of the Disputed Federalist Papers," Part II, *William and Mary Quarterly,* Vol. I, 1944, p. 236.

them. Kendall took care to find out what the people wanted. During the Bank fight with Nicholas Biddle, for example, Kendall made a trip to Baltimore, Philadelphia, New York, and Boston. He sounded out bankers and others on Jackson's plan to withdraw federal funds from the Second Bank of the United States and to place these deposits with state banks. Kendall made a favorable report upon his return, and the President withdrew the deposits. Kendall sought to keep open the lines of communication between Jackson and the people from whom he drew his support.

Although truly a pioneer, Amos Kendall was quite unlike most of his modern counterparts, particularly those who operate in Washington. As a youth on a bleak Massachusetts farm, he was shy and priggish. As an adult, he was no hail-fellow-well-met. When Kendall joined the influx of Jacksonian spoilsmen into Washington, this dour Yankee was appalled at the excesses of the nation's capital. The ladies laced too tightly and brazenly exposed their bare shoulders! During a fashionable reception, Kendall was seen to snatch a cup of coffee from a waiter, retire to a corner, and watch, with obvious disgust, the men crowding around the wine and whiskey on the sideboard. Nor was he an impressive personality in terms of dress and appearance.

But like some of today's practitioners, Kendall operated from backstage and preferred anonymity. Most of his work for Jackson was performed while he served in the rather obscure post of Fourth Auditor of the Treasury. Kendall could often be found late at night, sitting in his unpretentious office in the old Treasury Building, preparing messages, writing pamphlets, devising political war maps, or earnestly consulting Jackson's other advisers. On other nights he would be working in the White House. The President's White House bedroom was the scene of many night conferences of which Kendall was the chief scribe. It was there that Jackson and Kendall planned strategy, fashioned their verbal thunderbolts, and prepared speeches and state papers. From this backstage position, the unkempt but shrewd Kendall contributed much to Jackson's success, to American history, and to the beginnings of public relations.[13] Ex-President John Quincy Adams once said of Van Buren and Jackson, "Both . . . have been for twelve years the tool of Amos Kendall, the ruling mind of their dominion."

The first clear beginnings can be found in the Jacksonian era. This was the period in which the common man won the ballot and started the free public school. The literate public was enlarged. As the people gained political power, it became necessary to win their support. No longer was government the exclusive concern for the patrician few. "The new Democracy was heavily weighted with what gentlemen were pleased to call the rabble." With the rise

---

[13] For one example of Kendall's work, see Lynn Marshall, "The Authorship of Jackson's Bank Veto Message." *Mississippi Valley Historical Review*, Vol. L, December, 1963. For fuller view of Kendall's influence, see Arthur M. Schlesinger, Jr., *The Age of Jackson* and other histories of this period. Also, *Autobiography of Amos Kendall* (Micro-Offset Books, 1949, reprinted). To compare Kendall's role with that of James Hagerty, see "The White House: Authentic Voice," *Time*, Vol. 71, January 27, 1958.

of democracy in America came increasing rights for, and power of, the individual." [14]

THE STAGE IS SET BY
1900

The modern concept and terminology were little known in those days of young America. There were few coercions for the development of full-scale public relations in nineteenth century America. There were no means of mass communication on a national basis. Group relationships were relatively simple. People, on the whole, were rather self-sufficient and independent. Large-scale development was to wait for the twentieth century, after our history had passed through the watershed of the 1890's. But many of the generating forces had their origins in the last century. Of the threads that form the fabric, traced back through the 1800's, three of these—press-agentry, political campaigning, and business practices—merit a word. The roots of a practice so varied, of a concept so diffused, are to be found in many places.

PRESS-AGENTRY

It is a gross oversimplification to state flatly that public relations has evolved from press-agentry. Such a statement, however, has a degree of truth. Systematic efforts to attract or divert public attention are as old as efforts to persuade and propagandize. Much of what we define as public relations was labeled press-agentry when it was being used to promote land settlement in our unsettled West or to build up political heroes.[15] Elements of press-agentry are to be found in many public relations programs today but not as much as the critics of public relations assert. Mainly the press agents, beginning with Phineas T. Barnum and the theatrical press agents who followed, developed as an adjunct to show business and advertising. Box-office enterprises are the prime employers of press agents.

Amos Kendall's time brought an effective demonstration of the "build-up" when Jackson's opponents created the myth of Davy Crockett in an effort to woo the frontier vote away from Old Hickory. Crockett's press agent was Mathew St. Clair Clarke. The Davy Crockett legend was given an intensive if short-lived revival in the 1950's when Walt Disney featured that "yaller flower of the forest" in movies, TV programs, books, and records. Disney

14 T. Swann Harding, "Genesis of One 'Government Propaganda Mill,'" *Public Opinion Quarterly*, Vol. 11, Summer 1947, pp. 227-35. History of this now large governmental PR department.

15 See John Walton, *John Filson of Kentucky* (Lexington: University of Kentucky Press, 1956).

did not create the Crockett legend; he just cashed in on it. Davy was a boorish boob, not a brave hero. The Whigs, stressing his eccentricities, humor, and lusty pioneer spirit, turned him into a vote-getting buffoon. Books were turned out in the name of this almost illiterate man. When he was defeated for Congress, Crockett told his constituents that they could go to hell, and went off to Texas to die at the Alamo. This put a dramatic finish to his colorful legend.[16]

But the master of them all was Phineas Taylor Barnum—and he knew it. Barnum was born in 1810 and died in 1891. His life span covered a period of great importance in the evolution of public relations. His influence lives today. Barnum's most recent biographer, Irving Wallace, writes: "Barnum's showmanship was evident not only in a canny instinct that enabled him to give the masses what they wanted, but also in his ability to dictate to them a desire for what he thought they should want. . . . Every man has his star. Barnum's star was an exclamation mark." Promoter Barnum also employed a press agent—Richard F. "Tody" Hamilton. Dexter Fellows, a latter-day circus drumbeater, said that "Tody" Hamilton developed the art of exaggeration into a fine art. Fellows writes: "Chary as Barnum was of giving credit to anyone but himself, he has been quoted as saying that he owed more of his success to Tody Hamilton than to any other man." [17]

Barnum's most notable successses were in the build-up of Tom Thumb, the midget, the American tour of Jenny Lind, "The Swedish Nightingale," and the circus that long carried his name. When he died, he left an estate of more than four million dollars. Barnum, a master showman, was fully aware of publicity and used it cleverly. He knew how to exploit the news values of controversy, the bizarre, the fantastic. He knew the box office appeal of pure notoriety. He bought yards of newspaper space to hawk his wonders. But he got much more through fakery and staged events.[18]

The earliest known use of the term *press agent* is found in the 1868 roster of John Robinson's Circus and Menagerie. This listed, as the circus's third top executive, "W. W. Duran, Press Agent." It can be presumed that Robinson's competitors used press agents, possibly before he did, and that they were fairly common even at that early date. Their number today is legion. The showman led the way and others followed in an ever-increasing number. Success begets imitators. During the two decades before 1900, the art infiltrated from the show business into closely related enterprises. In due time it was in

---

[16] For accounts of Davy's build-up, see Marshall Fishwick, *American Heroes*, pp. 70-71; and Vernon Parrington, *Main Currents in American Thought*, Vol. Two, pp. 173-78.

[17] Dexter W. Fellows and Andrew A. Freeman, *This Way to the Big Show* (New York: Halcyon House, 1938), p 193.

[18] See *The Life of P. T. Barnum*, Written by Himself (Redfield, 1855), pp. 154-74; Harvey W. Root, *The Unknown Barnum;* James S. Hamilton, *Barnum;* Waldo R. Browne, *Barnum's Own Story*, a condensed version of his 1855 autobiography; and the most recent biography, Irving Wallace, *The Fabulous Showman: Life and Times of P. T. Barnum.*

almost every type of enterprise that needed to attract the public's attention. Book publishers, for example, found this new technique profitable in booming book sales.

"Buffalo Bill" Cody is another American folklore hero who owes his place in history largely to the work of press agents. Marshall Fishwick writes: [19] "Cody's principal hero-makers were Ned Buntline, Prentiss Ingraham, and John Burke. Also helpful were Nate Salesbury, Texas Jack Omohundro, Dexter Fellows, Courtney Ryley Cooper, and Johnnie Baker. To them belongs credit for making Buffalo Bill the most highly publicized figure in Western history. What they did was not easy; no one should underestimate their endeavors. More spectacular men had to be outdistanced. Mountains had to be made out of molehills."

In 1911, Will Irwin, a shrewd and observing journalist, wrote: [20]

> But while the theatrical press agent declined, a hundred, a thousand other kinds of press agents arose, unperceived by the public. The theatrical managers had shown how easy it was to get free news space—more valuable, generally, than any amount of display advertising—by a little ingenuity and much inside knowledge of the newspaper game. They had proved another thing—how smooth a good press agent can make the relations between a corporation or an institution and the prying, troublesome newspapers. Forthwith, there arose a new profession, numbering its hundreds, its thousands, and finally its tens of thousands. "Half the population is trying to get into the newspapers and half to keep out"—that is a maxim almost as old as the news era. But where the assault on the news columns had been a straggling, guerilla fight, it became organized warfare, full of strategies so subtle that the keenest and most conscientious news editor must be beaten in detail again and again.

As press agents grew in number and their exploits became more incredible —albeit successful more often than not—it was natural that they would arouse the hostility and suspicion of editors. It was inevitable that the practice and its practitioners would become tainted. This inherent suspicion remains as part of PR's heritage.

POLITICAL CAMPAIGNING

Public relations has long been an essential part of the political party's apparatus. Virginian John Beckley must rank among the first, if indeed not the first, of a long line of political propagandists and organizers who have made our political party system work. He was a devoted aide of Thomas Jefferson in building what was then known as the Republican Party but today is the Democratic Party. He was Jefferson's eyes and ears and his propagandist, "one of the leading party organizers of the 1790's." [21] However, development of

---

19 Fishwick, *op. cit.*, pp. 100-10.

20 Will Irwin, "The Press Agent: His Rise and Decline," *Collier's*, Vol. 48, December 2, 1911, p. 24.

21 Noble E. Cunningham, Jr., "John Beckley: An Early American Party Manager," *William and Mary Quarterly,* Vol. 13, January 1956, pp. 40-52.

modern political campaign methods and techniques, except insofar as these have been modified by television, are largely rooted in the last decade of the nineteenth century. Increasingly "the activities of the public relations man have become a significant influence in processes crucial to democratic government." [22] In the final two decades of the nineteenth century, techniques used by the political party managers changed with the changing American environment, then rushing headlong toward industrialization and urbanization. Between 1880 and 1900 the political campaign methods crystallized that still prevail. The campaign methods originated by Kendall and his fellow "Kitchen Cabinet" members had remained essentially unchanged after the rise of democracy and enfranchisement of the people, save for a few minor refinements.

The bitter, close race in the Tilden-Hayes presidential campaign jarred both groups of party leaders. They began searching for new ways to enlist the support of the rapidly growing host of voters in a population fed by high birth rates and immigration. The campaign of 1880 witnessed the introduction of campaign literature on a mass scale. This development stemmed, in part, from the growth of the press, improved printing presses, a more abundant supply of cheap paper, and the need to "educate" the new immigrants. This development, in turn, spurred the evolution of the party "literary bureau" into a real press bureau. *Munsey's Magazine* says that "campaign literature" was carefully prepared and read.[23]

> Expert and experienced political managers give their closest attention to this detail. Men who are learned as regard to the issues at stake, and who have that requisite of the successful politician which might be termed a knowledge of applied psychology, hold the blue pencil. Paragraphs, sentences, and words are weighed with reference to their effect on the mind of their reader. What will be of advantage to one part of the country may be useless or possibly harmful in other parts.

The hard-hitting Bryan-McKinley campaign of 1896 marked the first use of modern political campaigning methods. It set a pattern which served for 60 years. Both parties moved their campaign headquarters to Chicago for this epic struggle. From both headquarters there flowed a heavy stream of pamphlets, posters, press releases and other campaign propaganda now a standard part of the American political campaign. The 1896 pattern of campaigning was, for the most part, repeated in 1900 and continued in subsequent campaigns, with slight modification, until the introduction of radio broadcasting in the mid-1920's.

Full-scale use of television in 1952 and 1956 marked the beginning of the end of this historic pattern. As the population grew, the voters became more and more out of reach of the stump-speaker. Indirect methods of communica-

---

22 Stanley Kelley, Jr., *Professional Public Relations and Political Power* (Baltimore: The Johns Hopkins Press, 1956). Provides examples of current political PR tactics.

23 Luther B. Little, "The Printing Press in Politics." *Munsey's Magazine,* Vol. 23, September 1900, pp. 740-44.

tion were inevitably pushed to the fore. This trend started in the latter part of the nineteenth century. By 1900 the manager of the political press bureau, both national and state, had assumed most of the functions which characterize today's practitioner. Ivy Lee's first appearance on the national scene came as publicity man for Judge Alton B. Parker in the 1904 Presidential campaign.

THE BEGINNINGS
IN BUSINESS

The most fundamental development in setting the stage in our time was the wild, frenzied, ruthless development of industry, railroads, and utilities in the post-Civil War years. In the 25 breath-taking years from 1875 to 1900, America doubled its population and jammed its people into cities; went into mass production and enthroned the machine; spanned the nation with rail and wire communications; developed the mass media of press and magazine; replaced the plantation baron with the prince of industry and finance; and replaced the versatile frontiersman with the specialized factory hand. In all this we laid the foundation for the mightiest industrial machine the world has yet known. These were years of extraordinarily rapid and enduring change.

The rise of powerful monopolies, concentration of wealth and power, and the roughshod tactics of the Robber Barons and their imitators were to bring a wave of protest and reform in the early 1900's. Contemporary public relations, as a practice and as philosophy, was to emerge out of the melee of the opposing forces in this period of the nation's rapid growth. Goldman observes, "Shouldering aside agriculture, large-scale commerce and industry became dominant over the life of the nation. Big business was committed to the doctrine that the less the public knew of its operations, the more efficient and profitable—even the more socially useful—the operations would be." [24] As the autocratic railroad magnate E. H. Harriman told Clarence J. Hicks, "I don't want anything on this railroad that I cannot control." Bold exploitation of the people and of the natural resources of this rich, young continent was bound to bring, ultimately, protest and reform once the people became aroused. This was the era of "the public be damned."

Incidentally, there is considerable dispute about the origin of this often quoted remark. It frequently has been erroneously attributed to salty old Commodore Vanderbilt. If it was used at all, it was used by his son, William Henry Vanderbilt, in an interview with *Chicago* reporters aboard his private railroad car, October 8, 1882. When questioned about the public's interest in the removal of a fast New York Central train between New York and Chicago, young Vanderbilt was quoted as saying, "The public be damned. . . . I don't take any stock in this silly nonsense about working for anybody's good but our own because we are not. When we make a move we do it because it is in

---

24 Eric F. Goldman, *Two-Way Street* (Boston: Bellman Publishing Co., 1948).

our interest to do so. . . ." A few days later, in an interview with a reporter from the *New York Tribune,* Vanderbilt denied making such a statement. "I never used it, and that is all there is about it." Whether or not Vanderbilt used the phrase mattered little. The quote stuck with him because it accurately symbolized the attitude of the business giants of that day, men whom Charles Francis Adams described as a "coarse, realistic, bargaining crowd."

The first strong protest came from the National Grange, an obscure secret order known at first as "Patrons of Husbandry." The Grange had a sudden and spectacular growth. This spearhead of the agrarian revolt was largely responsible for passage of the Interstate Commerce Act of 1887, first of the Granger regulatory laws designed to curb the excesses of the new industrial era. This Act subsequently was influential in inducing PR programs in public utilities and carriers. After this peak, the Grange slowly receded in influence. Its protest strength flowed into other groups, such as the Farmer's Alliance, the Greenbackers, and the Populist Party. The people were on the march against the excessive abuses of Big Business in what Parrington called "a huge buccaneering orgy."

Historian Merle Curti observes, "Corporations gradually began to realize the importance of combating hostility and courting public favor. The expert in the field of public relations was an inevitable phenomenon in view of the need for the services he could provide. As early as the 1890's, George Harvey, a newspaper man and publisher, was engaging in public relations activities for Thomas Fortune Ryan and Harry Payne Whitney, well-known promoters and financiers." [25] Even before this, the Mutual Life Insurance Company had employed a man by the name of Charles J. Smith to manage a "species of literary bureau," in about 1888. According to one writer, "In ordinary times his (Smith's) activities have been general and rather unimportant, but in time of emergency they are enlarged; for instance, last September when the investigation began, he turned all his strength to preparing articles calculated to counteract the reports of the investigations sent out through regular news channels." [26]

In fact, there is evidence that these buccaneers of old utilized "press representatives" as early as 1869, when a congressional committee brought out that John Bigelow, editor of the *New York Times,* had dealt with James McHenry, a press representative of the notorious Fisk-Gould interests. In the latter half of the nineteenth century, the railroads were the intensive users of publicity men and promotional agents. Railroads developed the art of publicity to promote settlement along the iron rails reaching to the Pacific Ocean and to fend off rising tides of public criticism. In 1859 Charles Russell Lowell, a promoter for the Burlington Railroad, wrote: "We are beginning to find that

---

25 Merle Curti, *The Growth of American Thought* (New York: Harper & Row, Publishers, 1964), 3rd ed., p. 634.

26 "Manufacturing Public Opinion." *McClure's Magazine,* Vol. 26, February, 1906, pp. 450-52.

he who buildeth a railroad west of the Mississippi must also find a population and build up business. We wish to blow as loud a trumpet as the merits of our position warrant." [27] Ten years later the Burlington hired "Professor" J. D. Butler to promote Iowa and Nebraska lands through his "widely published entertaining and practical letters," and by means of "well-concocted circulars, Posters, and a judicious amount of advertising," which Butler was certain would produce "a big stampede of immigrants for these favored lands." [28] In 1877 Jay Gould hired Robert Strahorn, traveler, promoter, and publicist, to create a literary bureau and advertising department for the Union Pacific Railroad for the same purpose. This same period saw the growth of the lusty and brash advertising business. As James Harvey Young has written, "The well-greased engines of advertising and public relations that dominate Madison Avenue today had a humble beginning in the 19th Century in the promotion of pills and potions guaranteed to cure everything from corns to senility."

What was probably the first corporate public relations department, in the contemporary meaning of this term, was established by George Westinghouse for his newly founded electric corporation in 1889. Westinghouse organized his firm in 1886 to promote his then revolutionary alternating current system of electricity. Thomas A. Edison's Edison General Electric Company was already established with its direct current system of distribution. The now famous battle of "the currents" ensued. Immediately Edison, aided by his right-hand man, the astute public relations-minded Samuel Insull, launched a scare campaign against the Westinghouse AC system. McDonald records: [29] "Edison General Electric attempted to prevent the development of alternating current by unscrupulous political action and by even less savory promotional tactics. . . . The promotional activity was a series of spectacular stunts aimed at dramatizing the deadliness of high voltage alternating current, the most sensational being the development and promotion of the electric chair as a means of executing criminals." The State of New York adopted electrocution in 1888. The next year Westinghouse realized he had to get his story to the public, and hired E. H. Heinrichs, a Pittsburgh newspaper man, for this purpose. Heinrichs served Westinghouse as his personal press representative until the latter's death in 1914. Then, as now, it took specialized skill to gain a hearing in the arena of public opinion.

OTHER THREADS

Still other threads in the fabric were first woven in the 1880's. The American fund-raising drive, an important task in PR today, was born in the Civil

27 Richard C. Overton, *Burlington West* (Cambridge: Harvard University Press, 1941), pp. 158-63.

28 *Ibid.*, pp. 298-303.

29 Forrest McDonald, *Insull* (Chicago: University of Chicago Press, 1962), pp. 44-45.

Subject **re information as to service, rates &c.**

Wm. R. DRIVER, Treasurer.

W.H. FORBES, President.   THE AMERICAN BELL TELEPHONE CO.   THEO. N. VAIL, General Manager.

Nº 95 MILK STREET.

P. O. DRAWER 2.

Personal

W. A. Leary, Esq.   *Boston,* **Dec. 28th, 1883.**
    Iowa Union Tel. & Tel. Co.
        Davenport, Iowa.   *In reply to yours* ⌐

Dear Sir : -   *No.*

        Now that the Telephone business has passed its ex-
perimental stage, I would like to get your opinion upon points giv-
en below. This opinion to be based upon our existing relations,
and upon your own and your associates observation and experience
in your particular field : -

        Is the Telephone service as it is now being furnish-
ed, satisfactory to the public.
        Are the prices satisfactory to the public, consider-
ing the facilities and service that is given.
        Would it be advantageous to furnish the same ser-
vice now being furnished at any lower rate provided it could
be done.
        Is it possible in view of the contingencies of storm,
under ground legislation &c., to make any lower rate to the
public for same classes of service.
        Is it desirable, and what would be the most practi-
cable way, to provide a service at a rate which would be within the reach of families. etc,.
        Is it practicable to give different classes of ser-
vice within the same Exchange.
        What has been the tendency of the relationship be-
tween the public and the local Co's., for the past year ie.,
are the relations between the public and the Co's. improving.
        Where there has been any conflict between the local
Exchange and the public, what has been the cause of the dif -
ficulties, and what has been the result.

        A full and detailed reply from you by the 8th, of
January, would be of great service to me. Trusting that I am not
asking too much,

        I am,

        Very respectfully, &c.

        Theo. N. Vail

War. Jay Cooke, "the first to understand the psychology of mass salesmanship," conceived and executed the first American fund-raising drive. "A propagandist of truly heroic proportions," Cooke sold war bonds for the Union by first selling patriotism and building a militant public opinion. Many of his techniques reappeared in the bond drives of World Wars I and II. Also, by the time of the Civil War the United States Marine Corps was using advertising on a regular basis to attract recruits. And in the Spanish-American War of 1898, the work of Cuban propagandists did much to arouse American sympathies for Cuba and to discredit Spain. This junta used press releases and mass meetings to raise funds and promote support for the Cuban cause from 1895 on.[30]

---

[30] Emery, *op. cit.* (in footnote 7), p. 432.

Even professional groups were taking cognizance of public opinion more than a century ago. In 1855 the American Medical Association passed a resolution "urging the secretary of the Association to offer every facility possible to the reporters of the public press to enable them to furnish full and accurate reports of the transactions." And in 1884 the A.M.A. launched the first of its many programs to counter the attacks of the antivivisectionists. And evidence that *public relations thinking* is not brand new is shown in the letter of Theodore N. Vail, rare for its time, reproduced on page 31. The Association of American Railroads claims that it was the first business organization to use the term "public relations"—in 1897 in the *Year Book of Railway Literature.*

Additional Reading

Edward L. Bernays, *Public Relations*. Norman, Okla.: University of Oklahoma Press, 1952. Part One: The Growth of Public Relations.

Carl Berger, *Broadsides and Bayonets*. Philadelphia: University of Pennsylvania Press, 1961. Deals with Revolutionary War propaganda.

Ray Allen Billington, *Words That Won the West*. New York: Foundation for Public Relations Research and Education, 1964.

N. S. B. Gras, *Shifts in Public Relations*. Monograph reprinted from *Bulletin of the Business Historical Society,* October 1945, Boston. Traces evolution of PR attitudes in business.

Ralph V. Harlow, *Samuel Adams: Promoter of the Revolution*. New York: Holt, Rinehart, & Winston, Inc., 1923.

Robert Lindsay, *This High Name: Public Relations and the U.S. Marine Corps.* Madison: University of Wisconsin Press, 1956. Traces history of pioneering military PR program in U.S.M.C.

Siegfried Mickelson, "Promotional Activities of the Northern Pacific's Land Department." *Journalism Quarterly,* Vol. 17, December, 1940.

John C. Miller, *Sam Adams Pioneer in Propaganda.* Boston: Little, Brown & Co., 1936; Palo Alto: Stanford University Press, 1960.

Charles L. Mowat, "The First Campaign of Publicity for Florida," *Mississippi Valley Historical Review,* Vol. 30, December, 1943.

Irving Wallace, *The Fabulous Showman: Life and Times of P. T. Barnum.* New York: Alfred A. Knopf, Inc., 1959.

"What Mr. Vanderbilt Says," *Railroad Gazette,* Vol. 14, October 13, 1882. (See page 627 for an account of famous interview, and page 649 for his denial.)

James Harvey Young, *The Toadstool Millionaires.* Princeton, N.J.: Princeton University Press, 1961.

Chapter Three

FROM

1900

ON—

THE

REAL

BEGINNINGS

I believe in telling your story to the people. If you go direct to the people and get them to agree with you . . . everybody else must give way in your favor.—Ivy Lee.

Although the roots of today's practice extend deeply into the sands of time, the *definite beginnings* date from the early 1900's, when the United States entered the wholly new, exciting, and eventful twentieth century. The dividing lines may be blurred, but the growth of public relations practice can be traced through five main periods of development:

(1) 1900-1917—The era of muckraking journalism countered by defensive publicity, a period of far-reaching political reforms; (2) 1917-1919—World War I which brought dramatic demonstrations of the power of organized promotion to kindle a fervent patriotism, to sell war bonds, and to raise millions for welfare work; (3) 1919-1933—This period saw the principles and practices of publicity learned in the war put to use promoting products, to earning acceptance of changes wrought by the war-accelerated technology, to winning political battles, and to raising of millions of dollars for charitable causes; (4) 1933-1945—The period of the Great Depression and World War II, events profound and far-reaching in their impact, which advanced the art and extended the practice of public relations; (5) 1945-present—The postwar era which has brought a tremendous boom in public relations practice and in a maturing concept of its vital function in the administration of today's organizations of size and complexity.

The excesses of the large corporations, railroads, banks, utilities, and other elements of the business world fed the fires of reform and protest as America moved into the twentieth century. The popular revolt against

33

business was inspired in large part by the astute political leadership of Theodore Roosevelt, Robert M. LaFollette, and Woodrow Wilson in capitalizing on public opinion aroused by the writings of David Graham Phillips, Lincoln Steffens, Upton Sinclair, Ida Tarbell, and others. These muckraking journalists effectively exploited the newly developed national forums provided by the popular magazines, national press services, and feature syndicates. Regier says, "Muckraking . . . was the inevitable result of decades of indifference to the illegalities and immoralities attendant upon the industrial development of America." [1] The period extended, roughly, from 1900 to 1912. The muckrakers took their case to the people and got action, a fact which shrewd observers fully noted. The agitation before 1900 had been primarily among farmers and laborers. Now the urban middle classes took up the cry against corruption in government and the abuses of Big Business. The little fish did not enjoy being swallowed by the big ones. These writers thundered out their denunciations in boldface in the popular magazines, which now had huge circulations. The impact of the growing mass media was coming to be felt. [2]

The muckraker was a key figure in the Progressive movement, which found its strength in the journalism of exposure. "Before there could be action, there must be information and exhortation. Grievances had to be given specific objects. These the muckraker supplied. It was muckraking that brought the diffuse malaise of the public into focus." [3] The work was dramatically begun by Thomas W. Lawson's *Frenzied Finance* appearing as a series in *McClure's Magazine* in 1903. Parrington says that the success of the Lawson series "proved that the fire was ready for the fat" and that a host of writers "fell to feeding the flames." Growing newspaper circulations and ten-cent magazines provided the vehicles. Ida Tarbell's *History of the Standard Oil Company* was described at the time as "a fearless unmasking of moral criminality masquerading under the robes of respectability and Christianity." Upton Sinclair's novel, *The Jungle,* exposed the foul conditions in the meat-packing industry. Both produced violent public reactions. Such exposures gave Big Business a black eye, the traces of which still linger. The public wave of protest and reform brought strict regulatory legislation and a wave of "trust-busting." Businessmen, long in the saddle, were forced to take the defensive. The corporations, the good ones with the ruthless ones, had lost contact with their publics. For a while they sat helplessly by, inarticulate and frustrated, waiting apprehensively for the next issue of *McClure's Magazine.*

Business leaders, so long accustomed to a veil of secrecy, felt the urge

---

[1] For full story, see C. C. Regier, *The Era of the Muckrakers* (Chapel Hill: University of North Carolina Press, 1932). For a generous sampling of these articles, see Arthur and Lila Weinberger, eds., *The Muckrakers* (New York: Simon and Schuster, Inc., 1961).

[2] Vernon L. Parrington, *Main Currents in American Thought* (New York: Harcourt, Brace & World, Inc., 1930), Vol. 3, pp. 404-5.

[3] Richard Hofstadter, *The Age of Reform* (New York: Alfred A. Knopf, Inc., 1955), p. 185.

to speak out in self-defense but did not know how to reach the people. Their first instinct was to turn to their advertising men and lawyers. In the first stages of the Muckraking Era, many great corporations sought to silence the attacks on them from the press by the judicious and calculated placement and withdrawal of advertising. Thus, the newly established advertising agency was early brought into public relations.

What was probably the nation's first public relations counseling firm was founded "in the early nineteen hundreds" in Boston by George V. S. Michaelis, a man with a "brilliant and restless mind," and Herbert Small, "a Harvard man with a highly developed literary sense." They took in a Thomas O. Marvin as a third partner some time later. Soon "drawn into this interesting enterprise" was a young reporter from the Boston *Herald,* James Drummond Ellsworth, who would later collaborate with Theodore N. Vail in building the pioneering public relations program of the American Telephone & Telegraph Co. Known as The Publicity Bureau, its stated purpose, according to Ellsworth, was "to do a general press agent business for as many clients as possible for as good pay as the traffic would bear." [4]

The Publicity Bureau came into national prominence in 1906, when it was employed by the nation's railroads to head off adverse regulatory legislation then being pushed in Congress by President Roosevelt. Ray Stannard Baker reported at the time: [5] "The fountainhead of public information is the newspaper. The first concern, then, of the railroad organization was to reach the newspapers. For this purpose a firm of publicity agents, with headquarters in Boston, was chosen. . . . Immediately the firm expanded. It increased its Boston staff; it opened offices in New York, Chicago, Washington, St. Louis, Topeka, Kansas . . . and it employed agents in South Dakota, California, and elsewhere. . . ." Baker records that The Publicity Bureau operated secretly, "careful not to advertise the fact that they are in any way connected with the railroads." This firm effectively used the tools of fact-finding, publicity, and personal contact to saturate the nation's press, particularly the weeklies, with the railroads' propaganda. The campaign was to little avail, however, because the Hepburn Act, a moderately tough regulatory measure, was passed in 1906.

Other industries took the cue and turned to the specialist who could tell the business story in the press, the newspaperman. It was a matter of fighting fire with fire. Thus began the large-scale recruitment of newspapermen to serve as interpreters for the corporations and institutions.[6]

For the most part, these ex-newspapermen in the employ of business

---

[4] In unpublished manuscript, "Unforgotten Men." In Mass Communications History Center, Wisconsin State Historical Society, Madison.

[5] Ray Stannard Baker, "Railroads on Trial," *McClure's Magazine,* Vol. 26, March, 1906, pp. 535-44.

[6] See: "The 'Publicity Men' of the Corporations," *World's Work,* Vol. 12, June, 1906, p. 7703.

countered with whitewash and press-agentry. On the whole, they demonstrated little grasp of the fundamental problems in the conflict. There were some exceptions. One of these was Ivy Ledbetter Lee.

IVY LEE

The astute young Lee, son of a Georgia minister and Princeton graduate, while a reporter covering the business world, shrewdly sized up the situation. He saw the possibilities of earning more money in the service of private organizations who were seeking a voice. After five years as a reporter, Lee quit his poorly paying job on *The World* in 1903 and went to work for the Citizen's Union. This was an organization supporting Seth Low's campaign for mayor of New York. Lee's work in this post led to a job in the press bureau of the Democratic National Committee during the 1904 campaign.

Ivy Lee had observed that the business policies of secrecy and silence were failing. He concluded that in order to be understood, corporations must become articulate, open their books, and take their case directly to the people. *The New York Times,* years later, observed: "Lee brought something new to the business of publicity. When he was a young . . . newspaperman . . . there were numerous press agents in town who promoted the theaters and stage stars, but there was no specialist in publicity for corporations who conferred on terms of equality with the boards of directors of great corporations. His life spanned that change, and he had much to do with the change."

Ivy Lee teamed up with George F. Parker, former Buffalo newspaperman and veteran political publicist, some time after the 1904 Presidential election to organize a public relations firm in New York City. Parker directed the publicity for Grover Cleveland's three campaigns for the Presidency, but Cleveland was not wise enough to use him as a press secretary during his two terms as president. In 1904 Parker was recalled to political battle to direct publicity for the Democratic National Committee in the futile campaign to unseat President Roosevelt. The young Lee was hired to assist Parker. Out of their association and conversations during the campaign came a decision to form a partnership. Another pioneer, Pendleton Dudley, who opened his office in 1909, recalls: [7] "Older than Lee and more widely experienced, Parker had quite definite ideas as to the practical functioning of an independent press agency and a sense of emergency about starting one. . . . Several clients were secured and the partnership prospered modestly for a year or more." However, the relationship of Lee and Parker was neither a profitable nor a happy one, and the firm dissolved in 1908 when Ivy Lee became the Pennsylvania Railroad's first publicity agent. That year Parker set up another partnership with C. A. Bridge, but this firm left no records in its small wake. Parker

---

[7] Pendleton Dudley, "Current Beginnings of PR," *Public Relations Journal,* Vol. 8, April, 1953, pp. 8-10.

wound up his career by serving as secretary for press and publicity for the Committee of the General Convention of the Protestant Episcopal Church from 1913 to 1919.

Ivy Lee, while working as a news reporter in Wall Street in the early years of muckraking, had sensed business' need for an articulate voice in the court of public opinion. Yet, in the early years of his publicity work, he found business-men unreceptive to his ideas. The rising tide of protest against business gave force to his arguments. In 1906 a large industry—anthracite coal—sought Lee's help after taking a licking in public. He became spokesman for the corporations. This role was to make him rich and influential and to gain for him the title of "father of public relations." Lee explained to all his prospective clients that secrecy was the cause of suspicion. He said he would not "press agent" them. Instead, he would attempt to advise them on how to correct their policies toward the public and to provide for favorable notices in the newspapers. Ivy Lee wrote the platitudes while they were fresh.

Lee, using the occasion of his appointment to represent George F. Baer and his associates in the anthracite coal strike, issued a "Declaration of Principles" which was to have a profound influence on the evolution of press-agentry into publicity and of publicity into public relations. Eric Goldman observes that this declaration "marks the emergence of a second stage of public relations. The public was no longer to be ignored, in the traditional manner of business, nor fooled, in the continuing manner of the press agent." *It was to be informed.* Lee's declaration, mailed to all city editors, reads: [8]

> This is not a secret press bureau. All our work is done in the open. We aim to supply news. This is not an advertising agency; if you think any of our matter ought properly to go to your business office, do not use it. Our matter is accurate. Further details on any subject treated will be supplied promptly, and any editor will be assisted most cheerfully in verifying directly any statement of fact. . . . In brief, our plan is, frankly and openly, on behalf of business concerns and public institutions, to supply to the press and public of the United States prompt and accurate information concerning subjects which it is of value and interest to the public to know about.

This statement was revolutionary for its time. It offers a sound guide to effective press relations today.

Lee put this new approach to work in the anthracite coal strike. The work of reporters assigned to cover the strike was enormously simplified because all channels of communication were open. Although the press was not permitted to be present during the strike conferences, Lee did provide reports after each meeting. Lee was among the first to use the "handout" system on a large scale. Lee's success in getting a good press for the coal operators led to the retention of Parker and Lee by the Pennsylvania Railroad in the summer of 1906. Lee handled this account.

During this period Lee was using the term *publicity,* which, in his think-

---

8 Quoted in Sherman Morse, "An Awakening in Wall Street," *American Magazine,* Vol. LXII, September, 1906, p. 460.

ing, was PR; but his concept steadily grew, and his success grew with it. In December, 1914, at the suggestion of Arthur Brisbane, Lee was appointed as a personal adviser to John D. Rockefeller, Jr. At the time, the Rockefellers were being savagely attacked for the strike-breaking activities of their Colorado Fuel and Iron Company. Thus began a long career for him in the service of the Rockefellers. His starting salary was $1,000 a month. Contrary to popular belief, Ivy Lee was not hired by John D. Rockefeller. Nor did Lee originate the elder Rockefeller's practice of giving shiny dimes to children. In fact, Rockefeller, Sr., did not approve his son's hiring of Lee, but he adhered to his long-standing promise not to interfere with the son's decisions. In his long service to the son, Lee did, in fact, provide many services to the founder of Standard Oil. It was during the Colorado strike that Upton Sinclair dubbed Lee "Poison Ivy," a term that was to plague him all his life. That same year another pioneer, George Creel, then a crusading journalist, attacked Lee as a "Poisoner of Public Opinion." Although his work for the Rockefellers is the most publicized, Lee served a number of clients in the years from 1919 until his death in 1934. He was counselor to the Guggenheims and promoted their interests in the American Smelting and Refining Co., the Chilean Nitrate of Soda Educational Bureau, the John Simon Guggenheim Memorial Foundation, and the Daniel Guggenheim Fund for the Promotion of Aeronautics. The latter foundation contributed much to the growth of commercial aviation in the 1920's. Lee's role in promoting the philanthropies of the Rockefellers and Guggenheims has been too little noted. He had other clients, but much of the work was handled by his staff.

Ivy Lee did much to lay the groundwork for today's practice. Although he did not use the term until at least 1919, Lee contributed many of the techniques and principles which practitioners follow today. He was among the first to realize the fallacy of publicity unsupported by good works and to reason that performance determines the kind of publicity a client gets. He saw the importance of humanizing business and continually stressed the human element. "I try to translate dollars and cents and stocks and dividends into terms of humanity." In his efforts to humanize wealthy businessmen and to put Big Business in the best possible light, Lee propelled the growth of publicity departments and trained publicity advisers in many institutions. And, in his 31 years as a public relations man, Lee changed the scope of what he did from "pure agency" to serving as "a brain trust for the businesses we work with." This work, he told his staff shortly before his death, amounted to "a new profession." Ivy Lee made a substantial contribution by establishing and publicizing the idea that there is a potential of great service in public relations counseling.[9] Lee, one of the craft's most forceful spokesmen, made an occupation of public relations by his practice and by his preachments.

---

[9] See his obituary in *Editor & Publisher*, Vol. 67, November 7, 1934, p. 18. For Lee's fumbling effort to define his work, see "The Duties of an 'Advisor' in Public Relations," *Printers' Ink*, Vol. 140, July 7, 1927, pp. 73-74.

Lee's record, although substantial, is not free from criticism. When he died, he was under public criticism for his representation of the German Dye Trust, controlled by I. G. Farben, after Hitler came to power in Germany and the Nazis had taken control of this cartel. The record does show that he never received pay from the Nazi government directly. Lee was paid an annual fee of $25,000 and expenses by the Farben firm from the time he was retained in 1933 until his firm resigned the account shortly after his death in 1934. Just before his death, Lee explained that his relationship with the German I. G. Farben came about as a broadening of his relationship with the American I. G. Farben, a subsidiary of the German concern. Lee told a congressional committee: [10] "My relationship with them has been confined to advising the officers of the German Dye Trust as to what I considered to be American reactions to what had taken place in Germany and as to what, if anything, could be done about it." The record indicates that Farben hired Lee more in an effort to moderate the policies of the Nazi government than to function as a propaganda agent.[11] Lee's role in this case is still a matter of dispute. The propriety of American public relations firms representing foreign nations in this country remains a troublesome issue to this day.[12]

The same year that flinty George Baer hired Ivy Lee to help him battle John Mitchell's United Mineworkers, John D. Rockefeller came to admit the need of a publicity man to defend him in the public prints. Businessman Rockefeller never appeared to mind criticism, but Philanthropist Rockefeller was cut to his Baptist quick by the accusation that his philanthropies were a transparent means of buying public favor. When the "tainted money" issue flared anew in 1905, Rockefeller was hurt and angered. His philanthropic adviser, Rev. Frederick T. Gates, urged him to abandon his policies of secrecy. "While replying frigidly to Gates, Rockefeller gave way. He asked Gates to see (John D.) Archbold; and it turned out that he had sent Gates' letter to the head of Standard, and had frankly yielded the whole question." [13] This led to the employment of Joseph Ignatius Constantine Clarke, colorful Irish newsman, as "Publicity Agent" for the Standard Oil Company in 1906 at the then high salary of $5,000 a year. Clarke tried hard to refurbish the company's reputation. He served the parent Standard company until its final dissolution in 1914.

In this same period equally important public relations developments were

---

10 For testimony on this case, see *Investigation of Nazi and Other Propaganda: Public Hearings Before a Subcommittee of the Committee on Un-American Activities,* Hearings Numbers 73-NY-7 (Washington, D.C.: U.S. Government Printing Office, 1934).

11 *Trials of War Criminals Before the Nuernberg Military Tribunal,* Volumes VII and VIII, Case Six, *U. S. v. Krauch,* "The I. G. Farben Case" (Washington: Government Printing Office, 1953).

12 For a current look at this problem, see *Activities of Nondiplomatic Representatives of Foreign Principals in the United States,* Hearings before Committee on Foreign Relations, United States Senate, Parts 1-13, 1963 (Washington: U. S. Government Printing Office, 1963).

13 Allan Nevins, *John D. Rockefeller* (New York: Charles Scribner's Sons, 1940), Vol. II, p. 547.

taking place outside the business community. In 1904 Willard G. Bleyer, pioneer journalism educator, set up one of the first press bureaus in a university at the University of Wisconsin. The whirlwind high-pressure campaign to raise money for charitable causes was first fabricated in 1905 in Washington, D.C., by Y.M.C.A. fund raisers Charles Sumner Ward and Lyman L. Pierce in a drive to raise $350,000 for a Y.M.C.A. building. This initial whirlwind drive intensively demonstrated the power of publicity; for the first time, a full-time publicist was used in a fund drive. The Y's successful techniques were soon utilized in the annual appeals of churches, colleges, civic centers, and health and welfare agencies.

In 1908, the first of health associations to appeal for public gifts, the National Tuberculosis Association, established a Publicity Bureau. That same year the American Red Cross hired its first publicity man. The United States Marine Corps established a publicity bureau in Chicago in 1907 under Captain William C. Harllee, thus paving the way for today's large-scale public relations programs in our military services. There were undoubtedly others specializing in the field in these early years. Each appears to have broken his own ground. There was no sense or spirit of an organized calling in those days.

That publicity had grown to considerable dimensions in these first few years of the new century is reflected in the growing concern of newspapermen about the "perils of publicity." Don C. Seitz, business manager of *The New York World,* reported to the 1909 convention of the American Newspaper Publishers Association that the number of press agents was growing, that some were making from $6,000 to $12,000 a year—high pay in those years. "Everybody was employing them; even the New York Orphan Asylum was paying a publicity man $75 a month. The advertising agencies—Albert Frank and Company, Lord & Thomas, N. W. Ayer & Son, J. Walter Thompson—had set up publicity departments which took fees for their services, fees diverted from the advertiser's newspaper advertising budget. Automobile manufacturers were sending a page of material each day to the *World,* and the cement, food, insurance, utilities, and other businesses were equally busy." [14]

Another public relations agency that traces its origins back to the first decade of this century is the Hamilton Wright Organization. The first Hamilton Wright, after working many years for the Hearst papers, was hired to do "promotional writing" for the Philippines in 1908 during the tenure of General Leonard Wood. Wright formally organized his agency in 1920 when he established an office on Park Row in New York City. That year his son, now head of the agency, joined him. Their big account was Florida promotion for the Flagler System during the time that the railroad was being extended from St. Augustine to Miami. The son, Hamilton Wright, Jr., served for nearly 20 years as publicity director for the City of Miami. This agency

---

14 Edwin Emery, *History of American Newspaper Publishers Association* (Minneapolis: University of Minnesota Press, 1950). See pp. 125-30.

came to specialize in the representation of foreign nations in the United States. It came to national attention during the Fulbright Committee Hearings in 1963 for its work on behalf of Chiang's China and South Africa.

Pioneer Pendleton Dudley maintains, with considerable reason, that it is a gross oversimplification to explain the beginnings as a counterattack of Big Business against the muckrakers. He says that this conclusion is "hardly justified by the facts." Mr. Dudley admits that such attacks did play their part, but he holds that the dawning recognition of news and its force on public opinion was more basic. "On the side of business it was an awareness that news, in all its aspects, had become a fresh, strong determinant of public behavior" that induced the employment of publicity specialists.[15] Surely it is significant that virtually all the pioneers, from Amos Kendall on, had been recruited from the nation's newspapers. This substantiates the theory that the growth of the mass media was a basic factor in creating the need for the skilled communicator and intermediary with the press, a fact still evident today.

The part played by President Theodore Roosevelt in spurring the evolution also has been too little noted. The colorful, swashbuckling President was a master with the art and power of publicity. He used that knowledge and skill to gain his political ends. Observers at the time claimed that Roosevelt ruled the country from the front pages of the newspapers. One of Roosevelt's first acts upon assuming the Presidency was to seek an understanding with the working press. One veteran newsman, David S. Barry, later observed: Roosevelt "knew the value and potent influence of a news paragraph written as he wanted it written and disseminated through the proper influential channels. . . ." A *Harper's Weekly* article of that time was titled "Theodore Roosevelt: Press Agent."

With the growth of mass-circulation newspapers, Roosevelt's canny ability to dominate the front pages was a new-found power for those with causes to promote. He had a keen sense of news and knew how to stage a story so that it would get maximum attention. Not only did Theodore Roosevelt set patterns, but his skill forced those whom he fought to develop similar means. Using these skills, Roosevelt advertised and dramatized to the country a point of view that was new and exciting. Frederick Lewis Allen said that this was Theodore Roosevelt's "most vital contribution to American history." His success brought many imitators.

This period, 1900-1917, saw an intensive development of the skills by the railroads and the public utilities. These businesses, particularly the local transit companies, were the first to feel the blistering heat of angered public opinion and to be brought under public regulation. The Interstate Commerce Act had set the pattern. In a five-year period, 1908-1913, more than 2,000 laws affecting railroads were enacted by state legislatures and by Congress. From 1897 on,

---

15 Pendleton Dudley, *op. cit.* Among Dudley's first clients was Trinity Episcopal Church, then caught in the muckrakers' fire, which tends to refute his view.

Ivy Lee

Edward L. Bernays

George Creel

Paul Garrett

Arthur W. Page

John W. Hill

the term *public relations* appeared with increasing frequency in railroad literature and in speeches of railroad men. In 1909 the *Railway Age Gazette* pleaded
for "better public relations" in an editorial entitled, "Wanted: A Diplomatic
Corps." On June 26, 1913, J. Hampton Baumgartner, another pioneer, gave
a talk to the Virginia Press Association on "The Railroads and Public Relations." He was hired in 1910 to be "in charge of publicity and public relations of the Baltimore & Ohio Railroad." Baumgartner explained that railroads had, in response to the wave of agitation which had crystallized into
antagonism, "endeavored to establish closer relations with the public, chiefly
through the medium of the press and with its cooperation." The Pere Mar-
quette Railroad in 1916 set up a full-fledged department, an innovation
among railroads duly noted at the time.

One of the first known efforts to define the practice was presented before
the American Street and Interurban Railway Association in Atlantic City in
1907 by its "Committee on Public Relations." In 1912, James H. McGraw,
writing in the *Electric Railway Journal,* advocated the open-door policy for
utilities.[16]

> In the most acute and difficult public relations in which railway managers
> find themselves there is, I believe, always the inner conviction that if the merits
> of the case could be conveyed to the public and its law makers, mercy at least,
> and possibly justice, could be obtained. The only medium of such communica-
> tion is educational publicity.

Henry Ford pioneered in the ways of public relations as well as in the
making and selling of cars. He was quick to see the value of product publicity
in selling mass consumer goods. His work dramatized the worth of publicity
as a supplement to paid advertising. Practitioner David Lewis, who has
chronicled Ford's public relations story says: "The industrialist is revealed
. . . as perhaps the most astute self-advertiser in the whole history of a land
that has produced its full share of promoters and showmen." From 1908 on,
Ford and his associates sought publicity, in sharp contrast to their publicity-
shy business contemporaries of that era.

Ford sensed the value of racing events in publicizing performance of his
new gas buggies. The house organ, *Ford Times,* was started in 1908 "to introduce hints among members of the Ford organization." Ford was among
the first to use opinion surveys to give him guidance in marketing his cars. In
1912 he had 1,000 Model T owners queried as to why they had bought Fords.
Interestingly enough, 842 of them reported that they had bought the car on
the recommendation of a friend who had one. He organized Ford owners into
clubs, as another promotional device. Ford pulled out all publicity stops in
heralding announcement of his $5 a day for an eight-hour day in 1914, a story
that was to shake the industrial community and make him a world-known
figure.

The pattern for the early development is illustrated in a study of the

---

16 See article entitled "Publicity," Vol. 39, July 1, 1912, p. 151.

American Telephone and Telegraph Company, one of the first firms to develop a PR program. It organized its first press bureau in Boston, around 1890. It was officially termed a "literary bureau." In 1900 the tactless, ruthless John E. Hudson retired as its president. Theodore N. Vail returned as a director in 1902 and the policies today identified with A. T. & T. began to take shape. These policies were brought to the fore when Vail became president in 1907. A program was undertaken to eliminate public criticism through efficient operation. Consideration for the needs of subscribers was directed. A systematic method of answering complaints was put into effect. Unlike other utilities, Bell did not fight public regulation. Bell accepted it as a necessary price for monopoly. Vail and Ellsworth, working in cooperation with the N. W. Ayer agency, pioneered in the extensive use of institutional advertising.

WORLD WAR I
AND GEORGE CREEL

Contemporary practice first emerged as a defensive measure. But World War I gave it great offensive impetus. George Creel and his effective Committee on Public Information demonstrated, as never before, the power of mass publicity and the techniques of mobilizing opinion. Creel emphasized the positive approach. The Liberty Loan drives, although based primarily on advertising techniques, taught businessmen and other executives how public relations practices could be used effectively. The Creel committee trained a host of practitioners who took their wartime experiences and fashioned them into a profitable calling. Among these were Carl Byoir and Edward L. Bernays. Byoir, who at 28 rose to the associate chairmanship of the CPI, after a decade's detour in other endeavors, founded in 1930 what today is one of the nation's largest public relations firms. Bernays became the articulate advocate of public relations.

The Committee on Public Information was set up by President Wilson in response to a suggestion from Creel, a journalist friend and supporter of Wilson. President Wilson himself was master of the art and knew the value of using the agencies of communication. Creel naturally was chosen to direct this committee. The subsequent events are well described in Creel's book, *How We Advertised America,* and by Mock and Larson in *Words That Won the War.*[17]

> Mr. Creel assembled as brilliant and talented a group of journalists, scholars, press agents, editors, artists, and other manipulators of the symbols of public opinion as America had ever seen united for a single purpose. It was a gargantuan advertising agency the like of which the country had never known, and the breath-taking scope of its activities was not to be equalled until the rise of

17 James O. Mock and Cedric Larson, *Words That Won the War* (Princeton, N. J.: Princeton University Press, 1939), p. 4.

the totalitarian dictatorships after the war. George Creel, Carl Byoir, Edgar Sisson, Harvey O'Higgins, Guy Stanton Ford, and their famous associates were literally public relations counselors to the United States Government, carrying first to the citizens of this country and then to those in distant lands the ideas which gave motive power to the stupendous undertaking of 1917-1918.

Plowing new ground, Creel's successful demonstration was to have a profound impact on the American culture. As Bernays later commented, "It was the war which opened the eyes of the intelligent few in all departments of life to the possibilities of regimenting the public mind." Analyzing the influence of the Creel committee in spurring the growth of what it still termed "press agents," the *New York Times* commented in 1920: [18]

> Essentially the species, if not a war product, is one which the war has mightily increased. Liberty Loans had to be advertised throughout the country. Publicity did that. Five times, at short intervals, the newspapers of the nation stepped into line and "put across" to the man at the breakfast table, and in his office, in the factory, in the mine—in every phase of commerce and industry, in fact, the need of digging down deep into his pocket and "coming across." It worked. Beautifully and efficiently. Not only did he have a staff of press agents working immediately under him in a central office, but [Creel] decentralized the system so that every type of industry in the country had its special group of publicity workers. In this manner, more than in any other, were the heads and directors of movements of every type introduced to and made cognizant of the value of concentrating on publicity in so-called "drives."

It should be noted, however, that press-agentry and publicity, as distinguished from public relations, grew even more rapidly after the war. This growth was mostly a corollary, although the line of demarcation may be a fuzzy one. In the immediate postwar years, men who had gained experience under Creel or had observed the efficacy of Creel's techniques carried their knowledge back into civilian life. They began hammering out a new profession—even though it was still dimly seen.

BETWEEN TWO WORLD WARS

Vigorously generated by the wartime developments, this new specialty quickly spread. It showed up in government, business, the churches, social work—now burgeoning in the war's aftermath—the labor movement, and social movements. The victory of the Anti-Saloon League in gaining national prohibition provided fresh evidence of the new-found power. The coercions compelling the development of this practice had also been enormously multiplied. The process of industrialization and urbanization had been pushed several notches further during the war. Things began moving at a faster clip.

With the war over and his duties with the American Red Cross ended,

---

18 *New York Times,* Feb. 1, 1920, p. 9, col. 1.

Ivy Lee resumed his practice in a newly organized counseling firm, Ivy Lee & Associates. Included was T. J. Ross, who joined the firm in 1919 and became an influential figure in his own right. In 1961, when Ivy's son, James, retired from his father's firm, this agency took the name of T. J. Ross and Associates.

Among those vying with Ivy Lee for prominence and for business in the 1920's was Bernays, long a central and controversial figure in this craft, who retired in 1962. Bernays was born in Vienna but was brought to New York City by his parents when he was still an infant. Bernays' mother was a sister of Sigmund Freud. Later Bernays also became a nephew-in-law of the famous psychologist when Freud married a sister of Bernays' father. His first effort at press-agentry, performed for Richard Bennett's sexy play *Damaged Goods,* opened young Bernays' eyes to the power of publicity. Prior to World War I, Bernays worked as a press agent, serving, among others, the great Caruso. He worked for the Creel committee during the war. There his busy mind was envisioning the possibilities of making a life's work of "engineering public consent," as he terms it.

Bernays coined the term *public relations counsel* in his landmark book, *Crystallizing Public Opinion,* the first on public relations. Published in 1923, this book and others reflected the booming growth in this postwar period. Bernays broke more new ground the same year when he taught the first PR course at New York University. Bernays' book was preceded by one year by Walter Lippmann's classic *Public Opinion,* a book that has had a profound influence in this field. Lippmann reflected the awakening interest in the nature and power of opinion generated by the war. There were some 18 books on public opinion, publicity, and public relations printed in all the years prior to 1917, but at least 28 titles were published between 1917 and 1925. In 1921 the Library of Congress published a bibliography, the first one on the subject, *List of References on Publicity, with special reference to press agents.*

Equally influential has been the scholarly interest of social scientists which dates from this period. Here began the shift of interest from the power to the nature of public opinion and the role of communications in its formation. The work of social scientists in studying public opinion, analyzing propaganda, and observing the work of pressure groups in society has contributed much. Market research, social surveys, and public opinion polls gained headway during the postwar years. General Foods, a market research pioneer, set up a panel of homemakers in 1926 to test recipes for jams and jellies. The Lynds' historic social survey, *Middletown,* was made in 1925. The *Literary Digest* made its first presidential election poll in 1916. This poll had its heyday in the 1920's. Development of sound opinion-measurement methods was slow until the 1930's, but there were earlier beginnings.

Many other rapid-fire developments occurred in this postwar period. A number of new counseling firms were established alongside the existing ones of Dudley, Lee, and Bernays. In 1919 John Price Jones established his firm to direct fund-raising campaigns and to provide publicity service to corporations. Over the years, Jones made more money and gained more fame as a fund raiser than as a public relations counselor. When he started his firm, he billed it as "Organization and Publicity Counsel." He retired in 1956. In 1923 Harry A. Bruno, long-time aviation enthusiast and wartime flier, set up a PR in partnership with Richard Blythe after the airline that Bruno was working for went broke. Most of Bruno's early clients were makers of airplane motors and instruments, and he aided them by promoting aviation. Bruno broke into national prominence when he and Blythe handled the press relations for young Charles A. Lindbergh's historic flight across the Atlantic in May, 1927. Bruno's publicity and public relations projects did much to speed America's acceptance of the Air Age.

In 1926 William Baldwin, after serving an apprenticeship in a shipbuilding firm and as a fund raiser, opened a public relations agency that was to serve corporate and civil clients—many of the latter gratis—over the next 35 years. Baldwin recalls that there were only six firms listed in the Manhattan telephone directory when he started. The next year, 1927, John W. Hill, Cleveland newsman, started a firm in that city. In 1933 he formed a partnership with Don Knowlton. A short time later Hill moved to New York to found Hill & Knowlton, Inc. Knowlton remained in Cleveland to run Hill and Knowlton of Cleveland. The two firms, connected only by overlapping ownership, operated independently until 1964. That year Knowlton retired and the Cleveland office was sold to a successor firm.

Similarly, advertising agencies started moving into the field as product publicity became an important aspect of marketing. A few advertising agencies had set up publicity sections prior to the war. Now more were moving into this growing and lucrative field. The 1909 Seitz report noted that there were four agencies with publicity departments at that time. In the 1920's more developed this service for both advertiser clients and nonclients. Hower noted this in his history of the Ayer Agency, the pioneer in this development: [19]

> In some respects the Ayer agency entered the field of public relations about 1900 when it began to handle the advertising of such large concerns at the National Biscuit Company and the Standard Oil Company, for it soon had to take account of the attitude of the public toward these "big business" institutions. The agency strove to obtain goodwill principally by the use of advertising, but inevitably it was compelled to prepare publicity material as part of its regular work and also to prepare news releases. By 1920 the firm had a well-organized publicity bureau which became increasingly important during the next decade.

This period saw definite beginnings of institutional advertising as a PR tool. Probably the oldest continuous public relations advertising campaign is that of the Illinois Central Railroad which was started Sept. 1, 1920. These ads sought, in the words of IC's president, "promotion of a better understanding and closer relationship with the patrons of our lines." A latter-day successor, commenting in 1960 on the completion of 40 years' continuous advertising,

---

[19] Ralph M. Hower, *The History of an Advertising Agency* (Cambridge: Harvard University Press, 1939), pp. 297-98.

said: "We believe this program, which we have often termed 'an investment in understanding,' has done much to take the mystery out of railroading. Taking the public into our confidence has earned many friends for the Illinois Central through Mid-America." In 1922, the Metropolitan Life Insurance Company started its good-health campaign, a series that also is still going. In 1923 General Motors began to use advertising to sell GM as an institution. (GM did not set up a PR department until 1931, when it brought in Paul Garrett, another influential pioneer who retired January 1, 1957.) In 1921 the American Association of Engineers held its first national conference on public information. Later it published the proceedings in a book entitled *Publicity Methods for Engineers*. Another development of the early 1920's was the wholesale adoption of the Creel techniques by the notorious Samuel Insull and his cohorts in the utilities industry. Insull sparked a movement, beginning in 1919, to convince the American people of the blessings of his particular private ownerships.[20]

During the same period a more creditable development was taking place in higher education. A handful of major universities and colleges had set up press bureaus prior to the war. More did so in the early 1920's, generally as an adjunct of a capital fund-raising drive. In March 1915, T. T. Frankenberg, then publicity director for the Western College for Women, Oxford, Ohio, planted the first seed for the American College Public Relations Association. Frankenberg's idea of a meeting for "an exchange of ideas that might be helpful" to those in college publicity did not take root until April 1917. In that year he was able to stimulate sufficient interest to effect an organization, the Association of American College News Bureaus.

It is indicative of this period that this name was selected only after vigorous debate. A strong minority wished to be known frankly as college publicity workers. The more conservative members prevailed. The "taint" of publicity in higher education was avoided! The outbreak of war soon vitiated this movement. It was not until the 1920's that it came alive again. At the 1925 convention, the organization took on vigor and strength, reflecting the growth of the practice in higher education. Symbolic of the growth in ensuing years, the organization's name in 1930 was changed to the American College Publicity Association and in May 1946 to the American College Public Relations Association.

After World War I, the interest and utilization of publicity techniques spilled over into the new field of social work. This, likewise, had been given great impetus by the war and by the dislocations the war produced. As more and more money had to be raised to meet more and more needs of an urban

---

[20] For this unsavory page in PR history, see *Utility Corporations: Efforts by Associations and Agencies of Electric and Gas Utilities to Influence Public Opinion,* A Summary Report Prepared by the Federal Trade Commission, 70th Congress, 1st Session (Senate Document 92, part 71-A) (Washington: U.S. Government Printing Office). A popular summary of this probe is Ernest Gruening's *The Public Pays,* published in 1931 by the Vanguard Press. Also see Forrest McDonald's *Insull,* cited in Chap. Two (footnote 28).

society, there was growing recognition of the importance of publicity and of the need for trained publicists. Advancement of social work publicity was spearheaded by Evart G. and Mary Swain Routzahn of the Russell Sage Foundation. The Routzahns played a key role in the birth of the National Publicity Council for welfare agencies and of a Health Education Section in the American Public Health Association in the early 1920's. What was first a committee on publicity methods in social work became, in 1922, the National Publicity Council for Welfare Services. From its inception in 1922 until 1940, the Council was the vehicle of the Routzahns and was used by them to transport new ideas, new techniques, and missionary zeal to the novices in health and welfare publicity work. The Community Chest movement which burgeoned after the war also provided employment for a growing number of publicists.

Religious leaders, too, sensed the changing times. They saw the value and need of publicity and public relations in the service of the churches. In 1918, the National Lutheran Council launched a strong national church publicity program. Later that same year the Catholic Church, operating through the Knights of Columbus, organized a publicity bureau with John B. Kennedy as its director. *The New York Times* noted at the time, "They are quite frank in admitting that the 'biggest and most practical human lesson learned from the war is that nothing requiring organized effort can succeed without publicity and plenty of it.' " The quotes were attributed to Kennedy. The Y.M.C.A. and Y.W.C.A. had long had publicity staffs, and they formed something of a nucleus for the spread of organized church publicity.[21] Astute leaders everywhere were observing this "most practical human lesson from the war."

Propelled by the wartime lessons and the changing nature of the American environment, the practice moved full speed ahead until the stock-market crash in 1929. The ensuing Depression marks another milestone. Bernays writes of this period, 1919-1929: [22]

> At first, the techniques proven in the Great War were applied to organization drives for universities, colleges and hospitals. Later, industrial enterprises like General Motors, General Electric, American Telephone and Telegraph and others used them. Nationwide and even international publicity festivities took place. . . . Industry began to recognize the importance of public interest activities. Foundations, research institutions and general laboratories of individual businesses and of associations were conducted in the glare of publicity. . . . Industrial leaders groped, set the pace. Others followed as best they could. This period saw the initiation and growth of the independent public relations organizations. All of which set the stage for the revolution in public relations, started in 1929. The new trend has been marked by the idea that the private and public interest must coincide; that public relations activities must further this new orientation.

---

21 The Seventh-day Adventist denomination had opened a National Publicity Bureau in 1912 in what may have been the first organized church public relations program in the U.S.
22 E. L. Bernays, *Public Relations* (Boston: Bellman Publishing Co., 1945), p. 11.

The catastrophic Depression and Franklin D. Roosevelt's New Deal generated a fuller and broader development in many fields. Like his distant cousin before him, F.D.R. coupled strong leadership with consummate skill to harness the forces of protest into an effective political coalition. Roosevelt won his battles on the front pages and over the radio, a new medium which he used with matchless skill. Roosevelt's adroit moves in the public arena can be credited in large part to his unsung public relations mentor, Louis McHenry Howe. The astute, tough-minded Louis Howe served F.D.R. faithfully and effectively from 1912 until his death in 1936. He gave his life to being Roosevelt's right-hand man and did much to advance Roosevelt to the White House.[23] F.D.R.'s success in winning public support spurred the efforts of the conservative forces, particularly the business community, to counter his appeals. A new trend set in, marked by acceptance of an institution's or industry's social responsibility. It was increasingly realized that profitable public relationships could be built only by coupling responsible performance with persuasive publicity. Such a cataclysmic event as the Depression was bound to produce a sharp readjustment of values.

Events flowing from the Depression and the New Deal brought home to every group the need for building informed public support. The New Dealers soon found that this was essential to pave the way for their radical reforms. Government public relations had its greatest expansion under Franklin Roosevelt. School administrators were made to realize the dangers of an uninformed public as hard-pressed taxpayers chopped off "the frills" in education. The Depression brought a tremendous expansion in social welfare needs and agencies. These administrators, too, came to realize the need for better public understanding. Military leaders, looking apprehensively at the build-up of the Nazi and Fascist war machines, began to promote support for more adequate armed forces. Colleges and universities, caught in the web of financial woes, turned more and more to public relations to win contributions and to recruit students.

Business leaders turned increasingly to public relations men for help in fighting against Roosevelt's biting criticisms and his legislative reforms. There was a marked trend away from occasional and defensive efforts. There was a marked trend toward more positive and continuous programs executed by newly established departments. A growing labor movement, too, soon found that it had problems and needed guidance. Growth was stimulated all along the line by the social and economic upheavals of the Depression.

WORLD WAR II

The onrush of World War II produced more violent changes in our environment. It accelerated this trend. Once more the government led the way,

---

[23] For a balanced view of Howe's contributions to F.D.R.'s career, see Alfred B. Rollins, Jr., *Roosevelt and Howe* (New York: Alfred A. Knopf, Inc., 1962).

with a breath-taking demonstration of the power of an organized informational campaign. This time it was called the Office of War Information. The capable Elmer Davis was its director. Davis and the O.W.I. set the pace for extensive expansion of the practice in the armed forces, in industry, and in allied fields. More techniques were developed. Many more practitioners were trained in this gigantic program, which completely dwarfed the Creel committee.

In industry emphasis was put on PR to spur war production by promoting productivity and combating absenteeism. There were equally challenging tasks that could best be met by specialists. This, plus the excess profits tax then in effect, speeded organization of new departments in industry. War bonds had to be sold. Material and manpower had to be conserved. Rationing had to be imposed. Morale of those at the front and those at home had to be bolstered during the long, hard sacrifice of war. All these required intensive efforts. Lack of goods to sell and the need to keep the company name before the public spurred wider use of public-service advertising. Employee publications had their greatest growth during the war. In the expanded armed forces, thousands of men and women were recruited and trained in public relations. Everywhere more and more people discovered the value of the art. In World War II, practitioners were confronted with new challenges and new opportunities. That they proved their worth is indicated by the booming growth of the practice which later ensued.

The accelerating developments from World War II on have been the most extensive yet recorded. Reasons for this growth will be underlined in the next chapter.

Additional Reading

Roscoe C. E. Brown, "Menace to Journalism," *North American Review,* Vol. 214, November, 1921. (For reply and rebuttal to this harsh indictment of "press agents," see same publication, Vol. 215, February, 1922.)

Roger Burlingame, *Don't Let Them Scare You—The Life and Times of Elmer Davis.* Philadelphia: J. B. Lippincott Company, 1961.

James I. C. Clarke, *My Life and Memories.* New York: Dodd, Mead & Co., 1926.

George Creel, *How We Advertised America.* New York: Harper & Row, Publishers, 1920.

————, *Rebel at Large.* New York: G. P. Putnam's Sons, 1947. His autobiography.

John Gunther, *Taken at the Flood—The Story of Albert D. Lasker.* New York: Harper & Row, Publishers, 1960. Biography of America's pioneer advertising man, who made many public relations innovations.

John W. Hill, *The Making of a Public Relations Man.* New York: David McKay & Co., Inc., 1963. Part autobiography, part philosophy by one of PR's pioneers.

Peter Lyon, *Success Story: The Life and Times of S. S. McClure.* New York: Charles Scribner's Sons, 1963. Biography of the architect of the muckraking movement.

Evelyn Roat, "Current Trends in Public Relations," *Public Opinion Quarterly,* Vol. 3, July, 1939.

George K. Turner, "Manufacturing Public Opinion," *McClure's,* Vol. 39, July, 1912.

Henry A. Turner, "Woodrow Wilson and Public Opinion," *Public Opinion Quarterly,* Vol. 21, Winter, 1957-58.

"Utilities Abandon Propaganda Work," *Editor & Publisher,* Vol. 65, February 18, 1933.

S. H. Walker and Paul Sklar, *Business Finds Its Voice.* New York: Harper & Row, Publishers, 1938. (Reissue of articles in *Harper's Magazine* for issues of January, February, and March, 1938.)

Franklyn Waltman, "Corporate Public Relations Comes of Age," *Public Relations Journal,* Vol. 11, October, 1955.

Chapter Four

ECOLOGY—

THE

PR

ENVIRONMENT

The public relations specialist has been produced by the urgent needs of his time. His function will grow in scope and importance as the American environment accelerates in interdependence and complexity.

The function of public relations will continue to grow in scope and importance as the American environment accelerates in interdependence and complexity. And accelerate it will. Once the needs are understood, PR's purpose and place become clear. Moreover, as the nature of the function as a direct response to its environment unfolds, its inevitability and permanence can be easily seen.

Webster's Dictionary defines *ecology* as "the mutual relations, collectively, between organisms and their environment." Ecology, which deals with the interrelationships of living organisms and their environment, is used mainly in the life sciences. However, social scientists have found it an increasingly useful term to describe the interrelationships of environment and human institutions. We find it so in this effort to relate the practice to the environment which brought the developments summarized in Chapters Two and Three.

Any public enterprise, to prosper and endure today, must (1) accept the obligations of public responsibility imposed by an increasingly interdependent society; (2) find ways and means of communicating with unseen, remote publics over lines lengthened by physical distance and psychological difference and complicated by multiplying barriers to communication; (3) find ways of achieving integration into the community that the organization was created to serve. In point 1 we find the source of *public relations thinking* in management enterprises. In point 2 we find the reason for the growth of PR as a *specialized staff function*. In point 3 we find the *objective* of both the management philosophy and the specialized practice.

"THE BIG CHANGE"

The first six decades of the twentieth century brought an avalanche of· change that transformed the world beyond the wildest dreams of those who turned the calendar to this century when the buggy was the means of local transportation. America has steadily and swiftly moved from an agrarian society of small towns, small organizations, and face-to-face relationships. America has become an industrial society of big cities, big organizations, and impersonal relationships. Frederick Lewis Allen described this as "The Big Change." [1] *Fortune* has termed it "The Permanent Revolution," in which a free people broke the power of capital as their master and put it to work as their servant.[2] The net result of these complex forces has been the creation of a comfortable, fluid society of massive bigness, impersonality, and interdependence.

Today's world is a world of complex organizations, big structures, and societies of scale. These are the result of several basic trends. These trends—all of which have profound implications for public relations—include: (1) the world's population explosion brought about by an increasing birth rate and conquest of disease; (2) urbanization, which sees more and more people being jammed into large metropolitan complexes, creating new frictions and complex community problems; (3) the scientific explosion, which has propelled America from the Age of the Auto to the Age of the Atom to the Age of Aerospace in a few breath-taking years; (4) automation of production of goods, which profoundly affects the nature of work, requirements for work, and the problems of investment capital and marketing; (5) the rising level of education stimulated by rising requirements for specialized knowledge and rising social expectations in a middle-class society; (6) the social revolution in the United States, which is bringing integration in all phases of American life in fulfillment of the Constitution's pledge of equality for all; (7) separation of ownership and control in American industry, with the replacement of the entrepreneur by the professional manager who manages with precision and planning.

These continuing trends are bringing changes great in number and magnitude faster than society can successfully adapt to them. Progress comes through change. Gaining acceptance and adaptation to change is a difficult task. Tension inevitably accompanies change. The long, bitterly fought battle over "featherbedding" in American railroads is but one example. These ever-accelerating changes are still in motion. The problems they pose offer great challenge to those skilled in communication, mediation, and persuasion.

We have moved in some six decades to a segmented, stratified society of separateness. It is also a society dominated by science and technology. This

---

[1] Frederick Lewis Allen, *The Big Change: America Transforms Itself, 1900-1950* (New York: Harper & Row, Publishers, 1952). A readable, informative account of these changes.

[2] Editors of *Fortune, USA: The Permanent Revolution* (Englewood Cliffs, N.J.: Prentice-Hall, Inc., 1951).

has made the communications task ever more difficult. One writer put it in the extreme when he wrote that we have reached the point where there is no communication between "the masses" and "the elite." [3] A thoughtful publisher, Alfred A. Knopf, doubts that the activities of today's business corporation can be made meaningful to more than a handful of its shareholders, because the corporations "are all operating today in fields so highly technical that the average layman cannot understand what they are doing, much less its significance, no matter how simple the language." A communications researcher suggests, "Perhaps it would be best to give up the idea that the mass media can become reliable disseminators of science information, simply because they are not equipped to supply information and their audience is not equipped to handle it." [4] A philosopher, Charles Frankel, expresses a despairing sense "that events are outrunning the human capacity to understand them."

Your authors recognize the magnitude of the problem. This is why we believe that the practitioner will come to be more and more interpreter of the complexities of his organization and less and less a publicist.

In this "Big Change" was born the concept of *public relations thinking* and the functional application of specialized *public relations practice*. The fundamental consequences of this breath-taking and truly spectacular revolution have had great significance:

1. Interdependence that requires the cooperation and coordination of more and more persons to get a task done. This requisite cooperation and this coordination require, in turn, more and more communication with more and more persons about more and more matters.
2. The steady growth in the power of public opinion has come with the extension of government and popular control of that government; this power compels, sooner or later, adequate communication and satisfactory adjustment of conflicting interests.
3. The struggle to align people on the side of one's cause, client, or company has become increasingly competitive.
4. Communications have failed to keep pace effectively with the changing nature of our society, notwithstanding the unparalleled development of mass communications.
5. The swiftly accelerating pace of technology and its consequences have enormously multiplied the number of adjustments required within this environment; adjustments must be effected among widely separated people and organizations.
6. Maladjustments consequently multiply as social institutions lag perilously behind scientific and technological advances.
7. The sense of community is lost in our rootless, mobile society characterized by depersonalized urban, suburban, and exurban living.
8. Modern society requires the specialist for its administration and communications.

---

[3] C. Wright Mills, *The Power Elite* (New York: Oxford University Press, 1956). The late sociologist Mills took a much dimmer view of these changes than those found in Allen and in *The Permanent Revolution*.

[4] Percy Tannenbaum, "Communication of Science Information," *Science,* Vol. 140, May 10, 1963.

FROM ISOLATION
TO INTERDEPENDENCE

1. BIG BUSINESS.   In early America, industry was a simple thing. The iron-master of the Saugus Ironworks in Massachusetts in 1650 lived near the blast furnace, forge, and slitting mill. He attended to his own public relations with his few helpers. He did it on a personal, intimate basis as part of his everyday contacts. He did it in his face-to-face dealing with his customers, and in friendly chats with his neighbors going to and from work. He was his own director of public relations, just as he was his own production manager, sales manager, and controller. The New England cobbler who made shoes for people in his town and its environs dealt with his customers personally. They came to his shop to be fitted. They saw how their shoes were made. Any imperfections or any differences over price could be ironed out amicably across the counter. This cobbler employed one, two, or ten apprentices. He knew them and their families. He knew their problems. In the daily side-by-side associations there was little chance for misunderstandings. But as the cobbler's reputation for making good shoes grew, and as technology changed, his business grew.

The private-property system in production which began with early America's farm and forge has all but vanished in the vast area of our economy dominated by the industrial giants of today. The rise of the large corporation began with the railroad systems, but it is almost wholly a twentieth-century development. As Berle notes: "Many of these corporations have budgets, and some of them have payrolls, which, with their customers, affect a greater number of people than most of the countries of the world." [5] These giants are managed by what he terms "an automatic self-perpetuating oligarchy."

What was once a small business with a few personal relationships has become a large corporation. The large corporation is divided into separate operating units. The units are often decentralized away from the main offices. The giant corporation has been chopped into precincts. Often some of the precincts are in foreign countries. Gone is the owner who lived in the community. In his stead are literally thousands of *shareholders* scattered across the nation.

The job of administering the business has been taken over by specialists called *management*. These professionals live in one part of town and move in one social orbit. Their *employees* live in another part of the city and move in an equally narrow orbit. Today's managers know few of the thousands of

---

[5] In "Economic Power and the Free Society," a pamphlet published by The Fund for the Republic, December, 1957, p. 15. Also see: A. A. Berle, Jr., *The 20th Century Capitalist Revolution* (New York: Harcourt, Brace & World, Inc., 1954), and his *Power Without Property*, published in 1959 by the same publisher.

men and women whom it takes to make products and provide services for the mass market.

Today's *customers* are spread across the nation and around the world. They must be dealt with through a complex hierarchy of salesmen, distributors, and dealers. They must be persuaded to buy through mass-media advertising. We now have mass production, mass ownership, mass markets, and mass communication with a mass public.

General Motors, one of the world's largest enterprises, epitomizes what has happened. Organized in 1908, it produced its first 50 million cars in 46 years but, at present rates, it will produce its second 50 million cars in 12 years. GM accounts for 2.5 per cent of the nation's Gross National Product and makes more than half of all the automobiles sold in the United States each year. This industrial giant is owned by more than a million shareholders. GM provides directly jobs for more than 600,000 employees, who receive 3.5 billion dollars a year in pay. It buys the goods and services of some 30,000 suppliers and thus partially provides jobs for another 15 million people.

GM measures its profits in billions. It holds the power of economic life or death over more than 15,000 franchised car and truck dealers. With all these and a host of others, General Motors must do business. To do business, it must communicate. The communications between General Motors management, its shareholders, employees, suppliers, dealers, and customers must pass through a host of intermediaries and gatekeepers, up and down. The lines of communication between the GM president and the car dealer in Seattle are long and complicated. Some of the consequences of this were dramatized in congressional hearings several years ago. At these hearings disenfranchised GM dealers unburdened complaints to Congress which they had been unable to effectively communicate upward to GM's top management. This situation is not unique in GM by any means; it is an inevitable consequence of bigness.

A business' publics have grown beyond the scope of personal communication. Today business firms are known to a mass public by the images they project through the mass media and other means. These images are inevitably subject to distortion by intervening barriers. This is not just a problem for the large corporation. It is a problem for most organizations. For example, one of your authors has been dealing with one garage for six years, yet he does not know the managers in the front office nor do they know him. Our opinion of this garage's work has been communicated to its owners by returning a post card questionnaire on the quality of service received. The old personal relationships today are synthesized. This includes personal attention, the handshake, the chat on the street, the expression of appreciation for patronage— all the amenities that build and hold goodwill.[6]

2. BIG LABOR. Big Business has, in turn, produced Big Labor. To protect

---

[6] Harwood L. Childs, *An Introduction to Public Opinion* (New York: John Wiley & Sons, Inc., 1940). His chapter, "What Are Public Relations?" stands as one of the thoughtful discussions of PR's ecology.

themselves against the growing economic power of today's employer, a large share of industry's workers have banded together in labor unions. After much travail, America's work force has forged a countervailing power to that of Big Business. In the labor union the employee finds job security and, to some extent, a sense of belonging. It is not without significance that two out of every three industrial employees in the nation's 17 major urban centers are union members. Today more than 18 million workers are joined together in organized labor unions exerting a power far beyond their numbers. Organized labor is today the articulate voice of the nation's wage earners. The rise of organized labor intensified the need for and the problems of industry's relationships with its armies of employees.

Effective internal communication between the AFL–CIO president and the union member in St. Louis is just as difficult as it is between General Motors' president and the car dealer in Seattle. The Rosens found in their study of one large union that "the failure of communications seems particularly acute in both directions with respect to what is actually being done in the union." [7] In those unions which are democratically run, member participation in union affairs is a difficult problem. Like industry, labor too must demonstrate public responsibility and must communicate persuasively. Like industry, labor too has felt the lash of angered opinion when it failed to measure up to its public responsibilities or abused its tremendous power. This was demonstrated when Congress passed the Taft-Hartley Act to correct abuses which grew up under the Wagner Act and again in 1959 when Congress passed the Landrum-Griffin Act after a congressional committee exposed corruption and malfeasance in the Teamsters' Union and other unions.

Periodically labor unions stage strikes to gain their objectives in collective bargaining with employers. These strikes, however justified, often irritate if not injure the public and thus pose difficult public relations problems for the unions. Large strikes of long duration spread concern as to whether unions have grown too strong and whether their strength is applied without attention to the public welfare. It is harder for the public to see management's strikes against labor. Reflecting the integrated nature of our economy, a prolonged strike in a strategic sector can and often does create hardship for millions. For example, early in this decade a walkout of 664 crewmen on railroad ferries and tugs in New York harbor stranded 100,000 commuters, forced an embargo on export freight, and stopped virtually all main-line service on the New York Central and New Haven rail lines. To keep strikes in perspective, it should be recorded that only a tiny percentage of labor-management bargainings ever reach the strike stage.[8]

---

[7] Rosen and Rosen, *The Union Member Speaks* (Englewood Cliffs, N.J.: Prentice-Hall, Inc., 1955), p. 110. A study of one large union and the attitudes of its members toward their union and toward their employers.

[8] See A. H. Raskin, "Labor's Crisis of Public Confidence," *Saturday Review*, Vol. 46, March 30, 1963. For a view of the future, see his "Labor's Welfare State," *Atlantic*, Vol. 211, April, 1963. For a look at labor's PR, see Gerald Pomper, "The Public Relations of Organized Labor," *Public Opinion Quarterly*, Vol. 23, Winter, 1959-60.

3. BIG AGRICULTURE. America was born on the farm, but it moved to the city. In the last century, more than half the people lived on farms, mostly small ones. Large families produced mainly for their own needs. Land was plentiful, labor was cheap, and little capital was needed. The farmer's interests did not extend much beyond the county seat, where he went Saturdays to buy a few necessities and to visit. All this has changed and is still changing. In 1870, 53 per cent of our people were employed in agriculture. The 1900 census marked the first time that the industrial workers outnumbered those in agriculture. As late as 1933, when the New Deal came to power, 31 per cent of our people lived on farms. By 1960 this percentage had dropped to 10 per cent. It should be noted that, although the number of farm people is declining, the rural population is increasing owing to the increase of nonfarm residents. America's some four million farms produce more than enough food and fiber for the other 90 per cent of our people. In 1900 one farm worker produced food and fiber for himself and 7 others. Now one farm worker supports himself and 27 other persons. Agriculture is no longer so much an individual's way of life. It is a heavily mechanized and capitalized business.

These changes reach far beyond replacement of the old farm springhouse by a food freezer in the basement of the modern farm home. As an official of the United States Department of Agriculture points out: "The massive changes in farming are more than a shift from horse, mule, and human muscle to mechanical or electric power. They are a genetic revolution as well—witness the millions of acres of hybrid corn. They are also a managerial change of the first magnitude. Today's modern commercial farm is not just a face-lifted traditional farm. The skills required to manage its complex of technical, economic, and biological factors are of a high order." [9] The trend is clear. The independent farmer and his family are leaving the land. The homestead is vanishing. The business office is taking over. *Fortune* has said that agriculture today is comparable to "all industry, cartelized, subsidized, and rigidified," and "one of the most powerful blocs in American history."

These profound changes have brought a complex of interdependent relationships with people far removed from the American farmer. Today his economic livelihood depends on the needs and tastes of consumers in faraway markets. It rides on the political attitudes of these same consumers in the election booth. Today's agriculture is a delicate mechanism. What the government does is soon felt in every township, although the impact varies from area to area. Changes in consumer tastes, such as the recurring reducing fads, quickly radiate their effects out to the farm. Consequently, we see America's dairy farmers uniting in the American Dairy Association to spend millions of dollars annually on public relations. A far cry from 1900.

Today's farmer, a businessman rather than a yeoman, must communicate with consumers and voters far beyond the county seat. He must persuade the

---

[9] Phillip F. Aylesworth, *Keeping Abreast of Change in the Rural Community* (Washington, D.C.: U.S. Department of Agriculture, October, 1959), p. 1.

nation's voters to provide him with the subsidies, soil banks, and other help he insists that he needs. He must persuade the nation's consumers to buy his products. To meet these needs, the American farmer has need for, and through farm organizations employs, specialists.

4. BIG PRESSURE GROUPS. Pioneer forefathers retreated into the stockade for protection against marauding Indians. Today's citizens have retreated into trade, interest, and professional groups to protect and promote self-interests and beliefs—in short, to win public opinion to a group point of view. Given the complexity and the competitive pressures of today's society, the trade association, professional association, cooperative, labor union, and cause bloc— all pressure groups—are inevitable. There are more than 10,000 of these national, state, and local interest groups. They promote and protect every known interest and political view through persuasion, pressure, and politics.

Such groups are the inevitable response to the need for individuals or institutions with common interests to match the power of opposing groups. These pressure groups are, in large measure, a response to the growing power of public opinion and to the growth of Big Government. If the natural gas producers combine to control production and fight federal regulation, it is inevitable that the gas consumers will combine to resist. The interest group or association has two functions. *One is to stabilize the relationships of its members through internal self-discipline. The other is to present the group's case effectively in public.*

5. BIG GOVERNMENT. Government in the last century was a narrow instrument. Governmental needs could be handled to a large extent in the town meeting and at the state capital. This, too, has changed markedly. Industrialization, accelerating technology, urbanization, and the concentrations of economic and political power combined to induce Big Government in our time.[10] This is particularly true of the federal government. Government today—at the federal, state, and local levels—employs millions. It spends billions to regulate and service more and more of our daily lives. Government has steadily grown in strength and shifted in locus. Public decision making has ebbed from the town meeting to the statehouse to Washington. Likewise, because of the complexity of what government regulates and provides, decision making has flowed from the legislative branch into the administrative arm of government.

The growth of positive, powerful government began in the last quarter of the nineteenth century. It started gathering real momentum with President Theodore Roosevelt. It has continued to grow in size and scope to this day, regardless of the party in power. This growth and its multiplying regulation of our lives are a direct response to our environment and the needs it brings.[11]

---

[10] For a detailed picture of modern government, see James L. McCamy, *American Government* (New York: Harper & Row, Publishers, 1957).

[11] See John M. Gaus, *Reflections on Public Administration* (University, Ala.: University of Alabama Press, 1947). A valuable series of lectures that offer quick insight into the changed nature and function of our government.

Man invents the automobile, and a whole host of government activities are the result. Man unlocks the atom, and a giant Atomic Energy Commission is inevitable. Space exploration brings a NASA.

Because of the tremendous power gathered in government, and thus into the hands of voters, public enterprises have had to conform more and more to standards of conduct imposed by voters. Its growth has meant more and more relationships with those who wield its regulatory powers and dispense its favors. Handling these relationships requires the talents of specialists in public opinion as well as specialists in law.

The nature of government is such as to require that those who make the rules and provide the services must communicate with those who are affected by the rules and those who should get the services. Enforcement of a public health law requires public understanding and support of its purpose if it is to be effective. Promotion of soil conservation requires an understanding of its benefits and techniques by landowners if they are to cooperate. This takes skilled communication. The lines of communication between the citizen and the government official have been lengthened physically and psychologically. It is a long way from the Potomac to Puyallup, Washington. There is a big difference in the attitude toward apples of the bureaucrat in Washington, D.C., and the apple grower in Washington State.

This is illustrated in the extreme in the futile effort of an earnest citizen to communicate with his President in the White House. It is equally apparent in the effort of the President to escape the insulating barriers around him and to listen to the people. When President Woodrow Wilson started the White House Press Conference, March 15, 1913, he asked the reporters, "Please do not tell the country what Washington is thinking, for that does not make any difference. Tell Washington what the country is thinking." This need was reaffirmed by President Dwight Eisenhower on the 43rd anniversary of this informal, but important, link between the President and the people. He said, "I rather like to get the questions, because frequently they represent the thinking that is going on." President John F. Kennedy, perhaps our most public relations-minded president, greatly extended the reach and impact of the Presidential news conference by putting it on television. He used this and other means to communicate his views and program effectively to the voters. He also made a determined effort to keep in touch with the public through travel, wide-ranging contacts, public-opinion polling, and a sensitive reading of newspapers and magazines. In his less than three years in office before his assassination, John F. Kennedy made a deep imprint on the hearts and thoughts of Americans.

In facilitating two-way communications with the voters, the United States President has the help of a large staff of practitioners. Here again we see the environment compelling the development of specialists in opinion analysis and communication. The need is to bridge the gulf from citizen or corporation to the government and back from bureaucrats to citizens and corporations distant from the scene of decision. Big Government has become the largest single employer of practitioners. The United States Information Agency is, in fact, the nation's public relations agency in relaying our views and values to the world and world opinion back to the nation's policy makers.

6. BIG MEDIA OF COMMUNICATION. Growth of mass media has come as a result of advancing technology, urbanization, and the rising level of education and income. Mass communication is another important element of massiveness contributing to the depersonalization of society. It is more than coincidence that the extensive growth of public relations began with the emergence of large newspapers and magazines circulated on a national scale. In small-town, small-shop America, we could know people for their true worth. Today what we are and what we think are projected in a matter of minutes to vast, unseen millions by oversimplified images of us in the mass media. A headline says, "Housewives in Arms Over Coffee Price Rise." The resulting image is, inescapably, compressed and thus bound to be distorted to a degree. Unless people know what truly motivates us and what values we hold, they cannot truly know us. And if they do not know us, they are apt to misunderstand us, and we, them. "They know not England who only England know." Yet we make many decisions each day on the basis of these second-hand images in the mass media. And therein lies their power.

Justice Learned Hand once observed, "The day has clearly gone forever of a society small enough for its members to have a personal acquaintance with one another and to find their station through the appraisal of those who have first-hand knowledge of them. Publicity is an evil substitute and the art of publicity a black art. But it has come to stay. Every year adds to the potency, to the finality of its judgments." Today the people are "incessantly peering at us through the magnified, but sometimes distorted, lenses of journalists, broadcasters, and motion picture producers." [12] *The mass media of press, magazine, radio, television, and motion pictures have become the common carriers of decision-making information.*

We have learned through research that the images and words these media carry determine, within the limitations posed by intervening factors, opinions of people and, thus, their actions. Woodrow Wilson saw this, too. He said, "Unless you get the right setting to affairs—disperse the right impression—things go wrong. . . ." It has become vital to all concerns subject to public opinion to project a favorable image through the mass media. And the media will not do this without assistance and guidance. Consequently, the effort to control and influence the content these media carry to the people has become an intense and spirited one. Growth of mass media, more than any other one factor, has created the public relations occupation. It is *Fortune*'s opinion, "When all is said and done, it is the public-relations man's major job to help management deal with the various segments of that maddening and massive communication agency called the press."

---

12 Childs, *op. cit.*, p. 10.

CONSEQUENCES
OF THE "BIG CHANGE"

Significant and far-reaching consequences were bound to flow from changes as profound as those just described. Those consequences with significance for public relations were listed on page 55. Their significance for public relations can be described as follows:

1. **INCREASED INTERDEPENDENCE.** Our industrialization has made us small cogs in one great industrial complex. Each segment is dependent upon countless others unseen and remote. We all have a place on the American assembly line. A breakdown at any one point along this continent-wide assembly line quickly and directly affects all who man it. A steel strike in Pittsburgh quickly radiates its unhappy consequences to the automobile dealer in Phoenix. Little wonder that there has developed a strong public interest in labor peace or its unhappy opposite, labor strife. Loss of income on the farm is quickly felt in the unemployment of the man who makes farm implements. A slump in the buying of refrigerators soon has its consequences for the men who make steel. And so it goes. Individually, we are no longer masters of our fate. Hence, there is a compelling need for each component to be responsible to all others. If this responsibility is shirked, society finds ways and means of enforcing it.

This interdependence has enormously multiplied the number of personal and institutional relationships. If there is to be cooperation, coordination, and adjustment in the meshing of these complex and infinite relationships, there must be effective communication. A tremendous burden has been placed on the communications function. Complexity of content, occasioned largely by the scientific explosion, has added to this. Today we are confronted by a paradox—unparalleled facilities but increasing difficulty and complexity in communication. *Effective communication, essential to the functioning of an interdependent society, poses a task that can be met only by the skilled specialist.*

2. **GROWTH IN THE POWER OF PUBLIC OPINION.** Public opinion has long been an omnipotent force. Ortega y Gasset wisely wrote, "Never has anyone ruled on this earth by basing his rule on anything other than the rule of public opinion." It is this shadowy but nonetheless real force in society, *public opinion,* that is the source spring of public relations practice. Where public opinion counts for little, there is little concern for the state of one's public relationships. Any ex-GI or missionary who has served in New Guinea can confirm this. The Melanesians don't worry much about their PR.

That Americans are free to have opinions and to make them effective in shaping their destiny gives great force to public opinion. As the power of public opinion to influence the course of human affairs has grown, the efforts to manipulate and mold this force have likewise grown. That people are governed and guided by public opinion in much that they do makes the practice of public relations mandatory. In the early years of formalized public relations in 1910, Theodore N. Vail, then president of the American Telephone and Telegraph Co., said, "In all times, in all lands, public opinion has had control at the last word. Public opinion is but the concert of individual opinion and is as much subject to change or education. It is based on information and belief. If it is wrong, it is wrong because of wrong information and consequent erroneous belief. It is not only the right but the obligation of all individuals, or aggregations of individuals, who come before the public to see that the public have full and correct information." Once the power of public opinion as the supreme arbiter in public affairs and the thesis that opinion is subject to change are accepted, public relations efforts of *communication, persuasion,* and *adjustment* inevitably follow.

Many have paid homage to this power. None has stated it more vigorously than did Abraham Lincoln with his now classic quotation, made during a debate with Douglas, *"Public sentiment is everything; with public sentiment, nothing can fail; without it, nothing can succeed. He who molds opinion is greater than he who enacts laws."* Lincoln was echoing the Frenchman, Rousseau, who developed the term *public opinion* as it is used today. In his discussions of the general will, *volonté generale,* Rousseau said that "whosoever makes it his business to give laws must know how to sway opinions and through them govern the passions of men." A law without public support is but a relic in the statutes.

There is no more powerful office in the world than the Presidency of the United States. Yet President Harry Truman once observed, "You hear people talk about the powers of the President. In the long run, his powers depend a good deal on his success in public relations. . . . His powers are great, but he must know how to make people get along together." [13] His successor, President Dwight Eisenhower, said much the same thing, "We must mobilize public opinion to support and enforce highway safety. *Through such action, this problem, like all others to which free men fall heir, can be solved."*

Today's citizen, equipped with education, with access to information, and with organizations of strength, has considerable if not full power to enforce a public accounting on all institutions vested with a public interest: not only business, but government, social welfare agencies, labor unions, schools, churches, and the like. The citizen exerts this power with his consumer dollars, his investment dollars, his philanthropic dollars, and his votes. Perhaps most important of all, today's citizen has the means to communicate his views to others with like interests and thus build organized support to enforce group opinions. This power reaches its zenith in what David Riesman has called our *"other-directed"* society.

3. LOSS OF COMMUNITY. In Erich Fromm's opinion, man is today suffering from his sense of alienation—"his feeling of being cut off, shut out, adrift,

---

[13] William Hillman, *Mr. President* (New York: Farrar Straus & Company, 1952), p. 11.

fragmentary." The secretary in New York City, the rubber worker in Akron, the salesgirl in Chicago, and the timber worker in the Pacific Northwest share a sense of helplessness. They seek the security of belonging, the respect of personal dignity. The rapidity of our urban growth has accentuated this problem. Not until 1920 did urban residents outnumber rural dwellers. Since then, virtually all our growth has been in the cities. By 1980, according to forecasts of the Urban Land Institute, our population will be nearly four-fifths urban. Nearly three in five of these urban dwellers will by then live in suburbs. Although we huddle together in cities or flee in droves to Suburbia, we are more estranged from one another than ever before. A national longing for "togetherness" merely reflects this. The small town was also a neighborhood, but not today's large apartment building or urban housing project. Nor is neighborliness always found in Suburbia, where today more than a third of our people live. There, people do not, in the view of a thoughtful minister, meet heart to heart, but meet at cocktail parties in a superficial way.[14] The mechanization and automation of work have, likewise, depersonalized our society, leading to what Harvey Swados terms "the stultifying vegetativeness of the modern American work routine."

Today's citizen suffers a feeling of futility and frustration as he watches decisions being made for him by those beyond his reach. "There appears to be a tenuous line of communication between the governors of our society and the governed." Reflecting this, John Cogley asks this disturbing question: "Are our problems so vast, the technical aspects of modern life so tricky, access to the facts so slight, and the necessary knowledge so elusive that American democracy will become simply a matter of living one's private life and turning over the management of the public sector to professionals?" Much of public relations work involves efforts to supply this sense of "belonging" and a "line of communication between the leaders and the people."

We live in a world of fragments and factions forever splitting off, one against another. Consequently, we retreat into the protective arms of groups where "we belong," where we can find a sense of worth, of dignity. The result of this often is, not communication, but groups rebounding from groups. Our relations with other human beings are conducted through organized groups, nation to nation, corporation to union, farm cooperative to the market. Fruitful public relations can play its part in meeting the new and intense psychological needs of man. It can also serve society by helping to bring about a sense of communion in an integrated community.

4. **MULTIPLYING MALADJUSTMENTS.** The social and cultural lag caused by man's inability to adjust to the accelerating scientific and technological advances long has been a source of concern and comment. A tense world cowering in fear of atomic annihilation because scientists split the atom is a stark

---

14 For further information on Suburbia, see David Riesman, "The Suburban Dislocation," *Annals of the American Academy of Political and Social Science,* Vol. 314, November, 1957; and Robert Wood, *Suburbia: Its People and Their Politics* (Boston: Houghton Mifflin Company, 1959).

reminder of this inability. Today man is frantically trying to erect political institutions capable of controlling the scientific realities of atomic and hydrogen warheads coupled with intercontinental or submarine-launched ballistic missiles. The United Nations is such a vehicle. On this race all else depends. The maladjustments resulting from this social lag are to be seen in lesser but nonetheless critical ways. It can be seen in the continuing unemployment of unskilled labor, many of them young "school dropouts"; in the mounting populations in our mental and penal institutions; in the decaying blight of the central city ringed by new suburbs; in efforts to bring safety on the highways and in the airlanes; in the dislocations due to mechanization, automation, and changes in plant needs; and in countless other ways.

The swiftness of the changes has left a smaller and smaller span of time for adjustment to their consequences. Our great-grandfathers had a whole lifetime to adjust to the railroad and telegraph; our grandfathers had a lifetime to adjust to the automobile. Grandson whips across the ocean in a jet plane in about the time it took Grandfather to travel by car to the Big City. In the span of a decade or more, America's space industry became bigger than the nation's 60-year-old automotive industry. A corporate executive was predicting in the mid-1960's that "The United States space exploration effort will grow larger than the combined auto industries of the world to a business around 20 billion dollars annually." This generation has had to grapple with adjustments to mass communication, the automobile, the airplane, propeller-driven and jet, electronics, automation, atomic energy, earth satellites, and space travel, among others, since the turn of the century. James E. Webb, administrator of NASA, has predicted, "The thrust into space will change the ideas and lives of people more drastically than the Industrial Revolution."

Kenneth Boulding says it succinctly: "If the human race is to survive, it will have to change its ways of thinking more in the next 25 years than it has done in the last 25,000."

Lack of human ability to keep pace with this fast-flowing change has produced maladjustments aplenty. This harsh fact, too, has implications for the function of public relations, with its objective of adjusting an institution to its changing community. Furthermore, introduction of change brings the need for winning acceptance of new ideas, new products, new ways of doing things. For instance, as automation gains momentum, industrial practitioners once more have the task of convincing employees and the public that mechanization will ultimately increase, not diminish, the number and quality of jobs.

5. SPECIALIZATION. To perform the myriad tasks required in today's highly scientific, computerized society, specialists are required. The knowledge used in the management of today's large-scale enterprises is so vast, complicated, and abstract that few individuals have either the time or ability to master it. Instead each person tackles one small sector and masters that. Thus we have the specialist in data systems, personnel, or fiscal management, the corporate lawyer, the nucleonic engineer, the high-energy physicist, and the

astronaut. Each specialty has its own particular language, and this adds to our communications barriers.

The specialty of public relations has emerged in response to our changing environment. Discussing the increasing importance of the public relations specialist in American politics, Kelley wrote: "It is based on a solid demand. . . . More than anything else, public relations as an occupation owes its existence to the growth of the mass media of communication. Having committed themselves to the use of the mass media of communication for propaganda purposes, politicians and interest groups have found it an exceedingly complex problem to use them in such a way as to receive wide circulation for a point of view." [15] This is equally true in other sectors of society. This is the age of the specialist, and public relations is no exception to this trend.

---

[15] Stanley Kelley, Jr., *Professional Public Relations and Political Power* (Baltimore, Md.: Johns Hopkins Press, 1956), p. 202.

Additional Reading

Adolf A. Berle, *The American Economic Republic.* New York: Harcourt, Brace & World, Inc., 1963. An analysis of the American economic system.

Paul W. Cherington and Ralph L. Gillen, *The Business Representative in Washington.* Washington, D.C.: The Brookings Institution, 1962.

Marquis W. Childs and Douglass Cater, *Ethics in a Business Society.* New York: Harper & Row, Publishers, 1954. (Also available as a Mentor Book.)

John K. Galbraith, *The Affluent Society.* Boston: Houghton Mifflin Company, 1958.

David Riesman, *et al., The Lonely Crowd.* New York: Doubleday & Company, Inc., 1953. (Abridged from an earlier Yale University Press edition.)

Robert Heilbroner, *The Future as History.* New York: Harper & Row, Publishers, 1959.

Maurice R. Stein, *The Eclipse of Community.* Princeton, N.J.: Princeton University Press, 1960.

David B. Truman, *The Governmental Process: Political Interests and Public Opinion.* New York: Alfred A. Knopf, Inc., 1951.

Arthur J. Vidich and Joseph Bensman, *Small Town in Mass Society.* Princeton, N.J.: Princeton University Press, 1958.

Chapter Five

PERSUASION

AND

PUBLIC

OPINION

The power of public opinion must be faced, understood, and dealt with. It provides the psychological environment in which organizations prosper or perish.

Influencing the opinions of people is the practitioner's job. Basically, there are three means of getting people to do what you want—*pressure, purchase,* or *persuasion.* The United States draft law got men into the armed forces by *pressure* or *force.* When a vice king bribes policemen to wink at law violations, he gets compliance by *purchase.* The campaign of the New York Stock Exchange which raised the number of common stock owners from 6 to 16 million was one of *persuasion.* In public relations, persuasion is used. The basic objective of programs is either to *change* or to *neutralize* hostile opinions, to *crystallize* unformed or latent opinions in your favor, or to *conserve* favorable opinions.

Some years ago a number of harsh criticisms erupted in New York State against that state's welfare programs. To allay these criticisms, the State Charities Aid Association in New York set out to bring the critics face to face with the grim problems of poverty, illegitimacy, illiteracy, and so forth. This is a modern version of citizen inspection of the poorhouses of yesteryear. The project's basic plan was simple: to let the community leaders see and talk to people living "on welfare," to watch caseworkers cope with the complex problems they face every day. The pilot project was sponsored in ten New York communities and financed by a grant from the Field Foundation. Other communities later adopted the plan.

In these communities on a given day community leaders—particularly those most vocal about loafers, chiselers, and loose-living women—are

68

paired off with caseworkers. Critic and caseworker spend the afternoon visiting typical welfare recipients. These recipients are not tipped off in advance but when asked if the observer may sit in, they readily grant permission. Typical rather than "best" or "worst" households are visited. Then all visitors and welfare workers come together for a dinner and discussion of what has been seen during the day. This discussion often runs past midnight and the critics wind up with a different opinion about those living "on welfare." The State Charities Aid Association, after the pilot program, concluded: "This demonstration has proved its value in helping lift the fog of public suspicion about welfare." This is a *planned* effort to change what had been *hostile* opinion.

Public relations efforts to *create* attitudes where none exist is illustrated in the National Safety Council's campaign to get motorists to use seat belts. Basic research has indicated that universal use of seat belts would save 5,000 lives each year and would reduce serious injuries by one-third. Much of this educational effort meets the ingrained resistance of human habit. The Joint Seat Belt Committee, consisting of the National Safety Council, the American Medical Association, and United States Public Health Service, keep up a steady barrage of persuasive communication, using films, posters, public service advertising, news stories, TV documentaries, and spot radio announcements to get more motorists to use seat belts. Here the effort is to *crystallize* latent or unformed opinion.

The diamond has long been a standard of ultimate value, fluctuating little more than money itself. When sales charts disclosed a trend away from the use of diamonds in engagement rings a few years ago, the DeBeers Consolidated Mines Ltd. did something about it. To revive the concept of a diamond as a symbol of high fashion, publicity pointed readers and viewers toward the diamond that each TV, radio, and movie star received on becoming engaged. Fashion models were encouraged to wear diamonds with new gowns. Diamonds and St. Valentine's Day were linked in publicity. The jeweler was given special materials and booklets to use at service clubs and schools. All of these efforts had the objective of *conserving* favorable opinion.

The practitioner is striving constantly to start, lead, change, speed, or slow trends in public opinion. His problems are compounded of people's differences in outlook and opinion. The daily tasks of the staff are created by people who "don't understand us," who "won't cooperate," who "won't work as hard as they should," who "won't vote right," who "won't give as much as they should," and so on.

The term *public opinion* is a slippery one. Our ability to measure it is greater than our ability to define or manipulate it. Although the concept originated in the eighteenth century, it still has not been defined satisfactorily. *Public opinion* is difficult to describe, elusive to define, hard to measure, impossible to see. For this reason the concept is utilized less and less in the growing precision of social psychology, sociology, and political science. Most writers agree that the force of public opinion is perceptible, though the concept is vague. Certainly its pervasive power is easily felt. James Russell Lowell said, "The pressure of public opinion is like the atmosphere. You can't see it, but all the same it is sixteen pounds to the square inch." Another New Englander, Samuel Bowles II, added, "Public sentiment is a capricious, intangible thing, so hard to reach, so hard to manage when it is reached." The power must be faced, understood, and dealt with in a free country. *Public opinion provides the psychological environment in which organizations prosper or perish.* No one has better described it than did Lord Bryce: [1]

> [public opinion] . . . is a congeries of all sorts of discrepant notions, beliefs, fancies, prejudices, aspirations. It is confused, incoherent, amorphous, varying from day to day and week to week. But in the midst of this diversity and confusion every question as it rises into importance is subjected to a process of consolidation and clarification until there emerge and take shape certain views or sets of interconnected views, each held and advocated in common by bodies of citizens. It is to the power exerted by any such views, when held by an apparent majority of citizens, that we refer when we talk of Public Opinion . . .

A WORKING DEFINITION

There are countless definitions. Most scholars in this field agree that public opinion represents a *consensus* among a varying number of persons and that this consensus exercises power in the public-opinion arena. Each of the two words that make up the term *public opinion* is significant. A *public* is simply a collective noun for a group—a group of individuals tied together by some common bond of interest—and sharing a *sense of togetherness*. It may be a small group or a large group; it may be a majority group or a minority group. Ogle defines a *public* as "any group of two or more persons who demonstrate in any manner whatever that they are conscious of group solidarity." The term "public" is used frequently in public relations as a synonym for "a group." We talk about our "employee public," our "community public," our "alumni public," and so forth. There are literally an infinite number of smaller publics within the General Public.

An *opinion* is simply the expression of an attitude on a controversial topic. *Opinion* implies controversy and dispute, whereas *fact* implies general acceptance. The law of gravity is a fact; the justice of a "right to work" law is a matter of opinion. One man's fact may be mere opinion to another. An *attitude* is simply an inclination to respond in a given way to a given issue or situation. The terms "attitude" and "opinion" are often used interchangeably. This leads to some confusion. They are distinctly separate concepts, although there is a continuing interaction between inwardly held attitudes and outwardly expressed opinions. Wiebe thinks, "Opinions adapt attitudes to the demands

---

[1] James Bryce, *Modern Democracies* (New York: The Macmillan Company, 1921), pp. 153-4.

of social situations; but having adapted them, opinions appear to become ingredients in the constant, gradual reformulation of attitudes."

The attitudes of individual citizens provide the raw material out of which a consensus develops. Influencing an individual's attitudes is a prime task of the practitioner. Consequently, he must know the source of a person's attitudes, their organization as reflected in the person's value system and personality, and the processes which bring attitude change. All this is of basic importance in understanding the end product that we glibly label "public opinion."

There are two main streams of thought with respect to the determination of man's attitudes: (1) one school assumes man to be an irrational being with limited powers of reason and thus susceptible to emotional appeals; (2) the second assumes man to be a rational being with strong powers of reason and discrimination. The early advertisers who relied heavily on the power of suggestion and exploited fear appeals reflected a belief in the irrational man. Those who believe that Americans are but puppets at the end of the "Hidden Persuaders' " string reflect this notion. Those who adhere to the rational model of man put their reliance on getting adequate information to people. Our educational system, for example, is based on the rational model of man. Practitioners who put their reliance on two-way communication of information demonstrate their belief in the importance of intelligence and comprehension in the formation of men's opinions.

In fact, most persons are influenced by both irrational and rational reasoning. A person who smokes may ignore evidence linking cigarette smoking with lung cancer on one hand but go through a rational process in arriving at an opinion concerning a civic issue on the other. Either school of thought can point to evidence which supports its assumptions and undercuts the arguments of the other. There are elements of truth in both approaches in dealing with attitude formation and change.[2]

On the psychological level, the reasons for holding or for altering attitudes are found in the essential functions they perform for the individual in enabling him to cope with his situation. These are the functions of adjustment, ego defense, value expression, and knowledge. Daniel Katz, social psychologist, groups these according to their motivational basis: [3]

1. *The instrumental, adjustive, or utilitarian function.* . . . A modern expression of this approach can be found in behavioristic learning theory.
2. *The ego-defensive function,* in which the person protects himself from acknowledging the basic truths about himself or the harsh realities in his external world. . . .
3. *The value-expressive function,* in which the individual derives satisfactions from expressing attitudes appropriate to his personal values and to his concept of himself. . . .
4. *The knowledge function,* based upon the individual's need to give adequate

---

2 See Daniel Katz, "The Functional Approach to the Study of Attitudes," *Public Opinion Quarterly,* Vol. 24, Summer, 1960.

3 *Ibid.,* p. 170.

structure to his universe. The search for meaning, the need to understand, the trend toward better organization of perceptions and beliefs to provide clarity and consistency for the individual. . . .

In sum, this functional approach is simply an effort to understand the reasons why persons hold the attitudes they do.

In dealing with the formation and change of attitudes, the practitioner will find Leon Festinger's theory of *cognitive dissonance* of value. This theory is based on the fact that human beings demonstrate a great desire for consistency and congruity in their attitudes and, conversely, they find inconsistency between what they know and what they have done disturbing and discomfiting. Festinger states his theory thus: [4]

> Any time a person has information or an opinion which considered by itself would lead him not to engage in some action, then this information or opinion is dissonant with having engaged in the action. When such dissonance exists, the person will try to reduce it either by changing his actions or by changing his beliefs and opinions. If he cannot change the action, opinion change will ensue. This psychological process, which can be called dissonance reduction, does explain the frequently observed behavior of people justifying their actions. . . . When dissonance exists, dissonance-reduction attempts do occur.

Each individual accumulates his predispositions to think or act in a certain way from many places, many sources. A person's attitudes remain latent until an issue arises for the group to which he belongs. An issue arises when there is conflict, frustration, or anxiety. Thus confronted, the individual takes his stand and voices his opinion. For example, university students have latent attitudes about what are the proper hours for coeds to be in their dormitories or sorority houses at night. The dean of women issues an edict requiring coeds to be in an hour earlier. A conflict develops. These attitudes crystallize into opinions pro and con. The opinion expressed represents the sum of a person's attitudes on a specific issue in debate tempered by that person's degree of concern for group approval of his *expressed* opinions.

Now that we have taken the term *public opinion* apart, let us try to put it together. The individual opinions expressed by members of a group with a common bond—be it a city council or voters of a commonwealth—are loosely bunched under the umbrella concept, public opinion. This is not the opposite of private opinions. Rather, *public opinion is the aggregate result of individual opinions on public matters.* Public matters are those which affect groups of people, not isolated individuals. A public is a group of people affected by the same affairs. Publics cannot have and do not have opinions, because a public is not an entity in itself. *Public opinion is the sum of accumulated individual opinions on an issue in public debate and affecting a group of people.* Within this broad definition, McCamy sets up three main categories: [5]

---

[4] Leon Festinger, "The Theory of Cognitive Dissonance," in *The Science of Human Communication,* edited by Wilbur Schramm (New York: Basic Books, Inc., 1963), pp. 18-19 and 26. For a fuller discussion, see Festinger's *A Theory of Cognitive Dissonance* (New York: Harper & Row, Publishers, 1957).

[5] James L. McCamy, *American Government* (New York: Harper & Row, Publishers, 1957), p. 462. These categories are expanded in his chapter on public opinion.

1. Public opinion in its broadest sense is the whole way of life in the nation, or what social scientists call the "culture" of a people.

2. Public opinion is the prevalent mood of a people, or at least a considerable portion of them.

3. Public opinion is the collection of individual opinions in a group of people whose attention is directed toward a common subject, purpose, like, or dislike.

The tides of public opinion are forever ebbing in and out, beating against the boulders of public issues as they ebb and flow. These tides move at slow, almost imperceptible speeds, for the most part. They are propelled more by events than by publicity. In Galbraith's phrase, "The enemy of conventional wisdom is not ideas but the march of events." Public opinion encompasses attitudes and supporting behavior that polarize around an issue in public debate. When goals are accomplished, the supporting opinions tend to disappear. Public opinion on one issue can be displaced by opinion on another. The episodic nature of our news coverage facilitates this. As issues change, so does public opinion. In this process, the practitioner plays an influential role.

The process of opinion formation goes something like this:

1. A number of people recognize a situation as being problematic and decide that something ought to be done about it. They explore possible solutions and do some fact-finding.

2. Alternative proposals for solving the problem emerge, and these are discussed back and forth.

3. A policy or a solution is agreed upon as best meeting the situation recognized as problematic. Agreement and a decision to promote its acceptance lead to group consciousness.

4. A program of action is undertaken, and this is pressed until the requisite action is obtained or the group becomes weary of the battle and its members turn to other projects and other groups.

ROOTS OF OUR
ATTITUDES

Public opinion gets its power through individuals, who must be persuaded and organized. "Public opinion is but the concert of individual opinion." To deal effectively with this potent force, one must study it situation by situation, influence it individual by individual, group by group. This starts with the individual and the source of his opinions. This requires an almost endless exploration of heredity, environments, and the motivations of human behavior. People act on the basis of "the pictures in our heads" rather than in accordance with the reality of the world outside. What a person believes is true, *is true for him*. To understand him, we start by digging out the roots of these "pictures in our heads." [6] What goes into the composition of these pictures of a world out of sight, out of reach?

---

[6] The concept of the stereotype was introduced by Walter Lippmann in his now classic book, *Public Opinion* (New York: Harcourt, Brace & World, Inc., 1922). This book has stood the test of time and still offers a lucid insight into the nature of public opinion.

Harwood Childs classifies the factors that shape a person's attitudes into two categories—*primary factors* and *secondary factors*. Primary, in Childs' view, are the things we read, hear, or see. ". . . the channels of communication and what comes through them—the ideas, reports, news, representations that constitute our world of verbal symbols." Our interpretation of these symbols is shaped by the glasses through which we view them. The lens in the individual's glasses are ground by the secondary factors of environment—where we live, how old we are, how prosperous we are, and our biological, physical, social, and psychological heritage. The primary factors are *active;* the secondary factors are *latent.*[7]

The roots of one's attitudes are many and extend in all directions and depths in the soil of our culture. Researchers can dig up and examine each of these roots. They still cannot, with any certainty, determine the amount of vitality or degree of variation that each root contributes to the living plant. Which has the greater force on what one thinks and says—his heredity? His environment? His family or age associates? His church? His political party? The list of influencing factors is almost endless. The role each plays in relation to all the others is hard to calculate. It varies with each individual and each situation of conflict. The "pictures in our heads"—the symbols, codes, slogans, superstitions, and stereotypes that people live by—have their origins in many places.

The human personality has four primary determinants:

1. Biology or heredity.
2. Group membership, essentially one's environment.
3. Role, involving one's age, sex, social status, class, and color.
4. Situation, all the accidental things which affect people, which can make two brothers from the same environment turn out to be quite different.

In most attempts to enumerate and classify, the influence of heredity as against environment is a common starting point. From there such efforts take different pathways to answering the old question, "Why *do* we behave the way we do?" It is a question continually confronting the practitioner for a practical answer. Why do more people like coffee than tea?

OUR CULTURE. No man lives unto himself alone. To demonstrate this to oneself, all a person needs to do is to be *absolutely* alone for 24 hours. From the crib to the casket, he is influenced by others. The newborn child finds an elaborate civilization awaiting him. "He fits into historic institutions and is molded by them. The family, play group, school, church, city, state, and nation are organized ways in which the individual enters social relations. They make possible a richer life than could be attained if individuals lived in isolation. . . . The necessities of civilized life, in turn, compel us to maintain cordial and cooperative relations with our fellows. We group ourselves to-

---

[7] Harwood Childs, *An Introduction to Public Opinion* (New York: John Wiley & Sons, Inc., 1940). See the chapter, "Formation of Opinion."

gether to work, to play, to worship. Without society, with its cultural heritage, man would be a beast." [8]

These are the factors which determine a person's *mental set*—the screen upon which are cast the lights and shadows of what he reads, sees, or hears to form the pictures in his head. The basic institutions of family, church, school, and economic groupings grind the lens through which one views the world outside. They determine norms, standards, values. They transmit from one generation to another that which Bagehot named "the cake of custom." Man shapes these institutions and, in turn, is shaped by them. Public relations plays its role in this process.

THE FAMILY. The family, the germ cell of society, is the first molder of opinions. No person can escape the strong, formative influences of the family circle. Certainly Henry Adams was not recording a unique experience when he wrote that his father's character contributed more to his education than did the influence of any other person. In many, many ways, some overt, some subtle, the child acquires the parents' attitudes and outlook. A great many people, for example, inherit their political affiliation.

"Within the family is to be found the germ of all those potentialities which later ripen into love and hate, work and play, obedience and revolt, reverence and agnosticism, patriotism and treason. It is the matrix which molds the human personality and gives it the initial impetus and direction determining its goal and means to its fulfillment." [9] This influence is underscored by recent knowledge which indicates that many of our principal characteristics are acquired before the age of five. It is the family that bends the tender twig in the direction it is likely to grow.

Most of our social institutions serve mainly as reinforcing devices to re-inculcate the lessons the child learned in the family circle. The neighborhood, mother's bridge-club companions, father's fellow workers, the evening paper, the neighbors next door, and the breadwinner's economic status shape adult attitudes. Similarly, the family shapes the attitudes of the children.

RELIGION. One basic human trait binds nearly all people together. This is religion and the belief in a supernatural, universal power. Religion is a vital force. Both believers and nonbelievers are influenced by it. No effort to influence public opinion can omit or deny the strong influence of the church. The church is more influential in the formation of opinions than a mere survey of members might indicate. Religion is so important and pervasive that many Americans feel compelled to go through the forms though they may not subscribe to the substance. On the other hand, many religious persons have no formal church connection.

Religion has been a major influence in Western civilization. Who can doubt, for example, the Calvinist influence in shaping the ideals of industry, sobriety, frugality, and thrift which stem from America's frontier? R. H.

---

[8] Peter Odegard, *The American Public Mind* (New York: Columbia University Press, 1930), p. 31.

[9] *Ibid.*, p. 47.

Tawney held that the Protestant Revolution was one of the most decisive factors in the development of the capitalist ideology. He said, "Capitalism was a social counterpart of Calvinist theology." Who denies the indelible stamp placed upon American culture by Puritanism?

The influence of religion and dogma which permeates all strata of society is extended and underlined as the church increasingly turns to social issues in applied Christianity. Today clergymen—thought leaders—are active on many fronts in striving to generate and guide public opinion on social issues. The churches are concerned with teen-age gangs and with delinquent parents, with slum clearance, civil rights, and narcotic addiction. The important role which religion plays in shaping attitudes on public questions was clearly demonstrated in the 1960 Presidential election. As Theodore White concluded: "There is no doubt that millions of Americans, Protestant and Catholic, voted in 1960 primordially out of instinct, kinship, and past." [10] A University of Michigan research group concluded that "President Kennedy's Catholicism was clearly the biggest issue of the 1960 election."

SCHOOLS. A teacher's influence stops only with eternity. The influence and importance of the school in the public-opinion process is underlined in a state which regards an educated, enlightened electorate as indispensable to a free society. Whereas it seems that there has been some lessening of the influence of the family and church in recent decades, it appears that the schools have gained influence. More children than ever before are going to school. They are starting at an earlier age and attending for longer periods of time. Expanded and improved teaching methods, larger enrollment, and longer schooling account for the schools' increased influence.

Because of their key role in shaping tomorrow's citizens, the schools are getting increased attention from the practitioner. The philosophy or cause he represents strives for a greater share in the education of young people. This is reflected in diverse, greatly increased pressures on schools—with respect to what shall be taught, who shall teach, and what textbooks they shall use.

America deems it proper that the state shall have the right to take the child from the family and keep him in school until he reaches a certain age or a certain level of education. More and more parental responsibility is being shifted to the schools in the winter months and to the organized recreation programs in the summer months. In urban areas it is quite common for the child to leave the home for nursery school at the age of three, be enrolled in kindergarten at the age of four or five, and then be entered in the graded system at six. Any parent who has been bluntly told, "The teacher says you are all wet, Daddy. This is the way it is," does not need to be reminded of the impact of teachers and textbooks on a child's opinions.

ECONOMIC CLASS. Sometimes overlooked in exploring the roots of attitudes

---

10 Theodore H. White, *The Making of a President 1960* (New York: Atheneum Press, 1961), p. 356. This Pulitzer Prize-winning book provides a readable and useful case study of the making of public opinion in a presidential campaign. Recommended reading.

are *economic associations and status,* the individual's stake in the capitalistic economy. Although the "economic man" concept has been demolished, none would deny that economic motivation and influence are strong with most individuals. An individual's status as an unskilled laborer or as a management executive determines, in large measure, the way his attitudes are bent and shaped. Attitudes of the different income groups toward the role of government are proof of this..

The economic status determines, to a large degree, the particular social orbit in which people move. The pictures in a man's head will be shaped, too, by the nature of his affiliations. Is he a member of the National Association of Manufacturers, the AFL–CIO, or the unorganized "white collar" workers who now outnumber "blue collar" workers in America? One's place of work, pay, and security are vital factors in life. Their influence is large.[11]

SOCIAL CLASS. Somewhat related, but not necessarily so, is the influence of *social status.* Certainly one's position as a member of the yacht club set will determine outlook, sources of information, and opinions. Those who belong to art circles, have big boats, and travel abroad see events differently from those without these status symbols that characterize today's "smart set." It is important not to confuse income with social status. High income does not necessarily mean high social status, although it often does. Determining factors are family background, education, occupation, home, and neighborhood. Status influences every phase of one's life. It must be taken into account in persuasive communication.

David Riesman in *The Lonely Crowd* theorizes that there are three basic types in the American character structure, the "tradition-directed," the "inner-directed," and the "other-directed." The tradition-directed person is one whose conformity to the social order is assured by rigid adherence to the accustomed way of doing things. He "does what is proper." The inner-directed is one whose conformity is assured by early implantation through parents, elders, and teachers of goals and values which last throughout life. The other-directed person derives his character from the outside—from his contemporaries, peer groups, associates, friends, and the mass media. Riesman thinks that the "other-directed" character type is coming to the fore in America. This theory has important implications for those who would influence opinion. The inner-directed person has clearly formulated personal goals and relies relatively little on the approbation of others in reaching his decisions. The other-directed person who strives to "keep up with the Joneses" is more easily influenced. Thus it becomes important to know who the Joneses are.

Another factor increasingly important in shaping our mental set is one's race in these days of tension as the United States moves to full integration.

---

11 The pressures for conformity in the business and organizational worlds have been a favorite topic of William H. Whyte, Jr. See *The Organization Man* (New York: Simon and Schuster, Inc., 1957). Also Vance Packard, *The Status Seekers* (New York: David McKay Co., Inc., 1959).

SOURCES
OF MOTIVATION

Different people will respond differently to the same social pressures and persuasions. The appeals in incentives used will be effective to the degree that the individual has the necessary *motivational predispositions* to respond. These sources of motivation need to be taken into account.

PERSONAL MOTIVATION. All the reactions of the members of a group, a public, occur within the individual. Le Bon's *crowd mind* theory has been discarded. To understand the opinion process, we must study, too, the individual's emotional and physiological drives. All people have these basic drives in common—among them *self-preservation, hunger, security,* and *sex.* Our basic emotional needs include the desire for *affection,* the desire for *emotional security* or trust, and the desire for *personal significance.*

The whole sum and substance of human motivation is not bound up in those three brief terms. But we can set them close to the center of a good working concept of human nature. Practitioners must and do devise ways of meeting these basic emotional needs in their day-to-day programs—employee communications, for example. Consider the emphasis on awards, promotions, and clubs. In these basic drives the individual seeks physical and social security, gratification of his human desires, and protection of his ego.

GROUP MOTIVATION. Communicators have found it increasingly necessary to take into account the group to which individuals belong. People, with rare exceptions, do not live in isolation but in constant association with others. There are essentially two kinds of groups, *statistical* and *functional.* It is helpful to enumerate the target audience both ways. An audience may be classified by age, sex, income level, educational level, occupation, and so forth. This is useful because members of the same statistical group *tend* to respond in the same general way to the same communications. Such classifications help to identify common bonds of interest which may be used in building a bridge between communicator and audience.

But the *functional* group plays the more vital role. Functional groups are composed of individuals who come together for some common purpose. It may be a construction crew, a political club, or the congregation at a church service. People desire to belong to groups and to find a sense of social security. In an "other-directed" society, we take our cues from our group associates. The group's influence appears to be on the rise; or else, through research, we are merely learning more about the group role in opinion formation. *To belong to a group, we pay a price. We conform to its standards, its consensus.* There is evidence accumulating in social science research of common attitudes among those who "belong together."

Our individual attitudes, and thus our opinions, are maintained in association with small numbers of others. We influence them, they influence us.

An individual's relatedness-to-others has an important bearing on efforts to persuade him this way or that. For example, employers have found that workers will forego the increased pay possible under wage-incentive plans rather than be ostracized by their work group as "rate busters." To "belong" can be as strong an incentive as money.[12] Thus, whether you change a person's opinions or not will depend to some degree on the resistance or support which the person encounters in his group. We are learning more and more that these interpersonal relationships intervene in the mass-communication process.[13]

A group develops standards for its members' behavior. These standards are shared. They represent the behavior and attitudes that members expect of one another. "There are some things you just don't do in *this* group." To the degree a person is dependent upon his group he is *motivated* to conform. Also there will be found in groups "situational cues" which operate to arouse the motives related to conformity. Study of group dynamics and the group structure of our society is essential for the practitioner. The results of research can be summarized.[14]

1. A person's opinions and attitudes are strongly influenced by the groups to which he belongs and wants to belong.

2. The person is rewarded for conforming to the standards of the group and is punished for deviating from them.

3. People who are most attached to a group are probably the least influenced by communications which conflict with group norms.

It is important to note the distinction between the public-opinion process and the group-consensus process. Yet the distinction is not easily made. In the public arena, opinions form around a particular issue or a number of related issues, whereas the range of subjects on which the group demands conformity is broad indeed. A second difference is that the group interaction takes place among those who know each other well and are in frequent contact, whereas the public-opinion process involves those who may be in contact only the one time on the one campaign. Davison rightly concludes:[15] "The group opinion process is an extremely important component of the public opinion process but the distinction between the two must be maintained if public opinion phenomena are to be explained adequately."

12 See William Foote Whyte, *Money and Motivation* (New York: Harper & Row, Publishers, 1955).

13 See Elihu Katz and Paul F. Lazarsfeld, *Personal Influence: The Part Played by People in the Flow of Mass Communications.* This book introduced the two-step flow theory of mass communication and is essential reading for the public relations student. It will be referred to at several points in this book.

14 Condensed by Herbert I. Abelson for Opinion Research Corp. in *Some Principles of Persuasion*, 1956, and based on research of Katz and Lazarsfeld, S. E. Asch, H. Guetzkow, and Leon Festinger, *et al.*

15 W. Phillips Davison, "The Public Opinion Process," *Public Opinion Quarterly*, Vol. 22, Summer, 1958, pp. 91-106. Also reprinted in Christenson and McWilliams, *Voice of the People* (McGraw-Hill, Inc., 1962), pp. 6-20.

A NATION OF MANY
PUBLICS

It is a common mistake to think of The Public as one massive, monolithic assemblage. No money-spending, vote-casting, goods-buying unit of more than 120 million adult Americans waits as one vast audience to be molded into "public opinion." "We the People" consist of many publics, of many kindred interest groups, and of unorganized groups with like and unlike preferences in fashions, music, fiction, and so forth. Novelist Joyce Cary thinks the "mass mind concept" is our time's special bit of nonsense.

A check of consumer purchases will quickly show the risk in fashioning national campaigns for national audiences. A product may have great appeal in New England and yet be ignored in California. Many public relations failures in the past resulted from the assumption that public opinion could be molded from New York City down. Our efforts to communicate persuasively with The General Public are, on the whole, inefficient and often ineffective. The total public is complex, heterogeneous. Within this great mass are smaller publics which can be defined and thus influenced.

The number of different publics is theoretically the number of distinct combinations of individuals within a given community. The number of key publics for any one organization is relatively small and manageable. For **ex**ample, the university **PR** director is primarily concerned with these publics: trustees, administrators, faculty, nonteaching staff, students, parents of students, prospective students, alumni, donors, community leaders, and legislators. **On** these groups he beams most of his communication. *The publics in public relations are those groups with common interests affected by the acts and policies of an institution or whose acts and opinions affect the institution.*

Individuals form themselves into publics in various ways—politically in parties, religiously in churches, socially in clubs and lodges, economically in trade associations, labor unions, or farm blocs. An individual can and does belong to a long list of publics simultaneously. It is dangerous to classify people rigidly as "employees" or "customers" when, in fact, these people play many roles. We are *whole* individuals. A person's overlapping memberships in many publics lend stability to this mercurial force, public opinion. Citizens are continually forming, disbanding, and re-forming into publics holding specific views toward specific issues.

Americans are great joiners and intensively organize themselves from Cub Scouts to Old Age Klubs. This makes it easier to focus on and communicate with individuals joined in groups. *To communicate with individuals in groups, appeals must be significant and relevant to a particular group interest in a particular situation.* Schramm says, "The kind of roles we play and the value and attitudes we build around them are largely determined by the groups we belong to." A person's group relationships provide the setting for most of the communication he receives and transmits.

Today's citizen has many interests. He can be a voter, a taxpayer, a Methodist, a Mason, a Republican, a Rotarian, a war veteran, a merchant, a member of the Chamber of Commerce, an employer, a parent, a fisherman, and a consumer all in the same day. Each of these "memberships" involves a special allegiance. The issue at stake determines which allegiance prevails in a given situation. All have their impact on a person's underlying attitudes. One minute a man may be a pedestrian crossing the street and mumbling about "those crazy drivers." A few moments later he may be driving home from work and angrily honking his horn at "fool pedestrians who never watch where they're going." Both roles will come to bear in shaping this man's opinions on a new traffic law. Quite often, too, a person's allegiances collide. When new taxes are proposed to pay a soldiers' bonus, will the individual respond as a taxpayer or as a veteran?

Individuals also react in unorganized groups. Some describe this as "crowds"; others refer to "the mass." Persons sharing an attentiveness to the same thing at the same time may be said to belong to an *unorganized public*. Certainly, under conditions of today's society, mass behavior has emerged in increasing magnitude and importance. The excited squeals of teen-agers excited about the latest crooning idol are to be heard from Portland, Me., to Portland, Ore. There is mass advertising of mass-produced goods appealing to mass behavior. It makes people wear the same style clothes, drive the same kind of shiny, streamlined cars, and idolize the same TV stars. The strength of the "mass" influence is a matter of spirited debate in scholarly circles. Certainly it is an important influence on opinions, mores, and values.[16]

GOVERNORS OF OPINION CHANGE

As pointed out earlier in this chapter, the environmental factors of *culture, family, religion, schools, social group,* and *economic class* interact with the active, direct influences of what people *see, hear, or read—their experience.* The environmental factors provide the glasses through which we see and interpret the public scene. Our environment and our experience fuse. These primary factors of opinion formation and change lead to the intense competition for public attention. The struggle for men's minds is waged with slogans, symbols, and stereotypes in all media of communication, in our schools, plants, stores, and offices. *Pragmatic agreement on the factors of what people see, hear, or*

16 Herbert Blumer, "The Mass, The Public, and Public Opinion," in *New Outline of the Principles of Sociology,* edited by Alfred McClung Lee (New York: Barnes and Noble, Inc., 1946), pp. 185-93.

read as the primary forces influencing opinions leads to the inevitable struggle as to what the public shall or shall not see, read, or hear. This competition for men's minds becomes a battle of communication and censorship. Communication and censorship, or the lack of them, tend to regulate one's opinions and the rate of change.

COMMUNICATION. Social life is possible only through the ability to communicate, to transfer meaning between individuals. Group activity would be impossible without some means of sharing experiences and attitudes. Communication includes all the symbols of the mind, the means of conveying them, and the means of preserving them. To reach, to understand, and to influence another, a person must communicate. This is basic in the interacting process and *the nub of public relations.*

Today's public-opinion market place is loud with the babble of men and issues clamoring for attention and consent. Every group faces strong, strident competition. Each person has less and less time, attention, and energy to give to more and more things thrust upon him. His time goes to those things that seize his attention and seem to merit his support.

The primary factors of what we see, hear, or read—the factors that *activate* our opinions—are selected out of a welter of things to see, read, or hear. Newspapers, books, and magazines are showered down upon us in an endless torrent. Radio programs fill our ears from sunrise to bedtime. Television, the movies, bowling, and baseball compete for what little leisure time is left after we've earned a living and given some time to our families.

The importance of communication is underscored by the fact that *each individual acts on the basis of that which he knows or thinks he knows.* The world is a big and casual place. To the individual, it frequently appears a confused and chaotic place. Each person can know with accurate, first-hand knowledge only a tiny fragment of the world's affairs. Yet he must have opinions and pass judgment. For this reason, one's judgments are rarely based on research and logical deduction. They are, for the most part, borrowed expressions accepted on the authority of others—a "talker" in the neighborhood, a union leader, the local paper, advertising, the boss, a TV commentator, a faraway "expert," or a favorite uncle.

CENSORSHIP. Censorship represents an effort to influence opinions by *suppression* of what persons might see, read, or hear. *Opinions can be affected by what one does not know as much as by what he does know.* Opinions based on no facts, part of the facts, or all of the facts are likely to be quite different. Thus, the tool of censorship is used to create or obliterate an individual's opinions. Dictators know this well. So do "managers of the news."

There are two kinds of censorship. *Artificial censorship* is deliberately invoked at the source or along the lines of communication. *Natural censorship* is effected by barriers of physical, psychological, and semantic distance and difference. The latter derive spontaneously from the environment of organized society. They intervene at many points in the communication process. Not the least of these is the individual's self-imposed *censorship of attention.*

People see what they wish to see, hear what they wish to hear, believe what they wish to believe. Research indicates that changes in opinion over short time spans are small in relation to overwhelming barrages of information. *Opinions are the basis for selective exposure to information.*

It is easy—especially in the mass media—for people to avoid exposure to information. It takes only a flick of the dial or a flip of the page. We tend to expose ourselves to that information which seems to agree with us. Breaking through the individual's wall of isolation and insulation of fixed attitudes and limited scope of interest is not easy. Sales managers know this. Psychologists generally hold that emotional experiences far outweigh information in the shaping of opinion. If information is to have influence on attitudes and behavior, it must be related to one's sense of values. Value judgments are essentially tied to the emotional processes.

The values each individual gives a situation determine what he perceives. This brings us to a key point. *Nearly every problem in public relations has its roots in the difference in perception—two or more people viewing the same situation in different ways.* An individual's values stem from his heritage, his previous experiences, his sentiments, his likes and dislikes, his sense of obligation to others, his ideals, his goals, and his definition of self-interest. In short, his *mental set.* For each one of us reality is whatever our values permit us to recognize as reality. We constantly seek to reinforce our beliefs and our values by selecting those facts from a situation which are consistent with what we believe. We ignore those facts which conflict with our beliefs. The business executive reads *Business Week;* the UAW member reads *Solidarity.* The factors of *awareness* and *evaluation* guide each person in what communications he accepts and in what he censors. Communication and censorship govern the flow of opinion change.

GENERATORS
OF OPINION CHANGE

A host of forces and groups are constantly at work in promoting changes in old opinions and creating new ones. These *generators* of opinion keep the opinion process in a state of ferment and flux:

   a. Programs of industry, labor, agriculture, government, education, social welfare agencies, and so forth.
   b. Political parties.
   c. Pressure, professional, and interest groups.
   d. Propagandists for partisan causes.
   e. Press, including all mass media.
   f. Churches.

It is necessary to keep in mind the continuing interaction of all the forces and factors. Man is a creature of culture, yet creates his culture. Attitudes shape opinions. Expressed opinions, in turn, reformulate attitudes. The family influences the child, who, in turn, influences the family. The group norms guide the behavior of the group's members, yet the members determine the norms. The press, through its content and emphasis, builds and changes opinions. Yet the content and emphasis in the mass media are selected in response to the opinions of the audience. Men create and direct organizations. Yet, as Chester I. Barnard once noted, when the efforts of five men become coordinated in an organization, there is created something new that is wholly apart and different from the sum of the five individuals. The "organization" shapes their opinions as they guide it. Political parties generate opinions, yet they spread and shape themselves to appeal to the most people. The way our two-party system aggregates opinions was seen by Key: [17]

> Each party leadership must maintain the loyalty of its own standpatters; it must also concern itself with the great blocks of voters uncommitted to either party as well as those who may be weaned away from the opposition. These influences tend to pull the party leaderships from their contrasting anchorages toward the center. In that process, perhaps most visible in presidential campaigns, the party appeals often sound much alike. . . .

It is this host of variables interacting upon one another with varying effects that makes this mercurial substance so difficult to grasp. "At all times it is difficult to determine whether public opinion is leading or being led, followed or manipulated." The answer is, both. *Public relations programs guide and are guided by public opinion.* The process will remain more of an art than a science until we build up what is now the imperfect knowledge and science of the mind.

SOME "LAWS"
OF PUBLIC OPINION

Hadley Cantril some years ago worked out "some laws of public opinion" on the basis of intensive study of the trends over a decade. Cantril holds that trends, as recorded by the polls, support these generalizations: [18]

> 1. Opinion is highly sensitive to important events.
> 2. Events of unusual magnitude are likely to swing public opinion temporarily from one extreme to another. Opinion does not become stabilized until the implications of events are seen with some perspective.
> 3. Opinion is generally determined more by events than by words—unless those words are themselves interpreted as "events."
> 4. Verbal statements and outlines of course of action have maximum importance when opinion is unstructured, when people are suggestible and seek some interpretation from a reliable source.

---

17 V. O. Key, *Politics, Parties and Pressure Groups* (New York: Thomas Y. Crowell Company, 1958), p. 241.

18 Hadley Cantril, *Gauging Public Opinion* (Princeton, N.J.: Princeton University Press, 1947). See the chapter "The Use of Trends," pp. 220-30.

5. By and large, public opinion does not anticipate emergencies, it only reacts to them.

6. Psychologically, opinion is basically determined by self-interest. Events, words, or any other stimuli affect opinion only in so far as their relationship to self-interest is apparent.

7. Opinion does not remain aroused for any long period of time unless people feel their self-interest is acutely involved or unless opinion—aroused by words—is sustained by events.

8. Once self-interest is involved, opinions are not easily changed.

9. When self-interest is involved, public opinion in a democracy is likely to be ahead of official policy.

10. When an opinion is held by a slight majority or when opinion is not solidly structured, an accomplished fact tends to shift opinion in the direction of acceptance.

11. At critical times, people become more sensitive to the adequacy of their leadership—if they have confidence in it, they are willing to assign more than usual responsibility to it; if they lack confidence in it, they are less tolerant than usual.

12. People are less reluctant to have critical decisions made by their leaders if they feel that somehow they, the people, are taking some part in the decision.

13. People have more opinions and are able to form opinions more easily with respect to goals than with respect to methods necessary to reach those goals.

14. Public opinion, like individual opinion, is colored by desire. And when opinion is based chiefly on desire rather than on information, it is likely to show especially sharp shifts with events.

15. By and large, if people in a democracy are provided educational opportunities and ready access to information, public opinion reveals a hard-headed common sense. The more enlightened people are to the implications of events and proposals for their own self-interest, the more likely they are to agree with the more objective opinions of realistic experts.[19]

PRINCIPLES
OF PERSUASION

Research in the social sciences has brought, in recent years, some tentative principles of persuasion based on experimental research.[20]

1. To accomplish attitude change, a suggestion for change must first be received and accepted. "Acceptance of the message" is a critical factor in persuasive communication.

2. The suggestion is more likely to be accepted if it meets existing personality needs and drives.

---

[19] For sharp criticism of these "laws," see the chapter "The Behavior of Public Opinion," in Leonard Doob, *Public Opinion and Propaganda* (New York: Holt, Rinehart & Winston, Inc., 1948). Doob says it is premature to hazard a set of laws, and then proceeds to fashion some of his own.

[20] These are condensed from a number of sources, including: Herbert I. Abelson, *op. cit.;* Schramm's *Process and Effects of Mass Communications,* a reader; Katz and Lazarsfeld's *Personal Influence,* *op. cit.,* and Carl I. Hovland, Irving L. Janis, and Harold M. Kelley, *Communication and Persuasion* (New Haven: Yale University Press, 1953). All of these sources use the research of many people in arriving at these "principles." These books cite, too, the original research upon which they are based.

3. The suggestion is more likely to be accepted if it is in harmony with group norms and loyalties.
4. The suggestion is more likely to be accepted if the source is perceived as trustworthy or expert.
5. A suggestion in the mass media, coupled with face-to-face reinforcement, is more likely to be accepted than a suggestion carried by either alone, other things being equal.
6. Change in attitude is more likely to occur if the suggestion is accompanied by other factors underlying belief and attitude. This refers to a changed environment which makes acceptance easier.
7. There probably will be more opinion change in the desired direction if conclusions are explicitly stated than if the audience is left to draw its own conclusions.
8. When the audience is friendly, or when only one position will be presented, or when immediate but temporary opinion change is wanted, it is more effective to give only one side of the argument.
9. When the audience disagrees, or when it is probable that it will hear the other side from another source, it is more effective to present both sides of the argument.
10. When equally attractive opposing views are presented one after another, the one presented last will probably be more effective.
11. Sometimes emotional appeals are more influential; sometimes factual ones are. It depends on the kind of message and kind of audience.
12. A strong threat is generally less effective than a mild threat in inducing desired opinion change.
13. The desired opinion change may be more measurable some time after exposure to the communication than right after exposure.
14. The people you want most in your audience are least likely to be there. This goes back to the censorship of attention that the individual invokes.
15. There is a "sleeper effect" in communications received from sources which the listener regards as having low credibility. In some tests, time has tended to wash out the distrusted source and leave information behind.

Counselor Earl Newsom has compressed the relatively little known about public opinion into these principles: [21] (*Interpolations are ours.*)

1. *Identification Principle.* People will ignore an idea, an opinion, a point of view unless they see clearly that it affects their personal fears or desires, hopes or aspirations.

Your message must be stated in terms of the interest of your audience.

2. *Action Principle.* People do not buy ideas separated from action—either action taken or about to be taken by the sponsor of the idea, or action which people themselves can conveniently take to prove the merit of the idea.

Unless a means of action is provided, people tend to shrug off appeals to do things.

3. *Principle of Familiarity and Trust.* We the people buy ideas only from those we trust; we are influenced by, or adopt, only those opinions or points of view put forward by individuals or corporations or institutions in whom we have confidence.

---

[21] Compiled from two published addresses by Newsom.

Unless the listener has confidence in the speaker, he is not likely to listen or to believe.

4. *Clarity Principle.* The situation must be clear to us, not confusing. The thing we observe, read, see, or hear, the thing which produces our impressions, must be *clear,* not subject to several interpretations.

To communicate, you must employ words, symbols, or stereotypes that the receiver understands and comprehends.

Additional Reading

William Albig, *Modern Public Opinion.* New York: McGraw-Hill, Inc., 1956.

Floyd H. Allport, "Toward a Science of Public Opinion," *Public Opinion Quarterly,* Vol. 1, January, 1937. Still useful.

Bernard Berelson and Morris Janowitz, *Reader in Public Opinion and Communication.* New York: The Free Press of Glencoe, Inc., rev. ed., 1953.

Robert T. Golembiewski, *The Small Group: An Analysis of Research Concepts and Operations.* Chicago: University of Chicago Press, 1962. Useful introduction to research centered on the group.

Rex F. Harlow, *Public Relations and the Social Sciences,* New York: Harper & Row, Publishers, 1957.

Floyd Hunter, *Community Power Structure.* Chapel Hill: University of North Carolina Press, 1953. (Study of a specific city.)

————, *Top Leadership,* USA. Chapel Hill: University of North Carolina Press, 1959.

Joseph A. Kahl, *The American Class Structure,* New York: Holt, Rinehart & Winston, Inc., 1957.

Daniel Katz, ed., special issue, "Attitude Change," *Public Opinion Quarterly,* Vol. 24, Summer, 1960. (Also available in book form.)

Alfred McClung Lee, *How to Understand Propaganda.* New York: Holt, Rinehart & Winston, Inc., 1952.

Curtis MacDougall, *Understanding Public Opinion.* New York: The Macmillan Company, 1952.

Pierre Martineau, *Motivation in Advertising: Motives That Make People Buy.* New York: McGraw-Hill, Inc., 1957.

James N. Rosenau, *National Leadership and Foreign Policy: A Case Study in the Mobilization of Public Support.* Princeton, N.J.: Princeton University Press, 1963.

Oren Stephens, *Facts to a Candid World.* Stanford, Cal.: Stanford University Press, 1955. (See Chaps. 2 and 3.)

Chapter Six

THE

PRACTITIONERS—

STAFFS

AND

STATUS

The specialty of public relations will attain top professional status at an accelerated speed, but the distance to go is still substantial.—Dan J. Forrestal.

There are some 35,000 men and women engaged in the professional practice of public relations in the United States. Thousands more are employed in public relations agencies and departments as secretaries, technicians, and clerks. Additional thousands of persons handle public relations responsibilities as part of other jobs. It is difficult to arrive at precise figures in a field so fluid, with the many titles and with the variety of duties which characterize them. In 1960 the United States Census included for the first time the job classification, "Public Relations Men and Publicity Writers." Prior to 1960, public relations workers had been classified under the broad category of "Editors and Reporters." The 1960 Census recorded a total of 31,141 men and women employed in the civilian labor force as public-relations practitioners or publicity writers. Of this total, 23,870 were men and 7,271 were women. The Census figures are shown in Tables I and II.

These Census figures are open to some question and appear to be on the low side. For example, the Census does not include those in the armed forces; the Army, Navy, Air Force, and Marine Corps, collectively, have nearly 2,000 full-time public information officers. For another, the Census shows 1,222 persons under the "public administration" category, yet the U.S.I.A. alone employs more professional practitioners than this. No accurate figures on the number of persons employed in public relations tasks in our federal and state governments have been compiled, despite repeated efforts of legislative committees and scholars to do so. Nonetheless, these 1960 Census figures give the most accurate estimate of the size of this field that we have yet had. This census erased the commonly used round number of 100,000 quoted in trade talk for years.

In an effort to determine the rate of growth in public relations, the Census Bureau developed comparative figures from the 1950 Census which showed a 63.9 per cent gain in the number of practitioners over the 1950-1960 decade. The 1950 total was derived by a sampling procedure. These figures, too, are open to question, but they do reflect the solid fact that public relations is a growing field of endeavor and employment. The figures are shown in Table III. *Harper's Magazine* once described it as "our fastest-growing industry." Concrete evidence of growth abounds. Most of this growth is taking place inside departments in industry, government, education, health, and social welfare rather than in the public relations counseling firms.

Despite public relations' over-all growth, counseling agencies have remained rather stable in number and size over the past decade. There are an estimated 1,500 public relations firms in the United States, ranging in size from man and secretary to staffs of 100 or more. Eighteen years after the end of World War II, the two agencies that were the largest remained in this position but did not grow much in size. Today, it is probable that not more than a half-dozen PR agencies or advertising agencies employ more than 100 persons in public relations. Public relations agencies have not grown at the same

Table I

NUMBER OF PUBLIC RELATIONS PRACTITIONERS

	Experienced Civilian Labor Force			*Employed*		
Region	*Total*	*Male*	*Female*	*Total*	*Male*	*Female*
Northeast	10,468	7,628	2,840	10,131	7,416	2,715
North Central	7,308	5,809	1,499	7,191	5,742	1,449
South	6,621	5,234	1,387	6,527	5,164	1,363
West	6,744	5,199	1,545	6,514	5,036	1,478
Totals	31,141	23,870	7,271	30,363	23,358	7,005

(From U.S. Census Bureau. Extracted from Table No. 256, "Detailed Occupation of the Experienced Civilian Labor Force and of the Employed, by Sex, for Regions: 1960.")

rate as have advertising agencies in recent years. It is the belief of Chester Burger that the notion that one account executive can handle all aspects of a client's program has been largely responsible for the lack of growth in public relations agencies. He says, rightly, "the need has grown, but apparently, relatively few agencies have met the test." [1]

---

[1] In "Why Haven't PR Agencies Grown?" *Quarterly Review of Public Relations,* Vol. 6, Winter, 1961, pp. 17-22.

Table II

EMPLOYERS OF PUBLIC RELATIONS PRACTITIONERS

Male, Employed—Public Relations Men and Publicity Writers:

Total, 14 years old and over	23,358
Agriculture, Forestry, and Fisheries	68
Mining	116
Construction	287
Manufacturing (Total)	5,053
Furniture, and Lumber and Wood Products	118
Primary Ferrous Industries	175
Primary Nonferrous Industries	92
Fabricated Metal Industries (incl. not spec. metal)	247
Machinery (exc. electrical)	353
Electrical Machinery, Equipment, and Supplies	539
Motor Vehicles and Motor Vehicle Equipment	366
Aircraft and Parts	368
Other Transportation Equipment	74
Other Durable Goods	345
Food and Kindred Products	636
Textile Mill Products	50
Apparel and Other Fabricated Textile Products	31
Printing, Publishing, and Allied Industries	625
Chemicals and Allied Products	490
Rubber and Miscellaneous Plastic Products	84
Other Nondurable Goods (incl. not spec. mfg.)	460
Railroads and Railway Express Service	249
Trucking Service and Warehousing	174
Other Transportation	462
Communications	1,282
Utilities and Sanitary Services	861
Wholesale Trade	890
Food and Dairy Products Stores, and Milk Retailing	95
General Merchandise and Limited-Price Variety Stores	122
Eating and Drinking Places	66
Other Retail Trade	290
Finance, Insurance, and Real Estate	2,415
Business Services	4,056
Repair Services	62
Hotels and Lodging Places	133
Other Personal Services (incl. private household)	118
Entertainment and Recreation Services	873
Medical and Other Health Services	447
Educational Services, Government	630
Educational Services, Private	980
Welfare, Religious, and Nonprofit Membership Organizations	2,062
Other Professional and Related Services	276
Public Administration	1,222
Industry Not Reported	69

(U.S. Census. Extracted from Table 209, "Industry Group of the Employed, by Occuption and Sex for the United States: 1960.")

Table III

ESTIMATED RATE OF GROWTH IN NUMBER OF PRACTITIONERS

Public Relations Men and Publicity Writers

	1960	*1950*	*Per Cent Increase* *1950-1960*
Total	31,141	19,000	63.9
Male	23,870	17,000	40.4
Female	7,271	2,000	263.6

(U.S. Census. Extracted from Table 201, "Detailed Occupation of the Experienced Civilian Labor Force, by Sex, for the United States: 1960 and 1950.")

PRACTITIONERS' TASKS

Eight major job classifications of public relations work were developed in a vocational guidance survey conducted by the Education Committee of the Public Relations Society of America. These are:

1. *Writing.* Reports, news releases, booklet texts, radio and TV copy, speeches, film sequences, trade paper and magazine articles, product information, and technical material.
2. *Editing.* Employee publications, newsletters, shareholder reports, and other management communications, directed to both organization personnel and external groups.
3. *Placement.* Contacts with the press, radio, and TV, as well as with magazine, Sunday supplement, and trade editors, with a view toward enlisting their interest in publishing an organization's or a client's news and features.
4. *Promotion.* Special events, such as press parties, convention exhibits, and special showings; open house, new facility, and anniversary celebrations; special day, week, or month observances; contests and award programs; guest relations; institutional movies; visual aids.
5. *Speaking.* Appearances before groups and the planning requisite to finding appropriate platforms. The preparation of speeches for others, organization of speakers' bureaus, and the delivery of speeches.
6. *Production.* Knowledge of art and layout for the development of brochures, booklets, special reports, photographic communications, and house periodicals is required.
7. *Programming.* The determination of need, definition of goals, and recommended steps in carrying out the project. This is the highest-level job in public relations, one requiring maturity in counseling management.
8. *Institutional Advertising.* Advertising a company's name and reputation through purchased space or time is a function of public relations. Close coordination with advertising departments is maintained, and frequently the advertising-public relations responsibility is a dual one.

THE SIZE OF PR STAFFS

Public relations departments and agencies range in the size of their staffs. Similarly, organizational budgets range from a few thousand dollars to the multi-million-dollar budgets of General Motors, U. S. Steel, du Pont de Nemours, and other corporate giants. Counseling firms show a similar spread. Many are comprised of a man-and-wife team or man-and-secretary; more have larger staffs of specialists. The largest agencies are Carl Byoir & Associates, Hill & Knowlton, Inc., and Ruder & Finn. The advertising agencies of N. W. Ayer and Son, J. Walter Thompson, and Young & Rubicam have large publicity departments.

The trend is clear. The Gallagher Report, in a survey made in 1963, found that nearly 82 per cent of 344 corporate PR directors responding agreed that their companies were putting more emphasis on PR than they had five years before. Over this same five-year period, 56.6 per cent of all United States companies enlarged their PR departments and increased their PR budgets. Less than 3 per cent had cut the function down. The average company in this Gallagher survey had had a department 13 years and at the time of the survey had a professional staff of 11. The majority of PR directors reported directly to the company president or the chairman of the board. Nine out of ten PR executives said that they had very satisfactory access to top management. The average PR director studied in this survey earned $21,500 annually, although, in the companies with sales of a billion dollars a year or more, salaries passed the $65,000 figure. In 100 million-dollar to 500 million-dollar companies, the average is about $19,000.[2]

A survey of manpower and function among 166 product-making corporations by the Information Center Committee, Public Relations Society of America, showed these figures:

Size of Companies in Sales	Average Number of Persons in PR Dept.	Average Number of Persons Doing PR Jobs
Over $1,000,000,000	65	77
$500,000,000 to $1,000,000,000	20	26
$250,000,000 to $500,000,000	13	17
$100,000,000 to $250,000,000	12	13
$50,000,000 to $100,000,000	6	10
Under $50,000,000	4	6

THE SCOPE
OF THE FUNCTION

The variety of functions performed is indicated by the response of 108 organizations to the question: "What responsibilities might fall under the normal functioning of a PR department?" The question was asked in a survey by the Champion Paper Company, with these results:

---

2 *The Gallagher Report*, Vol. 11, July 22, 1963.

Responsibilities	*Number of Companies*
Press-Radio-TV	99
Employee Publications	50
Special Events	45
Policy Making	43
Miscellaneous Manuals and Leaflets	40
Editing and Writing	36
Annual Reports	34
Photography	33
Community Relations	31
Speakers' Bureau	28
Mailing and Distribution	20
Training and Education	19
Survey Research	19
Advertising	16
Movie Distribution	16
Stockholder Relations	15
Employee Relations	14
Contributions	11
Movie Production	11
Customer Relations	7
External Publications	1

As for variations in counseling firm functions, data collected by *Advertising Age* showed these "other services performed" beyond the clearly defined area of communications:

Legislative Work	Spot Assignments
Advertising Agencies Selection	Labor Relations
Institutional Advertising Planning	Stockholder Relations
Institutional Advertising Preparation	Trade Shows and Exhibits

The manpower and function survey of the Information Center Committee, PRSA, listed the following activities in the order that 166 PR staffs were doing these jobs as part of their going programs:

Activity	*Per Cent*
Press Relations	92.7
Product Publicity	92.7
Company Contributions	88.6
Community Relations	88.0
Publications	88.0
Photography	83.1
Speeches for Executives	82.5
School Relations	81.3
Investor Relations	70.5
General Internal Communications	60.2

The titles by which PR executives are known tend to confirm the variation and scope of the duties performed. Among counseling firms and advertising agencies, the titles are usually *counsel, counselor, consultant, agent,* or *account executive.*

In industry, the Champion Paper Company survey disclosed this roster:

Title	Per Cent
Director of Public Relations	56
Manager of Public Relations	13
Vice-President	11
Assistant to President	3
Assistant Vice-President	3
Vice-President and Director of Public Relations	2
Director of Industrial Relations	2
Director of Advertising	2
Corporate Director	1
General Manager	1
Assistant to General Manager	1
Sales Promotion Manager	1
Supervisor of Public Relations	1
Publications Editor	1

It is significant that in at least 70 per cent of the above list, the function is given an identity as "public relations" and obviously apart from advertising, as such, industrial relations, or personnel. In recent years there have been some noteworthy consolidations of PR and advertising and of PR and personnel, mainly in very large corporations. The preponderance remains on the side of separate identities for these specialized staff functions.

REMUNERATION

The variations in staff with respect to size, function performed, and titles do not mean that the professional practice has no shape or dimension. Rather, it means that the practice has had to be flexible. It has had to take on the talents and manpower to cope with the tasks assigned. It has not, being new, been able to select all tasks for itself. This reflects the fluidity of the concept. This flexibility extends to the income which practitioners receive, and to the manner in which they are paid.

Early in this decade, the Publicity Club of Chicago made a survey of pay ranges in public relations in that city. Eighty-eight employers of practitioners responded, reporting a salary range for public relations work from $4,000 to $50,000. Twelve positions were reported as follows: [3]

Position	Pay Range		Average
PR Director	$ 6,000 to	$50,000	$15,500
PR Writer	4,000 to	16,000	9,500
Assistant PR Director	5,000 to	30,000	11,500
Publicity Director	5,300 to	21,000	10,500
Staff Assistant	4,500 to	12,000	8,500
Account Executive	6,500 to	50,000	15,000
Editor	4,000 to	21,000	10,000
Radio-TV Manager	5,500 to	20,000	12,500
Industrial Relations Director	10,000 to	30,000	17,000
Fund Raising Director	7,500 to	15,000	10,000
Asst. Fund Raising Director	6,000 to	8,000	7,500
Community Relations Director	6,000 to	9,000	8,000

[3] Reported in *Blurbs,* club publication, January, 1961, p. 2.

In their study of the practice in Columbus, Ohio, Prof. Walter Seifert and William Moore found that practitioners' salaries ranged from $5,700 to $50,000. The majority of them, 67.5 per cent, earned from $5,700 to $12,000, whereas the remainder earned from $13,000 to $25,000, with the exception of one PR director, who received $50,000 a year.[4] The pattern of compensation characteristic of individual industries and organizations can be expected to apply to the pay of public relations workers. Variations according to geographic location will also be found, as a comparison of the Chicago and Columbus figures indicates. Workers in the nonprofit field are usually paid less than those in business and industry, and in the welfare field there is limited opportunity to climb higher than the $15,000-$20,000 range.[5] Women's salaries are generally less than those paid to men.

COUNSELING FEES

Counselors use several methods to charge clients for a sustained service or for a particular project. You can distinguish the more common methods by these definitions:

Fixed Fee. This is a one-cost contract. It is common with small or new accounts because it allows a fixed budget. The fixed fee tends to be a speculative and somewhat unpopular method so far as the counsel or agency is concerned. Frozen revenue, with not always fully predictable expenses, makes for uncertainty. The exception would be a long-established account where the job to be done is well known and the annual expenses can be accurately forecast.

Fixed Fee with Out-of-Pocket Bill-Back. This provides for a flat, one-cost contract for internal services. External trade services, such as modeling or printing, are billed back to the client at cost.

Fixed Fee plus Hourly Billing, Plus Out-of-Pocket Bill-Back. This provides for personnel time-charges, such as salary for specific job assignments, as a breakdown of internal costs. This is usually rendered in addition to an agreed monthly retainer fee. Outside services are then billed back at cost.

Fixed Fee plus Hourly, plus Overhead, plus Out-of-Pocket. This provides for a breakdown, not only of personnel time or salary charges, but also of overhead, to include rent, light, and accounting. There is usually an agreed monthly retainer to cover the cost of supervision and profit. Outside services are billed back at cost. Advertising agencies with PR departments, long adjusted to the idea of 15 per cent commission, tend to introduce the commission, as such, into billing procedure.

Although these four basic systems are used in establishing charging practices for public relations services, the actual cost to the client for such services varies considerably, based on five factors.[6] In a study of fees and charging prac-

---

[4] William C. Moore, "A Critical Analysis of Public Relations Practitioners in a Midwestern Metropolitan Area." Unpublished master's thesis, Ohio State University, 1962, p. 18.

[5] Public Relations Society of America, *Let's Consider Public Relations, An Occupational Guide* (New York: PRSA, 1963), p. 18.

[6] The Rubel Service, "Public Relations Charging Practices," published and distributed by Robert Associates, 862 Grove Street, Glencoe, Ill., Vol. 3, September, 1960, p. 498.

tices by public relations agencies, the Counselors Section of PRSA found a broad understanding that these elements must be included or reflected in a cost statement if the counselor is to stay in business: [7]

1. Cost of the staff used on the project.
2. Executive time and supervision.
3. Overhead costs.
4. Out-of-pocket costs—for example, telephone and travel.
5. A reasonable profit for doing work.

There are wide variations in accounting procedures and in arriving at client costs. For example, there are different ways used in determining the hourly value of individuals working on accounts. Some firms use cost accounting based on dollar salary cost per hour plus overhead and profit determined by mathematical formulas; some firms guess at their approximate cost, and then apply an arbitrary factor for all clients; others use different factors for different clients. There is equal variation in arriving at overhead costs. Some firms build time spent getting new business into overhead; others do not. Public relations agencies, generally speaking, need better cost accounting procedures and more common agreement on methods of charging clients.

THE WORKING OF A PR DEPARTMENT

Where there is no outside counseling, an internal department handles all four steps in the PR process. Operating on a budget, the staff undertakes fact-finding. They set up objectives and plan programs. They follow through with the necessary communications and events. They evaluate results. Many departments vary this pattern by hiring opinion research firms to measure public opinion and to evaluate results.

The work of the staff will in all probability be segmented. Someone will be designated to edit the house magazine, to handle the news service, to contact the press, to stage special events, to conduct the plant tours, to prepare speeches.

The alternative to dividing the tasks among the staff is to establish a Jack-of-all-trades group, assigning projects on a "who's not busy now?" basis.

In both of these setups there will be the need to retain some outside services, because either time or talent is lacking internally. Typical outside services would be the layout, artwork, printing, binding, and mailing of a fiftieth-anniversary booklet. The internal staff might have planned the book and its content and distribution and have written its copy.

Other examples could be the refreshments catering for an open house, the monitoring of press notices, radio and TV broadcasts, lecturing at a seminar, and the mimeographing and mailing of news releases.

---

[7] "Fees, Charges and Overhead in the Practice of Public Relations," A Study Report Sponsored by the Counselors' Section, Public Relations Society of America, December, 1961, pp. 7-8.

THE PR DEPARTMENT'S
ADVANTAGES

An internal staff practitioner has four factors working for him:

1. He has team membership.
2. He has knowledge of the organization.
3. He represents economy to the organization.
4. He is available constantly to his associates.

Team Membership is a great advantage. The confidence and support of team members go with it. This tends to overcome or to relegate into unimportance the natural antagonism toward any new function or person. At the same time, the close connection between the PR work and the chief executive office of the organization provides *first team* membership, rather than remote or insignificant membership.

Knowledge of the Organization means an intimate, participating knowledge that comes from being an insider. The staff man knows the relationships between individuals and their functions within the organization. He knows the undercurrents of influence, the key people, the conservatives, the harmful ones who put personal ambition and expedience ahead of the organization's interests, the articulate and the tongue-tied.

This kind of knowledge can be acquired by an outsider. But the insider is in a position to do most about it continuously. He can advise where needed, conciliate, and render services from within to induce attitudes and actions which will bring about harmonious relationships *inside* as well as outside.

Economy can result simply from residency in an organization, and from integration in an organization. For example, the PR department's bills for rent, heat, and light in a large organization are not expressed in a manner that looms large. They are expressed generally as a small part of an over-all cost for many departments and offices.

Similarly, for an event like a 100th anniversary, the PR department's activity is not a single, separate cost. It is part of a celebration cost. Perhaps the only separate departmental tasks are to prepare a booklet and to place a giant cake with 100 candles on the front lawn. Concurrently during the year the advertising department may run special ads. The Board of Directors may establish a scholarship in memory of the founder. All employees may be given a holiday on the birth date. These activities, to the publics involved, would all be PR. Only two, however, were in this instance charged or executed departmentally.

Availability of the staff practitioner has many facets. When things go wrong, he is not one minute from a face-to-face meeting with the organization's officials. As a deputy, he can be entrusted with delicate matters. When a senior executive resigns in a huff, the president wants a PR man on the spot who knows the background, understands the dangers of mishandling the news, and has credibility with the press. In such a situation the head of an organization would feel uneasy dealing through an outside PR man.

Availability means that the staff is on call for all departments, divisions, and decentralized units. The staff man can slip into and out of committees and meetings. He *belongs*. He is handy for consultation. He has both acceptability and authority.

His availability to perform service functions involves him in a broad range of PR-oriented activities. He may be asked to handle a tour of facilities for some foreign visitors who do not speak English. He may represent his organization on a local Civil Defense committee. He may advise an employee's family on the recovery of a lost child. He may respond for the organization on receipt of a citation. Or, he may make the arrangements for his president's vacation or for the wedding of his daughter.

A HOST OF
PERSONALIZED SERVICES

The personalized-service aspects of professional practice should be regarded seriously. They are numerous. They are important in the eyes of employers and clients. The outside counselor, too, becomes involved frequently. As an illustration, here is a list of some PR-oriented tasks. All these appeared on a practitioner's calendar during a few months of one year. They are typical.

Formation of letter-writing clinic for secretaries
Consult on athletic association by-laws
Devise program for golf tournament
Establish memorial fund
Arrange for employee's son to enter Soap Box Derby
Speak at "Press Club" of house magazine reporters
Donate prize for foremen's banquet
Judge beauty contest
Arrange loan of equipment for outing
Participate in three industrial exhibits
Review little-theater plays for local newspaper
Counsel on high school commencement program
Judge YMCA handicrafts exhibit
Arrange loan of helicopter to civic event
Supply sports celebrity to Little League banquet
Arrange for display of guided missile
Participate in survey on future housing

THE PR DEPARTMENT'S
HANDICAPS

The staff man's advantage of team membership, and his continuous availability, are handicaps on occasion. *He loses objectivity.* In being supported by the team, he tends to be conciliatory in his views. He is in constant danger of becoming a "yes" man. Much of his time is diverted from long-range planning to daily crises of small import. These handicaps add up to *domination and subjectivity.*

A Biblical saying describes the occupational hazard of the staff man. "A prophet is not without honour save in his own country and in his own house." At a glance that seems in strange contradiction with the support and deference often rendered him by teammates in an organization. It bears closer inspection because the support tends to become possessive in the manner of a bear hug.

The staff man *is* in his own country. He *is* in his own house. He is contained by all the emotional elements of belonging in an organization. He is harnessed to an office a large part of the time. In that office are a desk to catch the daily mail, a telephone to receive the daily calls, and chairs to accommodate the daily visitors from down the hall. As a result, the details preclude the benefits of regular outside contacts for refreshing stale viewpoints. The people with whom he exchanges opinions daily tend to look, to feel, and to talk the same as they did the day before. They place him in the middle of conflicts. There is the daily necessity of making innumerable small decisions that push from his mind the challenge of grappling with larger or more remote matters. *Availability exacts a price.*

As a part of the restrictive influences, the staff man's viewpoints on specific areas of communication trouble tend to be subordinated to the viewpoints of operating officials. The staff man must strive to hold to an objective viewpoint. This is never easy to do.

THE OUTSIDE COUNSELOR OR AGENCY

Public relations counseling firms in the United States range widely in size and scope of service. In addition, there are more than 200 advertising agencies offering public relations services to some degree.

The majority of counseling firms are engaged in public relations work exclusively. A growing number, however, are offering advertising, graphic arts, trade association management, and sales promotion services as well. There is a discernible trend toward specialization among public relations firms, for example, in financial relations, employee communications, and association management.

Most advertising agencies find it difficult to determine what, if any, public relations services to offer and how to effectively organize the PR function. N. W. Ayer pioneered in 1920, when it offered a publicity service for its advertising clients. In 1925, Albert Frank-Guenther Law took the next step when it expanded its operations to offer a full-fledged PR and publicity service. In the next few years, J. Walter Thompson, Young & Rubicam, and Benton & Bowles followed suit. By the mid-1940's, 75 agencies were providing publicity service for clients, according to an *Advertising Age* survey. In 1953 *Advertising Age* made another survey and concluded: "The role of the public relations department in the advertising agency is a strange one. Many topflight agencies billing over $5 million a year still do not have one. Many of those that do regard it purely as a service function."

In 1956 Marion Harper, of McCann-Erickson (now Interpublic), broke new ground by setting up that agency's public relations department as a wholly owned subsidiary corporation, Communication Counselors, Inc. Other agencies to follow suit included Benton & Bowles, Inc., with its General Public Relations, and Chirurg & Cairns, which set up Creative Public Relations. Harper ultimately folded CCI into Communications Affiliates, Inc., an Infopublic subsidiary, which includes market research, advertising and sales communications, and Infoplan, a worldwide public relations organization.

Today there are basically two kinds of advertising agencies—those offering some measure of PR service and those who shun it. Most agencies service only advertising clients; a few take on nonadvertising clients for public relations or publicity service. Most PR work in advertising agencies is spent in product publicity. Few agencies are adequately equipped to offer broad-gauge public relations counseling. A 1962 study of New York City advertising agencies by Public Relations Aids, Inc., found that 77 agencies (some 44 per cent of those queried) have either a separate PR department or a wholly owned subsidiary, or have set up an outside PR agency with interlocking ownership. Irving Smith Kogan asserts that "in spite of its growth, PR in the advertising agency business has had spotty success." [8]

Executive Report, a Prentice-Hall publication for top management, has predicted after making a special study that both public relations and advertising services will be taken over by agencies offering a complete communications service to industry by 1980. Marion Harper's Communications Affiliates was an effort to move in this direction. In a special report, *Executive Report* predicted that "the communications specialist will cut across artificial boundaries to solve the specific corporate problem most effectively." This publication predicted a need for an agency to which a client could take a total marketing or other communications problem and have it handled under one roof, coordinated through one account executive. *Executive Report* concluded: "We don't get Public Relations 1980 until the entire communications structure is unified. In part, most public relations agencies handle a variety of communications services. But all, to date, stop short of total communications service. . . ." [9]

A practitioner, William Safire, predicts the same thing in his *The Relations Explosion.* He thinks "relations services must change swiftly to meet the changing character of business." He predicts "A new type of communications method will develop. It will fuse together all the relations services to deal cohesively

---

8 In "Public Relations: Agency Stepchild," *Madison Avenue,* June, 1962, pp. 14-15 and 30.
9 Special study, "Inside Public Relations," issued by *Executive Report,* August, 1963. Published by Prentice-Hall, Inc.

with the publics that any business has to serve." [10] If Safire's predictions come true, the public relations, advertising, and marketing agencies undoubtedly will find the amalgamation painful.

Wherever public relations, advertising, and promotional services are mutually rendered, there is usually an effort to identify the firm as offering a "complete marketing service." This assumes that client organizations are invested with a marketing problem, whether it be an automobile, a safety campaign, better medical facilities, or charity.

Separate from counseling firms that offer a range of services, there are some which offer services of a highly specialized nature. Some offer only research, or employee communications advice, liaison in Washington, financial PR, press contacts, or product promotion. Diversification within a single agency to offer clients specialized services is also taking place.

Counselors find clients in a variety of ways. They send out literature about themselves. They solicit interviews. They use professional advertising. Perhaps the most effective means of acquiring clients is the endorsement of satisfied clients. The PR department of the advertising agency enjoys an advantage over the independent counselor in offering its services to those clients for whom it performs advertising. Occasionally, the advertising agency provides limited publicity or product-promotion services to advertising clients at no extra charge.[11]

Quite often it is the client, rather than the counselor, who does the seeking. This happens when the client has an emergency situation or imminent threat. This was the case, for example, when medical research reports linked cigarette smoking to cancer. Entering an emergency situation, the counselor has no choice. He must immediately try to correct the existing misunderstandings. Later on he can investigate the sources of the communication or performance breakdown and suggest preventive measures for the future.

In normal circumstances, the counsel will begin his service to a new client by exploring the health of the relationships between the client and those public groups on whom he depends. The initial exploration might take months. Whenever it is completed, one of three things can be expected to happen. The counselor tells the client that he finds no problem or threat of harm in communication of a magnitude to require outside assistance. Or, he tells him that the problems disclosed by the research are in a realm other than that of the PR field. Or, he tells him that there are problems which can be solved through the application of public relations techniques.

In the latter case, the counsel arranges to make a presentation of his findings. In this presentation are exposed: (a) the central core of the difficulty, (b) its current status in terms of harm to the organization, (c) related difficulties which must be considered, (d) ultimate alternatives to be faced,

---

10 Published by The Macmillan Company, 1963, with subtitle: "The Coming Boom and Shakeout in Corporate Relations."

11 For one example, see "Case History in Selecting a Public Relations Counsel," *Tide,* Vol. 30, October 26, 1956, pp. 24-26.

(e) desirable objectives, (f) a long-range plan shaped toward the objectives, and (g) an immediate program of actions involving anything pertinent, even if it involves the removal of a senior officer.

Not all of these factors in a presentation are exposed invariably at one sitting. The counselor, however, to establish a suitable working climate, must obtain an understanding on the full range before his firm's talents can be committed sincerely to the tasks.

The burden of proof for the effectiveness of advice and actions rests with the counsel. Many results are intangible, or even nebulous. Who can tell how many extra dollars for a charity drive came in because of the newspaper stories about the work of the charity during the year? Polls are helpful, but many of the common yardsticks are not appropriate. In oversimplified terms, the counsel submits reports of progress, holds periodic meetings with key people in the client's organization, and coordinates the program. As the counselor-client relationship matures, the shape of the client's enterprise most likely undergoes cloud-like variations. Communications programs are revamped, scrapped, or replaced. New ones are activated. Special devices are imagineered to deal with peculiar needs.

The counselor usually functions in one of three ways with clients:

1. He provides advice. The execution of plans is left to others.
2. He provides advice and undertakes full execution of plans.
3. He provides advice and collaborates with the client's staff to execute the plans.

Burger lists six reasons why outside agencies are retained: [12]

1. Management has not previously conducted a formal public relations program and lacks experience in organizing one.
2. Headquarters may be located away from New York City, the communications and financial center of the nation.
3. The wide range of up-to-date contacts maintained by an agency.
4. An outside agency can provide services of experienced executives who would be unwilling to move to other cities or whose salaries could not be afforded by a single firm.
5. An organization with its own PR department may be in need of highly specialized services which it cannot afford on a permanent basis.
6. The need in crucial matters of over-all outside policy for the independent judgment of an outsider.

THE COUNSELOR'S
ADVANTAGES

The greatest single advantage of the counselor to the client is his opportunity for *objectivity*. This is an advantage he enjoys over the staff man and

---

[12] In "Why Haven't PR Agencies Grown?," *op. cit.,* pp. 18-19.

the client. He need not be confused by the internal frictions of the organizations he serves. He need only be concerned with recognizing them and helping things run more smoothly. The fact that one vice-president's wife snubs another vice-president's wife is no cloud on his vision. He need not live with the day-by-day minutiae which plague his clients. He can stand apart from the complaints that reach the top official's desk each day and keep him so busy patching up communication chinks in the organization that he has no time to think through plans for a major overhaul. The counselor can conceive the overhaul without wasting time on the chinks. He is, in a phrase, a free agent.

A second advantage to the counselor is the *scope* of his operations and variety of skills. From an office in New York, Washington, or Chicago he can serve clients in Colorado, West Virginia, and Vermont. If that becomes impractical, he can open branch offices in major population centers. He can exchange services with firms in other cities. In cases of need, he can install sand-lot offices in Colorado, West Virginia, and Vermont. Reasonably intimate contact can be maintained through periodic meetings on the premises of clients. If that does not suffice, the counsel can help the client obtain a suitable staff director, or he can lend someone from his own staff.[13] At the same time, the counselor's central location in a metropolitan communications hub permits frequent and personal contact with the press, radio, magazines, and TV—the main means of external and outward communication for all clients. His contacts embrace the press in New York, Washington, Chicago, San Francisco, and Hollywood. Several firms offer publicity services on a United States network basis.

The staffs of large counseling firms or advertising agency PR departments might include news writers, magazine writers, trade journal writers, and speech writers. There might be radio and TV programmers, trained researchers, home economists, educators, sociologists, merchandisers, fund raisers, economists, engineers, political campaign experts, artists, and photographers.

Third in importance among the advantages accruing to a counselor is his *flexibility*. In the course of any year, a counselor will be confronted with communication problems of unbelievably varied nature. Typical would be a strike in a small town, a brutality case in a public institution, the introduction of a new product by a manufacturer, prospective legislation harmful to the interests of a trade association, and the inauguration of a new university president. The range of a successful counselor's services is wide. If the agency is a successful, substantial one, its range of experience is equally wide. In a sense, a public relations firm is a useful repository of living case histories. Each project adds to its fund of knowledge. Experience and versatility of staff make this possible. The counselor approaches the situations bolstered by past familiarity with them and the success or failure that attended previous encounters.

---

[13] For example, see James R. Hanson, "Prefab PR Department," *Public Relations Journal,* Vol. 12, April, 1956.

THE COUNSELOR'S
HANDICAP

The foregoing may make it sound as though the task of the counselor were simply to arrive on the premises. In the rendering of a counseling service—and this applies to almost all consultants—there is, with rare exception, an area of *antagonism*. That is the counselor's handicap. The antagonism toward outsiders is a natural human trait. The old guard resists change as a threat to its security. That goes for the new idea, the new approach, the new look. This resistance is common. It is almost a certainty in organizations that have been static for years.

An understanding of this resistance is a course of study in itself. Much the same kind of resistance is found in a household when a student son returns from one year of college and declares to his parents that they should remodel the house to include some of the modern devices found in the fraternity house or the dormitory. There is resistance—probably plenty of it. That does not mean that the idea is no good. It means that hostility comes naturally when changes of drastic or sudden nature are proposed.

The counselor, more often than not, is in the position of having to suggest changes designed to improve relationships. Whether the suggested changes involve policies, equipment, methods, or practices, the people responsible for them historically are alienated. Their realm is being "invaded." Their judgment is being "criticized." The offended ask, "What does *he* know about *our* business?"

Other handicaps for the counselor grow from this embryo. The insiders antagonized may attempt to discredit a counselor. He is labeled with the worst possible connotations of the term "outsider."

A finger of accusation might be pointed at the *superficiality* of the counselor's grasp of the organization's unique problems, the local angles of the problems, the historical contributions to success made by the policies and methods now being maligned. A finger of criticism might be pointed at the *costs* entailed in retaining the counselor's services and carrying out the program he proposes—with no guarantee that there will be concrete results.

THE DIVISION
OF RESPONSIBILITY

Regardless of variations in staff and scope, advantages and handicaps, all practitioners have the same philosophy of service. There are several natural questions. Is the counseling firm more or less effective than the PR department of the advertising agency? Than the internal PR staff? Are they all necessary? If so, in combination or separately?

In recent years there has been increased interest of counselors and advertising agencies in PR-oriented marketing services. This has been reflected by the internal PR staff's increasing role in product promotion and product publicity. Some professional resentments and frictions have grown. A few quotes will suffice to outline the situation and indicate the fervor of the feelings.

Corporate PR Executive: "It is not the proper job of a corporate public relations staff to devote its primary efforts to the direct selling of products or services. That is the function of the marketing or sales department.

"The primary job of the public relations man is to achieve broad public understanding of the manner in which his company operates to satisfy those for whom it was created to serve."

Corporate PR Executive: "Advertising and public relations can work together if each realizes . . . that the former is selling the products of industry, while the latter's job is to sell the institutions behind the products."

A Former President, PRSA: "Advertising is primarily an adjunct to the marketing effort. Public Relations is, on the other hand, an adjunct to marketing, to shareowner relations, to community relations, to employee relations, and to management: voice and eyes and ears."

New York Times Columnist: "The advertising agency is moving to a radically new concept of a full-scale marketing organization. In this type of operation advertising will be merely one function of the agency's work.

"Perhaps the biggest push behind the change is the fact that profits are shrinking under the setup calling for compensation on the basis of 15 per cent of media billings.

"Public relations people, unless they show the courage to reverse a trend . . . are faced with commercial suicide.

"Ad agencies are taking over more and more of the public relations work and 'downgrading' it by making it a publicity function of their operations."

Financial Editor: "Any concerted movement on the part of the advertising agencies to integrate their public relations and advertising business would be a step backwards in the over-all relationship of our corporations with the general public. It could only result in the public's interest being supplanted with the corporation's private interests—the increased sale of products."

Howard Chase, a counselor who has served as a staff director in a corporation, as head of McCann-Erickson's PR subsidiary, and now head of his own agency, rightly describes advertising and public relations as "un-identical twins." He has asserted: "While the target of both advertising and public relations may be a share of the human mind, the scope of advertising is limited, and will be limited, by the availability of purchasable media. There are no limitations on the scope and range of public relations. . . . It is my impression that recognition of these functional differences will gain wide acceptance in the years ahead at high executive levels." To date no single pattern of successful operation of a public relations agency within an advertising agency ownership has emerged. The basic difference which Chase suggests may be the reason.

THE TREND—
A HARMONIOUS TEAM

An effective working combination is the trend. The corporate publicity or product function being contested is but one segment of PR work. Certainly no advertising agency has claimed superiority in employee communications or civic events. Certainly, the matter of product promotion is not a major PR interest to the chairman of the Red Cross campaign, or to Cornell University. This division of responsibility would not concern a manufacturer of *capital* earth-moving equipment to the extent that it might interest the manufacturer of *consumer* garden tools.[14]

In practice, one-man crusades are less and less a part of the organizational concept. The team is the thing. It constitutes a logical trend in the specialization of industrial and institutional work. It is logical in the decentralization of industry, in the departmentalizing of government and the Armed Forces. Among corporations with products or services for mass consumption, complementing of counsel and staff is common. The same can be said of trade associations, trade unions, and welfare agencies, to name a few.

Exceptions are found among several very large corporate enterprises. In these instances—General Motors is a case in point—there is no regular outside counseling, but the internal staff is of such depth that its top level can devote itself to the counseling function. Other very large undertakings—Standard Oil Company of New Jersey, for example—are staffed internally in depth, yet retain outside counseling. Still a third setup provides for wide internal staff with outside counseling called in for special matters.

In organizations financed by public funds—the Armed Forces and state institutions—the general practice excludes expenditures for outside counsel, although the Armed Forces have used counsel for recruiting programs and perhaps other special government programs. The restraint seems more a consideration of politic usage of tax monies than a decision based on evaluations of the most effective approach to communications problems. Then, too, in these cases quite often specialized talent is already located somewhere in the organization, needing only reassignment and integration of efforts.

Two team organizations are common and both have been successful. One is a combination of outside counsel, either PR firm or ad agency, with a small internal staff to handle the localized problems. In the other organization, a large internal staff calls on counseling firms for advice in problems which need the outside viewpoint. In these two types of teams, each component aids the other. The outside counsel adds to the stature of the internal staff among

---

14 For typical patterns of organization, see "How Companies Run Their PR," *Tide*, Vol. 30, December 28, 1956; National Industrial Conference Board, *Public Relations in Industry* (New York: The Board, Studies in Business Policy, Number 80, 1956).

the top-echelon people in the organization. The internal staff aids the counselor by easing any antagonism.

There is no guaranteed combination. Public relations teams must be selected for each organization. They cannot be removed from one organization and slipped into another without some alteration. *Adaptation to the specific problems of each organization is a necessity.*

Additional Reading

Association of National Advertisers, *How Public Relations and Advertising Are Working Together to Meet Company Objectives.* New York: The Association, 285 Madison Avenue, New York 17.

Caroline Bird and Thomas D. Yutzy, "You Have to Manage Public Relations," *Harvard Business Review,* Vol. 35, Nov.-Dec., 1957.

Counselors' Section, Public Relations Society of America, *Public Relations and Public Relations Counseling.* New York: PRSA, 1962. 12 pages.

Bert C. Goss, "How Public Relations Counsel Works With Corporate Management," a speech given February 16, 1956, and published by Hill & Knowlton, Inc.

William J. Long, "Inside or Out?", *Public Relations Journal,* Vol. 12, May, 1956.

Alfred G. Paulson, "Profit Control in a Personal Service Business," *The New York Certified Public Accountant,* Vol. 33, January, 1963.

————, "Budgeting in the Public Relations Agency," *Quarterly Review of Public Relations,* Vol. 6, Fall, 1961.

————, "Fee Billing: A Return for the Effort Spent," *ibid.,* Vol. 6, Winter, 1961.

Irwin Ross, *The Image Merchants.* New York: Doubleday & Company, Inc., 1959. Profiles leading New York counselors.

Chapter Seven

THE

PR PROCESS:

FACT-FINDING—

THE

FIRST

STEP

"If we could first know where we are and whither we are tending, we could better judge what to do and how to do it."—Lincoln.

Organized practice is the continuing effort to bring about a harmonious adjustment between an institution and its publics. This adjustment requires, among other things, exchange of opinions and information. This does not just happen in today's complex society. It must be *planned* and *provided for*. This is the practitioner's job. He serves, in turn, the role of *listener, counselor, communicator,* and *evaluator* in this process.

The process has four basic steps:

1. *Research-Listening.* This means probing the opinions, attitudes, and reactions of persons concerned with the acts and policies of an organization, then evaluating the inflow. This task also requires determination of the facts regarding the organization. *"What's our problem?"*

2. *Planning-Decision Making.* This means bringing these attitudes, opinions, ideas, and reactions to bear on the policies and programs of an organization. This will enable it to chart a course in the mutual interests of all concerned. *"Here's what we can do."*

3. *Communication.* This means explaining and dramatizing the chosen course to all those who may be affected and whose support is essential. *"Here's what we did and why."*

4. *Evaluation.* This means evaluating the results of the program and the effectiveness of techniques used. *"How did we do?"*

Each one of these steps is as important as the others. Each one is vital to an effective program. Too often there is too little research, too little planning, and too much publicity. Emphasis on fact-finding and planning largely distinguishes public relations from straight publicity.

108

The program moves steadily forward in one *whole, continuing* process. The fluidity of the process does not permit a neat compartmentalization. As one has observed, the "public relations processes of analysis, synthesis, communication, and interpretation are continuous, spiraling, and overlapping processes."

One minute the industrial PR man will find himself called into the president's office and asked to ascertain, quickly, what the community's reaction will be if the company does not join the drive to keep the local professional baseball team. This requires *fact-finding*. Next he may go into a conference with the sales and advertising executives to devise plans for introducing a new product. This requires *counseling* and *planning*. He may break away from this huddle to keep a luncheon date with a reporter from the local paper for an interview on the firm's new pension plan. Here he serves as *communicator* and *interpreter*. In mid-afternoon he may hold a meeting

THE PUBLIC RELATIONS PROCESS

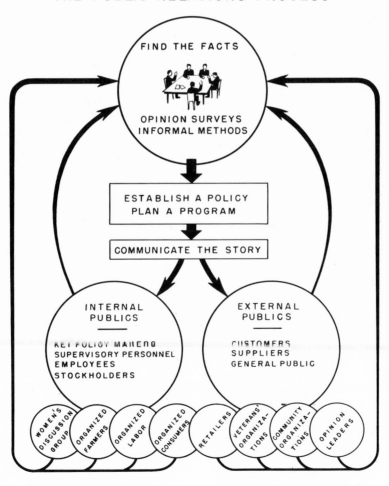

FIND THE FACTS

OPINION SURVEYS
INFORMAL METHODS

ESTABLISH A POLICY
PLAN A PROGRAM

COMMUNICATE THE STORY

INTERNAL PUBLICS
—
KEY POLICY MAKERS
SUPERVISORY PERSONNEL
EMPLOYEES
STOCKHOLDERS

EXTERNAL PUBLICS
—
CUSTOMERS
SUPPLIERS
GENERAL PUBLIC

WOMEN'S DISCUSSION GROUP
ORGANIZED FARMERS
ORGANIZED LABOR
ORGANIZED CONSUMERS
RETAILERS
VETERANS' ORGANIZATIONS
COMMUNITY ORGANIZATIONS
OPINION LEADERS

with his staff and representatives from Industrial Relations to re-evaluate the purpose and content of the employee publication. This requires *evaluation*.

So goes the day as the PR man participates in a going program. Between such tasks he may be answering a query from a financial magazine, arranging for a series of on-the-job safety pictures, cleaning up last-minute details for a Boy Scout drive, digging out material for a speech, or checking proofs on the forthcoming annual report.

In order to understand the process, it is helpful to break it apart and examine each phase. That is the purpose of this chapter and the three that follow. The *unity, overlapping,* and *continuity* of the whole process should be kept in mind as the parts are taken out of the running machine for examination.

The four-step process is illustrated in this problem which confronted Standard Oil's PR staff some years ago:

> Standard Oil decided to close its Mankato, Minnesota, sales division as part of a company-wide reorganization to gain more efficiency. This meant that 600 *employees* would have to move or find new jobs. The Mankato *community* would suffer a loss in income. Minnesota *customers* would be concerned about getting equally good service under the new setup. The *public* would be curious about the meaning and implications of this move.
>
> The first task was to marshal all the facts through research so that the decision could be explained and justified to those concerned. The next step was to plan announcement of the decision. Timing was an important factor. The news had to be broken swiftly before rumors started. Still, the news could not be released until plans were completed for its simultaneous release to all those affected. With plans completed, then came the task of communicating the decision in a manner calculated to gain understanding of the necessity and wisdom of the change.
>
> Materials included: a procedure memorandum to guide PR staff; a presentation script for meetings, letters to several different groups of employees, letters to all dealers, a news release, a statement on banking arrangements for Mankato banks, a general office letter, plans for meetings. The news was released through meetings, letters to all the different groups involved, and through the mass media. Finally, PR department *evaluated* its handling of this problem with an eye to improving its procedures when the next move out of a community must be communicated.

RESEARCH ATTITUDE
NEEDED

Public relations may be likened to an iceberg. Three-fourths of it is unseen below the surface. The one-fourth—publicity—that does show is too often taken for the whole iceberg. The unseen three-fourths—research, planning, evaluating—is generally more important in the long run. Because of the high stakes, executives must increase the precision of their decisions. Staff officers are expected to provide facts upon which sound administrative decisions can be made. Executives are coming to realize that an organization's human relations problems are just as specific and researchable as are other problems. This parallels the maturing fields of opinion measurement and public relations. *Methodical, systematic research is the foundation of effective public relations.*

Counselor John F. Moynahan offers this example of how research can be utilized to make sound plans and strengthen communication with a particular public: [1]

> A New York department store's earnings were running above the level of previous years and an extra dividend was indicated. The store's employees belonged to a militant union and the executives feared an extra dividend would create hostility among the employees. Accordingly, the advertising department prepared a brochure intended to gain the employees' "understanding" of management's view on profits. Just like that! Before the brochure was released, management wisely had an opinion survey made. The survey showed that most of the employees neither understood nor were impressed by the relationship of profits to gross sales, which was the main theme of the planned brochure. Depth interviews revealed that most of the store's employees thought of earnings in terms of the mark-up on the store's merchandise.
>
> This opinion survey had three benefits: (1) It helped management plan a more effective brochure; (2) It provided a guide for a continuing information campaign to employees; (3) It provided a base against which changing employee attitudes could be re-measured in the future.

The "research attitude" can be as valuable as the research itself. A great researcher who helped build the automotive industry, the late C. F. Kettering, once described this desired attitude in these words: [2]

> Research is a high-hat word that scares a lot of people. It needn't. It is rather simple. Essentially, it is nothing but a state of mind—a friendly, welcoming attitude toward change. Going out to look for change, instead of waiting for it to come. Research, for practical men, is an effort to do things better and not be caught asleep at the switch. The research state of mind can apply to anything. Personal affairs or any kind of business, big or little. It is the problem-solving mind as contrasted with the let-well-enough-alone mind. It is the composer mind, instead of the fiddler mind; it is the "tomorrow" mind instead of the "yesterday" mind.

1. RESEARCH PROVIDES MUCH-NEEDED EMPHASIS ON THE LISTENING PHASE OF PUBLIC RELATIONS AND GIVES SUBSTANCE TO THE "TWO-WAY STREET" CONCEPT. One of the vitiating weaknesses in the past has been a misplaced emphasis on publicity. Communication starts with listening. This requires humility and systematic effort. F. J. Roethlisberger asserts: "The biggest block to personal communication is man's inability to listen intelligently, understandingly, skillfully to another person. This deficiency in the modern world is

---

[1] In "Opinion Research: To Solve a Problem, Grasp an Opportunity," *Public Relations Journal*, Vol. 19, June, 1963, 26-27.

[2] In article by him, "More Music Please, Composers," *Saturday Evening Post*, Vol. 211, No. 32 (1938).

widespread and appalling. And not too much is being done about it." Too often what purports to be communication is simply opposing ideas passing each other in psychological space, for example, in a management-versus-labor bargaining situation in which each side is merely waiting to score points, not listening to the other's views. As Redfield stated: "One-way communication is ungratifying, unnatural, and cumulatively sterile in its effects."

Listening is not an easy task. Channels from the worker out in the plant or the car dealer in Seattle must be provided and kept open. Failure to listen leads to useless "communicating" on issues that do not exist to publics that are not there.

Before there can be rapport through communication, there must be empathy. Empathy is achieved by open-minded listening. As Thoreau put it: "It takes two to speak the truth; one to speak and another to hear." Public Relations is a *two-way* street. Both lines of traffic must be given equal right-of-way. Unless you know the values, viewpoints, and language of your audience, you are not likely to get through. These values and viewpoints can be learned only through *systematic* and *sympathetic* listening.[3]

2. RESEARCH PROVIDES THE OBJECTIVE LOOK REQUIRED TO "KNOW THYSELF." Public relations has been likened to a mirror, a mirror that reflects the public's image of the organization to its executives and reflects the image of the organization to the public. Opinion surveys, attitude studies, and audience research on what people *really know, really believe,* and *actually read or listen to* provide an effective safeguard against our human lack of objectivity. Today more wrong decisions are made on mistaken hunches of what the public thinks than on willful disregard of public opinion. Robert Burns said it so well:

> Oh wad some power the giftie gie us
> To see oursel's as ithers see us!
> It wad frae monie a blunder free us,
>   And foolish notion

The practitioner mirrors the publics of an organization by relaying the views and desires of those publics to its policy makers. To accurately interpret the publics of an institution to its policy makers, a practitioner must be able to look at problems from the *public viewpoint*. Objective research serves as a shoehorn for putting on the other fellow's shoes. It provides an effective stimulus to self-correction. Subjective assumptions of what "the public thinks" are risky.

3. RESEARCH EARNS SUPPORT FOR COUNSELING AND PROGRAMMING AROUND THE POLICY-MAKING TABLE. The research-based approach is apt to be the most effective in gaining consideration for the public relations aspect of organiza-

---

[3] For a specific example of the pay-off of two-way communications, see "The Dewey and Almy Chemical Co. and the Chemical Workers," *Causes of Industrial Peace,* edited by Clinton Golden and Virginia Parker (New York: Harper & Row, Publishers, 1955), pp. 100-20.

tional problems. Executives are a fact-minded lot. The surest way to counter a controller's idea of "what the people want," when he is wrong, is with surveys and case studies of similar situations. Clarence J. Hicks, pioneer in industrial relations, once said: "It is characteristic of a profession that recommendations are of value in proportion as they are intelligently based upon a thorough diagnosis of the individual case or problem." *The need is for research-supported diagnoses, not new medicines.*

4. RESEARCH REVEALS FESTERING TROUBLE SPOTS BEFORE THEY INFECT A LARGE BODY OF PUBLIC OPINION. Too often problems are allowed to define themselves in the form of a crisis. Too much effort goes into "fire-fighting" rather than "fire prevention." This is dramatized in industry when deteriorating labor relations present the problem of a strike or a lockout. Such situations usually have long histories. Sometimes neither party knows what caused the blow-up. Heading off "blow-ups" is part of the PR task. The earlier a complaint is caught, the easier it is to handle. Continuous fact-finding will uncover many problems while they are still small enough to permit quiet handling without a critical public looking on. The same attentive listening will permit the catching of rumors before they become widespread.

5. RESEARCH INCREASES THE EFFECTIVENESS OF OUTBOUND COMMUNICATION. To obtain the maximum effect in communication. and persuasion, each public must have special study and special treatment. Pimlott says: "This emphasis on the need to pinpoint the specific publics is one of the most useful contributions which public relations has received from the social scientists." Much of today's publicity effort is characterized by wasteful misses of the target audience due to lack of prior fact-finding. Dissemination of publicity is not the equivalent of communication. Research enables the practitioner to pinpoint his publics, discover their leaders, learn their values, viewpoints, and language. These he must know if he is to beam his message in on its target. *A public relations effort increases in effectiveness in proportion to the specificity with which it is directed to a group.*

6. RESEARCH PROVIDES USEFUL INTELLIGENCE—AN IDEA SERVICE FOR EXECUTIVES. An intelligence service is an indispensable auxiliary to an information service. Increasingly administrators rely on the public relations department as a central source of information on the organization, the public's image, the industry or field, and the social, economic, and political trends. Such demands are to be encouraged. This service enhances the effectiveness of the total program. To provide this service requires fact-stockpiling and information analysis. One of the most useful services is to interpret the changing social-economic-political environment to executives. Many executives simply do not have time to keep abreast. Research has two basic purposes: *First,* the collection and collation of facts which are used in planning a course of action and in determining channels and content of the informational program; *Second,* exploration of basic attitudes, opinions expressed, and information held by members of an organization's publics. Information gained in the latter type of research is generally used more for long-range planning.

The principle of fact-finding is not new. The increasing emphasis is: PR men and women have long been accustomed to spending a lot of effort ferreting out facts. In the past, however, there has been too much reliance on hunch and happenstance. As the social scientists produce more reliable research tools for exploring "the pictures in our heads," public relations is using these tools.

The typical practitioner heads up a small three- or four-man staff in an industrial or institutional organization. Quite often a department consists of a director and a "girl-Friday" secretary. In such setups there is little time or money for extensive research. This accounts, to a large extent, for uneasy reliance on the cheap, quick, and haphazard methods. Generally it is not lack of vision that prevents full use of these tools. It is lack of staff and money. This can be the falsest sort of economy. In the opinion of Franklyn Waltman, of the Sun Oil Company, "Research for the finding and development of facts is an absolutely essential ingredient of any sound public relations program."

Measurement and analysis of opinions range from the highly informal and impressionistic to the methodical and near-scientific. Progress in any specialized field is marked by its advance from impressionistic observation to objective testing with accurate measurement techniques. Opinion research provides guidance at four stages of the process. Opinion Research Corp. lists these as:

(1) *Current situation:* what people think today and why;
(2) *Basic principles:* how public opinion works;
(3) *Pretesting:* how people react to a given ad, article, argument, etc.;
(4) *Evaluation:* how people did respond and how attitudes changed, if they did.

WHAT ONE COMPANY DOES. In the Sun Oil Company, the public relations department has these responsibilities: (1) "to establish and maintain constant liaison with the managers of all departments of the company for the provision of counsel and assistance regarding their public relations activities and problems"; (2) "to conduct research in, and prepare reports on social, economic, and political subjects and trends from a public relations viewpoint which may affect the activities or interest of the company, the petroleum industry, or business generally"; (3) "to keep company officials promptly informed of currently published or broadcast statements relating to the company, the oil industry, and business generally." To meet these assigned tasks and to carry out its specific programs to build goodwill, the Sun Oil PR department established a research division—one of the first PR departments to do so. This PR research division performs various functions.

1. *Maintenance of a Library.* This library is directed by a trained librarian and houses standard reference books: general business and oil and chemical trade publications; works devoted to public relations practice and skills; reports on public relations programs; media analyses; public opinion and attitude surveys; definitive books on economic, financial, and other business subjects; a legislative

reference section, including printed sets of congressional hearings on the oil industry, current volumes of the *Congressional Record, Federal Register,* and services listing legislation pending in Congress and in the states; more than 2,000 file folders containing accumulated reference material from newspapers, magazines, and such sources.

2. *News Intelligence.* This section keeps track of what the daily and periodical press, radio, and TV are saying about the company, the industry, and business generally. News and editorial comment are abstracted from a representative list of daily papers in a *Daily News Digest* for top managers. Clippings and radio and TV reports are made widely available to PR staff and management. Each week the full PR staff reviews 50 weekly or monthly periodicals and abstracts items of interest. These are distributed in the company in a multilithed publication, *Periodical Highlights.* Annually the research section issues a *Company Encyclopedia,* a compendium of facts about company operations, history, etc. This is a desk bible for the several hundred managers who receive it. Another Research Division publication, *Petroleum Reference Sheet,* is a three-part document. It provides a weekly, monthly, and special case compilation of current statistics on oil industry operations.

3. *Special Reports and Surveys.* The Research Division prepares reports on specific public relations problems, such as "Government Controls Over the Oil Industry." It also sponsors periodic surveys on attitudes toward the company and toward the oil industry. Surveys are being used increasingly to learn more about the impact and effectiveness of programs. For example, this division periodically sponsors readership surveys of company publications. Also this staff is increasingly making pretests of communications materials before they are widely disseminated. The goal is to accomplish more at less cost per unit of results.

The value of a comprehensive research program as the one sure foundation upon which to build a public relations program is seen in the need for and use made of research by the United States Information Agency. The U.S.I.A. must tell America's story around the world to people of many cultures and many levels of comprehension—to people ranging from the illiterate *campesino* in Latin America to the toiler in Asia's rice paddies to the Western European intellectual. To communicate effectively with these and other peoples, the Agency needs a continuous, authentic, and up-to-date body of information about its audience. Here's the way U.S.I.A. goes about this task:

U.S.I.A. operates a Research and Reference Service, using many tested techniques and methods of audience sampling. The objectives of communications research are to: (1) discover the long-term values and aspirations of the world's peoples; (2) determine the current attitudes of the world audience; (3) study target groups which the United States is attempting to influence; (4) investigate channels and methods of communication; (5) examine the effectiveness of the Agency programs. The research effort is accompanied by a program of analysis and evaluation which combines all pertinent information. Evaluations are provided to U.S.I.A. policy and operating officers as a guidance in developing programs that are carried out in 105 countries around the world. In one five-year span, U.S.I.A. prepared 650 such studies. Also, based on its fact-gathering and opinion research, U.S.I.A. maintains communications fact books on all major nations. These are basic reference works and contain information on population, education, literacy, religion, language, communication channels, and target groups. A part of the research effort involves public-opinion polling abroad.

Obviously, only the large industrial and nonprofit organizations can afford to maintain research divisions of this scope. But every public relations job requires that these functions be cared for to some degree. Here's how.

FACT-FINDING

THE FIRST STEP: A FACT FILE. It has been said that all a man needs to become a counselor is a shiny office and a subscription to *The New York Times*. The grain of truth in this axiom emphasizes that it is important to collect, clip, and compile facts.

Locating, arranging, and analyzing information is important to a client or organization. Useful information is to be found in government publications, in libraries, trade publications, newspapers, industry reports, and a multitude of sources. The painstaking fact finder will be greatly rewarded when confronted with an immediate need for information. Such demands are many and often unexpected. When the boss wants some information, he wants it now! Keeping a current organizational "World Almanac" is a useful idea. A common starting point in the organization of a PR office is the building of a fact file of reference materials. Daily requests will tell what is needed.

In practice, the department becomes the central information bureau in most organizations. Queries which cannot be answered by other departments wind up in this office. Newspaper, magazine, radio, and TV men have come to expect the office to provide quick answers. Such demands are met and encouraged. Media men should be encouraged to rely on the office for authentic information. Such practice has many valuable consequences. For instance, a reporter's query often gives a running start on a crisis in the making. Such demands should be anticipated.

From fact files come ideas and information for speeches, pamphlets, special reports, institutional advertising, exhibits, special events, and background information for special projects. The department is responsible for assembling the factual content of its communications program. Often these items have to be whipped up in a hurry. For example, a PR department of a bank had to get out a brief history booklet in two weeks to help mark the millionth depositor.

This department should have the over-all responsibility for developing accurate facts regarding the company and industry policies, practices, and operations and for developing the dimensions of public relations problems on this basis. Increasingly, public relations departments are assigned the task of building and maintaining company or organizational libraries. Providing quick answers for tough questions can be a goodwill builder for the department, both inside and outside the organization.

DEFINING THE PUBLICS

Another essential part of research is in defining the publics. This involves, too, determining the effective channels of communication with each. Precise definition of a client's publics, their composition, and their prevailing attitudes goes beyond such simple enumeration as trustees, faculty, students, alumni, and so forth. Members of a given public are constantly shifting. *In public relations you must communicate with a passing parade, not a standing army.* De Tocqueville observed: "Each generation in a democratic society is a new people." Socrates knew: "Oratory is the art of enchanting the soul, and therefore he who would be an orator has to learn the differences of human souls—they are so many. . . ."

The publics themselves change from time to time. There is a constant shifting in age groupings, economic interests, political interests, and geographic residence. The latter is increasingly true in mobile America. Also, new publics are always coming into being. The past few years, a new American buying public has emerged with an interest in foreign-made cars.

Introduction of a new product may, in the case of a manufacturer, create a new buying public. Establishment of a new branch plant brings a new community public to be studied and understood. No two are exactly alike. Normally, regroupings take place gradually, almost imperceptibly, such as the changes in family living brought on by television. Other times, the shift comes with lightning-like swiftness—as when a whole nation is plunged into war or economic depression. Thus, it is imperative to keep current an accurate analysis of your publics and their sentiments.[4]

Such analyses will reveal the group leaders or *influentials* in each of your several publics. The importance of determining the real group leaders as against the presumed opinion leaders was underscored in Chapter 4. Too often in public relations there is a tendency to short-cut this task in an effort to "economize" by tagging lawyers, doctors, clergymen, bankers, as the sum total of leadership, or by assuming that a union leader is a leader in political or social affairs as well as in union matters. This short cut is full of risks. For example, barbers talk to union members more often than do their officers. So do bartenders. Persons may be influential in their groups and yet not prominent in the community. Each social stratum generates its own opinion leaders. Individuals look to different group leaders for guidance in different facets of their daily lives. Sighting respected group leaders requires laborious fact-finding. There is no short cut.[5]

In conducting this "publics" research, learn and recognize the interrelated-

---

4 For examples, see Glen Perry, "Which Public Do You Mean?" *Public Relations Journal,* Vol. 12, March, 1956.

5 For support of this view, see Katz and Lazarsfeld's *Personal Influence* and Floyd Hunter's *Community Power Structure, op. cit.*

ness of all these groups. The practitioner needs to know which of several appeals will be most effective with a specific public. He needs to gauge the reactions of this group and also of those that "listen in." What is said to one group may be heard by another. This presents a dilemma; the more you appeal to different groups in terms of their self-interest, as you must, the greater is the danger of offending other groups. *Often you have to choose which groups you want on your side.*

Systematic definition of an organization's publics is needed, too, to determine order of priority. And priorities must be assigned to an institution's almost infinite number of publics. Rarely does a practitioner have the staff and money to do all the things he thinks need be done. This Nicholas Samstag terms "the perpetual priority problem."

PUBLIC RELATIONS WORKS FROM THE INSIDE OUT. The place to start in defining the publics is at the heart of an organization—in its power structure. It is there that the essential character of an organization's relationships is determined. The key policy makers must be the first concern. Working out from this inner circle, there are junior executives, supervisors, employees, home communities, consumers, investors, donors, and all others. From these immediate publics, attention moves along a broad front of special-interest publics within the general public. These include labor unions, industrial associations, farm groups, political groups, women's groups, professional groups, educators, veterans, and similar common-interest groupings. These special publics will be discussed in Chapter 16.

SELECTING THE AUDIENCE. Research is used also to determine the best ways of reaching publics once they have been identified. This requires determination of channels of influence and communication. Pinpointing is essential if the message is to be designed in terms of the audience. This is required to gain the intended audience's attention. *It is not easy to attract the public's attention or to hold its interest.* Careless or casual determination of group and geographic boundaries is too common. *The more carefully you define the various publics, the more ways of reaching and influencing them will you discover. Research will best define the mutuality of interest that will serve as a bridge to carry your persuasive communication.*

LISTENING IS AN INTEGRAL PART OF A SUSTAINED PROGRAM. An able practitioner of another generation, Abraham Lincoln, knew the importance of listening. Lincoln once advised a friend: "Keep close to the people—they are always right and will mislead no one." He followed his own advice. Carl Sandburg in his biography tells how Lincoln, twice each week, set aside a period of his valuable time for conversations with ordinary folk, the housewives, farmers, merchants, and pension-seekers. He says Lincoln listened patiently to what they had to say, no matter how humble their circumstance or how trivial their business. An officer in the War Department once protested to the President that he was wasting valuable time on these unimportant people. Lincoln rebuked him, saying:

". . . no hours of my day are better employed than those which bring me again within the direct contact and atmosphere of the average of our people. . . . All serve to renew in me a cleaner and more vivid image of that great popular assemblage out of which I sprang and to which at the end of two years I must return.

"I tell you, Major . . . that I call these receptions my public opinion baths . . . the effect, as a whole, is renovating and invigorating." [6]

Prudence dictates the systematic listening to an organization's publics through scientific research. Yet many organizations still fail to utilize fully this tool. Why? Because: (1) Sound opinion research is expensive; (2) A time lag exists between the formulation of an opinion study and the time when the results are needed; (3) Management does not want to listen to the views of their publics; (4) There is a lack of knowledge about these research tools on the part of publicity-minded practitioners; (5) There is a lack of confidence in the precision of the research tools now available. Typical is this comment found in *Trends in School Public Relations:* "Two-way communication is slim in some school systems because superintendents are afraid of it. They see it as organized back talk and a potential threat rather than an essential tool of modern management. But in most systems, the two-way flow is a trickle because it takes a lot of effort and skill to obtain reliable feedback."

INFORMAL METHODS. Pioneers in this field lacked the precision tools that are available today to gauge opinion accurately. They were forced to fall back on what rough-and-ready means could be devised. Despite the development of the more accurate measuring sticks, reliance on the informal methods still dominates many programs.

This is due to lack of funds and to the necessity of making quick, on-the-spot evaluations. These informal methods include: (1) personal contacts by telephone or mail of persons you know; (2) advisory committees or panels; (3) analysis of an organization's incoming mail; (4) reports of field agents or salesmen on their evaluations of opinions about the organization; (5) press clippings and radio and TV monitorings on what has been said on a particular subject; (6) conferences of those involved in a particular problem or situation; (7) study of national public opinion polls to gain a sense of opinion climate and trends; (8) study of election and legislative voting which reflects public opinion on certain issues; (9) speeches and writings of recognized opinion leaders; (10) sales records.

These informal methods can be helpful. Recognize their weaknesses, however. Inherently they lack *representativeness* and *objectivity*—the keys to sound opinion research. Such methods can provide vital and significant clues to opinion trends and reveal sources of things people like and do not like.

PERSONAL CONTACTS. In 1893 Lord Bryce said, "The best way in which the tendencies at work in any community can be best discovered and estimated

---

[6] Carl Sandburg, *Abraham Lincoln: The War Years,* Vol. II (New York: Harcourt, Brace & World, Inc., 1939).

is by moving freely about among all sorts and conditions of men." Skill in sizing up the attitude of individuals has long been and always will be one of the prime qualifications of a counselor. There is great value in wide acquaintanceships with *representative leaders from all walks of life.*

It is a good practice to win friends in all publics. By probing, talking, listening, and analyzing as he moves freely about, the practitioner can learn a great deal. The politician has been doing this a long time. As Woodrow Wilson wrote Mrs. Crawford Toy: "Do not hesitate to give me any opinion with which you may chance to come in contact. That is the only atmosphere in which the mind of a man charged with public duties can properly or successfully function, the atmosphere of opinion." [7] Many practitioners consult regularly with such bellwethers as editors, reporters, ministers, labor leaders, bartenders, civic leaders, bankers, and housewives.

IDEA JURIES, PANELS. It is only a short step from asking friends and associates for their reactions to organizing idea juries or opinion panels. These range from *ad hoc* to highly formal arrangements. The degree of formality and continuity in these sounding boards varies a great deal. The jury panel is one of the most economical "polls." [8] Careful selection can provide a rough, working idea of opinion within these groups. Bringing such a group together for a lunch or dinner once a month can pay good dividends.

ADVISORY COMMITTEES. A variation of this informal device is the advisory committee. The honor of service on such a committee quite often will bring to an organization the services of an able group. An advisory committee can be helpful in preventing many a misstep. Nonprofit organizations can tap the aid of skilled PR people in this way. Formation of such a group for a college or Army installation can serve to win the interest and participation of influential persons in the community. Advisory committees create the opportunity for participation. Once interested and informed, members are likely to return to their own circles and carry the ball for the program. *But there is a price to be paid in using such committees.* Their advice must be given earnest consideration, or else the gesture will backfire. No one likes to serve as a show-window mannequin.

MAIL ANALYSIS. Another economical way of gauging opinions—one frequently overlooked—is a periodic analysis of an organization's incoming mail. The correspondence will reveal areas of favor, disfavor, and a lack of information. There is a tendency of letter writers to be critical rather than commendatory. This should be kept in mind in making such analyses. Letters often will hoist warning flags on sources of ill-will or service breakdown, or detect the boomerang effects of a program. *Letters reveal indications of opinion but they do not measure it.*

---

[7] For an article on Wilson's efforts to influence public opinion, see Henry A. Turner, "Woodrow Wilson and Public Opinion," *Public Opinion Quarterly*, Vol. 21, 1957, 505-20.

[8] For plusses and minuses on consumer juries, see S. Watson Dunn, *Advertising Copy and Communication* (New York: McGraw-Hill Book Company, 1956), pp. 494-98.

Specific mail responses can be significant, too. A district manager of a large Western oil company became concerned about the large number of inactive accounts among credit-card holders. He sat down and wrote them a personal, friendly letter. Thirty-four hundred letters were mailed and 1,100 responses came back, although no incentives or premiums were provided. An amazing response! Analysis of the letters revealed many implications for the program of that company.

FIELD REPORTS. Most concerns have salesmen, district representatives, or field agents who travel the organization's territory. These agents should be trained to listen. They should be provided an easy, regular means of reporting opinions encountered. In this way they can serve as the "eyes and ears" of an organization. Systematic reporting of opinions, complaints, and commendations should be included as part of their job. The PR department can promote this. Reports of such representatives tend to be optimistic, however.

For example, in an effort to measure the impact of a certain Progress Week, the industry's sales representatives in Bangor, Maine were asked for an evaluation. Forty per cent would venture no opinion. About half of those responding thought that the week's promotion had produced more favorable attitudes toward the industry. Actually, in a cross-section survey it was found that only 11 per cent of the Bangor population were inclined to be more favorable toward this industry. In this case only 12 of the 42 "grass-roots" observers were able to gauge opinions correctly. All impressionistic measurements must be studied with caution. Field reports can be helpful when the natural margin of inaccuracy is kept in mind.

Another way of determining impact on the public by an organization's personnel is through the use of "comparison shoppers." Retail stores have long hired shoppers to test the efficiency and courtesy of their sales clerks as well as to compare merchandise and prices of competitors. Other establishments dealing with the general public frequently hire "customers" to check on the performance of their personnel.

MEDIA REPORTS. Press clippings and radio-TV monitor reports—all available from commercial services—have long been used as yardsticks. These devices will indicate what is printed or broadcast. They cannot report, however, whether the message was read or heard and, if so, whether it was believed and understood. Newspaper clippings are useful in measuring acceptability of releases sent to the press, but they cannot measure *impact*. These services can be used to detect what is being disseminated about your organization or about a competitor. One hundred per cent coverage on newsclips is difficult to achieve, and returns from a particular service will vary.

The press, when used with extreme caution, can be a fairly reliable guide to current opinions, particularly those of protest and criticism. The wide disparity between the voting opinions of the people and the editorial opinions of newspapers is demonstrated in elections. This should warn against uncritical acceptance of newspaper editorial opinion. The same is true of radio and TV news commentators. Caution should be use in accepting interpretive reporting as reflecting public opinion. Mass media can be used as indicators, not as yardsticks.

MORE RELIABLE
METHODS

The surest way to learn opinions and underlying attitudes would be to sit down and talk things over face to face. This is not often possible. Instead, social scientists and market researchers have developed the technique of talking to a *small but representative* group in each public. *This is the sample survey.* Sampling is a great money saver. It is accurate when the sample is *representative.* It is built on the laws of mathematical probability.

By asking precise, understandable questions of a truly accurate miniature of a whole, public opinion can be measured with a high degree of accuracy. Just as the practitioner depends largely on the established channels to talk to the public, he surveys to listen to the public. Through such devices representatives of the public are encouraged to tell their story to the institution. These survey tools offer an effective means of facilitating an inflow of information and opinion. *Through these devices the practitioner interprets the public to the institution.*[9]

1. CROSS-SECTION SURVEYS. A carefully prepared set of questions is asked of a cross-section sample of a given public. The questionnaire builds a bridge between an organization and members of the public. There are three ways to draw the sample to be interviewed: (1) *probability sample*—in which people to be interviewed are chosen at random by some mechanical formula, such as every *n*th name on a list; (2) *area sample*—a form of the probability sample in which geographical areas are listed, for example, cities, then units to be surveyed are chosen at random; (3) *quota sample*—population in question is analyzed by known characteristics—sex, age, residence, occupation, income level, and so forth, then interviews are assigned by quota in the same proportions as these characteristics exist in the whole population.

All these methods involve a degree of sampling error. This can be kept within tolerable limits. Such surveys are made by many commercial polling firms. They can be arranged through one of several universities. The results obtained through cross-section surveys are more quantitative than qualitative in nature. They often fail to reflect the depth and intensity of opinions expressed by respondents.

2. SURVEY PANELS. Under this method, a panel of people is selected and is

---

[9] Discussion of the tools and techniques of surveys does not fall within the scope of this book. Suggested are such standard works as Mildred Parten's *Surveys, Polls and Samples,* Hadley Cantril's *Gauging Public Opinion,* and A. B. Blankenship's *Consumer and Opinion Research.*

interviewed several times over a period of time. The selection of participants is determined on a cross-section basis. Panels are used to learn what happens to people under varying conditions over a span of time. It is an effective device for controlled experiments. A panel could be used, for example, to measure the impact of a series of projects in community relations, or, to follow people's buying habits in a grocery store. Panels are difficult to administer, and it is hard to keep all members interested over a long stretch. Panel members, in time, also tend to become atypical rather than typical.

3. **DEPTH INTERVIEW.** This is a qualitative instrument to probe the attitudes underlying expressed opinions. It is an informal kind of interview. The respondent is encouraged to talk fully and freely. This method takes highly trained interviewers and skilled analysts. Elmo Roper says: "Because of the informal nature of this technique and the fact that the most productive depth interviews are those which give respondents the widest range of latitude for responding, one major problem in its use is how to evaluate its meaning." He thinks the really qualified depth interviewer is rare. The depth interview is one of the techniques used in motivational research, one of the newer tools in the marketer's kit.[10]

4. **CONTENT ANALYSIS.** This is a method of systematically coding and classifying the content of one or all of the mass media. This method can tell an organization what is being said and published about it and in what context it is talked about. Media content can be measured as to how much is descriptive, how much is favorable, how much is critical. Content analysis will show the pattern of mentions of an organization. Such analyses provide helpful clues to the kinds of information your publics are being exposed to, not necessarily what they consume and believe. It is also possible to couple content analysis with a sampling procedure and obtain from a sample of some 50 daily papers an accurate picture of nationwide dissemination of a given subject.[11] Content analysis also can be useful in periodically assessing content of informational output against stated PR objectives.

5. **MAIL QUESTIONNAIRES.** Use of mail instead of face-to-face questionnaires is economical. It is thus tempting to the ·penny-pinched practitioner. *The danger is that there is no assurance the respondents will be representative of the whole population.* In putting questions by mail, you lose the flexibility and interpretations possible in personal interviews. It is difficult to get an adequate response to many mail questionnaires. Many people have been polled in this fashion. There is some resentment. This economical device can be useful when used with due caution. It is most effective in soliciting opinions of homogeneous groups and where the cleavage of opinion is decisive—such

---

10 See Perrin Stryker, "Motivation Research," *Fortune,* June, 1956.

11 See Huntington Harris and Paul M. Lewis, "Some Methods of Measuring Press Attention." *PR,* Vol. 1, October, 1955; Wendell Coats and Steve Mulkey, "A Study in Newspaper Sampling." *Public Opinion Quarterly,* Vol. 14, Fall, 1950, 533-46. For brief introduction to this research tool, see Richard W. Budd and Robert K. Thorp, *An Introduction to Content Analysis* (Iowa City: Iowa University School of Journalism, 1963).

as of a group of employees on the question of overtime or night shift. This tool can be helpful in uncovering sources of criticism and praise. Space should be provided for additional comment at the end.

6. SEMANTIC DIFFERENTIAL. This is a relatively new technique of measurement, one easy and economical to use—thus, one of great utility for the practitioner who invariably faces a "budget problem" on research. The Semantic Differential was developed by Professors Charles E. Osgood, George J. Suci, and Percy H. Tannenbaum and is presented in full in their book, *The Measurement of Meaning.* It is designed to assess variations in the connotative meanings of objects and words, and is based on the premise that such meaning constitutes one of the most significant variables mediating human behavior. The procedure consists of having the subject rate one or more objects of judgment (or concepts) against a set of scales defined by a pair of adjectival opposites, with seven steps between them. For example, one could obtain an index of an individual's meaning of Lyndon B. Johnson by having the individual allocate this concept on a set of bi-polar scales, such as *strong-weak, active-passive, valuable-worthless, heavy-light, pleasant-unpleasant,* and so forth.

The respondent rates the central concept in terms of what it means to him on each of a set of such scales, the particular selection and number of scales being unfixed. The seven steps between the pairs of opposites allow the subject to express both the direction of his association and its intensity, with a neutral point in the middle. Thus, confronted with a scale such as

safe _____: _____: _____: _____: _____: _____: _____: dangerous,

the subject can indicate whether he regards the particular concept to be *very* safe or dangerous, *quite* safe or dangerous, or *slightly* safe or dangerous, with the middle point reserved for the feeling of either equally or neither safe nor dangerous. With such sets of scales, measures of the connotations of various concepts can be obtained from specially selected individuals or groups, representative samples of the public, and so forth. Similarly, there is no basic restriction on the kinds of concepts that may be judged—individual personalities, corporation images, and so forth. The generality of the technique is attested to by the wide range of uses it has had in its relatively short existence —in attitude measurement, linguistics, psychotherapy, advertising, and image profiles in public relations.[12]

OPINION RESEARCH IN PUBLIC RELATIONS

The oldest type of research of value is market research. Aimed at improving the distribution and marketing of consumer goods, it dates back

---

[12] For elaboration, see Osgood, Suci, and Tannenbaum, *The Measurement of Meaning* (Urbana: University of Illinois Press, 1957); and Charles E. Osgood's essay "An Exploration into Semantic Space" in Schramm's *The Science of Human Communication.*

more than 50 years. The pioneer N. W. Ayer ad agency started to make market analyses for clients as part of its regular procedure around 1910. Market research embraces consumer and product research and is of primary concern to production and sales in business. Yet much is learned in market research that is of value to the PR staff. Reliable methods of surveying consumer goods and tastes have been developed to measure potential markets and effectiveness of marketing programs. Market research is of immediate interest for product publicity and PR counseling on marketing projects. Accrued results offer much valuable knowledge and insight concerning American buying habits. This fact-finding will pay off with efficiency and economy in sales promotion. It will also provide information needed for better control of a product's destiny among retailers and consumers. Such research serves to eliminate waste, cut costs, and point the way to new markets for new products or for old ones designed anew.

Opinion research which probes attitudes and the complexities of human motivation is considerably younger. It dates largely from the early 1930's. The emphasis is as much on the development of more reliable methods as on the findings themselves. Even though it is barely of age, opinion research offers vast potentialities.

It should be fully understood that opinion research is not a substitute for decision making. It is only a guide to it. The role of public opinion research is put in focus by Angus Campbell of the Michigan Survey Research Center:

> Knowing your public is a difficult assignment. Leading your public is an even more exacting charge. Studies of public attitudes will give much more useful information to the administrator of public relations programs but they will not relieve him of the responsibility of leadership. . . . The growth and development of all . . . institutions depends on the initiative of [those] . . . who are not content merely to keep the public satisfied with things as they are.

Opinion measurement has been used by a few pioneer practitioners for decades, but extensive utilization of this tool has been a fairly recent development in public relations. American Telephone & Telegraph has been one of the longest and most imaginative users of opinion research. A. T. & T.'s first survey, using a formal questionnaire and sampling methods, was made in Detroit in 1926, and this was followed by a similar study in Pittsburgh in 1927. In 1929 A. T. & T. had a survey made in Milwaukee to get information on the effectiveness of Bell System advertising. All these studies were made by J. David Houser and Associates, one of the pioneer research firms.

In 1929 Bell set up an opinion research unit of its own. Since that time, this organization has been developing improved survey methods and assisting Bell subsidiaries with their own studies. These Bell polls have varied widely in scope and purpose. All have been aimed at facts about customer opinions, employee opinions, and public opinions needed for current operations and policy decisions. Since 1946, Bell has conducted periodically a Customer Attitude Trend Study; and since 1949, all the Associated Operating Companies have been conducting their own trend surveys. Early in its experience, Bell's opinion researchers learned: [13]

1. That customers were willing to give their opinions when asked.
2. That the information the company got by going directly to the customers made sense.
3. That this information was useful to public relations and operating telephone people.

Generally, extensive use of opinion polls and attitude surveys in public relations has accelerated since World War II. The trend is growing. This is illustrated in the intensive use made of polling by modern political leaders —John F. Kennedy, Richard Nixon, Lyndon B. Johnson, Nelson Rockefeller, and others. Too often, however, no one thinks of a poll until an emergency develops, such as an airliner crash in the neighborhood of an airport. When such crises arise—and if there is still time—a poll can be used to define clearly the problem and to suggest its solution. A poll can reveal who is angry, who is not, who has the correct information, and who is off base. It can demonstrate the relationships of information, misinformation, and dominant attitudes. It will isolate urges and identify motives. It may indicate the positive and negative symbols to which people will react in a given situation. Usually time does not permit crisis polls. The prudent practitioner uses surveys to head off problems before they crystallize into crises. Opinion research is most productive when used as a guide to long-range plans and for improving communication techniques.

Additional Reading

Robert O. Carlson, "The Use of Public Relations Research by Large Corporations," *Public Opinion Quarterly,* Vol. 21, Fall, 1957.
William P. Ehling, "Public Relations Research: A Few Fundamentals," *College and University Journal,* Vol. 1, Fall, 1962.
Pierre Martineau, "It's Time to Research the Consumer," *Harvard Business Review,* Vol. 33, July-August, 1955.
Ralph O. Nafziger and David M. White (eds.), *Introduction to Mass Communications Research.* Baton Rouge: Louisiana State University Press, rev. ed., 1963. The chapter on "Field Methods in Communication Research" is especially helpful.
Edward J. Robinson, "Research in Public Relations," *Public Relations Journal,* Vol. 17, January, 1961.
Wilbur Schramm (ed.), *The Science of Human Communication.* New York: Basic Books, Inc., 1963.
Claire Selltiz, Marie Jahoda, *et al., Research Methods in Social Relations.* New York: Holt, Rinehart, & Winston, Inc., 1962.

---

[13] From mss. of a talk given at the University of Wisconsin, April, 1962, by C. T. Smith, Market and Public Relations Research Administrator in A. T. & T.

CASE PROBLEM

Let's assume that you are serving as director of public relations of your college or university. The president has accepted an invitation to give the main talk at the annual alumni banquet during Commencement Week. He asks you to prepare a 30-minute speech (approximately 10 typewritten pages) on "The Problems Facing Higher Education Today." To carry out this assignment, you must:

1. Define your audience.
2. Determine themes to implement present and long-range objectives.
3. Assemble factual content through research.
4. Outline the suggested speech preparatory to a conference with the president on theme, tone, content, and so forth.
5. Write the speech.

Chapter Eight

PLANNING—

THE

SECOND

STEP

Planning requires a searching look backward, a deep look inside, a wide look around, and a long, long look ahead.

The second step in the process is the laying of plans. Once a particular problem is defined, then comes the decision of what to do about it. Effective plans, when they reach the action phase, become effective programming. As public relations matures, more emphasis is put on planning. Lack of thorough planning often leads into wheel-spinning busywork or into defensive spur-of-the-moment projects. Harried, hasty planning is makeshift at best. In times of crisis it tends to produce negative results. Prudent, long-range planning is more likely to result in:

1. An integrated program in which the total effort accumulates definite accomplishments toward specific goals.
2. Increased management participation and support.
3. A program emphasis that is positive rather than defensive.
4. Unhurried deliberation on choice of themes, timing, and tactics.

Planning is based on adequate fact-finding and the common-sense idea that people ought to know where they are going if they are trying to get somewhere. Even though the values of a planned program are clearly evident, there is still too little emphasis on this step. A survey made in Columbus, Ohio found that only 53 per cent of the practitioners were being guided by written objectives.[1] Why? These appear to be the main obstacles to public relations planning:

---

[1] William Carter Moore, "A Critical Analysis of Public Relations Practitioners in a Midwestern Metropolitan Area," Master's thesis, Ohio State University, 1962. A brief summary of this study is found in "Testing a Test City for a Public Relations Profile," by Moore and Walter W. Seifert, *Public Relations Journal*, Vol. 18, September, 1962.

1. Failure of management to include the practitioner in deliberations that lead to policies and programs.
2. Lack of clearly agreed upon objectives for implementing the public relations program.
3. Lack of time, which is stolen by the pressures of meeting daily problems.
4. The frustrations and delays which practitioners encounter in the endless task of internal clearance and coordination with other departments.
5. The practitioner's faith in the ultimate value of getting publicity as it develops in organization day by day.

Planning requires:

1. *A searching look backward*—to determine all the factors which led to the situation under study.
2. *A deep look inside*—in which the assembled facts and opinions are considered in the light of the institution's objectives and weighed as to their validity.
3. *A wide look around*—in which there is study of like situations in like organizations; political, social, and economic trends; and the mood of the times.
4. *A long, long look ahead*—in which goals for the organization and for implementing the PR program are set.

Planning starts with the realistic aims of the organization. It encompasses a determination of goals, of strategy, of tactics. It sets up objectives, or targets, at close and long range. It decides between preventive and remedial activities in specific situations and works toward an atmosphere that is as nearly preventive all the way through as possible. Then there is the *staffing* and the *action* or follow-through to implement the plans.

A public relations firm that specializes in political campaigns once set down this outline:

While there is no master blueprint which can be followed in successive campaigns, there is a fairly definite table of contents. This applies to each plan of campaign, and serves as a guide in drafting it. Here are some of the major requisites:

1. Careful delineation of the strategy which will be followed in every aspect of the campaign, and of the steps which will be taken in the development of that strategy so that the action moves forward with precision and reaches its peak of impact in the closing days before election.

2. Thorough appraisal and development of all the principal issues of the campaign, and agreement on the relative importance to be given each issue. This keeps the focus of public interest on the objectives and issues which have the most widespread appeal.

3. A complete outline of all the organization aspects of the campaign—the foundation and framework for the vast volunteer organization which will man the battle lines and carry the crusade personally to the voters.

4. Detailed plans for the use of all media—campaign pamphlets, newspaper and magazine advertising, direct mail, radio and television, billboards, moving pictures, newsreels, "literature" of all types, *et cetera*.

Note the sequence of planning, programming, and action.

A BACKDROP OF IDEALS
AND AIMS

Without ideals to form standards of perfection, there would be no important incentive toward the things that make up what we call "progress." Without some definite, attainable goals, there obviously would be little progress. Life would have no sense of direction. People would concentrate on procurement of the bare necessities. They would not seek to better their own lives or to help others. Thus, our constant process of linking ideals and goals gives promise of a better tomorrow. The process provides us both purpose and direction. It also imparts a certain drama to day-by-day living.

Organizations as well as individuals have ideals and goals that give purpose and direction to their functions. As a preface to the planning that goes into the organizational process, it is important to recognize these underlying motivations.

> *To gain rewards.*
> *To help others.*
> *To be supported within the organization.*
> *To be respected within the community.*
> *To deliver a necessary and a wanted product or service.*
> *To be free from needless outside restraints.*
> *To have an influence on public opinion.*

Problems involving an organization's public relationships, including breakdowns in communication, relate readily to one or another of these basic aims. In a business, for example, a common problem is economic distress. Sales drop, or something else, causes earnings to slip off. The business, in that case, is not *gaining rewards.*

In social welfare work, a problem arises if a charity cannot get volunteer workers to help solicit funds in the annual campaign. In that case, the undertaking is not *being supported within the organization.* For a military camp, a problem exists if the residents in the neighborhood resent it as an intrusion. In such a situation, the military is not *respected within the community.* Or, if congressional action were pending to ban women from military service, the organization would not be *free from needless outside restraints.*

In the perspective of an organization's basic aims, the specific problems threatening, or able to threaten, should be isolated for study. Three preliminary steps should be taken:

1. Determine by analysis the policy makers' attitudes toward publics with whom communication has broken down.
2. Determine with equal care attitudes of the publics toward the organization.
3. Block out the areas of common agreement and common interest. Work from these areas in devising a program to iron out differences and soothe the hostilities.

STRATEGY AND TACTICS

Planning takes two general directions. One is concerned with long-range programs to achieve the PR mission. These are defined by the institution's basic policies. Within this framework will be fitted short-term plans for specific projects. It is important to keep the short-range programming subordinate to the long-range plans.

The initial fact-finding and analysis compares with the "intelligence" function in the military. The planning compares with the strategy and tactics of a military campaign. Long-range planning relates to broad outlines of strategy; short-term projects, to the tactics that make the strategy work. All are interrelated. Strategy is a master plan for winning a campaign. Tactics cover skillful use of tools and techniques in winning the several battles that make a campaign.

Long-term planning jells in decisions on ultimate aims. Although aims are usually couched in broad phrases, one must guard against the tendency to permit them to become vague, vaporous generalities. *Formulation of aims is the task of management with aid from its communications specialists.*

Within the framework of basic policies and long-range planning comes the implementation. For example, The Parker Pen Company, as one of its basic policies, supports the idea of free-flowing world trade. Long-range planning looks to the day when the markets of the world will be open equally to the pen makers of the world. Meantime, to dramatize the desirability of this ultimate aim, projects in the company's home community have included a "Peso Pay Day" for employees, a "Path of Nations" across the front of its plant, a World Trade Fiesta in the community, and so forth. This programming pursues the company's long-range goal by keeping attention focused on the basic policy.

Parker officials found in this basic theme the guide to solving a difficult PR problem—How does a relatively small company compete with the giants of industry in an extravaganza like the New York World's Fair of 1964? After two years of planning talks, the firm set down these criteria which had to be met: tie-in with the Fair theme, "Peace Through Understanding"; people-participation rather than just people-observation; involvement of non-Fairgoers, too; an exhibit and pavilion that related to its basic business—selling pens. Parker's theme became "Peace Through Understanding . . . Through Writing," and it launched the biggest international letter-writing exchange ever attempted, using a computer to store and carefully match hundreds of thousands of names. Called the Parker Penfriend program, the company's dealers from all over the world helped collect names and thus won traffic to their stores by providing a welcome service. First letters were written in Parker's pavilion at the Fair, which became a catalyst for Parker to gain attention, then involvement, plus contributing in its modest way to world understanding. This is PR planning with a capital P.

THE TWO KINDS OF
PLANNING

Nugent Wedding, professor of marketing at the University of Illinois, has provided definitions of preventive and remedial programs.[2] In the past there has been too much remedial public relations—too much occasion for it—and too little preventive. Quite often a matter calling for remedial action provides the spark that touches off preventive planning for the future. More than one PR department has been born in a time of crisis.[3] Making good to consumers for a faulty lot of merchandise is a remedial action most manufacturers have experienced at one time or another. Usually that experience constitutes so much of a threat that plans are initiated for immediate corrective action. Controls are installed to minimize chances of a recurrence, such as periodic surveys that will provide advance detection.

The relationship of fact-finding and opinion surveys to planning can be seen in these examples.

The Association of American Railroads has been engaged in an intensive, long-term campaign to get relief from tight regulatory legislation imposed in a day when the railroads had a virtual monopoly of public transportation and often abused this power. The association's PR objectives were partially achieved with enactment of the Transportation Act of 1958. This victory brought a new public relations problem—"How was public concern to be maintained until the remaining problems were solved?" Basically, as its PR director, Handly Wright, saw it, the problem was contained in two questions: (1) Was the public at last aroused enough over the plight of railroads so that further action could be successfully pressed in Congress? or (2) Did the public believe that the railroads' problems had been solved, and that now they should get on with their work? To answer these questions, the Opinion Research Corp. was employed to make a nationwide opinion survey. Out of this survey came the association's planned campaign to concentrate on getting rid of work rules that required the railroads to hire more employees than were essential. The survey showed that one out of every three respondents thought "featherbedding" was the railroads' most serious problem.[4]

One city's United Givers-Red Feather organization failed to meet its fund-raising goal three years in a row. On advice of counsel, it sponsored an opinion survey. This poll revealed, among other things, that many persons thought that

---

[2] Nugent Wedding, "Public Relations in Business," *University of Illinois Bulletin,* Vol. 47, July, 1950, 32.

[3] For examples of "crisis" public relations, see "Shock Treatment for Parke, Davis," *Fortune,* Vol. 48, September, 1953; "Ford's Fight for First," *Fortune,* Vol. 50, September, 1954. For proof that the most careful planning does not insure success, see John Brooks, "The Edsel," *New Yorker,* Part I, November 26, 1960; Part II, December 3, 1960.

[4] In "Association of American Railroads," *Proceedings, Seventh Minnesota Public Relations Forum,* Minneapolis: University of Minnesota, 1959, 8-9.

the agency's new headquarters were much too large and luxurious. Most of this criticism was based on the erroneous belief that only the United Givers staff occupied the building. A corrective campaign to publicize the fact that this building provided offices for many of the Red Feather agencies was planned and undertaken. This included placing a large sign listing all agencies headquartered in the building on the front lawn. As the result of this and other information projects planned on the basis of the survey, the organization's fund drive went over the top the next year.

PLANNING STARTS WITH
A PLATFORM

After taking any remedial measures needed to cope with emergency problems, the practitioner is freed to develop a continuing program to improve conduct and communication. This broad-gauge effort will customarily be punctuated by projects along the way that speed the process and lend drama.

PUT IT ON PAPER. The over-all program should be set down on paper, in *the form that is approved by the governors of the organization.* Effective programming requires an agreed upon, clear-cut platform.

Without a platform, public relations is, in one practitioner's view, "in danger of becoming tremendously expert in selling a grab-bag package without having any clear idea of what our merchandise is." Surely *aimlessness* is one of the main factors vitiating much of the effort and expenditure in this field. Veteran counselor Paul Garrett years ago said: "Set down on a sheet of paper the policies of your company you would like the public to know about. Then build supporting projects." The values of such a platform are listed by Oliver Gale: [5]

1. Opportunities are legion. If a company knows what it wants—it can do a more intelligent job.
2. The public relations department and . . . the whole organization can devote their efforts in the same directions.
3. A written statement can be studied and accepted by top management and all departmental heads.

Arthur W. Page, architect of the Bell System's public relations program, said repeatedly that this is the first thing to be done in setting up a program. "This (statement of policy) is equivalent to saying to the public: 'We should like to serve you and we offer you the following contract which we think would be fair to all concerned and mutually profitable.' The statements of policy are hostages for performance." A corporation that pays lip service to free competitive enterprise through a series of advertisements and is then caught in a deliberate violation of the antitrust laws learns, the hard way, that its profes-

---

[5] Quoted in Conger Reynolds' article, "And What Is Your Public Relations Platform?", *Public Relations Journal*, Vol. 11, October, 1955.

sions of faith constitute a hostage. Mr. Page suggested a sound reason for public policy statements. There are also good reasons for having the basic policies of the enterprise known and understood internally. It invites support and collaboration from all hands. In expressing the position of the organization, the position of officials is also clarified. This is particularly important for the counselor.

Here is a typical statement of policies for the Merck Company. Note that this statement could well stand exposure to public scrutiny, yet it is phrased for the internal audience of the business.

First, we want to make sure that our company is a good organization to work for. In other words, we must start at home, building understanding and deserved goodwill among our workers, their relatives, and close friends.

Second, we must be a good citizen of our community. There are some things we and others need to do if we are to enjoy topnotch relations with our neighbors.

Third, we want to bring about greater understanding beyond the borders of our home towns of the scientific advances which are being made, and of the care exercised to provide quality and value in our products.

Fourth, we want the general public to know from our deeds that our motives are dominated by a genuine desire to serve. The American people are more "ends-minded" than "means-minded." They like to feel they know your goal and your results.

Elgin National Watch Company put down these broad-based objectives:

1. To help develop and maintain friendly relations with the retail jewelry trade.

2. To secure public and trade recognition of our leadership in the field of design.

3. To secure public and trade recognition of our leadership in the field of research.

In a survey conducted by Nugent Wedding among 85 business firms, the following objectives were mentioned most often: [6]

Objective	Per Cent of Total Respondents
Increased sales	57.6
Public understanding of the company and its policies	48.2
Building public or community goodwill	45.8
Employe contentment, reduced turnover, aid in recruiting new employees	21.2
Developing better understanding between management and employees as an aid to better production	20.0
Explaining the part played by the firm in the economy	20.0
Preserving the free enterprise system	17.6
Selling the company and the product to the public	15.3
Keeping employees informed about the company and its operation	12.9
Securing favorable legislation	11.8

[6] Nugent Wedding, *op. cit.,* p. 19.

In a more recent, though more narrowly based, study, A. Douglas Lyke found these the major objectives in 24 Chicago-area companies: [7]

1. To interpret the company, its goals, policies, practices, and types of business to the company's publics.
2. To interpret to management the attitudes and opinions of the publics about the company.
3. To anticipate, ferret out, and prevent internal difficulties that might cause trouble for the company.
4. To obtain customer acceptance of company products, increase sales, and obtain franchises by winning customer friendship or improving service.
5. To take care of several miscellaneous company functions which don't belong in other departments.
6. To guide management in making the right moves for the company.

CHECKLIST FOR PLANNING

Planning, its detail and procedures, too often appears as an abstract, academic sort of business. It can be overorganized and thus become quite theoretical. It can also lead to rigidity. Informal planning is realistic. Its danger lies in ignoring the necessity of planning altogether. There are a number of yardsticks which serve to measure programs as projects before they go into action. Well-planned programs should be:

1. *Sincere* in purpose and execution.
2. *Durable* and in keeping with organization's purpose and character.
3. *Firm,* positive in approach and appeals.
4. *Comprehensive* in scope and continuous in application.
5. *Clear and symbolic,* with simple messages.
6. *Beneficial* to both the sender and the receiver of the message.

In planning a program to advance organizational goals, it is important that the content be devised so that it tells, over a period of time, the institution's history, ideals, and achievements, publicizes its people, its policies, and its products or services, and projects its plans for a better tomorrow. Unless such yardsticks are used periodically, emphasis is apt to become disjointed under exigencies of the moment. *To touch all bases, program content must be planned and devised.*

By following a checklist, each press release or special event will bring progress toward the broad goals of good repute and wide recognition for public service. The DuPont Company measures each program project with an "analysis formula."

What is the objective this project is designed to gain or approach?
Is the objective sound and desirable?

---

[7] *Public Relations as a Management Function in Chicago-Area Companies* (New York: Public Relations Society of America, 1954), p. 99.

Are there collateral advantages?
Is the project feasible?
Can it be done with existing personnel?
Does it involve cooperation outside the department?
Is it counter to sound public relations policy?
Is it counter to company policy?
Is the expense too high in relation to possible gain?
Can it embarrass sales, production, research?
Where is the money coming from?
What are the penalties of failure?
Why do it now?
Why do it this way?
Who must approve the project?
Who must be informed?

PLANNING AND BUDGETING

Planning and budgeting for public relations go hand in hand. To prepare a budget for the next year, the department must plan ahead, and plans cannot be implemented without a supporting budget. Systematic budget-making requires planning in *advance* instead of on the spur of the moment. However, flexibility must be provided that enables a staff to capitalize on PR opportunities that cannot be foreseen. Budgets provide means of relating objectives with plans as these are shaped and limited by funds available. A sound budget includes all phases of management planning and results in a unified, agreed upon plan of action.

An example of how budgeting and PR planning go hand in hand is outlined by Robert H. Herrick of the Cleveland Electric Illuminating Company: [8]

I. The starting point is an *annual budget-planning report* to provide:
   1. Management with analytical information needed to modify and improve policies.
   2. Improved coordination for planning and to make possible a review of all plans to test consistency with the company's long-term plans and objectives.
   3. A common yardstick for the next year's progress by stating what is to be measured and defining standards.

   These reports are prepared in three main sections:
   1. A *progress* section, reviewing accomplishments of the past year. It covers progress compared with plans established in the previous budget-planning report.
   2. A *planning* section, where next year's plans and goals are stated and explained.
   3. A *budget support* section—narrative justification of the budgeted requirements for the forthcoming year. Specific plans are set forth and then translated into dollar costs.

---

[8] In "Planning and Budgeting—Siamese Twins of Public Relations," *Public Relations Journal,* Vol. 17, January, 1961, pp. 14-15.

THE PR MAN'S ROLE

The role of the counselor or staff director in the execution of programs is well established. His role at the earlier stages of fact-finding, analysis, and planning is not so clearly defined nor firmly established. Ideally, he serves as *analyst* in the investigating phase and as *adviser* in the planning phase. Once the program and its projects move into action, he becomes *advocate*.

There are two reasons which stand out above all others for the practitioner to participate in the preliminary as well as the action stages. *First,* it is here that he brings the public's needs, desires, and opinions to bear on the policy-making process. He cannot later on interpret the organization to its publics if the organization's officials are deaf to what those publics think and feel. *Second,* only by participation in the planning can he fully understand and interpret basic policies. *No one can effectively explain or execute something that he himself does not understand;* it makes little difference how skillful or adroit he may be. Without such understanding, his efforts to translate are likely to be vague. Possibly they may not even relate to basic goals.

In actual practice, the PR man is often confined to matters of publicity. All too often he cools his heels in the outer office while a major policy decision is formulated. He is called in and given a ten-minute briefing on the decision with a completely subjective analysis of why it was the "right" decision. Then he is told, in effect: "Now, you get your gang to explain in the newspapers why this decision was made and why it is the right one, so that we'll get the credit we deserve." Obviously, in such cases the practitioner is, and is expected to be, simply a paid apologist.

Odom Fanning illustrates the consequences of this. A group of university experimenters were studying underwater explosions in a government-sponsored research project, but no plans had been made to allay the predictable fears of residents in the nearby off-campus area that these would not be dangerous explosions. One night the scientists worked late. Their explosions shook the neighborhood, rattling windows and knocking pictures off walls. The alarmed neighbors called police. In due time the neighbors' fears were replaced by irritation at the university. For months the university's public relations director had urged the president to adopt an emergency plan in connection with this research project but to no avail. The president kept insisting, "We'll handle each emergency as it comes along." Fanning observes: [9]

> The president didn't realize that a lack of public relations planning on his part was accompanied by a widespread lack of public relations appreciation on the part of faculty and staff. So he discovered what many an executive in colleges, in industry, and in the government could have told him: Years of excellent public relations can be toppled in a moment under the stress of an emergency.

[9] In "Planning and Candor—Key Words in an Emergency," *Public Relations Journal,* Vol. 17, March, 1961, p. 23.

The extent of this problem in recent years was indicated in a series of talks by William M. Freeman, *New York Times* staff member who served for years as advertising and marketing columnist.

> How many men with a public relations title actually take part in management? . . . Public relations is an all-inclusive concept, defined as the effort to improve the relationship of a product, a person or a company with the public. Yet, when it comes to a showdown, "public relations" is watered down to publicity, the running of errands between the decision makers and the media selected to spread the news. If the public relations man is to be worthy of the title, he should be a full-scale adviser to management, and he should take part in the mapping of plans for improving the regard in which the management's product is held.
>
> Management is quite willing to let an advertising executive into the conference room. The advertising man commands rather more respect, possibly because his work in improving the relationship with the public can be measured rather more exactly.
>
> It is important to remember that public relations at the highest level uses advertising and publicity as techniques. The PR man is out in the cold because he isn't doing the job he says he is doing. PR people have only themselves to blame for this state of affairs. Instead of practicing public relations, many are merely using the title, and engaging in publicity, or press-agentry.

PROPER INDOCTRINATION

When a continuing program has been jelled at the policy level, it becomes necessary and desirable to indoctrinate the top echelons of executives in what is to follow. Otherwise, these important collaborators may wind up uninformed, like the counselor who is not allowed to participate in the planning. They would not be able to do their part. Nor would they be able to translate its importance into support from the people under their supervision.

The mechanical process of indoctrinating an organization is actually a test of personal skill in persuasion and coordinating. In this connection, some generally accepted tenets merit noting.

Starting with the top echelon of an organization, the basic problems should be explained in terms of the harm that can be done if they are left unattended. Then, the immediate remedial measures should be explained in relation to the long-term plans. The use of similar case examples is often very helpful. Surveys should be relied on to substantiate the plans. Personal opinion should be eliminated except as it applies to special knowledge already possessed. The program should be related to the climate in which the organization operates and hopes to enjoy in the future. It should be stressed that the activities to be undertaken will have a profound ultimate effect on public opinion. Explanations should be short and to the point. The practitioner should be *decisive,* a quality highly respected by managers and administrators.

Having gained the understanding and support of the top echelon, the next group to be tackled is that upper level of the organization where executive collaboration in news preparation and the like is necessary. Such collaboration can best be acquired through informal sessions in which individuals can air their views and talk things out. Quite often meetings are arranged in which the practitioner presents the programming, then throws open the meeting to discussion. Where this is done, a summary should be supplied afterward to all participants in the discussion. This can take the form of meeting minutes, a program timetable, a roster of projects, or a brochure explaining the plans. It is important for the future relationship that the programming agreed upon be a matter of record. Getting it down on paper tends to pin the details in the right places.

For an example of the whole process, assume that the A.B.C. Manufacturing Company, makers of parachutes, has decided to convert from the use of nylon to a new type of material called *Chemthin*. It is claimed to be better and is known to be lighter in weight and bulk. The raw materials for it are in free supply.

Assume, too, that the conversion idea originated years earlier. At that time the organization learned that the weight and bulk of standard parachutes were a source of concern to military officialdom and flight personnel alike. Consequently, a specific research program was activated. Chemthin was created and engineered by the A.B.C. Company as a private undertaking.

The prospect of introducing the new material posed problems involving relationships between the company and the military, the suppliers, the parents of flight personnel, and others. Long before the fabric was ready, the **PR** man or woman presented a carefully planned program of information **and** events. These were devised to gain a sympathetic understanding from certain publics and the enthusiastic support of others. The program was approved.

Indoctrination of the organization followed. The plans were explained down the line from executives through supervisors to employees in the offices and shops. Auxiliary channels of information were used. A letter went from the president to each employee's home. Everybody in the organization, by being fully informed, became a front-line participant in the conversion.

Next the practitioner opened the communication gate a bit wider. This might have been planned to happen in a rapid succession of events and news releases requiring no more than a working day or two for the full range. Or, it might have been planned to fan slowly out, first to the community, then to the national level.

In the dissemination of information externally, there were three basic components: (1) news, (2) media to carry the messages, (3) funds and staff adequate to get the job done.

Continuing the example, assume that it was agreed the informative phase should tell a story of research, product refinement, quality, durability, and safety. A thread was to emphasize that the company's action was in the public interest because it contributed to the national defense effort. The arrangements for external communication might have looked like this on paper.

COMMUNICATION VEHICLE	IMMEDIATE PURPOSE
First, a statement to the home town press.	To relieve any anxiety about the community's economic security due to the changeover.
Second, a statement to the national press.	To confirm publicly that the move served the national interest as well as private interests.
Third, a special letter to the shareholders of A.B.C. Company.	To reaffirm the confidence of investors in the stability of the company.
Fourth, special magazine articles telling about the development of Chemthin.	To impress on segments of the general public the safety and quality features of the product; to establish leadership.
Fifth, an A.B.C. Hardship Committee.	To deal with employee hardship cases due to temporary layoffs during conversion.
Sixth, a plant visit by military officials.	To point up the progress of conversion and to identify activities with the defense effort.
Seventh, a booklet on Chemthin.	To reassure soldiers, parents of soldiers, educators, scientists, students, and others who might inquire.
Eighth, an open house on completion of conversion.	To demonstrate the benefits to the community and to reaffirm the interdependence of company and community.
Ninth, public demonstrations of the finished product.	To prove the safety, quality, and value aspects of Chemthin.

Note that the specific target publics were those most keenly affected by what A.B.C. was doing. There were soldiers and parents concerned about safety, stockholders who bore the financial risk of the change, hometown residents whose livelihoods were linked with the ebb and flow of A.B.C.'s business, new suppliers whose materials would now be needed by A.B.C., and military officials and the general public shouldering the expense of the national defense effort.

THE TIMETABLE CAN MAKE THE DIFFERENCE

It will be apparent from a re-examination of the program just outlined that the chronology was deliberate, not accidental. One reason is that people rebel against any sudden change of drastic proportion without some kind of reassurance that everything is going to be all right. Mental digestion leading to acceptance of change is normally a gradual process in human nature. A second reason is that communication, to obtain a desired reaction, should move out in waves from its original source. It should preserve, insofar as possible, its original form and integrity. It should be accurate. The normal path of information is from those most intimately involved to those who are only incidentally interested. A third reason is that news or advertising naturally follows the logical sequence of happenings.

TIMING IS A KEY ELEMENT. The several elements of a program, such as Chemthin's, must be spaced and timed to produce the desired effect at exactly the right time. In political campaigns the strategists and practitioners strive to bring enthusiasm and support for their candidates and their cause to a peak the weekend before Tuesday's voting. Like timing is sought in fund-raising campaigns. However, such plans cannot be made in a vacuum. They must be related to the total situation in which actions and communication will take place.

For example, some years ago the United States Internal Revenue Service was rocked by a series of scandals. Headlines reporting cheating and fraud on the part of a few Revenue officials darkened the nation's front pages. In the midst of these exposés, the Commissioner of Internal Revenue sent a letter to the nation's taxpayers chiding them for their carelessness in making out tax returns. He sternly wrote: "Our National Defense Program demands much from us. It places a reponsibility on both you and me, as fellow taxpayers, to see that our taxes are correctly and completely paid." At another time such a letter might have produced the desired result. In the climate in which it was received, it produced a hollow sound and brought much additional criticism to an already harried commissioner.

The calendar offers many opportunities for positive timing. For example, the public relations director of Atlanta's schools wanted to get the public's attention focused on the serious school-dropout problem. She prepared a documentary entitled, "The Ghost Story—School Dropouts," and it was broadcast on Halloween night. Shrewd timing is also used to smother a story rather than have it spotlighted, or to smother an opponent's story. Franklin D. Roosevelt, probably coached by Louis M. Howe, in 1932 held the hearings on the ouster of Mayor Jimmy Walker of New York the same day that Herbert Hoover was accepting the Republican nomination. The Walker hearings, highly sensational, overshadowed the Hoover story on the nation's front pages.

Here are some other examples: A leading manufacturer of home appliances took advantage of the news lull on Christmas Day to announce a sharp price cut effective January 1. Many a husband eyeing a shiny appliance by the Christmas tree and thinking of the higher price he had paid, was resentful. Many said so. A leading steel firm announced that it was boosting the price of steel $4 a ton because of increased labor costs. Forty-eight hours later it released its annual report boasting of record profits. The coincidence of these two announcements brought public criticism that should have been expected. The time of the annual report was fixed. The price boost could have been delayed for a better psychological time. A few years ago the DuPont Company announced grants of nearly one million dollars to over 100 universities and colleges. This laudable act of corporate citizenship should have brought DuPont much favorable publicity. But the news was smothered. It was released the same day that the Ford Foundation announced a $500 million grant to educational institutions and hospitals. The public plaudits went to the Ford Foundation.

One of the many valuable guides that practitioners have learned from social science research is that *"Change in attitude is more likely to occur if the suggestion is accompanied by change in other factors underlying belief and attitude."* It is obvious that *the more we can make the environment give credence to our communication, the more likelihood there is of our message being accepted.* It is equally important to avoid, if we can, contradictions of our communication current in the environment in which they are received. Wilbur Schramm sums up implications of research on this factor in communications:[10]

> In general, (a) if we can make our messages appeal to individual needs and wants, (b) if we can provide or point out social support for the desired attitudes, (c) if we can *introduce our messages at such a time as will let them be reinforced by related events,* (d) if we can point out or provide a channel for action along the line of the desired attitude, and if we can eliminate so far as possible or point out ways of surmounting the barriers to such action—then we can be as confident as possible . . . of accomplishing what we want to accomplish with our suggestion.

PLANNING FOR
DISASTERS

It is usually possible to time an open house so that it will not conflict with local events. It is usually possible to announce a decision of national significance at a time when it will not be crowded off the front pages and the airwaves.

There is one type of event which cannot be forecast—a catastrophe. *But it can be planned for.* Every institution and industry is subject to the fate of a disaster and should plan accordingly. When it happens, time is a key element in the handling of communication. There is no time to plan cautiously and carefully a program of information. Plans made far in advance for calamity procedure must go into action. The on-the-spot planning which would normally be given weeks must be crammed into a few minutes, or a few hours at most.

A thoughtful and considerate handling of communications in such an emergency was demonstrated in the tragic Sioux City explosion some years ago. Eighteen employees of Swift & Company and three employees of commercial trucking companies lost their lives. More than 100 others were injured. Looking back later, G. C. Reitinger, Public Relations Manager of Swift & Company, reported the following activities in the communication phase of the Disaster Plan:

---

10 In *The Process and Effects of Mass Communication* (Urbana: University of Illinois Press, 1954), p. 214. A helpful volume of readings edited by Schramm.

1. Twelve executives, including two PR men, were sent by chartered plane from the main office in Chicago. They arrived within seven hours after the accident.

2. A brief statement was issued to the press emphasizing that the company's primary concern was for the welfare of the disaster victims and their families.

3. Full assistance was rendered to the press. That included an adequately equipped headquarters from which the press could work, availability of facts and figures on casualties, cooperation with photographers, and emphasis on the care and welfare of those affected by the tragedy.

4. Teams were organized to visit families of those who died, the hospitalized, and families of those seriously injured.

5. There were follow-up visits.

6. Financial aid was arranged for those in need.

7. Assistance was rendered in funeral arrangements.

8. Flowers went to funerals and to the injured in hospitals.

9. Facilities for paying wages and salaries were set up in a local bank. The accident occurred the day before pay day. Arrangements to pay all employees were set up two days later.

10. Assurance was given to all employees that they would be kept on the payroll.

11. Assurance was given to the community that the plant would be rebuilt.

12. A special message in a half-page advertisement appeared in Sioux City papers. The message was signed by the president, John Holmes, expressing appreciation for the help of all organizations and individuals. The injured were assured of the best medical care, and sympathy was offered to bereaved families.

13. Company executives visited every community official who had helped, including the relief organizations such as the Salvation Army and the Red Cross.

14. Handwritten notes from President Holmes went to the family of each person who had died.

15. Personal letters from the president went to those who helped in the emergency.

Cooperation with the press netted the company every consideration. There was no unreasonable sensationalism in reporting and photography. The community and the bereaved families of the victims were outspoken in their appreciation. Quick planning, but planning nonetheless, proved invaluable.

Standard Oil Company of Indiana experienced a like disaster at its Whiting, Indiana, refinery years ago, when a hydroformer unit exploded. Fragments of steel killed a boy, injured his brother, and smashed into nearby houses. In the refinery, steel fragments tore into storage tanks. Crude oil was soon ablaze in a 10-acre area. The fires lasted for eight days. Smooth, skilled handling of the events which followed the explosion and fires brought the company public understanding and its PR staff praise and awards. The underlying policies called for *consideration* for those affected and for complete *cooperation* with news media. The PR staff had *planned* for just such an emergency and thus was prepared to act swiftly.[11]

---

[11] John Canning, "The Whiting Fire, a Case History in Disaster PR," *Proceedings, Fourth Annual Minnesota Public Relations Forum* (Minneapolis: Minnesota Chapter, PRSA, 1955), pp. 18-24. Also see John T. Hall, "A Fire Made Them Famous," *Public Relations Journal,* Vol. 11, July, 1955.

Its first "Procedure for Reporting News of Serious Fires and Other Unusual Emergencies" was drafted in 1947. It has been revised periodically since that time. After outlining the procedure for reporting such emergencies to management and to public relations oficials—including names, phone numbers, home addresses, and so forth, in sequence, the SO memo as last revised carried this policy statement:

The general policy will be to receive all press and radio representatives courteously and to do everything possible to facilitate their getting the objective facts regarding the fire or accident.

Watchmen in particular should be courteous at such a time. They will generally be the first company representatives with whom reporters and photographers will have contact.

When press representatives ask watchmen at Refinery gates for permission to enter the Plant, as they always do at such a time, watchmen will tell them as politely as possible that watchmen do not have authority to grant such permission. They will suggest that for official information they go to the emergency press headquarters in the Personnel Office Section, Industrial Relations Div. Bldg., 1915 Front St., Whiting.

Reporters and photographers are not to be permitted inside the Refinery during emergencies.

There is to be no company interference with reporters and photographers at work outside Refinery fences. So far as our company is concerned, photographers have a right to take photographs from public highways, railroad property, and the like. Employees, particularly watchmen, are not to expose film or confiscate camera when photographers are working on property which does not belong to our company and is not inside Refinery fences.

Our representatives will not do any guessing or speculation. They will state only established facts.

In regard to monetary damages, they will make no statement until one has been authorized by the head of the Refinery or one of his superiors. . . . To inquiries regarding the cause they will reply with only such information as is clearly correct. Whenever the cause is in doubt, they will courteously request inquirers to defer their questions until there has been time to gather more information.

In proceeding cautiously in such matters, company representatives are to use their common sense and to be neither overly conservative nor too ready to jump to conclusions.

Whenever it is evident that the reporter is trying to make a sensation out of the incident, to represent danger or loss as being much greater than it is, our representatives are to endeavor tactfully to make him see the facts in their correct proportion. This is particularly necessary in case of oil fires, which are usually spectacular and look more dangerous than they usually turn out to be.

Additional Reading

Louis H. Bell, "Columbia's Magic Bicentennial Theme," *PR*, Vol. 1, October, 1955.
Edward L. Bernays, "What Every Executive Should Know About Public Relations," *Printers' Ink*, Vol. 240, September 12, 1952.
John S. DuBois, "Building the Company Image." *Public Utilities Fortnightly*, Vol. 61, Feb. 27, 1958.

Glen Perry, "Plugging Up the Holes," *Public Relations Journal,* Vol. 7, September, 1951.
Public Relations Society of America. "Budgeting the Public Relations Dollar." New York: the Society, 1960.
Edgar Stephens (pseudonym), "Programming for Public Relations," *Public Relations Journal,* Vol. 13, May, 1957.
William Taylor, "Long-Range Planning—Key to University's Celebration," *Public Relations Journal,* Vol. 18, July, 1961.
Burt Zollo, "Setting Your Goals." *Public Relations Quarterly,* Vol. 7, Summer, 1962.

CASE PROBLEM

You are an account executive in a local public relations counseling firm. You specialize in handling retail stores and in staging civic events. Your firm is retained on an annual basis by Duffy Enterprises, Inc., a realty and construction company. Your firm was hired because the Duffy firm is opening a new shopping center, The Eastgate, at the eastern edge of the city, in six weeks. You are assigned to the account. You don't have much time, but—

1. Study accounts of similar shopping center and like events in PR publications.
2. Assemble necessary "information" you need for planning.
3. Canvass and select, in cooperation with Duffy executives, an advertising agency to handle advertising for the opening.
4. Organize a Tenants' Committee to cooperate with you in planning and staging the opening celebration.
5. Draw rough plans for a gala opening of Eastgate to present to a conference of Duffy executives, other officers of your firm, representatives of the advertising agency, and the Tenants' Committee.

Chapter Nine

COMMUNICATING—

THE

THIRD

STEP

The fleeting attention today's citizen can offer is caught by those in whom he believes and who talk to him in terms of his self-interest in words that he can understand.

The dictionary describes communication as "intercourse by words, letters, or messages; interchange of thoughts or opinions." It would be difficult to think of anything that takes place, makes a sound or a gesture, that does not in some way communicate. Our social life abounds with communication, some of it overt, much of it unverbalized. The average American spends about 70 per cent of his waking hours communicating verbally—listening, speaking, reading, and writing. Truly, Americans live under a waterfall of words. This is inescapable in our interdependent society. Communications is the cement which holds society together.

The newborn infant's first cry communicates. It says, "I am alive." From then on through life a winked eye, raised eyebrow, smile, cupped ear, shaken finger communicate. Notice, however, that these simple human gestures are not in the form of actual words. Still, they inform eloquently. The same is true of sounds for which the audience forms words. There's no doubt what's going on when one hears a church bell, snap of a mousetrap, or thunder.

Building from sights, sounds, and sensations, one finds the means to express himself, to be understood, and to understand. In the process, words form the main carrier. The use of words, whether the communicating takes the form of a news release or an open house event, constitutes the first common denominator.

Words are symbols. There are words which serve as symbols for real

146

objects, *table, chair—thing words.* There are words which are symbols of abstract ideas, such as *freedom, love—nothing words.* Children are taught, for example, that a furry little animal with long ears and a short, fuzzy tail is a "rabbit." Once the word and the little animal are associated, the word will always evoke the image of that creature. Word symbols for real objects are readily understood with a high degree of agreement. Not so with symbols for abstractions.

Abstractions, like "free enterprise" or "military morale," have no simple or universally agreed on referents in the real world of objects. It is difficult for people to agree on an image of free enterprise when they cannot see, touch, hear, taste, or smell it. This difficulty goes right to the heart of the communications problem. *To communicate effectively, the sender's words must mean the same thing to the receiver that they do to the sender.* The more *thing* words and the fewer *nothing* words the communicator uses, the easier his message is to understand.

The word *communication* is derived from the Latin *communis,* meaning "common." *The purpose of communications is to establish a commonness.* There are three basic elements in communication: the source or *sender,* the *message* or symbols, and the destination or *receiver.* A breakdown can involve one or more of these three elements. Effective communication requires efficiency on the part of all three. The communicator must have adequate information. He must be able to present it in symbols the receiver will understand. He must use a channel that will carry the message to the receiver. The message must be within the receiver's capacity to comprehend. And it must motivate the receiver's self-interest.

When there has been no common experience on which to establish *commonness,* then communication becomes impossible. A sender can *encode* his message and a receiver *decode* it only in terms of his experience and knowledge. This explains a layman's inability to understand an Einstein and a non-baseball fan's bewilderment at the cry of "Bunt!" Common knowledge and experience provide the connecting links, like this: [1]

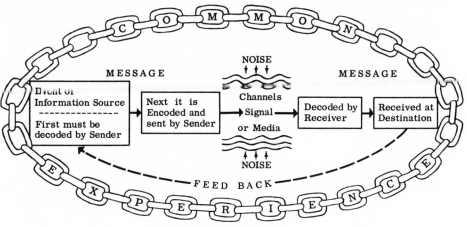

THE TWO-STEP FLOW
THEORY

In this seemingly simple process, there are a number of variables which intervene. Research, dating roughly from the 1920's, has successively isolated and identified these variables as: (1) exposure, access, attention given the communicator's message; (2) the differential character of the media of communication; (3) content of the message—its form, presentation, and appeals; (4) receiver's predispositions which cause acceptance, modification, or rejection of message; (5) interpersonal relationships of individuals as members of groups. Each one of these variables must be taken into account.

The most recent variable found to be influential is that of the receiver's interpersonal relationships. This has led to formulation of the *two-step flow of mass communication* theory.[2] Spurred by the performance of the Creel Committee in World War I, communicators in the 1920's developed a mass communications model which is now outmoded. This Model T vehicle was built on assumptions that: (1) the people were an atomistic mass of millions of isolated readers, listeners, and viewers eager and ready to receive The Message; (2) that every Message had a direct and powerful stimulus which would get an immediate response; (3) that there was a direct relationship between information and attitudes.

In short, the growing mass media were looked upon as a new kind of unifying force. This force would reach out to every eye and ear in a society characterized by an amorphous social organization and a loss of interpersonal relationships. This vertical theory of communication presumed that the Message from the Mass Media beamed down in a direct line to the newly urbanized, isolated, and lost individuals—"the image of the audience as a mass of disconnected individuals hooked up to the media but not to each other." [3]

The naïve notion underlying the obsolete Model T theory is seen in this advice given to professional publicists after World War I: "Although clearness and logical arrangement toward a climax are necessary in presenting arguments, the chief thing is to emphasize a supreme point by which . . . a prospect is 'swept off his feet.' " [4] Research and pragmatic experience have

---

1 This process is elaborated in Wilbur Schramm's introductory essay, "How Communications Works," in his *The Process and Effects of Mass Communications*, pp. 3-26.

2 For a full discussion of this significant theory, see Elihu Katz and Paul Lazarsfeld, *Personal Influence: The Part Played by People in the Flow of Mass Communications* (New York: The Free Press of Glencoe, Inc., 1955), pp. 15-42.

3 For later evaluation of this theory, see Elihu Katz, "The Two-Step Flow of Communication: An Up-to-Date Report on an Hypothesis," *Public Opinion Quarterly*, Vol. 21, Spring, 1957.

4 Herbert F. deBower, *Advertising Principles* (New York: Alexander Hamilton Institute, 1919), p. 91.

shown this image of the simple, direct effect of the mass media to be a great oversimplification. As Lazarsfeld says: "Paradoxical as it may seem, the closer one observes the workings of the mass media, the more it turns out that their effects depend on a complex network of specialized personal and social influences." [5]

Modern practice prefers a communications model which takes into account the *relay* and *reinforcement* roles played by individuals. This means less reliance on mass publicity and more on reaching thought leaders. Communications is both a *vertical* and a *horizontal* process. This was first noted in Lazarsfeld, Berelson, and Gaudet's study of the 1940 Presidential election when "it became clear that certain people in every stratum of a community serve relay roles in the mass communication of election information and influence." [6] To communicate effectively, more attention must be paid to the group, its grapevine, and, particularly, its leaders. These leaders tend to specialize in issue areas.

These leaders, whether operating at local levels or national levels, serve as the key link between the official decision makers and the general citizenry. In the view of the late V. O. Key, political scientist, these leaders—"the talkers, the persuaders, the speculators, the philosophers, the advocates, the opponents —mediate between the world of remote and complex events and the mass of the public." He thinks, properly, in our view, that the mass of citizens limit their participation in public affairs to supporting or vetoing the policy alternatives developed by the leaders. Practitioners must develop a more realistic model of the democratic decision-making process to guide their communications programs.

In relating recent research findings to America's communications efforts abroad, W. Phillips Davison lists these misconceptions that mislead communicators: [7]

1. That propaganda is an effective instrument for influencing opinion because the media govern the sentiments of mankind.
2. That propaganda should be aimed at a mass audience with mass attitudes as the primary target.
3. That propaganda should be directed at those who hold opposing opinions in an effort to win them over when, in fact, this is most difficult, if not impossible to do.

There are three fundamental facts the communicator must keep in mind: (1) That the audience for his communications consists of people. These

---

[5] In the essay, "Mass Media and Personal Influence," by Lazarsfeld and Herbert Menzel, in *Science of Human Communication*, edited by Wilbur Schramm (New York: Basic Books, Inc., 1963), p. 95.

[6] *The People's Choice* (New York: Columbia University Press, 1948).

[7] In "Political Communication As an Instrument of Foreign Policy," *Public Opinion Quarterly*, Vol. 27, Spring, 1963, 28-36. For a full analysis of what has been learned about effectiveness and limitations of mass media in influencing opinions, see Joseph T. Klapper, *The Effects of Mass Communication* (New York: The Free Press of Glencoe, Inc., 1960).

people live, work, and play with one another in the framework of social institutions. Consequently, each person is subject to many influences of which the communicator's message is only one. (2) That people tend to read, watch, or listen to communication which presents points of view with which they are sympathetic or in which they have a deep personal stake. Each person lives in the shelter of a cocoon of his own spinning that insulates him from the communications babble that beats in upon him all day long, a babble steadily increasing in intensity. (3) The response we want from our intended receiver must be *rewarding to him* or he is not likely to respond.

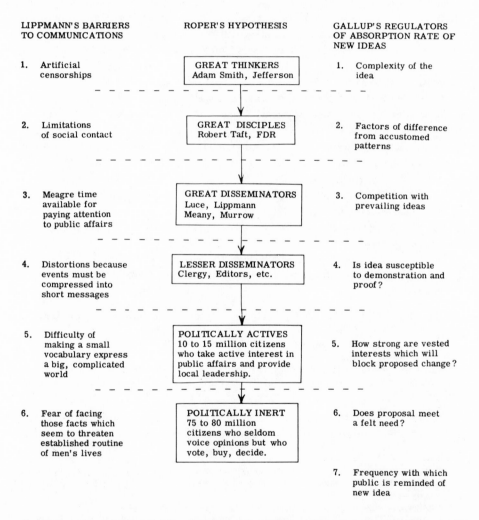

LIPPMANN'S BARRIERS TO COMMUNICATIONS	ROPER'S HYPOTHESIS	GALLUP'S REGULATORS OF ABSORPTION RATE OF NEW IDEAS
1. Artificial censorships	**GREAT THINKERS** Adam Smith, Jefferson	1. Complexity of the idea
2. Limitations of social contact	**GREAT DISCIPLES** Robert Taft, FDR	2. Factors of difference from accustomed patterns
3. Meagre time available for paying attention to public affairs	**GREAT DISSEMINATORS** Luce, Lippmann Meany, Murrow	3. Competition with prevailing ideas
4. Distortions because events must be compressed into short messages	**LESSER DISSEMINATORS** Clergy, Editors, etc.	4. Is idea susceptible to demonstration and proof?
5. Difficulty of making a small vocabulary express a big, complicated world	**POLITICALLY ACTIVES** 10 to 15 million citizens who take active interest in public affairs and provide local leadership.	5. How strong are vested interests which will block proposed change?
6. Fear of facing those facts which seem to threaten established routine of men's lives	**POLITICALLY INERT** 75 to 80 million citizens who seldom voice opinions but who vote, buy, decide.	6. Does proposal meet a felt need?
		7. Frequency with which public is reminded of new idea

1. Walter Lippmann, *Public Opinion*. New York: Harcourt, Brace, 1922, p. 30.
2. Elmo Roper, "Reaching the General Public." *PR*, Vol. 1, October, 1955, 1-6.
3. George Gallup, "The Absorption Rate of Ideas." *Public Opinion Quarterly*, Vol. 19, Fall, 1955, 234-42.

ROPER'S CONCENTRIC
CIRCLE THEORY

Gaining acceptance of an idea or point of view, then, is more than simply beaming it at an audience through a mass medium. There is still not sufficient evidence to be positive about how ideas are disseminated among Americans. Elmo Roper, after nearly 30 years of opinion research, formulated a hypothesis which he calls the "concentric circle theory." [8] Roper assumes that ideas penetrate the whole public very slowly. They do so by a process similar to osmosis. They move out in concentric circles from Great Thinkers to Great Disciples to Great Disseminators to Lesser Disseminators to the Politically Active to the Politically Inert. The flow of ideas as hypothesized by Roper is charted on the opposite page. This hypothesis assumes that American society can be stratified as indicated. It emphasizes the importance of using opinion leaders in the PR process. His theory squares with the findings of Lazarsfeld, Katz, and others. It deserves further testing.

The *rate of flow* in the transmission and acceptance of ideas is governed by many factors. These include the five variables listed on page 148. They also include the "Regulators of Absorption Rate" named by George Gallup on the basis of three decades of opinion research, also listed on the chart.

THE DIFFUSION PROCESS

The communications step in the process requires influencing opinion among both sizable and distant groups. The United States Department of Agriculture has been working at this task longer than most. The USDA has learned that getting new ideas accepted is not the simple process of discovering a new grain and publicizing it. It took 14 years to gain widespread adoption of hybrid seed corn on America's farms, for example. Out of their long experience and *evaluation,* agricultural sociologists have concluded that acceptance goes through five stages.[9]

1. *Awareness.* The individual learns of the existence of the idea or practice but has little knowledge of it.
2. *Interest.* The individual develops interest in the idea. He seeks more information and considers its general merits.
3. *Evaluation.* The individual makes mental application of the idea and weighs its merits for his own situation. He obtains more information and decides to try it.

---

[8] Outlined in "Who Tells the Storytellers?", *Saturday Review,* Vol. 37, July 31, 1954.

[9] This theory of the diffusion process has emerged as the result of research of many people over a number of years. It is summarized in Herbert F. Lionberger, *Adoption of New Ideas and Practices* (Ames, Ia.: Iowa State University Press, 1960); in E. A. Wilkening, "The Communication of Ideas on Innovation in Agriculture," in *Studies of Innovation and of Communication to the Public* (Stanford, Cal.: Institute for Communication Research, 1962).

4. *Trial.* Individual actually applies the idea or practice—usually on a small scale. He is interested in how to apply practice, techniques, conditions for application.

5. *Adoption.* If the idea proves acceptable, it is adopted.

STAGES IN THE ADOPTION PROCESS

AWARENESS Learns about a new idea or practice	INTEREST Gets more infor- mation about it	EVALUATION Tries it out mentally	TRIAL Uses or tries a little	ADOPTION Accepts it for full-scale and continued use
1. Mass media radio, TV, newspapers, magazines	1. Mass media	1. Friends and neighbors	1. Friends and neighbors	Personal experience is the most important factor in continued use of an idea
2. Friends and neighbors mostly other farmers	2. Friends and neighbors	2. Agricultural agencies	2. Agricultural agencies	1. Friends and neighbors
3. Agricultural agencies, extension, vo-ag, etc.	3. Agricultural agencies	3. Dealers and salesmen	3. Dealers and salesmen	2. Agricultural agencies 3. Mass media
4. Dealers and salesmen	4. Dealers and salesmen	4. Mass media	4. mass media	4. Dealers and salesmen

Used by permission from Herbert F. Lionberger ADOPTION OF NEW IDEAS AND PRACTICES, page 32.

They have concluded that information about new farm and home practices are communicated by these agencies in order of appearance: (1) mass media—radio, TV, newspapers, magazines; (2) friends and neighbors—mostly other farmers; (3) agricultural agencies—extension agents, vo-ag instructors, and so forth; (4) dealers and salesmen—purveyors of commercial products and equipment.

These media or agencies have a varying impact at each stage of the process. The mass media have their greatest impact and usefulness in creating *awareness*. For farmers and farm wives, at least, the mass media become less and less influential as the acceptance process advances toward adoption. In the *interest* stage, mass media still play an important part. But, to learn more, the farmer turns to agricultural agencies and friends. In the *evaluation* stage, friends and neighbors play the dominant role. In the *trial* stage, agricultural agencies, friends, and neighbors are all important. Dealers and salesmen are influential in this stage when commercial products are involved. The time span in each stage varies.

This diffusion model, developed on the basis of extensive research among rural families, was confirmed in a comparable study of how doctors in four communities responded to the availability of a new "miracle drug." Despite the differences between a new seed and a new drug, and between farmers and doctors, the results are quite comparable. Comparing the study that traced the adoption of hybrid seed corn and that which traced the adoption of the new drug, Elihu Katz concludes, among other generalizations, that: [10]

10 Elihu Katz' essay, "The Social Itinerary of Technical Change: Two Studies on the Diffusion of Innovation," in *Studies of Innovation and of Communication to the Public, loc. cit.,* pp. 5-35.

(1) Both studies plot curves of diffusion to map the spread of innovation, over time, within the social structure or various parts of it. The authors of the corn study inferred from the curve that interpersonal influence would appear to account for the observed pattern of spread. The drug study went one step further and, by comparing the curves for "integrated" and "isolated" doctors, could show that interpersonal influence was operative precisely where it would most likely be expected—among the "integrated" doctors.

(2) Both studies find that "information is not enough"—neither farmers nor doctors accepted the innovation upon first hearing. It was shown that there are media which typically inform a potential adopter about an innovation, and that there are media which typically "activate" or "legitimate" the decision to adopt. The former tend to be more commercial and more formal; the latter more professional and more informal.

Professor Katz properly warns, "Whether these generalizations apply equally to the diffusion of other innovations remains to be seen."

The research conclusions demonstrate that communicating a new idea or practice is a long, tedious task. Different media are effective at different points and in different ways. The influence of the innovator or influential leader is great in every community. It is important for the communicator to know what media and techniques to use at different stages and how to mobilize these influences effectively. Taken together, these theories provide a much surer approach. *Effective communication is expensive in time, in understanding, and in emotional control. The cost is higher than is commonly supposed.*

THE BARRIERS AND DISTORTION

Barriers to understanding and distortion of message exist in the communicator and the audience alike. Each person lives pretty much by his own symbols and stereotypes. There are social barriers, age barriers, language or vocabulary barriers, political and economic barriers. Finally, there is the constant roar of competition for people's attention.

People have impressions about everything that touches the consciousness. Lippmann has bracketed these impressions into four groups.[11] One is the person's approach to the world, the second is his stereotypes, the third his personal interests, and the fourth his image of the world. Everyone lives in a world of his own symbols. Public figures, for example, during their lifetime and afterward are known partly through a personality created by images fixed in the public imagination. Astronaut John Glenn and Prince Philip are good examples. Their families and associates know them as people entirely different from their public personalities. People who live on one side of town tend to know people on the other side of town or in remote cities in a half-fictional, half-imagined way.

---

[11] Walter Lippmann, *Public Opinion* (New York: Harcourt, Brace & World, Inc., 1922).

In communicating, nothing raises more problems than the fact that the audience has limited access to the real facts in any given situation. Access, as Lippmann has made clear, is limited by the six main factors listed in the chart. With limited access to the real facts, and with some information tending to confuse as much as it clarifies, people rely heavily on stereotypes. Specific and significant impressions become generalities.

From the cover of a magazine, for example, with a picture entitled "criminal," the person looking at it may pick out two or three sharply defined features. Perhaps he selects a low forehead, a squinting eye, a scarred face, or a mouth that curls at the corner. From then on, the impression may be so deeply rooted that he feels sure he knows the "criminal type" whenever he sees it. He can classify everyone, including his friends, as to whether or not they are criminal types. Indeed, he has classifications into which he can fit almost everyone he sees or hears about.

Lippmann emphasizes the sacrosanct regard that people have for stereotypes as "the core of our personal tradition, the defense of our position in society." Stereotypes tend, as a defense mechanism, to express the hopes of the audience. They form a moral code from which personal standards are derived. The PR specialist learns to recognize the influence and the presence of symbols and stereotypes in the seeming contradictions and contrariness of public opinion. *Stereotypes are used to counter stereotypes.*

Another system of barriers encompasses the superstitions, prejudices, and vanities to which we all cling. Considering superstitions alone, one man may laugh at another for his refusal to open an umbrella in the house. The same man who laughed at that superstition might well walk two blocks out of his way, however, to avoid letting a black cat cross his path. *We believe what we want to believe.* That is perhaps the best way to explain, in oversimplified terms, the grip that superstitions, prejudices, and vanities have on us.

THE ACT OF
COMMUNICATING

With such barriers and obstacles it would be disappointing, if not futile, to establish any single set of sure-fire rules. Such a set could appear perfect in principle yet be rendered ineffectual by an unseen characteristic of the audience. The timing could be bad. This was the case when a TV maker tried to push color TV before millions of Americans owned a black-and-white set. The audience could harbor an unspoken prejudice, such as confronts a Democrat campaigning in a Republican precinct. The wording of the messages could be such that it does not square with the images in the heads of the audience. Or perhaps the audience is not in a listening mood. Regardless of the specific barrier, results from standardization of programming are generally frustrating and futile.

Effective communication means tailor-made programming specially de-

signed for the situation, time, place, and audience. It means careful selection of media and technique. No program, simply because it worked once before in a given situation, can be carted about like a trunk full of clothes and deposited in every new situation of the same type. With rare exception, the clothes will not fit the second wearer. If nothing else, they'll be out of style.

All public relations problems, however, do have people as a common denominator and require some communicating to bring the people and their viewpoints closer together. This applies whether the program calls for news releases, institutional advertising, meetings, or any other tool of contact.

The barriers and the means by which intelligence is acquired point up the need for continuity in communicating. They emphasize the need for repetition of a consistent message in simple form. They urge careful selection of time, place, and method. They recommend the use of a variety of media that converge on the audience from several avenues.

NEED FOR BETTER COMMUNICATING

Only through communication that is answered by the audience with a reaction favorable to the communicator can there be a solid platform for congenial relationships. Accepting that premise, and placing it alongside today's lack of adequate effective communication, Wilbur Schramm has discerned the tremendous task to be done.[12]

> The typical community has become heterogeneous and massive. Industrialization and fast transportation have made more changes in social patterns in one lifetime than were formerly made in centuries. Individuals have increasingly been forced to delegate their affairs to groups, so that the world presents a scene of groups dealing with each other through paid advocates who are often interested more in victory than in agreement and understanding. Increasingly, individuals have had to depend on intermediaries to inform them, and to inform others for them. This dependence on second-hand communication has come ironically at the very time when technical skills have drawn far in front of social skills, and when we have begun to wonder whether quick and constant communication, wide and effective information, may not be the only way a civilized society can survive. That means we have to depend on the large media to cut through the differences, penetrate the groups, carry the information on technical skills and social adaptations, and contribute to the exchange of opinions and the creation of social consensus. The need is great and growing.

Today, the citizen is swamped and surfeited with causes and institutions. People are bombarded from all sides with pleas to listen, to buy, to give, to vote, to do this, or not do that. Faster living permits less and less attention to these pleas. The day-to-day demands of grubbing out a living, taking care of family chores, multiplying recreational pursuits, and fulfilling

---

12 *Communications in Modern Society* (Urbana: University of Illinois Press, 1948), p. 2. This is a book of 15 studies of the mass media, edited by **Schramm**.

growing civic obligations take most of the available time and energy. There is little time left to listen, less to read, and precious little to think.

The mass media are pitched to these facts of life. These media, though vested with heavy public responsibilities, are primarily private businesses. In order to compete successfully, they find it necessary to emphasize that which excites and entertains. In determining content, they tend to headline the values of the sensational, the controversial, and the amusing. Factual, less interesting information tends to be subordinated. Values are hitched more to emotion than to reason. It is a sad but real fact that readers and listeners are much more interested in sin than in virtue. A felon is better copy than a professor of Greek.

These mass media must appeal to the common denominators. Audience begets advertising; advertising begets revenue. The audience is attracted by the satisfaction of its wants. Such generalizations reflect current values of society rather than indictments of the media which serve it.

This matter of emphasis—the reference is more to the degree of emphasis than to total content—makes it necessary for all institutions invested with public interest to take the initiative in constructively telling their sides of the story to the public. The press will take the initiative to report strikes. Industry and labor must take the initiative in reporting peaceful, productive labor-management relationships. The press will take the initiative in reporting student escapades. The universities must take the lead in reporting the substantial, though unspectacular, educational achievements. The press will quickly and fully report the conflicts of political personalities. Government must provide the less controversial story of its constructive achievements and of its services.

As James Reston of the *New York Times* observed: "The Presidential campaign dramatizes the American habit of looking at everything in terms of personalities and in terms of triumph or disaster. . . . Meanwhile the great issues of world politics are not turning on who is in power or in any conflict between violent extremes. . . ."

These, obviously, are broad generalities. Many exceptions can be found. It is difficult to generalize on the press, for example, when the term embraces such extremes in philosophy as the *New York Times* and *Christian Science Monitor,* on the one hand, and the *New York Daily News* on the other. Similar extremes are found in magazines, books, radio, motion pictures, and television.

These media do afford readily accessible channels for the institution that chooses to tell its story candidly and constructively. This is proof of an urge and an effort toward a more significant and balanced content. There is ample evidence that news values are undergoing steady self-examination and revision toward a more significant and more responsible definition of what interests people. The transition, however, is a long way from complete. The point is sharply illustrated by one capital-city newspaper. It has four writers to cover spectator sports. It employs only one man to cover the state capital with its more than 60 governmental agencies whose functions and policies affect the lives of four million citizens.

Hence, the need to tell the story of an industry or institution is not so much born of the desire for "free publicity." It is the need to be accurately reported. Both motives are found behind current publicity efforts. Those who maintain that good deeds bring their own reward and recognition fail to see the urgent need of making themselves understood. Unless they make that effort, they run the risk of being misunderstood and misrepresented. Many misunderstandings can be traced not only to misinformation but also to the lack of information. This lack on the part of those with whom congenial relationships are sought can be the root of needless frictions and aggressions. *Informed support is strong, sure support.*

NEW PERSPECTIVES
NEEDED

There is the need to shift emphasis still more in terms of people's interests and mental capacities. The ideal is to keep publicity in perspective as a *part* of the whole process, but remain primarily concerned with the absorption of messages—the reaction. We must be more impressed by the *actions* that the audience takes than by the clippings and radio transcripts. The pounds of clippings and the hours of air time mean very little if the organization is still misunderstood. Our focus must be on the audience.

The facts of the story should be told *continuously, clearly, and candidly.* Those who seek to withhold the facts of their story must reckon with the practical certainty that the story will somehow be circulated. The negative aspects are more likely to be told if others do the telling.

Institutions are faced with the choice of doing their own telling or risking relationships that develop from gossip, rumor, and backfence and tavern conversation. In making that choice, the institution either succeeds or fails to invest itself with news interest. If the choice is in the affirmative, and a green light is given, it follows that, as a corollary, *everything newsworthy* about the institution becomes news. There is nothing but trouble and embarrassment ahead for the institution that tries to have the good things about itself invested with a headlining news value, and the bad things suppressed. The decision to undertake the communicating phase implies an all-the-way attitude.

SEMANTICS

Semantics is the science of what words really mean.

Word meanings change. Words are raised from the dictionary to popular usage. Other words wither away from neglect or are banished by abuse. In this text, this science of semantics can only be kissed lightly in passing. Space denies a full courtship. Don't be misled by that. The subject really deserves and gets more attention than that from men and women in public relations work. For, in communicating and interpreting, PR people live by words. They make their living by them. Practitioners seek mastery of word meanings both as users and as understanders. For communicators, there is no escape from what T. S. Eliot described as "the intolerable wrestle with words and meanings."

The basic importance of semantics must never be lost. In communicating, a person is constantly making decisions on word meanings. Stephen Fitzgerald put it very well by saying, "When you decide whether the refusal of men to work should be called a strike, a work stoppage, or a damnable crime against the people, you are making a decision in semantics."

In selecting words to use as weapons, the practitioner must remember that the same signs and word symbols have different meanings for different persons. There is no 1-to-1 ratio between a word and its meaning; more likely, the ratio is 1-to-50. Not only do signs and words have different meanings for different people; they have two different kinds of meaning—*denotative* and *connotative. Denotative* meaning is the common dictionary meaning generally accepted by most people with the same language and same culture. *Connotative* meaning is the emotional or evaluative meaning we read into words because of our experience and background. For example, all persons will agree that DOG *denotes* a four-legged, furry, canine animal. For most persons, the word DOG *connotes* a friendly, faithful pet and usually awakens nostalgic memories. To some people, however, the word DOG *connotes* a dangerous animal to be feared. Another example would be the term *bullfight.* North and South Americans fully agree on what the term denotes, but the connotative meaning of *bullfight* differs sharply in North and South America.

THE ROOTS OF MEANING

The source is the alphabet. It was man's greatest invention and has proved at times his most troublesome one. It repeatedly gets him into trouble with other people. Yet, the alphabet is potentially man's best means of getting along with other people.

By use of the alphabet, words and sentences are formed. The words and sentences express ideas and thoughts. Some of the expressions are troublemakers, and others give people hope of getting along with each other. One man calls another a string of names. That starts trouble. The two men fight physically. Next day they apologize and explain things to each other with the hope of getting along at least for a while. *All but the fist-fighting was done with words.*

As ideas and thoughts have become more and more complex, the language of words has broadened and grown more specialized. People have had to specialize language to talk about television, cybernetics, antibiotics, jets, automation, and atomic power. There will have to be more specialization in the years ahead to handle such things as earth satellites, microelectronics, and computers. Meantime, there are already special language arrangements for scientists, immigrants, deaf and blind people, musicians, and even baseball fans.

The specialization has not been restricted to language. People, themselves, in their work and outside pursuits have specialized. The old-time family doctor has become a dozen specialists. Then, there is the specialization of thought patterns. Once there were nice, broad philosophies as big and comfortable as a roll-top desk. Now there are many more smaller areas of thought categorized in pigeonholes for the precepts, concepts, principles, tenets, and the like.

THE PR MAN IS EXPECTED TO BE THE ANSWER MAN

Into the midst of the confusion walks the public relations man. Studying the words that leap out of people's mouths, stare up from newspapers, and smile out from a television tube, he's expected to react and then to be able to tell what those words mean . . . *not what they say, but what they really mean*. Then, he's expected to combine words that will correct the misunderstandings, educate where there is a lack of understanding, and, in general, clear up the confusion.

A cardinal premise in making the effort is that *you cannot tell anyone something he cannot understand. Rarely can you tell anyone something you cannot understand. You have to understand it first and then you have to make it understandable to the other person*. Whether you are dealing with one person or with a crowd, it's the same thing.

Public relations people must be tuned in on the various meanings of words used by all self-interested groups. The word *farmer* when used by a farmer is a compliment. It's not always a compliment when spoken by a city man. A "heel" is a different thing when tacked on a shoe or a man. There are several kinds of "Yankee." Ask a baseball fan, a Southerner, and a Connecticut farmer. Likely, you'll get three answers.[13]

Public relations people must be able to select and to transmit for various audiences words that will be received as kinfolk. Think of the harm that has been done, the confusion created, by legal language. A book could be written about the confusion which has been created by legal language. Perhaps a single illustration will be enough.

---

[13] For a list of key positive and negative words used in our war of words with Russia, see Edward W. Barrett, *Truth Is Our Weapon*, Chap. 10, "The Problem of Words."

Periodically, labor officials and management officials spend weeks talking out a new agreement on working conditions. Between them on the table at negotiation sessions is a contract. They're talking about the provisions in it. When it's all done, the union has a "new" contract, all properly drawn to stand up in court. *Not more than one of every hundred employees bound by that contract could understand all of it if they read it.* So, generally, they don't read it. They are told what it's all about in words they can understand. They're usually told in a manner that compliments the source, whether labor official or management spokesman. In one case it's "Here's what we got for you." In the other, it's "Here's what we are giving you." The chances are that the employee is no nearer a real appreciation of the issues and solutions than he is when he gets through filling out an income tax form or reading an insurance policy, a financial statement, or instructions for claiming unemployment compensation.

For example, here is an actual excerpt from the minutes of a labor-management Bargaining Committee meeting.

> It is agreed, in response to the request by the Bargaining Committee, to change past practice and policy so that in the future when an employee is absent from work on one paid holiday qualifying day on a leave of absence that includes that day, one of the excused absences as provided in the labor agreement may be used to cover such absence to qualify for pay for the holiday subject to the contractual paid holiday provisions, with the understanding that this agreement is in no way to be interpreted to mean that past practice and policy is changed to provide that an employee absent from work on a leave of absence on both qualifying days is to receive pay for the holiday regardless of remaining excused absence credit.

That may have made sense to the members of the bargaining group. They had been talking about it for several meetings. But it can't be transplanted, as is, for any other audience. To another audience it's just so much gobbledygook.

The same is true for the language of doctors, educators, the military, and government. Each has a special jargon not readily understandable to others —legalese, Pentagonese, educationese, and militarese. Then there are slangs, dialects, slogans, and exaggerations. The PR man must work with his cousins in the press, radio, television, and on the platform to help straighten things out for the public. Oddly, the straightening out process is not so much a matter of using only monosyllables as it is mastery in the use of words.

HOW DO WE GO ABOUT IT?

There have been, within a generation, several wonderful examples of word mastery. To name a few word masters in various fields, there have been Franklin Roosevelt, Ernie Pyle, Will Rogers, and Winston Churchill. There are a few women, too. In specialized fields of word usage, Stuart

Chase has made sense of complex economic matters. Paul de Kruif did the same with medical science. Some popular magazines do a marvelous job with fiction and features.

Of the communicators mentioned, Franklin Roosevelt—regardless of politics—had no equal. He always found the right word in a tight situation. He was particularly skilled in his radio projection, but radio appeal was not all of it. He knew words. For example, the Social Security Act was first drafted as an "Economic Security" bill, but F.D.R. knew "social security" would be more acceptable. A typical story comes from *Roosevelt and Hopkins* by Robert Sherwood.[14]

> Roosevelt was back in Washington for a momentous ceremony: the drawing of the first numbers under the Selective Service Act. This lottery would determine the names of the first 800,000 men—roughly five per cent of the total registrants—to be drafted into the Army. This would have been a tense, nervous occasion at any time; with the current state of the world, and with the word "warmonger" being thrown about so recklessly it was all the more harrowing. This was no moment for trick phrases. The nation was listening breathlessly for the broadcast announcement of the fateful numbers as they were drawn. With his marvelous gift for finding homely, old-fashioned words to fit new circumstances, Roosevelt did not refer to Selective Service as a "draft"—certainly not "conscription"—he called it a "muster" thereby evoking race memories of the rugged farmers of Lexington and Concord taking their flintlock muskets down from the fireplace. . . .

Winston Churchill had little resemblance to Franklin Roosevelt in choice of words for a mass audience. Churchill was dramatic in his "blood, sweat and tears," "the soft underbelly of Europe," and "the Iron Curtain," although he didn't originate them all. He, more than any other man, made "it's me" acceptable English. The fact that both Roosevelt and Churchill could draw an audience into a deep emotional kinship had to stem from something more than words or inflection. It did. Both men in their respective use of language represented the abstract symbols they embodied in the mass public conception. In their words and in their delivery, they lived up to their images.

In contrast with the symbols of these men was the symbol of Will Rogers. Here was the cracker-barrel philosopher with the hometown sense of humor. His mastery of words—and it was the same with characters created by Mark Twain and Irvin S. Cobb—had no roots in a standard English textbook. It had roots in every county seat and imitators in every county election.

Tagging your proposals with warm, favorable terms and the other fellow's with unfavorable ones is an important part of the communications contest. What one group calls a "program," an opposing group brands a "scheme." The proponent for paying farmers not to grow crops calls it a "soil bank." This couples two warm, respected words. Opponents call it a "subsidy." There's a difference in the impact of "sliding price supports" and "flexible

---

14 Robert Sherwood, *Roosevelt and Hopkins* (New York: Harper & Row, Publishers, 1948), p. 190.

price supports," yet both describe the same plan. Industries seeking tax postponements on new plants talk of "accelerated tax amortization." Critics of this law call it "fast tax write-off." Labor leaders plead the case for "union security" while industrialists plead for "the right to work."

The governor of New York pledges not to ask for higher taxes; he recommends an increase in "state fees" instead. The governor of Wisconsin vows never to sign a sales tax bill; he signs an "excise tax" bill instead. Neither semantic trick fools voters. The campaign for national prohibition made "saloon" a dirty word, so today those who drink do so in taverns and cocktail lounges. Incidentally, the drys were too wise to campaign for *prohibition,* a harsh word; they advocated "temperance." A great coup in semantics was coining the term "life insurance" to describe what could be called, just as properly, "death insurance." The latter would be harder to sell. Another ten-strike in PR semantics has been the successful effort of bowling promoters to change "bowling alleys" to "bowling lanes." And your ball no longer veers into the "gutter"; it goes into the "channel."

Words change from one context to another. "Progressive" and "education" when used separately are warm, solid American words. Put them together and you get the sneer term, "progressive education." Inept choice of a word can have unhappy consequences. A few years ago in a call-up of reserves, the Army referred to the casuals called to bring divisions to full strength as "fillers." This the troops resented. The railroads campaign against forced employment of more men than are needed as "featherbedding." The railroad unions counter with such terms as "dead man control" and a "full crew law." Today it is not good international PR to describe any nation as "backward." Such nations are "emerging" or "underdeveloped."

An excellent illustration of the importance of semantics in public relations is the United States Air Force's successful campaign to make "aerospace" a part of our language. The word was coined by Air Force publicists as what *The Reporter* termed "their secret weapon in the bitter interservice battle for the space dollar." If air and space were one, the public relations men reasoned, then the Air Force would eventually become the Space Force. The word is now used everywhere, by the National Aeronautics and Space Administration, in the want ads and on the press wires—a coup for Air Force public relations.

A flair for the picturesque, memorable term and a feeling for words are important requisites for the practitioner.

TWO SUGGESTIONS, FOR WHATEVER THEY ARE WORTH

There is a constant need to refresh the language of the day. Words wear out. They go out of style. They lose significance from repetition. They are discarded in favor of a fresh idiom. Whatever happened to the mania for *spelling things out* that swept business some years ago? Where's the *flapper* of the 1920's? Are we still *hep* to *jive?* Does the new contingent of service men abroad *fraternize?* Tired from overwork to a point where the intended meaning is vague and forceless are words like *revolutionary, new, security, democracy, hell,* and *damn.* Excessive use saps words of all meaning.

Aside from overwork, words suffer from their associations. The term *public relations* has wavered between good and bad on that score. It has kept company with press-agentry, has been seen trying to manipulate public opinion for no good end, and has included shoddy people in its roster. The word *propaganda* has the same problem. A perfectly good word in ecclesiastical use for centuries, it is today a nasty word. And a useless one.

Time changes word meanings. When a person said "Capitalist" in 1932 and 1962, he probably had two different kinds of persons in mind. He evoked different kinds of reaction. The word means different things to people in different parts of the world today. In fact, finding an acceptable term that accurately describes our competitive, dynamic economic system to people abroad has posed a tough semantic problem for Americans. For some years we've used *people's capitalism,* but that doesn't quite do it.

Don't condemn writers who coin words or fashion phrases to refresh the language. Not as long as the fresh way of saying something simplifies rather than complicates, and as long as it makes the process of reception more exciting. The writer who paraphrases an old saying, "The quickest way to a man's heart is a piece of beeksteak" revives the significance of a worn phrase. As for occasional foreign words, there may be no other way to show the exact relationship between two people than to say that they are "simpatico."

The light sprinkling of fresh words that are not in the dictionary but pop up in the news generally adds nouns or adjectives. Once in a while you run across a crossbreed that isn't a legitimate verb form, noun, or adjective. As an example of that: "My friend can put ideas to work. He's a real *imagineer.*" Or, another one: "The word imagineer is not used to confuse anybody. It's used to unclutter the language, not to *complexify* it." In the tricks that can be played with the language it makes a great difference whether the writer or speaker is careful and expert in what he's doing. Take those same two words, *imagineer* and *complexify,* and transmit them another way. For example: "My friend is an *imagineer* who has now lived seventy years. I have often heard him *complexify.*" The words don't come off right this time. They invite confusion. But when a professor uses *sportsuguese* to describe sports jargon, he gets through.

Some people have the gift of using the exactly right word without any straining. Others attain a knack. On the moist bank of memory, they keep a supply of fresh words ready to slip into the right thought when it comes along. Among writers and speakers the knack is expected. What a delightful surprise, though, when it is discovered in bank presidents, trigonometry teachers, chimney sweeps, or heavyweight boxers.

The knack can be cultivated to the extent of a person's imagination. If you have it in embryo, encourage it. Talk to yourself if necessary. Write down what you have said. Is it interesting? Entertaining? Is there anything daring? Anything different? Try it again, and this time leave a little bit unsaid. Don't sacrifice accuracy, but save a little room for the reader. Here's an example: "A vice-president should be nice to the guys waiting to see him in the reception room. Some day those guys might BE vice-presidents." You don't always say what will happen then. That's the part you leave for the reader to fill in.

Be imaginative and inventive. In using words to express meaning, use what appeals to you. Let personality come through. With all the need for imagination and daring, there is *the need for propriety*. That means a little more than restraint in using strong words. A particular danger is in the transportation of words from one language to another. Propriety reaches out to include the occasion. Guest Night at the Ladies' Aid is a bit different from Ladies' Night at the ballpark. The same speech will not do. There is a tendency for the popular language and the words in it to grow coarse. The tendency is toward facile writing and speaking. Propriety has a challenge in raising men's sights and thoughts by cleaning up their language.

SAY IT WITH SYMBOLS

Communication involves more than semantics; it uses symbols and stereotypes in large measure. The symbol offers a dramatic and direct means of persuasive communication with large numbers of persons over long lines of communication. Symbols have been used since the dawn of history to compress and convey complex messages to the multitudes. The Star of David and the Cross of Christ remind us of this. Most persons need the shorthand of symbols to deal with that which is abstract, diffuse, or difficult. In David Berlo's view, this is the age of symbol manipulation. "In our grandfather's day, most people earned their living by manipulating *things,* not by manipulating *symbols.*" The need met by symbols was explained by Lippmann years ago: "This problem of the acquisition of meaning by things or of forming habits of simple apprehension is the problem of introducing (1) definiteness and distinction and (2) consistency or stability of meaning into what otherwise is vague and wavering. . . . We tend to perceive that which we have picked out in the form stereotyped for us by our culture. . . ." [15]

The value and use of a venerated symbol is seen in the British monarchy. The British Commonwealth of Nations today is a free association of independent nations held together, not by legal ties, but by the symbol of the Queen of England. She symbolizes the traditional loyalties, the common in-

---

[15] In *Public Opinion,* pp. 60-61. Pelican edition.

terests, the traditional institutional forms held more or less in common, the family tie. The American flag, our cherished symbol, movingly and dramatically symbolizes all this nation stands for and means to us every time we see it. Think of the symbolic use we make of George Washington, Abraham Lincoln, of the Minutemen at Lexington and Concord, and of the Statue of Liberty in our patriotic and persuasive communications.

Symbols play an important role in the public relations and fund-raising programs of health and welfare agencies. Probably the best-known symbol of its kind is the Red Cross from which that agency takes its name. The Red Cross originated in Switzerland and created its symbol by reversing the white cross of the Swiss flag on a red background. Today the Red Cross flag is a welcome one wherever it waves, and this fact is exploited by its public relations staff. The upright sword of the American Cancer Society, chosen in a nationwide poster contest, was created to portray its crusading spirit. Another crusade, that of the National Tuberculosis Association, is symbolized by the Cross of Lorraine, a symbol that dates back to the Crusades. Another popular symbol is that of the Red Feather, used by our community chests and united funds. This symbol, created by a local community chest in 1928, was modified in 1955 to incorporate a large "U" to symbolize the merging of community chests with united funds.

One of the most effective symbols ever created is that of Smokey Bear, used by the United States Forest Service to promote the preservation of our forests. The idea originated within a group of foresters and advertising people who were concerned about the need to protect our forests during the war years of 1941-1945. After experimenting with drawings of deers, squirrels, and other small animals to carry fire-prevention messages, they hit on the idea of using a bear. A bear, with its human-like posture, its way of handling himself, its universal appeal to young and old, seemed ideal to build into a persuasive symbol. The Forest Service today has an artist who serves as "Smokey's caretaker" to make certain that drawings and pictures of him reflect the personality he is intended to convey. Smokey's personality, as determined by artists, has been changed over the years as various interpretations were fused into this one symbol. Although a created symbol, Smokey has had wide impact, especially among the young people of the nation. Smokey, shown here, keeps a half-dozen girls busy answering his mail every day, taking care of his Junior Forest Ranger program, and sending out his fire-prevention campaign material—not only in the United States but all over the world. In a typical year, some 23 million printed items bearing his imprint are distributed by the Forest Service.

Increasingly business corporations are emphasizing their symbols in an effort to create a sharper, more favorable public image. Even so, many business firms are wasting millions in advertising and public relations dollars by using corporate marks that do not truly or effectively represent their companies. An industrial designer advises that a corporate symbol should be selected on the basis of (1) memorability; (2) recognition; (3) appropriateness,

and (4) uniqueness. Surely the symbol should be distinct, different, and in character for the institution using it.[16]

THE 7 C'S OF COMMUNICATION

1. CREDIBILITY. Communication starts with a climate of belief. This is built by performance on the part of the source. The performance reflects an earnest desire to serve the receiver. The receiver must have confidence in the sender. He must have a high regard for the source's competence on the subject.

2. CONTEXT. A communications program must square with the realities of its environment. Mechanical media are only supplementary to the word and deed that takes place in daily living. The context must provide for participation and playback. The context must confirm, not contradict, the message.

3. CONTENT. The message must have meaning for the receiver and it must be compatible with his value system. It must have relevance to him.

---

[16] Symbols, design, and printing all play a part in projecting an institution's image. For elaboration, see Dean R. McKay, "IBM Shows How to Create a Contemporary Corporate Design Theme," *Public Relations Journal*, Vol. 18, November, 1961; and Russell R. Jalbert, "How to Create a Graphic Identity—and Save Money," *ibid.*, Vol. 18, April, 1962.

In general, people select those items of information which promise them greatest rewards. The content determines the audience.

4. CLARITY. The message must be put in simple terms. Words must mean the same thing to the receiver as they do to the sender. Complex issues must be compressed into themes, slogans, or stereotypes which have simplicity and clarity. The farther a message has to travel, the simpler it must be. An institution must speak with one voice, not many voices.

5. CONTINUITY AND CONSISTENCY. Communication is an unending process. It requires repetition to achieve penetration. Repetition—with variation—contributes to both factual and attitude learning. The story must be consistent.

6. CHANNELS. Established channels of communication should be used—channels which the receiver uses and respects. Creating new ones is difficult. Different channels have different effects and serve in different stages of the diffusion process.

7. CAPABILITY OF AUDIENCE. Communication must take into account the capability of the audience. Communications are most effective when they require the least effort on the part of the recipient. This includes factors of availability, habit, reading ability, and receiver's knowledge.

Additional Reading

Bernard Berelson, "Communications and Public Opinion," in Schramm's *Process and Effects of Mass Communication, op. cit.,* pp. 342-56.

David K. Berlo, *The Process of Communication.* New York: Holt, Rinehart & Winston, Inc., 1960.

Stuart Chase, *Power of Words.* New York: Harcourt, Brace & World, Inc., 1954.

S. I. Hayakawa, *Language in Thought and Action.* New York: Harcourt, Brace & World, Inc., 1949, rev. ed.

Carl Hovland, Irving Janis, and Harold H. Kelley, *Communication and Persuasion.* New Haven: Yale University Press, 1957.

Irving J. Lee, *How to Talk With People.* New York: Harper & Row, Publishers, 1952.

Carl R. Rogers and F. J. Roethlisberger, "Barriers and Gateways to Communication," *Harvard Business Review,* Vol. 30, July–August, 1952.

Everett M. Rogers and George M. Beal, *Reference Group Influence in the Adoption of Agricultural Technology.* Ames, Ia.: Iowa State University, 1958.

Rogers, Everett M., *Diffusion of Innovations.* New York: The Free Press of Glencoe, 1962.

William H. Whyte, *Is Anybody Listening?* New York: Simon and Schuster, Inc., 1952.

CASE PROBLEM

You are public relations director in an industrial firm which manufactures outboard and other small motors. Normally your firm employs 2,200 workers. Cancellation of a military order requires the firm to lay off 450 workers at the end of the month.

The personnel director works out plans for the layoff, which include a three-week notice to the men as a matter of fairness to them. Personnel also makes arrangements to try to find other jobs for them in the community and to provide the men laid off with a list of available jobs.

As public relations director, you are asked to work out a plan of communicating this information to company officials, foremen, union officials, the men, and the community. Your plan should include:

1. A timetable designed to squelch rumors and prevent confusion. ,
2. Themes and tone of announcement.
3. Wording of announcement to employees and to the local press.
4. Letter from the president to opinion leaders.

Chapter Ten

EVALUATION—

THE

FOURTH

STEP

Methodical research removes the guesswork from much of public relations practice. Evaluation is the common-sense of profiting from experience.

The final step in the process is to seek, through research, answers to the questions: "How did we do? Would we have been better off if we had tried something else?" Evaluation leads logically back into the first step. The two aspects of fact-finding are separated here to emphasize the importance of evaluation. One of the weaknesses of contemporary practice has been the lack of yardsticks to measure results. Evaluation of results deserves a larger investment of time and money. As practitioners invest more time and money in evaluation, they will improve their precision. As they improve the precision of their efforts, they will enhance their professional status. *Extensive feedback is essential to an effective communications program.* The obstacles are, obviously, those of time, money, and skill.

Executives are becoming more yardstick-minded. To keep costs down, managers must periodically re-examine the worth of each function. Administrators, particularly controllers, have a forceful way of asking: "What did we get for all the money your department spent?" Increasingly, in the opinion of Stanley Baar, practitioners "are being obliged to *prove* that the effort has produced measurable and valuable results and that the cost is fair and reasonable. . . ." He suggests four questions to answer in these periodic examinations: [1]

1. How much does this activity contribute specifically to the attainment of business goals? *What* specific goals?

---

[1] In article, "Yardsticks for Public Relations," *Public Relations Journal,* Vol. 13, April, 1957, 20 ff.

169

2. Are we getting our full money's worth for each expenditure?

3. Is the over-all cost offset by its accomplishments? Specifically *what* accomplishments?

4. All of our public relations expenditures—how much do we really need them, *and why?*

Evaluation takes one of two forms, *pretesting* and *posttesting*. The devices used in pre- and posttesting media, methods, and content are still in the experimental stage. Even so, they can provide helpful guides in shaping appeals and selecting channels. Successful advertisers have long used these methods. Practitioners, limited by access, time, and budget, must make every item in the program count. Scientific checks, before and after, will serve this end.

Pretesting before launching an expensive, crucial informational campaign is likely to prove economical in the long run. Posttesting will uncover mistakes that need not be repeated. It points the way to improved techniques. It is dangerous to rely on the number of clippings returned on a press release, the number of postcards received in response to a radio or TV program, and other equally rough indicators of impact.

Despite the broad developments in methods of evaluating program content and impact, professionals have been slow to adapt them to their needs. Westley Rowland reports: "A recent survey of 272 colleges and universities . . . revealed that few of them had developed any effective methods for evaluating their public relations programs." [2] A survey of results obtained among large users of public relations advertising revealed that only a few sponsors had made a serious effort to gauge the impact of the expenditure of tens of thousands of dollars. Baar found a like result when he surveyed 150 practitioners to determine yardsticks they used to measure the value of printed publications in PR programs. He says, "it became painfully obvious that comparatively few had the vaguest notion of the impact or effectiveness of the words in question. Millions for printing, but not a penny for evaluation!" Moore's Columbus, Ohio study revealed that only 42 per cent of the practitioners studied made systematic efforts of determine the effectiveness of their work. [3]

Researcher Charles R. Wright pointedly reminds: "Unread leaflets, unheard broadcasts, unviewed films—however abundantly and skillfully produced—have no chance of influencing an audience that is not there. And volume of output does not guarantee that an audience is reached." [4] *Evaluation research will forcefully remind the communicator that dissemination does not equal communication.* Research may be conducted by practitioners themselves or obtained through commercial research services—Opinion Re-

---

[2] A. Westley Rowland, "Do We Know How Well We're Doing?" *PR*, Vol. 1, April, 1956, 24-28.

[3] William Carter Moore, "A Critical Analysis of Public Relations Practitioners in a Midwestern Metropolitan Area," Unpublished Master's thesis previously cited, p. 28.

[4] In "Evaluation of Mass Media Effectiveness," UNESCO *International Social Science Bulletin*, Vol. VII, No. 3.

search Corporation, Elmo Roper and Associates, Dr. George Gallup, Psychological Corporation, Alfred Politz, Crossley S-D Surveys, Daniel Starch and Staff, and many others. Several major universities also do such research for profit and nonprofit agencies.

The need for "a merciless personal audit of the finished project" has long been recognized. Pioneer Evart G. Routzahn told the 1920 National Conference of Social Work: "After the returns are all in—when the last meeting has been held, the final distribution of printed matter made, and all activities of the immediate effort have been recorded as history—is the time to put yourself and your methods through the third degree . . . with prayerful solicitude that you will be able to untangle the lessons to be applied to the next project." His counsel has yet to be fully accepted.

PRETESTING

A careful precheck of material to be used in a project will pay off in detecting, beforehand, possible backlash effects. It will help in sharpening the understandability of the information for its intended audience. Sometimes an appeal or technique can boomerang with unanticipated, unfavorable results.

This can be avoided by making a response analysis. This means using a sample audience to observe immediate reaction to specific communication content. As an example, some years ago an organization promoting tolerance prepared a series of anti-prejudice cartoons featuring an unsavory character, Mr. Biggott. These cartoons were pretested on 160 persons to determine their understanding and reaction. The response analysis showed that the cartoon message was misunderstood by nearly two-thirds of the audience and that the message boomeranged for 33 per cent of the people.[5]

Catching potential boomerangs before they have a chance to do widespread harm is obvious common sense. A large insurance company published a series of articles in its employee publication on representative employees —a salesman, a stenographer, an accountant, and so forth. Its article on "The Management Man" boomeranged badly. The editors thought this was another routine article; how wrong they were! The article brought a heavy barrage of criticism, with these typical comments: "If this is the kind of a man——wants, I don't want   ;" "I didn't know you had to be an egomaniac to be a manager;" "Mrs.——is a snob;" and so forth. A cautious try-out can head off such unhappy consequences.

Also, there is need to pretest the *understandability* of messages. What may appear to be a simplification of an annual report may actually make it more

---

5 Cited in Patricia L. Kendall and Katherine M. Wolf, "The Analysis of Deviant Cases in Communications Research," *Communications Research, 1948-49*, edited by Paul F. Lazarsfeld and Frank N. Stanton (New York: Harper & Row, Publishers, 1949), pp. 152-79.

complex in the eyes of the reader. The symbolism chosen for a public relations document may represent perfect clarity to its creator, but be both uninteresting and unintelligible to the reader. Or the symbol may be inappropriate. The latter proved to be the case when the United States Information Service put on an exhibit in India. The first panel featured a painting of Christ delivering the Sermon on the Mount, and the caption expressed the exhibit's theme, "Man Shall Not Live by Bread Alone." India's hungry Hindus and Muslims did not respond favorably.[6] To get results, your appeals and symbols must be appropriate and must be understood.

A tough problem in industry is how to present effectively "sales-dollar" information to employees. Swift & Company was tipped off in a readership survey of its employee publication that its presentation of sales-dollar information was not getting across. The company decided to test several different presentations *before publication*. Swift's commercial research department, under the direction of R. W. Coffman, prepared four different copy treatments of the dollar income and outgo. These were tested for comparative effectiveness among employees of one plant. Mr. Coffman observes that Swift learned five things from this study: [7]

1. Each idea must add to a whole or unity. Each part must fit logically and add up to one or one hundred.
2. The number of ideas which can be successfully projected pictorially will not exceed four on any one page.
3. The association between the idea and the symbol must be simple and clear.
4. Copy must be short.
5. Labels and terms must be brief and familiar.

A cautionary note on the value of pretesting must be inserted here. The stream of public opinion rushes along swiftly. An idea which worked well on a pretest might possibly prove a fiasco upon widespread use because of the intervening time lag. Seasons change, and with them change people's buying patterns, recreational pursuits, interests, and so forth. The context of the public opinion market place can change markedly overnight with an unexpected news event. In using pretest results as a guide to communications program, you ought to be as certain as possible that present conditions are akin to those which existed during the pretest.

POSTTESTING

Posttesting is valuable not only in determining aftereffects of a specific program but in advancing professional knowledge. Through such research the rough-hewn principles now relied on can be proved true or false.

There are a number of maxims that are taken for granted in daily prac-

---

6 Arthur Goodfriend, *The Twisted Image* (New York: St. Martin's Press, 1963), p. 208.

7 See the article, "How's Your Impact?" in *Public Relations Journal*, Vol. 7, February, 1951.

tice. Research tends to cast some doubt upon their validity. One is, "What people know about a subject depends roughly upon the amount said or published about it." Several years ago an experiment designed primarily to find ways and means of extending support for the United Nations was carried out in Cincinnati, Ohio. A survey was taken to determine attitudes and level of information about the UN; then an all-out saturation information campaign was carried out over a six-month period. A postcampaign survey indicated no fundamental changes in the degree of support for the UN in Cincinnati, although the information level had been raised somewhat.[8] Such findings clearly indicate that increasing the flow of information does not necessarily spread information effectively.[9] Another PR maxim is, "If people know you better, they will like you more." Yet, studies of attitudes toward big business and toward several foreign countries have indicated the opposite.[10] Still another is, "The more employees know about their company, the better they will like it." Research has thrown doubt on this premise.[11] There hasn't been enough research to make flat generalizations about these maxims one way or the other. There is equal need to measure results of specific appeals, media, and methods.

Audience research can put you straight if you are using words that don't communicate. Rensis Likert cites this example: [12]

> A particular company spent a substantial sum (I was told it was over a million dollars) advertising that its refrigerator was "dual automatic." But after a year's effort doing this, only 14 per cent of the housewives could identify which refrigerator this was. "Dual automatic" is not a concept which is closely linked to the life sphere of most housewives. At the same time another company advertised that it guaranteed "Four years of trouble-free service" for its refrigerator. Trouble-free service entered the life spheres of housewives to such an extent that 60 per cent of housewives interviewed could identify this refrigerator.

MEASURING IMPACT

A specific program's effectiveness can be evaluated by measuring in terms of four dimensions. They are *audience coverage, audience response, communi-*

---

[8] From mimeographed reports, "Cincinnati Looks at the United Nations," Report No. 37; and "Cincinnati Looks Again," Report No. 37A. National Opinion Research Center, University of Chicago. These reports are no longer available, but this classic information experiment has been widely reported.

[9] For evidence of this generalization, see Herbert H. Hyman and Paul B. Sheatsley, "Some Reasons Why Information Campaigns Fail," *Public Opinion Quarterly,* Vol. 11, Fall, 1947. (Also in Katz *et al., Public Opinion and Propaganda,* a book of readings.)

[10] For one bit of evidence, see Burton R. Fisher and Stephen B. Withey, *Big Business As People See It* (Ann Arbor: The Survey Research Center, University of Michigan, 1951).

[11] Dallis Perry and Thomas A. Mahoney, "In-plant Communications and Employee Morale," *Personnel Psychology,* Vol. 8, Autumn, 1955, 339-46.

[12] In *Public Relations and the Social Sciences* (Ann Arbor: Institute for Social Research, University of Michigan, 1952), p. 13.

cations impact, and *process of influence.* Wright points up the importance of each of these measurements this way: [13]

> 1. *Audience Coverage:* To produce results you must first reach the audience. How large an audience is reached? What are they like? What proportion of the desired audience do they represent?
> 2. *Audience Response:* How do members of the audience respond? Does the content of the message strike them favorably or unfavorably? Does it arouse their interest? Does it bore them? Do they understand it?
> 3. *Communications Impact:* After an appraisal of these immediate reactions, you must consider the impact which a message has on its audience. What are the lasting, discernible effects upon people exposed to a message?
> 4. *Process of Influence:* What is the process by which a communication operates to influence its target audience? Through what channels of influence and mechanisms of persuasion does the message finally affect the individual? How effective is the program in setting into motion the social processes necessary to influence the opinions and behavior of its target audience?

EVALUATION TOOLS.   In addition to the fact-finding, formal and informal, described in Chapter 7, the practitioner has these evaluation tools. Each one is based on the principle of making a survey of a *representative sample* of the target audience in a systematic way.

1. READER-INTEREST STUDIES.   What people read in newspapers, magazines, employee publications, and so forth, can be measured through reader-interest surveys. This technique was developed in the 1930's by the Advertising Research Foundation and a few journalism schools. The ARF, supported jointly by advertising agencies, advertisers, and newspapers, has made more than 150 such studies. These provide a wealth of data.[14] (The ARF's *Continuing Study of Newspaper Reading* did not include nonurban readers and readers under 18. The results should be viewed with these facts in mind.) This tool is more a quantitative than qualitative measuring device.

A reader-interest survey is made by taking fresh, unmarked copies of a publication to a representative sample of the total potential reading audience. After the interviewer makes the necessary introduction and qualifying statements, he goes through the publication with the respondent, page by page. The respondent shows the interviewer items he has seen or read. These are recorded on an interview form by code number. At no time does the interviewer point out items to the respondent. The key question is "Did you *happen* to see or read anything on this page?" Checks on this method have proved that readers are honest in saying what they have read.

Published reader-interest studies offer valuable insights into what potential readers actually consume. In using the results of such studies, it is well to keep in mind this advice of a veteran magazine editor, "A magazine cannot be edited by arithmetic alone." Reader-interest results are guides, not mandates, for the responsible communicator. This research ought to be followed

---

[13] Wright, "Evaluation of Mass Media Effectiveness," *op. cit.*
[14] See Charles E. Swanson, "What They Read in 130 Daily Newspapers," *Journalism Quarterly,* Vol. 32, Fall, 1955, 411-21.

up, after a given interval, to determine the comprehension and retention of the material read by readers. Both methods will provide healthy reminders that *readership doesn't equal circulation* and *readership doesn't equal comprehension and retention*.

2. READABILITY TESTS. Yardsticks for the reading ease of printed materials have been developed. It is possible to grade a given message as easy to read at a given educational level, be it 7th grade or college senior. This yardstick enables the communicator to write his message for the reading ability of his intended audience. This should not be interpreted as "writing down" to people nor should a person's reading ability be equated with his intelligence. Making copy more readable definitely increases readership. This has been proved repeatedly. These yardsticks, too, should be used as guides rather than as commands to write inside a fixed formula.

It should be clearly understood that readability is only one aspect of getting readership. Equally important are *content, format, organization,* and *writing style.* These factors, coupled with the more fundamental understanding which the writer brings to his writing and the reader brings to his reading, all shape the reception and impact of the printed word. If used in this perspective, readability tests are helpful. There are four commonly used methods for measuring readability.

 a. *The Flesch Formula.* Dr. Rudolf Flesch's method is divided into two parts; Reading Ease Score is determined by the difficulty of words used. This is measured by the number of syllables in words and by sentence length. Human Interest Score is measured by the number of personal words per 100 words and the number of personal sentences per 100 sentences.[15]
 b. *The Gunning Formula.* Robert Gunning's formula measures reading ease by the average sentence length, number of simple sentences used, verb force, portion of familiar words, portion of abstract words, percentage of personal references, and percentage of long words.[16]
 c. *Dale-Chall Formula.* This one, developed at Ohio State, measures reading ease by analysis of average sentence length and the proportion of words outside the Dale List of 3,000 Words Most Commonly Used.[19]
 d. *Cloze Procedure.* This test was developed by Prof. Wilson Taylor of the University of Illinois and is somewhat different from the first three. It measures help provided the reader by the context of the total message. It can also be applied to auditory as well as visual communication. This method tests readability by giving samples of the material to subjects with every *nth* word left blank. Success of subjects in filling in missing words on the basis of other parts of the message measures the item's readability. The "cloze procedure" is aimed at measuring reader's comprehension of material as well as its readability.[18]

---

15 Rudolf Flesch, *How to Test Readability* (New York: Harper & Row, Publishers, 1951).

16 Robert Gunning, *The Technique of Clear Writing* (New York: McGraw-Hill Book Company, 1952).

17 Edgar Dale and Jeanne Chall, "A Formula for Predicting Readability," *Educational Research Bulletin,* Ohio State University, Vol. 27, January and February issues, 1948.

18 Wilson L. Taylor, "Cloze Procedure: A New Tool for Measuring Readability," *Journalism Quarterly,* Vol. 30, Fall, 1953, 415-33, and "Recent Developments in the Use of 'Cloze Procedure,'" Vol. 33, Winter, 1956, 42-48 ff.

Readability tests, when used in conjunction with reader-interest studies, will provide practitioners with useful guides for future projects.

3. RADIO AND TV AUDIENCE RESEARCH. There are seven basic methods for obtaining measurements of a program audience's size in the broadcast media.[19]

a. *The Diary*. This requires that some member (or members) of the household keep a written record or log of program exposure.

b. *The Recorder*. This method electronically or mechanically records automatically individual set tuning, including frequency or channel.

c. *The Personal Coincidental*. Personal interviews are made throughout the duration of a given program or time period. Respondents are queried regarding program exposure at moment of call.

d. *The Personal Roster Recall*. Respondents are shown a list of programs and stations. They are asked to indicate which they were exposed to during the measured time span.

e. *Personal Unaided Recall*. Personal interviews are made during which respondents are asked about program exposure for a preceding time span. Unlike the roster, the personal unaided recall uses no list of programs or stations. It depends entirely upon the respondent's unaided memory for exposure information.

f. *The Telephone Coincidental*. This method employs the same principles as the personal coincidental method except that interviews are made by telephone.

g. *The Telephone Recall*. This method employs the same principles as the personal unaided recall except that the interviews are made by telephone.

h. *Combination Telephone Coincidental and Diary*. This method combines broadcast exposure information obtained by the coincidental telephone method in one sample of homes with information obtained by the diary method in another sample of homes.

i. *The Combination Telephone Coincidental and Telephone Recall.*

j. *The Combination Telephone Coincidental and Personal Roster Recall.*

Among the leading commercial research organizations which use one or more of these methods in measuring audience size for clients are the A. C. Nielsen Company, American Research Bureau, Pulse, Inc., Trendex, Inc., and Sindlinger & Company.

Public confidence in the validity and honesty of audience research in radio and television got a series of jolts in 1963. Early that year the Federal Trade Commission obtained consent decrees from The Pulse, Inc., A. C. Nielsen Co., and American Research Bureau that these firms would stop claiming that their findings are 100 per cent accurate. In a series of public hearings weeks later, the House Commerce Committee presented evidence to show that radio and TV ratings were often based on faulty or dishonest research. Evidence presented indicated that the largest firm in this field was using a sample based largely on a now outmoded 1940 United States Census. This use violated the basic premise that a sample must be truly representative if research results are to be valid. Another commercial firm could not present records to support rating surveys it had sold to clients as documented

---

[19] *Recommended Standards for Radio and Television Program Audience Size Measurements,* p. 15. Copyright 1954 by the Advertising Research Foundation, Inc. Reprinted by special permission.

research. Still another admitted that it had fudged on the size of the sample needed for reliable results. One witness cynically remarked, "The industry doesn't want true figures, anyway." Chairman Oren Harris told one firm that its rating service "appears to me to be a con game." [20]

After these congressional hearings, both the Federal Trade Commission and the Federal Communications Commission expressed official interest and concern over the "ratings mess." These hearings made it clear that, in the heat of competition for the ratings business, many firms had cut the corners of research methods, with the result that their work was shoddy at best, dishonest at worst. This incident should warn practitioners that it is truly pound-foolish to expect a cheap buy in audience or opinion research.

4. PROGRAM ANALYZER TESTS. This is a mechanical device for recording an audience's reaction to a program while people are being exposed to it. Reactions are recorded in terms of Like, Dislike, or Indifference. The member of the audience indicates his preferences by pressing one of two buttons. These reactions are recorded on tape as the program progresses. Time lines on the tape serve to identify parts of the program to which the member is reacting. Through this device, responses of audience members to specific items of program content can be determined.[21] This device can be used to pretest PR presentations.

5. MEASUREMENT OF IMPACT. The real test of a communications program is its results. Did it pay off at the box office? The sales counter? The voting booth? Did the program bring about the desired reaction and action? Did your message result in the desired modification of a group's attitudes? Actual results offer a sure test. They deserve to be studied and analyzed. In addition to observation of results *apparently* obtained, there are other ways of getting at the impact.

a. *The Focused Interview.* This involves interviewing recipients of communication and getting them to relate their experience to various parts of a program.

b. *Impact Analysis.* This means studies to determine short-term and long-term effects of a given program. It includes determining the effects on individuals and on groups and subgroups. There are differences in impact to be studied in terms of time span and in terms of individual and group reactions.

c. *Experimental Studies.* The ideal way to measure the impact of a program is by comparing two groups which are exactly alike except for the fact that one group has been exposed to a program whereas the other has not.

---

20 Anonymous, "Is Pulse running a 'con game'? Rep. Harris Asks That Question, Then Puts Nielsen on Hot Seat," *Broadcasting*, Vol. 64, March 25, 1963, 34-50. For details on hearing, see "Hearings, Subcommittee of the Committee on Interstate and Foreign Commerce, House of Representatives," *Broadcast Ratings*, Part I and Part II. (Washington, D.C.: The Committee, Government Printing Office, 1963.)

21 See Tore Hollonquist and Edward A. Suchman, "Listening to the Listener," *Radio Research, 1942-1943*, edited by Paul F. Lazarsfeld and Frank N. Stanton (New York: Duell, Sloan, and Pearce, 1944).

The critical feature is in matching two groups so that they are identical in every respect save the exposure to a specific program. In such experiments it is essential to control extraneous influences. Results are obtained by surveys and by panel studies.[22]

OVER-ALL REVIEW OF PROGRAM

The research tools described above are helpful, but they measure only the bits and pieces, not the over-all program. The total effort must be kept in view. An important step is to review, periodically, the total program and to measure its results against the assigned objectives. Several PR "report cards" have been designed for this purpose. One practitioner offers these check points as a guide in periodically evaluating a going public relations program: [23]

1. *Objectives*—Are they clearly stated and understood throughout company? Are there areas in which agreement on goals is needed?

2. *Organization*—Are related public relations functions organized as a single unit, or scattered throughout various departments? Does the public relations director have adequate management backing to see that public relations responsibilities are considered throughout the company? . . . Is size and training of staff adequate to achieve desired public relations objectives?

3. *Content*—Do your programs and activities give adequate consideration to all segments of the public—customers, employees, stockholders, and the financial community, government groups, civic, educational, and community organizations, the press, and suppliers? . . .

4. *Measurement of Results*—Do you have adequate staff, budget and management backing to gauge results of your work? How do these activities compare with those of others in your industry and in other industries? Have you considered an outside specialist to review your public relations program?

5. *Control*—What steps have you taken to improve future public relations activities in the light of audit findings? What steps need to be taken during coming years?

Additional Reading

John M. K. Abbott, "Evaluating Public Relations Activities," *Public Relations Journal,* Vol. 15, March, 1959.

Keith Davis, "A Method of Studying Communication Patterns in Organizations," *Personnel Psychology,* Vol. 6, Autumn, 1953.

Leo Handel and Marjorie Fiske, "New Techniques for Studying the Effectiveness of Films," *Journal of Marketing,* Vol. 11, April, 1947.

Frank E. Hewens, "How to Audit Your Public Relations." *Public Relations Quarterly,* Vol. 8, Winter, 1964. Helpful guide.

---

22 For illustrative study, see Hovland, Lumsdaine, and Sheffield, *Experiments on Mass Communication,* Vol. III (Princeton, N.J.: Princeton University Press, 1949).

23 John T. Cunningham, "Evaluating Public Relations' Effectiveness," *Public Relations Journal,* Vol. 19, January, 1962, 21-23.

Robert Jones and Leslie A. Beldo, "Methodological Improvements in Readership Data Gathering," *Journalism Quarterly*, Vol. 30, Summer, 1953.

Darrell B. Lucas and S. H. Britt, *Advertising Psychology and Research*. New York: McGraw-Hill Book Company, 1951. (See Part V, Measurement of Advertising; and Part VI, Evaluation of Media Audiences.)

Claire Selltiz *et al.*, *Research Methods in Social Relations* (New York: Holt, Rinehart & Winston, Inc., 1959).

Frederick F. Stephan, "Advances in Survey Methods and Measurement Techniques," *Public Opinion Quarterly*, Vol. 21, Spring, 1957.

Charles E. Swanson, "Readability and Readership: Controlled Experiment," *Journalism Quarterly*, Vol. 25, December, 1948.

Elmo C. Wilson and Frank Bonilla, "Evaluating Exchange of Persons Program," *Public Opinion Quarterly*, Vol. 19, Spring, 1955.

Martin Wright, "Why Make a Communications Audit?", *Public Relations Journal*, Vol. 18, October, 1961.

CASE PROBLEM

1. Measure the readability of an employee magazine, handbook, annual report, or university brochure—by measuring samples of content, using:
   a. Flesch, Gunning, or Dale-Chall method.
   b. "The Cloze Procedure" method.
2. Compare results obtained by the respective methods used.
3. How does the reading level of the material square with the probable reading level of the intended audience?

Chapter Eleven

THE

TOOLS

OF

COMMUNICATION

Mechanical means of communication have their important places; but they are only adjuncts. None of them can take the place of personal man-to-man contact.—Wm. G. Werner

In his work the practitioner utilizes the printed word, the spoken word, and the image. He uses three avenues —*personal contact, controlled media,* and *public media.*

The importance of personal contacts and the part played by the people in communicating ideas already have been emphasized. The news media, through which the practitioner reaches the general public, are beyond the direct control of the practitioner. *For space and time in these media, he competes against all comers on terms set by the media.* The mass media pose special problems which will be discussed in Chapter 17.

In this chapter we shall examine, briefly, the following 16 tools. Their content can be controlled by the communicator at the point of origin. Their impact depends on the communicator's skill.

House Publications
Handbooks, Manuals, Books
Letters and Bulletins
Bulletin Boards, Posters, Billboards
Information Racks
Inserts and Enclosures
Institutional Advertising
Meetings and Conferences
Speakers' Bureaus
Public Address Systems
The Grapevine
Motion Pictures and Slide Films
Closed-Circuit Television
Displays and Exhibits
Open Houses and Plant Tours
Staged Events

These tools will be discussed in terms of *what they are.* Later on they will be discussed in terms of how and where they are used in specific situations.

THE PRINTED WORD

HOUSE PUBLICATIONS. Here is a standard tool, and one of the oldest. The first known company publication was the *Lowell Offering,* put out by the Lowell Cotton Mills in 1840—sort of a literary magazine. It was a far cry from today's carefully edited publication. *The Locomotive,* started in 1867 by the Hartford Steam Boiler Inspection and Insurance Company, has never missed an issue. The Travelers Insurance Company started its *Traveler* in 1865, but the name has been changed and publication halted several times. Aetna Life Insurance Company started an employee magazine in 1868, and Massey Harris lauched its *Triphammer* in 1885. National Cash Register Company started one in 1891.

Because of its versatility, the house publication has developed into a major medium. In the view of the *Wall Street Journal,* these publications have become "workhorses instead of just management megaphones of intangible value." They meet the common need of all organizations to tell their story through at least one medium, on paper, in their own words, in their own way, and without being interrupted. In each case, however, the sponsor must get the publication *read, believed.*

The idea did not catch fire at once. It smoldered, but it kept a spark alive through the depression periods. The growth of company publications came in these steps.

Year	Number of Company Publications
1921	335
1928	575
1930	280
1941	1,000
1945	5,000
1958	7,500
1964	9,000

Exact figures on the number of employee publications are not available. At least 7,000 can be definitely accounted for. It is the estimate of the International Council of Industrial Editors that publications sponsored by business and industry reach a total circulation of more than half a million per issue. Industry is investing well over $500,000 per year in this medium of communication to employees, customers, shareholders, dealers, and others. Of the some 7,000 company publications, 65 per cent are published for employees. These are estimates because, as *Fortune* says, "the house-organ publishing operation is so big and sprawling, no one has yet succeeded in measuring it."

The growing maturity and stability of this medium is reflected in the results of the ICIE's 1963 survey, which found that: [1] (1) more than half the

---

[1] International Council of Industrial Editors, *Operation Tapemeasure 1963.* Summary of ICIE's 1963 survey.

editors responding devote more than half their time to the publication; (2) a majority of them had been editors more than four years; (3) nearly 80 per cent worked on publications five or more years old; (4) salaries are increasing; (5) there is greater centralization of the editorial function,‛ with three-quarters of the editors reporting to either the president, vice-president, industrial relations manager, or public relations manager; (6) the great majority reported that their management's attitude toward them and their publications ranged from favorable to enthusiastic.

The company publication is so common in business circles that there is a tendency to think and talk about its usage solely in terms of business. There are thousands of publications put out by military units, governmental agencies, schools, colleges, welfare agencies, fraternal groups, and trade associations. Lumping these publications with those of industry, a safe estimate would be a grand total of some 9,000 such publications being issued on a regular basis in the United States.

There are three types of publications: (1) *internal;* (2) *external;* (3) *combination internal-external.* Most are published for employees or members of organizations. Some are designed for general public consumption or for such specialized publics as alumni, dealers, contributors, reservists, or community leaders. Some serve *both* inside and outside publics. The broader the audience sought, the more generalized the content must be. These publications are variously issued on a daily, weekly, bimonthly, or monthly basis.

In this staggering array of publications, there is little uniformity in format and approach. House publications take the format of daily newspapers, news magazines, and general slick magazines. Some are published as paid-for pages in local newspapers. There are slick-paper and newsprint publications; letterpress, offset, and multilith productions; special-cover, self-cover, and no-cover papers; four-syllable talk, picture talk, comics talk, cracker-barrel philosophy, preaching, personal items, gossip. Some publications stick to shop talk; some ignore it completely. Some have a mixture. A few sell advertising space. A few, such as A & P's *Woman's Day* and *Arizona Highways,* have paid circulations. A recent innovation is the use of records to carry the sponsor's message into the employee's home. These plastic records are also used by firms to send special holiday greetings to employees and customers.

Still another variation of the employee-magazine format is Buick's *Factory Whistle,* an hour-long broadcast each workday morning of news and information for Buick's 18,000 employees over a local radio station. Buick pays for the radio time. *Factory Whistle* gives the time, weather, and traffic advice and transmits news of personnel appointments, promotions, retirements, employee awards, sales, and production successes. All this is packaged within the format of a radio show.

The seven-year span between ICIE's two extensive surveys, *Operation Tapemeasure* and *Operation Tapemeasure 1963,* indicates that many firms are broadening the purpose of their publications. The study reports: [2]

---

2 *Ibid.*

Publication Audience

1956		1963
65%	Internal	62%
18%	External	12%
14%	Internal-External Combination	26%
3%	Other	—

The magazine remains as the most popular format; more than half of the 1,600 editors queried reported using this format. Twenty-seven per cent used the newspaper format; 11 per cent used the newsmagazine format; and 7 per cent relied on the newsletter. Comparison of the two surveys shows a marked shift from letterpress to offset printing. The composite publication, based on the 1963 survey, is a four- to eight-page magazine, 8½ by 11 inches in size, uses 8 point type, is reproduced through the offset process, and comes out on coated paper stock.

The content of house publications varies as much as the format. Two elementary editorial schools of thought predominate. One is that content should be what readers will enjoy, news about themselves, for example. The other is that content should be what the publisher wants readers to know; for example, news about the organization and its objectives. Some industrial editors argue strongly for presentation of management's views on controversial political issues. Others argue as vehemently that company organs should avoid the controversial. Some company publications, such as Goodyear's *Wingfoot Clan,* include union news; most do not.

A survey was conducted by *Dun's Review and Modern Industry* among 256 companies to find out where editorial emphasis is being placed. There were 102 respondents. The replies showed that the most popular subject matter was employee progress—promotions, service anniversaries, distinguished achievement awards. The two runner-up topics were announcement of new developments and policy changes, and company products and services.

Most editors strive for a workable compromise between what the organization wants its publics to know and what they want to read. Properly viewed, the house publication is a direct channel to specific publics, not a vaguely conceived "morale booster." To justify the expense and effort required, a publication must accomplish something useful for the sponsor.

Chit-chat publications are on the decrease; personal gossip, weddings, babies, pictures of big fish, transfers, and so forth, are being subordinated to the yardstick of useful information about an organization. There is growing realization that chit-chat accomplishes little for either reader or publisher. *A house paper has no intrinsic value.* Its only value is that put into it by the editor, guided by definite objectives. Intelligent editors do not confuse reader-bait with the purpose and substance of the publication. *The content of a publication determines its character and impact.*

There is a trend toward making the publication two-way. This means inviting questions and answering them in print. It has been a tough job to sell management on the idea, and an even tougher job to get readers to turn in questions.

A lamentable waste of money and manpower on ineffective publications is still widely evident. Much of this waste stems from the fact that organizations still do not have definite objectives for their publication and do not employ competent editors. In the 1956 survey of the International Council of Industrial Editors, only 38 per cent of the nearly 2,000 editors responding said that they were guided by definite objectives set by management. The 1963 survey did not cover this question. Sound journalistic principles in presenting *timely, interesting, useful information* should guide the editor along the right course.

Here is an example of how the employee magazine, given specific goals and skillful editing, can contribute to the success of an enterprise. Some years ago the *Milwaukee Road Magazine* alerted that road's employees to the need for an intensified sales campaign to bolster sagging freight revenues. The article started on the cover of one issue with a photograph of a determined salesman entering an industrial plant. The news peg for the article was the new sales kit prepared in the Traffic Department. In clear text and bright pictures, the article explained to each "salesman" the traffic tools used by the company; these were specifics—not a collection of bromides about "get out and get your shoulder to the wheel." Milwaukee Road employees, after reading this brisk, hard-hitting article, would be able to give everyone they met tangible reasons for shipping via Milwaukee. Moreover, they were made aware, subtly, of the road's battle for revenues.

In the average-budget PR setup, a most effective use of the house publication can be attained without straining for special effects. Four-color covers are not essential. The prime needs are for candor, intelligent selection of subject matter which combines the objectives of sponsor with interests of readers, simple format, and the constant purpose of helping readers learn as much about matters of mutual interest as they desire. Such a publication will almost assuredly break through barriers that isolate management from those who do want to think, to grow, and to share an understanding of the important things going on.

HANDBOOKS, MANUALS, BOOKS. There are three general types of booklets and pamphlets.

1. *Indoctrination booklets* welcome the new soldier, employee, society member, student, supplier, or visitor. Literature for the customer or product owner usually falls in the area served by the sales or advertising department. The beginner's booklet has the purpose of helping him to get off on the right foot. It tells him the rules of the game and the benefits of playing the game according to the rules. It seeks to instill a team spirit—the feeling that he has joined a winning combination.

2. *Reference guides* comprise a second type of handbook. These are useful to the seasoned member as well as to the neophyte. Reference handbooks concern themselves with details of a Group Insurance Plan, Pension Plan, Suggestion System, Hospitalization, Profit-Sharing, Housekeeping and Safety, Library Content, Recreation Program and Facilities, Contest Rules, Campus

Geography, and the like. Handbooks enable members to look up specific information easily. In content, they tend to be definitive and instructive. They save time and encourage appreciation of the values in membership. They quickly provide information actually sought by the reader.

3. *Institutional booklets* and brochures have subject matter devoted to the selling of an idea or a philosophy rather than a product or service. Typical are messages related to the free-enterprise system, military recruiting, educational facilities, or charitable work. In another category are reports of dedications, celebrations, awards, history, success, expansion, and developments in science or the arts. Some contain statements of position on national issues. Then there are the commemorative booklets and brochures on traditional anniversary occasions.

The format of booklets has the same wide variation as the house publication. The financial circumstances of the organization enter in, as do size of circulation, audience impression sought, and importance attached by officials to media and occasion. In most cases the circumstances are such that an organization wants its booklets to reflect both its success and its pride. The booklets tend to be lavish. Budgets tend to be secondary. There are, of course, exceptions. University bulletins that reveal progress in a field of research, for example, are quite restrained in make-up and content. The information, rather than the appearance, is the thing. Similarly, there is a pattern of uniformity established for military manuals.

There is no single method of distribution that has proved most effective for handbooks. Many organizations maintain libraries. Handbooks are seen in company cafeterias, reception lobbies, and club rooms and in wall racks. This distribution is often secondary, copies having been mailed or handed to prime audiences. Employees get their handbooks variously at their place of work or in the mail at home. Dealers receive theirs by hand from salesmen or in the mail. The government catalogs literature and makes it available at nominal cost from the Superintendent of Documents. Large corporations mail literature to the homes of interested people in their plant cities. Trade associations issue literature at conventions and by mail to members and thought leaders.

The important thing to remember about these tools is that they are *supplementary,* not primary. A handbook for the new employee is no substitute for the personal handshake, a thorough orientation, and a personally conducted tour of introduction. Many organizations use the "buddy" system for newcomers.

A related medium being utilized more and more is the full-length book tracing the history of an institution or industry or else one chronicling the biography of a founder. These books are written for business firms, universities, and trade associations. They are usually subsidized by the sponsor and published by a commercial publisher. The sponsor sees to it that copies are placed in libraries and freely distributed to the influentials of his publics. These sponsored books are high in initial cost but pay a long-term dividend if they are accurate, well written, and widely distributed. Placed in libraries, such histories become source material for writers and historians. Examples include *It Floats,* the story of Procter & Gamble, *Herbert H. Dow, Pioneer in Creative Chemistry,* and *Ford at Fifty.*

Another use of the book is to sponsor publication of paperbacks that plug the firm's products. American Machine & Foundry, for example, joined with Pocket Books in publishing *The A. M. F. Guide to Natural Bowling,* a book that plugs A. M. F.'s bowling balls and accessories. The Dennison Manufacturing Company, maker of party games and decorations, published *The Dennison Party Guide.* Gaines Dog Food sponsored a popular book, *Puppy and Dog Care.* Arrangements for such books vary. In some cases, the sponsor and publisher share publishing costs; in others, the sponsor merely agrees to buy a stipulated number of the books, thus underwriting its publication.

LETTERS AND BULLETINS. Individually written, individually addressed letters have long constituted the backbone of interorganizational communication. Printed letters are being used in increasing volume to establish a direct, speedy line of communication with specific publics. Letters are used on a regular or spot-news basis to reach employees, dealers, alumni, or workers in a fund-raising or legislative campaign. As the *Wall Street Journal* observes: "An increasing number of corporations are finding the old-fashioned letter an answer to communications problems, a fact that may seem somewhat surprising in this era of electronics, high-powered press-agentry, and glossy company publications."

In industry the employee letter has been developed as a supplement to the slower, less frequently published house magazine. It offers an opportunity for the chief executive to talk to the employee and his family in a "you and I" conversational, newsy approach. James M. Black, writing in *Factory Management and Maintenance,* gives six advantages for use of the company letter: (1) *inexpensive;* (2) *direct;* (3) *important-looking;* (4) *intimate;* (5) *quick;* (6) *informal.*

A main type of letter used for public relations purposes is written by the chief official of an organization or the chief of a division, for circulation among the members. The purpose is to establish a direct contact that spans the gap between the head man and all those who do not see as much of him as they would like to. Letters support the line communication. They insure the accuracy of line transmission. Content points up what is important and newsworthy in the organization's affairs. Letters give added importance to line communication by proving that the line is well informed.

Other letters go from organization officials to community opinion leaders, to members of selected professions such as medicine or teaching, to congressmen, suppliers, dealers, or the editors of newspapers. Common reproduction methods for letters include typewriter, multigraph, mimeograph, and printing.

More letters are mailed to the home than to business addresses. The home provides wider readership and a good climate for persuasion. There is a reluctance in some industrial quarters, however, to the sending of letters into employees' homes. This exists mainly where there is a tense labor-management relationship. The reluctance is due in part to the possibility that union officials might seek to interpret the technique as a measure to weaken their organization.

Typical content of letters for a business house would be policy statements, welfare programs, financial reports, product news, and economic education. As one example among many, the General Electric Company does an outstanding job in the use of printed letters. G.E.'s *Commentator* has gone to more than 258,000 employees and their families. *Employee Relations News Letter* goes to G.E.'s management people. Here are a few topics selected at random from issues of the *Commentator:*

What Is Communism?
Bigger Output—More Jobs—Higher Pay
Steeper Taxes—Less Earnings
Doing Our Best (to render service)
Doing Right—Voluntarily (to curb inflation)
Production—Yes, Inflation—No
We Must Be Neutral (in contest between national union and local officials)
We Report an Offer (negotiation with union)

Trade associations rely heavily on the circular letter to carry news to members. Charities take to the letter in the solicitation of funds. Most educational institutions at the higher level have a periodic "president's letter" for alumni and one for parents of students. Crusaders for a particular idea or philosophy use letters in broad public mailings.

More important than these printed letters issued periodically are the larger number of letters that comprise an organization's daily correspondence. The endless flow of letters that goes out daily from today's organizations constitutes an important, influential, but too often neglected means of communication. The importance of effective letters that evoke a pleased reaction, not irritation or confusion, is obvious. Yet too many organizations continue blindly in the rut of writing cold, stilted, hackneyed letters that do more to obfuscate than to clarify. Certainly one of the ways a person judges an organization is by the letters he receives in response to his requests for information or clarification or in response to a complaint. As American organizations get larger and automate more of their operations, the opportunities for personal contact grow fewer. The individually addressed letter, with a personal touch, is one of the few ways left. It should be more effectively utilized.

THE BULLETIN BOARD—POSTERS—BILLBOARDS. The application of bulletin boards is widespread: in college buildings, on the campus, in every department of factories and offices, in military installations, in public buildings, and in the larger retail stores. The bulletin board is here to stay. If there were no other reason, laws requiring the posting of an ever-increasing number of notices would preserve it. Daily news bulletins posted on bulletin boards are one means of coping with the speed of the organizational grapevine.

The bulletin board offers a good place to corroborate information that circulates through interdepartmental correspondence or instructions. It provides quick access to the internal public for spiking rumors and for making desirable information stick. The bulletin board gets regular attention if kept current and interesting. It needs to be serviced often so that the news on it does not get stale. There's a petty annoyance to a reader in seeing the same notice again and again after it has become history. Messages should be brief. Boards should be placed where traffic is heavy and the reading light is good. They should be at proper height for easy, eye-level reading.

In somewhat the same category as bulletin-board messages are the posters and placards placed on walls or columns of factory shops and offices. The theme of such posters is usually safety, housekeeping, economics, preparedness, or security.

Assuming that the messages are personalized and appropriate to the audience, the poster can do a job. In doing that job, it is important that these short messages be changed frequently and the phrasing be memorable. To keep posters from growing stale, one good system is to start with a series of them in various locations, rotating them regularly between the several stations.

Outdoor signs are used for institutional messages. Signboards are popular PR tools for the retailer or other organization at the community level. As you enter a city, you are likely to find on its outskirts a billboard with the message, "Welcome to Bedrock—The Home of Toddler Toys." The message has a promotional aspect, but, more important, it has an institutional aspect. Somewhere in the vicinity of that sign there may be signs telling where and when the local Rotary and Kiwanis Clubs meet. Banks, colleges, state institutions, national parks, and the service organizations use outdoor signs as a foremost tool. Billboards used for public relations purposes tend to escape the natural antagonism of the motoring public toward the corruption of the scenery.

INFORMATION RACKS. The information rack is used primarily for morale and employee education, with emphasis on economic education. It was started in 1948 by General Motors as "an idea cafeteria for offering mental and spiritual nourishment to employees." The idea caught on rapidly, and it was estimated 15 years later that 1,500 firms were using information-rack programs. Firms specializing in this service provide companies with booklets and reprints of magazine articles in wholesale lots which are distributed free to employees from these racks on a "take what you want" basis. The racks are usually placed in reception rooms and near plant and office exits so that employees may pick up a few on their way home. The usual procedure is to put out only enough booklets to cover 50 to 80 per cent of the total number of employees.

One supplier for these information racks suggests these values for the reading rack: [3] (1) The broad range of reading materials thus put in hands of employees tends to broaden the range of their reading and, consequently, their

---

[3] Moris T. Hoversten, "Information Racks in Business and Industry," *Public Relations Journal*, Vol. 17, April, 1961.

range of knowledge; (2) The voluntary pick-up has value to the employee, who has much communication forced upon him; (3) Home readership of these pamphlets and reprints gets the message to the wives and children of the employee; (4) It enables the firm to disseminate information on subjects the company would hesitate to take up in ordinary communication channels; (5) These booklets serve to reiterate and reinforce messages directed to employees through other channels; (6) It is a handy distribution medium that enables employers to get materials to employees quickly if need be. Granted these advantages, this supplier admits that most companies continue this reading-rack program pretty much on faith. The typical employer attitude is found in this quote: "If they are taking the material home and not leaving it around the plant, they must be reading it."

The booklets and reprints cover a wide range of subject matter—sports, hobbies, health, safety, how-to-do-it, economics, Americanism, and uplift material. Public relations and personnel practitioners hotly debate the worth of the considerable expenditure involved. The tool is too new to be evaluated as to its worth. In the words of one personnel director, "Reading racks are the ultimate in immeasurables." In a survey to determine extent and effectiveness of the reading rack, *Industrial Newsletter* found that, of 700 firms responding to its questionnaire, 60 per cent had made no evaluation of the rack's effectiveness. Another example of lack of evaluation!

INSERTS AND ENCLOSURES—STICKERS. There are no available statistics on the number of enterprises that use inserts with pay checks, dividends, and invoices.

With pay checks, printed inserts explain changes in method of payment or in the amount. They also deal with new deductions required by law, the firm's plans for the future, budget plans, food recipes, or the economic system. The insert may be used as a place to provide a breakdown of the pay check itself, showing the various deductions. A great many organizations have check blanks with added sections to show a breakdown between gross and take-home pay.

Along with invoices go explanations of new terms, datings, delivery schedules, allocation notices, materials problems, new product announcements, advertising plans, introduction of a new salesman in the territory, and so on. Quite often the enclosure with an invoice is in the form of a gummed sticker affixed to the invoice.

INSTITUTIONAL ADVERTISING. The one certain way to get publicity printed or broadcast is to buy space or time—to use advertising. The 12-billion-dollar advertising business was developed initially to sell goods and services. Increasingly, paid advertising has proved useful as a public relations tool. Such advertising is variously termed "institutional advertising," "public service advertising," and "public relations advertising." Advertising to disseminate information or promote opinion change was first used in the early 1900's and on a small, spasmodic basis until World War II. Ivy Lee bought full-page ads in the Colorado newspapers in 1914 to tell the Rockefeller side of the story in the historic Colorado Fuel and Iron strike. In World War II and in the decades since, advertising has been widely used on an increasing scale as a PR tool.

The large plus of advertising is that it enables the sponsor to tell his story in his own words when he chooses and to the audience he selects. The headline and story are written exactly the way the advertiser wants them to appear, either in print or on the air. On the minus side, the citizen instantly recognizes this as paid pleading. Audience resistance may thereby be raised to some degree. News does not carry this handicap.

Advertising as a tool of public relations is largely confined to industrial and business concerns because of the large expense it entails. Nonprofit public causes can, of course, hitch-hike by getting firms to finance advertising for a worthy cause. In such cases the advertisement does double duty. This kind of advertising has been found rewarding by many sponsors. The Sinclair Oil Company's advertising to promote and preserve the national parks and shrines brought that company much favorable public reaction and increased its business, too. The advertising industry's contribution to promotion of worthwhile causes through the Advertising Council has been especially noteworthy. Campaigns have promoted Religion in American Life; Better Schools; Forest Fire Prevention; Civil Defense and Safety; Higher Education.

This tool is a versatile one. Some occasions have been cataloged by George Hammond, president of the Carl Byoir firm: (1) community relations—plant openings, plant expansions, plant open houses, company anniversaries, annual statements, promotion of community activities, such as clean-up weeks, safety, community chest campaigns, and so forth; (2) labor relations, including the company's side in labor disputes; (3) recruitment of employees; (4) promotion of art contests, essay contests, scholarship awards, and so forth; (5) statements of policy; (6) proxy fights for company control; (7) consolidation of competitive position; (8) records of accomplishment; (9) product difficulty or public misunderstanding which must be cleared up immediately; (10) promotion or opposition to pending legislation; (11) consolidation of editorial opinion; (12) supplier relations; (13) celebration of local institutions, such as the press during National Newspaper Week; (14) presentation of industry or professional activities and points of view. As Hammond says, "These 14 suggestions only scratch the surface of possible uses."

Is It Effective? This is the big question. Concrete examples of its power in specific situations are multiplying, but there are also examples of failures. The use is still relatively new. There has been little research on its efficacy. Evidence to date indicates that *specific campaigns aimed at specific objectives by reputable sponsors are the most effective.* Ads with a "news" approach and using strong human interest pictures draw the biggest readership. Measuring the effectiveness of idea or opinion advertising is not easy.

Many are using this means to talk directly to the media gatekeepers by placing ads in the trade journals of press, magazine, and radio. Many have used this medium to place on record in convincing fashion their public relations policies for the benefit of the men and women in journalism.

*If you should desire to visit Caterpillar . . . regular plant trips are available Monday through Friday at 10:00 a.m. and 2:00 p.m.

behind the scenes at
CATERPILLAR

This is No. 16 in a series which tells about Caterpillar folks . . . what they do and how they do it.

FOREMAN BILL ROWE (left) is on hand to meet and welcome Lloyd Houze (right) and his family, Phyllis, Jimmy, and Charles. Lloyd is an automatic turret lathe operator in Building HH

PREPARING FOR a new family group are Bill Alberti, plant tour coordinator, and June Elliott, shown typing guest badges. Invitations come from the supervisors of each section and will continue until all employees have been invited.

IT'S A *Family Affair*

"Bill . . . I would like you to meet my family."

Introductions similar to this, between family and fellow employees, have been repeated literally thousands of times over the past sixteen months during Caterpillar's Family Visit program. To be exact . . . Caterpillar folks and their families who have been guests of the Company during this time have totaled more than 24,000.

For folks like the Lloyd Houze family, the visit program gives Dad a chance to conduct his own family tour. And especially, it gives him the opportunity to show his family what his job is and how he does it. Because Lloyd's job is important, like all jobs at Caterpillar, he takes pride in showing his family around. The story Dad tells . . . the movies they see . . . the folks they meet . . . all help the family get better acquainted with Caterpillar.

As one wife said after a plant visit, "Now I understand what my husband does at work and it's interesting to talk about his job."

Employee visits at Caterpillar are truly . . . *a family affair*.

CATERPILLAR TRACTOR CO.

ED NALLEY DESCRIBES his work on this external grinder to his wife while first shift employee, Walter Link, operates the machine.

IN THE THEATER, a brief welcoming includes a short slide presentation and a movie. Retired employees and families are also invited.

GOOD FOOD is the order of the day for Ron Sulaski and his parents. Visitors are guests of the Company for dinner in the cafeteria.

Rules for Effective PR Advertising. The public relations firm of Hill &.
Knowlton has formulated these guides for preparing effective copy:

1. Be frank, fair, and honest.
2. Tell your story directly to an individual in his own language.
3. Don't talk up or down to anyone.
4. Use simple, unvarnished words and facts so that every housewife in the
community will both understand and believe what you have to say.
5. Tell one story at a time—don't overload your copy.
6. Use figures sparingly—and only when illustrated by simple, everyday examples.

The use of paid advertising in public relations has been somewhat circumscribed by the ruling of the United States Internal Revenue Service that
costs of advertising designed to promote or defeat legislation or to influence
public opinion on pending legislation are not a tax-deductible business expense. This is true even though the proposed legislation may directly affect
the advertiser's business, industry, or occupation. The I. R. S. ruling, adopted
in December, 1959, does not permit deduction from gross income for tax purposes the cost of advertising designed to (1) influence members of a legislative
body directly or indirectly, by urging or encouraging the public to contact
such members for the purpose of proposing, supporting, or opposing legislation, or (2) influence the public to approve or reject a measure in a referendum,
initiative, vote on a constitutional amendment, or similar procedure.

The I. R. S. ruling was upheld by the United States Supreme Court. Advertising media, advertising associations, and the Public Relations Society of
America strongly protested the ruling, but to no avail.[4] In another ruling, the
Federal Power Commission disallowed expenditures for institutional advertising by private utilities as a factor in fixing the rates of that company. Neither
of these rulings disallows deductions for goodwill advertising.

THE SPOKEN WORD

MEETINGS. Here is a vehicle that brings people together face to face. This
medium not only provides an *opportunity to communicate* to a selected audience but also provides the *opportunity to listen.* The carefully staged meeting
results in *two-way communication.* As more has been learned, this tool has
come to the fore. Many firms, for example, are shifting the emphasis in employee communication from the printed and visual media to work-group and
plant-group meetings. Industries have found, too, that the surest way to reach
educators is to invite them in for conferences of one day, several days, or for
as long as three weeks. Such conferences are expensive, but if effective can
prove economical in the long run. *Meetings, to be effective, require purpose,
careful planning and staging, and skillful direction.*

---

4 "Political Action Ads Ruled Non-Deductible," *Editor & Publisher,* Vol. 93, January 2,
1960, 10.

The most impressive form of get-together is the mass meeting where corporate officials explain the annual report to employees, where the commanding officer explains to all troops why they are shipping out, where the college president tells the student body the decision to drop football, where the office manager announces plans for the move to another city.

In these meetings, exchange of viewpoints is very carefully handled. The question-and-answer portion, if there is one, is controlled so that the meeting doesn't drag, and so that any discussion sticks to the important features. Otherwise the discussion roams into other pastures, or it explodes in personalities. The mass meeting has been most effectively used in middle-sized groups of employees or members and in cases where the one-big-boss really runs the organization. Effectiveness depends, too, on the top man being a pretty good speaker.

Other meetings take the form of discussion groups with a round table or panel of from 10 to 35 persons. Among supervisory personnel, charity volunteers, and civic committees, these meetings are well attended even though held out of normal working hours. For the hourly employee, the buck private, or the student—the man on the bottom rung of the ladder of success—such meetings are usually scheduled as a part of the work program. To avoid any inference of "captive audience," attendance should be voluntary.

The staging of such meetings is often the task of the PR staff. There are several check points:

1. Comfortable facilities.
2. "Breaks" in the middle of long sessions.
3. Exhibits, displays, charts, graphs, and films wherever suitable to the subject-matter.
4. Refreshments if participants give up their spare time.
5. An opportunity for everyone to get into the act even if it's only through a note pad and a pen.
6. Press notice for the occasion with credit to the departmental people who were responsible for it.

There are many excellent case studies. The following are business examples, but the adaptation to other types of undertakings should be a simple one.

Standard Oil Company (N.J.) sponsors annually the Jersey Roundtable, a three-day conference of some 25 university teachers from all parts of the country and a like number of top-level Standard Oil officials on problems and philosophy of the industry.

Motorola, Inc. has a 15-man Advisory Council of elected, middle-management people. They meet alternate Monday evenings, study corporate problems, and submit reports to the senior Board of Directors.

Sergeant and Company, New Haven, Connecticut, stages group discussions to determine workers' attitudes toward the personnel program.

Elgin National Watch Company, Elgin, Illinois, conducts field tours for employees.

Carrier Corporation, New York, has an institute of business lecture series followed by small-group discussions.

Pitney-Bowes, Stamford, Connecticut, holds job-holders' meetings for all its employees.

Sharp & Dohme, Philadelphia, has an annual meeting for all employees with officials to discuss industrial economics.

Thompson Products Company, Cleveland, has a foreman training program.

General Electric provides face-to-face reports to supervisors on the business outlook for the future.

SPEAKERS' BUREAU. The speakers' bureau is a *planned* means for providing speakers at service club luncheons, evening cultural group meetings, schools, and special events such as annual Chamber of Commerce meetings, graduation exercises, dedications, anniversaries, celebrations, and fetes for visiting celebrities. The requests for various areas of subject matter provide great latitude. Common among them are current events, business conditions, foreign travel, and the arts. The speakers' pool is also valuable in trade relations for the manufacturer, in civil relations for the military, and in general public relations for the government department, the educational institution, and the social agency.

There are few organizations of any size without some officials who can get on their feet and talk interestingly for a few minutes. There are, however, some commonly practiced alternatives. One is to engage outside public speaking specialists and pay their fees to fill engagements on the organization's behalf. Another alternative is for the organization to call on its friendly associates, such as PR counsel, management or legal counsel, nonresident director, or advertising agent, to fill engagements in its behalf. In all cases the kind of talent available determines its use. Practitioners are frequently called on to research speech material or to prepare an outline or a complete manuscript. In other cases, the public relations department collects appropriate material and functions as a speakers' library in the organization.

Here are four points worth remembering:

1. Select and coach the line-up of speakers with some care.
2. Select topics of broad interest which serve the needs of the potential audience and carry the organization's story.
3. Provide speakers with helpful visual aids—flip charts, flannel boards, slide films, etc.
4. Promote and publicize the availability of the speakers to get maximum mileage.

PUBLIC ADDRESS SYSTEMS. The industrial use of public address to link the boss in the front office with the man at the bench and to pipe music into working areas has a strong appeal. The public address system deserves more experimentation in PR communication among working groups because of its immense effectiveness in promotional work among crowds. Many practitioners will be taking a second and a third look at this tool in the generation ahead. There is a growing awareness of its advantages as well as its limitations. The PA system can be made mobile; the messages can be relayed. Along with closer examination and more consideration of this tool goes a working knowledge of tape and wire recorders, the turntable, and telephone relays.

THE GRAPEVINE. The grapevine is not a formal tool of communication. It is informal, but, like Orphan Annie, it really gets around. Keith Davis, Indiana University, reported in the *Harvard Business Review* the example of an industry official's wife who had a baby at 11 P.M. By 2 P.M. the next day, 46 per cent of the plant management group knew it. It is a potent line of transmission. The grapevine is the channel that carries information much more exciting than the truth. Sometimes it is actually harmful or threatens to be. Rumors of layoff, of friction among officials, of product and service trouble, or of bad blood between factions can be harmful. The· word travels far beyond the local group; it becomes more and more distorted. The hints of trouble tend to breed trouble wherever there happens to be a chip on anybody's shoulder.

The grapevine cannot and will not be eliminated without drastic change in human nature. People are going to talk out loud, and they're going to whisper. It's normal. Gossip is normal. Participation in it is a prized vanity; it's an escape valve for pent-up emotion; it's a facet of "belonging." The PR staff usually stays tuned in on the grapevine. When the gossiping and rumoring are harmless, nothing is done about them. When real trouble brews, the gossip is squelched by the release of full facts on the topic. Once in a while, a counterrumor or an exposé of the facts among the natural leaders of an organization is sponsored to offset a harmful rumor.

THE IMAGE

MOTION PICTURES AND SLIDE FILMS. Since its inception before the turn of the century, the motion-picture film has been used in efforts to inform and persuade. In 1897 Dewar's Whiskey and Columbia Bicycles showed films on outdoor screens in New York City. In 1911 General Electric started using films, and U. S. Steel followed suit the next year. Other firms pioneering in the use of PR films include Ford Motor Company, Caterpillar Tractor Company, International Harvester, and A. T. & T. Recent years have seen an amazing growth in the use of films for public relations purposes. Indications are that the future will see an acceleration in this trend. The basic factors which gave television its great potential have long been used in the motion picture as a tool to transmit ideas, stimulate imagination, and produce action. The conviction, "I saw it with my own eyes," is hard to refute. This is the age of TV, pictorial journalism, and the 16mm motion picture. A tremendous audience awaits the timely, skillful film presentation of a sponsor's story. The motion picture provides an *effective, economical* means of reaching selected groups with real impact. Although the initial costs of production and distribution may appear high, the cost-per-viewer is the proper yardstick to use. The film's use in PR is steadily accelerating. United States Steel figured out that of the films in their library, one, on the average, was shown every seven minutes of every working day to an audience of about sixty people.

The strengths of the motion picture are commonly accepted.[5] (1) It combines the impact of sight, sound, drama and movement, color, and music with group enthusiasm. (2) It attracts sustained, exclusive attention to a message for the length of the showing. (3) It can present certain meanings involving motion. (4) It clarifies the time factor in any operation or series of events. (5) It provides a reproduced record of events. (6) It presents processes that cannot ordinarily be seen by the human eye. (7) The camera can bring the past and the distant to the viewer. (8) It can enlarge or reduce objects and can use cartoons to dramatize abstractions.

It is estimated that there are more than 600,000 16mm film projectors owned by organized groups meeting regularly—schools, colleges, churches, clubs, fraternal organizations, and labor, veteran, farm, and women's groups. These outlets, coupled with possible showings of sponsored films on TV stations and in commercial theaters, provide unlimited potential. All these outlets welcome showings of informative and entertaining sponsored films. Schools and colleges are emphasizing the use of visual aids from kindergarten to graduate school. Churches and clubs are equally eager for good programs, which films can provide. One distributor of sponsored movies says that its list of film users now totals more than 181,000 groups.

The potential inherent in good films is steadily expanding because of increased opportunities of reaching larger audiences through television, in the nation's theaters, and in schools and colleges, where the emphasis on visual education steadily increases. This potential is being utilized. The first year of this decade, 5,400 sponsored films were made, 1,700 more than had been made in one year, five years earlier. Most of these sponsored movies are made for corporate firms, but many are produced for governmental agencies, trade associations, and nonprofit organizations.

One large reason for this growth is the willingness of TV stations to use commercially sponsored films at no cost. For example, hundreds of TV stations have shown a film produced by Goodyear Tire & Rubber Company showing a series of speed tests of custom cars on the Utah salt flats. There is no mention of the Goodyear name, but the camera is frequently focusing on the Goodyear name on the tires and on the shirts of the service crews. Other examples of films designed for school and club use and also shown on TV would be General Mills' "A Visit With Betty Crocker," Kraft Foods' "The Romance of Cheese," and Kimberly Clark's "How to Catch a Cold," which features its Kleenex. The latter film, produced by Walt Disney, has been seen by nearly 170,000,000 persons, according to its sponsor. Most TV stations operate on limited budgets and cannot afford to produce documentary films. Consequently, TV program managers welcome films that are interesting and timely, that fit the program time slot, and that are not too blatant with the commercial plugs.

---

[5] Association of National Advertisers, Inc., *The Dollars and Sense of Business Films* (New York: ANA, 1954). Condensed from pp. 38-51. A useful, documented study.

The growing use of PR films in the motion-picture theaters parallels the drop in Hollywood's output of cartoons and other short-length movies. Hard pressed by TV competition, movie houses are much more receptive to free program material than they once were. Theater managers insist that such films be entertaining, however. "Rhapsody in Steel," a powerful documentary tracing the development of steel, has been exhibited in most of the nation's movie houses. This 23-minute film was produced by United States Steel at a cost of $400,000. An even more ambitious film was that made by Coca-Cola at a cost of half a million dollars. This film, "Wonderful World," had a cast of 1,057 persons and was filmed in 31 different countries. To shoot the movie, three camera crews for nine months ranged over most of the world. More than 1,000 prints were made, and the sound track was recorded in eight languages.

These are the spectaculars, but the vast majority of PR films are produced by smaller organizations on more modest budgets. The typical PR film runs from 23 to 25 minutes in length and ranges in cost from $25,000 to $75,000 to produce. One university made film on mental retardation at a cost of $1,000 that won wide understanding of this problem and also won several film-festival awards. Nonprofit agencies with limited budgets do find ways and means of using films. The St. Johns, Michigan, schools PR director produced a 25-minute film telling the schools' story at a cost of $700. The film, shown before local civic, service, and P.T.A. groups, brought much favorable comment. The director said that all you need are "a rented 16mm camera, a good supply of color film, a little imagination, and lots of spare time." The Dad's Club of a Des Plaines, Illinois, township high school took on the production of a school film as a project and came up with a 30-minute film with musical background and narration.

Given the potential viewing audiences assembled in front of their TV sets, in movie houses, and in schoolrooms, these costs can be nominal indeed. Successful films that get wide showings are dramatic and entertaining and keep the commercialism subdued.

Keeping pace with its expanded use, the number of firms producing sponsored films has mushroomed in the past 20 years. It is estimated that there are 50 such firms. The breadth and quality of service that these firms offer vary greatly. Sponsors should use care in selecting a film producer. Costs of production likewise vary greatly. The A.N.A. survey of business films found that costs of 157 films studied ranged from $1,732 to $426,000. The median cost was $25,800. Translated into costs-per-viewer, A.N.A. found that nearly 87 million viewers saw 46 films for an average of 26 minutes at an average cost for production and distribution of each film of $87,264. This communication was achieved at a cost of 4.6 cents per person. Showing nine of these films on TV brought the cost per viewer down to 1.6 cents for those films.[6]

Films are distributed through film producers which provide this service, through educational film libraries, through firms specializing in this service,

---

[6] *Ibid.*, pp. 32-33. Such costs are higher today.

by the sponsor, or through a combination of two or more of these channels. Firms and libraries charge a small fee for this service; sometimes this is paid by the sponsor, sometimes by the requesting group. There are more than 2,000 16mm film libraries in the United States which provide ready channels for distributing sponsored films.[7]

Because of the expense and effort involved in a good film, the practitioner should weigh carefully the purpose of the film, channels of distribution available, and the potential audience. After he has decided that the film is worthwhile, he should mull over these questions.

1. What is the most important thing this film is expected to do?
2. What secondary points are to be made? Will they crowd film?
3. What sources for research and information are available?
4. How long must the film be to do its job? Color or black-and-white?
5. Treatment? Comic? Documentary? Entertainment? Serious?
6. Music? Needed? What kind? Recorded? Special? Cost?
7. Is there a deadline? Shooting time? Weather?
8. Can we do it? Should we hire a professional firm?

Similarly, there is a growing use of slide films and strip films, especially by agencies unable to afford motion-picture films. Nonprofit agencies find the slide film of value in their fund-raising efforts.

CLOSED-CIRCUIT TELEVISION. This tool, developed as a by-product of commercial TV, offers great potentialities. By means of a closed circuit, leased through A.T.&T., live pictures and sound can be piped from an originating point to one or more receiving locations across the country for viewing by selected audiences. This type of TV is not transmitted to stations for broadcasting to home viewers. It is simpler and less expensive than broadcast TV. It combines the power of TV with carefully designed programs for specific, invited audiences. It is as private as a telephone conversation.

The cost of staging a program or conference through closed-circuit TV is relatively high. It can, however, be more economical than staging a conference or convention in one city. This tool, too, can be a great time saver for busy executives. Robert G. Dunlop of the Sun Oil Company reported that "Our firm saved $125,000 by using closed-circuit TV to introduce a new gasoline to dealers, distributors, and employees in 30 cities throughout the country as compared with separate dealer meetings before." Another oil company staged eight meetings simultaneously for the same purpose at a cost of $10,000. Use of this medium permitted "instantaneous break of a new product to all people in the field at the same time."

Dentistry and medicine are being taught through this medium. Firms use it to make annual reports to shareholders and staffs, or to hold sales meetings. Political parties use it for fund-raising dinners and rallies. Educational institutions use it for teaching. More and more universities and colleges, pressed by

---

[7] For a list, see U.S. Department of Health, Education and Welfare, Office of Education, Bulletin No. 11, *A Directory of 2002 16mm Film Libraries* (U.S. Government Printing Office, 1951).

mounting enrollments, are using closed-circuit large-screen TV to reach students across campus and across the state. The United Fund and Community Chest campaign has used this medium to kick off its annual fund drive by assembling the volunteers in groups across the nation. Where no TV outlets were available, kinescopes of the program were shown to the workers.

The Ford Motor Company utilized this medium to stage an electronic press conference when it introduced its Falcon. Some 2,000 newsmen were assembled in hotels in 21 cities to participate in a two-way closed-circuit TV press conference. This event took months of preparation and the mechanics were handled by Theater Network Television, one of the firms providing such service.

Canadian National Railways held a coast-to-coast press conference by closed-circuit TV to announce sweeping changes in its passenger-train services. Reporters were linked by two-way broadcast lines and TV monitors from Newfoundland to British Columbia. The high costs and the difficulties caused by differences in time are the major obstacles to the use of this tool on a nationwide and frequent basis.

DISPLAYS AND EXHIBITS. In almost every factory, there is a reception room, a showroom, a museum, or an employees' lunch area. In every college there is the equivalent of an "Old Main," a Students' Union, a museum, or a visitors' room. Every branch of military service has its sites to perpetuate its memories, receive its guests, and show its progress. These places are natural areas for displays and exhibits. For anyone who has ever taken a plant tour or visited a World's Fair, it is redundant to detail the content of such exhibits. The point to be made is that preparation and servicing of such displays usually fall in the province of the PR staff.

In addition to the stationary or permanent displays, such as the Ford Rotunda, there are temporary exhibits in the community, like GM's Powerama. There are national industrial shows, state and county fairs, and traveling displays. Some business houses have exhibits of materials, processes, or products which they lend to their customers and their suppliers for use in special showrooms of their own. The National Guard has equipment which it can put on display or wheel out for parades and local events. Occasionally a university takes a dramatic show to other cities. The welfare agencies usually are anxious to take part in exhibits where the nature of their work can be dramatized.

Users of exhibits should remember that the objective is "to invoigle the footsore visitor (1) to stop in front of the display; (2) to remain long enough to look at the material; (3) to be stimulated to immediate or future action." Lynn Poole of Johns Hopkins University says that an exhibit to accomplish this must be something: (1) *different* that (2) creates an *action* and (3) promotes good *humor* while (4) stimulating *participation*. The eye-getting, communicating exhibitor provides unusual, fresh ideas with a sense of showmanship.

EVENTS. The handling of visitors is another direct-contact vehicle. Its most prevalent use is in open house events and in the day-by-day handling of plant tours. The idea behind the careful handling of visitors is to merchandise an organization's facilities and its practices. Open house events attract the community. Plant tours catch outside friends and relatives, vacationers, youngsters in school, foreigners here to absorb industrial know-how, customers, and people who are just plain curious and haven't much else to do with their time.

Sponsors of these events have been quick to seize on them as opportunities to make friends at home. Most people are good hosts in their own houses. They work at it. A large proportion of these events come off well. The use of these tools is rapidly increasing, and there have been a growing number of circumstances urging their usage. New plants and installations have opened. Old ones have been renovated. New products have been abundant. Organizations have reached important milestones. In short, there has been much to show off and much to talk about.

Techniques have become quite elaborate. Clever invitations, special transportation, celebrities, souvenirs, exhibits, motion pictures, and refreshments figure among the enticements. Then, too, the events regularly make news locally and nationally. In the community, an open house is a good story of civic spirit that the press welcomes. When visitors drop in from afar, their own hometown papers are glad to get word. If they are prominent citizens of some town, a photograph is in order.

STAGED EVENTS

Almost every city has some kind of annual occasion all its own when everybody in town pitches in to make a staged event a whopping success. Perhaps it's the opening of the Christmas shopping season, Milkman's Day, Pickle Harvest Festival, Dollar Day, Fashion Parade, Founder's Day, Help Your Neighbor Day, Junior Government Day, Vets Holiday, Community Auction, or All-Sports Parade. Of all occasions, the most universally observed are anniversaries and milestone developments, such as inaugurations, dedications, and personal tributes.

These events are wonderful. They are crowd days. People shed their routines and some of their inhibitions to turn clown, auctioneer, beauty contest judge, auxiliary cop, hog caller, past champion pie eater, trombonist, or flag bearer for a few hours. People rediscover the idea that the grindstone is not everything in life. On these occasions the people in town who make most of the money the other 364 days of the year spend some of it freely. And the hot-dog vendors who don't make money the other 364 days get a break on this day.

Local planning and staging bring together, as a central committee, representatives of the mayor, the town's leading industrialist, the high school band, the Junior Chamber of Commerce, the owner of the local pony ranch, and the winner of last year's cake-baking contest at the county fair. These people, or others just like them, do the deciding on committees to select the marshal for the parade, judges for the floats, the precise moment at which the band strikes up with *God Bless America,* and who are to take turns making speeches. There are committees to select committees, and then subcommittees. A great many people in town have some little function to perform in order for the whole show to come off.

When the event finally happens, it is remarkable if several little things don't go wrong. PR men usually hope that they will. Ideally, somebody snitches the prize-winning pie; the mayor sleeps through the speeches; some kid hits the parade marshal's horse with a B-B gun; a store window gets pushed in; the visiting celebrity turns out to be a boyhood chum of the new hotel manager. If all these things happen, the occasion is a success. For days after, there will be much to talk about. Communication will continue to bring together people who have had nothing to say to each other for years. Everyone will have felt a community kinship in the event, in the elbowing that took place, and in the delightfully human foul-ups.

Additional Reading

Russell N. Baird and Arthur T. Turnbull, *Industrial and Business Journalism.* Philadelphia, Pa.: Chilton, 1961. See the section on "Company Publications."

Walter J. DeLong, "Weyerhaeuser: A Nine-Year Record of Corporate Advertising That Pays Off," *Public Relations Journal,* Vol. 18, May, 1962.

Robert O. Dunn, "Ford Motor Company Captures Animal Film Audience of 64,000,-000," *Public Relations Journal,* Vol. 18, December, 1961.

E. W. Earl, *Bulletin Boards.* National Industrial Conference Board, 1953. (Studies in Personnel Policy No. 138.)

Ronald Goodman, "New Look at a Vital Medium: The Company Booklet," *Public Relations Journal,* Vol. 18, July, 1961.

William C. Halley, *Employee Publications.* Philadelphia, Pa.: Chilton, 1959.

Kenneth B. Haas, *Preparation and Use of Audio-Visual Aids,* 3rd ed. Englewood Cliffs, N.J.: Prentice-Hall, Inc., 1955.

Rudolf Modley and D. Lowenstein, *Pictographs and Graphs: How to Make and Use Them.* New York: Harper & Row, Publishers, 1952.

R. Newcomb and M. Sammons, *Developing Effective Supervisory Newsletters.* New York: American Management Association, 1956.

C. T. Smith, "Measuring Effectiveness of Your Business Films," *Public Relations Journal,* Vol. 18, December, 1962.

Arthur L. Gaskell and David Englander, *How to .Shoot a Movie Story.* New York: Morgan and Morgan, 1959.

Harold P. Zelko, *Successful Conference and Discussion Techniques,* New York: McGraw-Hill Book Company, 1958.

CASE PROBLEM

You are in charge of written communications for the Apex Manufacturing Co. This firm employs 5,000 employees in a city of 35,000. It makes high-quality industrial pumps with a good reputation. Existing written communications consist of: (1) monthly two-color magazine of 32 pages, mailed to employees' homes; (2) bulletin boards. You have an assistant, a photographer, and a secretary.

Six months ago Apex experienced a drastic shake-up in management. The company has slipped and is losing its competitive position. Salesmen are finding it difficult to meet quotas. Wage negotiations will get under way in three months, and the union expects to ask for a 15 per cent wage hike. Apex's wages are higher than those of competing firms, yet it has been the policy not to discuss these matters with employees. To cut production costs, Apex is installing new machinery which will cut down on manpower requirements. Rumors of layoffs are beginning. The accident rate has been climbing in the past year. There is unrest in the plant and in the community. Apex's situation is really not critical, but this is not generally known because the situation has not been explained to employees and the community.

The new president wants to change this. He wants to lay the company's cards on the table, but he cannot increase the communications budget at this time. He puts the problem to you and asks for a two-page memorandum on your recommendations. *Your recommendations must* (1) be within the present budget; (2) be effective within a six-month period; (3) be detailed sufficiently to give the president a clear idea of their objectives and your method of attack; (4) list the priority of actions. Your job with Apex may depend on the worth of the program you recommend.

Chapter Twelve

INTEGRATING

THE

FUNCTION

*He who wishes to travel far spares his
mount.*—Racine

The public relations function must
be fully integrated into the organization. In the words of H. A. Batten:
"Unless the business is so organized
and administered that it can meet at
every point the test of good citizenship and usefulness to the community, no amount of public relations
will avail." Public relations cannot
be compartmentalized. Public relations specialists cannot work in a
vacuum. Their work and counsel
must be integrated into the operations of the organization as it deals
with people day in, day out.

The task of effectively integrating
public relations in the daily work of
an organization is a vital one. The
first task of the practitioner is to earn
and hold broad, enthusiastic support
for the public relations concept
within his organization. As one PR
man put it: "I find that I can afford
to spend up to 75 per cent of my
time, if necessary, to persuade my
associates as to what I do in the
remaining 25 per cent." Unless this
is done, there will be conflict, not
coordination and cooperation. Conflict begets friction and frustration.
Friction slows motion, frustration
breeds ulcers.

Where the function is new, it is
a matter of getting off on the right
foot. Where the function is established, the need is for helpful collaboration with other departments.
Integration applies whether the PR
setup consists of outside counseling,
an inside staff, or a combination of
the two. Successful integration of the
PR function depends far more on the
personalities involved than on principles of administration.

Effective integration is not easy.
It must be pursued through *patient*

203

persuasion and helpful service to all members of the team. The PR function is still relatively new in many organizations. Its place and purpose in administration remain to be clarified through experience. Often there is a natural lack of understanding of how this new function meshes with older ones. Responsibility for achieving integration rests with the PR man. He should strive to:

1. Assure PR-mindedness of organization officials.
2. Obtain written definition of authority and responsibility.
3. Gain confidence and cooperation of associates.
4. Indoctrinate the entire organization in principles and programs.
5. Provide service to other departments, staff and line.
6. Develop a desire and opportunities for mutual participation in the program.
7. Promote a communication philosophy of candor.

A sound approach to this timeless task is offered in a paraphrasing of Ordway Tead's counsel. The job of the public relations executive in influencing and educating top managers is the most difficult of his tasks. To do it, he needs proper status, a personality which commands respect, easy access to top executives, and a sustained concern for all the educational influences he can bring to play upon his colleagues. These educational efforts should not be confined to only the top brass; they should extend to middle-management and line people. The task will be examined in this chapter. First, however, there is need to have a realistic perspective of the practitioner's position in the organization.

EVERYTHING, NOTHING, OR SOMETHING

There is no unanimity even among practitioners on a single proper function in the strata of all the organizations served. The role performed and the stature enjoyed vary from client to client and from one institution to the next. Both are decided within each organization. The wide variety of assignments, ranks, and titles has given rise to confusion, and many contentions of public relations spokesmen intended to clarify have tended to confuse still more.

The bystander hears that public relations is "an operating philosophy," that it is *"the* function of management," or that it "embraces all the relations between an organization and its publics." The occasional strident demand for a bigger voice, or a more universal voice, in policy-making affairs has irritated some management people, misled some others, and made many shy away from the function.

At least two of the unfortunate results of the confusion and the element of controversy merit more consideration. *First,* the confusion of public relationships as an *end* result leads, inevitably, to the idea that public relations is everyone's job. This breeds the notion that no expertness is required, that everyone identified with an institution or group can and does handle public relations. *Everybody's job becomes nobody's job.*

Second, the lack of fixed boundaries for the working area of the public relations man leads to friction and conflict with the older, more solidly entrenched staff functions. This also is unfortunate. To be effective, the specialist, whether an advertising man, a psychiatrist, or a public relations man, needs cooperation. It is primary. The title and the rank of the specialist tend to be secondary.

Because of the failure of some managers to firmly fix the place and delineate the scope of the function, some practitioners become embroiled in jurisdictional disputes. Bird and Yutzy concluded after their study: [1] "The failure of public relations which draws snide comment is, we believe, a simple failure of management to manage it. All too often, a company buys public relations without knowing what to do with it, where to put it, or what to put into it."

Lacking absolute boundaries, it can be said that the function of public relations is *not* to manage or to administer an institution. The practitioner is *not* in charge of all the institution's relationships. He is *not* qualified by training to be an expert in everything.

Final clarification of the PR position on the organization chart cannot be expected to emerge suddenly or by virtue of statements supporting the importance of the function. It can be expected to emerge gradually, in direct proportion to its usefulness as a staff function.

Reflecting a basic insecurity, some practitioners spend much time fretting about the proper place of the function on the employer's organization chart. Such time will be better spent in demonstrating competence in assisting management. Too many persons think that "the organization chart is the quintessence of management, the very end-all of industrial engineering." Debunking the myth of the organization chart, sagacious Clarence B. Randall, former head of Inland Steel, had this to say: [2] ". . . to know who is to do what and to establish authority and responsibility within an institution are the basic first principles of a good administration, but this is a far cry from handing down immutable tablets of stone from the mountaintop. . . . It is not the preparation of the organization chart that I condemn, but its abuse: this blowing up of its significance to a point where guidance ceases and inhibition sets in."

This perspective is important. Managers determine basic policies. PR specialists work with them on matters having a strong impact on public opinion. They may be called on to counsel on other matters. Administrators make major decisions, authorize major moves. When communication is an integral part of the decision, the PR specialist should participate. Au-

---

[1] Caroline Bird and Thomas D. Yutzy, "You Have to Manage Public Relations," *Harvard Business Review,* Vol. 35, November-December, 1957.

[2] In *The Folklore of Management* (Boston: Little, Brown & Co., 1959), p. 24.

thority should be delegated to him for implementation needed in those actions which depend on communication for their effectiveness.

IT STARTS WITH
MANAGEMENT

The management of an enterprise determines the scope, place, and, to a large degree, the effectiveness of the staff function. Clarence J. Myers, when president of New York Life Insurance Company, said: "When it is all said and done, a company's public relations office will only be as useful to management as management wants it to be. If management thinks of the public relations operation in a small way, then it will occupy a small place in the company's scheme of things, and its contribution will be small. If management thinks it is important, then it will occupy a prominent place and its contribution will be significant."

Awareness of the importance of public opinion is characteristic of today's generation of organization executives. The importance of the function and its directing specialist have been recognized in corporate management, in military command, in government, in education, and in all other fields. Louis F. Hamele in an exhaustive study of public relations' place in corporate management found evidence to support this generalization. After a detailed study of a representative sample of American corporations, he concluded: [3] (a) Corporate management has recognized the essentiality of the public relations function, and as a consequence has placed the function in the higher levels of the organizational structure; (b) Corporate management has recognized the specialized nature of the function, and as a consequence has practiced sound organizational principles by the establishment of separate public relations departments, headed by a specialist.

Hamele's findings were substantiated in a similar study by Prof. Robert W. Miller of Columbia University. In a nationwide survey of 182 corporations, 39 per cent reported that the person in charge of public relations is a member of the policy-making group. More than one-third of these corporations reported that the person in charge of PR was a vice-president. As Miller notes: [4] "This represents a significant change in the role of corporate public relations over the last 15 years." The *Wall Street Journal*, in a reappraisal of public relations, observed: "Over the past decade or so, there's been a steady succession of major corporations which have relaxed their earlier tight-lipped policies and developed effective programs to keep the public accurately informed of their activities." [5]

---

[3] In "Public Relations, Its Place in Corporate Management." Unpublished Master's thesis, University of Wisconsin, 1962.

[4] Reported in a mimeographed news release, Columbia University, July 3, 1962. Also in *Editor & Publisher,* July 14, 1962, p. 39.

[5] John F. Lawrence, "Public Relations Reappraisal," *Wall Street Journal,* August 13, 1963, p. 12.

Full-fledged acceptance of the mature concept of this function was underlined when the late President John F. Kennedy issued a revised definition of the mission of the United States Information Agency in 1963. This directive was the cumulative result of nearly 20 years' troubled experience and unremitting effort to define and clarify the role of this nation's public relations agency for winning understanding abroad. America's overseas information program, dating from the Office of War Information in World War II, went through many hectic reorganizations, changes in name, and frequent changes in directors before it achieved the full acceptance and adequate authority reflected in President Kennedy's memorandum. In his directive, the President added the responsibility of counseling to the agency's long-established communications function.

There are still many executives and practitioners who have yet to understand and implement the mature concept of public relations in the administration of today's complex organizations of size. Nonetheless, the trend is clear and unmistakable.

THE ROLE OF THE
STAFF MAN

Public relations is a staff function. Thus, its practitioners need to understand *the staff role* in administration. The line–staff principle of management originated in the military but has been extended to most organizations of size. In industry, finance, engineering, production, and sales are the main *line functions; staff functions* embrace personnel, planning, public relations, and advertising. The staff official to *assist* the chief officer became necessary as organizations increased in size and complexity, pushing the administrative burden beyond the time or capabilities of any one man.[6] Line executives have the authority and responsibility to see that the work gets done, but they need assistance in the form of plans, advice, and suggestions from staff executives. *The job of the staff officer is to support and assist the line officer.*

Staff work is the art of collaboration, and staff people justify themselves by their total educational effectiveness. The burden is on the staff man to have the ability and willingness to assist line officers on *their* problems and to help *them* arrive at *their* solutions. Robert Sampson says staff people need "(1) a sense of business organization and operations; (2) an understanding of people, their functions, their relationships; (3) an acceptance of managers as full-scale managers; (4) a humility about their contribution in their limited role; (5) a desire to relate themselves helpfully and dynamically

---

[6] For elaboration on this point, see Lyndall Urwick, *Profitably Using the General Staff Positon in Business* (New York: American Management Association, 1953).

to the ongoing management process." [7] The PR counselor must keep this basic objective constantly before him—*the continuity of the organization and its survival as a healthy entity.* All efforts must be bent in this direction.

The staff function embraces both *advisory* and *operational* tasks. In the advisory role, the PR officer *analyzes public opinion* and *counsels* line and other staff officers on the *public relations aspects* of organizational policies and problems. In the operational role, he handles the organization's communications *outside* the line function. In mature programs, the function embraces both. In too many cases, it is limited to communications.

Management and staff men have a right to expect certain things from each other. *Management should expect:*

1. Loyalty of PR official to organization he serves.
2. Help *for* management in exploring the public relations aspects of its decisions.
3. Skill in making principles articulate, in interpreting, in explaining, and in enlarging understanding of the organization.
4. Inspiration for all members of the team in doing their best and in providing service with a smile.
5. Influence to restrain line and staff people from saying or doing anything detrimental to the organization's welfare.

The PR staff man should expect:

1. Positive public relations leadership from management.
2. A definite PR policy supported by management.
3. A definite PR plan embracing all policies and programs.
4. A budget to do the job that needs to be done.
5. Funds for adequate public relations research.

The public relations aspect of each problem confronting an organization should be given due consideration—but no more than this—along with all other aspects of a particular problem or a proposed policy. The staff man can ask for no more than this. A standard operating procedure is the best way of insuring this. Here, for example, is the Summary Sheet which accompanies all policy matters as these are routed for clearance in the Department of the Army:

SUMMARY SHEET						
				(DA Memo 340-15)		
TO				FOR	FROM	
DCSLOG	COA	CLL		APPROVAL	AGENCY	TELEPHONE
DCSOPS	ACSI	CHIEF OF STAFF		SIGNATURE		
DCSPER	ACSRC	___ S OF A___		COORDINATION	GRADE & NAME OF CONTACT OFFICER	
CRD	TAG	SECRETARY OF THE ARMY				
FILE REFERENCE		SUBJECT			DATE	
IMPLICATIONS (The implications checked below are involved in this action. are discussed below or in a seperate inclosure. and have been considered in the final recommendation.)						
☐ CONTROL PROGRAM	☐ MANPOWER	☐ BUDGET	☐ LEGAL			
☐ CONGRESSIONAL	☑ PUBLIC RELATIONS	☐ MORALE	☐ SECURITY	☐ NONE		

---

[7] Robert C. Sampson, *The Staff Role in Management* (New York: Harper & Row, Publishers, 1955). A useful book on role, uses, and pitfalls in staff work.

CLARIFY THE FUNCTION

Foremost of the measures to be taken is to clarify for the management group what PR is supposed to do, where it fits, and how it will go about its chores. Such understandings work two ways. The function is protected from having doors politely closed in its face, and the executive group is reassured that PR is not going to take over the files and feed them to the newspapers.

The following is a statement of responsibilities and functions sent around to the officials of a very large company when a Department of Information was activated.

> The responsibilities and functions shall be:
> 1. To serve as the central source of information about the company and as the official channel of communication between the company and the public.
> 2. To bring to public attention, through appropriate media, significant facts, opinions, and interpretations which will serve to keep the public aware of company policies and actions.
> 3. To coordinate company activities which affect the relations of the company with the general public or with special public groups.
> 4. To collect and analyze information on the changing attitudes toward the company of key public groups.
> 5. To plan and administer informational programs designed to fulfill most effectively the responsibilities outlined above.

In the same company, the placement of the Department of Information under a Director responsible to the President was announced. Outside counsel retained by the organization developed the statement and worked with the internal staff.

Here is a more specific statement of responsibilities in another organization:

> 1. Formation and conduct of a public relations program for the company in the areas of consumer relations, trade relations, shareholder relations, community relations, employee relations, and any other areas in which responsibility is assigned.
> 2. Supervision of company magazines.
> 3. Review of all published documents of the company from the standpoint of their public relations implications.
> 4. Preparation and/or approval of all news and feature articles, photographs, and other expressions of the company transmitted to all media of communication not involving the use of paid time or space.
> 5. Preparation of consultation on statements or speeches of company officers and executives, as requested.
> 6. Counseling with personnel officials of the company, in an advisory capacity, on matters pertaining to employee relations, with a view to helping express company policies and to help explain the company's problems.
> 7. Promotion of sound relations with plant communities by cooperating with local press media, civic and social organizations, schools, and churches.
> 8. Work with management and legal counsel in governmental relations work, as directed specifically by the president. This may include working with legal

counsel in preparation and distribution of company statements to governmental agencies and to interested segments of the consumer and trade press.

9. Cooperation with the marketing division, in an advisory capacity, in planning and executing programs designed to improve relations with the retail trade.

10. Any other duties assigned specifically by the president.

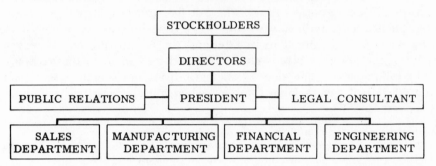

A setup in a business organization of one or two thousand employees with a consumer product or service might look like the accompanying diagram.[8] With outside counseling and internal staffing to be considered, there are many departmental variations. On the opposite page are examples taken from a National Industrial Conference Board report.

WHERE THE PR
FUNCTION FITS IN

The relationship of the function to other departments varies with organizations and their objectives. Often it is a matter of history. One major firm has the PR staff reporting to the treasurer because years ago the first PR man was hired to edit the annual report. More often it is a matter of personalities. No flat rule can be set down as to how the function ought to be organized or where it should go on the organization chart. The function has "no customary position."

The National Industrial Conference Board found in its survey of business firms that "the principal factors affecting the place of public relations in the company are: attitude of top management towards public relations; age of function within company; type of market for company's products; size of company; general organizational policy of the company." The NICB concluded, "When public relations is highly regarded to warrant its being organized as a separate department, the executive in charge usually reports either directly to the chief administrative officer of the company, or to a vice-president in charge of a group of staff functions."[9] Of the other staff

---

8 For examples of how the function is organized in different firms, see National Industrial Conference Board, *Public Relations in Industry* (New York: The Board, Studies in Business Policy Number 80, 1956).

9 *Ibid.*

C.I.T. Financial Corporation Public Relations Department

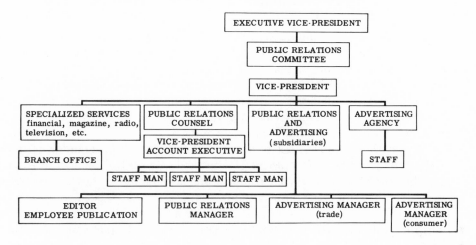

Sylvania Electric Products, Inc. Public Relations Department

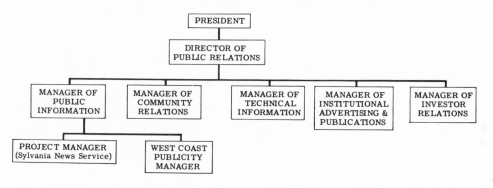

Underwood Corporation Public Relations Department Organization

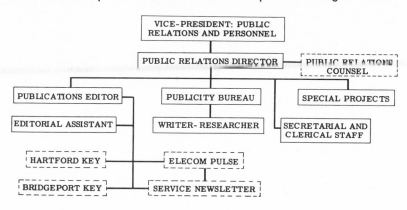

functions, PR staffers work most closely with personnel, industrial, or employee relations and advertising. These functions intertwine and overlap in varying degrees.

Sometimes, at the outset, a practitioner may find himself in the middle of a conflict between officials in an organization. One or the other of the officials may place him in that position on purpose. Many a sincere PR man has expended himself on the barricades of organizational politics. Sometimes the department finds itself in direct conflict with another department.

Particular sources of internal friction are the departments of *advertising, personnel,* and *legal counsel.* Such disputes are costly to all concerned, especially to the employer. Each function needs the support and cooperation of the others if each is to discharge effectively its obligation to the team. It must be emphasized that such conflicts are not common—they are the exception, not the rule. In most organizations, they have been resolved. But because the potential for conflict is inherent in the fluidity of the public relations function, practitioners should be aware of it and understand the reasons for it.

The conflict between public relations and legal counsel is an ancient one. In the days of the Muckrakers, corporate executives more often turned to their lawyers to "fix things" than to the emerging public relations specialist. Some still do. Ivy Lee felt strongly about this: [10] "I have seen more situations which the public ought to understand and which the public would sympathize with, spoiled by the intervention of the lawyer than in any other way. Whenever a lawyer starts to talk to the public, he shuts out the light." Even in this day we can expect conflict when one corporation counsel asserts: "I am prepared to defend the position that the truly competent legal counsellor to the public relations division should be expected to express his opinion not only on matters of factuality which have potential legal impact, *but even on matters of good taste, logic, honesty, yes even at times on the persuasiveness of your copy.*" [11]

Such invasions of the public relations domain must be repelled. On the other hand, there are many areas in which the close coordination of legal and public relations counsel are essential. Such cooperation is particularly urgent in the area of labor contract negotiations and in that of legal actions, e.g. an antitrust suit. There must be coordination and clearance on such matters as booklets explaining fringe benefits to employees, announcement of new facilities, location of new plants, and so forth. In one survey, public relations men reported that they found legal issues involved in their work about half the time.[12] As organizations—corporations in particular—deal with an ever more complex environment and the expanding scope of government,

---

[10] In his *Publicity, Some of the Things It Is and Is Not* (New York: Industries Publishing Company, 1925), pp. 58 and 59.

[11] William Barron, labor relations counsel for General Electric, in address before 10th annual conference of PRSA in Philadelphia, Pa., November 18, 1957.

[12] Albert Blaustein and Sidney Gross, "Working With Lawyers," *PR,* Vol. 1, July 1956.

they will need the combined talents of cooperating legal and public relations counsel to guide them.

The relationships between public relations and personnel and/or industrial relations are many. The risk of friction is high because of the overlap in these functions. The problem can be sensed in the varied ways in which authors of textbooks on management define the two functions. One, for example, outlines the objectives of a personnel program as: [13]

> (1) the improvement of the service rendered by the enterprise to society through building better employee morale, which leads to more efficient individual and group performance; and (2) establishment in the minds of those associated with the enterprise (employee, stockholder, creditor, customer, and public at large) of the fact that the enterprise is rendering the best service of which it is capable. . . .

On the other hand, as practitioners learn that it is the way an organization's personnel deal with their many publics that shapes the public's attitudes, the more practitioners seek to influence employee attitudes. Control of employee communications is the most frequent bone of contention between these two functions. Increasingly this is being allocated to public relations, which has the communications specialists on its staff. Such a transfer breeds the kind of resentment reflected in this wry comment of the personnel director of the Idaho Power Company: "Far be it from me to claim kinship with public relations experts in the utility field. They obviously are a fraternity of specialized souls far above my poor power to add or detract from the vexing dilemmas they enjoy today." [14]

In a study directed by one of your authors, a survey of a representative sample of American corporations showed this breakdown of specific tasks which are often bounced from one function to the other: [15]

Public Relations Dominant

Annual reports
Open house, plant tours
News releases on labor negotiations
Maintenance of biographical data on key employees

Personnel Dominant, PR Not Involved

Suggestions systems
Bulletin boards
Reading racks

[13] L. P. Alford and H. R. Beatty, *Principles of Industrial Management* (New York: The Ronald Press Company, 1951), pp. 637 and 640.

[14] R. H. Sessions, "Let's Be Sensible About Public Relations!", *The Electrical World*, Vol. 149, April 21, 1958.

[15] A survey conducted in 1959 by Scott M. Cutlip and Leroy Johnson to ascertain trends in the patterns of organizing the public relations, personnel, and advertising functions. Questionnaires were sent to public relations and personnel directors in 73 representative business firms, chosen on the basis of size, type of business, and geographic location. Seventy-four per cent of the selected sample responded. This study was financed by a grant from the University of Wisconsin Industrial Relations Research Center.

New employee orientation
Exit interviews
Service awards
Recruitment programs
Pay inserts
Christmas parties

Personnel Dominant, PR Advisory

Employee attitude surveys
Employee meetings
Safety-promotion material

Responsibility Split:

Employee publications
Employee newsletters
Liaison with civic bodies
Manpower for local fund drives, *e.g.,* United Fund
Conducting career days

The above distribution represents the dominant pattern found in this representative sample of 35 corporations and is based on questionnaires sent to and returned separately from personnel and public relations departments of these firms. The varying patterns of allocation of these tasks and the common interest of both personnel and public relations in them indicate the potential for conflict between these two staff functions unless clear, logical lines are drawn by management. When these specialists do collide, the top manager must thoughtfully ask: "Is it any wonder that management sometimes displays lack of understanding of human relations when the two departments of management that should be most concerned with this problem do not even understand each other?"

The basic conflict between public relations and advertising was discussed at some length in Chapter 6. Here the tussle is usually over control of public relations advertising and over product publicity, in the case of business concerns. This jurisdictional dispute is not found in nonprofit organizations, but disputes involving the spheres of personnel and legal counsel are.

One quite useful means of absorbing these conflicts is to form a public relations policy committee or consulting group which includes the opponents. The public relations counselor or staff director assumes the role of coordinator, executor of decisions, or secretary to the group. Others in the group tend by majority persuasion to forgo individual oppositions. The clash of personalities generally gets lost in the shuffle, for the moment. That is not to say that the formation of policy groups has no advantages to integration other than in removing personality barriers. There is much to recommend such groups, on occasion, in bringing together the best minds available —all the specialists—to thresh out problems affecting the whole organization. They can swap ideas and the best solution will emerge. More than that, when it's all done, everyone is committed to the joint decision.

A main consideration in the formation of guiding groups is to keep them small enough so that they will not collapse of their own weight. Only those persons intimately concerned with communication should be brought in. And only matters that involve all participants in the group should be brought up for joint discussion or decision. For example, the treasurer of a university does not want to give up an entire morning to discussing a policy covering how often the campus lawn should be mowed. Nor, for that matter, would the superintendent of grounds relish the idea of that particular subject, which he considers his exclusive domain, being tossed on the table for the opinions of uninvolved officials. Finally, in guiding group discussions toward a decision, a coordinator should lead off with the areas of common agreement, not the points of probable conflict.

A number of the nation's major corporations, in an effort to eliminate overlap and conflict, have combined the public relations and personnel functions into one department under one director or vice-president. The General Electric Company led the way in 1956, when it merged public relations and its expanding employee-community relations departments under one vice-president. This enlarged department was re-titled Staff Relations Services in 1958. Other firms wrapping the two functions together under one head include: General Foods, Eli Lilly, Calumet Hecla, Texaco, Inc., Kennecott Copper, Quaker Oats, Equitable Life, and the Pennsylvania Railroad. Other firms have combined public relations and advertising for the same reason.

The Cutlip-Johnson study found a greater number of public relations departments merged with the advertising function than merged with personnel. One-fourth of the companies surveyed reported this organizational pattern. However, the majority of firms rely on informal exchange between these departments on a coordinate level. Close cooperation by specialists of competence and cordiality are by far the most effective solution to these jurisdictional disputes.

The internal relationships of the function are illustrated in this cataloging of Boeing's director of public relations and advertising: [16]

BOEING AIRPLANE COMPANY

The director of public relations and advertising has the following relationships:

To: The President

He is accountable to the president for interpreting and carrying out his responsibilities and will fulfill any additional responsibilities assigned him by the president.

To: Public Relations Manager—Wichita Division

He will arrange for receiving reports and other coordinative information to assist him in carrying out his responsibilities for policy direction over the public relations manager—Wichita Division. He will develop with the public relations manager—Wichita Division an understanding as to what material in the form of press releases, publications, or speeches should be cleared through his office prior to release

To: Vice-president—Industrial Relations

On matters of industrial relations, particularly in connection with the publication

---

[16] NICB Report, *Public Relations In Industry*, p. 9.

of BOEING NEWS, he will coordinate general policy concerning employee relations with the vice-president—industrial relations.

To: Vice-president—Finance

He will coordinate reports to stockholders with the vice-president—finance, and
the secretary.

To: Director of Sales

Coordination will be achieved with the director of sales on general policy of
product promotion and customer relationships.

To: Assistant to the President

He will coordinate with the assistant to the president as to general policy on plant
visits, use of the plant public address system, and management development
activities.

To: Others

He will maintain liaison with the directorate of public information, United
States Air Force; Aereospace Industries Association; Seattle Chamber of Commerce; and other civic organizations and committees.

As it all adds up, management or administration in large organizations
is properly a team. Specialists have their places determined by the relative
worth of what they contribute. On the team, the top official is the spokesman. He constitutes the frontispiece or symbol. To outsiders he is "the
company," or "the organization." Surrounding him, the executive group,
together with outside consultants, form the character and personality of
the organization. This group is the "they" whom employees or members
refer to without names. "They" in the Army are the people who, according
to junior officers, always pass the buck to them. "They" in industry are the
people who make the rules.

Somewhere within or alongside this group, the practitioner with his staff
has a position and performs his specialty. Sometimes he has an office ad-
joining the top official. Sometimes he is located a little closer to the rank
and file. This is secondary. His function is rendered impotent only when
it lacks facilities for contact with the top echelon and for participation
within the power structure.

THE PRACTITIONER'S
PERSONAL TASK

A public relations man can be prejudged harmfully if his personal standards are something lower than those he prescribes for others. A public relations man's personal principles and conduct loom large in the effective
integration of his function. He and his staff must set the example.

He must gain the confidence of the thoughtful and influential people
in the organization. He must learn their language, their problems, their
thinking. He must enjoy at least the neutrality of all others. Respect for
him and his judgment must reach from the top of the administrative stem
down past the supervisory levels. The confidence of top management quite

logically derives in part from the respect that people on down the line have for him. If he lacks that respect, the chances are that he can't be very useful in management affairs. No man who has to take responsibility and exercise authority can be universally popular, but a PR man should never give up trying.

To gain respect, *the effective public relations man must operate through channels, keep his promises, preserve matters given him in confidence, and seek no partiality. He must lick his own wounds privately.*

A PR man must have a bit of the crusader's fervor about him. His function is young. His own enthusiasm, coupled with results that back it up, will go far toward instilling a *public relations mindedness* throughout the organization. The public interest, goodwill, prestige, and a good press can become everybody's concern without robbing the PR man of his function. That has been achieved adroitly in some companies. When the president makes a speech, everybody can prove that what he says is right. The spirit is such that ideas for programs are being volunteered. Everybody wants to get into the act. Personal popularity is much more difficult for the outside consultant to accomplish than for the staff man. The counselor is not on the premises daily to cultivate acquaintanceships. His visits are largely consumed by meetings with a relatively small number of people. He must make the most of his opportunities.

THE JOB STARTS WITH INFORMATION

Before an initial program is planned, the public relations man goes back to school, so to speak. He becomes a student of his environment. It may be that he has research performed by outside firms. But in his personal contacts, he is a researcher. He seeks out old-timers on the premises. He draws them out about their experiences. He listens to learn of changes in attitude and policy that have taken place through the years. He studies all the departments in the organization and their relationships to each other. In the process he learns the motivations of the departments and their insecurities.

The leg work is important in such personal research, but no less important is the desk work. The public relations man examines complaint letters from outsiders and testimonials, too. He reads the files on internal grievances, resignations, important meetings. He goes through employee handbooks, statements of policy, typical letters going out, bulletin board notices, the organization's history, financial reports, and various brochures. He digs around in the file morgue and in the legends, the lore, and the keepsakes of the organization.

In his search the public relations man, of course, is looking for past or potential causes of breakdown in the communications of the organization with its publics. The search takes him walking. He walks around the hometown, the camp, or the campus. As he goes, he listens. He listens in the barber chair, at the corner grocery, in the bank, on the golf course, waiting for the bus, and across the back fence.

THE INDOCTRINATION PROCESS

The public relations man, necessarily a learner, is at the same time a teacher. He plants seeds of thought where needed. In the sowing, there are several ready-made vehicles.

1. Clippings of news about the organization and about its competitors can be routed among department heads.
2. News stories to be sent out should be cleared with the persons and departments involved. Copies of releases to executives not involved will prove to be a courtesy appreciated.
3. Professional publications can be routed with marginal notations for the attention of interested individuals.
4. Personal notes of congratulations and compliments can be sent concerning the civic activities of members in the organization. The same for condolences. Not only are the notes indicative of thoughtfulness, but they also serve to remind others that it is effective to do likewise.
5. Participation in community welfare campaigns or civic enterprises can become the internal public relations man's hobby. Again, here is an example for others.
6. The house publication can emphasize, without heavyhanded promotional technique, that public relations is everybody's job. This is an old, well-worn theme. It has endured because its ultimate truth appeals to everyone's innate desire for participation. It can easily be demonstrated how the contacts of the purchasing agent, salesman, soldier on leave, or student does a public relations job for the organization he represents.

   The house publication can become an effective integrating force through constant and adroit development of the idea of mutual participation. In its own editorial staffing the house publication can include numerous reporters appointed through the organization, a voice-of-the-people column, a column of suggestions, by-lines for contributors, and the enclosure of sincere questionnaires seeking guidance from readers.
7. Activities can be encouraged to bring together groups having objectives and functions in common. As prototypes, there could be a Better Letter Writing Clinic for business correspondents, a Leadership Forum for military noncoms, a Civic Council for Students, a Customers' Service Panel for utility office people, a Newcomers' Welcome Committee for the Chamber of Commerce, and Outing Clubs for members of a retail association.

RENDERING SERVICE

Within organizations there are many opportunities for personal service by the public relations counselor or director. Minor as they may seem, they are important to the recipients. They make the public relations staff valuable to others, personally. This does not imply ingratiation, but rather, a policy of service.

For instance, many a man is committed to give a speech who cannot put his thoughts well on paper. Consider the brilliant scientist who tries to put scientific terms into a vocabulary suitable for a group of small-town businessmen. That's where the public relations specialist comes in. He has a sufficient grasp of science and an acquaintance with the language of the layman. Speech-writing often gives the access to the top brass that he needs and seeks.

Another service is in liaison between departments and their publics, on occasion. Visualize the predicament of the people in a credit department confronted by irate customers who arrive on the premises with chips on both shoulders. The internal public relations staff can offer diplomatic service.

A third type of service is rendered in assisting reticent but capable people to participate in employee and community activities. A typical situation is that of the newcomer who wants to meet people of similar social interests and wants to be of service in community affairs. The public relations internal staff can handle introductions.

Then, there is the service of helping the introverts in the organization to have a share in some of those things that the extroverts take for granted. The public relations man exercises great influence on the content of the house publications, the committees for employee events, and the staging of parties, conventions, and awards occasions. He can look out for the men and women who might otherwise get lost in the shuffle.

The "service" approach is effective, and limitless. For example, here are some ways public relations can assist, suggested by a former public relations executive of Procter and Gamble.[17]

1. In a buying department, in the way it builds friends among suppliers even where it can't place orders.
2. In a sales department, whose management wants the customer to speak of the company as "fine people to do business with."
3. In a legal department, where, alongside sound law, the constant admonition of the head counsel concerns public opinion.
4. In an employment department, where unsuccessful applications are not rejected like lightweight cattle at the stockyards.
5. In stockholder relations, where the shareholder is not by inference told to count her many blessings and be silent.
6. In a financial department, where a thoughtfully planned policy of contributions to health, education, and welfare causes is considered not an inescapable tax on the treasury, but a means of building valuable goodwill.
7. In a traffic department, where people remember that the employees of the carriers can be customers and friends of the shipper.

---

[17] William G. Werner, "Can We Measure Up?", *Public Relations Journal,* Vol. 10, January, 1954.

8. In an adjustment department, where a patron helped is considered more important than an argument won.

9. In correspondence handling that signs letters—even form letters—that breathe warmth, friendliness, and understanding.

10. In a manufacturing department, where employees realize that sloppy shipments or disregard for plant-city neighbors have a direct bearing on a steady flow of orders.

11. In an advertising department, where, beyond the question, "Will it sell goods?" the question is asked "Will it make friends for the company?"

12. In executive echelons, where a contribution of time and experience toward leadership in public-interest causes is considered not only a civic responsibility, but also a valuable public relations function.

THE LIMELIGHT

In the course of a year in most organizations, there is a variety of news of internal and external interest. In the ferreting out of news, each facet of the enterprise, each department, should be explored. This is particularly helpful to the outside counselor. It helps him to be known favorably throughout the organization. The planned information program, using a wide variety of news outlets, can include releases about all phases of operations, all departments. On page 221 is a partial list of the news items released during the year by one business concern. Note the various departments within the company which shared the limelight.

COMPLETING THE
INTEGRATION

A significant indication that public relations-mindedness is permeating the whole structure appears when people begin to say to each other that candor in communication is the best policy. That means that people realize the organization is clean. There's nothing to hide. Why hide anything? Moreover, it means that they have complete confidence in the PR staff to place the company in the right light, publicly.

With the appearance of this important symptom, the public relations man or group can actually apply complete candor in the communication structure, wherever it may have been lacking. The various groups sharing in the organization can be told anything they want to know. Outsiders can be helped to get any kind of look into the organization that they want.

The exposure to public gaze of a clean organization, operating in the mutual interests of itself and its publics, does not mean that all there is to say about the organization should be blurted out. In business there are competitive considerations. In the military there are security considerations. In institutions there are rigid ethical considerations. Common sense is the yardstick.

News Releases	Departments Mentioned
Announcement of spring advertising campaign	Sales, Advertising
Announcement of average wage in factory	All plant employees
Announcement of new technique in window trimming	Sales Promotion
Monthly meetings of supervisory people to hear outside speakers	Factory supervisors, union officials
Visit of foreign distributors to home-town plant	Export
Results of beauty contest among girls in office and plant	Factory, Office, Sales Promotion
Installation of plant safety devices	Factory Management, Personnel
Company participation in local industrial exhibit	Public Relations, Foremen, Beauty Contest Winners
Announcement of special promotion	Sales, Advertising
Announcement of company annual report	Production, Sales, Research, Finance
Attendance of engineers at industrial institute	Factory engineering
Award of product to high school valedictorian	Factory official
Bus-load of employees to neighboring festival	Factory assembly and others
Signing of a union contract	Factory management, union officials
Comparative figures on employment locally in plant	Factory employees
Visit of officials from foreign subsidiary	Management Export
Announcement of new product	Sales, Advertising, Promotion, Factory, Design group
Promotion of executive	Sales, Field force
Announcement of sales meetings	Field force, Divisional Sales Managers
Establishment of welfare fund	All employees
Human interest—employee father of three children born same day of different years	Factory employees
Article on proper care of product	Service
Policy statement allocating merchandise	Sales, Management
Plans for convention participation	Sales
Announcement of trend to higher-priced products	All employees
Disclosure of new material used in product	Research
Article on company aircraft	Administration
New display device	Sales Promotion
Factory methods	Factory management
Instructions on wrapping gift parcels for soldiers overseas	All employees, Office Management
Viewpoint of Latvian employee	All employees
Retention of prominent designer	Sales, Design group

Additional Reading

David Finn, *Public Relations and Management.* New York: Reinhold Publishing Corp., 1960.

Howard F. Harris, "When Management Asks . . . ," *Public Relations Quarterly,* Vol. 8, July, 1963.

E. Paul Harvey, "Organization and Practice of College PR," *Pride,* Vol. 1, December, 1958.

F. Rhodes Henderer, *A Comparative Study of the Public Relations Practices in Six Industrial Organizations.* Pittsburgh, Pa.: University of Pittsburgh Press, 1956.

John W. Hill, "Corporation Lawyers and Public Relations Counsel," *The Business Lawyer,* American Bar Association, Vol. 14, April, 1959, pp. 587-608.

Public Relations Society of America, "Report of the National Research Committee: The Organization of Public Relations in Health and Welfare Organizations," 1953.

Earl Newsom, "The Care and Feeding of Bosses," *Public Relations Journal,* Vol. 14, February, 1958.

Charles H. Prout, "How to Organize and Run a Corporate Public Relations Department," *Public Relations Journal,* Vol. 19, February, 1962.

CASE PROBLEM

You were employed six months ago to organize a PR department in the John O. Jones Co., a 40-year-old firm manufacturing heavy pipe, tanks, and other products made of steel. This firm set up a separate department when it entered the consumer goods field with a new product. Your staff consists of a press relations director and a secretary. Your function is new in this old, solid, and rather conservative firm. The firm has had excellent employee relations over the years, is known as a maker of quality products, and has always made a profit. In your initial fact-finding, you did find that it had the reputation in the community for being a dangerous place to work and a plant with a high accident rate. You learned that this is based more on hearsay than on fact.

You get a call at 9:30 A.M. from the local daily that an employee has been killed in the plant an hour ago. The reporter says the ambulance crew told him that the man was crushed by a heavy pipe. He asks for details. You ask time to check and promise to call back. You go to the safety supervisor. He blows up and insists that no details of the accident be given to the press. He insists on taking you to his boss, the personnel director. The personnel director—on the same level of authority with you—backs up his safety supervisor. What do you do now?

Chapter Thirteen

THE

EMPLOYEE

PUBLIC

The underlying cause of industrial peace is the basic desire of the parties to share information and make joint decisions rather than the type of machinery which they employ to achieve such ends.—Frederick Harbison and John R. Coleman.

The term *internal public* as used here means the people working in an organization—the governors and the governed. They are the managers, employees, members, teachers, and associates for organizations variously engaged in business, government, military defense, education, or social welfare. This chapter will deal with communication between the administrators and those who are employed. *Employee relations* is the short-cut term used to describe this internal relationship. Its use should not be construed in terms of business alone. Employee relations are a prime concern of management in every field.

THE BASIC
RELATIONSHIP

Reaching the internal public is not difficult. The working relationship brings about daily communication. Besides that, there is a wide variety of auxiliary tools. The effectiveness of the auxiliary communication depends to a greater extent than generally admitted on whether or not the working relationship is a good one; that is, whether the audience is receptive and responsive. *Before there can be effective employee communication, there must be a climate of belief.* This is built—or destroyed—by the day-to-day actions of those in authority.

Common sense says, then, that practitioners need to know about the kind of working relationship that exists. Each organization is, within itself, a productive or service unit with production or service responsibilities. *It is also a social unit, with social responsibilities.* Burleigh Gardner wrote relating this basic fact to organizational structure.[1]

> Any concern may be considered as a human organization of people in functional relation to one another. Each person has a place in this structure; he has duties and responsibilities, he has certain relationships with others, and his work has a place in the total pattern of work.
> This social system is a well-knit unit in which the function of each has direct and indirect effects upon the others.
> Because it is such a closely integrated system of cooperative effort it is important that everyone concerned with increasing its effectiveness . . . have an understanding of the nature of such a system and of the problems of maintaining effective cooperation within it.

Consequently, in any approach to the internal public, the social needs as well as the economic needs must be acknowledged and satisfied. A pay check falls far short of being the only thing an employee wants, although its importance should not be unduly minimized. Howard Wilson lists the social or psychological needs of man as: [2]

> 1. *Need to belong.* Man wants to identify himself with other people, he wants to be part of a group stronger than himself.
> 2. *Need for accomplishment.* Man wants to feel that he is making progress toward worthy goals; goals within his capabilities.
> 3. *Need for self-esteem.* Each man develops his own sense of worth, his own standard of pride and dignity.
> 4. *Need for acceptance.* Man must feel that he is accepted by the groups with which he identifies himself.
> 5. *Need for security.* The interdependence of modern life has sapped the once proud quality of self-reliance. Modern man is insecure and thus needs greater assurance of security.
> 6. *Need for creativity.* Too often in modern life the skill function has been taken from man and given to the machine. Without the chance to be creative, egos of men suffer.

Providing satisfying work for our multiplying millions of workers is becoming an ever greater problem in our automated, productive society. It is a problem for which there is no easy solution. Eric Fromm asks: [3] "Is man, during the next hundred years, to continue to spend most of his energy on meaningless work, waiting for the time when work will require no expenditure of energy? What will become of him in the meantime? . . . Is not work such a fundamental part of man's existence that it cannot and should never be reduced to almost complete insignificance?"

Those who would effectively communicate with employees must find ways of seeing work from their view. One who did this is Harvey Swados, writer and teacher, who went to work on an auto assembly line. He discovered how

---

[1] For elaboration, see Burleigh Gardner and David Moore, *Human Relations in Industry* (Homewood, Ill.: Richard D. Irwin, Inc., 1955). A useful reference.

[2] "The Psychological Needs of Man," *PR*, Vol. 1, October, 1955.

[3] In *The Sane Society*, New York: Holt, Rinehart & Winston, Inc., 1955.

little we Americans really know the texture of each other's working lives. He writes: [4]

> It came as something of a shock to discover that the one unifying force among all those men, so different from one another in ethnic background, educational attainment, and personal ambition, was hatred of their work. . . . I was doubly surprised that my middle-class friends found it difficult to accept this. . . . My friends of the middle class were frankly ignorant of the working lives of their fellow-Americans. . . . But when they heard what I had to say, they found it very difficult to accept it. . . ."

Another who did the same thing is Patricia Cayo Sexton, also a college teacher, who found that "the worker's world—as one lives in it—is very different." As a result of her three years in a Dodge plant, this sociologist concluded that "such phrases as 'powerful unions' and 'enlightened management' seem to me to convey very little of the essence of life on the assembly line." [5]

Equally tough problems must be faced in dealing with the expanding numbers of white-collar workers. Today nearly half of the employed civilian labor force are salaried personnel, yet these persons are too often overlooked in employee communications. Among the salaried people, the upward mobility of the college graduate has been slowed and the scramble for status has intensified. By 1970, according to *Fortune,* college-trained men between 25 and 34 will represent one-fourth of the total work force in that age group. *Fortune* reasons: "The time is at hand when a fair number of college-trained men must already be working at jobs to which no high status attaches." An employee communications consultant suggests that "it is imperative that business organizations take a long, searching look at their salaried employees" and the ways of communicating with them.[6]

These needs are felt by industrial and social service workers, soldiers and sailors, teachers and tellers, barbers and bartenders. Peter Drucker says that the corporation, as America's representative social institution, must satisfy two minimum requirements: "It must give status and function to the individual, and it must give him the justice of equal opportunities." One could have a college in mind and say the same thing.

Status and function require that each person have importance in his or her job despite the necessity for the jobs to be subordinated. They mean that the floor sweeper in a factory realizes and feels sure that his job is worthwhile in the over-all scheme of things. The same is true for the filing clerk in the large office. All jobs have importance.

Parallel with this realization, there must be an understanding of the

---

4 In "Work As a Public Issue," *Saturday Review,* Vol. 42, December 12, 1959, pp. 13-15 and 45.

5 In "The Auto Assembly Line: An Inside View," *Harper's Magazine,* Vol. 224, June, 1962, pp. 52-57.

6 William Scholz, "Salaried Employees: Challenge and Opportunity," *Personnel Journal,* Vol. 40, November, 1961, pp. 266-68.

reasons why one job merits status different from another. One factory worker may be required to wear a uniform. Another may be permitted to wear whatever he chooses. One executive may have a more sumptuous office than another. One secretary may work in a private office and another in a stenographic section. Understanding of the reasons for these symbols must replace envy of them. Along with this understanding there must be support of the promotion system in which advancement from one job to another is possible and desirable.

Provision for the satisfaction of equal opportunity requires that each person's capabilities be known and measurable. It is not required, nor is it desirable, that all persons have equal opportunity for advancement regardless of their capabilities. It is not required or desirable that opportunities be opened in directions where people have unequal aptitude or training. An effort should be made to help the individual advance as far as possible in directions for which he is qualified. He cannot have a lasting working satisfaction if he is denied avenues of advancement, or the hope of advancement, either socially or economically.

Giving the individual status, function, and opportunity establishes a wholesome working relationship. It satisfies the need of everyone for security, importance, individuality, and the friendship and esteem of others.

All this is good. All is ideal. But a practical approach must take into account that the supply of tangible forms of status, function, and opportunity is not unlimited. The realistic approach must recognize that the United States economic system is one of *rewards* in return for something—usually, time or effort in the form of productivity.

EFFECTIVE COMMUNICATION HAS A VITAL ROLE. Maladjustments and frustrations breed in large organizations. The lack of social integration leaves many workers asking: "Where do I fit?" "What does my boss think of me?" "How can I be a success?" Communication which answers such questions helps reduce anxieties, create security, and bring job satisfaction. But such meaningful, two-way communication becomes ever more difficult—from university president to student, from general to troops, from department head to field agent. Yet the glut and maze of communication grows. One large corporation estimates that it uses 12,000 sheets of interoffice stationery a day!

GAINING ACCEPTABILITY

Mutual confidence of employer and employee in each other is essential to the success of any enterprise. To paraphrase L. M. Keys: The main asset of any enterprise is the confidence of the men in their leaders, the confidence of the leaders in their organization, and the confidence of both in their product or service. Without such faith, there can be no permanent success.

In industrial organizations with collective bargaining agreements, such faith must embrace these fundamentals for industrial peace and productivity:

1. Full acceptance by management of collective bargaining.
2. Full acceptance by unions of private ownership and operation of industry for a profit.
3. Strong unions that are democratically and responsibly run.
4. No company interference in union affairs.
5. Both parties demonstrate mutual trust in all dealings.
6. Neither party takes a legalistic approach in negotiations, which should be problem-centered, not issue-centered.
7. Full sharing of information and widespread consultation on matters of mutual interest.
8. Prompt settlement of grievances as these arise.

Many employers do not have to deal with unions. Nonetheless, they must gain acceptability by following the same basic approach of full sharing of information, consultation on matters of mutual interest, and prompt settlement of grievances. Enlightened corporate management has taken most of the thrust out of organized labor's efforts to unionize all employees by providing voluntarily what the unions used to get through the power of collective bargaining. Union membership has been stabilized at approximately 18 million members for many years, although the nation's work force has been growing. *Fortune's* Daniel Bell ascribes this relative loss of strength by unions to "the increased sophistication of management, and because in this period of relatively full employment wages have been high in nonunion as well as unionized plants." Nonprofit agencies can write a comparable set of fundamentals.

The process of earning acceptability for the manager or administrator is not complex. There are three components. One is an expressed interest in the employees' or members' affairs. The interest must be genuine, not simulated. It must be humane. It must be attentive to the employees' expressed desires and fears. It must be studious.

The second component is in the actions taken as a result of what is revealed to be necessary in the problems of the employees. This implies no actions that are foolhardy or that consist of giving away something for nothing. It means, specifically, an overhaul of personnel policies wherever employees' or members' affairs are neglected. This gives positive action to the employer's genuine interest. Good intent is supported by deeds. An interest in employee health is backed up by actions providing for sanitation, safety, and medical services.

The third component is a *free and candid flow of information between management and employee.* The flow uses the line organization and auxiliary tools. The purpose is to strengthen the wholesome working relationship. In practice, this requires an exchange of differing viewpoints. It requires efforts to reconcile the differences for the best interests of all. It requires a collaboration in realizing workaday satisfactions.

In analyzing the reasons for the long and harmonious relationships in the Marathon division of American Can Company, two specialists found this to be a key factor: "The company early established with its employees and with the unions when they arrived, a reputation for absolute integrity and a willingness to sit down and talk about any subject." [7]

An organization which takes these factors into account can get through even the most unpleasant situations. Take the way the George D. Roper Corp., Rockford, Ill., handled a layoff of 450 workers. This firm had a military contract which was suddenly cut back. To gain time to ease the blow to the employees, the firm obtained a 30-day extension on the cutback. This enabled it to give the men three weeks' notice and thus time to look for other jobs. Personnel and employee communicators went to work to collaborate on *planning* the layoff and its announcement.

A detailed plan of breaking the news was worked out. Efforts were made to line up other jobs for the men. Round-the-clock interviews were arranged for 900 other employees who had to be shifted to other jobs in the plant. Union officers were called in to help iron out complaints and to work out problems of seniority. When layoff day came, the news was broken by this timetable: 8 A.M.—plant foremen; 9 A.M.—union representatives; 10 A.M.—office supervisors; 10:30 A.M.—notices went up on plant bulletin boards; 11 A.M—news released to press, radio, and TV outlets in Rockford; 12—a letter from the Roper president was put in the mails, timed to explain the layoff to workers' families the following day.

By that date the company's personnel people had completed 1,300 interviews. The 900 men to be kept were ready to step into their new jobs. Of the 450 let out, more than 200 had other jobs in Rockford within a week, owing largely to Roper's help. The final move was formation of the "Roper Veterans Club" for 21 employees who had passed or were near retirement. This club has been used to help retired employees find part-time jobs if they want them. It also has provided all retired employees an annual dinner. The reaction of employees—both those kept and those laid off—was most favorable.

Most organizations put their personnel policies down on paper. It is wise to do so. The forms vary, but the intent is uniform. Having the attitudes of management down on paper constitutes a bid for acceptability. Administrators must remember that *these policies become a binding contract* in the employee's eyes. Such policies should be widely communicated. There is a resultant awareness of management's attitudes on the part of employees or members. Here is a typical list.

WESTERN ELECTRIC
(Ten Commandments of employee relations)
1. Pay all employees adequately for services rendered.
2. Maintain reasonable hours of work and safe working conditions.
3. Provide continuous employment consistent with business conditions.
4. Place employees in the kind of work best suited to their abilities.

---

[7] Clinton S. Golden and Virginia Parker, eds., *Causes of Industrial Peace* (New York: Harper & Row, Publishers, 1955), p. 222. This is a valuable compilation of 13 case studies of good management-labor relationships.

5. Help each individual to progress in the company's service.
6. Aid employees in time of need.
7. Encourage thrift.
8. Cooperate in social, athletic, and other recreational activities.
9. Accord to each employee the right to discuss freely with executives any matter concerning his or her welfare or the company's interest.
10. Carry on the daily work in a spirit of friendliness.

Tone-of-voice in policy statements can be almost as important as what is said. The employee will interpret the attitude of management almost as much by the manner in which he is told as by what is provided in a policy. For example, the response to the granting of a privilege can be considerably lessened if the announcement sounds like a threat against anyone who abuses it.

A QUESTION OF LAW

For employers of union workers there is a troublesome legal question of how far management can go in its employee communications without violating the Taft-Hartley Act. This question, not fully resolved, was raised when a Trial Examiner for the National Labor Relations Board found the General Electric Company guilty of unfair labor practices and cited its communications with employees during a bargaining period as evidence. The case is in litigation. This is the background.

Since 1947, General Electric has followed a firm policy *vis-à-vis* its unions, and it has backed this policy with an intensive program of employee communication. The program was formulated largely by L. R. Boulware after he took charge of GE's employee and community relations that year. He later brought PR into his domain. Union critics labeled the program "Boulwarism." GE's stated purposes for this wide-ranging, hard-hitting program is: (1) Integrate and motivate the management team; (2) Develop supervisors as leaders of their people; (3) Build employee confidence in management. An industrial relations writer identifies "Boulwarism" by these characteristics: [8]

1. Management has a tendency to bypass the union and communicate directly with its employees on day-to-day problems.
2. Management attempts to win its employees' allegiance in competition with the union by convincing them that it is sincerely interested in their welfare and is doing its best to promote it.
3. Management follows a policy of firmness in negotiating with the union; for example, giving out a statement of its best and final offer with a deadline for acceptance and a warning that there will be no retroactivity for any later settlement.
4. Management communicates its offers directly to its workers and the public, independently of the union.

---

8 Robert N. McMurry, "War and Peace in Labor Relations," *Harvard Business Review,* Vol. 33, November, 1955, p. 48.

It was the latter that brought a citation for unfair labor practices from Trial Examiner Arthur Leff, who based his ruling on what lawyers call "the totality of conduct" doctrine. Leff found, in part: [9]

> Note has . . . been made of the great mass of employee communications to which GE employees were subjected during the period following the IUE convention, as well as of the apparent purpose of the communications to impair employee faith and confidence in the motives of the IUE top leadership, to induce a form of vote more to the Company's liking, and to impress upon employees the finality of the Company's position and the futility of strike action. . . .
>
> During the same period, the Company in its communications continued to plug hard on the merits of the company offer. The communications did not always confine themselves to arguments that had been presented to union negotiators. In some instances the Company elaborated its arguments far more fully to employees than it had at the bargaining table. In some others, the Company presented arguments to employees that it had not presented at all to the union negotiators. . . .

This ruling raises the tough and vexing question, How far does the employer's right of free speech extend in competing with the union for the allegiance of his employees? Section 8 (c) of the Taft-Hartley law reads: "The expressing of any view, argument, or opinion, or the dissemination thereof, whether in written, printed, graphic or visual form, shall not constitute or be evidence of an unfair labor practice under any of the provisions of this Act, if such expression contains no threat of reprisal or force or promise of benefit." What constitutes "threat of reprisal or force or promise of benefit" will never be an easy question to resolve. Professor Jack Barbash has wisely said, "It is the configuration of factors—the interweaving of the words themselves, the form in which communicated, the quality of the union-management relationship, the character of the community—which determines whether there is promise of reward and threat of reprisal or not." Barbash holds, rightly, that "the circumstances more than the words deserve the weight of consideration" in answering this thorny question.[10]

Resolution of this legal dispute will have an important impact on employee communication. The whole issue raises many questions. One commentator notes: [11] "One key issue is whether a company can take its case to its employees directly. If it cannot, then the whole structure of employee communication changes, for central to this problem is the question of a company's right to tell its workers where it stands on all issues affecting operations: working conditions, pay, profits, job security, management's position on a union's proposal."

Beyond the law, communicators must remember one basic fact: Neither

---

[9] National Labor Relations Board, "General Electric Company and International Union of Electrical, Radio and Machine Workers, AFL-CIO, Cases Nos. 2-CA-7851." Issued by NLRB, April 2, 1963, p. 47.

[10] In "Employer 'Free Speech' and Employee Rights," *Labor Law Journal*, April, 1963, pp. 317-18.

[11] L. L. L. Golden, "What Can You Tell Employees?", *Saturday Review*, Vol. 46, August 10, 1963, p. 50.

management nor unions can sell a bad case with good communication. General Electric is quite correct in asserting that "the public increasingly and properly expects more maturity and responsibility on the part of both management and union representatives in collective bargaining." [12]

COMMUNICATIONS IN PERSPECTIVE

Over the past 20 years, American business has steadily increased its emphasis and expenditure on employee communications. The growth in number, size, and use of these tools is reflective. Too often "communications" are held out as the panacea to cure all the ills, frictions, and aggressions which breed conflict inside organizations. In this period there has been too much communication about communication. Management is quite concerned about its communications. Many companies have created special departments and have launched, periodically, intensive hurry-up campaigns. Most firms have active, large-scale programs. Communication specialists have multiplied. Nonprofit organizations have followed the lead of industry in headlong pursuit of this wonder drug. Millions of man-hours and of dollars are being spent. A lot of these are wasted.

This mounting barrage of employee communication is based on these premises: (1) the need to "re-educate" employees in the values of America's competitive, capitalistic system, on the premise that they have become, somehow, ignorant of or hostile to the system; (2) that there is a correlation between the amount of information a worker has about the company and his attitude toward his company; (3) that there is a correlation between a worker's attitudes, or morale, and his productivity; (4) that employees who know the "facts" will be more reasonable at the bargaining table.

The validity of these premises is open to doubt and will remain so until there has been more *evaluation*. Much of the propagandistic political-social-economic education efforts of management have been shrugged off by workers as irrelevant and irritating propaganda. Industry's massive indoctrination campaign has had something of a benumbing effect on the intended audience. In Peter Drucker's opinion, most of these campaigns have failed because of these *mistaken* assumptions: (1) that employees consider the same things to be important and relevant that management considers relevant and important; (2) that employees are hostile to the free enterprise system.

The second premise is equally questionable. Two researchers who tested the assumption that "good communications bring about high morale" concluded: "There is no significant relationship between employees' attitudes toward their company and their knowledge about the company." [13] Likewise,

---

12 General Electric's *Relations News Letter* for September 21, 1961.
13 Dallis Perry and Thomas A. Mahoney, "In-plant Communications and Employee Morale," *Personnel Psychology*, Vol. 8, Autumn, 1955, p. 339.

there is no firm proof that there is a relationship between worker morale and productivity. Two psychologists, after reviewing research testing this premise over a period of 20 years, concluded: "It is time to question the strategic and ethical merits of selling to industrial concerns an assumed relationship between employee attitudes and employee performance." [14] There is evidence to the contrary in both cases. The fourth one is difficult to test.

The reader should not leap to the conclusion that *all* employee communications programs are wasteful or ineffective. The findings are too fragmentary for that. To the contrary, there is solid evidence of effective employee communications contributing to the successful operation of all kinds of enterprises. Shadows of doubt are cast here to bring the matter into reasonable perspective. For the efforts that have failed, there are two questions: Did it fail in expecting too much of mechanical media? Did it fail in use of the media? The answer to both probably is: in varying degrees.

THE PR MAN'S ROLE

Seldom does the PR function embrace making and executing personnel policies. Exceptions exist. In most organizations, the staff is not *directly* involved in labor negotiations, employee recruitment, promotion, counseling, and training. However, the department has a large stake in productive, pleasant internal relationships. It can contribute much. The PR role in employee relations includes: (1) an over-all concern for the success of the enterprise; (2) the attitudes employees reflect in their role as ambassadors of good or ill will for the firm in their relationships with customers, community, and other publics; (3) responsibility for creating an environment favorable to the personnel, industrial relations function; (4) responsibility for encouraging and implementing two-way communication between managers and men.

Too often the emphasis in employee communications is on "selling" workers. Channels for an *upward flow* of employee opinion must be created and utilized. The employee must have adequate opportunity to tell: (1) what he would like to know about his job, his company, and related matters; and (2) what he would like management to know about himself and the things that are bothering him. The PR man should work to promote an understanding of the employee view inside management. Tactfully and without getting out of channels, he should encourage managers to *listen* to what employees have to say.

The staff can provide skilled assistance by sponsoring employee attitude surveys, promoting use of the suggestion system, putting on "Why I Like My Job" essay contests, providing a Q.-and-A. box in the employee paper, and other means.

---

14 Arthur H. Brayfield and Walter H. Crockett, "Employee Attitudes and Employee Performance," *Psychological Bulletin,* Vol. 52, September, 1955, p. 421.

The practitioner's primary task, as it is usually defined, is to provide persuasive, informative auxiliary communications to support line communication. Employee papers, letters, bulletin boards, and suggestion systems *supplement* but do not *supplant* the working communication system. This task requires skill, tailored tools, and, above all, *good ideas coupled with good timing*. To do this job, the staff must work closely with personnel and/or industrial relations and must be informed on what is taking place on the line. He must know management's employee objectives if he is to promote them effectively.

The competent practitioner can make a substantial contribution to productive employee relationships. One industrial relations writer, George S. Odiorne, sees these benefits in utilizing PR skills in employee communications: [15] (1) Public relations people have a facility with verbalizing and writing; (2) PR people add color, vigor, style, and impact to their messages; (3) the PR section is staffed with people who have creativity and imagination, and these qualities show themselves in the ingenuity and *élan* which go into communicating information; (4) Many personnel people are not specialists in communications, whereas PR people are.

Odiorne also warns against these pitfalls which ensnare some practitioners when they move into employee relations: [16] (1) Failure to develop a clear image of who is "the employee"; (2) The PR department may tread dangerous ground in being too strongly antiunion; (3) Failure to know substance of employee relations; (4) Tendency to indulge in "class" forms of communication and to see management as a class of people rather than an activity which is necessary for the success of everyone in the organization. In short, the benefits which the PR man can bring to employee relations are lost if the expertise is "rooted in inexperience and unrealism."

THE PERSONAL CONTACT IS SUPREME

The basis and framework of any communication program is the line organization.

Procter & Gamble, which has a long record of good employee relations, holds that communications is a matter of having sound policies to pass on to employees and of receiving their reactions through man-to-man communication. At P. & G., employee communications is viewed as a personal function, not a mechanical one. It makes each member of supervision wholly responsible for communications in that portion of the operation assigned

---

15 In "Public Relations and Industrial Relations," *Personnel Journal*, Vol. 38, March, 1960, pp. 366-69.
16 *Ibid.*

to him. To his people at P. & G., each supervisor *is* the company management.[17]

THE FOREMAN

The foreman or supervisor has an increasingly important and difficult position in large organizations. He has counterparts in the top sergeant, the office supervisor, and the ward captain in a charity drive. He has an important role in internal communications, but he must be *trained* for it. The foreman-worker relationship is crucial, for it is here that management's objectives and worker attitudes intersect. Auxiliary communications *must support, not undercut,* that relationship.

In sizable organizations, the people in the offices and shops seldom see the firm's administrative officials and only occasionally see the factory manager or office manager. The foreman and the supervisor have become the first link with management. These two key jobs constitute the counterpart of the factory boss in those days when most shops were small and everybody saw the boss every day. Consequently, foremen and supervisors are objects of strong emotional attitudes.

The custom in modern management is to grant the foreman and supervisory people full membership in the factory managerial team. Common today are foremen-training programs in economics, labor law, and human relations. There has been a marked salary adjustment upward. There is participation in high-level consultation and action groups. Finally, there are social clubs and events bringing foremen into the executive circle. The National Management Association has done much to strengthen the foreman through the formation of Foremen's Clubs and through its PR program.

THE EMPLOYEE
COUNSELOR

Employee counseling is another vehicle for achieving face-to-face communication. Pioneer exploratory work in this field was done at the Hawthorne (Chicago) Western Electric plant. The employee counselor was an outgrowth of Elton Mayo's historic Hawthorne studies of three decades ago which had a profound effect on human relations. Many industrial firms today have counselors whose job it is to hear out employees, to let them get things off their chests privately. Many organizations without a full-scale employee counseling program retain the services of consultants in industrial psychiatry or psychology. In the armed forces, the work performed by the classification

---

[17] See William G. Werner, "Person to Person," *Public Relations Journal,* Vol. 12, April, 1956, pp. 3-5.

sections, the Inspector General's office, and chaplains comprise a counterpart. In education, there are faculty advisers and student counselors. In social work, the caseworker counsels on a personal basis. Counseling provides an effective means of clearing away trouble.

PARTICIPATION IS THE KEY

An ounce of meaningful participation can be worth a ton of pamphlets. Organizations are learning this. There is a consequent shift to group discussions. An affiliate company in the Bell System made a study of its presentation of a rate-increase request to its employees. This affiliate found that *participation-type* meetings were the most effective in getting this complex story to employees. The company's researchers found that "belief and knowledge were best in situations where employees said they had a 'whole lot' of discussion." Straight presentations with little or no discussion were much less effective.

This controlled study followed extensive research on employee attitudes in the parent Bell System by an outside research team. From this, American Telephone & Telegraph learned that: (1) When people get a lot of satisfaction out of their work, they reflect their feelings to outsiders, and they are more effective on the job; (2) Often important information fails to reach an employee because of employees' *lack of interest* or *lack of involvement;* (3) Employees want an opportunity to ask questions and express their ideas in small meetings.[18] Out of this has come Bell's program of regular work-group meetings.

Situations in which employees can fully participate can: (1) provide means of two-way communication, including feedback of employee questions, mistaken notions, and so forth; (2) provide individuals with means of self-expression and tap the creative ideas latent in any group; (3) uncover opposition and obstacles to plans before they are put into effect; (4) encourage a sense of responsibility for the decisions made and thus pave the way for change. There is a price to be paid for these returns; the employees' views must be heard and given due weight. *Participation cannot be just a sounding-board operation.*

An aircraft manufacturer was losing large sums because 53 per cent of its daily production of fins for jet motors was being rejected. In the motors then in production, there were 9,000 fins costing $50 each in each motor. A 53 per cent rejection rate was appalling. The company put on a hurry-up campaign of communications and exhortations to cut this waste. Rejections declined slightly. Desperate, the firm brought supervisors and men together

---

18 John W. Cogswell, "Telephone Employees and Public Relations," *Bell Telephone Magazine,* Spring, 1955.

to decide how the problem could be licked. When solving the problem became a cooperative effort, the acceptance rate went up. Eventually it reached an acceptance of 89 per cent. The savings added up to $300,000 in one year!

People's resistance to change poses tough problems. Textile firms have to make frequent changes in designs and products, and thus in jobs. The Harwood Manufacturing Company learned from its records that, after a change in operations, 38 per cent of the operators recovered their standard rate of production. The other 62 per cent became chronically substandard or quit. It made a controlled study using two groups. The group which was given *total participation* in planning and effecting the change was back to pre-change efficiency in 14 days. Then it progressed to a production rate 14 per cent above the former one. Members of the nonparticipating control group dropped off in production about 20 per cent and improved little beyond their early efficiency ratings.

Opposition to incentive systems is often a tough nut to crack. One firm cut through the fear of the "speed-up" and succeeded, after years of vain attempts. It did it by sharing savings with employees and by permitting full participation in working out the plan.

There are many ways of strengthening the line organization through group participation. This includes self-administered activities: music groups, parties, sports teams, outings, hobby clubs, credit unions, or contests. Selection of such activities, weighing one against the other, is of secondary importance. Final selection will, by and large, reflect the interests of the spark plugs in the organization.

Suggestion systems and various kinds of awards for safety, good housekeeping, and length of service comprise a form of participation. The PR aspect is to bring winners into the limelight. Usually, awards are made on a special occasion in the presence of many associates. If not that, the house publication or the local newspaper calls appropriate attention to the individual honored. Suggestion systems, to work, must be *promoted*. They won't function on their own power. Some personnel men argue that the use of a suggestion system indicates a weakness in line communications. But many firms use this device effectively even though it is expensive.

Participation of employee representatives in the actual conduct of management-level affairs, although outside the PR orbit, is another vehicle. This area, long considered sacrosanct, has had some test invasions. Committees without power are common. Student councils to talk about their own problems are common. But the most provocative development in industrial relations in employee-management participation is the Scanlon Plan, named for its author.[19] The core of the plan is a joint union-management productivity proposition through which union members get bonuses for tangible savings in labor costs. Its supporters hold that the Scanlon Plan's success is

---

[19] For details on Scanlon Plan, see "Enterprise for Everyman," *Fortune,* Vol. 41, January, 1950, p. 55.

due to the fact that workers participate in the real thing. *Participation must be used with sincerity and not as a manipulative device.*

OTHER AUXILIARIES
TO THE LINE
COMMUNICATION

Employed with skill and in place, other *auxiliary* tools of employee communication contribute much. Use of the auxiliaries must be coordinated. One must reinforce the others. Their content must be beamed on specific objectives. For industry, Professor Wayne Hodges sets these over-all goals:

1. To promote unity, as defined by a sense of identity, of common purpose, of common loyalty, and of common benefit under the enterprise system.

2. To promote an understanding of management's problems, needs, duties, obligations, principles, and practices—and faith in the goodwill behind all these.

3. To maintain an atmosphere and a means conducive to genuine two-way communication.

4. To provide a permanent company record of actions and affairs not legally documented.

5. To inform employees concerning the role of their company and of themselves in community affairs.

Among the auxiliary tools of internal communication are:

House Publications	Pay Enclosures
Bulletins, Handbooks	Bulletin Boards
Letters	Surveys, Polls, Contests
Information Racks	Special Events

Contrary to the opinions of some, *tangible* results can be and are accomplished with these tools. Take these examples:

In a 1,300-man cellophane plant, a study indicated that power consumption could be substantially reduced. Management used the employee paper to spearhead a plant-wide power-savings program. Suggestions from employees were invited. The number of employee suggestions was double the number in the same quarter the year before. Management gave the paper most of the credit for resulting power savings, estimated at $100,000 a year.

New York Central's *Headlight* promoted a "weight marathon" to encourage employees to double-check freight weights to insure against losses in railroad revenues. In one year the railroad collected on an additional 770,312 pounds of freight because of this drive in the employee publication.

In a 3,000-man chemicals plant, when steps were taken to modernize a routine process, rumors began to fly to the effect that this conversion would result in wholesale layoffs. The full story was put before employees through the plant paper. Supervisors reported that rumors and speculation abated rapidly once the story was published.

The Standard Register Co. uses regular mailings to employee families to guide them in building financial security. One mailing offered a booklet, "How to Avoid Financial Tangles," at a discount price. Seventy per cent of the employees bought this booklet after getting the offer in the mail.

In another plant, supervisors reported to management a common problem, grumblings by employees that the cafeteria prices were too high. The company was making money. An illustrated story gave a complete breakdown of cafeteria costs. It showed that the firm was paying out $1.02 for every $1 taken in. The complaints disappeared in short order, supervisors reported.

Thomas J. Lipton, Inc. used its 3,500-circulation, semimonthly newspaper to improve the safety record of its car-fleet salesmen and other employees. The fleet accident rate went down, though the fleet grew 26 per cent and mileage increased 52 per cent. The insurance rates went down, too!

Examples could be multiplied many-fold. In using these tools, the practitioner should strive to keep the content *employee-centered*. It should be related to such specific goals as increased productivity, full use of fringe benefits, reduction of waste, reduction of accidents, reduction of absenteeism, elimination of misinformation and rumors, encouragement of employees to be *informed* ambassadors.

SOME OTHER HINTS

The audience of a house publication should be checked periodically by survey to see what material is being read or bypassed, what new problems may be puzzling readers, and, in general, how well the publication is doing its job.

Most people like to answer questions. Readers will rarely feel offended by surveys or polls. In fact, they are more likely to be flattered by the attention. In making surveys useful for house-publication editing, questions can reach far afield from the content of the publication. Questions about the cost of living, the housing situation, and community welfare are not out of order. The replies give guidance in writing that provides a service.

Letters to employees' homes should be personalized. If the circulation is so large that they must be printed, then by all means there should be the signature of an individual rather than an organization.

Bulletin-board space should be used as though it cost money. In a factory, space taken up by a note that says "Tillie, meet me at Joe's Saloon at five o'clock. . . . Sam" is not used to the best possible advantage of the employer and all employees. In an Army Camp, bulletin-board space used for the twenty-second or thirty-fourth verse of poetry about somebody's exploits on a furlough does not serve the over-all interests of military life nearly so well as notices about athletic programs. Bulletin-board material should be brief. It should be changed frequently. It should be timely and should employ illustration.

Handbooks, annual reports for employees, and other booklets should have the tone of voice that management wants with its people. An excellent way to handle preparation of this literature is to form an employee editorial board.

The use of enclosures with pay checks is an underdeveloped tool. The audience is probably in a receptive frame of mind, and the cost of including a message is very small.

Above all else, remember this: *Employees should neither be overlooked in disseminating information nor should they be overloaded with information.*

Additional Reading

American Management Association, *Building a Balanced Communications Program.* New York: AMA, 1954. (General Management Series 170.)

M. J. Dooher and Vivienne Marquis, eds., *Effective Communication on the Job.* New York: American Management Association, 1956.

C. J. Dover, "The Three Eras of Management Communication," *The Journal of Communication,* Vol. 9, December, 1959.

Robert Newcomb and Marge Sammons, *Employee Communications in Action.* New York: Harper & Row, Publishers, 1961.

Paul Pigors, *Effective Communication in Industry.* New York: National Association of Manufacturers, 1949.

Douglas McGregor, *The Human Side of Enterprise.* New York: McGraw Hill Book Co., 1960. Presents the Scanlon Plan.

Willard V. Merrihue, *Managing by Communication.* New York: McGraw Hill Book Co., 1960.

Charles E. Redfield, *Communication in Management: The Theory and Practice of Administrative Communication,* rev. ed. Chicago: University of Chicago Press, 1958.

Harriet O. Ronken, "Communication in the Work Group," *Harvard Business Review,* Vol. 29, July, 1951.

Perrin Stryker, "A Slight Case of Overcommunication," *Fortune,* Vol. 49, March, 1954.

CASE PROBLEM

You are employed on the PR staff of Jones & Jones, makers of children's toys. The firm employs 2,000 persons, about 75 per cent of whom are women. Most employees ended their formal education in high school. The work is fast and tiring, but not heavy. Because of growth, the firm has decided to move from the downtown congestion in Your City to a suburb 15 miles away. The new location will require additional travel but will afford easy parking. Many employees don't have cars. Assume that employees will resent the change. You are given the task of working out an announcement program that will "sell" the employees, the community, and the nearly 1,000 stockholders, mostly in Your City, on the move.

Draft a detailed plan, including themes, timetable, and so forth, for making this announcement which you can submit to the PR director, who, in turn, will submit it to top management.

Chapter Fourteen

THE

STOCKHOLDER

PUBLIC

A company's best interests are served by managements that supply shareholders with complete, current information during bad times as well as good.

The emergence of the stockholder— or shareholder or shareowner, as some industrialists prefer to call him—as a prime PR target was dramatized in the epic battle for control of the New York Central Railroad some years ago. In sharp contrast to the day of the nineteenth century when Commodore Vanderbilt gained control of NYC by bluff, tricks, and threats, the modern NYC battle was mainly a struggle by opposing public relations staffs. This battle was waged in the arena of public opinion, with news releases, paid ads, letters to stockholders, use of proxy solicitors, and similar tools.[1]

Where he was once given little or no attention beyond the payment of dividends, today the stockholder is courted for his investment money, his votes, his ideas, and his patronage as a consumer. Stockholder relations has become an important aspect of corporate public relations. The shareowner insists upon it. One corporate executive says: "Many managements had to be literally knocked on the head by violent, widely publicized proxy fights for the control of valuable industrial and commercial properties to become aware of the importance and power of the shareowner."[2]

Not too many years ago, the president of a firm told a stockholder

---

[1] For overview of several spectacular battles in the mid-1950s, see Charles M. Williams, "Stockholders' Rebellion," *Harvard Business Review*, Vol. 33, July-August, 1955, p. 21. For a novel based on the fight for control of Montgomery Ward, see *The Man Who Broke Things*, by John Brooks.

[2] Emery Cleaves, "Good Stockholder Relations—The New Order of Business," *Public Relations Journal*, Vol. 11, October, 1955, p. 28.

intrepid enough to inquire what the company made in its plant, "We make money in it!" Today his son who succeeded him says, "We're going to tell the stockholders everything we can about Scovill." Gone is the day when Standard Oil's John D. Archbold would say, "Private corporations should not be required to make public items of receipts and expenditures, profits and losses." Today's corporate leader observes: "To gain the favorable opinion of those whose money finances our businesses, management now makes an effort of which it would never have dreamed a generation ago."

Closely allied programs are directed to the small but vital public of 30,000 men and women in the securities business. These twin programs are often combined under "financial public relations." The purposes of a soundly conceived financial program are: (1) to achieve and maintain a fair evaluation of the company's securities in the market place; (2) to provide well-priced share-money; (3) to meet competition in the nationwide financial community; (4) to prevent misunderstandings and maintain the loyalty of both share-owners and financial opinion leaders.[3]

Financial public relations has been one of PR's growth areas in corporate practice. A PR counseling firm lists these reasons: (1) Nearly 50,000 publicly owned corporations are bidding for the attention of the investor through newspapers, financial publications, and security analysts; (2) Few daily newspapers carry more than one page of financial news, thus making the battle for space an intensive one, with the nonlocal corporation at a disadvantage; (3) The same 50,000 companies compete for the time and favor of the security analyst, whose decisions are crucial in the investor's choice of stock to buy; (4) The average analyst covers a minimum of 350 companies, and his required research leaves little time for attention to messages of other firms; (5) Nearly 50,000 companies issue SEC-required annual reports, which flood in upon potential investors and analysts with little chance of getting read.

INDUSTRY'S NEW OWNERSHIP

There are nearly twenty million stockholders in this country, more than double the number of a decade ago. The number is steadily increasing as American business strives to broaden its ownership and as the adult population grows. In 1962 17,010,000 persons owned shares in 6,300 companies. This total represents a fantastic increase over the total of 6,490,000 shareowners counted in the first survey in 1952. Much of this growth is due to the spread of investment clubs. The New York Stock Exchange has spearheaded this effort with a large-scale program aimed at building wide public understanding of stock ownership. The Exchange program has been reinforced by the

---

3 Harold M. Gartley, "Financial Public Relations," *Public Relations Journal,* Vol. 13, April, 1957, p. 3.

large brokerage houses in their advertising and public relations programs. Industry woos the stockholder and the potential stockholder in order to: (1) get needed expansion capital; (2) give more people a stake in business' well-being; (3) gain the part-owner as a customer and as an ambassador of goodwill.

The growing number of stockholders gives substance to "people's capitalism," which we use to describe our economic system. The small stockholder, once brusquely treated, today is the object of much PR effort. This growing army of stockholders includes an increasing number of employees. Many firms have programs which permit and encourage employees to buy their company's stock. Industrialists are divided on the merit of such plans.

These million owners of industry cannot be picked out of a crowd. They do not look alike, act alike, or dress alike. They are not unified in their opinions. The only thing that a group of 500 stockholders has in common is an interest in the affairs of the company in which they have stock. With little likeness among stockholders, effective contact with them takes on some of the aspects of communicating with the general public. Still, there is that one common bond of interest. In that sense, they are intimately involved with their firm's success or failure. Effective contact has a *potentially* intimate aspect to it.

The financial security of a corporation—indeed, the job security of its management—is in the hands of the shareholders. If management fails to deliver a return on invested funds, the investment may be withdrawn. Or if stockholders become dissatisfied with management, they may turn the managers out. This latent power of the stockholder is occasionally dramatized in spectacular publicly fought battles for stockholders' proxies. Management must have the confidence of stockholders in order to move ahead with its plans for the enterprise. However, the power of the stockholder in the American business system can be vastly overrated. Only on rare occasions does his vote really count, as Adolf Berle has made abundantly clear. But Berle adds: [4] "Nevertheless, the body of shareholders having votes do at least assent that the power of the corporate institution shall be, or continue to be, vested in these particular men; and they do have a clear interest in the process." The important shareholders are the holders of large funds—such as insurance companies, pension trusts, and so forth.

The average stockholder probably owns less than a hundred shares of stock in any company. Fifty shares of stock give him as much personal interest in the welfare of his money as would 5,000 shares. Yet he has appeared apathetic in proving his interest. He doesn't always bother to answer proxies, seldom shows up at the annual meeting, and sometimes doesn't even peep when a dividend is passed. This is not true apathy. It's simply that the small stockholder feels his voice is a faint one and that he's not an expert in the

---

[4] *Power Without Property* (New York: Harcourt, Brace & World, Inc., 1959), p. 105. A realistic appraisal of the stockholder's role.

business in which he has invested. He is barely able to make sense of the accountant's language in the annual report, and he's busy earning a living.

Still, there is a lot of evidence that the stockholder would like a better liaison between himself and "his" company. Survey after survey shows that. This has also been underscored in rather dramatic fashion by the sympathetic kinship many stockholders have for Lewis D. Gilbert. Gilbert has become the champion of the small stockholder, and since 1933 he has been showing up regularly at annual meetings to pose tough questions for management.[5]

Considered a nuisance at first by nearly all business officials, Gilbert's "sin" has become a "virtue" to many of them. He has given guidance to management in detecting blind spots of information and revealing complaints. He has provided management justification to undertake a more aggressive approach to good relationships. The Gilbert crusade has attracted followers. A PR counsel, Mrs. Wilma Soss, organized the Federation of Women Shareholders. (More than 50 per cent of shareowners are women.) Once she appeared at the annual meeting of U.S. Steel dressed in a Gay Nineties costume to satirize that firm's antiquated custom of holding its meetings in out-of-the-way Hoboken, N.J. Gilbert issues an annual report of "Stockholders' Activities at Corporation Meetings" which catalogs stockholder complaints.[6]

Plain John Q. Shareholder is also speaking out at the annual meeting. This is "when the boss has to step out from behind his cordon of secretaries and offer himself up at the annual stockholders' meeting as the main course in the year's first barbecue," as *Time* exaggeratedly put it. A woman asks the president of Texaco, Inc., why he doesn't fight harder to preserve the oil industry's depletion tax allowance. A man asks the president of IBM why the company is enlarging its collection of early scientific models instead of paintings. The trend is for the annual meeting to be more accessible, more businesslike. More and more security analysts attend.

ADMINISTRATION OF
STOCKHOLDER RELATIONS

Policies relating to stockholder relations are the province of top management. Sometimes there is a committee with board members and officers taking part. Responsibility for execution and implementation of policies follows a normal course of delegation. Quite often there is a division of responsibilities among the firm's secretary, the treasurer, and the public relations man.

Administration and execution naturally vary widely, depending on the size of the firm's stockholder roster. In small companies, policymaking is not often a very formal process. Perhaps it is no more than a discussion between

---

[5] See John Bainbridge, "Profile—The Talking Stockholder," *The New Yorker*, Vol. 24, December 11 and December 18, 1948.

[6] Published annually by Lewis D. and John J. Gilbert, 1165 Park Avenue, New York 28, New York.

the secretary and the president. Execution could be simply the actions of someone in the president's office or the advertising department to handle matters agreed on by the president and secretary.

In any event, the handling of stockholder relations necessarily involves several people. The president may sign welcoming letters to new stockholders —letters possibly written by a public relations man based on information supplied by the firm's secretary. The annual report may contain a message written by the president and containing financial data compiled under supervision of the treasurer. In the report may be photographs and promotional copy devised by the advertising department. Along with it might be a questionnaire developed in the PR department. Press releases might be handled by an outside counsel. Still another outside firm might undertake to round up proxies on an important issue.

THE GOALS

Regardless of who does what in stockholder relations, everybody will be trying to bolster faith in the performance of the company. Before stockholders can respond, they have to be fortified with full information of what's going on inside the company. They have to know that their interests are protected. The geographical and occupational gaps have to be spanned by more than a regularity of dividend checks. Stockholders in large corporations should be encouraged to feel that they are close to the company, that their voices count.

These goals have been recognized for years by a great many managements. Good stockholder relations, wherever they exist, are jealously maintained. The important realization is that there can be no relaxing in the future. The satisfied stockholder is an asset. Why? Because he says nice things about the company. He buys its products or services. He tells his friends they ought to buy them. He tells them to invest in the firm. In short, he's a sandwich man for the firm. On the grand scale, he is one public body with every reason to understand and to support the free competitive system of enterprise. Stockholders can be a source of ideas, too. For example, the Glidden Co. marketed a stick shortening which was first suggested by a woman stockholder.

USING THE TOOLS

The first direct contact which management can establish with a stockholder is at the time the stock purchase is made. A *letter of welcome* from a top official serves to invite a rapport. The letter can enclose a copy of the most recent financial report or a booklet telling the history of the firm. It can offer to supply any information wanted personally, issue an invitation to visit the firm's offices or factories, pave the way for a sample product sent separately, submit a questionnaire, or merely extend a polite and friendly word of welcome.

The keystone of any program is the *annual report*—the report card of business. This tool has grown to large dimensions and has been brought to a high degree of technical excellence. Much of this is due to the public relations emphasis in business. Some of the credit belongs to *Financial World,* which has stimulated improvement through its yearly survey and annual "Bronze Oscar of Industry" awards for the best reports. Despite the improvements in readability and graphic presentations, nagging doubts remain about the typical corporate report's effectiveness. One practitioner says: [7] "But for all the cost, and for all the earnest endeavors of those who wrote, edited, and approved these publications, and for all the importance of the subject matter, nobody—or almost nobody—will read them."

A comprehensive study made some years ago by the then Controllers Institute is even more discouraging. It found: ". . . when it comes to reading financial tables and forming his own conclusions about the soundness and prosperity of the company in which he owns stock, the typical stockholder loses interest—and his bearings!" The Institute report elaborated: "He (the stockholder) is oppressed by the complexity of financial data and frightened by what seems to him the incomprehensibility of accounting language." [8] The *Wall Street Journal* asserted a few years ago that stockholders find annual reports "a confusing jumble." One *Opinion Research Corporation* survey found that some 37 of every 100 stockholders do not even try to read them. There undoubtedly would be vehement stockholder protest if corporations did not issue annual reports that were both accurate and attractive in format. The fact is that the diversity and technological complexity of today's corporation are difficult to explain in simple terms.

Historically, the first annual report was published by the Borden Company in 1858 at the end of its first year of business. In 1903 U.S. Steel "rocked the caverns of corporate secrecy" when it published the first modern, informative annual report for its 1902 year. Judge Elbert Gary's trail-blazing was heatedly criticized by his fellow directors and by corporate officials who thought it was risky to take stockholders into management's confidence. All this is changed now. The annual report has become an important project for most firms over the past 20 years. It is required by law and by stockholder demand.[9]

Here are some hints for preparing the annual report. It ought to include: a distinctive cover design to attract interest and reflect corporate character; a brief executive summary at the beginning; a table of contents; identification

---

[7] Reynolds Girdler, "18,000,000 Books Nobody Reads," *Saturday Review,* Vol. 46, April 13, 1963, p. 71. At the time, Girdler was vice-president for public relations and advertising of Sinclair Oil Corp.

[8] Quoted in the Girdler article.

[9] For interesting reading on annual reports, see John Brooks, "From Dance Cards to the Ivy League Look," *The New Yorker,* Vol. 33, May 18, 1957, pp. 74 ff.

of managers; a narrative review of the year told in terms of specifics with pictures and charts to illustrate it; a breakdown of the sales dollar; comparative operating and financial statistics tabulated over a 10-year span; information on owners of the company and employees—who they are, what kind of work they do, how they fare with the company; the firm's advertising and public relations programs; future growth, plans, and prospects; and an audited statement of income, financial condition, and number of stockholders. The effective report is:

1. WRITTEN IN READABLE MANNER. "Readable" means putting accounting language into lay terms and symbols. The ability of others to comprehend can be judged by the practitioner's own ability when it comes to accounting terms. How exciting is it to read about depreciation, depletion, amortization, lower of cost or market, unconsolidated subsidiary, and sinking fund? One widely accepted way of simplifying the reading problem is the Functional Operating Statement.

2. ATTRACTIVE. The use of illustrations, graphs, personalities, and color merits careful consideration. The extent to which this material can be applied will depend in part on the amount of circulation and in part on the nature of the firm's products and services.

Certainly a small mailing list of 1,000 persons might make it impractical to put out a four-color, 32-page, slick paper booklet, particularly if the company's products are steamboat whistles. Conversely, a homespun, two-sheet, multilith, one-color report to 15,000 stockholders of a firm making home appliances might be ill-advised. In this case, the 15,000 stockholders would be potential customers.

3. FRIENDLY. An annual report does not make common sense when it talks in stilted terms or vagaries, or when its appearance and format stand aloof from its audience. After all, it is the management's report to its bosses. The way to help the bosses approve of the report—apart from showing a good result for the year—is to put a smile on the face of management. Without that, the bosses are likely to think that the business is being managed with no more personality than runs through the pages of the report.

Some firms have published their annual reports as paid ads and as special supplements in daily newspapers. Most promote dissemination of the report and its highlights through annual report advertising.

In a study of 217 companies, the National Industrial Conference Board found that some 60 per cent issued *interim reports*. Interim reports usually take the form of letters signed by the president or board chairman. Letters bring the progress of the company up to date since the last report. Quite often topics involve events of a newsworthy nature, such as a labor stoppage; or they deal with materials problems, expansion plans in gestation, new-product introductions, changes in top-level personnel, or the situation in relation to the over-all economy. *Readership of interim reports is high.* They are generally brief. They have an air of news or urgency about them.

There is correspondence with stockholders to be handled. Some people submit thoughtful suggestions or make sincere inquiries about products, sales, processes, or research. Some others ask child-like questions about the current market price of the stock, the number of shares they own, the total number owned by people whose first name is John, or by people over fifty. Some are chronic gripers.

Among the specifics that stockholders are most likely to complain about, the N.I.C.B. study listed eight.

1. High executive salaries
2. Pension plans for executives
3. Ownership of stock by management
4. Cumulative voting
5. Women directors
6. Selection of public accountants
7. Size of dividends
8. Discounts on products

Responses from stockholders can function as a splendid communications tool. The responsive letters have the great charm of being personal. Each one gives a stockholder an intimate contact with the company and an actual participation in its affairs. Perhaps it is this aspect that causes so many corporation presidents to handle personally the responses to stockholder letters.

Shareholder meetings are the means of contact expected to enjoy the greatest amount of experimentation and refinement in the future. Meetings have that undeniable value of face-to-face encounter in which personality, voice, fact, kinship, and compromise all lend significance.

Large turnouts for annual stockholder meetings do not occur often, but attendance is increasing. Stockholders are scattered through the 50 states and beyond. The expense of attendance is disproportionate to the average stockholder's investment.

Some measure of the distance problem has been alleviated by the issuance of post-meeting reports. These take the form of meeting minutes, an informal letter from the president or board chairman, or a question-and-answer résumé. A few firms, notably General Mills and General Electric, have undertaken a solution of the problem with regional meetings. They have taken management to the population-hub areas where many can attend conveniently. Still other companies have sent representatives to call on selected stockholders, financial analysts, investment counselors, trust officers, and business-page editors. Western Union, with offices everywhere, has had an extensive program of personal calls on shareowners by local company representatives.

The *Wall Street Journal* has reported these complaints from stockholder meetings. After some years one firm cut out the custom of serving light lunches because stockholders complained loudly about the expense, yet other companies have been criticized because they did not serve lunches "like other companies." At one firm's meeting, stockholders complained about lack of samples and raided displays around the meeting room. Another firm's meeting overflowed the meeting room, and loudspeakers were provided to anterooms, but there were no microphones for these stockholders to use in asking questions. At an electric company's meeting, the film projector caused a short and lights in the building went out—ironical in this context. Another firm planned to give plastic ice buckets to shareowners attending its annual meeting—but grossly underestimated the number who would attend and was painfully caught short. Stockholder meetings, like any other, must be carefully *planned*.

A good minority of the larger corporations have put out special publications for stockholders. Extremely satisfactory results have been reported. *Stockholder publications* fall into three broad groupings. Some are issued regularly with somewhat the same continuity of format and content as employee house publications. Others are issued spasmodically, in booklet form, to point up some specific body of information bearing on the relationship between stockholder and the company. Then there are publications prepared for employees, dealers, or other groups which are circulated among stockholders on the premise that they, too, would be interested.

The stockholder as a potential customer has been mentioned earlier. Among the specific tools harnessed to the task of persuading purchase of products are samples, discounts, sales-promotional literature, and special packages or services. The American Chicle Company gives an assortment of its chewing gum to stockholders at Christmas. General Mills makes a special food assortment available at a special price. The Scott Paper Company and Ray-O-Vac welcome new stockholders with a sample.

The latch is always out for stockholders. Principal occasions are anniversaries and the opening of new or remodeled facilities. There need be no special occasion, however. More important is the need for a warm little red carpet to be rolled out whenever a stockholder does turn up. Planning for such visitors should include a handshake with a top official, an opportunity to get thoughtful questions answered by qualified specialists, a tour of installations, and a fitting souvenir of the visit. The open house is sometimes used.

Assuming that the receipt of a dividend is a happy contact with a shareholder, many companies use *dividend enclosures* to get in a sales pitch. That is not the outside limit of subject matter for enclosures. There is plenty of room for imagination. Enclosures offer a suitable medium for a series of messages devoted to the inseparability of free enterprise and popular government, for a one-by-one exhibition of products, for photographic likenesses of management people, for branch plant or departmental operations, and a host of others.

THE FINANCIAL
FRATERNITY

A survey of the Ferro Company showed that more than 50 per cent of the company's stockholders relied on the recommendation of someone in the financial community in deciding to purchase their stock.

This is typical. It explains in considerable measure why large corporations court the bankers, brokers, and security analysts. A prevalent approach, beyond those discussed above, is the appearance of corporate officials before regional groups of the National Federation of Financial Analysts Society and Investment Clubs. The PR staff man is frequently called on to prepare the material for presentation.

William G. Maas, president, Investment Analysts Society of Chicago, in a talk before the Chicago Chapter PRSA, gave these *do's* and *don't's* in such presentations.

Among the Things to Avoid Were:
 Long corporate history
 Rehash of annual report
 Enumeration of plants and properties
 Industry statistics
 Flag waving about free enterprise
 Sales talks

Among the Subjects That Should Be Discussed:
 Current sales
 Interim statement
 Sales breakdowns by divisions, types of operations, and customer classifications
 New products and their potentialities
 Plant expansion and modernization
 Management
 Existing problems
 Forecasts

A NOTE OF CAUTION

In financial public relations, the practitioner must be mindful of the regulations of the Securities and Exchange Commission which impose specific prohibitions upon persons involved in the sale of securities. These regulations are explained in S. E. C.'s Release No. 3844, October, 1957, entitled "Publication of Information Prior To or After the Effective Date of a Registration Statement." A practitioner, interpreting this S.E.C. regulation, makes these points: [10]

 1. The publication of information and statements, and publicity efforts, generally, made in advance of a proposed financing, although not couched in terms of an express offer, may in fact contribute to conditioning the public mind, or arousing public interest in the issuer, or in the securities of an issuer in a manner which raises a serious question whether the publicity is not in fact part of the selling effort.
 2. The release of publicity and publication of information between the filing date and the effective date of a registration statement may similarly raise a ques-

---

[10] Robert D. Eckhouse, "How Does It Look to the SEC?", *Public Relations Journal*, Vol. 15, May, 1959.

tion whether the publicity is not in fact a selling effort by an illegal means: that is, other than by means of a statutory prospectus.

3. A collateral problem is presented by the fact that the dissemination of information, other than that contained in a prospectus, prior to or during a distribution may tend to affect the market price of the issuer's securities artificially.

4. Information of a misleading character, gross exaggeration, and outright falsehood have been published to stimulate an appetite for securities, which could not have been included in a statutory prospectus.

5. Many previous cases in which PR practitioners have been questioned reflect an unawareness of the problems involved or a failure to exercise a proper control over research and public relations activities in relation to the distribution of an issue of securities.

Because of abuses by a few practitioners, the Public Relations Society of America, acting at its 1963 convention, tightened the PRSA Code with reference to financial publicity. That same year PRSA's president urged the S.E.C. to amend its regulations to prohibit public relations agents from trading upon "inside" knowledge.

Additional Reading

Anonymous, "SEC Reports on Public Relations' Impact on Securities Markets and Public Investors," *Public Relations Journal,* Vol. 19, June, 1963.

Corliss D. Anderson, *Corporate Reporting for the Professional Investor.* Auburndale, Mass.: Financial Analysts Federation, 1962.

Herman S. Hettinger, *Financial Public Relations for the Business Corporation.* New York: Harper & Row, Publishers, 1954.

Elizabeth Marting, ed., *A Company Guide to Effective Stockholder Relations.* New York: American Management Association, 1953.

Clayton S. Scott, Jr., and Frederick N. Robinson, "A Positive Approach to Annual Meetings," *Public Relations Journal,* Vol. 15, April, 1959.

Hal D. Steward, "A Sound Stockholders Program," *Public Utilities Fortnightly,* Vol. 59, March 14, 1957.

T. C. Thomsen, "The Care and Feeding of Financial Analysts by Public Relations People and Vice Versa," *Public Relations Journal,* Vol. 14, October, 1958.

CASE PROBLEM

The Ajax Company, for many years a producer of industrial hand tools, has undergone diversification in separate divisions producing power tools, children's toys, and metal kitchenware. The diversification, in five years' time, has increased sales from $6 million annually to $40 million. The stock is closely held by less than 1,000 persons. Management would like to broaden the stock ownership. Plan a program to achieve this, using whatever vehicles in this chapter seem best suited. Keep the costs of your program in mind, and justify them.

Chapter Fifteen

THE

COMMUNITY

PUBLICS

Community relationships—inescapable for industries or institutions—are a something-for-something proposition.

Community relations work runs the gamut of problems and opportunities. It is here that many practitioners find their most challenging and most satisfying work. Community relationships—inescapable for industries or institutions—provide a composite of public relations in capsule form. These are the tenets.

1. There is *increasing interdependency* of organizations upon the cooperation and esteem of many people, either in groups or as individuals. This works both ways. An industry, for example, cannot prosper without manpower, adequate municipal services, and freedom from strangling regulation. A community cannot live and grow without industries to provide expanding opportunities for its people. Ask the utility firm which has lost its municipal franchise! Ask businessmen in a community which has lost its biggest payroll!

2. The *continuous, interacting flow of the opinion process* starts at the top of an organization and flows downward through the ranks and then out into the community. A firm cannot have rewarding community relationships without healthy employee relations. Workers reflect community attitudes on the job and reflect job attitudes in the community where they live and play: one role reacts on the other. The "whole man" goes to work each day and returns home each night.

For example, in the study of industrial peace between the Nashua Corporation, Nashua, New Hampshire and its workers, observers found a close correlation between community attitudes and attitudes of employees toward the firm. This com-

251

pany provided steady employment and high wages. Its workers were telling their friends: "They don't keep after you all of the time if you mind your own business." Or "They have a good union. The place is run by good management. My friends say if you stay there, there are chances to get ahead." This reputation gives "the Card Shop," as it is known locally, "the cream of the labor market" in the opinion of its employment manager.[1]

3. A positive effort to build favorable community relationships is not *do-goodism*. It is a profitable investment of the money and time it takes. Community relations is a *something-for-something* proposition, a calculated casting of bread upon the waters.

The community provides a plant with good employees, fair political weather, transportation facilities, housing for its employees, schools for their children, churches for their worship, health and hospital facilities, recreational and cultural facilities—a good community in which to work and live. In a tight manpower market, the community is often the decisive factor in job choice.

In turn, the community expects that the business will provide people with good jobs at good wages, pay fair taxes, make local purchases, contribute to worthwhile causes, take leadership in community affairs, and behave as good neighbors.

The same things could be said for a university, an Army post, or an Air Force base. In the year 1956, the University of Wisconsin dedicated a $1,500,000 sports building as a memorial to veterans of the Civil War! This was done to mute the aroused protests of the Sons of the G.A.R., a small organization, and a few Civil War buffs who argued that erection of the building on a Civil War campsite was a desecration of hallowed ground. In this day of the jet plane, the Air Force and commercial airlines have more than their share of community relations problems.

4. Sound relationships are not built upon gifts, gimmicks, or publicity alone. Good relationships are the product of *responsible community citizenship adequately publicized*. Elmo Roper found in a survey of community attitudes toward the "best" company in Terre Haute, Indiana, that: "The 'best' company in Terre Haute actually turned out not to pay the highest wages or to build the most playgrounds, but it did create the greatest number of opportunities and, therefore, 'did most for the town.' " This firm made its mark as a good employer "by paying good wages, by keeping management accessible to the workers so that grievances don't fester, and . . . by being an expanding, going concern that provides opportunities for jobs and advancement—and *letting everybody know it*."

In what he admits is an oversimplification, Wayne Hodges says that there are two schools of industrial community relations: [2] (1) the "community-centered" or personal service school in which company presidents, and hence

---

[1] Golden and Parker, *Causes of Industrial Peace,* Harper & Row, Publishers, 1955, p.190.
[2] In *Company and Community* (New York: Harper & Row, Publishers, 1958), p. 42. This is a useful book with illuminating case studies in industry-city relationships in Syracuse, New York.

their administrative staffs, assume great responsibility for the development of the city and its institutions; (2) the "company-centered" school, concentrating exclusively on education of citizens in "basic economics" and on the use of public relations techniques to develop community attitudes favorable to the profitable operation of business and industry. As Hodges notes, "Each school holds vague reservations about the other." Few organizations today, profit or nonprofit, embrace the idea of isolation from the community.

THE MAKE-UP OF COMMUNITY OPINION

The local community is a miniature of the entire public. An organization has in its own hometown a panel or jury whose judgments predict the opinions and interests of the national spectator. *This is where national opinions are born.* An apt definition of the community in terms of its motivation has been provided by Dwight Sanderson. "The community includes not only individual persons but the organizations and institutions in which they associate. The real community is the devotion to common interests and purposes, the ability to act together in the chief concerns of life."

Today community life is organized along the lines of interest groupings, whether the interest is in lower taxes, higher wages, a new civic auditorium, attraction of industry, cultural facilities, or whatever. These groupings come and go, shift and overlap. Each community is different and ever-changing. This calls for constant cataloging of the *influentials* in community affairs. This requires programs tailored to fit the specific community—its people, history, and problems.

Community opinion itself is a complex thing. There are many conflicting self-interests. Almost any two people you want to pick will agree on one matter and oppose each other on another. Varied self-interests have much to do with behavior and opinion. At the community level, we see them extended through the individual into various groups of which he is a member, a patron, or a sponsor.

The first step in community relations is to tag the decision makers. Persuasion of these key individuals usually facilitates persuasion of their followers. *Each stratum in the community develops its own leaders.* The nominal leaders may not be the real leaders. In one town the mayor is a leader, in another, he is a puppet. Identification of opinion leaders requires probing.

Each city has a relatively few people who make the crucial community decisions. Floyd Hunter found this in his study of the Atlanta, Georgia power structure. Other researchers have found the same thing. Beneath this top hierarchy of policymakers for the community, those influential in civic affairs were ranked by Hunter: [3]

---

[3] Floyd Hunter, *Community Power Structure* (Chapel Hill: University of North Carolina Press, 1953), p. 109. For insight on power structure in a small town, see Vidich and Bensman, *Small Town in Mass Society* (Princeton, N.J.: Princeton University Press, 1958).

First Rate: Industrial, commercial, financial owners and top executives of large enterprises.

Second Rate: Operations officials, bank vice-presidents, public relations men, small businessmen, top-ranking public officials, corporation attorneys, contractors.

Third Rate: Civic organization personnel, civic agency board personnel, newspaper columnists, radio commentators, petty public officials, selected organization executives.

Fourth Rate: Professionals such as ministers, teachers, social workers, personnel directors, small business managers, higher-paid accountants, and the like.

Hunter was focusing on those who make community decisions. This is a concern of the practitioner. But of equal concern to him is the building of favorable attitudes in the city toward his enterprise. A favorable climate of opinion is compounded of many elements, many forces. A program is designed to win the favorable esteem of the *whole community,* esteem which holds your organization as worthwhile, a good place to work, and a good neighbor. Millard Faught classifies the "prime movers" in building such a climate:

1. Employees' or members' families.
2. The press, radio, and TV, their editors and reporters.
3. Thought leaders, including clergy, teachers, city officials, prominent retailers and professional men, union officials, bankers, civil workers, and industrialists.
4. Organizations, including city planning commission, welfare agencies, youth groups, veterans, fraternal, and service groups, cultural and political action bodies.
5. Crusaders, such as protest groups, petitioners, voice-of-the-people, special events, and the rumor factories.

THE BASIC APPROACH

Before thought leaders or the community at large can be persuaded in a specific direction or as a unified force, there has to be an understanding of the town's mutual interests by the would-be persuader. It is necessary to know what the community wants for its well-being, what part it expects each organization to contribute toward that, and how it measures those contributions. The interests of the community will all fit somewhere in these ten elements:

1. Commercial prosperity
2. Support of religion
3. Work for everyone
4. Adequate educational facilities
5. Law and order
6. Population growth
7. Proper housing and utilities
8. Varied recreational and cultural pursuits
9. Attention to public welfare
10. Progressive measures for good health

Accepting these elements as the scope of community interests, the communicating organization must somehow identify itself with them. It must show how it serves those interests. As a starting point, the underlying attitude of the organization must be one of a sincere interest in serving.

Organizational policies constitute a positive expression of attitude. They form the framework of a "personality" with which the organization is endowed in local opinion. The singular personality may be, in fact, composed of decisions rendered by a management policy committee. Most likely, the opinions will attach themselves to the personality of the head man. He becomes the symbol. People tend to identify actions and attitudes with people, not with buildings in which people live or work.

Beyond attitudes and personality, there is the factor of *participation*. The organization cannot stand aloof from the parade put on downtown by the local merchants or the town meeting discussing a new city auditorium. Nor can the top brass in the organization neglect a responsibility to get into the blood stream of community life. *Community relations cannot be delegated* to one man or department. Participation requires a costly investment of executive time. In his study of community relations in Syracuse, N.Y., Hodges found that "ten to fourteen hours a week, more than half that spent at luncheons and evening sessions, was about par for the most active executives; and six to ten hours a week was fairly common in these managements." [4]

Executives have a choice of participating in *angelic* activities, such as heading the United Givers drive, the Red Cross chapter, or the Y.M.C.A., or of becoming involved in *controversial* projects, such as slum clearance, survey of community health facilities, integration, and school bond referenda. Some leaders do both. Community progress takes leadership and seldom comes without some controversy. The rebirth of Pittsburgh, Pennsylvania, is an example.[5] The effort of Chicago to change its image of mobsterism is another. One of the authors of this book has for years headed the Communications Advisory Committee for the Economic and Cultural Development of Chicago. This committee has worked hard to revise Chicago's image.

Every enterprise has a stake in the condition of the city's physical plant, the quality of service provided by government and social agencies, the effectiveness of civic agencies, and the availability of community resources and facilities to improve the physical, mental, and moral health of the citizens. Most firms and institutions recognize this. Union Carbide is one. If it finds a lack of cultural activity in a community, its people will help organize a symphony orchestra or a small-theater group, or sponsor a lecture series. If it finds school facilities inadequate, it will lend its specialists as part-time teachers or provide classroom equipment.

Finally, there is the obligation of *continuous communication*. Private enterprise and public enterprise are both public. The affairs of an organization which mix with the affairs of a community are properly public domain. Silence on internal matters that affect the community is eyed by the home-

---

4 In *Company and Community, op. cit.,* p. 2.

5 A. Steinberg, "New City Called Pittsburgh," *Reader's Digest,* Vol. 66, May, 1955, pp. 83-86.

town people with great suspicion. It is as if the person or organization had something to hide. Holding back bad news is self-defeating. One DuPont official has observed: "Bad news doesn't necessarily have a bad effect. You gain the sympathy and understanding of the community. And getting the facts out quickly avoids incorrect stories and damaging rumors." Officials of a chemical plant in Memphis, Tenn., learned this the hard way. Many persons were taken ill when deadly chlorine gas escaped from a ruptured pipeline. The victims were hospitalized but the company made no public explanation. The story became "news" when the State Board of Health closed the plant until the danger had been eliminated. A company official subsequently admitted to the community: "Chlorine brought the wrath of God down on our heads. Perhaps we were lax explaining what we were doing here and we realize things that are unknown can create fear and suspicion about our activities."

The doors, the financial reports, and the policies of almost all sizable undertakings are open for inspection. Indeed, enlightened management anticipates community questions with answers.

A community looks around its own confines first for its news and opinions on grand-scale matters. The *New York Times* and the *Washington Post* have facilities for a more thorough coverage of national affairs than does the county-seat newspaper. Thoughtful analyses of national happenings come right into the home through the radio and television. Still, the hometown newspaper and the local prominent spokesmen carry more day-by-day weight than the most highly paid outside sources.

This emphasizes the extreme importance of the hometown audience to business, government, and social welfare. Opinions formed at the community level are expressed up the line to the national level. The actual formation of opinions takes place in the local environment.

Businessmen, state officials, military leaders, and social agency heads have come around more and more to the idea of communication programs individually tailored within the community rather than modeled after a single pattern cut in Washington or New York. There is much more work to the local tailoring, but there is a vastly more satisfactory result.

If each business house seeks and gains acceptability of itself in its hometown, public opinion of business nationally will follow suit. That makes sense. In almost every city in the United States there is one or more industrial enterprise whose actions and attitudes locally determine pretty largely how the people in town feel toward the United States business system. Utilities nationally are judged by the behavior of the hometown power and light company. Manufacturers as a group are judged by what the local machine tool company does or fails to do. The Armed Forces are judged by observations of the nearest camp, base, or station. So it goes. *People judge the whole by the parts they know.*

In looking to a good reputation locally, the utility and the manufacturer are helping the national reputation of the free enterprise system. The local utility branch or manufacturer delivers a bloc of favorable opinions in much the same manner as the county political party chairman delivers a bloc of votes.

Let's look at how these fundamentals are translated into specifics by well-managed concerns. These elements are present in the "something for something" community relations program of the Ansul Chemical Company, a firm with 583 employees in Marinette, Wisconsin, a city of 15,000. Its dynamic president, Robert C. Hood, holds that a company must be a good industrial citizen "by determining its citizenship responsibilities and how to meet them." Here's a thumbnail sketch of Ansul's CR program.[6]

1. **COMMUNITY AT LARGE.** An emergency rescue squad available 24 hours a day at no charge to anyone in the community; participation in activities of Marinette Chamber of Commerce; a daily radio program which carries free social and civic announcements for all local groups; large fire demonstration to highlight Fire Prevention Week each fall; plant tours and open houses; weekly advertising support of "Go to Church" campaigns; periodic community advertising.

2. **COMMUNITY THOUGHT LEADERS.** Regular mailing of company publication, special tours for specific influence groups; special mailings, such as company annual report or an outstanding national publicity "break."

3. **LOCAL PRESS.** Immediate dissemination of company news, both favorable and unfavorable; equitable, although modest, advertising support of all local communications media; impartial timing of news breaks, invitations to press to attend company functions; 24-hour-a-day availability to press; elimination of pressure to run company stories "as is."

4. **CIVIC ORGANIZATIONS.** Regular and proportionate donations to local charities; use of daily radio program; speaker's bureau, both for regular addresses and to fill emergency needs; free movies, projection equipment, and operator for use by nonprofit groups; plant tours and fire demonstrations for civic clubs.

5. **STUDENTS, FACULTY, SCHOOL OFFICIALS.** Plant tours by business, chemistry, and other school classes; regular advertisements in school yearbooks and newspapers; use of daily radio program by faculty; cooperation and leadership on Business-Education Day.

6. **MUNICIPAL EMPLOYEES, OFFICIALS.** Free fire equipment and recharging supplies to fire and police departments; use of fire test field for training and demonstrations; first aid training of firemen and policemen by Ansul Rescue Squad; availability of Ansul fire equipment for emergency use; personal leadership in city council, police and fire commission, civil defense, other municipal agencies; absence of pressure on tax assessments, zoning, special ordinances, and so forth.

7. **LOCAL MERCHANTS, INDUSTRIALISTS.** Mailing of *Ansul Fuse Plug;* avoid-

---

6 Chamber of Commerce of the United States, *Effective Employee and Community Relations, A Report on Ansul Chemical Company* (Washington, D.C.: The Chamber, 1956). (Sketch condensed from pp. 22-23.) An instructive report on what a small firm can do.

ance of "pirating" employees from local business and industry; brief congratulatory letter when businessman is honored or promoted; welcoming visits to new merchants or industry officials; salutes to other industries in the company's employee publication.

8. NONEMPLOYEE LOCAL STOCKHOLDERS. Mailing of *Ansul Fuse Plug;* special mailing of periodic information about the company's progress; invitations to visit plant.

Ansul believes that building a reservoir of goodwill in its local community in these ways has helped to bring about dollars-and-cents returns:

1. Equitable tax rates, assessments, and other municipal actions which tend to regulate a company's operations.
2. Availability of labor, skilled and unskilled. People prefer to work for a company that's liked and respected.
3. Public support in case of trouble—labor difficulties, layoffs, accidents, plant disasters.
4. Increased employee productivity. Employees tend to reflect favorable community attitudes.

TRANSLATING ATTITUDES INTO ACTION

When all is said and done, the organization hopes to be known as a good outfit to be with—a successful operation in which citizenship and neighborliness are practiced. Getting that across is a big task in deeds and publicity.

The good outfit to be with is the one that knows how to make a profit while paying good wages. Nobody wants to work long for a company that doesn't know how to make a profit. In the case of a nonprofit organization, the "good outfit" would be one that has no serious trouble getting public funds and in paying its bills. There's no security in working for a business that cannot show a profit or get the funds it needs to grow.

Then, the good businessman is the one who hires his help locally and doesn't import the kind of workers who turn out to be undesirable residents. Instead, he uses the local employment services to find people. He pays the going rates, but he doesn't pay so much that the retail merchants downtown can't afford to pay comparable wages.

The good employer makes the work as steady as possible. If he finds himself shorthanded in rush seasons, he does not pirate workers from other establishments in town. He gets nonworking members of local families to fill in. He attracts desirable people from other towns to move into his hometown.

When it comes to repairing the premises of the organization, remodeling, or buying replacement supplies, the good outfit gets as much of the work done by local people as possible. It buys as much of its supplies as can be purchased locally at fair prices. It calls on the local plumbers, electricians, office supply houses, hardware merchants, and automobile dealers. This is particularly important for military installations. Even so, it should be clearly understood that today community relations is more a frame of mind than a practice of buying goods from the local merchant in this day of free-flowing world trade.

The good employer lives with his business. Absentee ownership in this period of decentralization is understandable. But the local managers should have the authority to make the same decisions as the owner would if he lived in town. There are still too many large organizations whose branch managers cannot approve a twenty-dollar contribution to the local Red Cross.

Contrary to the envious looks that local enterprises often cast at the large branch plants in town and their high-budget community relations programs, the hometown organization has many advantages over these outsiders. A good program doesn't necessarily cost a lot of money. Professor Wayne Hodges observes: "Because every city differs from all others in its pattern, structure, and needs, a CR-minded local management must become an integral part of its plant community in order to understand it and work with it intelligently. In this sense a locally owned company has an inherent advantage. But the outside company, if it puts emphasis on *community responsibility,* can do equally well." [7] Hometowners are built into the community power structure. Outsiders have to work their way in.

Citizenship for the organization means that it does not try to dominate community decisions. Citizenship means observing the local laws without seeking special privilege. It means helping the town's elected officials. The community expects citizenship to be demonstrated through widespread participation in city improvement programs, housing problems, land reclamation, and the like. The company offers support to charity fund drives and moral support to the work carried on by local welfare agencies, school programs, and mercantile groups. Occasionally, the organization will be expected to offer some of its facilities for community undertakings such as conventions, evening meetings, and transportation. Cooperation is expected in matters of safety not only on the premises but nearby in reducing pedestrian hazards. And the good citizen is expected to cast his ballot.

The citizenship expected of the organization is pretty much for the top people in the organization. When it comes to civic projects, they're expected to be aboard and, again, without throwing their weight around. This is an area in which the official of an organization works alongside a wage earner from another organization. They have a common goal and a comparable status in civic work. They are joint participants on charity drives, the school board, the mayor's antipollution committee, or the tree planting project for the parks.

Practicing good citizenship is not the simple matter it appears. Take the matter of contributions to the community's United Fund each year. This fund supports worthwhile agencies, its budget is determined by community leaders, and the contributor does not have to face the difficult task of deciding who's deserving and who's not. Then, say, for example, the American

---

[7] Wayne Hodges, "Community Relations Is Community Responsibility," *PR,* Vol. 2, January, 1957, p. 23.

Cancer Society withdraws from the United Fund appeal. Now what do you do? Support the United Fund principle and antagonize the cancer society's membership? Or do you give to both and thus antagonize the United Fund believers? Such questions can lead to a reappraisal of a company's contributions program. As Calvin Kytle, a thoughtful practitioner, suggests, "These root questions are tough, and sometimes painful, because all of a sudden you're wrestling earnestly with problems that are inescapably ethical in nature." Ultimately you come to the basic question: *"Does* business have a social responsibility, or is its only and proper concern the art of turning a profit?"

Financial contributions are but one way that a business expresses its interest in a community. Another, and obviously more hazardous, is by taking, or not taking, stands on public issues. Here, too, the guidelines are fuzzy and the reactions sometimes violent. This many business leaders who have taken the lead in bringing racial equality to their communities have learned. Even support of a useful, public-spirited organization can bring an unexpected public backlash. This the Ford Motor Company and Sears & Roebuck discovered a few years ago when the Committee on Economic Development, a forward-looking business group, issued a report suggesting that 2,000,000 farmers should quit farming and take jobs in industry. The National Farmers Organization picketed Ford dealers and Sears stores in many cities throughout the Midwest in protest to this CED report. Ford and Sears officials had served on the committee drafting the report.[8]

Neighborliness means more than the president of an organization tipping his hat to the policeman when he runs through a red light. It means more than a speaker's bureau to accommodate the local service club meetings. There are expectations that the organization will make its plant, campus, or camp as attractive as is practicable, that it will keep its trucks off people's lawns, that it will not smoke up, smell up, or dirty the neighborhood without first doing everything it can to avoid such nuisances. Those expectations include provision for parking facilities, waste disposal, smoke filters, noise controls, traffic planning, and safety devices.

Smoke and stream pollution are common causes of irritation and ill will among community neighbors. These problems can be turned into public relations opportunities. After World War II, International Harvester built a new plant outside Memphis in open country. As inevitably happens to plants, air fields, and so forth, the surrounding fields were in time covered with homes and people living in them. IH recognized that its smoke and soot would soon become a problem and that it could not solve it by telling these people "We were here first, you had no business to move so close." The company took these steps.[9]

---

[8] For an example of what happened to one businessman who went into public service, see Hal Bruno, "Birth Control, Welfare Funds, and the Politics of Illinois," *The Reporter,* Vol. 28, June 20, 1963.

[9] James Robert Massey, "Smoke Can Lead to Understanding," *Public Relations Journal,* Vol. 10, September, 1954, pp. 13-14.

1. Company representatives rang all the doorbells in the affected neighborhood to talk over the problem with the housewives.

2. Samples of the offending dirt were taken from lawns and clotheslines. Then letters were written to the homeowners telling them that Harvester's powerhouse smoke was responsible.

3. The women were promised that Harvester would search for a solution. No promises of fast relief were given.

4. Harvester went to work on a solution and kept these women informed each step of the way. It put gas burners in the foundry cupolas, sprayed its coal with oil, put a warning bell in its smokestack, planted a park-like buffer zone of trees and grass. These items cost $70,000 and alleviated the problem. It kept up its search for a solution and after three years found a type of air control equipment which would solve it. This was put in at a cost of $71,900.

5. When the solution had been found, the company called in its plant neighbors and community leaders. It explained the new equipment and thanked them for their patience and understanding.

In the end, Harvester came out with good neighbors who thought highly of a firm that would be considerate of its neighbors. James Robert Massey concludes from this experience that:

> Industry can turn bad into good when smoke mars their community relations by (1) recognizing the serious public relations aspects of the situation; (2) being willing to spend the money necessary to provide relief, and (3) *maintaining frank, honest, and consistent communications with the community.*

Industries and institutions face what a paper maker describes as "unremitting pressure from government for an ever higher degree of pollution abatement." The enlightened industry meets this need voluntarily. The Public Service Company of Colorado, a utility, has spent 2.5 million dollars to eliminate smog-producing smoke from its huge power-station boilers because "We want to do our part to keep Colorado a beautiful and attractive place in which to live." The utility's announcement came when the Colorado legislature was considering bills to alleviate air pollution. The *Denver Post* observed: "PSC has shown that enlightened business leadership need not wait for a political solution to this problem." Indeed, it is far wiser not to.

There are less costly ways of dramatizing a firm as a good neighbor. The post-prom activities of high schoolers have become quite a problem in many communities. Teachers in West Allis, Wisconsin, home community of Allis-Chalmers, contacted the Rotary Club to see if a planned post-prom party could be arranged. Out of this came the Allis-Chalmers' student post-prom parties held now for a number of years in its clubhouse. It has brought A-C much community praise.[10]

Another facet of neighborliness is in being host to the city's special visitors, holding open house on occasion, providing plant tours on request, and being available for visits from city officials. Beyond being a host, the good neighbor takes part in exchange visits with merchants, educators, farmers, and other segments of the surrounding community. He attends other organizations' open

[10] Quentin J. O'Sullivan, "Student Post-Prom Parties," *Public Relations Journal*, Vol. 8, 1952. These parties were continuing to pay PR dividends for Allis-Chalmers in 1964.

house events, makes speeches in the city on invitation, and receives callers with courtesy on the telephone, at the front door, in the private office, and in the shop. If the official of an organization happens also to be a parent, he invites the children's teacher into his home. If he belongs to a cultural group, he gives it sincere attention, not merely dues.

Neighborliness means functioning as a partner in city recreational programs, milestone events, local holidays, and pet projects of civic groups. There is also the desirability of making awards recognizing the accomplishments of those whom the community wishes to honor.

No skeletons in the closet means having no secrets. The local press, radio, and TV should have access to all information which the townspeople feel necessary to their satisfaction. Exceptions, of course, are pieces of information that could be damaging for competitive, legal, or security reasons. As a good reporter, the organization is expected to supply information to its own employee first, to its community second, and to the outside public third. The good reporter makes a point of knowing what the local press considers news. The main thing is to pursue a policy of candor and at the same time keep a check on the reactions to the news.

APPLYING THE
AUXILIARY TOOLS

Open house and plant tours
Extended house-publication circulation
Direct-mail literature
Institutional advertising
News
Civic participation
Speaker's bureau
Discussion groups

There is an immense variety of ways in which these tools are used. Some firms award scholarships locally. Sears, Roebuck, among many others, does this. Others train local youths for a career. The Bulova Watch Company has a school to train disabled veterans in watch repair. Many firms put on a Business-Education Day. General Motors brings noted speakers into a plant community on occasion for special events. Organizations foot the bills for local baseball leagues or new hospitals. National Cash Register donates space and supplies for local youngsters to have their own gardens.

The open house has the advantage of bringing large numbers onto the premises of the organization. Its weakness lies in that such large numbers do not have the opportunity for much personal discussion about interests they share.

The size of attendance suggests keeping arrangements for refreshments and personal services to a minimum. Hosts should go all out for devices which will facilitate pleasure and ease for the guests. In this latter category should be exhibits which can be seen quickly, ample guides or signposts leading to appointed areas, seats for overflow crowd, and a carefully supervised method of regulating traffic. Of great advantage is the *participation* of employees. Many guests are relatives and friends of the rank and file. Participation as hosts gives employees a renewed pride in their working group.

The *plant tour* has as its most important feature the planning which precedes it. It is conducted as a special event, such as Business-Industry-Education Day or as a routine system to handle daily visitors. *Planning* must include these factors:

1. An itinerary which is logical in telling the story.
2. A duration that accommodates the comfort of the tourist. Many tours are too long and arduous. If the tour requires great walking or undue exertion, there should be a break somewhere along the way and seating facilities.
3. Competent guides who not only understand the various phases of the operations, *but can put them into words which laymen can understand.*
4. A running story which shows the interlocking of the organization's interests with those of the community.
5. Some sort of simple gesture at the end of the tour to make the occasion memorable. It can be a pause for refreshment, a handshake with the president, a sample of the product or one of its raw materials, an opportunity to operate a unique machine or device, or a pamphlet about the organization.
6. Above all, a plant visitor should be handled with enthusiasm.

Extended house-publication circulation is worthwhile. Little additional news matter is needed for the employee publications to be of interest throughout the community. Among the readers close at hand are the people waiting a turn in the doctor's office, the barbershop, and the airport. Similarly, employees' activities are followed keenly by the clergy. Organizational activities are a matter of concern to merchants and to city officials.

Actually, there is no area of the community in which the house publication is not welcome. With the addition of such features as safe driving hints from the chief of police, comments on city-wide events, articles dealing with legend and lore, and perhaps a listing of future special events, a real service is performed without conflicting with the purpose of the daily or weekly newspapers.

Thought leaders can also be reached by occasional *letters from officials* of an organization. These are quite helpful, especially in anticipating rumors and quieting hurtful conversation. Topics in such letters are generally maintained at a high level of discussion. There should never be any intent to force thought leaders to serve the interests of the organization. Rather, the intent should be to place them in a better-informed position to serve the interests of their constituents.

A great deal more persuasion can be achieved through opinion leaders. The tendency is to pay all attention to the clergy, doctors, lawyers, teachers, city officials, and bankers. Quite often, that's a case of people who have the same general philosophy confirming that they agree with each other. The

Caterpillar Tractor open house for barbers suggests that other audiences might have a good-sized hand in formulating community opinions. Barbers have the attention of all male residents for a half-hour, once every two weeks or so. Bartenders have a nightly audience. Then, there are the hairdressers, the local librarian, the auctioneers, the mailmen, the milkmen, and the hotel desk clerk. All of these people are in a position to influence others. All of them talk with the audience that organizations need to win over.

Plant city advertising is becoming more and more popular. Plant city advertising is one answer to the problem of absentee ownership. It also serves a helpful purpose to the organization with employees who are swallowed after working hours by the remote sections of the city and have little contact with each other.

The stigma of impersonalization often attaches itself to paid advertising space. The reaction is that the organization did not have to air its views or fight its battles in that manner; it could have come closer to the people without resorting to advertising space. Organized labor is inclined to interpret such advertising, when subject matter touches industrial relations, as an act of bad faith—especially if it is used in time of crisis or strikes. Reactions depend on the use, not the medium.

To praise or discourage the use of the tool would be an unsafe generalization. There are many specific cases of success and failure. One success is a series by the Armco Steel Corporation, Middletown, Ohio, in a house publication with spill-over readership through the community. The headlines indicate the context, with notes by the authors.

This Slot Machine Always Pays Off—in Cash (picture of time clock)
A Boy Who Needs $10,000 (amount invested in business per employee)
The Spade That Dug a Fortune (used to break ground for expansion)
Baby, You've Got a Future at Armco (planning for future)
Armco's $1,000,000-a-year Fishing License (retirement plan)
The Man Who Brings Us Paydays (plug for salesmen)
Henry, How is Armco Doing? (family's stake in company)
A Million Dollars from a Cornfield (monthly payroll at plant)
No Future in the Buggy Business (moving ahead for the future)
Bought Any Steel Mills Lately? (rising costs)
If Every Hen Laid Two Eggs a Day (plug for productivity)
A Sure Way to Get a New Pair (shoes pictured, plug for building surplus)

The *hometown news* is a large biceps in the local program. It cannot be said accurately that the PR man exercises a control over this tool. He doesn't. But the local press, TV, and radio want news. They don't have to be sold on the idea. Local news builds circulation and listening audiences. The doings of any major organization are news. Organizational news comprises a service to the newspapers, radio, and TV.

Quite apart from the desire and need to cover the news, the local press takes pride in the community and is dedicated to the town's growth and prosperity. What helps the community helps the newspaper and the organization. What helps the newspaper and the organization helps the community.

The interrelation is a close one. Recognition of that fact is a realistic one. It is well rooted.

A CHECKLIST

Many organizations periodically use a checklist to evaluate their program. Among them, this one for the United States Army is excellent.

1. *Command Policy.*

a. Are the commander and his senior staff officers and subordinate commanders sold on the necessity for a sincere and consistent attitude toward the community?

b. Has a definite community relations program been outlined?

c. Is the community relations program under the direction of a qualified officer?

d. Has the community relations program been explained in detail to the senior staff officers and all subordinate commanders?

e. Does the commander take into confidence the officer directing the community relations program?

f. Has the officer in charge of community relations been given the opportunity to study and overhaul command policies and activities so that the command will always be on the right and ethical side of any argument?

g. Is the command in its operations guilty of any of the more common community complaints against a military installation:

(1) Local tax dodging.
(2) High accident rates.
(3) Misconduct of military personnel.
(4) Waste of taxpayers' money.
(5) Failure of military personnel to participate in community projects and activities.

h. Does the command know what the public in the local civilian community thinks of it, its policies and its personnel?

i. Is there available an analysis of the community itself, its problems, its weaknesses, and its civic ambitions?

j. Have all points of citizen contact been checked for good community relations practices—the gate guards, military police, the telephone switchboard, the employment section of the Civilian Personnel Office, etc.?

k. Have all members of the command, particularly the officers and senior non-commissioned officers, been urged to take active part in community projects and activities?

l. Have all military personnel received an orientation on the local community as well as on the command community relations program?

m. Is there a continuing program to make members of the command more community relations-minded?

2. *Publicity.*

a. Have arrangements been made to assure local press, radio, and television of a 24-hour source for command information?

b. Are command news releases written in good news reporting style, without padding, and angled for community interest?

c. Do local press, radio, and television reporters have easy access to the command and its senior officers on reasonable notice?

d. Does the commander hold frequent press conferences for the purpose of announcing important changes in command policies or activities?

e. Are local reporters invited to visit the command frequently on both a group and individual basis?

f. Are local news media representatives invited occasionally to command social functions?

3. *Requests for Speakers.*

a. Has a routine been established for prompt handling of local requests for speakers?

b. Are military personnel given adequate assistance in preparation of speeches and of charts and other visual aids when asked to address more important gatherings?

c. Have several officers been selected because of their speaking ability to represent the command at meetings and gatherings not of sufficient importance to require the time of the commander or other senior officers?

d. Are all speech manuscripts cleared through one office for protection in matters of policy?

4. *Open House and Tours.*

a. Is an open house held by the command at least once a year?

b. Does the command have an established plan for proper handling of visitors who "just drop in"?

c. Does the command have a souvenir booklet to give visitors to remind them of their visit to the command?

d. Is everything possible being done to encourage local schools and community groups to visit the command?

e. Are business and professional clubs being encouraged to occasionally hold their weekly luncheons at a military installation?

5. *Contributions to Local Charities.*

a. Has the command made a careful study of local charities and annual community drives to determine its proper share of responsibility?

b. Does the command cooperate with local charity campaigns in other ways than by monetary contributions?

c. Has the command made any attempt to spearhead any such community drives with the initial gift?

d. Do any officers of the command serve on the boards of local charitable organizations?

6. *Community Relations Plan.*

a. Is the community relations plan a flexible one geared to the changing needs and interests of the local civilian community?

b. Are command policies and the programs predicated on them explained frankly and in detail both directly and indirectly through all channels of communications to the opinion leaders in the community?

c. Are all members of the command kept informed on the changes in and development of command policy so that they can assist in disseminating accurate information in the person-to-person contacts in the local community?

d. Is the community relations program completely humanized and personalized? In other words, the command must be interpreted to the community in terms of the attitude and character of all the individuals who are a part of its organization.

e. Does the community relations plan take into account coordination and cooperation with organized groups in the local community?

f. Has a Community Relations Committee been organized by the command to maintain the interest of the command and to create new ideas and projects to keep the program active?

g. Is there an active program to make each member of the command feel that he is a community relations representative for his unit? Every member of the command must be brought to realize that, while the command community relations program is outlined and instituted under the direction of the command's information officer, he alone is powerless to make it succeed. Each member of the command must be ready in every way to play the role of a community relations representative with sincerity in carrying out the over-all program.

Additional Reading

Anonymous, "Closing Down the Plant: A Case History," *Public Relations Journal,* Vol. 13, February, 1957.

Anonymous, "Skirting Company Town Pitfalls," *Business Week,* Sept. 14, 1957. (How Kaiser Aluminum moved into Ravenswood, W. Va.)

James A. Blay, "How We Moved 8 Communities and Kept Their Friendships," *PR In Canada,* Vol. 2, February, 1959.

Albert S. Fulling, "Community Public Relations Defeats Proposed Jersey Jetport," *Public Relations Journal,* Vol. 18, March, 1962.

Edwin C. Kepler, "The New Scope of Community Relations," *Quarterly Review of Public Relations,* Vol. 6, Winter, 1961.

Esther C. Lawton, "What Should Management's Policy Be Toward Participation of Employees in Community Affairs?", *Personnel Administration,* Vol. 20, November-December, 1957.

J. C. Long, "Princeton University Programs Friendship," *Public Relations Journal,* Vol. 17, November, 1961.

Louis B. Lundborg, *Public Relations In Your Local Community.* New York: Harper & Row, Publishers, 1950.

John T. McCarty, "The Image in Your Community," in Lee H. Bristol, Jr., ed., *Developing the Corporate Image.* New York: Charles Scribner's Sons, 1960.

Wilbur J. Peak, "Community Relations," chapter in Philip Lesly, ed., *Public Relations Handbook.* Englewood Cliffs, N.J.: Prentice-Hall, Inc.

U.S. Civil Service Commission, *Community Relations: A Guide for Federal Agencies.* Washington, D.C.: the Commission, 1958. Management Series No. 12.

CASE PROBLEM

You are public relations director for a medium-size manufacturing company. You have a publications editor and secretary for assistants. The firm is located near one of the better residential districts on the outskirts of an industrial city. To encourage more two-way communication, you introduce a question-and-answer page in the monthly company magazine which goes to people in the community. In announcing this feature, you encouraged readers to submit questions to the magazine with the promise that these would be answered in the next issue. The plea brought in a large batch of questions.

Nearly 20 per cent of the questions asked by community neighbors concerned the odor emanating from the plant. Although management knew the odor was strong at times, it was common to all manufacturers of the same product. It was not thought offensive or objectionable to many people. Management thought the community had learned to live with the odor. These questions bothered them. Yet virtual elimination of the odor would require equipment costing $250,000. The company is in the midst of a large expansion program for which every available dollar has been earmarked for the next 18 months.

Management turns to you in its bewilderment, and you are asked for a recommendation. What do you propose?

Chapter Sixteen

SPECIAL

PUBLICS

Any time more than two Americans meet on the street, one of them is sure to begin looking around for a gavel to call the meeting to order.— Will Rogers.

The American Public is ever growing, moving, changing. So is the American Mood. Every three seconds of the working day, a baby is born. Each day the equivalent of a town of 11,000 persons is added to Americe's expanding population. This means more babies to be fed, clothed, and provided with toys; more children to educate; more young couples setting up homes which they must buy or rent and furnish; more people to buy cars and more highways for them to travel on; more people to open bank accounts, buy life insurance, take vacations, and use governmental services. And more targets for communications!

Based on the assumption that present fertility rates by age will continue to 1975, the Bureau of Census projects the population of the United States in one estimate as follows:

	(In Millions)
1965	190.3
1970	204.6
1975	221.5

Americans are the most restless people on the face of the earth. United States Census reports show that an average of 30 million Americans have moved each year since 1947. This movement means the shifting, far and near, of millions of families with everything they treasure—from pitchers to pianos. Car-equipped, mobile Americans are constantly on the go—for vacations in the South, in the North, in the East, in the West. And abroad, too.

Americans are moving from the cities to suburbs and exurbs. Some of them are moving back to the Central City from Suburbia. Others

269

from farms to city. Marriage prospects, social customs, hobbies, social groupings, and buying habits of our times are being radically changed by the most
prosaic of men—the daily commuter. The spread to the suburbs and beyond
is breaking up concentrations of population with common bonds of nation-
ality, race, or custom. Increasingly, our people are rootless people. Also,
people are living longer. This means more people to be guided in the difficult
period of life—retirement. More people to be provided for in the Golden
Years. By 1975, it is estimated, there will be 20½ million persons past 65
years of age.

These basic trends have profound significance. Communication with this
massive, mobile Big Public would be nigh impossible—except for one thing.
Americans have an unmatched penchant for organizing themselves into
groups. Today's busy, busy citizen is organized and "committee-ed" almost to
the point of frustration. Each organized activity represents a common bond
of interest. *Practitioners use these common bonds as channels of communication and approaches of mutual interest.* In the craft, these groups are labeled
"Special Publics."

One of the first chores in public relations is to identify and establish
liaison with an organization's special publics. These may be many or few.
Effective communication with the whole public is made economical and effective by this public-by-public approach. Americans are a many-sided people.
They organize themselves into men's groups, women's groups, children's groups,
parent's groups, labor unions, trade associations, professional groups, religious
groups, service clubs, insurance groups, media groups, safety groups, transportation groups, ad infinitum. The membership and focus of these groups are
constantly changing.

The American's urge to join and identify himself with the group is old
and indestructible. De Tocqueville observed more than a century ago: "The
Americans of all ages, all conditions, and all dispositions constantly form associations." Despite the impact of TV and other distractions of modern living
on "lodge night," the number and membership of castles, camps, clans, circles,
chapters, conclaves, groves, hives, aeries, and nests continue to grow.

Some 125 million Americans hold membership in 275,000 different fraternal
and social organizations. These orders range in size from the multi-million-
member Masons down to a handful in the Liberty Boys of '76. Some are billion-dollar concerns, others have grocery-size budgets. Many employ PR men.
All are targets of PR programs. These groups have conventions, meetings,
publications, and officers who provide channels of communication and influence with their members on matters of interest to them. Fraternal groups
represent just one aspect of organized America.

Many persons are nonjoiners. Millions of Americans are not members of
any voluntary association, civic or church group, union or veteran organization, according to one National Opinion Research Center survey. Most
influentials are joiners, and these are the persons whom the practitioner seeks
to influence. Sociologists Charles R. Wright and Herbert H. Hyman report

that "the persons most likely to join organizations are those who are married and have children, who are interested in public affairs such as public school or city planning problems, who have a high 'socioeconomic status' as measured by level of income, home ownership, and education."

Increasingly, practitioners target their messages to special publics through these organizational channels that reach into every segment of the population. This trend is being speeded by increased knowledge of the opinion-molding process and by the budget limitations confronting most practitioners. Typical is this delineation of special publics by the Sixth United States Army, headquartered in San Francisco: (1) civil organizations; (2) trade and industrial associations; (3) veterans organizations (Army alumni); (4) youth groups; (5) women's clubs; (6) clergy; (7) educators; (8) communities. Army commanders and information officers are advised: [1] "The most efficient system by which the Army can retain and increase support of its publics is by working through the leaders of those publics."

SOME OF THE
SPECIAL PUBLICS

1. TEACHERS, STUDENTS, ADMINISTRATORS. More than 50 million members of The Big Public are primarily concerned with going to school, teaching school, or administering schools. In 1964 education was a full-time occupation or a time-consuming avocation for nearly 30 per cent of the population.[2] Teachers and students, from the elementary grades to graduate schools, are the objects of an increasing amount of educational material designed to shape the attitudes of tomorrow's citizens. Federal and state agencies promote conservation and health. Insurance companies promote safety and fire prevention. Manufacturers promote their industries and the capitalistic enterprise. *Worthwhile causes* find this important schoolroom audience increasingly receptive to *educational* aids and materials.

2. GOVERNMENT OFFICIALS. The increasing size and scope of Big Government and its increasing impact on the activities of every organization make it a key public for most concerns, especially business firms. From the President of the United States down to members of the county and town boards, elected and appointed government officials are the focus of much persuasion and pressure. What this powerful array of officials, elected and appointed, thinks and decides is often measured in dollars and cents. A government agency can grant or take away an airline route, a TV station license, or a tax rebate. It can build a power dam or let a privately owned utility build it. Government, with its billions to spend, is the nation's biggest customer.

---

[1] United States Sixth Army, *Information Officers Bulletin* (Presidio of San Francisco, Calif.: The Sixth Army), 16 April 1962.

[2] "The Magnitude of the American Educational Establishment," *Saturday Review*, Vol. 46, September 21, 1963, p. 63.

In coping with the far-reaching power of government, organizations must deal with many officials, persuade many persons, and clear numerous hurdles. More than 100 agencies of the Federal Government alone regulate one or more aspects of business firms. Forty-three separate bureaus deal with business activities in foreign trade; 60, those in manufacturing; 41, those in labor relations; 62, those in transportation regulation. The same holds true for the legislative branch. In a typical session of Congress, there were 52 committees operating which filed 1,520 Senate Committee reports and 1,328 House Committee reports; the Congress enacted 45 internal revenue laws, 38 appropriations laws, and 191 laws affecting business; a total of 1,927 were enacted in all. The same extent and complexity of federal relationships confront other organizations. Today, for example, both private and state universities are getting a large share of federal support, and these grants and contracts involve countless relationships with many federal agencies. The same thing goes on at the state and local levels of government. Such figures underline the number and importance of relationships with the *government public*.

More and more, practitioners are involved in efforts to influence government bureaucrats and legislators. This is true of practitioners both inside and outside of government. Much of this comes under the emotion-charged word *lobbying*. Lobbying today, as one writer notes, "is no matter of some florid operator buttonholing a Senator or Representative in the anteroom of the Capitol." Rather, as a lobbyist vouches: "The times are complicated. The problems are big. You've got to have more than an idea and a handshake. You've got to have a well-documented case. You're dealing with sophisticated men." [3] The issues are complex—as complex as a trade expansion act, legislating sugar quotas, medical insurance for the aged, and farm support programs. Increasingly it is the practitioner's task to counsel top management on long-run government economic, education, and research policies that might affect his organization.[4]

A House committee has termed lobbying a "billion-dollar industry," and each year nearly 1,000 lobbyists register with Congress as required by law. Several organizations spend more than $100,000 annually on this aspect of public relations. The stakes are high, the pressures intense, the relationships many. Behind the massive array of decision makers at all levels of government are some 15 million politically active persons in the two major parties. Government relations can be as direct as a lobbyist buttonholing a legislator or as broad as building nationwide support for reduction in the tariff. As government's rewards and regulations multiply, so will the relationships with its officialdom.

---

[3] Frederic W. Collins, "Another Potomac Army: The Lobbyists," *New York Times Magazine*, April 23, 1961, p. 100.
[4] See Paul W. Cherington and Ralph L. Gillen, *The Business Representative in Washington* (Washington, D.C.: The Brookings Institution, 1962). A report of a round-table discussion by 19 Washington representatives on their job as they see it.

3. WOMEN. The "hand that rocks the cradle" is increasingly clasped by those with goods to sell, stocks to promote, and votes to win. The 1960 Census recorded 91 million females, nearly 3 million more women than men. More of these women are working; more of them are taking part in public and civic affairs. Wise men never "underestimate the power of a woman."

It is often claimed, though not documented, that women do 85 per cent of the nation's buying. The majority of corporate stockholders are women. Women make up one-third of the nation's work force. Employers know that the wife's attitude follows the husband to work. Political leaders have recognized the woman's role in winning elections. Approaches to this powerful bloc can be a feminine angle in a mass-media message, a feature in an employee magazine, or a plant tour for the wives. Or the approach can be through the scores of women's organizations.

Combined, United States women's clubs represent a membership of some 40,000,000—mostly middle- or upper-level women. Many of these are community, political, religious, and educational influentials. Women's organizations include Altrusa International, National Federation of Business and Professional Women, American Association of University Women, the League of Women Voters, D.A.R., W.C.T.U., Zonta International, and scores of others. The importance of this public is providing increasing opportunities for women in PR work. It takes a woman to know a woman!

4. VETERANS. The United States has more than 23 million veterans, who, on some issues, exert a pressure beyond their numbers. Of these, more than 15 million served in World War II and 962,000, along with 4,520,000 others, served in the Korean conflict. The remainder served in other wars or during time of peace. Nearly half of the federal government's employees are veterans. With their families, veterans represent nearly half the adult population.

The veteran's voice is heard through his organizations—the American Legion, Amvets, American Veterans Committee, Veterans of Foreign Wars, and smaller ones. These organized groups embrace a minority of those eligible for membership. They provide a direct channel to men with war service who are "veteran-minded." The veteran influence can be exaggerated. Military service is the common experience of a majority of adult males today, not the uncommon thing it was prior to World War II. Hence, there has been a diminution of men thinking as veterans.

These and other members of the public move in and out of these and a host of other specialized publics. Composition of The Big Public can be cataloged in many ways. It depends on the issue at stake. Predominant interests of people vary with sex, age, occupation, residence, marriage status, income bracket, church affiliation, and so forth. Beyond these general population groups, each industry or institution has its specialized publics within its Big Public. For a school system, these would include school board, superintendents, principals, teachers, pupils, parents, public officials, taxpayers, readers and listeners of local media, and so forth. Space does not permit detailing the ways and means of dealing with this almost inexhaustible list of special publics. We shall discuss two as being illustrative—*educational relations* and *a manufacturer's trade relations.*

EDUCATIONAL RELATIONS

More and more organizations are beaming their message at what *Time* terms "the plastic minds" of young people. These efforts are channeled through youth groups and through the schools. Primarily the latter.

Organized youth groups which afford a channel of contact include Boy Scouts, Girl Scouts, Sea Scouts, Camp Fire Girls, 4-H Clubs, Future Farmers of America, Boys Clubs of America, Y.M.C.A.'s, Y.W.C.A.'s, and industry-sponsored Junior Achievement groups. The organized activities of such groups provide many opportunities for sponsorship, contests, granting of awards, presentation of programs, tours, displays, and books. Support of these activities demonstrates social responsibility and bids for future customers or supporters.

The most direct example of this approach to youth by business is Junior Achievement. Founded decades ago by Horace A. Moses and Theodore N. Vail, it has been carried on by countless business leaders to show young men by actual participation just how the competitive enterprise system ticks. The Junior Achievement program calls for adult businessmen to function as advisers to companies formed by teen-agers. In these junior corporations, boys and girls 15 to 21 sign up for jobs, sell stock, and undertake a corporate business. The jobs are rotated, everybody gets paid if the enterprise clicks, there are directors' meetings, stockholder meetings, and all the problems and procedures of a corporate enterprise.

Classrooms from kindergarten to university provide access to the key public of teachers and students for nonprofit agencies promoting the causes of safety, health, conservation, wholesome recreation, and good citizenship. Business and the professions have developed large-scale *educational* programs to create understanding of the American business system, to promote consumer education, and to recruit talent.

The once deep gulf between the worlds of education and business is steadily being bridged. Vehicles are corporate support of education, business-sponsored educator conferences, provision of internships and summer employment for teachers, provision of specialists as part-time teachers, visits by teachers to industry, visits by businessmen to schools, and similar projects. Better rapport and closer collaboration on matters of *mutual interest* are the happy result.

Industry assistance to schools and colleges takes such varied forms as: [5]

---

[5] Richard A. Stimson and C. Colburn Hardy, "How to Develop an Educated Approach to Business-Sponsored Materials," *Public Relations Journal*, Vol. 19, September, 1963, p. 20.

1. Grants and scholaships—often related to plant community relations, recruiting, or research.

2. Personal participation—furnishing guest lecturers, encouraging company people to serve on school boards and advisory groups.

3. Plant tours, including annual business-education days.

4. Loaning or donating supplies and equipment.

5. Supplying information and photographs to textbook authors and publishers.

6. Instructional materials distributed free or at nominal cost.

Business-sponsored materials for schools—booklets, pamphlets, movies, and other teaching aids—have become big business. The volume is steadily mounting. Practitioners find teachers and professors receptive to *honest, useful* aids which are truly *educational* rather than propagandistic in nature. *Teachers welcome useful information; they rightfully resent indoctrination.*

Printers' Ink suggests two criteria to guide those providing educational materials for schools:

1. Commercially sponsored teaching materials must contribute positively and effectively without distorting the educational program approved by the responsible educational authorities.

2. Commercial supplementary teaching materials must not promote product or service sales. The name of the donating firm should appear, but not with an emphasis or repetition that subordinates the educational content. There should be no boastful claims, no efforts to persuade, no urges to buy or try.

Practitioners should approach collaboration with educators in a spirit of cooperation and helpful intent. Efforts to infiltrate the nation's schoolrooms with partisan pleading will backfire. Mary Jane Burton thinks: "Some of these 'aids' are clumsy and even dishonest, a nuisance to schools and largely a waste of money for the sponsors." She follows these "rules of the road" in preparing sponsored materials for schools.[6]

1. Keep "advertising" to a minimum.

2. Avoid unfair slanting or bias.

3. Plan materials to fit the curriculum.

4. Keep materials easy to read.

5. Make them interesting.

Preparation of these materials is a task that the practitioner is seldom equipped to tackle unaided. He needs the help of teachers. Increasingly teachers are being employed on a part- or full-time basis to guide these programs. One educational program which attracted wide duplication was General Mills' health and nutrition project. This program can serve as a guide. From its inception, school administrators had an important role in this program. It was directed by a former school superintendent. The consulting service of the National Association of Secondary-School Principals was utilized. There was active participation by educators and nutrition specialists. The General Mills program was divided into four parts.

---

[6] In an article, "Sponsored School Materials Are 'Coming of Age,'" *Public Relations Journal,* Vol. 13, April, 1957, p. 9.

1. TESTING. More than 100 test schools, from Minnesota to Georgia and ranging from rural one-room schools to city schools at all grade levels, were used to experiment with techniques, to try out the program, and to *evaluate* its effectiveness.

2. TEACHER TRAINING. General Mills sought to show teachers how nutrition could be woven into regular classroom studies without disturbing the curriculum or the school organization. Demonstration programs for teachers were conducted at selected colleges and universities.

3. TEACHING AIDS. These were planned and developed by educators, nutrition and health specialists, and classroom teachers. They represented the framework for an inclusive nutrition and health program. These included a handbook, teacher's guidebook, wall posters, pupil leaflets, parents leaflets, nutrition guide, the story of cereal grains, an outline of a suggested program, a film, and evaluation devices.

4. PROMOTION. The program was promoted by *advertising* in 16 educational, agricultural, home economics, and health publications; by *direct mail* to key persons; by *personal contact* with key groups and individuals; by *presentations* to groups on city, county, state, and national levels; by *exhibits* at education and health conventions; and by a *publication* regularly circulated among some 28,000 educators.

There are other means of reaching this large, influential group of opinion makers and future citizens and customers.

BUSINESS-EDUCATION DAY. This is an educational relations tool of tremendous potential. B-E Days bring teachers and pupils to industrial plants and business firms for a close look and conferences. (The National Association of Manufacturers calls it Business-Industry-Education Day.) The idea started in 1946, when a Michigan State University professor took a group of school administrators on a flying tour of Michigan industries. The idea spread rapidly. The Chamber of Commerce of the United States, the N.A.M., and other trade groups vigorously promote it. Astute school administrators have turned the idea around to bring business leaders into the schools on Education-Business Days. It can work both ways.

B-E Days have several potentials. They (1) impart a better understanding of business policies and operations and the role of business in the economy; (2) give insight into teacher and teen-age opinions, and into the degree and validity of information these groups possess about business; (3) produce helpful suggestions for improvement of business relationships; (4) provide follow-up opportunities for plant tours, providing speakers for school assemblies, and placing exhibits in schools.

Earl B. Steele counsels B-E day sponsors: "Place the emphasis on those features which serve the real needs of the schools, teachers, and the students and those which develop a better understanding of our competitive system." [7] Such programs, like all others in PR, must be *mutually rewarding*.

---

[7] Earl B. Steele, "PR Opportunities of B-E Day," *Public Relations Journal*, Vol. 11, May, 1955, pp. 12-13. Useful pointers.

CAREER DAYS. This has become a standard spring event in most high schools. Such days offer another means of reaching tomorrow's citizens and employees. Community leaders are anxious to keep oncoming talent in the community. Industrialists, editors, and engineers seek to attract young people into their callings. In these programs, businessmen, professionals, and scientists describe the many careers open to students. The Miami Beach Chamber of Commerce has added an extra twist to this idea. It sponsors a "Boss for a Day" program for high school seniors. This provides them with a close look at work in stores, professional offices, and business establishments.

The Evansville, Indiana, Manufacturers' and Employers' Association stresses career guidance in its educational relations program. In an effort to encourage young people to enter Evansville industry, this association published a 192-page book, *Your Career Opportunities in Evansville Industry*. This was a *collaborative effort* of a Technical Committee, representing industry, and an Editorial Board of five educators. Plenty of copies are made available through the high school libraries. The book includes a "Dictionary of Job Opportunities in Evansville Industry." The book is used as a text in a 10-week freshman course. This association also has sponsored a contest among high-schoolers for the best *career-planning notebooks*.

CONFERENCES. Industry-sponsored conferences which bring school teachers and university professors into the business for joint conferences are growing in number. Standard Oil of New Jersey, DuPont, and International Harvester were among the pioneers. These conferences, conducted without strings, can be mutually rewarding. Efforts at high-pressure indoctrination backfire.[8]

For example, the chemical industry of Delaware collaborated to get the opportunities in science known to high school students. These firms sponsored a "New Frontiers Day" at the University of Delaware. Every secondary school in the state, public and parochial, was represented by at least one teacher. Most sent two. Executives and scientists told of the opportunities and demands for young men and women in the chemical industry. To permit the teachers to attend, the companies provided chemists, engineers, and physicists as substitute teachers for them. This provided a two-way impact.

SUMMER JOBS/INTERNSHIPS. An increasing number of industrial and professional organizations are providing summer employment for school teachers and university professors. This program has great potential for development of *rapport*. It provides the teacher with a realistic view to impart to his students. It provides those outside the academic world an opportunity to learn the educator viewpoint. Professions, newspapers, advertising, agencies, and business firms are providing an increasing number of summer internships. Some firms lend executives to colleges as visiting professors.

The critical shortage of scientists and science teachers has been one spur for this increasing exchange. An executive of the National Science Teachers Association thinks: "When approached with no more caution than is required

---

8 For one example, see Frederick S. Allis, Jr., "How Business Antagonized Some Teachers," *Fortune*, Vol. 50, September, 1954.

in any public relations activity, hiring teachers in science-related summer jobs promises rich rewards in increased understanding of the common problems of education, business, and industry." [9] Union Carbide has found that this program "achieves better community relations." A teacher who spent a summer with Monsanto Chemical Company reported he could better "interpret the opportunities and types of openings for both trained and untrained employees." Some industries are also sponsoring summer refresher courses for high school teachers at universities.

TRADE RELATIONS

On either side of the organization there are groups linking it with the general public. One group consists of suppliers. The other group consists of tradesmen who take the finished product or service to the consuming public. These groups are closely associated with the organization, yet they are not an integral part of it.

In the main, this middleman public is the concern of business organizations. But much of what can be said about a manufacturer and his suppliers or his retail dealers applies in principle to relationships between, let's say, a hospital and its suppliers on the one hand and its fund-raising committee on the other.

In a sense, employees within an organization comprise its family. The middlemen on its outskirts comprise its in-laws. They are wedded to each other by necessity but not always by choice.

THE BASIC RELATIONSHIP. A candid approach must concede that the business relationship between an organization and its dealers or suppliers is sometimes pretty fickle. Considering that the United States business system thrives on competition, this is as it should be. Goodwill between these groups quite often relates to consumer demand more than to any strong tug of economic brotherly love.

Manufacturers, for example, incline to buy from suppliers who give them the quality of goods specified at the lowest price possible. They like them for doing that, but the price and quality—not the friendship—come first. *If price and quality are nearly equal, however, then the supplier who has the manufacturer's goodwill can expect the nod.*

Suppliers, in turn, incline to woo the large user, the sure-pay customer, and they want the best price they can get for their goods. *When there are plenty of customers and a scarcity of goods, the customers who have the supplier's goodwill tend to be favored—particularly if they are good bets for the long haul.*

An association between a manufacturer and a supplier can go on amicably

---

9 John H. Woodburn, "Summer Jobs for Teachers Equals Public Relations Dividends," *Public Relations Journal*, Vol. 11, June, 1955, pp. 13-14.

for a year or for generations, with periodic expressions of goodwill. But let a competitive supplier come along with a more attractive proposition which the long-time supplier cannot match, and the association will be likely to cease. Or if a new manufacturer makes overtures to the long-time supplier about quantity and price which his old friendly manufacturer cannot or will not match, there will probably be some changes made.

The relationship between manufacturer, supplier, and dealer in normal times thrives on the economic law of supply and demand, with the asking and getting prices right in the middle.

The manufacturer who builds the mousetrap that consumers clamor for will usually find some dealers to stock and sell his product, although they may not like him heartily in the process. Some of the manufacturer's competitors might even have mousetraps of equal quality and might be nicer people to do business with. Chances are the dealers will also stock the slow-selling mousetrap for that reason. But dealers cannot risk their own success by failing to give the consuming public what it wants. They move and are moved, like everyone else, by public opinion.

Development of the discount house as a major outlet for consumer goods has re-emphasized the manufacturer's need to build solid consumer support for his products. This newcomer in the distribution system puts an additional premium on consumer confidence. It makes preselling of paramount importance. A discount house customer views a lineup of some 15 washing machines, say, as he ponders his purchase. There's little dealer sales pitch. The perplexed buyer probably will fall back on the trade name he has come to trust. In fact, the strength of the discount house depends on handling the highly regarded brand names. The discounter trades on the manufacturer's reputation.

Manufacturers tend to vie strenuously for consumer support FIRST, and for dealer support SECOND. Both are highly desirable. The former usually is more potent than the latter. *Together they are an unbeatable combination at the market place.*

Dealers, for their part, tend to be cordial with all manufacturers' representatives. They have seen the changing tides of consumer preference. They cannot be entirely sure which of several competing trade names will be top-dog a year hence. Good business sense dictates meantime that they refrain from playing favorites to a point where they hurt their own businesses. In general, their merchandising support—if not always their moral support—reflects today's consumer preference. It is reflected with careful accuracy in their inventories, window and counter displays, local advertising, and the facts revealed to them by the turnover and profit margin of various items or services. The exceptions they make are largely in giving a whirl to the innovation, the brand-new gimmick, the promotional item or idea which could become a sensation.

Few realistic practitioners quarrel with this basic relationship. It is part of the nature of a competitive business system. Competition is one force that makes the system tick. The result, as DuPont says in its advertising, has been "better things for better living." Any other system might thrive only at the expense of the consuming public. Certainly that would be true if a tightly restricted competition discouraged invention, improvisation, or risk.

In any case, the realistic approach to communication with these groups must recognize that dominant factors are the exciting tenets of good sales promotion, horse-trading, and expediting. This in no way precludes a public relations-mindedness. Other things being equal, goodwill wins the decision. That fact chalks off a definite big area for the practitioner to work on. It is difficult to draw a blade between the functions of sales promotion, good trading, and goodwill in these relationships. They are a *collaboration*.

THE ROLE OF COMMUNICATION. The relationship between buyer and seller starts with an organization's policies. Why? Because policies express attitudes. They determine actions. Here are several policy regions in trade relations that can win or lose goodwill in normal times.

1. *Discounts*. Are discounts comparable with competition? Are they equitable on some announced basis? Are they constant, or are they reduced when sales are high and increased when sales slip?

2. *Pricing*. Is there any price protection? Is merchandise marked plainly? Are price or service-charge changes explained in advance? Are changes capricious?

3. *Credit and Collections*. Are the practices reasonable? Are policies executed with impartiality and with tact? Are practices in tune with the times, or are they inflexible? Are bills paid promptly?

4. *Dealerships-Distributorships*. Is there a franchise agreement? If so, is it honored, or is it a meaningless bit of paper? Are dealers picked carefully or at random? Are market areas oversaturated with dealerships, or is there a consideration of old accounts?

5. *Contracts with Suppliers*. Are they carried through, or are they frequently abused?

6. *Cooperation-Support*. Among suppliers is there any avenue for counseling on common problems? Do suppliers have access to an understanding of a buyer's future plans and needs? Do suppliers' representatives have to cool their heels for long periods in the outer office because of bad scheduling on the part of the purchasing man's staff? Do supplier representatives see the right people, or do they get lip service and a brush-off?

As for dealers, are there sincere training programs provided by the manufacturer for their sales or service people? When dealers visit the manufacturer's home office, do they see people of equal stature, or are they palmed off on underlings? Does the organization say sweet things to dealers' faces but show disregard for them in its policy structure? Does the organization send representatives to those association meetings in which dealers are interested? Are there private deals for the big dealers and nothing for the little dealer?

References here are concerned mainly with trouble spots in normal times.

The public relations lesson is that cultivation of goodwill is a full-time, continuing process. *Providing effective, open channels for two-way communications between a firm and its distributors and dealers is basic.*

Additional Reading

Anonymous, "How One Firm Strengthens Its Local Science Program," *Management Methods,* Vol. 15, November, 1958.

Anonymous, "Dealer's Morale," *Business Week,* May 25, 1957. (How one company handles dealer complaints with an appeal system.)

Byron H. Christian, "Telling Business' Story on the Campus," *Public Relations Journal,* Vol. 12, December, 1956.

Mary June Burton, "Specifics for Schools: An Opportunity for Corporate Sponsors," *Public Relations Journal,* Vol. 18, November, 1962.

Sally Dickson and Joyce Clark, "The Image and Schools and Women's Clubs," in Lee H. Bristol, Jr., ed., *Developing the Corporate Image.* New York: Charles Scribner's Sons, 1960.

Mabel Flanley and Sally Woodward, "This Business of Women," *Public Relations Journal,* Vol. 11, October, 1955.

Eugene Gilbert, *Advertising and Marketing for Young People.* Pleasantville, N.Y.: Printers' Ink Books, 1957.

Thomas Ward Miles, "Telling the Industry Story to Congress," *Public Utility Fortnightly,* Vol. 60, December 5, 1957.

Robert Wilson, "7 Million Pairs of Ears," *Public Relations Journal,* Vol. 15, September, 1959. (Ways of reaching school children.)

CASE PROBLEM

For nearly 30 years a company making furniture specialties enjoyed a reputation for quality products. Five years ago a wealthy promoter obtained control of the firm. He began a systematic program to inflate the stock, which had substantial public distribution. He reduced the quality of the products materially but maintained high-quality prices. He stepped up appropriations for advertising and publicity. As a result, several quarterly reports showed soaring earnings. The market price of the company's stock mounted. When it got as high as the promoter thought he could push it, he sold out his holdings and severed his connection with the company. By the time a new management took over, the stock was selling for one-third its recent high, distributor and dealer complaints were multiplying, and sales were starting to slip.

The new management recognized the importance of swift action. It has hired you as public relations director. What do you recommend be done?

Chapter Seventeen

THE

GENERAL

PUBLIC

It is not what you write that counts, it is what you get others to read.— George Horace Lorimer.

The economical, effective avenue of contact with the general public is through the mass media: newspapers, magazines, trade journals, radio, and television. To handle this part of his job, the practitioner must understand the role of publicity, these media, and those who control access to them. This chapter will be divided into two parts. The first will treat the role of publicity in public relations. The second will discuss the media. Chapter 18 will outline principles for successful relationships with the men and women who work in these media. Press relationships deserve this emphasis.

THE ROLE OF PUBLICITY

Publicity is an important—but not all-important—part of public relations. Successful publicity, on a long pull, must be grounded in works that the public defines as good and motives that the public accepts as honest. As Cantril suggests, "opinion is generally determined more by events than by words. . . ." But there must be words and images, too —or else the good works are apt to be overlooked or misinterpreted by those with differing purposes or by those separated by distance. There can be quite a difference in impact between an act carefully explained and one that is not. A utility can simply go ahead and tear up a city's streets to put in larger gas mains to provide better service. Or it can manifest concern and consideration for the inconvenience and noise and dramatize this work as proof of a desire to provide the community with better service. Publicity is not a cure-all, but effective communication can get results.

Publicity's role must be understood in the larger framework of the whole public relations-communications process. It cannot be used for any length of time as a substitute for good works or for desirable corrective action. It can only serve as a spotlight to focus attention on good works and to clothe institutions with personality. In publicity practice, the operator of the spotlight naturally tries to put highlights on the good and to soften the unfavorable with shadows. But the publicist must always remember that there are other operators with spotlights in a position to cast a revealing glare in the dark corners of any institution or industry. As indicated earlier, *publicity is an all-or-nothing proposition*. Public interest in an organization cannot be turned on and off like a water spigot.

The objective of publicity is to make something or somebody known. The desire to be known stems from competition and from the mass media's partial failure, in terms of news coverage and values, to keep pace. The increased effort to make one's voice heard above those of others encourages an overemphasis on publicity. Publicity has its role in the public relations process, and it certainly has its consequences. Publicity used as one means of attracting attention to one's wares and citizenship is a forceful tool.

Publicity is potent but not omnipotent. One says: "We live in an age of publicity. What we buy, what we do, what we think, and what others think about us are influenced by publicity. This is not only true of people. It is also true of products, corporations, government and nations. . . . Publicity makes you buy Fords or Plymouths, makes you buy tickets to a fight or a ball game, makes you vote the Democratic ticket, makes you want to take a train ride or spend your last dime, makes you feel patriotic." [1] This is an oversimplification. Publicity is no miracle drug. It will not, by itself, sell goods, raise funds for a charitable cause, or win elections. These things take a good product, a good cause, and a hard-working organization. It can provide a voice to convey ideas to the people.

There are testimonials galore to the accomplishments of publicity. "Miss America" is one. The Rose Bowl Game is another. The "Blood Bank" is still another. When it was publicized that a United States President was eating beef bacon for breakfast, beef bacon sales skyrocketed and pork bacon sales slumped. One November, *The Reader's Digest* published an article about the Tracer Company of America, an organization which locates unclaimed bank accounts, legacies, and so forth. By the following May, this firm had received 438,000 letters as a result of this one article. A number of businesses trace their start to similar publicity breaks. These success stories can, of course, be matched by examples which misfired, or, worse, backfired.

Political and social history is replete with examples of the "big build-up." The techniques are many and varied, and most of them are easily mastered. This open sesame to "easy success" has led practitioners, on occasions, into

---

[1] From foreword by Don Francisco in Herbert Baus' *Publicity* (New York: Harper & Row, Publishers, 1942), p. 3.

an exaggerated idea of the power of being "known." Teamsters Union leader Jimmy Hoffa has gotten to be known pretty well. But he doesn't profit from the exposure. That's another side of the publicity rectangle. Getting an institution known by having it mentioned frequently in the press and on the air is a relatively simple and standardized procedure. "News" situations are fairly easy to contrive. Contrivance is a common practice.

Lavish testimonial to publicity breaks down, however, when one stops to consider that simple exposure of an institution to public gaze does not mean absorption of information, or support and understanding, by the public. There's a big gap between being heard and being appreciated. Contrast, for example, the public image of Kathryn Granahan, whose name is publicized on every dollar bill, with that of J. Edgar Hoover, who is selective in the publicity he gets. The public image of Hoover is proof of the power of good performance coupled with shrewd, dramatic reporting of that performance.

In using and in evaluating the publicity tool, it is important to keep in mind the total *two-step* mass communications process. Publicity items in these media soon become conversation pieces in offices, taverns, barber shops, and living rooms. Publicity provides a means of introducing your message into the word-of-mouth communications web. The publicity task should be approached with these thoughts in mind: (1) too much publicity can be, in fact, poor public relations; (2) it is the *content* and *absorption* of that content, not the amount of publicity, that eventually registers in public opinion; (3) publicity disseminated is not equivalent to information received; (4) publicity inevitably reflects the character of the institution it seeks to promote; (5) not all publicity that an institution receives originates within its control; (6) not all public relations activities result in publicity, nor should everything be so designed. In fact, there are times when avoidance of publicity is wisest. For example, when a large insurance company opened a 3,000-unit apartment project on a biracial basis in central Chicago, a highly volatile area, it chose not to use publicity. The decision proved wise, as the move came to be accepted without a single incident.

THE MASS MEDIA
OF PUBLICITY

A READY-MADE AUDIENCE AWAITS. The mass media reach into every home in the land. They influence every literate person. The mass media appear to represent an easily used tool for bringing ideas and information to the public. This concept can be delusive. Just because the media exist and can convey your message does not necessarily mean acceptance of or action upon your message.

Sound practice requires extensive knowledge and full understanding of these media; it requires a first-hand acquaintance with the men and women who staff them; it requires a keen insight into the potentialties and limitations of each medium. The practitioner must know which specific medium or media to use. He must know, too, the rules of the game. He must have a *planned* program for use on a coordinated basis, using one to reinforce and supplement the others. Walt Disney's skillful promotion is a good example. He uses his TV programs to promote his motion pictures and uses both media to promote the sale of his books, records, Disneyland, and other ventures.

NEWSPAPERS. When a person thinks of publicity, he almost instinctively thinks of the newspaper. The American press—daily and Sunday newspapers, weekly and semiweekly newspapers, Negro newspapers, labor newspapers, religious newspapers, collegiate newspapers, scholastic newspapers, and foreign-language newspapers—are read by virtually every literate person. Publicity in the press, day in and day out 52 weeks a year, forms the strong backbone of any informational program. A person who cannot be reached through a newspaper is not likely to count for much. The press provides a day-to-day continuity that no other medium provides. "Reading the newspaper" is as much a part of an American's daily habits as eating and sleeping. The influence of the press is incalculable. As an example, take this item from the wires of *United Press International.*

BERKELEY, CALIF.—(UPI)—An elderly St. Paul (Minn.) man dying of cancer changed his will and left $21,000 to the University of California cancer research program *after reading newspaper articles about it,* the university disclosed Saturday. (The italics are ours.)

The newspaper is the moving force of current history. Justice Felix Frankfurter once said: "The unconscious, and therefore, uncritical absorption of print is much more powerful than any skeptical alertness which most readers bring to print. To an extent far beyond the public's own realization, public opinion is shaped by the kind, the volume, and the quality of the news columns." Professor Emery gives the reason: "The power of the press is not in its persuasion by opinion, but in its dissemination of information and its arousal of interest in important issues hitherto submerged in public apathy."

The *strengths* of the newspaper are many. Newspapers are produced in local communities and are indigenous to those communities. They have a first-hand intimacy with their local publics. The local Y.M.C.A. can reach its community public through its local newspaper. The State Department of Health can reach its statewide publics through the daily and weekly newspapers of its state. A commercial concern with regional distribution can reach its regional publics by a regional selection of newspapers. Similarly, a national organization, such as the N.E.A., can reach that national audience through all newspapers. The number, locale, and variety of newspapers enable the publicist to pinpoint the geography of his publicity with precision.

There are other advantages. Newspapers reach more people more often than any other medium. A person buys his newspaper as something he wants, not as something thrust upon him. Newspapers constitute a medium of sustained interest and information. Readers are generally the interested, influential people. Because they reach their readers daily, newspapers are the most acceptable medium for a cumulative publicity build-up and thus are especially valuable in promotional campaigns. Newspapers are read at the reader's leisure and convenience. This is in sharp contrast with the broadcast media, where a program missed is gone forever.

The average reader has great confidence in "his" newspaper. It makes a lot of difference to a lot of people "to see by The Journal" instead of "to see by the propaganda of Watzit's Institute." The newspaper also serves well as the foundation of publicity in other media. The newspaper is used to build an audience for a speech and to report the speech for those who do not hear it. The newspaper is used to whet the appetite of radio and TV listeners and thus to increase the size of the audience. It is also used to publicize movies.

The value of utilizing newspapers to build audiences for radio and TV shows can be seen in these facts. In a typical television season, some 400 companies will sponsor, with varying degrees of participation, several hundred network TV shows. These shows require multi-million-dollar investments. The network publicity staffs will provide routine promotion for these shows, but they cannot do an effective, intensive job for each and every sponsor. Counselor George Hammond observes: "To a corporation investing such sums in an entertainment medium it is only sound business practice to spend the thousands additional that are needed to assure the maximum audience." [2] The smart sponsor will use newspaper publicity to push his message beyond the confines of the TV page and beyond the major marketing areas.

The newspaper also has its *limitations.* One important limitation is that the average reader reads only a portion of his daily newspaper. The typical reader spends some 20 minutes reading one-fifth to one-fourth of the editorial content of his newspaper. Thus it is a mistake to assume that publicity in the press is publicity received by all readers. Basic though newspapers are to a publicity program, they cannot carry the information task alone. The press must be used in close coordination with other channels of communication. Another limitation is imposed by the press' fetish for speed and the resulting haste with which newspapers are put together. This pressure of speed leads to many inaccuracies and fragmented, superficial coverage—a fact of life that the practitioner must cope with.

As of 1964, there were 1,754 daily newspapers in the United States with circulations totaling more than 58 million copies. There were 550 Sunday newspapers with circulations of more than 46 million copies. Although the number of daily newspapers has stabilized in recent years, newspaper circulation has climbed slowly, though not always in proportion to the population increase. Most newspapers are monopoly newspapers. (Fewer than 60 cities have competing daily newspaper ownerships.) American newspapers—from the mass-circulation giants down to the small dailies of 3,000 or so circula-

---

2 In "How to Back Up the Television Advertiser," *Public Relations Journal,* Vol. 18, March, 1962.

tion—vary a great deal in content, character, and audience. Yet all have a fairly standardized concept of what makes news.

Knowledge of newspapermen, of newspaper practice, and of newspaper-reader interests and habits will enable the PR practitioner to use this medium effectively. The PR practitioner who works with the press needs a few indispensable tools. He ought to read regularly such professional publications as *Editor & Publisher, The Journalism Quarterly, Nieman Reports, The Columbia Journalism Review,* and *The Quill.* Among the essential reference books in every office must be the *Editor & Publisher Yearbook* and N. W. Ayer & Sons' *Directory of Newspapers and Periodicals.* These annual directories give detailed information on the names, locations, circulations, staffs, and so forth, of newspapers.[3] They should be used to *keep mailing lists up to date—a chore not to be neglected.* Outmoded and inaccurate mailing lists are a common source of complaint by newsmen.

In 1963 there were 8,158 weekly and semiweekly newspapers in the United States with a total circulation of 23,433,718. These weeklies claimed an estimated readership of 93,734,872.[4] These newspapers offer an effective, direct, and intimate means of reaching the people of the small towns and farms, who are often the source of grass-roots opinion. The weekly newspaper reader is a loyal reader who reads his paper through. Most experts agree that the weekly newspaper exerts a far great impact on opinions in ratio to circulation than does the average daily newspaper. And these opinions count. This group exerts the dominant power in most state legislatures and has repeatedly demonstrated great power in Congress. Henry Beetle Hough, "Mr. Country Editor," counsels:

> It is well to abandon the fiction that ambition necessarily leads to the city, and the corollary that the people of the nation as a whole can be influenced by the old cliches and city symbols . . . as to the small town press, which is naturally important in any public relations thinking, it has a right to be judged functionally and not mechanistically or by fictitious or unrelated standards. Ordinary realism suggests the wisdom of relating it to its own purposes and environment, and not, by comparison, to magazines and city papers which rest upon different premises and different needs.

The public relations practitioner hedged in by the skyscrapers of the city should not forget the people of small-town America, or the weekly newspapers that shape their opinions.

There are two standard directories that can be used as ready reference tools on names, locations, publishers, and so forth, of weekly newspapers: The Ayer's *Directory,* previously mentioned, and the *National Directory of Newspapers,* published annually by American Newspaper Representatives, Inc., the

---

[3] Also helpful are: *Press Intelligence Directory* (Washington, D.C.: Press Intelligence, Inc.); and *The Working Press of the Nation* (Chicago: The National Research Bureau, Inc.). Both are guides to news outlets.

[4] *43rd National Directory of Weekly Newspapers,* p. 8. This annual directory is published by American Newspaper Representatives, Inc., 404 Fifth Avenue, New York City.

weekly papers' united advertising organization. Most state press associations also publish directories.

Labor journalism has developed extensively and matured considerably over the past 20 years. The exact number of labor newspapers is difficult to determine. Just about every union has its own magazine or paper. Recent estimates place the total at about 200 labor papers and magazines circulated on a national basis in addition to hundreds of regional and local ones. Their total circulation is variously estimated from 16 to 20 million. It is safe to assume that every union member receives at least one labor newspaper. To get a story into a union member's newspaper increases its acceptability to him. Naturally, the information must be of special interest and must square with the policies of organized labor.

The following labor publications and press services offer important outlets for stories with a labor angle:

> *AFL-CIO News:* A weekly paper published by the AFL-CIO, 815 16th Street, N.W., Washington 6, D.C.
>
> *AFL-CIO News and Mat Service:* A mimeographed version of material prepared for the *AFL-CIO News.* It is sent to a list of official labor papers three times a a week.
>
> *AFL-CIO American Federationist:* A monthly magazine published by the AFL-CIO, 815 16th Street, N.W., Washington 6, D.C.
>
> *Labor:* A weekly labor paper published by the Railway Brotherhoods, 400 First St., N.W., Washington, D.C.
>
> *Press Associates, Inc.* (PAI): A labor news and mat service, 312 Pennsylvania Avenue, S.E., Washington, D.C.

There are approximately 100 Negro newspapers and magazines which serve the specialized interests of Negro citizens comprising more than 10 per cent of the population. Negro papers are primarily interested in the advancement of their race. Any information related to this cause and to the activities of Negroes will find these media receptive. These newspapers have their own publishers association and are served by the Associated Negro Press news service. The Negro market is one of increasing significance.

THE PRESS WANTS NEWS. This vast array of newspapers wants one thing from the publicist—*NEWS!* The press is not interested in providing people and programs with publicity. News and entertainment features are the lifeblood of these publications. Although there is no precise definition, most journalists agree that news, essentially, is any material that an editor deems timely, of interest, or of consequence to his readers. The content of a newspaper provides the editor's definition of news.

The bulk of today's publicity output never appears in print. Large batches of publicity flood the newsrooms of our daily and weekly newspapers only to wind up in wastebaskets. To be specific, in studies made at the University of Wisconsin, it was found that: (1) out of approximately 300 releases received in a five-day period by a typical morning newspaper, 242 were rejected; (2) out of 339 publicity releases received in a five-day period by a typical evening newspaper, 218 were rejected outright, 32 were used as received, 42 were rewritten and used; (3) out of 113 publicity releases, totaling 363 pages, received in one week by a typical weekly newspaper, exactly *three* were used.

More recently, another researcher studying the input and use of publicity releases in five Milwaukee news media collected a total of 1,789 rejected releases in one full week. On the other hand, he found that, of the nonwire, nonsyndicated segment of the *Milwaukee Sentinel*'s news content, some 30 per cent of this came from publicity releases or phone calls. The *Milwaukee Journal* got 24 per cent of its nonwire, nonsyndicated news content from public relations sources. The public relations content for WTMJ-TV was found to be 12 per cent in terms of number of news items and 13 per cent in terms of air time. For WTMJ radio, it was about 10 per cent and 16 per cent, respectively. Twelve per cent of the items on the Wisconsin state AP wire came from publicists.[5] The lesson is clear: If the editor thinks the story newsworthy, he'll use it.

The reasons for these wholesale rejections are valid and well-known, yet the waste of effort and resulting irritation to editors continue. Professor James Julian surveyed 61 editors to determine the main reasons why more releases are dumped into wastebaskets than are used in print. He was given these reasons, in order of frequency:

Limited local interest
No reader interest at all
Story poorly written
Reasons of policy
Disguised advertising
Material obviously faked
Apparent inaccuracy in story
Duplication of release
Material stretched too thin

Providing newspapers with news, pictures, and features of value and of timely interest to readers not only brings publicity but *builds good press relations as well.* James R. Sutphen, who served as city editor on the Bergen, N.J. *Evening Record,* points the way to successful publicity practice with sound advice: "Daily newspapers labor continually under two serious shortages, lack of space and lack of time. There never is enough space to print all the news; there is never enough time to gather it, edit it, and publish it. So any aid they can obtain that will save space or time is welcome. . . . A responsible daily newspaper deals in only one commodity, news. Whatever agency helps editors and reporters obtain news accurately, completely, swiftly, they appreciate. Whatever agency blocks obtaining the news accurately, completely, and swiftly, they resent. Press relations is as simple as that."

Not to be minimized or overlooked in publicity is the photograph. This is an age of pictorial reporting. Reader-interest studies consistently show

---

5 Lt. Col. William Schabacker, "Public Relations and the News Media." Unpublished master's thesis, University of Wisconsin, 1963. For a brief account, see "PR News Content of Media Measured," *Editor & Publisher*, Vol. 96, June 8, 1963.

pictures at the top of the heap. Stories can be told dramatically and effectively in pictures. Good pictorial reporting will get a story in when a straight news story won't be accepted. Newspapers and magazines never have enough really good pictures.

AVENUES OF APPROACH. There are many different avenues in getting publicity into print. Each one has its special uses and its peculiar stop-and-go lights. Each one has a place in the going program. Knowledge of which avenue to use in a given instance and of the bumps and smooth places along each thoroughfare is a requisite.

The two major press associations or wire services, *The Associated Press* and *United Press International* provide daily newspapers and news magazines with the bulk of their straight news and much of their feature material. For

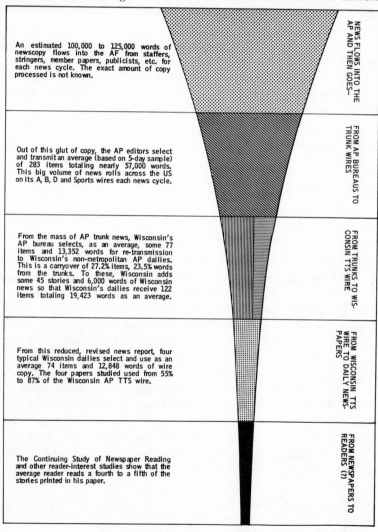

An estimated 100,000 to 125,000 words of newscopy flows into the AP from staffers, stringers, member papers, publicists, etc. for each news cycle. The exact amount of copy processed is not known.

NEWS FLOWS INTO THE AP AND THEN GOES—

Out of this glut of copy, the AP editors select and transmit an average (based on 5-day sample) of 283 items totaling nearly 57,000 words. This big volume of news rolls across the US on its A, B, D and Sports wires each news cycle.

FROM AP BUREAUS TO TRUNK WIRES

From the mass of AP trunk news, Wisconsin's AP bureau selects, as an average, some 77 items and 13,352 words for re-transmission to Wisconsin's non-metropolitan AP dailies. This is a carryover of 27.2% items, 23.5% words from the trunks. To these, Wisconsin adds some 45 stories and 6,000 words of Wisconsin news so that Wisconsin's dailies receive 122 items totaling 19,423 words as an average.

FROM TRUNKS TO WISCONSIN TTS WIRE

From this reduced, revised news report, four typical Wisconsin dailies select and use as an average 74 items and 12,848 words of wire copy. The four papers studied used from 55% to 87% of the Wisconsin AP TTS wire.

FROM WISCONSIN TTS WIRE TO DAILY NEWSPAPERS

The Continuing Study of Newspaper Reading and other reader-interest studies show that the average reader reads a fourth to a fifth of the stories printed in his paper.

FROM NEWSPAPERS TO READERS (?)

high reader-interest value, spot news of state, regional, or national significance, the wire service offers the most economical and effective outlet. Publicity with a "local angle" of local interest can be more properly directed to the individual newspaper where that local interest exists. Getting a story on the wires assures immediate and widespread coverage. It also increases the acceptability of your copy. Publicity that comes clacking in over the wire service printer or Teletypesetter tape is no longer "publicity." It is news! A well-written wire story can reach newspaper readers across the nation at little cost.

Feeding material to the press via the wire services generally means that it will be rewritten and compressed. Fat and puffery will be squeezed out. What starts out as an 850-word release in Washington, D.C. may wind up as a 50-word story in a Wisconsin newspaper. There is a steady compression and deletion of the tremendous bulk of material fed into the news wires as news progresses from Berlin, Germany, to Boise, Idaho. This is shown in the flow chart which was based on a five-day analysis of the content and flow of news in the Associated Press from trunk wire to state wire to daily newspaper.[6]

The Local Daily Newspaper

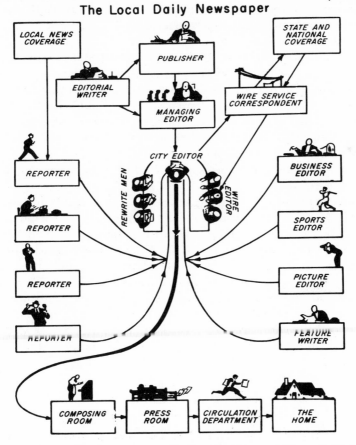

6 For details on this study, see Scott M. Cutlip, "Content and Flow of AP News—From Trunk to TTS to Reader," *Journalism Quarterly,* Vol. 31, Fall, 1954.

Each of the two press services operates with national trunk wires, regional wires, and state wires in the United States. Each has its general headquarters in New York with bureaus and clients around the world. The best approach to the wire service is through the nearest bureau or "stringer" correspondent. With the spread of Teletypesetter wire circuits and the growth of wire transmission of photographs, the importance of using the wire services has greatly increased. The mailed release or mailed picture is, by the same fact, less and less effective. With the advent of TTS, the wireheads have become the key to effective newspaper publicity.[7] Some agencies provide news releases on TTS tape.

In the nation's major news centers, many practitioners use commercially operated publicity wires to speed their releases to the city's newsrooms. Today in the newsrooms of New York City, Chicago, Los Angeles, San Francisco, Boston, Detroit, major Canadian cities, and London, England, publicity wire teleprinters stand alongside the bank of clattering wire news machines. These PR teleprinters are bringing to the newsroom publicity releases fed into a teletype system in a central midtown office. The first such publicity presswire service started in New York City by Herbert Muschel in March, 1954, now serves 27 news outlets in Manhattan. Its success quickly brought similar services in other major news centers in the United States, Canada, and England. In Chicago the PR News Service, operated by the City Press Association of Chicago, also offers messenger service for photos and bulky packages to the city's newspapers and wire services.[8] These publicity wires, for a fee, provide the client with swift transmission of his news, simultaneous release to all media (which eliminates charge of favoritism), and lend a flavor of news to the release, at least as the newsman is accustomed to perceiving news.

Another large portion of newspaper content is supplied by the feature, photo, and specialized news syndicates. Here, as in the case of the wire service, placement of a picture or a feature with a syndicate assures wide, economical coverage ˙and increases the acceptability of material. For example, the feature service, NEA—Newspaper Enterprise Association—serves some 800 daily newspapers in the United States and Canada and supplies colored comics to 386 Sunday and weekend papers. In addition, nearly 500 weekly papers use its features. A typical feature service, NEA provides pictures, comics, sports features, news features, woman's page features, columns, editorials,—in fact, everything a newspaper needs, down to fillers. Material can be channeled to the press through such syndicates as NEA, King's Feature Service, United Features, Central Press Association, McNaught's, and many others.

---

[7] See Walter Gieber, "Across the Desk: A Study of 16 Telegraph Editors," *Journalism Quarterly*, Vol. 33, Fall, 1956.

[8] For more PR wires, see Victor J. Danilov, "The News Wire Story," *Public Relations Journal*, Vol. 16, December, 1960; Thomas Babinski, "Canada News-Wire," *PR in Canada*, April, 1961; Philip N. Schuyler, "Business Publicity Flows to Media via PR Circuits," *Editor & Publisher*, Vol. 93, July 30, 1960.

A complete list of feature and specialized syndicate outlets for publicity is published annually in the *Editor & Publisher International Yearbook*. The 1964 edition, for example, listed 265 general feature services. Many of them deal in a specialized type of news, such as *Science Service, Religious News Service,* and *Fine Arts Features.* A story carefully targeted on the right syndicate will get a nationwide ride.

In dealing with the daily newspaper, the publicist quickly learns the importance of dealing with the specialist in the newspaper office. If it is a sports event that he seeks to promote, he works directly with the sports department. If it is a straight news story of local interest, he deals with either the city editor or the reporter on the specific assignment. If the publicity program is aimed at the feminine reader, then he channels material through the woman's editor or the society editor. It is helpful to remember that no two newspaper organizations are exactly alike. The same titles often mean different things on different newspapers.

The publicist should be especially alert to the publicity possibilities of the Sunday newspaper, which, in many ways, is much different. The Sunday newspaper generally gets a longer, more intensive reading on a full day of leisure. It tends to emphasize feature material—copy without a time element —more than the daily paper does. Special features and pictures without a time peg are supplied early in the week. Because of the now standard five-day work week, news is relatively scarce on Sundays and Mondays. Thus, newspapers are more receptive to material on these publication days. The publicist must also know and use the Sunday supplement magazines, such as *This Week, Parade,* and *Family Weekly.* The combined circulation of these "Sunday magazines"—some are distributed with Saturday papers—is approximately 34,000,000. Their content tends to be more magazine than newspaper. All are edited within a few blocks of each other in midtown Manhattan, and all of them try to straddle the magazine and newspaper worlds. Most of these supplements prefer to put their own writers on a story, rather than to take one from a publicist. They are eager for tips and story memos. Through them you can reach the major market centers of the nation.[9]

THE MAGAZINE MARKET. The broad array of American magazines, from the giants such as *Reader's Digest, Life, Look,* and *McCall's* to the trade journals such as *Woman's Wear Daily* and *Furniture Digest* to the hobby magazines such as *Yachting,* provide another effective publicity medium. The number, variety, and circulations of magazines are almost limitless. There are more than 950 general consumer magazines in the United States. Of these, 40 per cent are edited for general appeal; 10 per cent provide news and commentary; 6 per cent are aimed at the woman; 18 per cent are for farmers and farm families; and 26 per cent are comic magazines designed for children.

---

9 See William A. Hachten, "Sunday Magazines: End of an Era," *Columbia Journalism Review,* Vol. 2, Summer, 1963.

Within each of these categories there is wide variation. In addition to these general magazines there are thousands of trade and specialized publications.

There is a magazine or periodical catering to every known interest, vocation, and hobby of the American. For the promoter of pet foods, for example, there are these possible outlets: *All Pets Magazine, The Aquarium, Audubon Magazine, Cats Magazine, Our Dumb Animals, Popular Dogs,* and so forth. To reach the larger, more influential market of women consumers, voters, and shareholders, there is a strong group of women's magazines. For the young girl there is *Seventeen,* reaching a group with much spending power; for the woman in her twenties, there is, for example, *Glamour;* for older women, the publicist can use the channels of *McCall's, Ladies Home Journal,* and *Good Housekeeping.*[10] The readers of each magazine have distinct, non-interchangeable characteristics. This enables the publicist to aim his message accurately at a specific group—a fundamental of effective communication.

Opinion leaders read many magazines. The survey, *Public Use of the Library and Other Sources of Information,* records that "seven out of ten adults report reading at least one magazine regularly." Lazarsfeld and Kendall reported in their book, *Radio Listening in America,* that 61 per cent of persons interviewed read at least one magazine regularly. Magazines provide more durable information than do newspapers. The magazine reader has the opportunity to read, reread, discuss, and debate the information gleaned from this source. There is a trend in general magazines away from fiction and entertainment features toward more investigative and interpretative reporting of current issues. The vitality and force of magazines in shaping opinions, fashioning clothes, designing houses, setting standards for profession or business, and enlisting political support have been demonstrated since the first two American magazines were published in January, 1741.

Somewhat apart are the news magazines which want information of a spot-news nature and which emphasize the time element, except for special features in "the back of the book." From these the practitioner builds a series of specialized mailing lists to reach his particular publics. Publicity placement should be preceded by a careful analysis of the publication's readers, its editorial formula, its advertising content, and the market it serves. As Clay Schoenfeld, both a magazine writer and practitioner, counsels: "The best hint on how to communicate with a particular magazine audience is the magazine itself. If the editor weren't communicating well he wouldn't be in business." The smart publicist studies the magazine's topics, style, policies, trends, format, and so forth, and then translates this knowledge into slanting his pieces for a particular publication.

The practitioner can build a working list by using the resources of Ayer's *Directory, The Writer's Market* (published annually by *Writer's Digest,* a

---

10 See Robert E. Doherty, "Our Class-Conscious Women's Magazines," *Nieman Reports,* Vol. 17, September, 1963.

magazine for free-lancers), and Bacon's *Publicity Checker,* also published annually, and the directories of Standard Rate and Data Service.

Magazine publicity is supplementary to press publicity. In working with mass-circulation magazines of general interest and those dealing with broad groups in our population—women's magazines, men's magazines, and so forth —the publicist generally does not submit prepared material. Rather he works on a tip or query basis when he has something which would have reader appeal for these broad audiences. He submits story outlines or feature suggestions. If one is accepted, he then works with the magazine's staff or free-lance writers in its development. The job here is one of selling an idea and then providing cooperation to writer and photographer, who build the idea into an article.

An avenue of approach often used, but sometimes overlooked, is that of dealing with a free-lancer. Free-lance writers who sell to the national magazines are interested in "a real *account* of an institution, a man, or an event which possesses at least one of these three qualities: (1) national importance or significance; (2) elements of struggle, conflict, contest, or drama; (3) anecdotal enrichment and entertainment value." It is common practice to give a free-lancer a good story to develop. The free-lancer gets a check; the publicist, a publicity break in a magazine. The Society of Magazine Writers, 520 Fifth Avenue, New York City, maintains a referral service through which PR officials can tap a pool of professional writing skill for special projects.

For the smaller, more specialized publications, such as trade journals and professional publications, it is practical to submit prepared news items and feature material. If newsworthy for that specific audience, they are likely to be used in the form in which they are offered. Publicity in the trade journals can be highly productive. Practitioners are putting more emphasis on these outlets. Consider these examples: A manufacturer publicized a new brake installation manual in the automotive trade press and got 2,000 orders for the book; a photo-spread on new lighting fixtures in *House & Home* brought requests for catalogs from 1,500 home builders. Trade-journal readers form a highly motivated and sharply defined target.[11]

THE RADIO AUDIENCE. Radio broadcasts are a part of our daily life. Radio exerts strong influence. Radio broadcasting has adjusted itself to TV and reasserted its place in the mass-communications net. Radio offers a wide range of possibilities to the publicist. It reaches the breakfast table and living room, rides to and from work in the car, invades the bedroom, and goes along to the beach, to the woods, and even on fishing trips—a flexibility that TV finds hard to match. Its influence permeates every segment of society. Radio is a vital part of the American scene. It is a mobile medium in mobile America.

Radio's versatility is indicated by these examples. Texaco's long-term sponsorship of the Saturday afternoon Metropolitan Opera broadcasts has

---

11 Janet Laib, "The Trade Press," *Public Opinion Quarterly,* Vol. 19, Spring, 1955.

brought it the loyalty and patronage of opera fans—most of whom are affluent and influential in their communities. These broadcasts reach some 2 million music lovers in the United States and Canada over a special network of 115 United States stations and 36 Canadian stations. Texaco's opera network includes both independent and network-affiliated stations—which illustrates how radio outlets can be tailored to a sponsor's market. Texaco views this program as a public relations vehicle, and thus holds its commercials to the bare minimum. As one writer observes: "The commercials have a public relations impact that a hard pitch would destroy." [12]

Eastern Air Lines, like other carriers, was long plagued with the problem of its switchboards becoming jammed with calls from thousands of passengers and would-be passengers, all telephoning at the same time for information on departing and arriving flights. This communications jam resulted in irritations and lost customers. Eastern found its solution in radio. Eastern started *Flite-Facts*—announcements of approximately one minute each hour, seven days a week, from 6 A.M. and continuing 19 times through the day until midnight on one station in each of Eastern's ten key cities. To increase the reach of this program, Eastern made available, on loan, some 1,000 radios to the persons responsible for booking transportation in the large firms on its routes.[13]

Radio's vitality is reflected in the following figures. More than 98 per cent of American homes—some 56 million in number—have radios. Most have more than one. More than half our cars have radios. In 1964 it was estimated that there were more than 150 million radio sets in use in the United States. These sets can receive programs up to 18 hours a day (a few stations operate around the clock) fed from more than 3,900 AM stations, 1,000 commercial FM stations, and 150 educational FM stations. Radio stations are to be found in comparatively small towns of 5,000 population as well as in the large urban centers. Radio is ubiquitous. Though a mass medium, it possesses the qualities of a direct, personal touch as it uses the spoken word, for the most part, to convey its message.

Arthur Godfrey, who has used radio effectively, put his finger on this *intimate* quality of radio in describing the turning point in his career. ". . . lying in that hospital listening to the radio, I realized for the first time how really intimate the medium is and how ridiculously ineffective most of the speakers were . . . they were not *talking,* they were *reading,* and therefore convincing no one. . . . I decided I'd do things differently. . . . When I face a mike I have a mental image of only one person listening to me and I talk to that one person."

Today's radio fare is largely built around music, weather, news, and sports, all heavily loaded with commercials. The disc jockey is a central figure

---

[12] L. L. L. Golden, "Ask the Man Who Listens," *Saturday Review,* Vol. 46, May 11, 1963, p. 60.

[13] Malcolm A. McIntyre, "How Eastern Keeps Its Seats Occupied and Its Phone Unoccupied," *Broadcasting,* May 14, 1962, p. 22.

in this program mix. Radio flourishes on conversation, debate, discussion, and talks. The increased emphasis on news and discussion-type programs—such as N.B.C.'s Weekend Monitor format—opens up many possibilities for the publicist. Although radio offers a blanketing medium, it can also be used to select certain class or specific audiences—as in the case of Texaco's Metropolitan Opera broadcasts.

One researcher has pointed out that ". . . although total program audience must always be of primary concern, a dissection of this audience is a tremendous value to many who would influence certain strata. Actually, the 'radio audience' is no more a homogeneous whole than is the population of the United States. It is composed of many 'cells' which can be stratified not only by economic group but also by geographic region, community size and character, family size and composition, etc." If you want to reach influentials, you sponsor classical music; if you want to reach a rural audience, you play hill-billy music. If you want to reach today's lively, knowledgeable teen-agers, you do it through their favorite disc jockey. If you want to reach the broad span of the general public via radio, your best bet is the frequent newscast.

There are also many drawbacks to the use of radio. One publicist warns that ". . . it cannot hold our audience for us, if our program doesn't warrant attention. Nor can it protect us from competition from other and better programs broadcast at the same hour. . . . Reaching the listener in the home has its drawbacks as well as its advantages. The telephone bell, the arrival of visitors, the baby's wail from the nursery—any or all of these can break in on your time and whisk your listener away. . . . A dropped stitch or a trivial question from Junior can compete for your listener's attention—and almost always win."

Radio is primarily a medium of news and of entertainment. Its use as a public relations tool must be approached within this context. The ways to reach the radio audience are (1) through news and informational programs; (2) with programs of entertainment which will successfully compete with other program fare; and (3) through the feature programs, such as advice for the housewife, and the like. Methods of using radio include furnishing news, arranging for broadcast of special events, obtaining free "public service" time from the station for programs or from the sponsors of commercial programs, or by the purchase of paid time for your message.

Nonprofit organizations must depend primarily on public service programming. Public service time is seldom prime listening time, but it is not without value. In nonprime times, the competition of other stations is not so stiff, and you can still reach sizable audiences if your program fare attracts and holds listeners. In any event, radio requires a good bit of money in script and production costs as well as air time. These are the main possibilities in public service programming:

1. Special programs based on interviews, group discussions, demonstrations, and so forth, either in a series or in a one-time-only presentation,

2. Similar but shorter presentations inserted as "participating" features of other programs,
3. Brief spot announcements made at various times during a broadcast day. With radio's local format, the opportunities for free spots is much greater than it was formerly,
4. Personality spots made by on-the-air personalities, such as disc jockeys, farm directors, or directors of women's shows,
5. News items sent directly to the station or fed in by way of the station's news service,
6. Editorials prepared by the station endorsing your program or campaign.

Those who would use the broadcast channels to reach the public must bear in mind that stations are business enterprises operated to make a profit for their owners. Just as the newspaper has space to sell, the broadcaster has only one commodity, *time,* to sell. Except for bona fide public service announcements, the broadcaster ordinarily cannot afford to air free advertising. Thus, it is essential that the PR man seeking to use these outlets send genuinely *newsworthy* releases—written in the special style and format preferred for on-the-air delivery—to the news directors of stations or networks. United States broadcasters are complaining increasingly about the flood of so-called "news" releases and other efforts to get free air time. The publicist who gets his release back from a station or network along with an advertising rate card usually has no one else but himself to blame.

Every listener survey shows news broadcasts at the top or near the top of the list of programs preferred by most listeners. By providing news for the radio newscast, the publicist can get a wide hearing for his story within the audience limits of a given station or set of stations. Radio newsrooms want news prepared for radio, not carbon copies or mimeographed copies of newspaper releases. They want news written for bulletin presentation. Radio news editors want all difficult names and words phoneticized for the announcer. A 100-word story is the headline story on the newscast. Radio must cover the world in 13.5 minutes; sometimes it does it in 4 minutes! Radio wants news written for the ear, not for the eye. Radio news must be informal, conversational, brief, to the point—and, above all, accurate! Once spoken, errors cannot be recalled and corrected. One never gets exactly the same audience twice in radio. Radio newsmen expect and deserve equal treatment in the release of news and in the coverage of special events. Good results in radio news can be obtained by supplying tape-recorded interviews and news events.

Theodore Koop of CBS Radio counsels practitioners, ". . . for radio's sake, please call them news releases and not press releases. . . . The wordage of releases received in a single mail may equal those of a novel. Yet CBS Radio News in Washington, for instance, broadcasts only about 8,500 words a day. . . . It is obvious that most releases are written by former newspapermen who think in newspaper terms. Many of them are only vaguely aware that radio and TV news have special requirements. . . . For radio and TV, the publicist must be content with hitting the high spots."

An essential part of the working library includes, among the reference works, *Broadcasting,* the weekly journal of radio and television. The annual yearbook number, *Broadcasting Yearbook Issue,* lists radio and television stations and provides detailed information on these media and the markets they serve. It is possible to get monitored transcripts on what radio and television are saying about one's clients. There are firms that provide "listening" service and will monitor specific stations or specific programs for a fee.

In working with the broadcast stations, the practitioner should know and observe the regulations imposed by federal law, particularly those 1960 amendments to the Federal Communications Act outlawing payola, plugola, and the rigging of question games.

TELEVISION. The communication phenomenon of the century, television, has great force and scope as a publicity medium. Outstripping all other mass media, TV grew to full size in one decade—the 1950's. A medium which permits the use of the printed word, spoken word, pictures in motion, color, music, animation, and sound effects—all blended into one message—possesses unmeasured potency. It offers a vast range of possibilities for telling a story, from a terse, 60-second film clip on a TV newscast to a one-half-hour or one-hour documentary film.

Television has grown in scope and impact with incredible rapidity. It was developed on an experimental basis prior to World War II. The F.C.C. authorized commercial TV to start July 1, 1941, but its full development was held back by the entry into World War II. Several stations went on the air soon after the war, but because of the problem of finding sufficient channels, the F.C.C. froze all station applications from 1948 to 1952. From 1952 on, TV has grown rapidly in number of stations, size of audiences, and in perfection of its broadcast techniques. In 1964 there were more than 51,590,000 TV sets receiving programs broadcast from 653 TV stations. In addition to the 571 VHF and UHF commercial stations, there were 82 educational TV stations authorized or on the air. No medium has ever developed so rapidly in size, scope, and strength.

TV's sharp impact on public opinion has been repeatedly and dramatically reflected in recent Presidential elections. The 1956 Presidential campaign marked a definite break from the campaigning techniques which had been in vogue since late in the last century. The major candidates and parties relied heavily on TV to get their message across to the nation's voters. This was particularly true of Eisenhower, the winner. The Democratic candidate for vice-president that year the late Estes Kefauver—had won his national fame through a series of dramatic televised crime hearings.

TV's power was clearly demonstrated in the 1960 election, when President John F. Kennedy turned the TV debates with his opponent, Richard M. Nixon, to his advantage. The "Great Debates" which brought the two contestants into direct confrontation in four nationally televised debates marked an important new development in American politics. If, as Theodore H. White suggests, "the TV debates did little to advance the reasonable discussion of the issues," they did give the voters a sense of participation in this contest. Dr. George Gallup estimates that a total of 85,000,000 Americans watched one or more of the debates. Pollster Elmo Roper estimated that 57 per cent of those who voted believed that the TV debates had influenced their decisions. President Kennedy himself testified following the election, "It was TV more than anything else that turned the tide." [14] His judgment is confirmed in research that found "the first debate appears to have set the pattern of change, with Kennedy's TV image becoming more favorable, while Nixon's becomes less favorable." [15] Ironically, Nixon had saved his political life in the 1952 campaign with a dramatic TV appeal. TV's cost, its impact, and its demand for colorful, photogenic personalities have raised serious implications for the nation's political processes.

TV viewers generally like the program fare they are getting on television and rate the TV news shows as reliable. Two nationwide surveys by the Elmo Roper firm, one in December, 1959, and one in November, 1961, found that "more people get their news from newspapers than from television, by a narrow margin, but they believe what they see and hear more than what they read." [16] The percentage of those who believe television news most increased by 10 per cent over this two-year period. Thus the publicist who gets his story told on the TV news program gets it told by a credible source.

A more comprehensive study, published in 1963, concluded: "The average American viewer spends hours a day in front of his TV set and finds it a relaxing and pleasant—now an integral—part of his daily life: certainly not without important costs, but by and large, in his judgment, well worth them. . . . The programs, on the whole, he considers good—somewhat better than satisfactory. . . . He would like TV to be more informative and educational but certainly not at the expense of entertainment. Aside from the day's news and weather—which he watches regularly—he rarely uses the set as a deliberate source of information." [17] Like radio, TV is primarily a news and entertainment medium and should be approached within this context.

Television has impact and realism, is welcomed into the home, and is readily available as a publicity medium for practitioners who will take the time and trouble to learn how to use it. Increasingly a larger portion of TV time is being given to news broadcasts and news-documentary programs. These programs offer many opportunities to the alert publicist. Local stations find news coverage costly and welcome an assist from the PR man who can provide TV newsworthy film.

---

14 Quoted in Theodore H. White's *The Making of a President, 1960* (New York: Atheneum Press, 1961), p. 294. An excellent work, full of valuable information for the practitioner.

15 "Candidate Images," a chapter by Percy H. Tannenbaum, Bradley S. Greenberg, and Fred R. Silverman in *The Great Debates*, edited by Sidney Kraus (Bloomington: Indiana University Press, 1962), p. 281. A collection of research papers analyzing this historic use of TV.

16 John Tebbell, "What News Does the Public Believe?", *Saturday Review*, Vol. 45, March 10, 1962. Also to be found in the report, "The Public's Attitudes Toward Television and Other Media," published by Television Information Office, 1962.

17 Gary A. Steiner, *The People Look at Television. A Study of Audience Attitudes* (New York: Alfred A. Knopf, Inc., 1963), pp. 228-29. A voluminous report on a far-reaching study of attitudes toward this powerful new medium.

A United States Department of Commerce survey found that "All surveys indicate that television, in terms of (a) audience identification of the sponsor, (b) remembrance of, and understanding of, the sales point of the commercial, and (c) sales results produced, has greater sales producing impact per person reached than any other advertising medium." Other media dispute these conclusions.

On using TV as a PR tool, Sydney H. Eiges offers this counsel.[18]

> Networks have the glamour, the star appeal and the high-budget programs, but in public relations thinking, television should also be considered as a service provided in hundreds of communities by individual stations. Each of these stations is essentially concerned with its own community. . . . Identifying a story with that of the community at large arouses the interest of the local station and wins its cooperation. . . . Planning a campaign on a local basis can often be more productive than aiming only at networks which are of necessity more difficult to crack. Material and ideas should be aimed specifically at individual communities or regions. Stations should be approached individually and personally.

A local-station TV executive offers these tips to practitioners seeking time on local TV stations: (1) Approach the right person in the station. (2) Have a definite plan to discuss. (3) Have an idea with audience appeal, so that the station won't lose its viewers while your program is on the air. (4) Program idea must be within the station's capabilities. (5) Don't forget to say "Thanks." For the local nonprofit agencies without money and manpower, TV news and hitchhiking spot announcements offer the cheapest and easiest ways to reach the TV audience.

Thus far, TV has developed these formats for its programming: (1) Studio productions—musicals, comedy, drama, vaudeville, puppet shows, audience-participation shows, and so forth; (2) Remote broadcasts of sports events, public events, political conventions, congressional hearings, and so forth; (3) Films—old or reissued Hollywood movies, special documentaries, and films prepared for other audiences. As it has developed its own pattern of programming, TV has borrowed heavily from radio, journalism, Hollywood, and the stage. Selling story ideas to TV producers, getting personalities on the audience-participation shows, getting plugs on the conversation-type shows (for example, NBC's *Tonight* show), and providing film for news and documentary programs are the most common ways the publicist uses to insert his message into this powerful medium.

The expanded news-magazine type news program on TV, on both network and local stations, offers additional opportunities to organizations. On these 30-minute news-magazine programs there is need for short features as well as for spot-news film. The increased use of the documentary format enables organizations to "sell" program ideas to TV producers and sponsors that will carry their message to a large nationwide audience that believes what it sees on TV. One major obstacle to widespread use of TV as a publicity

---

18 Sydney H. Eiges, "The Sky's the Limit . . . ," *Public Relations Journal*, Vol. 11, October, 1955, p. 146.

medium is the heavy cost of preparing and producing programs. Here, as in the case of films, the cost of per-person impact rather than initial outlay should be weighed. Using TV will grow in cost as color becomes more common and as stations insist on getting TV film clips in color. Yet, Lynn Poole, director of public relations for Johns Hopkins University, has demonstrated with the *Johns Hopkins Science Review* that TV programming is within reach of the nonprofit institution and that educational programs can get and hold listeners.

Additional Reading

Ernest F. Andrews, "To Make Television Filmclips Tell Company News—Know the Territory," *Public Relations Journal,* Vol. 19, December, 1963, pp. 28-31.

Anonymous, " 'Pipeline' to Media Is Cutting PR Waste," *Editor & Publisher,* Vol. 93, February 6, 1960.

Bacon's Publicity Handbook. Chicago: R. H. Bacon & Co., 1955.

Erik Barnouw, *Mass Communication: Television, Radio, Film, Press.* New York: Holt, Rinehart & Winston, Inc., 1956.

Lee Feldman, "The Public Relations Man as City Editors See Him," *The Quill,* October, 1961.

Stewart Harral, "21 Points to Watch in Choosing Media," *PR,* Vol. 3, January, 1958.

Michael Horton, "What Television Can Do for Your Image," chapter in Lee H. Bristol, Jr., *Developing the Corporate Image.* Charles Scribner's Sons, 1960.

Joseph T. Klapper, *The Effects of Mass Communication.* New York: The Free Press of Glencoe, Inc., 1960.

Howard Stephenson, "Magazines as Media," chapter in Howard Stephenson, ed., *Handbook of Public Relations.* New York: McGraw-Hill Book Company, Inc., 1960.

Clay Schoenfeld, *Publicity Media and Methods.* New York: The Macmillan Company, 1963.

Bernard Ury, "How Much Publicity in Public Relations?", *Public Relations Journal,* Vol. 16, June, 1960.

CASE PROBLEM

Your university is sponsoring for the fifth summer a four weeks' course for utility-company middle-management executives. This is one of several such courses your school sponsors annually to provide the refresher training demanded by businessmen. Enrollment is limited to 35. Companies represented include telephone companies, Bell System affiliates and independents, gas, power, and light companies. Enrollees this year include accountants, engineers, sales managers, power superintendents, telephone district managers, and so forth. Those enrolled for this year's course come from Spokane, Seattle, and Bellingham, Washington; Boise, Idaho; Butte, Montana; San Diego, San Francisco, and Los Angeles, California; Denver, Colorado; Salt Lake City, Utah; St. Louis, Missouri; and Shreveport, Louisiana.

You have been asked by the Dean of the College of Business Administration to publicize this event in the daily and weekly press, trade journals, and house publications. Prepare a list of publicity outlets to cover your community, your university's region of influence, the enrollees' hometowns, and the trade journals in the fields represented. Use directories cited in this chapter as your sources.

Chapter Eighteen

PRESS

RELATIONS

Good press relationships are earned through honest, helpful news service provided in an atmosphere of mutual respect and candor.

Press relations represent an important part of the practitioner's daily work. The practitioner's standing with the media managers shapes and limits his accomplishments. Their confidence in him is one of his valuable assets. This is too little appreciated. He should constantly bear in mind that, although clients or employers come and go, the press and its gatekeepers are here forever. It is also important to understand the fundamentals. (In this discussion, the term *press* is used broadly to include all mass media.)

THE MAN IN
THE MIDDLE

To be effective in his role as go-between, the practitioner must have the full confidence of his organization and of the press. This is not easy. Their interests often conflict. Organizations want news reported in a manner that will promote their objectives and will not cause them trouble. The press wants news that will interest readers and viewers. Executives complain: "Why does the press always sensationalize things?" "The papers never get things right." "You can't trust reporters." "I didn't say that at all." "Why do reporters enjoy stirring up trouble?" Newsmen counter-complain: "That organization will never come clean." "They won't give us the real news, only a lot of puffs." "They won't let you in to see the men with the news." "What are they trying to hide?" Both sides have a point. The man in the middle must *patiently* bring each side around to understand the problems and viewpoints of the other. This *is* public relations!

303

It is important to keep in mind the underlying conflict of interest which always hovers in the background of this relationship. This basic difference between the publicist advancing a particular cause and the newsman representing the public point of view is a healthy thing. It should be so viewed by both parties. This clash of interest is often emotionalized beyond all proportion. But it does exist and is to be reckoned with. The irritation of the press is understandable. It is all too often flooded with uninteresting, poorly written releases. Too often the publicist drowns a few facts in a sea of words in an effort to get more news space. Or a newspaperman may encounter a tightly drawn press-release curtain put up by an inept practitioner. On the other hand, the press often fails to recognize the service provided in filling a void in comprehensive, constructive news coverage.

The basic conflict lies in the never-ending struggle of the press to keep clear water flowing in the news stream and money coming into the cash register. The other side is the effort of institutions and industries to get their story told accurately and constructively. It might be helpful to list the grievances on both sides of the fence.[1]

These are the complaints most often heard from the press:

1. Attempts by practitioners to color and check the free flow of legitimate news.
2. Space grabbing for "free advertising" with consequent loss of revenue to media.
3. Attempted "influence" and pressure methods of getting into news columns; indirect and sometimes direct bribery of reporters.
4. Gross ignorance of media's editorial requirements; no conception of what news is or how it should be written.
5. Raiding news staffs of experienced men with the lure of higher salaries.

Countercharges most frequently listed by the practitioner include:

1. Failure of the press to do its whole job; failure to increase its reportorial staff to keep pace with the expanding list of socially significant activities demanding news coverage (in the fields of industry, finance, education, medicine, and so forth).
2. The press' slowly changing definition of news which puts emphasis on conflict and minimizes the socially constructive events—the press' sensationalism.
3. Failure to treat news as news regardless of the source; that the attacks on publicity are only lip service to rationalize a basic money motive.
4. Failure to discriminate between the honest, helpful practitioner and the incompetent.
5. Increasing dependence of the press on the function it so frequently and lustily condemns.

PUBLICITY PRINCIPLES

Good relationships can best be achieved by the practice of a few basic principles: (1) *Shoot Squarely;* (2) *Give Service;* (3) *Don't Beg or Carp;* (4) *Don't Ask for Kills.*

---

[1] Victor J. Danilov, "Business Editors List PR Likes and Dislikes," *Editor & Publisher,* Vol. 90, September 14, 1957. Also: Charles Seller, "Small Daily's Handout Heave Exposes Failure of Publicists," *ibid.,* Vol. 91, September 6, 1958.

SHOOT SQUARELY. It is not just an academic nicety to counsel that "honesty is the best policy" in dealing with the press. It is plain common sense. The press men and women are alert, intelligent, critical, and, with very few exceptions, honest. They can spot a phony or shady practice a mile off. They see so many of both. It is their job to get the news. And they generally get it, one way or another. Anyone who tries to thwart or block them through trickery, evasion, and censorship will encounter tough opposition. A publicist may win the battle in such instances, but he is likely to lose the war. The press fires the last shot. Unless a practitioner has the confidence and goodwill of the media gatekeepers, his value to an employer is close to nil. This confidence is compounded of a record of *accuracy, integrity,* and *performance.*

Newspapermen are shrewd, understanding, and sophisticated people. They know the hokum of circus publicity. They play along with it only because they, like all Americans, love a circus. They recognize the inflated and artificial news pegs in the publicity output of a local charity or civic event, and they still use the stuff. They understand and appreciate the position of the man charged with making the most favorable presentation of his cause that the facts will allow. His stuff may be rewritten or tossed aside. If he is candid, he won't lose their confidence. If a publicity representative tries to short-cut, however, or to suppress what the newspaper or TV man considers legitimate public news, he will anger and forfeit the confidence of the press.

Out-and out dishonesty is shortsighted and stupid. The first rule for sound publicity practice is to *be candid and cooperative.* The open-door policy is best. Holding that "the day-to-day stories about us in your local newspaper and on the air publicly measure Quaker's success at being a good business citizen," the Quaker Oats Company advises its staff: "The public, particularly in our plant communities, has a right to know anything about Quaker which is not confidential, as production figures are, for reasons of competition. And the press and radio wants to tell as much of Quaker's story as it considers newsworthy."

General Mills tells its employees: "You represent a company that is honest, ethical, progressive, and has nothing to hide. In the event of an accident or other emergency, see that the newspaper gets the actual facts as quickly as humanly possible." Aware that "railroads have made more newspaper enemies as a result of obstructionism at wreck scenes than in any other way," the New York Central System sets a policy: "Whenever and wherever an accident occurs, it is company policy to permit full access to all reporters and photographers. . . ." New York Central knows that "no amount of obstructionism ever succeeded in stopping a story about an important wreck." Ivy Lee realized this sixty years ago, but there are still executives who insist on trying to suppress accidental details.

Here are some examples: (1) An Eastern plastics maker had a major explosion. Plant officials admitted newsmen to a plant meeting where they were allowed to wait but were told nothing. Reporters finally got the story from the hospitals, and in many cases they were the first to notify families of injured workmen. (2) A Midwest chemical plant call for fire protection while plant workers repaired a break in a chlorine gas line accidentally became exaggerated into a major poison-gas threat. School children were sent home as radio broadcasters flashed warnings. Plant officials, knowing the danger to be slight, could have eased this anxiety, but when the press called, they were not available!

The *Wall Street Journal* reports this example: A Cleveland company refused reporters' requests for a statement on how the company was doing during a period of slack demand. Shortly after, there was a rumor on Wall Street that the company was going in the red in the current quarter. It took a quick statement to the press pinpointing the less severe extent of the decline in earnings to halt an unjustified tumble in the price of the company's stock.

Despite the unhappy consequences which almost inevitably follow attempts to suppress bad news, executives—human as they are—persist. In a state hospital a woman about to undergo surgery was killed when the anesthetic was exploded by a static spark. Hospital administrators persuaded the local press to suppress the story because of its possible effect on other surgery patients. Within 24 hours the community was rife with gruesome rumors spread by the family, friends, nurses, and interns. The story, in three days, reached a metropolitan paper, which broke it on page one. The story rode high on the front pages of the state press for almost a week. The hospital was sharply criticized for its efforts to suppress a tragedy for which, in the beginning, it was blameless. And as is usually the case, *the rumors were worse than the published facts.*

In sharp contrast to this example was the way a Milwaukee hospital handled a similar story a few years later. It quickly made available to the press an accurate and complete reporting of the death of a child in an anesthetic accident. The story was carried through two news cycles and then dropped. Public confidence in the hospital and respect for the medical profession were, if anything, enhanced. When a suppressed story is exposed, it is played far beyond its normal news value. And the suppressor is thought to be guilty of wrong because he tried to hide it. Executives must be counseled against efforts to suppress, to abuse the "off the record" tradition by using it as a gag, or to bottle up news to which the press has reasonable claim. Governmental agencies are being continually criticized on this score.

A perfect illustration of the folly of news suppression is seen in the celebrated case of Army Private William S. Girard, who killed a Japanese woman while she was picking up scrap metal on an Army range in Japan. Because an Army officer made the mistake of trying to suppress this unfortunate incident, the Girard Case became a serious political issue between the United States and Japan, brought our government great embarrassment, and brought the Army unfavorable publicity around the world. What would have been a small, routine one-day story was turned into an unfavorable banner-line story that lived for months.

Such efforts to balk newsmen breed attitudes reflected in this memo of a Detroit news bureau chief to his home office:

> The motto of the _____ corporation's press relations staff, according to one of them, is "We'll give you anything but information." He said it in jest, but the harsh fact is that too often this slogan is observed. _____ guys are, with few exceptions, personable, pleasant fellows. . . . But try for facts and you're up against a wall. Let it be quickly said that _____ is not alone in this regard. . . . The essence of each group's system is this: Avoid answering a question at all if possible. If not, give as vague and inconsequential an answer as possible. And always strive to keep the P.R. man in between the primary source and the newsman.
>
> . . . This very quickly forces the conscientious and resourceful reporter into a couple of courses. He can battle the system frontally and spend all his time and energy fighting with public relations men in an effort to see the people he wants to see. This, in my opinion, is not the best course in Detroit. . . . The better method is to sneak around them. This system, however, has some real limitations.

Another fundamental principle is that *a publicist cannot favor one news outlet at the expense of others.* When he gets caught, he risks the confidence and goodwill of other news outlets. The publicity tune has to be played straight across the keyboard. This is not easy in a hornet's nest of stiff competition, newspapers against newspapers, or newspapers against radio and TV stations. The safest rule is that spot news should go out as fast as possible. Let the news determine the cycle in which it breaks. News and feature material for which the time peg can be fixed should be alternated evenly between the competitors. As a corollary of this, the publicist must protect a newsman's initiative in going after a story. If a reporter gets a tip on a story and asks for the information, it belongs to him. The same information should not be given to other outlets unless they come after it. This, too, will even out on the long pull. It is a policy with which no reporter can justly quarrel.

GIVE SERVICE. The quickest, surest way to gain the cooperation of media men and women is to provide them with *interesting, timely stories and pictures* that they want *when they want them* and in the *form in which they can readily use them.* Successful press relations are built on a foundation of service. Newsmen lean on and cooperate with the PR man who willingly responds to a midnight call for a picture and biographical sketch of an executive who just died. News is a highly perishable commodity and occurs around the clock. Newspaper and newscast deadlines must be met around the clock. *The PR man, likewise, must be on call around the clock.*

What does the press want? The *Syracuse Post-Standard* bluntly tells practitioners: "We don't want your publicity. We do welcome your *news.*" William M. Hines, Jr., Sunday editor of the *Washington Star* explains: "We want ideas, truth and assistance." Ernest K. Lindley of *Newsweek* advises: "We want reliable news and reliable background information. . . . We're interested in new developments, new products, new services, new enterprises, new methods of doing business." John Cameron Swayze counsels: "If you have a story a commentator likes, he'll take it. Have all the facts of the story ready when you suggest it. Know a man's deadlines."

DON'T BEG OR CARP. Nothing irritates media men and women more than a publicist who begs or carps. If the material is not sufficiently newsworthy to earn space in print or time on the air, it is not likely to attract interest in the audience. The editorial people get and hold their jobs by knowing what interests people. Don't beg to have stories used. Don't complain about the treatment of a story if it is used. Don't ask editors to serve as clipping bureaus by asking for tear sheets. One exasperated city editor expressed the irritation produced by these amateurish approaches when he wrote:

> Please, mister, if that's a handout in your hand, just give it to me. That's all there is to it. If we can use it, I'll ask a reporter to rewrite it. If we can't use it, I'll throw it away. Don't hold it under my nose and read it to me with your finger tracing every line. I can read. . . . And don't suggest that we have a little talk about it. I haven't got time for conferences. . . . No use standing there. There are 16 more press agents waiting to see me.

Too many people who deal with the press try to be "editors" on the assumption that they know as much about defining or writing news as the editor or reporter. Too many executives insist on trying to frame news releases as they would like to have them appear in print or on the air. They refuse to accept the fact that this is the newsman's job.[2]

Standard Oil Company of New Jersey tells its managers: "Don't try to be an editor." Johns-Manville advises its executives: "Should a reporter give you a copy of a story to check, review the story for factual accuracy only. Otherwise don't attempt to edit your pet phrases into the copy. Don't try to be an editor. From your viewpoint, facts are more important than the language." The reporter and the newscaster are the judges of how such material may be most effectively presented.

The admonition, "Don't Beg," also covers a warning against trying to pressure publicity into news columns and newscasts by using advertising as a wedge or weapon. There is nothing an independent journalist resents more than to have the publicist work through the advertising department. In most cases, it won't work and will bring only resentment. Advertising belongs in the advertising department, and news—if it is news—will get in the news columns or newscasts. As Johns-Manville counsels in its press handbook: *"The press should not have to beg for news and Johns-Manville should never beg for free space."*

Despite the predictable backfire, some organizations try, from time to time, to use advertising as a club to gain favorable treatment. Some business firms try to work out a publicity-for-advertising deal as a price of placing ads. On occasion they are successful. In most cases the media willing to make such a deal are not effective vehicles for either publicity or advertising. A more com-

---

2 Robert B. McIntyre, "Good Press Relations Is Key to Good PR," *ibid.*, Vol. 95, May 26, 1962. For reminder of PR's stake in the press, see J. H. Smith, Jr., "PR's debt to Journalism as a Practitioner Sees It," *The Quill*, Vol. XLX, January, 1962.

mon headache for the practitioner is in restraining executives who lose their tempers and withdraw advertising in retaliation for publication of unfavorable or undesirable news.

Even the pros make this mistake once in a while. A few years ago the *Wall Street Journal* published six months in advance of the usual unveiling the details of the new car models of the Big Four car makers. The same day General Motors cancelled $11,000 worth of advertising scheduled for that paper. GM also took the *Journal* off its news-release list. This hasty action brought severe criticism from the press. *Editor & Publisher,* voice of editors, said that General Motors' "sledgehammer retaliation through advertising dollars and control of news releases seems to us to be far below the dignity of such a mammoth corporation and more befitting the pique of a corner druggist." General Motors, in calmer wisdom, shortly restored its advertising in the *Journal* and called the matter closed. This happens every so often. A Colorado brewery pulled its advertising from a newspaper which editorially criticized its labor policies and then put it back with due apology. A Portland, Oregon, department store did the same thing. Such instances underline the need for a "church-and-state" relationship between the public relations and advertising functions.

DON'T ASK FOR KILLS. A publicity man has no right to ask a newspaper, magazine, or radio station to suppress or kill a story. To any newsman this is a crude insult. It is asking media men and women to betray their trust. It seldom works and brings only ill will as a reward. *The way to keep unfavorable stories out of the press is to keep situations which produce such stories from taking place.* There are occasions when it is perfectly legitimate to request a delay in publication or to explain to the press any part of a story that might be damaging to the public interest. If there are valid reasons, cards should be laid on the table, face up. The newspapers will cooperate 99 times out of 100. If more than two people know a story, the chances of suppressing it are almost nil.

These principles or "rules of the game" can serve to establish profitable press relationships. One editor once told a group of PR people that the press wants *honesty, speed, brevity, confidence.* Another newspaperman advises: "Be frank, be as cooperative in giving bad news as the good, realize that what your organization does affects a good many people in the community and they have a right to honest reports about your activities." Good press relations flow from the unreserved acceptance that the public has a right to public information. *Good press relationships must be earned.*

THE PRESS CONFERENCE

Frequently used as the occasion for the release of news and as a vehicle to cultivate good press relations is the press conference. There is no better way to give out a story simultaneously to all media, provided the subject is newsworthy. When is a press conference justified? The best practical answer is, "Seldom!" Nothing could be more embarrassing to an educator, businessman, military or civil official than to find, on exposure to the press, that his viewpoint or his announcement contained scant news value. Both he and the press should be spared that. Generally, important controversial matters such as labor-management disputes, political pronouncements, and major industrial policy changes suggest a conference because a discussion, rather than a one-sided statement, is in order. In contrast, matters which constitute no public issue can usually be handled without calling a special meeting of the press. In this category could be such matters as the introduction of a new consumer product, the appointment of a new college president, or the results of a charity campaign for funds.

There are, of course, many types of exceptions. A special event, lavish with drama, may not be a public issue. But the crowd, the spectacle, and the opportunities for feature and photographic angles make it desirable that it be covered personally rather than be reported. The same applies on occasion for celebrities, human tragedies, and highly technical or scientific matters.

Who should be invited to a press conference? As a rule of thumb, everyone representing the press who will not go away disappointed should be invited. If ever in doubt about a particular news medium, it is well to make advance inquiry of that medium. For local events of national significance, the local press should always be given the same welcome and courtesy extended to visiting members. In today's network of news media, the local press is usually linked up importantly with a national or international association.

As host for the conference, there should be an executive or official of the organization functioning an spokesman. On hand also should be experts and specialists capable of being interviewed in depth concerning the particular news matter at hand. All members of the organization participating in the conference should be briefed in advance on the most probable questions that will be put by press members. That will facilitate the answers, provide complete accuracy, place the organization in a favorable light, and put everyone at ease.

How should guests be invited? Invitations should be oral whenever possible. If written, they should be informal and friendly. A telegram sometimes lends a touch of urgency to an invitation.

What equipment should be on hand? For a spot-news break, telephones should be handy and representatives of the wireless services should be standing by. Typewriters, paper, and working space will most likely be needed. For discussion groups, when the news does not have the same urgency, comfort is a prime consideration.

Kits containing information and photographs involved in the meeting should be passed out at the beginning of the press conference, preferably with time to examine them, so that reporters can know what questions they want answered. If the story is complex, exhibits or demonstrations are very much in order. They tend to lighten heavy news substance and enable reporters to interpret in language that readers can readily understand.

The conflicting requirements and spirited competition between reporters from radio and television as against those from the print media pose a difficult problem for the sponsor of a press conference. Space requirements and the distractions of TV cameras, lighting equipment, and so forth, make it difficult to accommodate both electronic and print media reporters in the same conference. Whirring TV cameras that muffle the interviewee's words and block reporters' view of the speaker and the eagerness of some reporters to be seen on TV are common causes of complaint by veteran news reporters. Many PR men have developed the practice of having two conferences, one for the electronic media, one for the print media.[3]

One final note: The *press conference* should not be confused nor mixed with the *press party*. Newsmen prefer not to mix their work and their fun. There is a time and place for each.

PREPARATION OF NEWS

In preparing news for the press, radio, or television, the questions Who?, What?, Where?, When?, Why?, and How? should be answered. Preferably, they should be answered in the first sentence or the first paragraph, then details may be given.

As an example, (who?) John Jones (what?) died (where?) in his home at 10 Main Street (when?) at six o'clock Wednesday evening (why?) of a heart attack brought on by overwork. (How?) He had returned home in midafternoon complaining of a difficulty in breathing and was dead when the doctor arrived.

To assure accuracy in transmission, news copy should be typewritten. Changes of text should be clearly indicated following the accepted rules of marking manuscript. Typewritten copy should be written on plain white paper of the standard 8½ x 11-inch size. Text should be double- or triple-spaced. Paragraphs should be indented at least five typewriter spaces. Only one side of the paper should be used. If text runs more than one sheet, the word "more" should be placed at the bottom of each sheet except the last one, and page numbers should be used. The name, address, and telephone number of the person supplying the news should be written on the manuscript so that it can be verified readily by the publication if desired.

The release must be tailored for its medium. Write news stories for newspapers; terse, radio-style releases for radio, and TV news scripts for TV. Specialized headings are helpful cues to editors.

---

[3] For the way Kennedy Airport met this problem, see "Airport Reporters Defend a Principle," *Editor & Publisher,* Vol. 90, September 14, 1957.

PHOTOGRAPHS

In a wide variety of news, a photograph is invaluable. Quite often the photograph is, in itself, the news. If ever in doubt, a photograph should be included with the news story. The *matte-finish* still picture or one- to two-minute film clip is almost a must for television news. TV is primarily a visual medium. TV releases call for pictures, pictographs, screen slides, and film clips. The matte-finish photos for TV use should be horizontals in the ratio of 4 units of width to 3 units of height. This age of pictorial journalism has put a new premium on the good publicity picture.

One successful practitioner counsels: "Good pictorial coverage is . . . the key. Photographers should never be assigned 'to get some pictures.' Pictures are an intrinsic part of any story, not a by-product. The two basic approaches that we have found to be in greatest demand by the print media are: the 35 mm human-interest approach that attempts to capture reality through the use of natural lighting and an unposed look at the subject matter; and the elaborately prepared, posed and lighted 'setup' shot that depends for its impact on sharpness, clarity, and dramatic composition."

Photographs should be used by the publicist for what they are—*an economical, effective means of reporting a story.* Take, for example, the publicity photograph (shown on p. 313) set up by a noted British firm to dramatize the strength of its renowned bone china. Wedgwood's public relations department arranged for this truck to be balanced on four china teacups to demonstrate their strength. The Tower of London added the authentic British background. Such a photo was bound to get wide coverage—as this one did. Another example of imaginative use of photos to get publicity was that of a transit company which took a night photograph of all its buses, lighted and arranged in the form of a Christmas tree, as a way of saying "Merry Christmas" to its patrons through the local newspaper. Photographs are especially effective in conveying the needs and values of welfare services. One such user is the Cincinnati Family Service Agency, whose photographer says: "Photographs 'spell out' a story more quickly, clearly, and powerfully than any other means of communication, perhaps because of their inherent capacity for conveying mood and evoking emotional response." [4]

Generally, the less descriptive matter needed to amplify or to explain the photograph, the better the acceptance will be. The best photographs of dramatic events are those that need no explanation beyond identification. An example would be a scene showing a wrecked car photographed from such an angle that the reader could see the street marker at the corner, the clock on a nearby store, a body in the street, and the upset bicycle nearby. That tells almost the entire story except for the name of the victim.

---

[4] Margaret R. Weiss, "Communicating a Community Service," *Saturday Review*, Vol. 46, September 14, 1963.

Photographs of groups of more than six or eight people discourage publication because of the space required for identification. Activity implied in a photograph will give it greater interest. This sometimes eliminates the need for identifying all persons.

People being photographed have great trouble with their hands and feet. If standing, they don't know what to do with their hands. If seated, their feet seem to get in the way. Objects held in the hand and objects placed in front of the feet tend to relieve the awkwardness.

Rarely will an experienced photographer provide for publication any type of reprints other than glossy ones. No other kind should be submitted for publication unless specifically requested. Many publicists use a standard-sized print, say 7 x 9 or 8 x 10, to effect savings.

A saying nearly as old as the press is that babies, animals, and pretty girls are sure-fire news pictures. A minority of projects are involved with the interests of these three subjects, but by clever arrangements it is quite often possible to tie in one of them with the actual subject of the news.[5]

---

[5] "Pictures, Publicity, and Placement: A Former Photographer's Views," *Public Relations Journal,* Vol. 18, December, 1961.

ESSENTIALS OF
GOOD COPY

Possible sources of publicity material, steps involved in its preparation, and possible outlets are outlined in the chart on page 315. Although this outline applies to industry, it may be easily modified to serve a nonprofit institution, such as a college. Essentials of good publicity copy are essentials of good news writing. A few reminders can serve as a checklist.

CONTENT. Will the information or news really interest the intended audience?

Does the information answer every reasonable question that readers or listeners may ask?

Is the significance of the information explained in terms of audience?

Is the copy sufficiently newsworthy to survive stiff competition for public attention?

Will the information further the objectives of our institution? Is it useful?

Does the publicity accurately reflect the character and nature of the institution it represents?

Are the facts, names, and dates ACCURATE? Are technical terms explained?

STYLE AND STRUCTURE. Will the lead catch and hold the busy reader's attention? Will it produce a bright, eye-catching headline? Is the lead terse, to the point?

Do the facts of the story support the lead in fact and spirit?

Is it readable copy, stripped of superlatives? Good news copy must be CURT, CLEAR, CONCISE.

Has padding been stripped from the copy? (If you don't do this, the editor will!) Is the copy subject to the charge that it is an effort to get "free advertising"?

Is the information presented as dramatically as possible with this set of facts? Squeeze all the news value you can into your story, but don't exaggerate!

MECHANICS. Is copy legible, double-spaced, each page or ad correctly marked, end of story indicated?

Is source of release fully, correctly given? Easy for editor to check back with source if necessary?

If a fixed time is intended for release of story, is it plainly indicated on the outgoing release?

Is top third of first page blank, for editors who write heads directly on copy?

Is copy of genuine interest to readers of each publication slated to receive release? If not, don't send it.

Would the information be of genuine interest to an audience not provided for in present list? If not, what other outlets should receive copy?

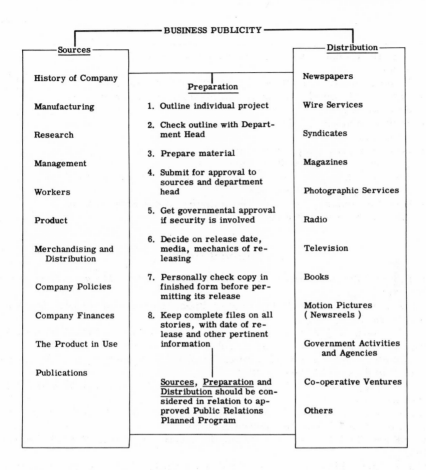

Will the release reach intended outlets while information is still fresh, timely?

If you can answer these questions affirmatively, your copy should pass muster with the toughest-minded news editor. If you can't, you had better take another look at your story. *News is* anything *timely* that is *interesting* and *significant to readers* in respect to their personal affairs or their relation to society. The best news is that which possesses the greatest degree of this interest and significance for the greatest number.

AN EDITOR'S SCORECARD

On the basis of its *fact-finding* to determine editors' attitudes toward the press relations practices of business, Opinion Research Corporation has drawn up this score sheet by which an organization may measure its performance in the eyes of the press.

	(check one)	
	YES	NO
1. Does the company have a sense of what is newsworthy and what is not?	___	___
2. Is the company generally willing to give out information?	___	___
3. Can we rely on the company's word–are they honest in their dealings with us?	___	___
4. Is there someone in the company we can go to when we need information?	___	___
5. Is the company aware of *our* problems–deadlines, reader interest, how a release is written, etc.?	___	___
6. Are we well acquainted with the company–do we know their people and do they know us?	___	___
7. Does the company ever take the initiative–not always make us dig out the news ourselves?	___	___

Additional Reading

John Brooks, "Business Parties . . . and the Free Loader," *Harper's Magazine*, Vol. 208, April, 1954.

"Business Papers Use Only 20 Per Cent of Press Releases," *Advertising Age,* Vol. 25, August 23, 1954.

Marion Cracraft, "If I Were a Public Relations Man Trying to Get Along with Newspapers," *Public Relations Journal,* Vol. 11, May, 1955.

Davis Douthit, "Nationwide Insurance: Problem in Sponsoring a Television Program," *ibid.,* Vol. 19, August, 1963.

Stephen E. Fitzgerald, "Public Relations from the Inside," *Nieman Reports,* Vol. 16, January, 1962.

Sondra K. Gorney, "All-Out Service Provides for Large-scale Press Coverage," *Public Relations Journal,* Vol. 16, November, 1960.

"How to Handle Press Contacts During an Emergency," *ibid.,* Vol. 18, September, 1962.

Carroll A. Lake, "Planning Makes a Press Tour Click," *ibid.,* Vol. 14, January, 1958.

Don Ross, "Do You Hear Gripes with PR Applause," *Editor & Publisher,* Vol. 95, January 6, 1962.

CASE PROBLEM

A nationally known chemical manufacturer opened a plant in the hills of a Southeastern state. The location was chosen on the basis of labor supply, raw materials, tax rates, and humidity conditions. Shortly thereafter, in an interview with local editors and wire service reporters, a top company executive said: "One of our major reasons for locating here–and thus one of our contributions to this community–was to help raise the standard of living of these hillbillies."

The story was widely reported. A storm broke. Nationally known natives of the state wrote burning letters to the newspapers. A syndicated columnist wrote a column, half in anger, half in fun. The governor, senators, and other politicians got into the act with duly indignant protests. People in the community expressed bitter resentment.

As public relations director, what do you recommend be done to remedy or repair this situation?

Chapter Nineteen

PUBLIC

RELATIONS

FOR

BUSINESS

Modern management recognizes that respect, goodwill, and faith in its business must be earned.

Public relations is most commonly associated with business. It is in business that it has had its most extensive and intensive development. Widespread adoption of the practice testifies to the importance that industrialists attach to good relationships and public notice of them. The basic concept is that the public interest is served in the successful operation of business. The foremost effort in industrial practice is to interpret, and thus help "sell," the corporations or industries to the various public groups from which they draw their success.

The interpreting involves exposure which identifies the company with nonprofit causes on occasion. It means exposure which influences decisions on public issues or legislation. It means personalizing and popularizing management as managers and spokesmen. It means enhancing a favorable corporate image, or a favorable industry montage, by exposing acts of industrial statesmanship. It involves exposure that promotes the sale of products or services.

Of the near 4,000,000 businesses in the United States, more than 95 per cent have fewer than 50 employees. Generally, those businesses with less than a quarter-million dollars in assets are classed as "small." The number of small firms is constantly in flux. New ones are started every day; almost an equal number are liquidated daily. *Public relations-mindedness, or its lack, often provides the crucial difference.* Public relations, not just a luxury for large corporations, is a practical necessity for the small business. Goodwill is a requisite for *any* business.

Big Business provides the muscle

for the free enterprise system. Small Business supplies its nervous system. N. N. Foote says: "The power of the consumer to express his wants in his own way will increasingly become a means of restoring communication between himself and the producer. This implies that all who play a part in the function of distribution must see themselves not merely as merchants but as channels of communication. . . ." [1]

PUBLIC RELATIONS
FOR INDUSTRY

At the close of World War II, the vast industrial production machine reverted to peacetime pursuits. Industry found its hands full of labor-management problems, legislative problems, civic problems, and competitive problems. Big Business decided in 1946 that its publics felt unduly adverse toward it. Some of this assumption was no doubt an expression of conscience. But there was little conscience in such major evidences of disfavor as bitter work stoppages, restrictive legislation, and opinion-survey results.

To counter the apparent ground swell, industry in 1946-1947 embarked on a promotional-educational campaign to make itself "popular." The prototype campaign on behalf of "free enterprise" was spearheaded by the National Association of Manufacturers. The techniques used were to advertise and otherwise publicize the idea that there was a cause-and-effect relationship between the free enterprise system and the high standard of living attained in America.

The multi-million-dollar campaign was not effective in any measurable way, although it did teach many in industry, including PR people, that an abstract idea could not be sold in the same way as a bar of soap. The notion persists with some businessmen that industry still is not telling its story. For example, the head of the articulate and powerful American Petroleum Institute lamented some years ago that business was "tongue-tied." Almost ten years later, a Kennecott Copper Corporation official echoed: "American business has failed rather spectacularly to tell and sell the advantages and merits of the economic system we call free enterprise." There's little evidence to support such contentions.

For a decade or so, there has been much concern voiced by businessmen about the "corporate image." Some of this is legitimate concern for building a climate more favorable to business' growth and profit making. Some of this worrying represents an attempt to rationalize self-doubts and uneasy consciences. Probably the first use of the term was in an article, "The Mass Image of Big Business," which appeared in *Harvard Business Review* in 1955.

---

[1] From the essay, "The Autonomy of the Consumer," in *Consumer Behavior*, Lincoln H. Clark, ed., Vol. 1 (New York: New York University Press, 1954). One in a useful three-volume series.

David Finn records: "Consolidated Edison was a pioneer among companies trying to change their image. In 1957, Lippincott and Margulies, industrial designers, reported that Con Ed had changed from a 'firm which had a personality problem if one ever existed' to 'a friendly, informal, progressive,' company. It accomplished this . . . through a new 'jolly' trademark, new 'bright' company colors, a new 'cheerful' sign . . . and 'a really new kind of ad. . . .'" [2] The corporate image must be built of more substantial stuff.

More fundamentally Finn, a counselor, thinks:

> The recent interest of organizations and public figures in images—besides compensating for self-doubt and rationalizing overweening ambition—is thus also an expression of the search for meaning in a confused period of history. The fact that corporate images have turned out to be just another fictitious wardrobe for the Emperor who still walks naked in the streets is not important. The image is so tenacious, not because it dresses up the organization, but because it answers a basic need for finding a convincing purpose for the corporate enterprise.

A newspaper reporter, Bernard Nossiter, thinks the Corporate Conscience has been invented by businessmen to assure us that all is well although the perfect competition theorized by Adam Smith has long since disappeared. Nossiter's point "is not to argue that businessmen are greedy, hypocritical, or irresponsible. Rather it is to suggest that corporate executives, by training and outlook, are ill-equipped to make difficult judgments in the swampy area of social responsibility." [3]

After analyzing several massive efforts on the part of business to sell "free enterprise" and to develop a greater appreciation on the role of profits in our economic system, *Fortune's* William H. Whyte came up with the conclusion that better understanding depended on closer participation between each corporation and its particular publics in matters of mutual interest. Common experience was just about the only sound basis for understanding. Whyte had part of the answer, but there was more to it.

INDUSTRY WAS IN THE DARK

Industrialists, with professional practitioners bending their ears, came to another conclusion, which altered the shape of public relations planning. It was that they did not possess very much really useful information about what special groupings such as employees, hometowners, or stockholders actually thought about the bigness of industry, its power, the corporate leaders and their personal integrity, or the wisdom of their views on politics, education, health, and welfare, nationally or locally. *There was need for more inbound communication from industry's publics.*

---

2 In "Stop Worrying About Your Image," *Harper's Magazine*, Vol. 225, June, 1962.
3 In "The Troubled Conscience of American Business," *Harper's Magazine*, Vol. 227, September, 1963.

There was a third conclusion of significance in shaping contemporary practice. It was that no industrialist was going to be very successful in persuading others to his views on matters other than engineering, production, finance, and marketing until he *earned* authority in other fields—particularly in the field of human values. Industrialists realized that such authority could come only from the publics themselves, and only on the basis of the performance which preceded preachments.

Periodically businessmen are painfully reminded that bad corporate behavior on the part of a few hurts all—in the market place and in the legislative chamber. When firms are caught fixing prices, they not only run afoul of the antitrust laws, but they make a mockery of preachments glorifying "free enterprise." All business suffered when 29 electrical equipment companies admitted rigging their prices in a collusion that spanned seven years. One writer said: ". . . the electrical conspiracy is but one instance in a disheartening pattern of hundreds of similar antitrust violations of many industries." [4] Polls taken by Opinion Research Corporation in the wake of the electrical price-fix case found an increase in public worry about the power of big corporations.[5]

Violation of the public welfare brings lasting damage to business and weakens the credibility of its communications. All business suffers when a congressional committee exposes profiteering in the sale of drugs; when the Federal Trade Commission discovers and publicizes fraudulent advertising; when the Pure Food and Drug Administration catches business selling products harmful to people's health; when the medical profession attacks the tobacco industry for its efforts to get young people to smoke. It is the total performance of the business community that will shape "the corporate image" over the long pull.

A RETURN TO
FUNDAMENTALS

As a result, there has been a noticeable return to the fundamental of "deeds first, and words last." To decide on a course of deeds, professionals led industrialists to fact-finding. The depth studies have shown some interesting and encouraging results. A typical study was that by Social Research, Inc., and reported by Burleigh B. Gardner and Lee Rainwater. Another was the Fisher and Withey study, *Big Business As the People See It.*

Gardner and Rainwater studied the "middle majority" or mass market,

---

[4] Harvey Bresler in a book review in *Saturday Review,* Vol. 45, March 10, 1962, p. 18.

[5] The electrical price-fix story is recorded in two books as well as in the periodical press of that period. See John G. Fuller, *The Gentlemen Conspirators* (New York: Grove Press, 1962); John Herling, *The Great Price Conspiracy* (Washington, D.C.: R. B. Luce, 1962). Thoughtful businessmen know that several generations of students will be directed to these books.

totaling 65 per cent of the population, as distinguished from the factory wage earner. This middle majority was discovered to have five definite favorable attitudes toward Big Business.[6]

1. Big Business is seen as the pace setter of the American economy.
2. Only Big Business can handle the job of production.
3. Big Business is good because the mass production techniques provide goods of uniform quality and at a low cost.
4. Big Business is good because it invests heavily in research and development.
5. Big Business provides many jobs and greater opportunity to work.

Although granting Big Business these virtues, the middle-majority person as well as the factory wage earner has serious anxieties. He is uneasy about the beneficence of Big Business. He feels that this is beyond his control. He fears the possibility that the power of Big Business will be used against him. He is anxious for evidence that business leaders take his interests to heart, and that they take their economic and social responsibilities seriously.

Fisher and Withey, likewise, found no clear-cut stereotypes but a mixture of attitudes. They concluded that ". . . a large portion of those regarding the 'good' effects as more important lodge considerable criticism against big business activities, desire its power reduced, and favor government control. The data clearly indicate, also, that many good points in big business functioning are seen by those who stress the 'bad' effects." The net sum found in this study was that "evaluation of big business arouses . . . a general tendency to stress good points." [7]

Later opinion surveys indicate that during the last decade "public opposition to government control of the economy has definitely weakened," and that, "because the inroads of government into the economy are a gradual process, people see no reason for alarm." Businessmen are far more concerned about government intervention in the economy than is the average voter. Businessmen see government as the umpire who sees that rules of fair play are observed in the market place; the public is receptive to having the federal government shoulder the burden, particularly on widely publicized needs.[8] The public is pragmatic, not doctrinaire—rural citizens did not want "public ownership of utilities," they wanted electricity on the farms. Faced with this problem, business leaders should ponder Adolph Berle's thought: [9]

There is no passionate desire to have the instruments of production in the hands of the state: there is a vivid and very active desire to have the production needed by the community available on terms which the community recognizes as substantially fair. There has been considerable public suspicion of concentra-

6 Burleigh B. Gardner and Lee Rainwater, "The Mass Image of Big Business," *Harvard Business Review*, Vol. 33, November-December, 1955.

7 Burton Fisher and Stephen B. Withey, *Big Business As the People See It* (Ann Arbor: University of Michigan Survey Research Center, December, 1951).

8 *The Public Opinion Index for Industry*, "Free Enterprise in America—1962" (Princeton, N.J.: Opinion Research Corporation. Copyright, 1962).

9 In *The 20th Century Capitalist Revolution* (New York: Harcourt, Brace & World, Inc., 1954), p. 57.

tion of power in great corporations; but then there has also been considerable public apprehension of undue centralized power in the government.

Industry has traditionally thought that its own destiny must rest finally on what it does or fails to do in the interests of the consumer, for the consumer public includes all other groups. There is growing awareness that this is an incomplete answer.[10] Satisfying the interest of the individual solely as a consumer does not suffice. The individual is a many-sided person. He is complex. He wears several hats alternately. One is labeled either *employer* or *employee,* another *Republican* or *Democrat,* and still others *tenant, taxpayer, parent* or *soldier,* as the case may be. With a multiplicity of roles, he has a multiplicity of contrasting convictions and anxieties. He is an economic being, a social and political being. Approached while in the role of a consumer, he is very much in the driver's seat. Industry is dependent on him. Approached in the role of tenant or employee, he is dependent on industry.

Thus, there is the paradox of the same person in several roles, reacting differently in each one. At work, he shows the anxieties explained above, uneasy and insecure about the power of the employer over him. At the close of work, however, he goes grocery shopping and, as free choices, he buys a Swift ham, a can of Heinz beans, a box of Wheaties, a bar of Lifebuoy, a package of Wrigley's gum, a carton of Camels, and scores of other products made by large businesses whose very size and potential power frighten him during the working day.

Meanwhile, industry is taking steps to better prepare its managers for dealing with people in a complex society. Nothing illustrates this better than the shift of emphasis in Executive Development Programs. Business' demand for executive training courses for its people from universities is nearly insatiable. These programs are moving from techniques to broader topics.

The emphasis is no longer purely on refining and perfecting the economic reflexes of the man destined for increasing managerial responsibility. The emphasis is on rounding out the man's personality and broadening his scope of informed interests. There is positive effort to inspire his interest in human and cultural values so that he will seek reasonable opportunities for public service.

The concept is that industry's managerial need in the future will not be for the technician. It will be for the well-balanced human being able to decide what should be done and what should be said. It will be for the man sensitive to trends, capable of research and forethought, of adjustment to change. Finally, he must be a good listener as well as a good communicator and persuader.

Social responsibility in management is an expanding concept. Fewer businessmen year by year look upon it as a nuisance obligation. More businessmen welcome a measure of public responsibilities inside and outside their busi-

---

10 For a critical view, see John Kenneth Galbraith, *The Affluent Society* (Boston: Houghton Mifflin Company, 1958).

nesses as a means of fulfilling personal satisfactions. The concept is getting more implementation and less lip service. As an *Wall Street Journal* has observed: "The fastest growing element in U.S. public service today is the personal participation of businessmen." This trend is being encouraged by industry and cheered by the organizations benefited.

One of the most useful aspects of public service work is that it serves to keep the executive in touch with his community. One of the difficult problems for the corporate decision maker today is to avoid being entrapped in "the ivory towers of business" and thus lose sensitive touch with public opinion. The businessman becomes so enmeshed in the problems of personnel, production, promotion of goods and services, and profits that he gets precious little time to read, to mix with others outside his narrow circle—in short, "to keep in touch." This, increasingly, is the responsibility of his public relations counselor. One who did "keep in touch" was Clarence Randall, long-time head of Inland Steel. He saw the problem clearly: [11]

> Responsibility breeds isolation. As a man's authority increases, so do the barriers that cut him off from direct contact with the world about him. . . . After he reaches the top, he is seldom seen in public, and seldom heard. He becomes a myth. . . . The consequence is that when the great storm comes, as it does sooner or later to every large corporation, and he is driven out into the turbulence of public opinion, he may not be ready to go on deck.

A perfect illustration of this is to be seen in the shock and dismay which officials of U.S. Steel suffered when confronted by an angry and articulate President of the United States after that corporation raised its prices in April, 1962. This showdown in the public arena between the large steelmakers and the President stands as a classic in public relations. U.S. Steel's move to boost prices after concluding a wage agreement with its steel unions was widely publicized as a public relations blunder.

The merits of the issue aside, it is quite clear that U.S. Steel's management did not anticipate the fierce public battle that ensued and caused it to back down on its price increase. This may have been the fault of management in not using the counsel of its PR staff; it may have been the fault of the PR staff in either not anticipating President Kennedy's explosive reaction or in failing to advise management that it would be opposed and criticized in the price move. The consequences are easier to discern. Roy Hoopes, in a book-length account of this public battle, thinks the mistake came from management's insulation and introspective thinking.[12]

Today's businessman is expected to keep in touch with his community and to serve it, both as a businessman and as a citizen.

11 In "Business, Too, Has Its Ivory Towers," *New York Times Magazine,* July 2, 1962.

12 In *The Steel Crisis* (New York: The John Day Company, Inc., 1963). For articles viewing the battle from the PR viewpoint, see Richard Austin Smith, "Behind U. S. Steel's Blunder," *Fortune,* Vol. 66, August, 1962; Anonymous, "Big Steel's Blunder: How Big?", *Printer's Ink,* Vol. 279, April 20, 1962. For a brief account of this dramatic public-opinion struggle, see Wallace Carroll, "Steel: A 72-Hour Drama . . . ," *New York Times,* April 23, 1962, pp. 1 and 25.

THE ROLE OF THE
PRACTITIONER

In recent years there has been an actual increase of programs to publicly demonstrate industry's public-spirited side. These programs have not taken place in a vacuum of silence. Variously, the creation of them, the public notice about them, the interpretations of reactions to them, and often their execution have been in the province of the practitioners. Little wonder that the *Wall Street Journal* in 1962 termed public relations "one of the fastest-growing phases of corporate activity." [13]

Interestingly, at the same time that the industrialist has been addressing his personal attention more to his public responsibilities, he has focused his PR man's efforts more and more on the economic responsibilities of the enterprise. Thus we have the image of the managerial executive heading a drive to get out the voters, and his public relations executive or counsel in a marketing huddle concerning the introduction of a new product.[14]

The opportunities of the practitioners in product promotion have been plentiful. As a result, much of the contemporary growth of the function personnel-wise has been due to added staffing for efforts related to marketing. Meanwhile, there has been no lessening of the practitioner's communications responsibilities in the longer-established areas.

HOW IS IT GOING?

The yardsticks used to measure industry's PR troubles a decade ago were work stoppage, restrictive legislation, and any apparent ill will in the plant community or financial circles. Applying those yardsticks now, there has obviously been an improvement. There are fewer labor strikes, more labor-management cooperation on problems in the work place and in the world market. The fear of Bigness, as such, has occasioned no great wave of public censure or demand for new antitrust legislation. Generally speaking, the "precinct system," in which each enterprise worries particularly about industrial spokesmanship and citizenship in its plant community, is improving the acceptability of industry nationally.

As the newer generations take over the management of industrial enterprises, demonstrably more public relations-mindedness is manifested. Monroe

---

13 For the changing role and requirements of the practitioner, see Earl Newsom, "Business Does Not Function by Divine Right," *Public Relations Journal*, Vol. 19, January, 1963.

14 For a detailed look at the social responsibilities of business, see Howard R. Bowen, *Social Responsibility of the Businessman* (New York: Harper & Row, Publishers, 1953); and Marquis Childs and Douglass Cater, *Ethics in a Business Society* (New York: Harper & Row, Publishers, 1954). (Also in a Mentor Book.)

J. Rathbone, president of Standard Oil Co. of New Jersey, speaks for modern management when he says, "We never do anything of importance without first considering in great detail the public relations aspects." Wise managers will do no less.

It would be misleading to attribute the improvements solely to the greater emphasis on positive PR programs of action coupled with the willingness of the industrialist to listen and be guided by public opinion. There has been a climate, both economically and socially, which has worked in industry's favor. Foremost, the nation has enjoyed unparalleled prosperity. This has reflected itself in family comforts and luxuries. People are not prone to complain or demand change when they have full stomachs and savings in the bank. Additionally, there have been no exceptional stresses of national proportion in the relationships between employers and employees, management and stockholders, corporation and townspeople, manufacturers and suppliers or customers. A sharp and severe economic recession could substantially alter this favorable image.

Time alone, and public opinion, will condone or condemn the character of industry's motivations. At this point, however, public relations has become highly competitive. Several large corporations of the magnitude of a DuPont or an American Telephone and Telegraph have discovered a practical value in the act of PR leadership itself. Ingenuity in devising new programs, projects, or techniques, and the pioneering tryout of them, have news value. A PR journal will hail a new communications project such as a televised directors' meeting or a new public benefit such as a paid holiday for each employee on his birthday as loudly as a medical journal will proclaim a new vaccine.

Competitors within an industry vie with each other's PR projects as heatedly as they do with advertising themes or mechanized production methods. The fact that industrialists have come to regard public service as a necessary ingredient of the competitive formula for success should not be censured summarily. The net results are beneficial. That is, they are in the public's best interests. In the contemporary history of industry, no public group has had to relinquish any major benefit acquired. Whether industry's part in this has been inspired by a conscience or a growing desire to serve—the service is no passing fad. The habit pattern is becoming reflex.

This is in good time, too. Ahead for industry are complex problems, sociological and otherwise, of diversification, decentralization, and automation. Beyond these are the growing public demand that industry expand fast enough to employ the increasing number of young people pouring into the job market, and that it do its hiring without regard to race or religion. There will be alterations involving the revision of organizational and occupational setups which have been in effect for generations. No doubt creative talent will devise appropriate communications devices. Meantime, here are summaries of some current activities which demonstrate the variety and scope of industrial PR.

IDENTIFYING WITH
NONPROFIT CAUSES

The obvious identifications are donations of money, equipment, time, and effort to charitable agencies. This is particularly a phase of plant-city relations. The changing aspect is that "giving" has become less a tax consideration and more a public-responsibility consideration.

Less obvious is the relationship of *industry and higher education,* as the student population grows, generation by generation. The Council for Financial Aid to Education cites five motives for corporate support of higher education.

1. The need and desire to insure the continued flow of educated personnel into business and industry and the nation at large.
2. Maintenance of the dual system of American higher education—gift-supported and tax-supported.
3. The determination to maintain and strengthen the socioeconomic environment in which free enterprise can function most effectively.
4. The practical value to a company, in terms of public relations values of goodwill and prestige, of gifts made in its role of corporate citizen.
5. Promotion of the general welfare of State and Nation.

The corporation is increasingly identified as a substantial giver to higher education, both to its capital fund drives and in response to its students need for aid. In 1963, for example, of the some 700 million dollars given in student aid in the United States, 40 million dollars came from private and corporation programs. Annual corporate giving to education has passed the $200,-000,000 mark. All told, United States corporations give more than a half-billion dollars a year to charitable causes.

In another area of the relationship between industry and education with public relations overtones, there has been industry's attack on the engineer shortage.

1. Underwriting employees in science and engineering courses
2. Equipping engineering school labs
3. Exhibiting in schools to attract the likely candidates
4. Lending teachers to vocational and other schools
5. Arranging plant tours for likely candidates
6. Providing summer jobs for engineering faculty
7. Providing work-and-study programs for students
8. Establishing fellowships and scholarships
9. Sponsoring cross-pollination meetings with science teachers

In the realm of *public service identification,* there is growing variety. Allis-Chalmers, on the occasion of Thomas Edison's birthday, presented "a biography in sound" honoring the inventor on a national television network. Industry has long supported Keep America Beautiful, Inc., whose mission is to preserve the nation's scenic beauty. Programs seek to create public efforts for cleaner surroundings. One of the slogans is "Don't Be A Litterbug—Put Me in a Trash Container." The Carling Brewery Co. also used an intensive antilitterbug campaign in Vermont to win itself goodwill and to help stave off legislation outlawing the throwaway bottle or can.

A number of corporations are lending support to the fine arts as a means of identifying themselves with the public welfare. Such programs earn goodwill among thoughtful, culturally minded persons. Corporate interest in art takes many forms—provision of exhibit space in corporate lobbies or department store windows; purchasing art for corporate offices or for donation to museums and universities; support of costly programs on television; and sponsorship of community art shows. One of the pioneers, Container Corporation of America, began its fine arts program in 1937. Its advertising campaign, "Great Ideas of Western Man," featuring the work of outstanding artists has become widely known. Container also has a traveling exhibit.

S. C. Johnson & Son, the wax maker, assembled the works of 102 American artists to be shown around the world in a cooperative venture with the United States Information Agency. This great collection cost Johnson $750,000 and is entitled, "Art: USA: Now." F. H. Johnson describes his interest "as sort of an act of faith in American art and, at the same time, an experiment by a business firm in international relations on a people-to-people level." Hallmark, the card maker, sponsors art competitions and annually gives the Hallmark Art Award to encourage "painters of promise."

Standard Oil Company of New Jersey has won wide acclaim in cultural circles for its sponsorship on television of the "Play of the Week"—an 18-week series of serious two-hour dramas; its "Age of Kings," a 15-week series of Shakespearean dramas; and, more recently, its "Festival of Performing Arts." L. L. L. Golden observes that these "programs filled a great void, made deep impressions, and brought results which have set the course for future television advertising by the country's leading oil company." [15]

Bamberger's Department Store in New Jersey initiated a program to bring the great artists appearing in nearby New York City to New Jersey audiences that has "won the respect and applause of audiences and performers alike." It first sponsored performances of the Ballet Russe in Newark, where the response was so enthusiastic that the department store has kept the program going. Bamberger's pays all promotional expenses and prints most of the programs as its contribution to the community's cultural program.

In sum, businessmen have found art provides a useful promotion. [16]

PERSONALIZING MANAGEMENT AS SPOKESMEN

Nothing indicates management's desire to bridge the communications gap brought on by Bigness better than the manner in which managers have come to grips with human relations problems. The industrial manager has long participated in making policy concerning employee relations and community

---

15 In "Art and Public Relations," *Saturday Review*, Vol. 46, March 9, 1963.

16 See "Business and Art," *Prentice-Hall Executive Report* (Englewood Cliffs, N.J.: Prentice-Hall, Inc., 1962).

relations. In recent years, however, he has increasingly taken the policies into the shop personally, and he has defended them articulately. Seldom in recent years has the businessman dodged the facts that mechanization displaces people, that safety must be sold, that taxes must be paid, that people must be allowed to participate, and that retirement and unemployment are everybody's problem.

Candor, and face-to-face communication, have become commonplace. When Motorola, Inc. took a major step to realign its topside structure into clear-cut divisions, and on another occasion when it reassigned a large area of military electronics activity from one locality to another, the several hundred key personnel involved were assembled in group meetings. The president, Robert Galvin, explained what was to happen and why, and answered all questions unrehearsed.

Rubbing elbows with employees is back in favor, despite all the difficulties posed by decentralization. Murray F. Gill, board chairman of Kansas Gas and Electric, gave it a novel touch when he visited a generating station to compliment 65 employees on their spotless safety record of 10 years. He put on a chef's hat and apron and broiled steaks for the entire group. The president of State Mutual Life Assurance Company couldn't chat with each policyholder about his company. But, to give a personal touch, he sent each one a paperback phonograph record on which he discussed operations.

Recognition, training, and promotion are prime vehicles in developing productive employee loyalty. Service pins and plaques, banquets and outings, and publicity in the house publication are standbys. The trend is to *training-for-advancement programs.* General Electric, for example, in one year conducted over a thousand courses in factory skills. Within this framework, 1,990 high school graduates took part in the Apprentice Training Program, 1,800 college graduates enlisted in the 10 programs available to them, and 6,551 employees availed themselves of courses in the professional work of managing.

The employee's natural desire for *direct participation with management* and owners has found a mutually satisfactory solution in profit-sharing. More than 10,000 companies have *profit-sharing plans.* One of the best-known programs is that of Eastman Kodak. In this plan Eastman employees receive wage dividends in addition to regular pay. The amounts are based on an employee's earnings over a five-year period, and are related to the amount of dividend declared for owners of common stock. In 1962 the Kodak wage dividend totaled $53,600,000 spread among some 47,500 persons.

Another participation vehicle is *stock ownership.* Many corporations have plans which invite and encourage stock purchases. Chrysler Corporation adopted such a plan in 1956. It is called a "Thrift-Stock Ownership Program" and provides for salaried employees to contribute up to 10 per cent of base salary for stock purchases. The company contributes a share, from 40 to 60 per cent of the employees' savings, depending on the company's ratio of earnings to net sales.

The *Suggestion System* is not new. Its success tends to depend on how effectively it is "sold." The selling, of course, rests partly with the PR function. Ford Motor Company has had a plan in effect for more than 15 years. Its success is attested by the fact that more than 165,000 suggestions have been put into effect, and more than $11,000,000 has been paid to employees for them.

Safety is a never-ending project area—where employees must be persuaded against a natural inclination to take chances. Among the more imaginative projects undertaken recently was that of the Gates Rubber Company in Denver. It was called "Wives' Weekly Jackpot." Each week a wheel was spun, an employee's name was drawn, and his wife was telephoned. She was asked this question, "How many days since the last lost-time injury on your husband's team?" She could know the answer only if her husband had checked the bulletin board on the way home. For the right answer, she got $1. A second question concerned the most recent weekly safety newsletter. For the right answer, she got $10 worth of groceries. In a very nice way, Gates succeeded in getting wives to prod husbands on safety.

The American Car and Foundry Company has used its *house publication, Rolling Stock,* to promote safety in a way that contrasts sharply with the usual reports of safety contests and records. In *Rolling Stock* a headline boldly says, "Suppose You Were Blind." The article is about an employee who offered to be a guinea pig by blindfolding himself for an hour or so. Then he tried futilely to do some of the everyday things, such as tying shoelaces, combing hair, eating breakfast, lighting a cigarette, playing with the baby, and walking out the front door.

There is no escaping the fact that mechanization and automatic processes generally displace people initially. Preorientation here seems the best approach. The Pacific Mutual Life Insurance Company started three years ahead of delivery date to tell its people about what a computer would do in electronic data processing. Along with education went the opportunity of training for job upgrading. The staff also became sidewalk superintendents at the installation of the computer, and their families attended an open house. All in all, the transition did eliminate some jobs, but it did not cost Pacific any valuable, transferable people.

The matter of *retirement* is an increasingly important aspect of management's relations with its employees. There is the now accepted responsibility of making adequate financial provisions for veteran employees' retirement. Beyond this, there remains for the employees the emotional problems of adjusting to the idea of not working daily and of drastically scaling down a living standard. The solution of the problems will not come through any communications gimmick. However, any palliative which holds any degree of promise should be used. A large number of palliatives may prove sufficient where each one individually is inadequate. Public relations can assist personnel functionally in this area. Many companies have organized Retired Employees clubs. The functions have been to bring together those who have retired from their jobs, and to help them to slow down the initial shock of retirement. At club meetings films and talks are provided on company activities, plant tours are engaged in, and participation in civic activities is arranged.

PROMOTING SALES

Advertising and sales promotion take a direct approach to the customer, offering him product or service advantages, at a price. Public relations efforts sometimes take the same direct approach to the consumer, extolling the virtues of a product or service insofar as its newsworthiness will permit. This is seen in product announcements and customer testimonials.

More prevalent, however, is the indirect publicity approach, in which are demonstrated and extolled the virtues of the corporate or industry entity behind the product or service. This is seen in news about sales and earnings, customer warranty and service, expansion plans, awards, and personnel appointments and promotions. The area is as vast as the imagination. A classic example was the Carl Byoir firm's work for Libby-Owens-Ford. They induced the use of more glass in home architecture, popularized better lighting, got auto men to stress the safety feature of more visibility, and obtained publication of a book which glamorized glass.

The Bicycle Institute of America coined a slogan, "The New Golden Age of Bicycling." They plumped for bike paths for safety, then for more use of the paths for health and recreation. Publicity stressed slim waistlines, muscle tone, good circulation and fresh air, picnics, and riding clubs. Finally, there were Junior Training Clubs, local bike ordinances, Safety Clinics, and "The Bicycle Song." Bicycle use has been increasing.

U.S. Steel sponsored "Operation Snowflake" to stimulate sales of major appliances for Christmas. There was advertising, but there was also a "Kitchen Planning Book" by an architect-designer. Newspapers received a four-page folder of editorial material and suitable halftones to feed the homemaker's interest in the latest conveniences. Brand Names Foundation, Inc. is sponsored by manufacturers of products whose brand names have earned a following. A slogan, "You're always satisfied most with a *Brand* that's made a *Name* for itself," appeals to consumers to pick known brand names, and to dealers to promote them rather than unknown brands.

Chesapeake & Ohio and Nickel Plate Road took the initiative several years ago to militate for "through sleeping car service coast to coast." Obviously, this was a great convenience to travelers, who formerly had to change trains in the middle of the night. The campaign used advertisements, letters, and news statements.

The musical instrument industry revived itself by forming the American Music Conference. This body comprised a promotional office from which material was beamed at school children and school music programs. A clip-sheet went monthly to the press. There were also slide film presentations, comic books, special magazine features, and an annual contest for the best use of a musical theme by an advertiser. On behalf of Sylvania, a committee of prominent citizens confers Television Awards on individuals and organizations who have made outstanding contributions to advancing the quality of TV programming.

One corporate practitioner, Robert Fegley, suggests these ways in which the public relations function can help promote sales: [17]

1. Increase brand preference by building understanding of the manufacturer as a maker of quality products. Surveys show a definite correlation between a consumer's view of a company and his purchases.

2. Convert PR audiences into customers; *e.g.*, see stockholders as customers as well as stockholders. Promote products in stockholder literature.

3. Establish a favorable identity in a new market to pave the way for acceptance of a new line of goods or services.

4. Build understanding of the firm's role and service to society by using its products or services as examples in literature, speeches, and so forth.

5. Build public demand for your products; *e.g.*, the maker of sewage filtration equipment promotes a "clean waters" campaign to eliminate stream pollution, which requires installation of new sewage plants.

6. To overcome public opposition to new products, new methods; *e.g.*, the PR campaign on the part of utilities and electrical equipment manufacturers to overcome public fears about atomic power plants being located in urban areas.

The most important contribution the practitioner can make to sales is to help the company appraise the needs of its customers and make that appraisal known to the management.

INFLUENCING DECISIONS
ON PUBLIC ISSUES

The obvious in this area are industry's widely publicized testimony and lobbying in antitrust, tariff, and tax legislation hearings and industry's steady drumfire against further encroachment by government upon industry's freedom. Efforts in this area can be as simple as battling with the Internal Revenue Service over what constitutes legitimate business expense when entertaining a prospective customer, or as complex as winning tariff reductions to enable the United States to adjust to Europe's Common Market. Or the efforts can be as local as a rezoning request or a bond issue for a new school.[18]

Increasingly the idea has taken root in the business community that the businessman belongs in politics—from the precinct level on up. As a matter of history, businessmen have been politically active since the Civil War.

---

17 In a speech given in Chicago, October 10, 1963.

18 See Robert E. Lane, "Law and Opinion in the Business Community," *Public Opinion Quarterly*, Vol. 17, Summer, 1953; for a clue to business' political goals, see Marver H. Bernstein, "Political Ideas of Selected American Business Journals," *ibid*.

Nonetheless, the conviction has been growing in some sectors that the businessman has too long held aloof from politics, with the result he has been outpointed by other interests in the community. Not all businessmen buy the notion that the corporate executive, Main Street merchant, or the business itself should be identified in partisan political struggles. Thomas Reid, of the Ford Motor Co., is among those who argue: "It is rather for them (businessmen) to be active and articulate in working for the kind of government under which our free enterprise system can grow and prosper." [19]

At the least, business firms can well afford to encourage their employees to participate in community affairs, including politics, and to encourage financial support of the party of the employee's free choice. The Internal Revenue Service has ruled that firms may deduct certain expenses incurred in promoting public interest in elections so long as such efforts are impartial.

INTERNATIONAL
PROGRAMS

As the world shrinks in size, communications-wise, and its commerce expands, an increasing number of business firms are expanding their programs to include relationships around the globe. International PR, a relative newcomer, is getting increased emphasis. As Arthur Reef points out, "there will soon be no place on earth which is not reached by modern transport and no people on earth who are not reached by some form of modern communications media." Corporations operating abroad have the obligation to further not only their own interests but also those of the United States and its aspirations for a free, peaceful world. To serve in this field, practitioners must broaden their backgrounds and their horizons. The fundamental that each program must be tailored to its specific public applies with special force in dealing with peoples in other lands. Every country is different. Each one has its own customs, taboos, pride, prejudices, and unique way of doing things.

For example, a ground-breaking for a new American plant in Turkey goes like this: The Moslem religious leader cradles a sheep in his left arm. He chants a prayer. The crowd draws closer. Then he slaughters the animal and lets the blood run down into the excavation. Finally, he tosses in a gold coin. The ground-breaking ceremonies are over. Now the American firm can proceed with its construction.

Americans have long been blessed with plenty of land, and some may tend to fail to realize the scarcity of land in crowded Western Europe or Japan, for example. Here's one firm that did not. "A well-known office-machine company planned to create a new plant in the Netherlands. The firm needed

---

[19] For a contrary view, see Michael D. Reagan, "The Seven Fallacies of Business in Politics," *Harvard Business Review*, Vol. 38, March-April 1960.

some of the country's drastically scarce land. A wrong area choice could have produced strong resentment. After consultation with government ministries, a site partially covered with water was selected. The manufacturer not only built a plant, but contributed to the continuous Dutch task of reclaiming land. Tactful public relations helped promote this example of good citizenship and good community relations." [20]

According to *Printer's Ink,* most international public relations experts agree on these rules for conducting successful overseas businesses: [21]

1. You are guests of the country. Act as a guest should.
2. The profits of your enterprise are not solely yours. Your local "national" employees and the economy of the country should also benefit.
3. Don't try to win over your new customers by completely "Americanizing" them.
4. Although English is an accepted language overseas, a fluency in the language of your international customer goes further in making sales.
5. Contribute to the country's economy and culture with worthwhile public relations projects.
6. Train the executives you choose to act properly overseas. This goes for their wives, too.
7. Don't conduct your business from the United States. Staff your offices with nationals who know what they're doing and supervise the operation from home.

The rapid growth of international trade in a world shrunk by supersonic airplanes and satellite communication makes it essential for corporations operating in foreign lands to get public relations counseling from nationals in those countries. This is true for the Japanese firm selling goods in the United States and for the United States firm selling goods in Japan. It takes one who knows the nation's culture, political structure, religious composition, and so forth, to effectively translate your program and policies into terms that will be understood and applauded in other lands. The increased importance of PR abroad has led to expansion of counseling services operating on an international basis.[22]

American firms expanding their holdings abroad in order to compete in the growing battle for international trade face a tough, twin-sided problem. The problem is sensitive on both ends. At home, overseas expansion is criticized for contributing to the adverse gold flow and for the loss of jobs in a nation with millions of unemployed workers. Abroad, the host country is apt to take the position that its resources are being exploited by foreigners and the country is losing control of its own destiny. This problem will require mature public relations counseling for years to come.

---

[20] "Making Friends and Customers in Foreign Lands," *Printer's Ink,* Vol. 274, June 3, 1960.

[21] *Ibid.*

[22] David L. Lewis, "International Networks: PR's New Golden Age," *PR,* Vol. 2, October, 1957. Also, Arthur Reef, "International PR for American Companies Abroad," *ibid.,* Vol. 5, January, 1960.

Additional Reading

Stephen Baker, "The Art of Building a Corporate Identity," *Public Relations Journal,* Vol. 18, 1962.

John Brooks, "Annals of Business: The Edsel," *The New Yorker,* Vol. 36, issues of November 26 and December 3, 1960.

Allen H. Center, *Public Relations Ideas in Action.* New York: McGraw-Hill, Inc., 1957. (Case Studies.)

Walter J. DeLong, "Weyerhaeuser: A Nine-Year Record of Corporate Advertising That Pays Off," *Public Relations Journal,* Vol. 18, May, 1962.

Theodore V. Houser, *Big Business and Human Values.* New York: McGraw-Hill, Inc., 1958.

Theodore Levitt, "The Dangers of Social Responsibility," *Harvard Business Review,* Vol. 36, September-October, 1958.

Tom Mahoney and Rita Hession, *Public Relations for Retailers.* New York: The Macmillan Company, 1949.

Bernard D. Nossiter, *The Mythmakers: An Essay on Power and Wealth.* Boston: Houghton Mifflin Co., 1964.

CASE PROBLEM

You are director of public relations for a publicly owned company of 1,000 employees, headquartered in a small town of 15,000 people, manufacturing a variety of specialty lighting devices ranging from street stop lights to airport beacons and simple flashlights. The total sales volume is $25,000,000 annually. The budget for public relations is $50,000, exclusive of $50,000 which the company allocates among various health, welfare, and educational organizations, and the minor expenses of the house publication.

Your company is the dominant industrial factor in this community. No other firm employs more than 300 people. Your company is among the top three in your field of products. Outline a comprehensive year's program for the gross $100,000 which will provide favorable exposure of your management among employees, community, and industry; which will favorably identify your company with nonprofit causes, demonstrate industrial statesmanship broadly, and aid in the promotion of your products.

A clue—keep in mind that your products all contribute to *safety.*

Chapter Twenty

UTILITIES,

CARRIERS,

BANKS

Planned public relations is usually a stepchild of conflict. Nine chances out of ten somebody on the other side is working at the problem as hard, if not harder, than we are.—Kinsey M. Robinson.

Public relations problems of business enterprises that sell services should be viewed separately. These enterprises include utilities which provide light, heat, water, power, and telephone service, public transportation, and banking services. These privately owned firms provide vital public services and thus are invested with great public responsibilities.

Utilities enjoy freedom from competition in their assigned areas of service. This protection, in turn, necessitates governmental regulation of rates and services. Because of their public nature, such businesses are constantly confronted with the threat of government ownership. Electric companies, particularly, face competition by government-operated and cooperatively owned utilities which get governmental support.

Federal, state, and local governments have been in the power business for decades. Municipally owned water and transportation systems are common. There is constant pressure for expansion of government operation of public utilities, particularly when these involve natural resources. The public power issue has long been one of the explosive issues in American politics. This battle is being fought again as America puts the atom to work.

Within this combination of circumstances, the approach to good public relationships differs somewhat from the approach in organizations in which competition, first and last, tends to determine rates or prices, territorial boundaries, and earnings. Somewhat apart from public utilities are transportation and banking. The nature and extent of governmental

335

regulation in their case differ from the case with utilities, as do the franchises granted. All share public responsibility, governmental regulation, and close public scrutiny.

To approach the public relations problems in these firms, one needs a clear idea of their public service philosophy. They sell *courteous, efficient, dependable service*. Legally, they have been adjudged to "affect the public interest" and are subject to the regulatory measures of the Interstate Commerce Commission, the Federal Communications Commission, the Federal Power Commission, the Civil Aeronautics Board, state public service or public utility commissions, and other agencies.

In public opinion, generally, they are regarded as noncompetitive monopolies. Utilities prefer the term, "natural single supplier," but they have not made it stick. There are some elements of competition. Buslines, railroads, and airlines compete for passenger traffic. Truckers, railroads, and airlines compete for freight business. Gas companies compete, to an extent, with electric companies. There is little competition in the telephone business, dominated as it is by the giant American Telephone & Telegraph Co. and its affiliates. Independent companies operate some 15 per cent of the nation's telephones. Although franchised and regulated, banks are increasingly competitive.

In this situation, these organizations can hold their franchises, prosper, and press back the incursion of government ownership in the future only by satisfying consumers today. With those consumers they deal directly and personally.

PUBLIC UTILITIES

Utilities are among the oldest and most experienced users of public relations. This has its roots in the history and the nature of the enterprise. Inefficiency and indifference to the public interest in the early 1900's by local gas, traction, and electric companies brought public protest—and public ownership of many. Utilities were the first businesses to be brought under public regulation. Wise leaders accepted this as a concomitant of monopoly franchises. Others fought regulation with questionable methods. At the end of World War I, which brought public operation of the railroads, the movement toward public ownership was gaining strength.

In the 1920's the utility industry was given a black eye by the dubious operations of the Insulls and their kind.[1] Local utilities were bought up and merged into large holding-company operations. Their officers were remote from the people served, and this led to indifference to customer service. In the 1930's, public opposition was bred by the tardiness of many companies in extending the benefits of electricity to farms and less prosperous areas. Intervention of the government was the consequence.

---

[1] See N. R. Danielian, "From Insull to Injury," *Atlantic Monthly*, Vol. 151, April, 1938.

The Tennessee Valley Authority and the Bonneville Power and Rural Electrification Administrations were created. These spurred advocates of public ownership. Counterparts developed at the state and local level. In Nebraska, under George W. Norris' leadership, a state monopoly of electric power was created. It operates today. The issue of public ownership remains alive. This issue has carried over into the determination of control of atomic energy.

By and large, in this generation, most privately owned public service organizations have kept their houses in order, improved their services, told their story well, and built a fortress of respect. There are exceptions, of course. Occasional puffs of suspicion blow across the industry when flagrant and manipulative practices are exposed. The Dixon-Yates affair and lobbying abuses in connection with the natural gas bill of 1956 are examples.

Considering their history, it is not strange that today enterprises that sell service are often the most completely organized of all industry to do an effective PR job. In these enterprises, the function usually speaks with more authority than in other industries. Public relations counseling and direction are usually placed at the top level. More than that, PR-mindedness is encouraged to run like a blood stream throughout the personnel roster.[2]

This emphasis is sparked by several aggressive, hard-hitting national organizations. These include the American Gas Association, the National Association of Electric Companies, the Electric Companies Advertising Program, the Edison Electric Institute, and the Electric Companies Public Information Program, known in the field as PIP.

The National Association of Electric Companies is not to be confused with the ill-fated National Electric Light Association, which was dissolved in the mid-1930's after its unsavory propaganda activities had been exposed in Congress.[3] The new N.A.E.C. was organized in 1945 and carries on a sustaining program for the industry as a whole. Its primary emphasis is on promoting support for private ownership of the nation's utilities. It is registered under the Lobbying Act and represents a substantial segment of the industry before congressional committees. It promotes PR programs within member companies. Stated objectives for individual utilities are set down by N.A.E.C.:

I. The company is a business-managed, taxpaying company, soundly financed and efficiently operated.

II. The company provides good and reliable service at fair rates which have been steadily reduced over the years.

III. The company's profits are reasonable. Income, after material costs of operation and taxes, is fairly apportioned as to wages for employees, dividends for stockholders, and investment for future growth and expansion of the business.

---

2 Nugent Wedding found this true in his study, "Public Relations in Business," *University of Illinois Bulletin,* Vol. 47, July, 1950.

3 For documentation, see Ernest Gruening, *The Public Pays: A Study of Power Propaganda* (New York: Vanguard Press, 1931); and Carl D. Thompson, *Confessions of a Power Trust* (New York: E. P. Dutton & Co., Inc., 1932).

IV. The company is a "good citizen." It has faith in the community it serves. It is interested and active in promoting the welfare and development of that community.

V. The company is progressive, forward-looking, and striving to improve its services.

VI. The company is a good one to work for, and a good one with which to do business.

The Electric Companies Advertising Program is a cooperative effort to place advertising in national media and to prepare advertising materials for local use. The focus of this advertising campaign is to promote private ownership and fight the REA coops.[4] The Edison Electric Institute is the industry's fact-finding and research arm. It serves as a check point for those supplying information to the public. The national information program is carried largely by PIP. It is directed by a Steering Committee of industry executives who determine policy and authorize expenditures. These policies are implemented by the PIP program, which includes the following activities:

1. Provides information and background material to press and radio reporters, editors, commentators, and writers.

2. Refutes misstatements and misconceptions.

3. Supplies news material, special studies, and recommendations for use by local companies.

4. Acts as a clearinghouse for ideas and experience of practical value to companies.

5. Stimulates and assists in the development of regional programs that help bring about further unity within the industry.

6. Works with associations and firms in other industries which have a common aim in resisting government encroachment.

7. Assists member companies in the solution of specific public relations problems.

8. Maintains a Washington office and, through other offices of counsel, seeks to inform companies of trends affecting the industry.

9. The job of watching trends in public opinion is handled by an opinion research firm.

These national groups, each guided by counsel, are useful in reaching national audiences and in stimulating projects in member companies. These programs collide head-on with those sponsored by advocates of public or cooperative ownership of utilities. Somewhere in between the two are the attitudes of millions of consumers who judge by their own personal experience when a courteous serviceman promptly responds to an emergency call, when a bus runs late, when rates are boosted, or the local paper editorializes. *The primary responsibility for earning public favor rests with each specific company serving specific communities.* The job starts in the local community.

PLANS AND PUBLICS. Programming stems from policy structures easily interpreted in good and popular actions, wide-open channels, and rewarding

---

[4] "Electric Company's PR Advertising Switches Public to Business' Side," *Printer's Ink*, Vol. 244, August 7, 1953.

reactions. In the area of employee relations, stockholder relations, and consumer relations, information programs seek understanding on these points:

1. Good management, efficient operations, fair tax payments
2. Widespread ownership, through all economic echelons
3. Good citizenship
4. Constantly improving services
5. Fair rates to customers
6. Reasonable profits, fairly distributed
7. Complete honesty, high ethics
8. Leadership in defending American capitalism
9. Quality in products and in services
10. Full information to employees, the community, and the nation

Mentioned specifically in the excellent handbook of the National Association of Electric Companies were 25 tools for communication and education as the instruments of a sound policy structure:

Employee Relations	Stockholder Relations
Personal Indoctrination	Simplified Reports
Supervisory Training	Interim Reports
Employee Reference Handbooks	Letter of Welcome
Employee Magazines	Departure Letter
Profit Reports	
Motion Pictures	
Bulletin Boards	Consumer Relations
Suggestion Systems	
Open House for Families	News Releases
Length-of-Service Awards	Institutional Advertising
	Educational Advertising
Community Relations	Cultural Programs
	Public Speeches
Civic Development	Pamphlets
Civic Participation	Motion Pictures
Employee Training in PR	Active Participation in Association

Of all the tools, advertising merits special mention because it is so admirably adapted to the mass audience of utility customers and voters. The highly successful program of Pacific Gas and Electric Company has been based on newspaper advertising. This tool was credited with weathering the danger of ill will once when drought conditions slowed up the power output and Northern California residents had more than their share of brownouts and power difficulties PG&F told its story in ads. It has also used advertising to introduce new uses for gas and electricity, to show what the firm means to the area as the largest single taxpayer in California, to remind users that its rates are among the lowest in the nation, and to emphasize the merits of the free enterprise system on a practical basis.

Another effective user of advertising has been the Indianapolis Water Company. In 1953 a Texas group bought this utility. Shortly thereafter the company raised its rates. These two events, one following the other, brought strong public criticism. This was reflected in increasingly unfavorable customer attitudes. The company took a public opinion survey. This fact-finding, based on 1,000 personal interviews, unveiled these uncomfortable facts:

1. Four out of every ten people felt that water rates were excessive.
2. Approximately one-fourth believed that profits were too high.
3. More than one-third thought that the company should be municipally owned.

On the basis of this survey, an intensive program was undertaken. Newspaper advertising was chosen as the primary pipeline. The emphasis was not on justification of current rates, but on winning long-range support. Thirteen ads were produced, each published twice in the three Indianapolis dailies over a year's time. The *theme* was "Here is a company devoted to public service and civic betterment." Ads were heavy on photographs, light on copy. The total campaign was effective. In a year's time, another survey found (1) a 15 per cent reduction in the number of people who felt that the company should be municipally owned; (2) a 30 per cent reduction in the number of people who felt that profits were excessive; (3) a 60 per cent improvement in awareness of the company's advertising by its customers.

The service-selling firms have brought the use of the institutional advertising tool to a high plane of excellence. Giving impetus to this has been an annual contest sponsored by the Public Utilities Advertising Association. Utilities are bracketed in the contest according to the number of customers. There are a liberal number of award winners.

However, the right of utility companies to use advertising to influence public opinion has been brought into question. In 1957 the Internal Revenue Service ruled that the cost of advertising "for lobbying or attempting by propaganda or otherwise to promote or defeat legislation" was not an allowable deduction for tax purposes. Subsequently the Federal Power Commission ruled that advertising "political in character" was not an allowable expense in figuring operating costs for rate-making purposes. The Commission's ruling was upheld by the United States Supreme Court late in 1962. The Federal Power Commission followed this in 1963 by prescribing new accounting rules which require utilities to isolate "political expenditures" from other "nonoperating expenditures." This could presage further elimination of public relations activities from the rate-making base. Utility companies argue that public relations advertising is a legitimate business expense to perpetuate their economic survival by influencing public opinion.

EMPLOYEES COME FIRST. Employees represent the first line. Loyal, informed employees provide the kind of service that wins customer approval. They disseminate the kind of information that brings public understanding. Good employee relations pay off when the chips are down. As an example, when advocates of public ownership promoted an election to decide ownership of the National City, California water system, the utility used every avenue of communication to tell its story and to retain ownership. The private utility won by a vote of 3 to 1. In the opinion of the manager, "The greatest single factor was the work and attitude of our employees. They put on one of the greatest exhibitions of word-of-mouth campaigning and company loyalty that I have ever seen."

Employees must be more than loyal. They must be informed. A president of the Washington Water Power Company advised fellow utility executives: "More utility executives must insist that our employees—these salesmen of ours who make thousands of calls each year—be taken into our confidence. We ought to discuss with them at least once a month what progress they are having in this endless task of making friends." Employee information programs make a difference. In Company Number 1, a thorough program of employee information is carried on. In Company Number 2, very little is done to inform employees about their jobs, their business, and the industry of which they are a part. In a survey among employees of these two companies, the following proportions answered that "I never talk with others about these things."

	Company 1	*Company 2*
Public ownership	15%	31%
The company's relations with government agencies	13	35
The company's stand regarding one of the federal power agencies	12	31
The company's relations with the REA's	12	26
The company's effort to attract new industries to the area	12	21
Taxes paid by the company	15	31
The company's profits	19	32

CUSTOMERS COUNT, TOO. A planned program of customer relations will bring in more of the customer's dollar and more goodwill. Competing hard for the customer's dollar also tends to make a utility look more like a competitive business than a monopoly. This is one of A.T.&T.'s "secrets." Foremost among the firms with good customer relations is the Detroit Edison Co., one of the few utilities which still gives away free light bulbs. This company keeps 500 employees and 47 service trucks busy replacing bulbs and fuses, installing lead-in wires for electric stoves, fixing appliances, and performing other helpful services which build goodwill—and business. Detroit Edison sells its average home customer 2,168 kilowatt hours per year, twice as much as a comparable company.

R. H. Sessions, personnel director Idaho Power Co., thinks, with reason, that customer relations is the key to public relations. He prefers to call public relations "consumer understanding." He says, "Consumer understanding will be achieved only when we personally are willing to take time out to talk face-to-face with each of our customers." [5]

A GOOD EXAMPLE. The American Telephone and Telegraph Company, founded in 1885, took its cue from Theodore N. Vail. He set down the basic premise that his company welcomed public regulation as an opportunity to

---

[5] In article, "Let's Be Sensible About Public Relations," *Electrical World*, Vol. 149, April 21, 1958.

be of service.[6] Commencing with Mr. Vail's presidency in 1907, the organization worked hard for progressive improvement of its equipment and services, for rate reductions, and for the development of a complete public service attitude in the functions of all employees. When Walter S. Gifford became president, public relations was integrated throughout the various operating divisions as a distinct and vital function. First director of the extensive department was the late Arthur W. Page. In his 20 years as public relations director of A.T.&T. Page not only constructed that utility's far-reaching PR program but pioneered many of today's commonly accepted precepts.

One of the definitive statements attributed to Mr. Page was that the first step to be taken was for the management to set down on paper its PR policy. That policy, whatever it contained, said to the public: "We should like to serve you, and we offer you the following contract, which we think would be fair to all concerned and mutually profitable." There is enough substance in this behavior pattern at the management level to explain why public relationships are good. As every A.T.&T. man knows, however, the biggest reason for success is that there's a public relations-mindedness permeating the internals of the organization. It may start at the top, but it rubs off on employees all the way down the line. One way of putting it into words was expressed by Arthur Motley, of *Parade* Magazine:

> Everybody talks about the A.T.&T. and what a wonderful public relations job they have done. But this fundamental is too often forgotten. A.T.&T.'s superiority lies in the training they give their people who meet the public at the place where the public has relations with A.T.&T.—the telephone. You are all familiar with the telephone operator with a smile in her voice—the girl who makes you forget the wrong number. She was trained for that. She is a sales person, yes. In the long run, that is the greatness of A.T.&T.'s public relations, not the fact that they ran a few very attractive, well-written advertisements in my magazine or somebody else's.

In its long-range thinking, A.T.&T. has recorded four public relations cornerstones on which to erect the lasting structure:

> 1. Public opinion will control the course of the business.
> 2. The direction that public opinion will take will depend first on the quality of telephone service and then on the facts about the service that people are given to think about.
> 3. The company is continuously obliged to give the public full and candid information about the business.
> 4. If the public is given all the facts all the time, it can be relied upon to reach sensible conclusions.

The job that A.T.&T. has done is not an exclusive opportunity reserved for the giants in industry. The Bell System starts making its friends at the hometown level. The same kind of job can be done by the hundreds of small,

---

[6] See Norton E. Long, "Public Relations of the Bell System," *Public Opinion Quarterly*, Vol. 1, October, 1937, Also, Connie Jean Conway, "Theodore Vail's Public Relations Philosophy," *Bell Telephone Magazine*, Vol. 37, Autumn, 1958.

localized service organizations of all types in the nation. There's just as much in it for the little fellow in his own back yard as there is for the big guy nationally.[7]

CARRIERS

The task for common carriers—airlines, bus lines, railroads, local transit systems—is two-sided. One basic objective is building public support for favorable legislation and allocation of route franchises; the other is building passenger and freight revenues. In the case of the airlines, the emphasis is on passenger revenue; for the railroads, the main concern is freight revenue. Government at all levels is inextricably involved in public transportation through the laws it makes, the subsidies it provides, the franchises it grants, and the terminal facilities it provides.

These prizes spur stiff competition for public opinion. Some of the hottest battles have taken place in this arena. The competition for passengers is equally spirited. Although licensed and regulated, components of the United States transportation system are fiercely competitive. Support for a particular form of transportation is promoted through the work of such trade groups as the Association of American Railroads, the Air Transport Association, and the American Trucking Associations. All have intensive PR and advertising programs.

Over the years, there has been confusion, conflicting policies, and contentions of favoritism and unfairness in the granting of government favor. Meantime, the citizen user of transportation is relatively unconcerned about these governmental policies. He is vitally concerned about *his* transportation. He is alternately pleased or displeased, depending on whether he gets the accommodations he wants when he wants them, whether the cost of travel is fair, and whether he is well or ill served during his trips.

In recent years traveling has been made easier, pleasanter. As transportation now looks to the customer, airlines compete with each other; railroads compete with each other and with the airlines. The bus lines figure in, too, especially for shorter trips as short-line rail service declines. The railroads offer the customer greater speed than interstate bus lines and more conveniences than the airlines. The buses offer greater economy and frequency. The airlines offer greater speed than any of the other carriers, many conveniences, and considerable glamor.

All three build their programs on the factors of courteous service, safety, comfort, constantly improving technical equipment, and a host of extras. As a result, there are in newsprint, advertising, pamphlets, and on the air the persuasions of pretty, efficient hostesses and stewards, the latest luxurious rail

---

[7] For one example, see "Florida Power & Light," *Fortune,* Vol. 41, April, 1950; and for a follow-up see "How We Did It," *Public Relations Journal,* Vol. 11, December, 1955.

Diesel car, the double-decker air-conditioned bus, the new timetable, the latest menu, the safety record or award, the special excursions, more comfortable seats with more leg room, and so on.

But it takes more than pretty pictures in travel folders and Champagne flights to satisfy travelers. It takes competent, courteous service. Bernard DeVoto, in one of his last essays, caustically wrote: "Giant strides in public relations are making the life of the traveler in the United States more laborious every year. . . . You have to work against increasing stupidity, inefficiency, arrogance, and public-relations applesauce and it is getting to be a tough job. But year by year the advertising brochures get more beautiful." [8] More recently Sydney J. Harris, widely syndicated columnist, wrote: [9]

> If large organizations . . . would spend less money on publicity, promotion, and 'public image,' and transfer these funds to communication—with the public and with their own employees—they might find some startling results in terms of profit and goodwill. Flying back from Florida last month, more than a hundred passengers on our flight were detained a half-hour at the baggage counter when our bags mysteriously refused to show up. The wait itself was not so terrible— but the attitude of the airline personnel made enemies by the score. Nobody would tell us a thing. . . . At the present time, the airlines are about as bad as any group in communicating with the public. It seems pointless for the airlines to spend millions in wooing travelers and then to create so much ill will by refusing to give information.

These sharp jabs remind us that publicity must be underwritten by deeds, and also, the popular misconceptions of what constitutes PR. Although the service on all lines has improved, customer complaints still bob to the surface. Airline passengers tell of luggage lost or sent to the wrong place, luggage damaged by manhandling, foul-ups in reservations, delayed flights, and snippy treatment.[10] These things happen to editorial writers, too. The *Louisville Courier-Journal* complains: "In the case of schedule delays, the passenger is not to be trusted with the truth; he is not to be told, for example, that a plane in New York or Chicago hasn't even taken off, thanks to engine trouble, and won't be in for five of the six wasted hours he hangs around the lounge." The *Philadelphia Bulletin* chimes in: "Airline timetables are more optimistic than realistic." The *Milwaukee Journal* adds: "A little more attention to adequate ground personnel and to accurate information, freely, honestly and quickly given, would soothe many a ruffled temper."

The railroads, long the butt of complaints, are still told about wooden trestles, high fares, dirty cars, old stations, tasteless food, poor safety and on-time performance, and rough road beds. Bus lines catch it, too, for failure to

---

[8] In "The Easy Chair," *Harper's Magazine*, Vol. 210, February, 1955.

[9] Syndicated column as printed in *Wisconsin State Journal*, March 27, 1963. Copyright. By permission.

[10] For other examples, see Richard Witkin, "Riders Criticize Airlines' Service," *New York Times*, February 26, 1956, p. 1 ff.

meet schedules, missed connections, bothersome fuel fumes, and grimy, littered waiting rooms. Keeping travelers on time is a tough job. Delays cannot be avoided. *But they can be explained.*

The public relations problems in this field are easily seen in the case of the airlines. With the coming of jet passenger planes, the pressure for good PR has intensified. The airlines must greatly increase their passenger volume to make the heavy capital investment required for jet airliners pay off. Their community relations problems have been intensified by the noise factor imposed on cities served. The increased volume and speed of air traffic require vastly improved air control measures by government. The heavier, faster planes require larger runways, bigger airports. These the people, through government, must provide. And as airport-to-airport trip time shrinks, the time and inconveniences of getting from city to airport will loom larger.

Even tougher problems lie ahead for the airlines. To condition the public to airplanes flying twice the speed of sound will be the next PR task facing world airlines, in the opinion of Harold B. Miller, PR director of Pan American World Airways. He predicts, "Within the next 10 years supersonic airplane cruising speeds will be well over 2,000 miles an hour. New York and London will be only an hour and a half apart." [11] Such profound changes pose many problems for the airline practitioner.

BANKS

Bankers, generally, lagged in adopting the public relations approach in their dealings with the public. In recent years progressive banks have moved rapidly to recover business lost to other financial agencies and to erase the traditional stereotypes. Disappearing is the old-fashioned banker of granite mien and high-button-shoe ways of doing business. Gone are the gloomy, forbidding interiors and grilled cages. Today banks, savings and loan associations, and small loan firms aggressively compete for the customer's business and for the investor's savings. Bank PR programs pursue new objectives:

1. Increasing business by improving service.
2. Telling the story of banking in general and of one bank in particular.
3. Strengthening the bank's position in the community.

A secondary objective is promoting an opinion climate favorable to reasonable regulation of privately owned banks. Banks are so numerous and their functions so competitive that any threat of nationalization seems vague indeed. Yet a survey made for a Philadelphia bank just a few years ago showed that one-third of those interviewed favored government ownership. This remains a latent though not serious problem for banks. Public opinion

---

11 "Pan Am Sees Mach 2 Succeeding Jet PR," *Editor & Publisher*, Vol. 94, February 25, 1961.

supports the idea that funds are completely safe in the hands of the home-town banker. This is due to improved management, government policing, and Federal Deposit Insurance. The continuance of public temper in strong opposition to nationalization of banking is a secondary task in PR planning for banks.

Of more direct concern are the degree and kind of public regulations imposed on banks. Financial institutions, of necessity, are subjected to tight governmental controls. Governmental relations comprise an important aspect of practice in this field. Frequently banks join forces to oppose what they consider unreasonable or unnecessary controls. Less frequently, but periodically, banks divide into opposing camps and do public battle. One group seeks to block branch banking, another seeks to open it up. One group of banks seeks a law to compel closing on Saturdays, other banks oppose the legislation. Building support to promote or defeat legislation is not an infrequent bank task.

But the main goal is building business to improve earnings. This is done by demonstrating that Bank A is a more efficient, more pleasant place to do business than Bank B. Successful banks are accomplishing this by providing an expanding list of high-quality services, demonstrating good citizenship, and lending the warm, personal touch to money transactions. *Service is a bank's only product, and the quality of that service is the primary determinant of people's attitudes.* Customers are influenced as much by the manner in which a bank does things as by what it does.

A large New York City bank found it necessary to increase charges on regular checking accounts—the kind that usually require some minimum balance. It did not inform its customers of the higher rates. At the end of the month many customers became exasperated when they could not get their checkbooks to balance. Bewildered and irate, they began to query branch managers. The managers, with no printed announcements on hand, had to explain the charges verbally. A bank spokesman explained that the bank "did not publicize the revision because only a few customers whose balances ran rather low would be affected and an announcement would only serve to confuse the majority."

A Milwaukee Braves fan mistakenly handed a ticket seller a good-luck silver dollar he had carried for years. After the game he discovered the loss of his cherished talisman. He contacted the Braves' management. The day's receipts had already been taken to the First Wisconsin National Bank. He turned to the bank for help—and found it. Fortunately, the deposits were still unchecked. Bank clerks spent hours sorting out the tremendous piles of cash until they found the cherished silver dollar. It was returned to an appreciative owner—and new customer.

The outworn stereotype of the flint-hearted banker is crumbling through such kindly, human acts. The Hanover Bank of New York was commissioned to sell the horses of William Woodward, Jr., whose stable included Nashua, sold for $1,251,200. A 12-year-old girl wrote the bank this letter:

Dear Sirs,
    I read in the papers today that you are going to sell Nashua and his friends. If you have a horse no one will buy, I would like to. The horse will have a good home, one and one-half acres of woods and fields and loveing care. I would like a horse that would grow old with me. My sealed bid is $24.03. . . .

The upshot of this letter was that a towhead fifth-grader who loved horses got her horse—bought and presented to her by the bank's officers. And the bank got priceless publicity in a *New York Times* feature story.

This human touch is reflected in other ways as banks strive to build a warm, favorable image. For years bank advertising was lampooned for its stodgy, conservative, and dull character. More recently it has taken on a new look. As *Editor & Publisher* observes: "Where the emphasis was once on ponderously selling the dignity of the institution rather than its services, today's bank promotion, by all past standards, fairly sparkles with friendliness, informality, and human interest. . . . The trend is to informative, down-to-earth copy featuring light but pointed illustrations."

But stereotypes die hard. The public relations counsel for the American Bankers Association made a recent survey and found "in most persons' mind, a bank is a formal and forbidding place, bankers are rich, hard-to-know stuffed shirts, and tellers usually are unhappy and underpaid." There are some bankers who are not convinced that the traditional concept of banks as somewhat austere, quasi-public institutions should be altered very much. But by and large, bankers are showing considerable enthusiasm for convincing people that there's warmth behind the cold marble façade.

This is reflected in increased sensitivity to public opinion. Bankers are using, in increasing number, opinion measurement. The Pennsylvania Company for Banking and Trusts learned by this means that people thought "banks made it too difficult to borrow money" and that "they made too much profit on their transactions." It then shaped its program accordingly. Many banks have adopted the retail store technique of hiring "comparison customers."

One state association has made a "Public Opinion Forum" a regular feature of its conventions. Representative lay citizens are invited in to express "What We Think of Banks." At one convention, bankers heard these criticisms:

    "Banks would have fewer clerical mistakes if they'd offer better pay for that kind of work."
    "Most laboring people won't go into a bank unless they're in dire necessity. You put them on exhibition by making them stand there at a rail and discuss their business in the open."
    "Interest on savings accounts is too low."
    "There's too much standing in line, and 'express windows' should be set up."
    "Service charges are a mystery, and banks should explain how they're calculated."
    "Banks don't explain in simple terms how they operate. For example, they don't make clear that a full day's work is being done even though the doors are open only for banker's hours."

"You are too eager to give advice on things about which you are not qualified —especially legal questions."

Banks are moving, individually and collectively, to eliminate the causes of valid criticism and to clear away mistaken impressions. Impetus for this is being provided by the American Bankers Association, the Association of Reserve City Bankers, the Financial Public Relations Association, the U.S. State Savings and Loan League, and the National Savings and Loan League. The ABA provides services to nearly 15,000 members through its 34 departments. It has long had a Council on Public Relations. The Financial Public Relations Association promotes PR-mindedness and provides many assists to bankers. It annually sponsors, in cooperation with Northwestern University, a School of Financial Public Relations. It maintains a projects library from which members can borrow detailed blueprints of successful programs. The other associations provide similar help to their members.[12]

Employees. Loyalty of employees, priceless in any business, is vital in banking. In many cases this loyalty has reached peaks where employees have used a tangible means of showing how they felt. In the First National Bank of Orlando, Florida, employees paid the cost of an ad headlined, "Why We Like to Be Members of the First National Family." Such loyalty is obtained first by fair wages, insurance protection, liberal time off, cash bonuses for new business, considerate treatment, and opportunities to advance. This is the base in any business.

Banks in growing numbers have adopted training programs to enable employees to understand the economics of banking, to provide skilled service, and to make friends across the counter. This training job must be worked at, day in and day out, year after year. Public relations can be used, too, in recruiting new employees—an increasingly difficult problem for many banks.

Customers. In the competitive scramble for customers, banks no longer aim their pitch solely at the head of the household. They go after the children and the housewife, too. The Bank of America intensively promotes children's accounts and sends messengers around to schools to collect the youngsters' pennies. It has more than a million children's accounts. Ten years ago, Bankers Trust of New York City was almost entirely a businessman's bank with four branches. Today it is bidding aggressively for the consumer's business through a string of 42 branches and an intensive PR-advertising campaign.

Banks are making it easier to do business with them. Many are open as much as 12 hours a day. Some have nighttime hours. Many provide for 24-hour deposits. Branches, where legal, are established in suburbs. For the customer who must do his banking by mail, there are simplified mailing enclosures and a streamlining of procedures generally. Even the décor is changing toward open counters, modern lighting, comfortable chairs, and ready access to officials. A Pearl River, New York, bank even put in a sidewalk window with a pretty teller. Drive-in TV banking is becoming commonplace.

To woo customers, many little extras are being provided. These can

---

[12] These trade associations are sources of helpful information on PR programming.

make the difference between Bank A and Bank B. A Long Island bank, for example, maintains in its lobby a bowl filled with nickels for customers to use in parking meters and an umbrella rack for people caught downtown when it rains. This bank employs a woman as a new business representative who calls on families as soon as they move into the community. It even helps newcomers find handymen to unpack and arrange for utilities. It sends officials to give talks in the local high school and sponsors essay contests in the grade schools. To lure new customers, some banks give away ballpoint pens, tickets to ball games, and serve free coffee.

Community. A considerable portion of the bank's work is done outside the building. A considerable part of its services are rendered in the life stream of the community. The ten-point community program suggested by the American Bankers' Association tells the story succinctly:

1. Draw up a plan to guide your activities.
2. Delegate the responsibility to an individual.
3. Try to develop some one program in which you are the prime mover.
4. Cooperate in all worthwhile community programs, regardless of sponsorship.
5. Offer your bank building for community meetings and displays of community projects.
6. Encourage (and pay for) staff membership in community organizations.
7. Develop staff speakers and encourage public speaking by bank people.
8. Donate to all worthy charities and causes, with the help of an equitable plan.
9. Avoid partisan politics, but lend your weight to moral and public issues.
10. Do the unexpected, by taking active part in affairs of churches, schools, and charities.

It has become the usual thing rather than the unusual today to find officials and employees of banks doubling as campaign managers for charity drives, as board members of the Chamber of Commerce, as advisers in local building projects, as crusaders for new industry, as deacons of the church, and as collaborators in programs bringing together agriculture, labor, and business. In the time left over, bank officers can be found making personal calls on depositors and supporting association activities at the national level.

In the use of communications tools, the average bank is the farthest advanced of small businesses and is a replica in miniature of large industrial concerns. The range of tools is so wide that the following list has importance mainly in its chronology:

Internal	*External*
Employee indoctrination and training through instruction, lectures, films, and pamphlets	Participation in community affairs
Employee staff publication	Local newspaper and radio advertising
Interior decoration, manners, and service extras	Local news
Lobby and window displays	Direct mail, statement enclosures, holiday cards, calendars
Employee incentives and contests	Open house

Of these tools, advertising is being used most intensively. Bank advertising has skyrocketed. The figures tell the story. In 1946, banks spent $22,000,-000 on ads; ten years later, in 1956, they spent $82,000,000. In 1963, the annual expenditure for bank advertising passed the $200,000,000 mark. Advertising is no longer confined to straight institutional ads in newspapers. Today banks use radio and TV and even sponsor sports shows, although the newspaper remains the primary medium. The ABA's advertising department offers this formula for effective bank advertising: (1) get attention; (2) offer a benefit; (3) prove your case; (4) create desire; and (5) get action. The ABA deserves much of the credit for the increased use and effectiveness of bank advertising.

IDEAS IN A HURRY. Case histories of ingenious PR projects for banks are numerous. The Detroit Trust Company had a series of radio forums known as Women's Town Meeting to provide women—and interested men—with an insight into free enterprise economics. The California Bankers Association undertook to educate itself in the economic education programs of others as a preface to sponsoring one on its own behalf. Valley National Bank of Phoenix sends to the bank's depositors and friends a quarterly four-page calendar of events of interest in the community.

The Investment Bankers' Association sponsored a correspondence course at the college level, through the University of Chicago. The course delved into financing, securities, marketing, and investments. The Republic National Bank of Dallas made the directors' room in its new building available for meetings of civic groups. The New Jersey Bankers' Association sponsored a PR school at Princeton for bankers to study principles and procedures. National City Bank of New York sent ten young and promising employees on a six-week camping tour to see industry in action in the East, South, and Middle West. This was an annual event. Campers went by truck, saw mines and factories, and got the feel of free enterprise in action.

Every so often a story crops up in the day's news reporting discovery of a cache of money which a person fearful of banks had hidden in the attic or family trunk or buried in the back yard. Usually banks let these items pass without comment. When workmen digging beneath a Troy, Ohio, feed mill found $350,000 which the owner had buried there because he didn't trust banks, a New York City bank reacted with imagination. It issued a news release pointing out that "If the money had been deposited in a bank and had earned interest at an estimated rate of three per cent, compounded quarterly, the interest alone would have amounted to $356,361 in the 18 years the money had been buried." It also suggested that, had the money been invested in stocks, it would have grown to more than two million dollars—a telling lesson on the value of banks.

Citizens & Southern National Bank of Georgia stages a "Customer Appreciation Day" on Valentine's Day. Valentines are sent to everyone who has had any dealings with the bank in the previous year. Persons dropping in at any of the bank's 26 offices that day are handed chocolate candies by antebellum hostesses. The Peninsula State Bank, Long Island, is careful always to send flowers to the opening of a local shop. Its customers may expect a note or a card when they go on vacation. These "extras" can be mighty influential when a person decides where to do his banking.

Some ideas don't work. One bank bought big advertisements announcing its left-handed checkbooks for port-sided writers. But few persons were interested. It has lots of left-handed checkbooks on hand.

Additional Reading

Alexander B. Adams, "How a U. S. Bank Advertises to Dispel the Myth of Materialism," *Public Relations Journal,* Vol. 18, October, 1962.

Albert R. Beatty, "Adventures in Railroading," *Public Relations Journal,* Vol. 11, August, 1955.

Financial Public Relations Association, *A Management Guide To Public Relations.* Chicago: The Association, 1963. Prepared by Members of FPRA's Research Committee.

Gordon Gilmore, "Public Relations of TWA's Twentieth Anniversary," *Public Opinion Quarterly,* Vol. 13, Fall, 1949.

Hubert Kay, "There's No Stopping REA—Or Is There?", *Fortune,* Vol. 67, February, 1963.

David L. Lewis, "Underground Public Relations: A Success Story from London," *Public Relations Journal,* Vol. 13, June, 1957.

Robert Lindquist, *The Bank and Its Publics.* New York: Harper & Row, Publishers, 1956.

Raymond C. Miller, *Kilowatts at Work: A History of the Detroit Edison Co.* Detroit: Wayne State University Press, 1958. A company history of a PR-minded utility.

Charles W. Pine, "Responsibilities of Financial Institutions in Community Relations," *Public Relations Journal,* Vol. 19, May, 1963.

James F. Stafford, "Why Utilities Must Advertise," *Public Utility Fortnightly,* Vol. 59, April 25, 1957.

United States Senate, 84th Congress, Special Committee to Investigate Political Activities, Lobbying, and Campaign Contributions, *Oil And Gas Lobby Investigation Hearings.* Washington, D. C.: U. S. Government Printing Office, 1956.

CASE PROBLEM

You are PR director for Jet Airlines, Inc., one of the nation's largest. Your company has been flying jet liners on its main routes for several years. Top executives tell you that plans have been made to extend jet-airliner service to smaller cities. This will include University City, which has had a prior unhappy experience with jets. Some years ago the Air Force shared occupancy of the municipal airport with commercial planes. The noise of the jets, coupled with the crash of one at the edge of the city, led to vehement, widespread public protest. The municipal airport is in a congested area. The Air Force built a new airbase beyond the city and moved to it two years ago.

Introduction of jet passenger service to University City will require that city to spend additional funds to lengthen two runways. It will also require that community acceptance be gained for the coming of the jet liners. The new service starts in three months. Your bosses tell you to work out a plan to pave the way for introduction of the new service in University City. List steps you would take and themes you plan to use in a public relations program to get acceptance for this move.

Chapter Twenty-One

WELFARE

AGENCIES,

HOSPITALS,

AND

CHURCHES

Welfare workers can meet critics on at least equal grounds if they do their jobs well and tell the public about their work in everyday English.
—Arthur P. Miles.

The fields of social welfare, public health, hospitals, and churches are expanding. The growing number of nonprofit agencies—either tax- or gift-supported, or both—is almost staggering. The practice of public relations runs the gamut from charitable organizations to social work agencies to health foundations to hospitals to libraries to religious bodies to governmental agencies in this field. These are served, in like range, with no formal programs at all, with simple promotional publicity, or with full-scale departments.

Generally, the concepts and practice in the nonprofit field are enlarging. These agencies and activities are supported, to a large extent, by public giving and taxation. Most are staffed by a small corps of paid professionals directing large groups of volunteer workers. Some use lay citizens only as consultants and board members. Public welfare departments in government are an example of tax-supported organizations. The primary PR objectives are:

1. To raise funds to keep going and growing as needs enlarge.
2. To broaden and maintain volunteer participation.
3. To win public acceptance of new ideas and new concepts, many of which are highly controversial.

The agencies for social work, health, education, and religion add up to a tremendous industry when measured by money collected and spent. In addition to churches, colleges, and hospitals, it is estimated that there are 500,000 gift-supported agencies. The Community Chests and Councils of America represent nearly 2,100 chests and united funds in the United States and Canada. In

1962, these community funds raised and spent more than 500 million dollars to support more than 26,000 local and national services during 1963. These cold figures represent an untold amount of promotion and participation in some 2,100 campaigns. Take just one state—Michigan: More than 100,000 volunteers worked to raise over 33 million dollars from some 4 million contributors in 166 Michigan communities. This sum finances 940 welfare agencies that reach 7 million men, women, and children.

Philanthropic giving passed the 10-billion-dollar mark in 1964. In 1962 an estimated 9.3 billion dollars was given to philanthropic causes, an increase of 600 million over the previous year. Contributions from the individual citizen represent more than 80 per cent of the philanthropic dollar given by all sources, according to the American Association of Fund-Raising Counsel. More than one billion dollars came from the more than 5,000 tax-free foundations. Over the 11-year period from 1950 through 1960, Americans increased their investment in the nation's philanthropically supported institutions at a faster pace than either personal income or the gross national product advanced. Little wonder that experts in this field predict that by 1970 Americans will be giving some 15 billion dollars a year to religious, health, welfare, and educational agencies. One fund raiser observes, "We're nearer the floor of giving than we are to the ceiling." And there will have to be more such giving if the needs of nonprofit agencies are to be met. Much of this giving will come only in response to planned, effective public relations programs.

But these nonprofit agencies need more than funds. They need public understanding and citizen participation to attain objectives which are partly educational, partly remedial, and partly palliative. From the viewpoint of the practitioner, this vast range of social welfare activity has three important aspects.

First, there is the possibility of a career that offers deep satisfaction in the service of one's fellow man. It is one of broadening opportunities, especially for women. However, the financial rewards are comparatively smaller. *Second,* as the social responsibility concept evolves for profit-making concerns, practitioners in industry give an increasing amount of time and talent to these public causes. *Third,* as the agencies multiply and competition for funds intensifies, the pressure on profit-making institutions likewise mounts. The decision as to which agencies to support and which requests to decline has become a tough problem for corporations, business firms, and labor unions.

The importance of expert public relations practice is slowly but surely being recognized in this diversified field. Progress has been a bit slower than in other fields, particularly at the state and community level. The emphasis has been on publicity and promotion rather than on education. The cramp of funds has been a large factor in slowing full-scale programs. That, however, is only part of the trouble, according to Sallie Bright, **veteran social agency practitioner:**

The recognition of public relations as a proper and necessary function in the administration of social welfare agencies is not universal. The social welfare agency which includes public relations in its administrative plans as a service to be staffed and budgeted along with other agency services is still the exception rather than the rule. However, it can be said with reasonable certainty, based on scattered but unmistakable evidence, that there is a slowly increasing tendency on the part of the social welfare field to regard public relations as an integral part of its work.

Considering that these two fields have grown up in the same era, it is difficult to fathom why, until recent years, the two have not been more closely related. Whether the practitioner goes directly into this field or not, he will find himself working in it from time to time. Every practitioner is expected to take his turn in serving the Community Chest, the Red Cross, the Y.M.C.A., the Boy Scout Council, the Cancer Society, the Child Guidance Center, and all the rest. Knowledge of social work's objectives, services, and problems is an essential part of the practitioner's mental furniture.

WELFARE AND HEALTH AGENCIES

THE PERSPECTIVE. The work of welfare, health, and religious agencies is society's response to the consequences of its social disorganization. Social welfare work is the affirmative answer to the question: "Am I my brother's keeper?" It is an outgrowth of the conflicts and maladjustments produced by America's high-speed urbanized living and a shedding of the notion of "survival of the fittest." The need to help those needing it dates from ancient civilizations. The humanitarian urge to give aid and comfort to those needing it is deep within us all. Social work is in the process of maturing into a professional calling. Caught up in the turmoil and tension of today's divided world, it is in the midst of difficult problems and on the threshold of great opportunities.

Social workers are casting off their defensive shells and struggling for their rightful place. This broad field, as it develops skill and acceptance, is facing up to its responsibilities to the whole public. It is more alert to the need for an intelligible accounting of its work to all citizens. Public relations concepts are in a stage of transition.

A retarding influence is the tendency of social workers to scurry into shells of privacy when the public seeks information. If agencies accept gifts from the public, they are obligated to report it. Information should be given, provided that it does not violate the confidential relationship of agency and client. The press, for example, is competent to judge good taste in publication—with some exceptions, of course. Newspapermen resent censorship. Garbled stories more often arise from withholding the facts than from incompetent reporting.

This issue comes to a sharp focus in the matter of access to confidential relief records. The press insists on such access as an essential safeguard against waste, inefficiency, or other misuse of relief funds. Social workers insist, with equal vigor, that the confidential relationship between the agency and client must be preserved and protected. Without reference to the merits of this controversy, it will continue as a tough problem until it is resolved, one way or the other. As to general information, budget totals, and so forth, certainly publicly supported agencies cannot be immune to public examination.

E. R. Leibert, counsel for the Health Information Fund, regards "the concept and status of public relations within the organization" as a serious problem, and he voices a common plaint:

> The executive heads and policy-making groups of most nonprofit organizations have not yet accepted public relations in principle or in practice as equal in importance to other major operating divisions. . . . Executives often think that public relations people in nonprofit organizations are interested only in volume publicity. . . . There is an aversion to publicity in most nonprofit organizations. In some it amounts to a "cancer complex." . . . Finally, many nonprofit agencies do a good job and would like to interpret their services but simply do not know how. They are aware of this and are open to the public relations approach but need help. . . .

The development of public relations in this field has been spearheaded by the National Public Relations Council of Health and Welfare Services and the Department of Social Work Interpretation of the Russell Sage Foundation. Fund raising on a mass scale became big business after World War I. The writing of persuasive messages and the mapping of campaigns became, more and more, a highly specialized task. This brought the professional publicist to philanthropy. Evart Routzahn launched his drive for recognition of this function when he read a paper, "Elements of a Social Publicity Program," at the National Conference of Social Work in 1920.

Spontaneous response to his demand for "a new type worker in the social welfare field . . . trained in the technique of expressing social information in ways that will attract attention" led, ultimately, to formation of the National Publicity Council for Welfare Services in 1922; this title was changed in 1939 to Social Work Publicity Council, and then to National Publicity Council for Health and Welfare Services in 1943. In January, 1961, the title was changed again, this time to National Public Relations Council of Health and Welfare Services. These changes of title reflect the growth in this field. The Council, headquartered in New York City, publishes a twice-a-month newsletter, *Channels,* sponsors conferences and workshops, and provides counsel to its member agencies. Its work speeds the advance being made in this field.

Complete public understanding of social workers and their endeavors is yet to be achieved. Much of the criticism of welfare agencies stems from general misunderstanding, but workers in the field have to accept a great deal of responsibility for creating these misunderstandings, in the opinion of

Arthur P. Miles, professor in the University of Wisconsin School of Social Work. He lists these fountainheads of criticism: (1) intellectual confusion of the social sciences; (2) confusion over what should be held confidential in the public welfare field; (3) gobbledegook of social workers; (4) anti-intellectual trends in America.[1]

Social agencies have yet to capitalize fully on full and frank accounting of their affairs to the public. Too many old-timers in this field demonstrate an attitude of "our noble motives and good works need no reporting to the donor citizen." There is need to distinguish between mass publicity-promotion campaigns once a year to raise funds and continuous, candid reporting week in, week out.

Agencies are constantly working against deep prejudices, deep fears, and ignorance. These bodies are particularly vulnerable to rumors and gossip because of such fears and ignorance. The American Red Cross has repeatedly proved its dedication to humanity. Yet it is frequently the victim of malicious rumors. Many of the charges lightly bandied about by Korean veterans are updated rumors common after the Spanish-American War. A child welfare agency must be steeled against the day when a newspaper will make a sensational crusade out of the agency's withdrawal of a child put out for adoption before the end of the probationary period. The answer to such unfounded, emotional attacks is to establish credibility through performance and to build enduring support based on education rather than emotion.

Nonprofit agencies require appreciation and tolerance for the plight of today's citizen, pounded by the multiplying demands of this cause and that agency for funds while his tax bill to pay for like services continues to rise. There is also need to realize that each person can give only so much time to the doorbell-ringing chores he is asked to perform by a multitude of agencies. *More effective two-way communication will bring the desired rapport between agency and citizen.*

A convincing demonstration of this principle was provided by the program of the State Charities Aid Association in New York to bring the critics of public welfare face to face with the grim problems of poverty, illegitimacy, and illiteracy, outlined in Chapter 5.[2]

THE PROGRAM. Welfare agencies start out in an enviable position to win goodwill. Their sole reason for existence is to help people. The agency can gain ready entry to mass media and opinion leaders. It presumably has no selfish axe to grind. There are, however, organizations born to promote legal or social reform—Planned Parenthood, for example—which run head on into solid blocs of opposition. Those agencies and causes which are highly controversial have a more difficult path.

On the other hand, social agencies are "selling" intangibles. The Com-

---

[1] For a sharp critique of today's social worker, see Marion K. Sanders, "Social Work: A Profession Chasing Its Tail," *Harper's Magazine*, Vol. 214, March, 1957.

[2] *Is It Safe? Is It Wise?* . . . Undated pamphlet, State Charities Aid Association, 105 East 22nd Street, New York City, circa 1963.

munity Chest has widely proclaimed, "Everybody Benefits, Everybody Gives." Still, many people regard these agencies as existing for the "other fellow." Much of the service provided by social agencies is shunned because "it's charity." Many who could use the services of these agencies simply do not know of their availability. There is difficulty in making concrete presentations of the tangible benefits derived by the individual citizen. This difficulty is compounded for the charitable and family service agencies because of the confidential relationship that must exist.

Some social agencies have drifted into a heavy reliance on the "fear technique," exploiting the emotions in their fund drives. This approach may raise funds, but it doesn't serve well in the long run. The trend is in the direction of more positive appeals, but fear as a primary motive is being cast out too slowly by some agencies.[3] Use of emotional appeals has served to cloud the purpose of the agency in the public mind and to blunt its educational objectives. For example, people must be motivated to get periodic cancer check-ups, but not frightened into an attitude of hopelessness.

More showmanship, less fear-mongering is emerging in social work. An example of what imagination can do to displace the "fear technique" is offered in the showmanship of Detroit's Torch Drive. The Detroit community fund, on its annual lead-off, has staged a parade worth seeing, one that brings out millions of Detroiters. This event does a job.

There are many other problems peculiar to this field. For one thing, there is the unflattering, untrue stereotype of the social worker. For another, there is social work jargon, full of clichés and meaningless abstractions. As one editor commented, "trying to catch such phrases as 'intergroup consciousness,' 'the weaving of the profession of social work into the community fabric,' ad infinitum, is like trying to catch a jellyfish in a net." More serious is the fuzzy notion in some quarters that these agencies are tax-supported. This is caused by the blurring lines between voluntary work and government programs in the same area.

Another problem is an overemphasis on publicity. This field pours out an endless flow of publicity. The national headquarters of such agencies as the Community Chests and Councils, Red Cross, Boy Scouts, Camp Fire Girls, the health foundations, and the others have strong, competent publicity staffs. These headquarters staffs promote national coverage in mass media. They also feed a steady stream of ideas and materials to the local units. At the local level, publicity is handled more often than not by volunteers with purely amateur standing. Many agencies could profit by putting more emphasis on the communication of ideas and less on getting publicity.[4]

3 See Helen R. Bitterman, "Slogans in Welfare," *Public Relations Journal,* Vol. 10, July, 1954.

4 For a case study in national organizations, see Harold P. Levy, *Building a Popular Movement* (New York: Russell Sage Foundation, 1944). (The Boy Scouts.) For a glimpse of Girl Scout PR, see Natalie Flatow and Harriett Philmus Pitt, "World's Biggest Public Service Campaign: 50 Golden Girl Scouting Years," *Public Relations Journal,* Vol. 19, July, 1963.

An example of the way in which the headquarters PR staffs assist local units is illustrated in the technique of Camp Fire Girls, Inc. Each year the organization's small staff at New York City headquarters has developed a newsworthy theme for its annual birthday. One year it was "Make Mine Democracy," an economic education program. Another year it was "Discovery Unlimited—An Adventure in Creative Living," a program devoted mainly to better understanding of crafts and arts. For each birthday program, the headquarters group has provided guidance kits to all the local councils, plumped the theme in its magazine, *Camp Fire Girls,* and climaxed the event with a network radio broadcast on the birthday date. The press is fully briefed on the details. The Camp Fire Girls stepped up this program for their 50th birthday with a Golden Jubilee Celebration which had four goals: (1) to increase public understanding of the organization; (2) to update and enrich the program; (3) to render an outstanding service to the nation; (4) to pay tribute to the vast body of dedicated volunteers across the nation. These goals were accomplished with a public relations staff of five professionals, two of them part-time, and four clerical assistants.[5]

Leadership from national and state headquarters, coupled with follow-through at the local level, makes an unbeatable combination. The California Division of the American Cancer Society brought out more than 186,000 California women to see showings of a film, "Breast Self-Examination," during a seven-week period. The success of this project was attributed to planning and local follow-through. Here are the steps the Society followed in putting the film project across:

1. *Set the objective*—analyze what it involves, make the goal realistic, and consider the problems to be met.
2. *Set a time schedule and keep to it.*
3. *Know the materials needed* (films, promotion, press releases).
4. *Know the facilities needed* (auditoriums, projectors).
5. *Know the organization needed*—the committee to oversee the program's operation, the subcommittees responsible for specific items.
6. *Know the people needed*—analyze requirements for the chairman of the over-all projects, the skills that should be included on the committee, number needed, and so forth.
7. *Approach personally, whenever possible, those whose help you want*—pick the right person to make the personal approach.
8. *Assign people to the job they can do best*—they'll do it better and get more satisfaction out of it.
9. *Involve all important people and groups from the very start of planning,* so that it will be their problem also—prepare each person for the job he is to do.
10. *Give everyone involved a chance to analyze and evaluate the project and let each person know you appreciate what he does*—build a bridge to the next project on which you want him to help.

Although the problems may differ from the Community Chest to Family Wel-

---

[5] Elizabeth M. McStea, "Camp Fire Girls Builds on 50-Year Foundation," *Public Relations Journal,* Vol. 19, June, 1963. A case study.

fare Service to Red Cross to National Probation and Parole Association to Girl Scouts, the principles of programming are the same.

THE YEARS AHEAD. Welfare agencies must tightly link their programs to educating the public to accept enlightened social concepts in fields such as mental health, crime and correction, child welfare, and the problems of aging. *Planned, consistent programs* are required to break the barriers of public apathy, superstition, and the deadweight of indifference on these fronts. For example, only enlightened opinion will bring acceptance of sound rehabilitation and parole procedures in the field of crime and corrections. To counter opinions blended of vengeance and sloppy sentimentality, corrections leaders must persuade the public of the values of modern prisons and the supervised return of prisoners to society. What can be accomplished is dramatically illustrated in the progress made in mental health over one decade.[6]

The expanded range of activity and the mounting public bill for philanthropy have been financed in an inflated war-and-defense economy. In an economic headwind, social agencies will be hard hit. The demand for their services multiply in time of financial depression, but sources of funds contract. Even with all the gains made, the pull on the citizen donor is still none too strong. Even in an economy loaded with cheap money, there is a strong tendency "to let George do it."

The tab for this vast range of social work no longer can be paid by the rich man or by the corporation. It is from the upper and middle income groups that donor-supported agencies must get the bulk of their budgets. It is in the middle income group that a strong sense of responsibility must be built. The alternative is to transfer the burden to government. Then all will pay through compulsory contributions in the form of taxes. The donor-supported, volunteer-manned agency has an important place in democracy. It must be maintained in the years ahead. Leaders of these agencies must strive even harder to muster enduring public support through public relations, support that will endure in good times or bad.

PUBLIC RELATIONS
FOR HOSPITALS

THE PERSPECTIVE. America's hospitals are thrust more and more into the public spotlight. They are in great need of broad public support. They are gradually becoming sensitive to the importance of good public relationships. Medical men and hospital administrators, once coldly aloof and sternly professional, are developing a "public opinion consciousness" under pressure. Stung by such adjectives as "indifferent," "complacent," "smug," and even "arrogant," medical professionals, assisted by specialists, are coming to accept

---

6 Harry Milt, "Taking the Skeleton Out of the Closet," *Public Relations Journal,* Vol. 12, August, 1956.

public relations as an essential part of medical practice. There is, of course, a way to go in building universally good relationships. But progress in this field has been marked.

Public relations for medicine is spearheaded by the growing number of practitioners serving the American Medical Association, the American Hospital Association, the American Nursing Association, Blue Cross, and similar groups at the national, state, and local levels. There is still too much effort expended, however, in justifying rather than correcting the irritants. Medical PR needs to be more concerned with the "diseases" which blight relationships than with their "symptoms." There is also need for closer coordination of the several active PR programs in the health field.

The advance made in hospital public relations in recent years is shown in a survey made at the University of Missouri in which 24 out of 27 state university hospitals responding had public relations departments. Significantly, none of the programs was in existence 20 years prior to the date of the survey: 18 of the departments had been organized within the previous decade. Twenty of the 24 directors were college graduates; 11 of these were journalism majors. Half of them had had prior newspaper experience. These 24 directors reported a wide variety of duties, but "two responsibilities seem to be basic. These include the release of information to the mass media and the preparation and supervision of production of publications. Other duties are as diverse as conducting tours for visitors and directing programs in postgraduate education." [7] On an average day, you can find more people than the combined populations of Boston and Cincinnati resting in United States hospital beds, plus some 45,000 newborn infants. The odds are that each of these infants will be confined in a hospital at least four times during its lifetime. More and more people are requiring and getting hospital care. The public is "hospital conscious" as never before.

"People do not have to be sold on the hospital; they want more hospital care. They do not have to be sold on doctors; they only want more of them and more opportunity to use them. What bothers the people the most is the problem of financing their health needs. Unless this problem is met, the rest will not matter very much." [8] And this problem of costs is the central one facing hospitals, too. Hospital deficits are swelling as the average deficit per patient is multiplied by an ever-growing stream of sick folk entering hospitals. These deficits must be made up by either contributions or taxes. Despite shorter average patient stays in hospitals, bills are up. Hospitals receive much criticism from state insurance commissioners, labor unions, employers, legislators, and other public spokesmen. Most of this criticism is because of hospital charges, even though three-fourths of the population now has some kind of hospital insurance. Demand for broader-based support comes

---

[7] Joye Patterson, "A Study of Communications Programs in State University Hospitals," Multilithed Report, 1962.

[8] William S. McNary, "PR and the Health Industry," *Public Relations Journal*, Vol. 10, September, 1954, p. 11.

in the face of the highest patient rates in history. Alden Mills has written: [9]

> The voluntary hospitals have been expected to care for a larger number of free patients or patients who pay less than cost. . . . Increasing costs of operation have been particularly marked in the voluntary hospitals. These institutions have always been regarded as the pacemakers in hospital administration. . . . This country needs the leadership that they can provide. . . . To the voluntary hospital, adequate understanding, goodwill, and respect are today vital. . . . Lack of public support and generous respect may be fatal to voluntary institutions.

The tax-supported municipal and state hospitals, likewise, are confronted with multiplying demands for treatment and the provision of new and expensive facilities. In either type of hospital, public support determines the answer to these problems. There is increasing political activity to combat what the medical profession bitterly labels "socialized medicine" and the ever-persistent antivivisectionists. A natural reaction is adaptation of public relations practices to the needs of the medical profession.

In explaining the philosophy of the Lancaster, Pennsylvania, General Hospital, Meryl Ruoss, PR Director, told the hospital staff:

> We are a community hospital. As such the destiny of our hospital is to be determined by the needs of our community. Such needs are established by the expression of opinions by the individual citizens of the community. So that these expressions be well-grounded and accurate, it is a community hospital's duty to at all times maintain a close liaison with the people. This entails a free and frank sharing of information and problems with the people by the hospital. . . .
>
> Like other leading industries, our hospitals were established upon the ideals and magnanimous financial contributions of a few people. But even as those industries are now recruiting their capital from thousands of small investors, so are the hospitals becoming dependent upon every citizen in the community for support. Stockholders expect dividends. A hospital's board of directors votes its citizen supporters dividends of community health and protection. To merit continued support on this broad base, they must also determine that the public shares in the hospital's hopes, fears, and aspirations.

Such an enlightened philosophy is unfortunately far from universal. Hospital administrators have been prodded in large measure by the growing signs of public dissatisfaction. Some years ago Edward L. Bernays conducted an opinion poll among the leaders of 1,000 national organizations to determine the attitudes of opinion leaders toward hospitals. Bernays' poll found considerable dissatisfaction with many features of hospital service:

1. Rates and method of payment for hospital service—there is a general agreement that this should be cut, particularly for the middle class.

2. Physical appurtenances should be improved, with attention to the psychological impact of drab surroundings.

3. There should be more doctors.

---

[9] *Hospital Public Relations Today* (Berwyn, Ill.: Physicians Record Co., 1964). Standard **work** in this field, now updated.

4. Patients should be treated more humanely.
5. There should be many more nurses. There should be higher standards for nurses and means of attracting them should be developed.
6. Social service is poor and needs improvement.
7. Outpatient service should be improved and expanded.

In presenting the views of John Q. Citizen toward hospitals, Frank Sinclair, former *Milwaukee Journal* writer, told a public relations conference of hospital administrators:

> Why is it necessary to awaken a patient a couple of hours before breakfast to wash his face? . . . He says that if it is a question of hospital routine or patient comfort, the hospital should make its routine fit the patient. . . . Why does it sometimes take many minutes for a nurse to answer the patient's light? . . . We've all seen nurses standing in the hallway talking and ignoring call lights. . . . Too many hospitals are drab.
>
> A more homey atmosphere is wanted. . . . Hospitals are too noisy. . . . Why can't more quiet be given the very ill? Hospitals that demand payment for care weekly or even at the end of the hospital stay, demonstrate a commercial quirk. . . . I know of one case where a husband was called upon to pay in advance before his wife was given a blood transfusion. . . .
>
> I've had people tell me that hospitals have become so professional that they are too impersonal, too cold and distant. . . . Some persons feel that hospitals overcharge on certain items. . . . The public can see no reason why any doctor who holds a license to practice medicine, and is capable, should not practice in every hospital. After all hospitals are tax-free because they support humanity.

The sum of all this is that hospitals, from the smallest community to the largest, need continuing programs directed by trained practitioners. The medical profession needs the intermediary in dealing with the public more than most groups do. Mills argues, possibly with some exaggeration, that "Without any attempt at melodrama, one can safely state that hospitals in the United States today face the most serious crisis in their history. The intelligent use of public relations programs may spell the difference between continued growth and stagnation."

THE PROGRAM. In no field of public relations is painstaking attention to detail and bird-dogging of loose ends more important. An individual's hospital experience is charged with emotion. The opportunities for irritations and ill will abound. On the other hand, the opportunity to gain everlasting devotion is unequaled. Every citizen is reached by the service of his community hospital at least once in every eight years. The basic requisite is considerate hospital service at reasonable rates. This means good medical care and efficient administration. In many hospitals, there is a broad gap between "public relations" and patient care. Hospitals, like others, must learn that good performance should precede the news of it.

Couple this principle to a planned program, and the hospitals have the means to meet their problems. Essentials of such a program are given in one planned for the Lancaster, Pennsylvania, General Hospital:

> EMPLOYEE RELATIONSHIPS. Orienting an employee in the initial interview, providing a tour of the hospital, and giving him a personnel brochure.

Informing employees through a weekly publication, movies, bulletin boards, panel discussions, and pep talks in pay envelopes. Providing employee incentives and understanding through a clearly established wage scale, a vacation policy in fact, a security program, and employee council as a channel of communication between management and staff, and plans for a termination interview. Using employees to tell the public the hospital story includes placing employee's family on mailing lists, hospital tours for families, and use of employees as speakers.

VOLUNTEER GROUPS. Informing members of the board of directors by providing full orientation, putting them on all mailing lists, and utilizing them as speakers and hospital representatives before public groups. Also providing appropriate recognition for their service. Keeping the volunteer auxiliaries thoroughly oriented, informed, and imbued with a sense of participation in hospital projects. Seeing that "Gray Ladies" are likewise given orientation, receive all hospital information, and are rewarded for their services.

MEDICAL STAFF. A contented staff essential to the best service and growth of the hospital. Definite and sound staff organization with working liaison between staff and hospital board. New staff men thoroughly oriented. Staff stimulated to help create means for the patient to better bear costs. Staff members continually made aware of variety of hospital problems. Staff, internes, and residents kept fully informed and educated as to importance of public relations consequences of their work.

PATIENTS. A voluntary hospital is a public utility. Patients are part of the society which owns and controls that utility. Demand the best of service. . . . Enter the hospital with a "combat mission" attitude. Their hospital experience a highly emotionalized one. Utilize this advantage. Admission interview to allay fears of hospitalization and financial worries. Understanding and appreciation of patient concept by all employees essential. The hospital interpreted to the patient, and convalescence is proper time to begin. Patient and visitors convinced that hospital is working in patient's interest. Services for visitors provided. Preadmission contacts also opportunity to win patient's understanding and goodwill.

In response to vociferous patient criticisms, many hospitals are junking the custom of 5 A.M. reveille, speeding admission procedures, dropping requirement of payment in advance, providing tastier food, and creating more pleasant surroundings. More medical people are coming to agree with Dr. Anthony J. J. Rourke, former president of the American Hospital Association, that "hospital rules must be set up for the benefit of the patient, not for the hospital or the doctor or the nurse." A writer found in a 100-hospital survey that those most affectionately regarded treated their customers as human beings, not as "symptoms with relatives attached." [10]

Typical of the new approach in hospital public relations is the attention given expectant mothers by Chicago's Michael Reese Hospital. Two months prior to expected delivery, the hospital sends the expectant mother (1) a letter confirming her room reservation; (2) a preadmission registration form which keeps admission delays to a minimum; (3) information about a special birth announcement service sponsored by the hospital's Woman's Board; (4) gen-

---

[10] Milton Silverman, "Are Patients Human Beings?", *Saturday Evening Post,* Vol. 228, October 1, 1955. Laden with examples.

eral hospital instructions, policies, and services; (5) a folder about the availability of radio and TV sets with earphones. This is the positive approach.

HOSPITALS AND THE PRESS. Doctors and hospitals, because they care for the sick and the injured and those who die, are a vital news source. This direct, daily relationship with these media holds great potential and poses equally difficult problems. Hospital administrators who maintain cordial cooperation with the press are virtually assured of access to the community through these media. A hostile newspaper or radio station can blast a hospital's reputation by the factual reporting of an unfortunate mistake which cost a life. Such things do happen. Take the case of a Woonsocket, R.I., hospital. The newspaper, using subtlety and restraint, told, with devastating effect, the story of how a missing oxygen-tank wrench cost the life of a prematurely born baby.

As acknowledged in one hospital-doctor-press code: [11]

> The community has a right to information about its hospital facilities and services. . . . It is the hospital's obligation to supply this information accurately, promptly, and willingly. . . . Each hospital should name authorized spokesmen to be available at all times (24-hours-per-day coverage) to answer inquiries from news media. News-media representatives should have the telephone numbers indicating where the appointed spokesmen will be available for information either day or night. After naming spokesmen, the hospital staff should be informed that the task of handling news has been assigned to specific persons. Others on the staff should not release information but should refer all inquiries to those named to perform the news function. Hospital telephone operators should be fully instructed to refer inquiries from news media to the authorized spokesmen—quickly, politely, and efficiently.

There is a gap between what the press wants for publication about personal injuries and illnesses and what the medical profession feels it can ethically reveal. The same is true in the matter of medical research and hospital innovations. The press demands for news run smack into the medical profession's code of ethics and the private relationship of doctor and patient. Hospitals, in turn, are circumscribed by doctors' attitudes and ethics. Leaders in both groups have been striving to gain agreement on mutually satisfactory procedures to govern these relationships.

A number of codes have been worked out between press and the medical professions at state and local levels over the past few years. These codes are more guides than rigid rules. Such agreements recognize the press' obligation to report medical news adequately and accurately. Hospitals recognize the related obligation of serving as a cooperative news source. Both should be guided by three major considerations: [12]

> 1. To safeguard the private rights of the individual, so that no hospital patient will be caused unnecessary embarrassment or discomfort or be made the object of scorn or ridicule.

---

[11] State Medical Society of Wisconsin, *A Guide for Physicians, Hospitals and News Media* (Madison, Wis.: The Society, 1960), p. 3.

[12] Chicago Hospital Council, *A Guide to Ethical Hospital Press-TV-Radio Relationships* (Chicago: The Council, 1956).

2. To report the news accurately, authoritatively, promptly.
3. To cooperate sincerely in all relationships.

PUBLIC RELATIONS
FOR CHURCHES

REALLY NOT NEW. An increasing number of church bodies are embracing the practice. But there is still some tendency among the clergy and lay leaders to shy clear of anything as "modern" and "secular" as "public relations." Such churchmen ignore the past. From the earliest recorded history, religion has been spread by missionaries and travelers, hymns and sermons, parchment scrolls and books. The first book printed was Gutenberg's Holy Bible. The term *propaganda* originated in the Catholic Church in 1622 to describe the act of propagating the faith. Public relations, in reality, is but a new name for activities centuries-old in the churches. It was St. Matthew who long ago said: "Let your light so shine among men that they may see your good works and glorify your Father which is in Heaven." And it was St. Paul who wisely advised those who would communicate with their fellow man: "Except ye utter by the tongue words easy to be understood, how shall it be known what is spoken? For ye shall speak into the air."

The major religious bodies have large, strong PR staffs in their national headquarters spending sizable sums on films and other media. The current emphasis is, in part, an effort to catch up with the refinements and the emphasis in industry, labor, government, and education. Donald C. Bolles observes: "The inventive genius that gave us newspapers, radio, television, films and magazines is being utilized by the churches to make its voice so powerful that it may rise above the din of daily life and point the way for all to a Christian sanctuary." The religious revival and return to the church of millions over the past few years is not unrelated to this growing PR awareness among the clergy and churchmen.

Adoption of public relations techniques to bring the church to the people and the people to the church is dramatized by Evangelist Billy Graham, who employs a PR staff. The *Wall Street Journal* reports: "A Billy Graham crusade is based on public relations, meticulous attention to detail and almost down-to-the-minute advance planning." More and more churches and religious agencies are determined to regain communion with those who have strayed from their folds. This trend will broaden and deepen. Religion's problems are born of the sense of "lost community," the intense competition for acceptance of ideas, and competition for membership.

The church can make a choice in the matter of continuing publicity, but it has no choice in the matter of relationships with society. Everything about a church is open to public view—its attitudes, needs, purposes, deficiencies, mistakes, and achievements. Each contributes to collective opinion. Churches are not immune to the power of public opinion.

THE PROGRAM. So that "the whole Gospel might be brought to the whole world," churches are making increasing use of the mass media to express their spiritual message and views on social issues. In its public relations tasks, the church faces obstacles peculiar to it. Harral lists these as the main ones: [13]

1. The intangible nature of many religious activities;
2. The sacred nature of many activities, which demands a dignified approach;
3. The problem of showing the practical worth of religious values;
4. The problem of interpreting a program that follows a more or less traditional pattern; and
5. The difficulty of knowing at which level to project ideas so that they will appeal to persons of all ages.

In outlining a program for Protestant churches, one lay leader recommends that a plan of action should cover these points:

1. Ascertain what the church is today.
2. Decide the case of each major church need.
3. Recognize the trend of the times.
4. Recognize the changes in needs and new church methods of organization, administration, and service affecting members and support.
5. Broaden member participation and understanding.
6. Enlarge and inform all church constituencies.
7. Cultivate wisely new and old church friends, especially members who do not give.
8. Plan on short- and long-term giving or stewardship.

This leader made these suggestions to implement this programming:

1. A committee should be appointed to consider implementing with the pastor new ideas and new plans to win support.
2. A church council should be arranged, with leaders drawn from every organization in the church.
3. Associates or friends of the church should be brought in for counsel and consultation.

There has been a rather distant and sometimes strained relationship between pulpit and press. Much of the current stress centers on improving the relations by telling the story of religion within the framework of standard news values. In the nineteenth century, the church relied mainly on the religious press to carry its message to the public. It has been estimated that "in 1840 three-fourths of all the reading by the American people was religious." A century later, it was safe to say that the religious press's impact —in terms of copies published—was closer to one-tenth that of the secular press.[14] As the consequences of this shift in reading finally dawned on the clergy, they got busy. News media are responding to this effort.

The re-examination of news values, spearheaded by the Associated Press

---

[13] Stewart Harral, "Public Relations for Religion and Religious Groups," in *Public Relations Handbook* (Englewood Cliffs, N.J.: Prentice-Hall, Inc., 1962), pp. 369-377.

[14] For a close look, see Lekachman, Marty, Deedy, and Silverman, *The Religious Press in America* (New York: Holt, Rinehart & Winston, Inc., 1963).

Managing Editors, is giving religion increased news value. The field of religious journalism is widening. As the mass media shed their traditional concept of religious news as church announcements, so must the clergy. As one newspaper editor once wrote: "Our newspaper, and I think it is generally true of others, is trying to improve its religious news. But, as in any venture, it is the old story of cooperation. The church news is measured in terms of cooperation between newspaper and clergymen." Religious news has moved from the obituary or church page to the front page.

FUND RAISING

THE BIG EFFORT. There is a strong thread running through the warp and woof of these fields. It is the eternal problem of raising sufficient funds to enable the agency, church, or hospital to keep going, one year to the next. Fund raising dominates the practice in all these fields. Sometimes it dominates the agency itself. Much of the thinking, planning, and publicizing in social, health, and religious agencies is tied to the coin container and the collection box. There is fierce competition.

Philanthropy is "big business" in the United States, one of the biggest. To raise the money required takes a lot of publicity, promotion, organization, committee hours, and door-to-door canvassing. John Price Jones reminds us: "Fund-raising is public relations, for without sound public relations no philanthropy can live for long. . . . It takes better public relations to get a man to give a dollar than it does to convince him to spend a dollar. Favorable public opinion is the basis upon which American philanthropy has been built. . . ." [15]

Some of this giving is spontaneous. By far, most of it is in response to carefully organized and promoted campaigns directed by professionals. Professional fund raising, a field closely allied with public relations, developed in the wake of World War I, when the potential of American philanthropy was realized for the first time. It has been estimated that, year in and year out, professional fund-raising agencies help raise 25 cents of every philanthropic dollar. These professional fund raisers may serve as counselors to an organization's staff or they may fully staff and direct the campaign. Ethical fund raisers work only on a fixed-fee basis, not on percentage of money raised. Generally, the professional fund raiser is brought in for one time capital fund drives, although some agencies retain them on a continuing advisory basis. The professional brings with him the accumulated experience of many drives. The organized fund drive, born in the Y.M.C.A. movement, dates from the early 1900's.[16]

15 *The Engineering of Consent*, edited by Edward L. Bernays (Norman, Okla.: University of Oklahoma Press, 1955), p. 159.
16 For the full story, see Scott M. Cutlip, *Fund Raising in the United States* (New Brunswick, N.J.: Rutgers University Press, to be published in 1965).

PROFESSIONAL OR AMATEUR? There is no pat answer. There are advantages and disadvantages either way. The decision will depend on the organization and its environment. The professional can furnish expert knowhow, skilled personnel, carefully screened donor lists, large libraries, and proven procedures. On the other hand, the fact that an outside firm is sharing in the proceeds can hurt the cause among prospective donors. The local, indigenous staff, sparked by zeal and enthusiasm, if expertly counseled by public relations practitioners, often can do an equally good job.

The most generally used adjunct in either case is the volunteer solicitor.[17] Volunteer fund raising has the advantage of broadly extending individual participation and thus increasing the opportunities for goodwill. There is a simple formula for raising money. It is to "ask enough people to ask a lot of other people to ask for money." It is also difficult to make broad generalizations about the ratio of campaign costs to total funds raised. Two axioms of business apply in most cases: (1) The ratio of costs to receipts gets smaller as the campaign goal gets larger; (2) A noncontinuing operation costs more per dollar raised than a continuing one.

The professionals pretty well agree that it is impossible to run a campaign for funds at a cost of less than 5 per cent of the total goal, and they regard 12 per cent as a safe maximum. If costs appear to run over 15 per cent, it is time to take another look. A recurrent source of criticism for some of the national health groups is that campaign costs eat up as much as a fourth of the money contributed. Most experts agree that publicity and promotion should be allocated at least a fourth of the total campaign budget.

PRINCIPLES ARE THE SAME. Whether the campaign is directed by a professional firm or the internal staff, the principles are the same. In most cases, however, it is unwise to leave the public relations planning and the publicity to amateurs, however zealous they may be. John Price Jones said: "Fully 50 per cent of all the time and effort in the average fund-raising enterprise is in the field of public relations. Public relations in fund-raising demands a greater proportion the entire effort than is required in industry." A successful campaign is compounded of a good cause, thorough fact-finding, careful planning, and skillful communication.

The American Association of Fund-Raising Counsel suggest that these steps must come before there can be a successful fund drive:

1. *The house should be put in order:* the service program tested for effectiveness and efficiency; business management checked; investment policies scrutinized; governing boards and officers reviewed; the family assayed.
2. *The needs should be studied and documented:* what the institution proposes to "sell."
3. *The public relations should be "right":* a clear indication of favorable opinion is an essential prerequisite.

---

[17] For a scholarly study of the volunteer, his role and motivations in fund raising, see David L. Sills, *The Volunteers: Means and Ends in a National Organization* (New York: The Free Press of Glencoe, Inc., 1957).

4. *The governing board should lead the way:* support given cause within the family.

5. *The area to be served should be defined.*

6. *Some estimate of total cost should be drafted.*

Common forms of fund-raising appeals include direct mail, sale of seals, benefits such as bazaars, balls, and dinners, radio and TV appeals and marathons, newspaper promotions, and direct door-to-door canvass.[18] An effective use of the door-to-door method has been the March of Dimes porchlight campaign. Another fund-raising device, employed by the Red Cross, Chambers of Commerce, and others is the membership campaign with various classes of membership. The annual membership drive is the backbone of several agency PR-fund-raising programs. It brings a sense of "belonging" and participation. This is why many organizations are reluctant to give up their separate drives and merge into united appeals.

The John Price Jones Company, one of the pioneer firms in this field, has codified its fund raising into 25 principles of successful fund raising. These are: [19]

Principles of Preparation

1. The five essentials of a successful campaign are a strong case, effective leadership, conscientious workers, prospects willing and able to give, and sufficient funds to finance the campaign during the preliminary period. These five essentials should be weighed with scrupulous care before outlining a plan of campaign.

2. Committee work and publicity work should be mapped out in advance. The correlation of these two lines of activity, all designed toward bringing a trained and enthusiastic worker face to face with a sympathetic and well-informed prospect, is fundamental to the success of any fund-raising effort.

3. The cost of a campaign, within reasonable limits, should be estimated in advance.

4. All campaign activities should be given a time limit. Dates provide the only insurance for a proper correlation of committee work, list work, publicity, and canvassing.

Principles of Committee Work

1. The originating group, whether a committee or a board of trustees, should be a representative body.

2. The necessity for strong leadership is inversely proportional to the strength of the appeal.

3. The effectiveness of the group is conditioned by the degree to which individuals will accept personal responsibility.

4. The activity of the originating group determines the activity of all subordinate groups: the originating group is the inevitable yardstick both for giving and for working.

5. Committees are more responsive critically than creatively. In asking any group

---

[18] For ways by which small groups raise money, see Helen K. Knowles, *How Groups Raise Funds* (Freeport, Me.: The Bond Wheelwright Co., 1961). For abuses in fund raising, see Ralph Lee Smith, *The Bargain Hucksters* (New York: Thomas Y. Crowell Company, 1962).

[19] In an undated pamphlet issued by John Price Jones Company.

for ideas on a plan of action, for suggestions on a list of prospects . . . give each member of the group a copy of a plan.

Principles of Public Relations

1. The case must be bigger than the institution. The first object of publicity is to sell an idea; the second, to sell the means for its accomplishment.
2. Printed material should appeal both to the emotions and to the intellect.
3. Publicity must have continuity.
4. Publicity should proceed from the general to the specific. Interest in an idea proceeds from an appeal of general application.
5. Cheap publicity material is expensive. Quality in publicity pays dividends.
6. Publicity should be positive and not negative. Effective publicity always plays up elements of strength.

Principles of Operation

1. A campaign should not only solve immediate financial need, but should lay a firm foundation for the future.
2. Solicitation should proceed in six steps: listing, rating, assignments, cultivation, canvassing, and the follow-up.
3. Effective canvassing answers five questions—why, where, who, what, and how.
4. Campaigns should periodically reach a climax point. The climax is essential in arousing concentrated interest.
5. All canvassing, even for special gifts, should be conducted in an atmosphere of universality. "What are others doing?" is the common query of all prospects, large and small.
6. Campaigns should be conducted under a steady and constant pressure.
7. The time to be spent on a campaign varies directly with the size of the goal and inversely with the popularity of the appeal.
8. The direct appeal for help should be made when the interest is at its peak.
9. Ask for ideas, not for money. The canvasser should first interest his prospect in an idea.
10. There are four tests of the effective operation of a campaign: quality, quantity, cost, and time.

The American Red Cross has developed the technique to a fine point of perfection. A former executive, Howard Bonham, worked out the following time schedule of operations for putting a membership drive over.[20]

1. Planning Period. Choose campaign planning or steering committee; board selects campaign chairman; chairman and board analyze last campaign; develop plan, organization, publicity chart, and time schedule; prepare list of membership prospects, plan division tasks, set division quotas, organize advance gifts division early; plan general public relations program; interpretation, emphasis, theme, questions and answers; appoint division chairman, set up card files of prospective workers; get out preliminary publicity; plan instruction meetings for workers.

2. Preparation Period. Constitute chairmen, division leaders, and other leaders as campaign operating committee; have this committee meet frequently to promote and check; division chairmen select captains; captains select workers; check campaign supplies and set up campaign office; complete plans for industrial canvass, begin industrial and advance gifts calls; complete enlistment of

20 Howard Bonham, "How to Conduct a Membership Campaign," in *Your Public Relations*, Glenn and Denny Griswold, eds. Reprinted with permission of Mrs. Denny Griswold.

team workers in all divisions, conduct active speaking campaign before clubs and organizations; follow through on calls for advance gifts; hold planning and instruction meetings for all workers, perhaps by divisions, launch intensive publicity campaign, bring to a climax a week before the "kick-off"; hold opening rally, dinner, or "kick-off" meeting.

3. Solicitation Period. Begin general solicitation, all together, on the appointed day; maintain full-scale publicity; campaign leaders check daily with workers through the chain of command; if weak spots are found, apply a stimulus; hold report meetings as scheduled; employ clean-up methods to ensure full coverage; send returns to report meetings or campaign headquarters promptly, hold victory meeting, report to the public, thank all who helped.

Even a cursory scanning of this blueprint will indicate the hours upon hours of planning and preparation and the amount of energy required. Such a well-organized campaign for a good cause will get members—and money. In planning the public relations part of the campaign, Jones counsels keeping these objectives in mind: (1) Appeal to the broad general public to create an atmosphere of universality, and (2) Endeavor to reach individuals for a direct response.

Additional Reading

Helen C. Baker and Mary S. Routzahn, *How to Interpret Social Welfare.* New York: Russell Sage Foundation, 1947.

Robert H. Bremner, *American Philanthropy.* Chicago: University of Chicago Press, 1960.

Richard Carter, *The Gentle Legions.* New York: Doubleday & Company, Inc., 1961. A study of the national voluntary health organizations.

Margaret M. Fellows and Stella A. Koenig, *Tested Methods of Raising Money for Churches, Colleges, and Health and Welfare Agencies.* New York: Harper & Row, Publishers, 1959.

Clayton T. Griswold and Charles H. Schmitz, eds., *How You Can Broadcast Religion.* New York: National Council of Churches of Christ, U.S.A., 1958.

Abel A. Hanson, *Guides to Successful Fund Raising.* New York: Columbia University Bureau of Publications.

Harold P. Levy, *Public Relations for Social Agencies.* New York: Harper & Row, Publishers, 1956.

National Recreation Association, *Communications and Public Relations.* New York: the Association, 1959.

Willard Pleuthner, *More Power for Your Church.* New York: Farrar, Straus & Company, 1952.

Ralph Stoody, *A Handbook of Church Public Relations.* Nashville. Abingdon Press, 1959.

CASE PROBLEM

For many years now, University City's United Givers Fund has followed the conventional pattern of concentrating its publicity on the annual fund drive, which takes place the last two weeks of October. This fund embraces 26 nonprofit welfare agencies. Reliance for year-round educational efforts has been placed on the volunteer publicity chairmen in each of the 26 agencies. Because last year's fund appeal fell slightly short of the announced quota, fund officers have done considerable probing to determine the possible reasons. Among other things, they found a lack of public understanding of the needs of the individual agencies and of the relationship of the United Fund to such institutions as the local Y.M.C.A. The new chairman appointed a year-round public relations committee.

The purpose of the committee is "to evaluate public opinion and develop a program of activities which will create better understanding, goodwill, and acceptance by both the general public and special publics—agency boards, agency staffs, clergy, clients, givers, governmental leaders, labor leaders, business leaders, media personnel, etc." You have been called in as the public relations consultant to this committee of laymen. After the necessary fact-finding, including a study of the Community Chest, draft a year-round public relations program for the fund and its constituent agencies which will utilize available manpower and be most economical. The fund employs one woman to handle its publicity at present.

Chapter Twenty-Two

GOVERNMENTS

AND

CITIZENS

A popular government without popular information or a means of acquiring it, is but a prologue to a farce or tragedy, or perhaps both.—James Madison.

As the impact and extent of government increase, the need for adequate communication between public official and citizen becomes more urgent. Yet inescapable forces tend to drive them farther and farther apart. This problem is being met, to some degree, by public relations. Government has become increasingly a matter of administration. A vast machinery of commissions, boards, bureaus—*bureaucracy*—has grown up to meet our complex problems. The development is quickened in a nation mobilized to discharge its leadership in a divided world. This trend raises vital questions concerning the relations between people and their government. One of our crucial problems is to handle today's problems effectively without destroying popular government.

Government today—federal, state, and local—is so complex and often so remote that citizens tend to become apathetic and bewildered. Who can assert informed opinions as to the exact number of billions of dollars and kinds of weapons required to provide adequate military security? Who can assert, with confidence, the solution for difficult, delicate problems in foreign relations? It is hard for the busy, self-centered citizen to become interested in things which he cannot easily understand.

The gulf between the citizen and his government tends to deepen as decision making moves away from him. Centralization and concentration of government produce a vitiating sense of remoteness. Government too often appears to the citizen as but a bundle of entanglements among special-interest groups. Public housing, for example, has appeared to

373

be more a private fight between the real estate interests and the low-income groups than a significant public issue. Citizen apathy, well termed the "loss of citizenship," is sharply etched in each election by the millions of Americans who do not vote. There are other evidences of a default in citizenship, and other reasons for it.[1]

The maze of government needs to be explained, interpreted, and clarified. Each person has only a small amount of time and attention to give .to his government. Today's citizen needs a system of communications that will give him the same voice and understanding that his forefathers acquired in the town meeting. By the same token, today's administrator needs the face-to-face relationships that his predecessor of years ago had. He dare not lose the common touch. The bureaucrat must guard himself against isolation and insulation from the people of Punxsutawney and Prairie du Sac whose lives he so profoundly affects. This is an age-old problem, but one greatly magnified by the accelerating changes of today's Space Age. In the view of a political scientist: "As governmental functions increase in number and complexity, the need for sympathetic interpretation of government action becomes more and more pressing . . . government now needs the cooperation of the interests affected to accomplish its purposes, and the general public needs to know what the government is trying to do." [2] This obligation of government is being recognized—by administrative action and by legislation.

Effective administration must grow out of the lives and problems of the people rather than be imposed from above. Skilled, conscientious practitioners can contribute much to solving these urgent problems. Zechariah Chafee, Jr. said: "Government information can play a vital part in the cause of good administration by exploring the impact of new social forces, discovering strains and tensions before they become acute, and encouraging a positive sense of unity and national direction." [3]

Reasonable people, in government and out, agree that there is real need and ample justification for a more effective transmission belt. In the words of one practitioner: *"Democracy will live where there is free communication of dependable information."* This problem raises anew a question posed by Aristotle centuries ago: "The environment is complex and man's political capacity is simple. Can a bridge be built between them?"

This is an old question but one possessing a new urgency today. In a real sense, as one observer points out, "while we Americans are many times as numerous as we once were and necessarily confront vastly more complex problems, our source of information and means for popular participation in

---

[1] For some of the reasons, see Morris Rosenberg, "Some Determinants of Political Apathy," *Public Opinion Quarterly,* Vol. 18, Winter, 1954-55.

[2] J. A. Corry, *Elements of Democratic Government* (New York: Oxford University Press, 1958), pp. 291-93.

[3] In *Government and Mass Communications,* Vol. II (Chicago: University of Chicago Press, 1947), p. 736. These two volumes, by-products of the Commission on Freedom of the Press, provide helpful background reading.

the democratic dialogue are being ever more limited." This writer, John Cogley, of the Center for Study of Democratic Institutions, goes on to ask: "Do our growing bureaucracies, our galloping technology, our bigness, and the headlong advance of science make government of the people, by the people, and for the people irrelevant?"

The answer must be a resounding *No*. Much of the meaningful dialogue required to make democracy work today is shaped and phrased by the public relations practitioner. This imposes a civic obligation on him as he becomes, increasingly, the intermediary between the candidate or the public official and the citizens. As political campaign costs mount and the skills of persuasive communication become more specialized, we find the practitioner playing an ever more important role in our campaigns and in our government. Political publicity is one of the oldest phases of the practice, but it never had the scope, shape, and reach that it has today. The public dialogue begins with the political campaign. Kelley observes: [4]

> Political campaigns are the principal institution in which this interaction between politician and electorate occurs, and the most striking role of the public relations man is that of a campaigner. The particular kind of campaign activity with which he is most often concerned has, in terms of the theory . . . of democratic government, an importance all its own. For the public relations man is occupied with directing the course of public discussion as it relates to the selection of government officials and the settlement of controversial issues of public policy.

PR'S ROLE IN GOVERNMENT

Certainly, the foundation stones of Aristotle's bridge must be informative, candid, continuous reporting by government and more accessible channels to government for all citizens, not just those with an "in." The rise of the service state has had many profound implications. Some of these were sketched in Chapter 4. Two are of special concern here.

First, governmental power has steadily ebbed from the community to the statehouse to the federal government. Important decision making has likewise shifted from the more responsive legislative bodies to less accessible regulatory and administrative agencies. The result is to make government increasingly remote from the voter's reach. Trying to get a piece of information, to have a problem solved, or to make a need known, the frustrated citizen often gives up in despair. He fulminates against "red tape." Or else he turns to a lawyer, lobbyist, legislator, public relations man, or a political fixer. This new relationship is not satisfactory. This is demonstrated by widespread suspicion and distrust of government, attacks on bureaucrats (the word itself

---

4 Stanley Kelley, Jr., *Professional Public Relations and Political Power* (Baltimore, Md.: The John Hopkins Press, 1956), p. 3. Recommended reading.

has become an epithet), protests against the ever-mounting tax bill, and finally default of citizenship by millions. It also breeds, inevitably, influence peddlers who gnaw at the vitals of government.

Second, the mass media are grappling with the task of reporting under the heavy hand of news values fashioned in frontier days and with too few reporters. In days gone by, news of government was a relatively simple matter of personalities, oratorical political campaigns, trust-busting, and the like. It was an entirely different problem from that of reporting world affairs, atomic energy, mental health, space travel, controversies over matters affecting physical health, conservation, and other complex subject matter. Interpreting the complexities of government requires trained specialists and takes more time than deadlines often permit. Much progress has been made by the media in government reporting over the past decade.

But there is still need for government to strengthen and supplement today's reporting by the press. *Time* has observed: "The shortcomings in coverage (of Washington) are not always the fault of the reporters; they are due to the size of the job. In three decades the Federal Government has swollen like an explosion. And there just aren't enough reporters around to do a thorough job." Many editors dispute this. An editor of the *Milwaukee Journal* once naïvely asserted: "If reporters had free run of departments in Washington and could keep in contact with the fountainheads of information, a much better job of covering 'big government' could be done with perhaps even fewer men than are now there."

Governmental activities embraced by the term "public relations" have developed naturally. They are part of the administrative system evolving in an effort to bridge the gap between popular and bureaucratic government. The objectives are *active cooperation in action programs* (for example, soil conservation); *compliance in regulatory programs* (for example, public health laws); and *voter support for the incumbent administration's policies* (for example, foreign aid). The justification for government public relations rests on two premises: (1) A democratic government is obliged to report to its citizens; (2) Effective administration requires citizen participation and voter support.

THE OBJECTIVES

These are the generally agreed upon objectives for a planned, continuing program in government.

1. To win consent for new laws and new reforms dictated by the needs of an everchanging, technological society. This involves a deep, fundamental shift in our theory of government and has dangerous implications.
2. To overcome apathy and bewilderment toward new and complex functions of government; also, to provide reliable information for the voter seeking to make an intelligent decision at the polls.

3. To keep the citizen informed of the services and the functions provided so that he may participate and gain full benefit from them.

4. To give the citizen usable devices for relaying his views and opinions to the administrator without employing intermediaries.

5. To interpret public opinion to the law enforcement agencies in order that regulations will be realistic and acceptable.

6. To crystallize public sentiment and pave the way for noncoercive compliance. This requires convincing the citizen of the need for the administrative rules and assisting him in understanding them.

7. To build a reservoir of support for an agency which it may tap when the going gets rough; to have friends in time of need when a conflict develops with other agencies, with the legislature, or with the public.

The most fully developed aspect is that of government information or "propaganda," as it is called by its opponents. James L. McCamy has classified government publicity according to the following objectives.[5]

1. *To distribute publicity among or for clients of the agency.* The need of the Veterans Administration, for example, to reach all the holders of "G.I." insurance policies; or the need of state department of agriculture to inform all seed growers of a change in seed testing standards; or of a city garbage department to explain a change in collection procedures.

2. *To catch and hold the attention of the large public.* The need of a public welfare department, for example, to explain and justify to the public at large a drastic revision in its mental health program, or the necessity of the U.S. Department of Agriculture to explain to the public the reasons behind a soil bank program or to try to win a wheat referendum.

3. *To influence legislation.* This is the most suspect and controversial use to which government publicity can be put. In a sense, as McCamy points out, all government information has an indirect influence on legislation. There are occasions when direct influence on legislation is the aim, whether it is a state university campaigning for its budget or a technical agency urging a law to conform with newly discovered scientific facts.

4. *To reply to attacks upon an agency of government.* This use is fraught with the danger that the reply will only propel the publicity of the attack. It is a use which should be employed sparingly. Yet there are times when there is no alternative.

5. *To avoid publicity.* This takes the course of either passively keeping quiet or deliberately withholding news. Instances of proper use of this purpose could be envisioned in the F.B.I., or in a government board mediating a labor dispute, or a State Department formulation of a delicate diplomatic bargain with other countries. There is great danger of abuse in this.

6. *To report, without a particular objective, the routine news of government.* This is the catch-all which covers a conscientious reporting of the news as it develops within a department without any planned or preconceived purpose in mind. The bulk of governmental information work falls in this category, which covers changes in department personnel, procedures, etc.

These objectives involve debatable practices when viewed within the framework of a government of checks and balances. McCamy points out: "Administrative publicity in the past and now has been useful in the process

---

[5] In *Government Publicity* (Chicago: University of Chicago Press, 1939). Although out of date as to specific data and out of print, this remains a useful work.

of administrative leadership. Presidents and their assistants have gone to the public on many important issues, sometimes to enlist public pressure on Congress and sometimes to explain to the public the program advocated by Congress and the executive leaders." In actuality, most of the impetus for public relations programs in governmental agencies comes from the need to marshal public support for the money and measures that must be voted in the legislative branch. Bureaucrats engage in lobbying just as surely as businessmen do, despite the myth that governmental bureaucracy is neutral. Peter Woll, who made a study of American bureaucracy, writes: [6]

> . . . through what might be called undercover devices, the bureaucracy engages in extensive lobbying and propaganda activities. . . . Administrative agencies function to a considerable extent as freewheeling interest groups, and in their use of propaganda activities they are no exception. They not only seek to apply pressure at critical points in the political process, but also strive to maintain a favorable image of themselves before the public generally and before specific groups which they consider important in the battle for political survival.

HOSTILITY TO THE FUNCTION

The public relations function has been established longer in government than in any other field of practice. Yet it has not been as effectively used as it might be. Government practitioners face more hostility and suspicion than do practitioners in most fields. This hostility stems from three fundamental conflicts of interest embedded in our democratic government. These have a long history.

1. The continuing struggle between the press fighting for "the people's right to know" and the officials of government, who insist upon discretion in deciding what public business should be exposed to public scrutiny.
2. The unrelenting struggle for balance of power between the legislative and executive branches of government. This contest is present whether it is between mayor and council, governor and legislature, or the President and Congress.
3. The continuing struggle for power between the major political parties. The "out" party fears the power of an army of "propagandists" in keeping the "ins" in and the "outs" out.

Beyond these conflicts there is the inevitable association of government information programs with that dirty word *propaganda*. Americans have long been deeply suspicious of anything labeled "propaganda." Suspicion and distrust have been intensified as this power device has been used in other countries to gain and hold despotic control. Thus, public suspicion of information as "nothing but propaganda" is especially strong when the information comes from government. After a thorough study of this field, Professor Donald Krimel drew these conclusions.[7]

---

[6] In *American Bureaucracy* (New York: W. W. Norton & Company, Inc., 1963), pp. 134-35.
[7] From his Ph.D. thesis, "The Public Communications Function of the Federal Government" (Madison: University of Wisconsin Library, 1955).

The idea that governmental propaganda can be and should be eliminated stands in the way of open, careful, and efficient use of this administrative tool. In addition, negative stereotypes attached to governmental propaganda also are attached to governmental information services by persons who understand no distinction between the two kinds of activity. These negative stereotypes are a major deterrent to more effective use of the whole of governmental public relations.

Also involved in this opposition is the double standard which many citizens have for government and for private enterprise. The public generally accepts the right and propriety of business to publicize and advertise even though the customer pays for it. On the other hand, many people regard government information work as a waste of tax dollars. Citizens generally see no need for government to hawk its wares. There is no way of telling just how deep-seated and widespread this citizen attitude is. The average person is probably unaware of the problem at all. However, some politicians think that they get votes when they flay "government propaganda."

FROM THE PRESS

It is the continuing task of the press to ferret out and publicize the actions of public officials. Officials, in turn, insist that not all acts should be open to public view. One day a small Midwest daily will editorialize about the danger of "governmental press-agentry." The next day a metropolitan newspaper will assert that "the amount of federal money and manpower devoted to publicizing government . . . has reached staggering proportions." Another day New York State newspapermen will join in a "move to tear apart the paper curtain which shields government officials at Albany from inquiring reporters." And on still another day a Florida weekly editor will announce "a boycott of all state agency handouts." Periodically there are magazine articles about "How Government Pressure Boys Squander Your Money" and blasts from radio and TV commentators. This historic conflict runs from the village school board to the statehouse to the federal government. It reached a new level of intensity in the past decade.

The conflict stems from the growth of government at all levels and, at the federal level, from the uneasy tensions and recurring crises of the Cold War. Decreasing access to news of government is thought by many newsmen to be the major threat to freedom of the press today. This alarm is frequently and stridently sounded by newsmen in their meetings and in their journals. For example, the Report of the 1963 Sigma Delta Chi Advancement of Freedom of Information Committee proclaims: [8] "Your Committee must report that genuine freedom of information is at its lowest ebb today in the

---

[8] Published in the fall of 1963 by Sigma Delta Chi, Professional Journalistic Society, Chicago, Ill., p. one. V. M. Newton, Jr. has long served as chairman of this committee. His alarms are not always shared by fellow newsmen.

history of our Federal Government. This can be summed up briefly . . . as follows: 1. Secretary of Defense Robert S. McNamara and his public relations director, Arthur Sylvester, have created an oligarchy of control over the release of all news emanating from the Department of Defense. . . . 2. All the rest of the Federal Government falls back on the mushy claims of 'Confidential' and similar excuses in spreading the blanket of secrecy over the records of government." Veteran Washington newsmen do not support such unwarranted charges. Whether there is, in fact, such decreasing access is open to doubt. Nonetheless, the government's efforts to "manage the news" are a source of deep concern to professional journalists.

Three professional groups—American Society of Newspaper Editors, Sigma Delta Chi, and Associated Press Managing Editors—have given much attention to this problem by making studies and issuing reports. At the federal level, the attack has been on the abuse of security classification to hold back news which the press insists the public is entitled to know. At the state and local level, the campaign has been to get laws requiring all agencies to hold open meetings and to maintain open records. The complexity of this problem and its meaning for freedom of the press have been well defined by Cross, Wiggins, Cater, and Rourke.[9]

The age-old conflict between press and government broke anew September 25, 1951, when President Harry S. Truman issued an Executive Order (No. 10290) giving all civilian agencies of the federal government authority to classify information which these officials might deem to affect the nation's security. In effect, it gave the head of every governmental agency authority to act as his own censor of what was to be made public. Truman told department heads that the order "must not be used to cover up mistakes by any official or employee of the Government." But its use for these purposes was inevitable. Truman's order was quickly and vigorously denounced by the press and set off the sustained newspaper campaign for the "public's right to know" that has been carried to the present day.

Even so, this Presidential order has been maintained in force in modified form by Presidents Eisenhower, Kennedy, and Johnson. Eisenhower issued Executive Order 10501 November 5, 1953, reducing the number of agencies empowered to use this classification authority. President Kennedy, in Executive Order 10964, September 20, 1961, further modified the basic directive by setting up an automatic declassification and downgrading system. Thus, as a congressional committee notes, "over the years . . . there has been significant progress toward resolution of the conflict between the necessity for a fully informed public in a democratic society and the importance of protecting defense information to help preserve that society." [10]

---

[9] For helpful background reading, see Harold L. Cross, *The People's Right to Know;* James Russell Wiggins, *Freedom or Secrecy;* Douglass Cater, *The Fourth Branch of Government;* Francis E. Rourke, *Secrecy and Publicity;* and Herbert Brucker, *Freedom of Information.* It was Brucker who introduced the phrase "managed news," in this context.

[10] United States House of Representatives, *25th Report by the Committee on Government Operations,* "Safeguarding Official Information in the Interests of the Defense of the United States" (Washington, D.C.: U.S. Government Printing Office, 1962), p. 13.

The continuing campaign against secrecy in government has been led by Congressman John Moss of California and his House Subcommittee on Government Information since the mid-1950's. This House of Representatives committee, through its investigations and its airing of newsmen's complaints, has provided a clearer picture of government information programs and knocked down many unwise restrictions. Moss thinks that the "major cause of the restrictive situation is a 'papa knows best' in federal agencies." More realistic are the reasons inherent in human nature and in the realities of politics. Executives find it more comfortable to do their jobs without the public looking over their shoulders. Subordinates find it safer to suppress information than incur the boss' wrath for releasing it.

When the Moss Committee started its campaign against secrecy, it found executive agencies using three legal justifications for not releasing all information sought by the news media: (1) The President's executive order giving authority to many department heads to classify information on the grounds of national security; (2) President Eisenhower's letter of May 17, 1954, to Secretary of Defense Wilson (written in connection with the famed Army-versus-Senator McCarthy hearings) holding conversations and documents involving strictly the executive branch to be confidential; (3) the public records law (5 U.S.C.A. 1001-1011) dating from 1872, which provides, among other things, "matters of official record shall be made available (to the public) . . . except when required to be held confidential." The Moss Committee and newsmen singled out the last statute as being most responsible for executive secrecy and set out to get it changed.[11]

In 1958 Representative Moss introduced in Congress a bill to spell out the idea that this housekeeping law "does not authorize withholding information from the public or limiting the availability of records to the public." Newsmen vigorously supported the measure and ten executive departments opposed it. The bill was passed and signed into law by President Eisenhower. However, in a report issued in 1960, the Subcommittee on Government Information admitted that its amendment had not served as an effective check upon executive secrecy.[12] In 1963 Senator Edward V. Long of Missouri introduced in the Senate a bill which would compel agencies in the executive branch to publish in the *Federal Register* the sources where reporters and other persons can get information about their activities. It would provide for legal recourse to force disclosure.

In these clashes between newsmen and governmental agencies the public relations man, inevitably, is caught in the crossfire. Typical of this conflict is the battle over "management of the news" that boiled up in the wake of the Cuban Crisis of October, 1962. This crisis brought the nation to the brink of nuclear war and posed an information-security problem for which

---

11 See the article by a one-time chief counsel of the Moss Committee: John J. Mitchell, "Government Secrecy in Theory and Practice: 'Rules and Regulations' As an Autonomous Screen," *Columbia Law Review*, Vol. 58, February, 1958.

12 See *Twenty-Fourth Report by the Committee on Government Operations*, 86th Congress, 2d Sess., House Report No. 2084, July 2, 1960, pp. 36-37.

there were no clear, meaningful precedents. During the crisis, Assistant Defense Secretary Arthur Sylvester, a veteran newsman, issued a directive to control all press contacts in the Pentagon. A few days later, the State Department followed suit, but that agency later rescinded its order in the face of strong press criticism. The Defense Department did not. Sylvester added fuel to the flames by arguing the right of the nation, when confronted with nuclear war, to "manage the news" in its self-preservation. Countless charges and countercharges flew back and forth in the well-publicized "news management controversy" that ensued.[13]

Editors agree to the need for protection of military secrets but argue that such orders are misused by officials to cover up the latter's blunders. Nonetheless, serious conflicts over "the public's right to know" remain. The Moss Committee points up two security problems that remain to be solved: [14] "There are strict penalties for failure to protect a document which may have an effect upon the Nation's security, but there are no penalties for those secrecy-minded Government officials who abuse the classification system. . . . The other problem, which seems to be no nearer solution today than when it was first posed by the committee . . . is the lack of an effective procedure for appeals against abuse of the information classification system." President Kennedy assigned the appeals job to his Assistant Special Counsel, but this incidental assignment to a busy assistant did not prove satisfactory.

Newsmen hold that there is an equally strong trend toward increased suppression of government information at the state and local levels. Closed meetings of state and local boards are a frequent item of editorial protest. Efforts to break down the news barriers by the news media have been more successful at these levels, where no national security matters are involved. Sigma Delta Chi's Freedom of Information Committee has spearheaded a campaign to get open meetings and open records laws passed in the states. As of 1963, it could boast that 28 states had adopted one or both of its recommended statutes since it initiated its campaign in 1952. As of 1963, 37 states had general open records laws; 29 states had general open meetings laws. Those that do not, in the committee's view, give "ample proof that American politicians across the country still have an abiding love of secrecy." The government practitioner is caught in the vortex of these infrequent but heated controversies.

The newsman's point of view is reflected in this "Declaration of Principles" adopted by the American Society of Newspaper Editors: [15]

---

[13] These articles are typical of the spate of writings in this row: Arthur Krock, "Mr. Kennedy's Management of the News," *Fortune*, Vol. 67, March, 1963; Hanson W. Baldwin, "Managed News, Our Peacetime Censorship," *Atlantic Monthly*, Vol. 211, April, 1963; John Lofton, "The Press Manages the News," *The Progressive*, Vol. 27, June, 1963; "The News Management Issue," special issue of *Nieman Reports*, Vol. 16, March, 1963.

[14] *Twenty-Fifth Report by the Committee on Government Operations*, 87th Congress, 2d Sess., *op. cit.*, p. 13.

[15] Robert U. Brown, "ASNE Spells Out Broad Scope of the People's Right to Know," *Editor & Publisher*, Vol. 90, July 20, 1957, p. 9.

To exercise this right (to know) citizens must be able to gather information at home or abroad, except where military necessity plainly prevents; they must find it possible to publish or relate otherwise the information thus acquired without prior restraint or censorship by government . . . . they should have freedom to distribute and disseminate without obstruction by government or by their fellow citizens. . . .

The members of the American Society of Newspaper Editors . . . are doubly alarmed by measures that threaten the right to know, whether they involve restrictions on the movement of the press to sources of news and information at home or abroad, withholding information at local, state, or federal levels, or proposals to bring within the purview of the criminal statutes those who do not place security of the nation in jeopardy but whose only offense is to disagree with government officials on what may be safely published.

The press lacks the resources to report comprehensively and constructively all the affairs of government. First, there is lack of manpower to cover the multiplying agencies and activities in government at all levels. A press service attempts to cover a state government of more than 60 separate agencies with a two- or three-man staff on a 40-hour week. Obviously this is an impossible task if the reporters are to dig below the surface and get the real news. Second, there is the outmoded set of news values which puts the spotlight on the negative, controversial, and wrongful aspects of government. For example, the press will quickly mobilize to report in detail a state prison riot. The lack of an effective parole program, lack of adequate penal facilities, and the mismanagement which led to the riot are not reported prior to the outbreak.

Ernest K. Lindley, veteran Washington reporter, said: "By and large the government information agencies have been invaluable to the Washington newsgatherers and therefore to the public. Without them, the comprehensive coverage of government affairs would be impossible." The working press in city hall, state capital, and Washington know that government information men are essential and they seldom share the bombastic views of the editor. As one veteran public relations man in Washington put it: "I have never found the working press to be hostile. The publishers and editors sometimes talk hostile, but the reporters, correspondents, and commentators want and ask for and use the public information services of the agencies."

The skilled, specialized reporter qualified to interpret the scientific and technical aspects of government today is rare and expensive. Such talent is beyond the payroll of most news agencies. On this point, Fred F. Merwin pleads for new horizons on public affairs in the news rooms." [16]

(1) Recognition that democracy is a positive, not a negative, or even a neutral, force; (2) understanding of the purpose and meaning of the service state; (3) willingness to believe that there are good things in government along with bad; (4) appreciation of the fact that there is a place in democracy for positive propa-

---

[16] In "The Reporting of Public Affairs," *The Annals,* The American Academy of Political and Social Science, January, 1942, Vol. 219.

ganda disseminated through private channels; (5) determination to record the unfolding drama of government in an intelligent, honest broad manner.

Such positive standards need not replace the press' watchdog search for the bad and nefarious in government. There is room and a need for both. There must be balanced perspective.

FROM LEGISLATORS

Attacks on the function by legislators are less frequent but perhaps more vitriolic than those of the press. This opposition comes from both the legislator engaged in a struggle for power with the executive branch and from the legislator of the minority political power seeking majority control. Legislative investigations are not frequent. But they are effective in intimidating or driving government information men underground. Legislative opposition and fear of the function has led to tangible legal restrictions.

This conflict is born in our government of checks and balances. The legislative body cannot view calmly the skillful use of public relations by the executive to achieve his legislative goals. On the other hand, the executive cannot dispense with them and do his job. Millard Faught suggests that "Congress would do far better to recognize honestly the facts and to make intelligent and integrated provision for the proper function of publicizing government activity than to be incessantly trying to bottle up administrative publicists." Pimlott writes of this conflict: [17]

> The controversy over the limitations which should be set upon federal government public relations springs from the fear lest programs undertaken in the name of administrative efficiency should result in an excessive concentration of power in the Executive. This fear is shared by Congress, the states, and pressure and other groups which, though unrecognized by the Constitution, compete with the constitutional organs in the de facto exercise of power. What is more, government public relations threatens the member of Congress not only in Washington but in his constituency, where he has traditionally been the chief medium of communication with the capital. The controversy over government public relations is one facet of the perennial controversy over a strong central Executive.

The legislative branch everlastingly hammers away at secrecy in the executive branch while, at the same time, condoning its practice in legislative committees. Typically, the Moss Committee Report for 1963 reads: "In the great majority of the cases covered by this report, the Congress has been successful in overcoming impediments to the flow of information from the executive branch. . . . The increasing readiness of the Congress to assert its right to know has become a vital counterpressure against the bureaucratic penchant for secrecy, for unrestricted congressional access to executive branch

---

[17] J. A. R. Pimlott, *Public Relations and American Democracy* (Princeton, N.J.: Princeton University Press, 1951), p. 72. Part II of this book has thoughtful discussion of government PR.

information is basic to the effective operation of the 'check and balance' principle which underlies our system of government." [18]

On the state level, a senator will slap an expensive booklet on the desk of a department head and ask, "What right do you have to spend the taxpayer's money to pressure us into spending more of his money for you?" In Michigan a few years ago, the governor was called "in and down" by a legislative committee because he was "sending political propaganda to local newspapers in order to put the legislators on the spot." A detailed look at the legislator's point of view may be found in the reports of the Harness Committee of the 80th Congress and of the Moss Committee.

There is the legislative view that "the enormous governmental propaganda setup is not only a gross waste of the people's money, but, over and beyond that, makes for the destruction of the proper exercise of the legislative functions of government." This has led to legislative restriction, circumvention, and under-the-table practices which are wrong and wasteful. Much of the waste and ineffectiveness which can be justly ascribed to government PR is directly attributable to legislative restriction. This hostility also causes many competent men to shy away from government practice. *Public relations should be a legitimate, aboveboard function of government.*

Four specific legal restrictions tend to confuse and cloud the practice in the federal government. The 1913 law came after the United States Civil Service Commission advertised for a "Publicity Expert" whose ". . . affiliations with newspaper publishers and writers is extensive enough to secure publication of items prepared by him."

1. An act of Congress, passed in 1913, forbids the spending of money for "publicity experts" of any part of an appropriation unless specifically appropriated by the Congress. (*See* 38, Part I, U.S. Stat. 212.)
2. The "gag law" of July 11, 1919 prohibits the use of any part of an appropriation for services, messages, or publications designed to influence any member of Congress in his attitude toward legislation or appropriations. (*See* 41 U.S. Stat. 68.)
3. The law, also passed in 1919, but not strictly enforced until 1936, requires that all duplicating of material, including multilith and multigraph, must be done by the Government Printing Office or at least farmed back to the department for reproduction by the G.P.O. (*See* 40 U.S. Stat. 1270.)
4. Restrictions on the privilege of executive departments and independent establishments in use of the free mail frank prohibit any executive department mailing material without a request therefor. (*See* Title 39, U.S.C.A. Sec. 321n.)

Any one of these measures, strictly enforced, could virtually paralyze an information program. It would not be hard to interpret, for example, a quite

---

[18] United States House Committee on Government Operations, *Availability of Information From Federal Departments and Agencies* (Washington, D.C.: U.S. Government Printing Office, 1963), pp. 9-10. Also for report of Harness Committee, see House Report No. 1073, 80th Congress, 1st Session, *Fourth Intermediate Report* of the Committee on Expenditures in the Executive Departments (U.S. Government Printing Office, 1947). *Hearings* reports of this committee provide specifics.

legitimate informational release as "designed to influence" a member of Congress. The barest of facts can influence a person's opinion. Although the legislative rule on printing has much merit, it causes much lost time and waste motion. The 1913 law has led to the parade of titles which cloak and camouflage the practitioner in the federal government. "Public Relations" as a job title is avoided.

The same situation exists to a lesser degree at the state level. A number of states have had or do have legislative restrictions. Legislative opposition— often coupled with executive disapproval—leads to the same cloaking under innocuous titles in state government. One survey found that in at least four states the information function was completely covered up. In six other states with public relations personnel, there were no public relations titles or civil service classifications for such positions. In 18 states reporting public relations as a staff function, there was some degree of conformity in title and function. Although the function is not extensively utilized in municipal government, it is usually accurately titled.

This necessary emphasis on the hostility and restrictions which surround government public relations may have produced a distorted picture. Despite this opposition, the practice has steadily grown in concept, in ethics, and in practice. City councils, state legislatures, and the Congress go right on voting money for it. The press continues to use the information and services provided. Public relations in government has grown apace with the practice in other fields. Its necessity and usefulness in government make this inevitable. The maturity and skill of government practice is exemplified in the accomplishments of James Hagerty as President Eisenhower's press secretary. He served as one of the President's key policy advisers, kept the public informed about the President's activities and health, and skillfully projected the President's views to the citizenry. Eisenhower's Presidential assistant, Sherman Adams, vouched that Hagerty was largely responsible for the complexion of that administration. A mature practitioner concluded, after making a scholarly study of Hagerty's eight years in the White House: "It is the business of any public relations man to influence the complexion of any organization which he serves. There is little doubt that Hagerty did this, and he served both the President and—through the press—the public very well." [19]

Underneath the editorial bombasts and legislative scrutiny are solid questions of public policy that must be kept in mind. Public relations, as a staff function, must be justified on the grounds that it will not give undue power to the executive branch of government and that it will provide the public with useful information. Most vital of all is it that the programs do not interfere in the slightest degree with freedom of speech and freedom of information. The opposition must have full opportunity to oppose, counter, and criticize.

---

[19] Colonel Gordon A. Moon II, *James Campbell Hagerty's Eight Years in the White House* (Thesis, University of Wisconsin Library, 1962), p. 307.

So long as all sides have equal access to the citizen, there can be no real danger to freedom from the "government propagandist." [20]

NUMBERS EMPLOYED

No accurate figures are available on the number of practitioners employed in government. The necessity for camouflaging titles and the difficulty of determining where information ends and public relations begins in government have blocked efforts to get an accurate head count. In 1952 it was estimated there were 2,625 full-time employees and part-time employees equivalent to 1,007 full-time people in executive departments; some 8,000 employees in the U.S. Information Service; and another 3,285 civilian and military personnel performing the function in the armed forces—a total of 15,457. Civil Service records for 1954 showed 5,211 specialists on information and editorial writing. This figure did not include the CIA, FBI, AEC, and a few smaller agencies. No accurate count has yet been made of the number of federal employees performing this function. The Moss Committee undertook the task anew in 1963. A like difficulty exists in trying to collect and collate a full picture of the practice in state and local governments. There are few reliable data in this area of PR, thus suggesting opportunities for the scholar.

It should be noted that the employment of practitioners in the federal government is not limited to administrative agencies. Most congressmen employ a public relations aide as administrative assistant or as a secretary. Congressmen use news releases, recorded radio and TV broadcasts, weekly news letters, and other means of keeping their name and views before the voters back home. This reflects the increased stress on PR in politics. Stanley Kelley observed: "The activities of the public relations man have become a significant influence in processes crucial to democratic government."

GOVERNMENT PRACTICE

The practice varies widely from local to state to the federal level and from department to department. It is a long way from a city explaining to voters where its tax dollar comes from and where it goes to the United States Department of Agriculture's informational system radiating from Washington to 3,000 county agents. In government there is the one-man-plus-secretary operating on a simple publicity basis to the complex, far-flung mission of the

---

20 For differing views on this fundamental point, see Chapter IX in McCamy's *Government Publicity* (cited in footnote 5); E. Pendleton Herring, *Public Administration and the Public Interest* (New York: McGraw-Hill, Inc., 1936); and the article by Harold W. Stoke, "Executive Leadership and the Growth of Propaganda," in *American Political Science Review*, Vol. 35, June, 1941.

United States Information Agency, which serves as America's PR arm around the world. The necessity, potential, and difficulties inherent in government practice are sharply illustrated in the U.S.I.A.'s stormy history.

From World War II on, the United States as leader of the free world has been concerned with the problems of international communication, particularly with getting the people of other nations to understand our way of life and our fervent desire for peace. America's overseas PR program has two main objectives: (1) countering Soviet propaganda and bringing other countries to a fuller and more friendly understanding of American policies; (2) making technical knowledge available to assist underdeveloped countries. In the words of the Smith-Mundt Act of 1948, this agency has the responsibility of presenting to the world "a full and fair picture" of the United States. While trying to accomplish this, the agency has been subjected to several reorganizations, repeated budget cuts, sharp congressional attacks, and undercutting from inside and outside goverment. It had nine different directors in the 13 years 1945-1958. The U.S.I.A. has no lobby to defend it from its critics.

Under Edward R. Murrow and Carl Rowan in the 1960's, the U.S.I.A. achieved a stature and stability more commensurate with its heavy responsibility. Accept the premise that peace begins in the minds of men and you accept the need for a stronger, more adequately supported agency to tell America's story abroad and to interpret other peoples to Americans, particularly to our top policy makers. To achieve its purposes, the U.S.I.A. employs all the aboveboard techniques of modern mass communications: press, radio, film, television, libraries, books, the arts, exhibits, and, most important, personal contact by its officers overseas. At 239 posts in 106 countries throughout the world, some 1,300 Agency officers are hard at work as spokesmen for America.

U.S.I.A. operates an international wireless file which radios some 10,000 words daily in several languages to these overseas posts, where it is adapted for local use. This wire news is used to supplement and balance that transmitted around the world by AP and UPI. Similarly, a constant flow of photos—some 750,000 prints and 160,000 copy negatives a year—is kept moving to the field for use in local publications. The agency produces four major magazines in Washington, and U.S.I.A. posts overseas produce 62 other magazines in 25 languages, as well as 20 newspapers, wall posters, and other periodicals. U.S.I.A. operates libraries and distributes American books by the millions of copies. Best known of U.S.I.A. programs is the Voice of America, the radio broadcasts carrying the U.S.A.'s message to the world in 36 languages 761 hours weekly to an overseas audience numbered in the millions. It also makes and widely distributes films and exhibits to tell our story. Professional practitioners have assisted U.S.I.A. through participation in its "People to People" program.

On the domestic front, the United States Department of Agriculture is one of the government's oldest and most intensive users of public relations. The department's director of information told a Senate committee in 1960 that his staff of 232 practitioners produced 3,600 news releases in one 12-month period. This figures out to more than 10 a day, not counting Sundays and holidays. The U.S.D.A. staff also produced 600 different printed publications, distributing more than 34 million copies. The agency supplied radio and TV stations with material every week and sent out 6,000 photographs to news media. Other Agriculture Department divisions also have information staffs. In all, the U.S.D.A. employs some 300 practitioners in Washington plus many more in field offices across the country. An increasing part of the U.S.D.A.'s assignment is to win public understanding of agriculture among the fast-growing urban population.

In most government programs, the emphasis is on disseminating information. Less attention is given to opinion analysis and policy making. Krimel gained the impression in his study that "the agencies of the Federal Government which carry on broad programs are almost entirely lacking in systematic, modern means for opinion measurement." Yet the Bureau of the Census and the Division of Special Surveys in the Department of Agriculture pioneered in opinion sampling. One of the pioneers was Dr. Rensis Likert, who directed surveys for the Bureau of Agricultural Economics before organizing the social science research program at the University of Michigan. He reminds administrators: [21] "The acceptance and support that a program receives depend not only upon its soundness and how well it meets the needs of the public but also on the understanding that the public has of the program. Fundamentally sound programs have failed because of misinformation and ignorance on the part of the public."

The same forces—press and legislative critics—that compel government agencies to camouflage their work as to cost and numbers employed also hinder full utilization of the research tools. For example, when the National Aeronautics and Space Administration announced a grant of $131,000 to a university to study the dissemination of science news, the New York *Herald Tribune* damned this as a "Master Stroke of Stupidity." That newspaper saw the proposed study as "another sample of our survey craziness." In the face of such vitriolic criticism, NASA backed down, and the study, a needed one, was not made.

Several agencies, including the armed services, do use surveys despite these criticisms. Not enough do. Information sections in many agencies regularly provide their colleagues with editorial opinion digests, with the result that many executives tend to think that press opinion *is* public opinion. By and large, however, government agencies rely on political channels to bring in the people's views.[22]

There are wide disparities in planning. In many agencies the information official is a strong and able personality. He will earn an influential voice in

---

21 In "Opinion Studies and Government Policy," *Research Frontiers in Human Relations,* Proceedings of the American Philosophical Society (Philadelphia: The Society, 1948), p. 345.

22 See Harry Alpert, "Opinion and Attitude Surveys in the U.S. Government," *Public Opinion Quarterly,* Vol. 16, Spring, 1952.

the agency's policy making. Hagerty was an example. More frequently, the information man will be relatively remote from the policy level. He is thus hampered in effectively interpreting the public to the agency, and vice versa.

Informational programs in government generally take the form of (1) a campaign on particular topics—for example, revision of the state's deer-season law; (2) a steady play on a central theme for a long period of time—for example, conservation of the natural resources; (3) issuing news without any specific objectives—for example, a personnel change. There is a tendency to place too much stress on formalized communications and not enough on actual face-to-face communications. One state highway commission takes great effort to prepare an attractive, readable annual report. The same commission ignores a red-tape licensing procedure that irritates large numbers of citizens in the annual license "rush."

All communications must be understandable. A major weakness in government informational programs, generally, is continued use of gobbledegook, still the trademark of the bureaucrat despite all the fun that has been poked at it. There is urgent need for plain English and conversational writing in government correspondence and communications. Government jargon is a real obstacle to meaningful communication. Stripping it away involves more than readability: it is equally a matter of attitude. Agencies tackle this problem periodically. Some years ago the Internal Revenue Service brought in Dr. Rudolf Flesch. More recently the General Services Administration hired a former college English teacher to show the government's 750,000 letter writers how to write less like government letter writers.

The government practitioner uses the conventional tools of personal contact, annual reports, bulletins, films, publicity, education, consultation, and demonstrations. Many would do well to emphasize personal contacts, consultation, and educational programs. Not to be overlooked in the dissemination of government information is the practice of "leaking" information to get it into public debate without revealing its source. "Leaks" through press officers and "plants" at informal dinners with a few chosen Washington correspondents are being used increasingly in the capital. Legislators as well as administrators use this technique. It can backfire badly, and frequently does.[23]

There are many examples of skilled programs and useful techniques to be found in government, some borrowed, some homegrown. The public relations-minded John F. Kennedy made many PR innovations to promote his political fortunes. One was the introduction of the Regional White House Conference, which took federal officials to key cities of the nation for public conferences on current government problems. These conferences served the double purpose of publicizing the Kennedy administration's view and of subjecting top officials to public opinion as reflected by the discussions which took place in these rather lively conferences.

---

23 See Douglass Cater, "Government by Leak," *The Reporter,* Vol. 12, April 21, 1955, and United States House Committee on Government Operations, *Government News From Anonymous Sources* (Washington, D.C.: U. S. Government Printing Office, April, 1964).

The State of New York has borrowed industry's open house. One year the state held Open House Week, putting out the welcome mat for its 17 million residents to visit some 500 state offices and institutions. Employees provided guided tours, showed films, gave talks, and provided literature on their work. Some years ago the Kentucky Department of Revenue used a PR program to pave the way for a needed overhaul of its 55-year-old tax laws.[24] Another good example is the story of Ralph Gates, who, as governor of Indiana, took "the state capital to the people" in the manner of a corporation taking its annual meeting to the stockholders.[25] John Reynolds, when governor of Wisconsin, borrowed and modified this idea by holding his budget hearings in the various state institutions as a way of dramatizing the needs of Wisconsin's colleges, mental hospitals, and penal institutions.

What a government program may embrace and what it can accomplish can be illustrated in the pioneering program of the City of Philadelphia, which has modernized its government as well as its downtown district. When Joseph S. Clark, Jr. took office as mayor under a new city charter, he recognized the need for a full-scale PR program. He held it essential to tell a coherent story about government and to give citizens a sense of participating in their government. He took the authorized city representative's position, conceived originally as a ceremonial job, and converted it into the top PR job. A new PR program resulted.[26]

1. A Bureau of Public Information and Service was created. Three media specialists were employed to supplement, not supplant, the work of local reporters. These men were assigned to cover every department. The bureau issues an average of 20 releases a week.

2. A TV show, "Tell It to the Mayor," was initiated on one station. It was an unrehearsed audience participation show in which citizens presented complaints to the city government. Another regular TV program, "Mayor's Report to the People," was carried alternately each month by one of the city's three TV stations. Special TV programs were also set up from time to time.

3. The old annual report format was overhauled and a popular annual report published and distributed as a supplement to local newspapers. The last annual report prior to establishment of the Bureau cost $41,000 for 50,000 copies mailed to a select list. The 1954 report had a press run of 1,500,000 and reached nearly every home in the city at a cost of $35,000.

4. Several motion pictures were produced. One was a 20-minute sound and color fire-prevention film. Another was a 30-minute sound and color film on Philadelphia's housing problem. In 1956 a traffic-safety film was produced. These got wide local showings.

5. A variety of pamphlets were printed. Among them were "Guide to City Council," "The New City Government," a summary of the new Housing Code, and a series of program statements by the service departments.

---

24 Lawrence A. Cassidy, "State Taxes and Public Relations," *Public Relations Journal,* Vol. 7, June, 1951.

25 Paul Ross, "The State Capital Goes to the People," *Public Relations Journal,* Vol. 12, November, 1956.

26 Condensed from Walter M. Phillips, *Toward a New Program of Public Information and Ceremony by the City Government of Philadelphia.* A four-year report dated October, 1956.

6. Ceremonies were arranged to dramatize completion of capital projects. Whenever possible, the program included "open house" for Philadelphia citizens. Other civic events were staged to get citizen attention and participation.

7. Efforts were made to promote civic pride in the City by arranging for publicity in national media with considerable success. The nationwide program included a celebration of Benjamin Franklin's 250th birthday.

8. To provide for an inflow of citizen views, the PR department promoted establishment of the Mayor's Office for Information and Complaints. The bureau gave considerable time to assist the Complaints office on public relations details and to develop publicity which would bring this new service to the public's attention.

9. The Bureau has provided much service and counsel to other city departments. It staged a series of seminars to assist department heads in their relations with the local media. It organized a Public Relations Council so that department heads could meet periodically and discuss mutual PR problems. It initiated several programs aimed at improving employee morale. It started a house publication, but did not get funds to continue it beyond the trial period.

This program was carried out in the first four years with an ultimate staff of 11 professional and 7 clerical persons and a budget of approximately $165,000.

Additional Reading

Leo Bogart, "Measuring the Effectiveness of an Overseas Information Campaign," *Public Opinion Quarterly,* Vol. 21, Winter, 1957-58.

Douglass Cater, *Power in Washington.* New York: Random House, 1964.

Dick Fitzpatrick, "America's Campaign of Truth Throughout the World," *Journalism Quarterly,* Vol. 28, Winter, 1951.

T. Swann Harding, "Information Techniques of the Department of Agriculture," *Public Opinion Quarterly,* Vol. 1, Winter, 1937.

Donald G. Hileman, "State Advertising: Tourist and Industrial," *Journalism Quarterly,* Vol. 34, Spring, 1957.

Lawrence S. Hobart, *Governor's Press Secretary: A Profile of Paul Weber.* Ann Arbor, Mich.: University of Michigan Bureau of Government, 1958. Papers in Public Administration No. 25.

Lee K. Jaffee, "Public Relations—the New Government Service," *Public Relations Journal,* Vol. 11, October, 1955.

William J. Lederer and Eugene Burdick, *The Ugly American.* New York: W. W. Norton & Company, Inc., 1958. A broad-axe bludgeoning, in the form of a novel, of our overseas public relations program.

Clark R. Mollenhoff, *Washington Cover-Up.* Garden City, N. Y.: Doubleday & Company, Inc., 1962.

Dan D. Nimmo, *Newsgathering in Washington.* New York: Atherton Press, 1964. Chapter II especially pertinent.

Cabell Phillips, "Torchlight, Train, Television," *New York Times Magazine,* September 18, 1960, Section 6.

Jack Redding, *Inside the Democratic Party.* New York: Bobbs-Merrill Company, Inc., 1958. Story of the 1948 Presidential campaign as seen by Truman's PR man.

Bernard Rubin, *Public Relations and the Empire State.* New Brunswick, N. J.: Rutgers University Press, 1958.

Pan Dodd Wheeler and Cliff P. Greenwood, *A Municipal Public Relations Program That Works.* Knoxville: University of Tennessee, 1954.

CASE PROBLEM

You are public relations director for the State Department of Public Welfare. Its division of corrections long ago decided that the state boys' school was grossly inadequate and a dangerous firetrap. The State Board of Public Welfare launched a PR campaign three years ago to win legislative support for a new facility in a better location. After three years of effort, the State Legislature appropriated six million dollars for a new reformatory. The Board of Public Welfare, in collaboration with the governor, decided to locate it in a state forest. This would provide attractive surroundings, isolation from cities, and constructive work for the boys. When this decision is announced, conservation groups, headed by the Izaak Walton League, issue vehement protests and threaten court action to block the move. The community in which the present reformatory is located organizes a committee to keep it there. Conservation groups start a public campaign to force the governor and welfare board to reverse the decision. The much-needed new reformatory appears to be in jeopardy. The director of public welfare and the head of the corrections division turn to you to ask: "How do we head this thing off?"

What are your recommendations?

Chapter Twenty-Three

PUBLIC

SCHOOLS

The progress of the school as an institution of democracy depends upon the support of the public it serves.

"Education is the bulwark of democracy." This platitude has been worn threadbare by educators. Nonetheless, the nursery school-to-university American educational system—public, parochial, private—is the bedrock of the democratic faith. Horace Mann's pioneering cry, "Schoolhouses are the republican line of fortifications," never carried more force than it does today. Thomas Jefferson proclaimed: "Educate and inform the whole mass of people. They are the only reliance for the preservation of liberty." To meet this great responsibility, education must be bulwarked by understanding and support.

Education is a major enterprise. Enrollment in public and private schools and colleges of the United States in 1963 exceeded 51 million students, more than one-fourth of the population. The rising birth rates are expected to boost this total to more than 60 million students, kindergarten through college, by 1970. Nearly two million teachers and administrators serve in our elementary and secondary schools. Roughly, 50 per cent of the nation's families have children in some kind of school. For the nation as a whole, more than one-third of local taxes are used for schools. An increasing percentage of state-collected taxes are, likewise, spent for education. Also, an increasing amount of federal tax money is being channeled to the education enterprise. In higher education, there are some 2,000 colleges and universities with 345,000 faculty members and approximately 4,500,000 students. The net result is that virtually every citizen is touched directly by schools in one way or another. The relationships of education with the

394

people are many, direct, and diverse. The opportunities for frictions, misunderstandings, and communication breakdowns are equal in number.

The urgent need for the understanding and support of education has brought increased recognition and enlarged practice of public relations in recent years. Education public relations is expanding in scope and concept. The literature on this field of practice is voluminous. The problems in the immediate years ahead promise to be tremendous. Education offers the practitioner a challenging field.

EDUCATION—A JOB
FOR ALL

The key to sound relationships is development of the idea that education is the job of all citizens. In achieving this, *educators must take the public into partnership,* using wisely the tools of persuasion, information, and co-operation. Much progress has been made in the past two decades, despite war, years of neither peace nor war, and mounting enrollments. This progress must be hastened and broadened if schools are to be equipped for the tremendous tasks ahead. Responsibility rests primarily with the educator. He is increasingly aware of this.

Americans have unbounded faith in education and a strong desire to provide education for all who seek it. American faith in popular education is older than the nation. It was demonstrated as early as 1642, when Massachusetts passed a law calling for universal education. In fact, there have been disturbing signs that Americans expect too much from education. Many presume education to be the panacea for all the ills that beset them.

One tends, too easily, to turn to schools for relief from weaknesses, for protection against enemies feared. If the accident rate zooms up, people demand safe driving courses. If juvenile delinquency breaks out in a community, people insist that the schools do something about it. Threatened from without and within by communism, people turn, frightened, to the schools for courses in "Americanism." They advocate loyalty oaths for those who teach and inquire earnestly into the content of textbooks.

On the other hand, the schools measure American aspirations. The expectations are great, as Walter Lippmann has observed.[1]

It (education) promises to solve the problem which is otherwise so nearly insoluble—how to educate rapidly and sufficiently the ever-expanding masses who are losing contact with the traditions of Western society. The explosive increase of the population in the past hundred and fifty years, its recent enfranchisement during the past fifty years, the dissolution, or at least the radical weakening, of the bonds of the family, the churches, and of the local community have combined to make the demand upon the schools almost impossibly big.

---

[1] In *The Public Philosophy* (Boston: Little, Brown & Co., 1955), p. 73.

The American's support of education in the abstract is unstinted and unwavering. His support and understanding in the specific situation is not nearly as certain or well informed. Many schoolmen, to their sorrow, have too often taken public support for granted. They have assumed that the public would foot a bigger and bigger bill for an ever-expanding program and plant. They have assumed that the public comprehends objectives and methods—despite ample evidence to the contrary. Or worse, in rare instances, they have assumed that courses and teaching methods were none of the public's business.

Educators' influence in improving education rests upon their ability to guide public opinion and to be guided by it in meeting society's needs. Failure to establish this cooperative partnership frequently results in defeats of bond issues needed to provide more classrooms and more teachers. Terry Ferrer, an education writer, puts it succinctly: "Much of the school financing opposition, much of the recurring criticism about education stems wholly or in part from an uninformed public." Miss Ferrer recognizes the fact that the mass media cannot provide this information unaided, and she urges a year-round school PR program as imperative.

Lack of this cooperative partnership is also the source of much of the unbridled criticism of teaching methods and curricula content. In recent years public forums have resounded with stinging criticisms of education. A book attacking the teaching of reading, *Why Johnny Can't Read,* was a national best seller in the 1950's. In the 1960's, Vice-Admiral Hyman G. Rickover's book, *American Education—a National Failure,* was widely sold and discussed. He aimed his shots at course content, curricula, and teaching methods. In the words of one educator: "Critics have loudly denounced the schools as godless, Communistic, unAmerican, unenlightened, and subversive." [2]

Former university president Robert M. Hutchins has said: "One reason why educational institutions are vulnerable to economy drives and Red scares is that the purpose of education is not generally understood." Yet Hutchins frequently criticizes the practitioner whose skill is needed in building such understanding. Evidence abounds that the public does not fully understand modern educational methods and objectives. Too much attention has been focused on the sideshows—athletics, baton-twirling, extracurricular activities, social events—and too little attention on the show in the main tent.

Evidence of the need for and value of effective two-way communication between schools and the taxpayers who support them abounds in two exhaustive studies carried out by Stanford University under the sponsorship of the United States Office of Education. These studies, directed by Richard F. Carter, were based on interviews with community leaders in 82 school districts in the nation and interviews with a representative sample of voters in

---

[2] For a sampling of these critical books, see Rudolf Flesch, *Why Johnny Can't Read;* Hyman G. Rickover, *American Education—A National Failure;* Arthur E. Bestor, *Educational Wastelands* and *The Restoration of Learning;* Arthur Lynd, *Quackery in the Public Schools.* For one rebuttal, see Paul Woodring, *Let's Talk Sense About Our Schools.*

four widely spread cities. These studies found, among other things:[3]

1. The voter thinks schools are good in general, but he criticizes them in particular areas: frills, too much play, curriculum, and discipline.

2. The voter thinks the most important tasks of schools are to teach the fundamentals—reading, writing, spelling, and speaking—and to instill loyalty to the United States. He also thinks that these are the tasks done best.

3. The voter thinks the least important tasks of the schools are to teach about the local region, to afford enjoyment of cultural activities—art and music—and to provide industrial arts.

4. The voter's evaluation of the local schools, his evaluation of school costs, and his pride in the schools are most closely associated with likelihood of voting, and of voting favorably.

5. About half the voters show no evidence of any participation in school affairs and no interest in such participation. About a third of the voters participate actively. The more the voter participates, the more knowledge he has of school performances.

These public relations fact-finding studies provide sound guidelines for the school practitioner and should be studied with care.

Never was the need for strengthening the schools greater, a need underscored by at least three factors. *First,* in the battle for freedom and peace, United States citizens face problems of unequaled perplexity and difficulty. The need for educated, informed citizens capable of charting a safe course for the nation was never greater. One of the prime functions of education is to develop informed citizens equal to their responsibilities. *Second,* because our system is grounded in free education, schools represent the first point of attack. This requires vigilance and common sense to safeguard against subversion and against being crippled by the well-intentioned but ignorant zealots.[4]

Third, the educational system, from kindergarten to university, is confronted with a critical lack of classrooms and qualified teachers. The accelerated birth rate, from World War II on, has swamped present facilities and staffs. There are more young people, more of them going to school, and more going longer. In 1963 there were some 40 million pupils in public schools. In 1973 there will be some 48 million children enrolled. For a typical city of 100,000 population, this means one new school building every year for the next ten years. This continuing enrollment boom also will require a comparable increase in the number of teachers who must be recruited for this task. Both requirements impose a heavy burden on public relations

---

3 Richard F. Carter, *Voters and Their Schools* (Stanford, Calif.: Stanford University Institute for Communication Research, 1960). Findings summarized on pp. 4-16. Also see his companion study, *Communities and Their Schools,* published the same year by Stanford's School of Education. Both are helpful.

4 For several examples of misguided efforts to censor what is taught and read in our schools, see Jack Nelson and Gene Roberts, Jr., *The Censors and the Schools* (Boston: Little, Brown & Co., 1963). For two others, see "Hell Breaks Loose in Paradise," *Life,* April 26, 1963; and Joseph A. King, "Books and Banners: A Case History," *Saturday Review,* Vol. 46, November 9, 1963.

Unless these staggering needs for more classrooms and more teachers are met, there will be more overcrowded classrooms, more unqualified teachers, more half-day sessions, and shorter terms. This, of course, means less than an adequate education for tomorrow's citizens. To persuade taxpayers to vote the money required for the new buildings and to pay salaries which will attract enough teachers is a task of the first order. It means, in short, that America's schools have the biggest job in their history. As one officer of the P.T.A. said, "The only solution is to overcome an amazing public apathy toward the problem. The people must realize that if America wants high-quality education, it must pay for it."

The magnitude of the problem is becoming clearer as educators step up their public relations efforts. Nationally, advances are being spearheaded by the nation's political and educational leaders, the National Education Association, and its affiliate, the National School Public Relations Association. This organization has grown rapidly and done much to elevate the status of the public school practitioner. Even with the tremendous gains of the past two decades, this progress is neither broad enough nor fast enough to meet the critical challenge. The task is to reach each individual citizen and convince him that the problem is his personally.

THE PURPOSE

The Depression of the 1930's provided some pretty rough jolts for educators. It was a period of sharp and often reckless retrenchment. When aroused taxpayers made cutbacks in schools, they attacked not the least useful activities, but generally those they understood the least. As the taxpayer association steamroller passed over them, schoolmen began to realize their failures in public relations. They ruefully admitted that, if the required economies were made on the basis of emotion and misunderstanding, they, not the taxpayers, were at fault. The depression years demonstrated how little most people understand their schools.

A new generation of administrators learned much the same lesson the harsh way after World War II. The years 1945-1960 saw a number of communities refusing to vote the tax monies required for sufficient classrooms and trained teachers; a number of communities refusing to consolidate small, uneconomical districts into larger, more feasible school districts; and a number of misguided but successful attempts to throttle the freedom of teachers.[5]

Yet, even in this day, there is disturbing evidence that not all school boards and administrators recognize the need for a planned program to build

---

[5] For a case study showing the cost of a failure in public relations, see David Hulburd, *This Happened in Pasadena* (New York: The Macmillan Company, 1951).

public support. For example, a study made in Wisconsin in 1963 showed that few Wisconsin school districts follow a planned policy for disseminating information. This study, based on a questionnaire sent to a representative sample of Wisconsin's 395 districts containing both secondary and elementary schools found: [6]

1. Few Wisconsin public school districts follow a predetermined information policy. Concern for such a policy may be increasing, but, as yet, most school districts handle communications problems as they arise.

2. Most school districts have some method of allocating informational duties, but in many cases communicating seems to be looked upon as just another duty to be performed.

3. The attitudes of school district administrators are not always on the side of the people's right to know.

4. The most frequently used channel of communication of the school districts is written press releases, whether or not an information specialist is employed.

5. Only three school districts in Wisconsin employed full-time PR practioners. Many schools use teachers on a part-time basis to handle publicity. Most specialists replying in the study said that they needed more time to do their PR tasks, particularly for external communications.

A somewhat comparable study of public relations attitudes and practices in ten school systems around Boston led Professor Albert J. Sullivan to a comparable conclusion. He found the sound view that "the prime objective of public relations for schools is mutual cooperation of all segments of the community" was neither widely held nor widely practiced in the Boston area. He writes: [7] "Educational public relations in its best sense envisions intercommunication and mutual cooperation. Too often this view, in practice, becomes diluted: one segment does all the 'communicating,' the other segments are conceived as receivers or listeners, or at most, as groups to be persuaded to some action." Professor Sullivan, rightly, laments the lag in educational public relations. He cites three reasons for this lag: (1) The philosophy of education that motivates much of American public school education has blocked it; (2) There has not been sufficient realization of the need; (3) There are not sufficient numbers of educators trained in public relations.

In an earlier study, John Moran found in a survey of 200 school systems that most of them had no organized program.[8] On the other hand, Roy Carter's survey of California found that half the superintendents in California daily-newspaper towns had a person on their staff to prepare pub-

---

6 Digested from a master's thesis, "Public Information Policies and Practices of Wisconsin High School Districts," by Timothy J. Burke (Madison: University of Wisconsin Library, 1963). Unpublished.

7 In an article, "What's Wrong With School Public Relations," *Quarterly Review of Public Relations,* Vol. 7, Fall, 1962, pp. 21-29.

8 A survey of 200 school systems indicated that "90 per cent viewed public relations as just another term for publicity." See *Public Relations Journal,* Vol. 9, December, 1953, p. 12.

licity releases. Full-fledged departments were less common.[9] An increasing
pattern, especially in large high school districts, is employment of a journalism-
trained teacher to teach journalism, supervise the student newspaper, and
"handle school publicity." Over all, there is marked progress in developing
full-time programs; the question is whether the progress is fast enough. There
are occasional setbacks. In 1963 the Cleveland, Ohio, school board wiped
out the public information and publications department in a misguided
economy move.

The purpose of school public relations programs should now be clear.
Few people have even a superficial knowledge of the virtues or shortcomings of the schools they support. Consider, for example, the emotional out-
bursts that can be aroused by the stereotype "progressive education." Or the
absurd falsity of the stereotype of the teacher as a stern spinster. In fact,
married women now outnumber the unmarried teachers about 5 to 2, and
married men teachers outnumber unmarried men teachers 8 to 2.[10] Or ponder
the problem of a taxpayer weighing a tangible tax bill for a new school
building against the unseen cost of going without a new building. One of
the tough problems lies in the fact that the social cost of inadequate education cannot be demonstrated concretely.

The average citizen has only the vaguest notions as to what constitutes
"good education." That there still remains a tremendous job for education
is repeatedly demonstrated. When the issue of district consolidation or construction of a new building is under debate, the exhortation still rings out
that "reading, 'riting, 'rithmetic was good enough for me and it's good
enough for my children." This, essentially, was the appeal of *Why Johnny
Can't Read*. Taxpayers watch their tax bills go higher and higher. They
question the need and ask hard questions. They are entitled to answers.

Most people accept the obligation to support schools at their present
level. Developing adequate support for more funds and needed changes
requires public persuasion. The problem is one of demonstrating that the
modern, consolidated school with a modern curriculum is essential to meet
today's needs. Then, there is the problem of safeguarding the integrity and
freedom of those who teach and those who learn. Schools are social, public
institutions with broad impact. Consequently, they are subjected to conflicting pulls and tugs. Public education touches the group nearest everyone's heart—children. This is especially true in our child-centered society.
Education performs a vital function. Its officials and teachers are public
servants, paid by taxpayers. It is subject to searching public scrutiny, suggestions, and criticism.

These are the common problems of American educators. Schools in the
South and in the Border States face even tougher problems born of geography

---

[9] Roy E. Carter, Jr. "The Press and Public School Superintendents in California,"
Journalism Quarterly, Vol. 31, Spring, 1954.

[10] For the new look, see Earl H. Hanson, "What Does Marriage Do to Teaching?" in
NEA Journal, Vol. 52, November, 1963.

and history. A comprehensive set of objectives has been set down by experienced school administrators.[11]

1. To inform the public about the work of the schools.
2. To establish confidence in the schools.
3. To rally support for proper maintenance of the educational program.
4. To develop awareness of the importance of education in a democracy.
5. To improve the partnership concept by uniting parents and teachers in meeting the educational problems of children.
6. To integrate the home, the school, and the community in meeting the needs of the children.
7. To correct misunderstandings as to the aims and objectives of the schools.

Inside these continuing, long-range objectives fall more specific, short-range objectives determined by current needs. For example, in the years just ahead, these would be specific, short-term objectives: (1) greater financial support to meet the increased pupil load of the next 20 years; (2) higher teachers' salaries and teacher tenure to attract more qualified people to public school teaching; (3) equal pay for elementary and high school teachers; (4) improvement of teacher training; (5) improved facilities; broadened, more realistic courses of study; and (6) needed expansion of school plants.

PUBLICS AND PROGRAMS

The chief executive of a school system is responsible for planning and directing the program. He needs skilled assistance. In too many systems public relations is left to individual schools with no central direction and coordination. *A public relations program requires direction,* and the superintendent must provide it.[12] He must:

a. Accept personal responsibility for planning and coordinating the PR program.
b. Adapt his leadership activities to his ability and personality and to community expectations.
c. Merit community recognition and acceptance by performance and competence.
d. Delegate the proper public relations functions and commensurate authority to staff assistants without relinquishing his own responsibility.
e. Make effective use of available technical assistance from staff members and laymen in the community, and assign specific responsibility to specific persons.
f. Encourage and expect the staff of each school in his system to maintain good public relations in its own service area.

A school program, like any other, starts with the system's policies and performance. These are determined by the superintendent and school board.

---

[11] American Association of School Administrators, *Public Relations for America's Schools,* 28th Yearbook (Washington, D.C.: The Association, 1950), p. 254. Though old, still a useful reference.
[12] *Ibid.,* p. 17.

The board members occupy a strategic position in the program. They determine the educational policies upon which the program must be based. The board is the intermediary between the public and the professional administrators.

School board members need to be conscious of their PR responsibilities as a board and as individuals. It is essential that a board agree on an adequate statement of public relations policy. The board must serve its function of interpreting the community to the school staff and, in turn, interpreting the ideas and policies of the staff to the community. Influential, articulate board members are a valuable asset to a school system.

Many school boards bring suspicion, criticism, and ill will by insisting on a "closed door" at board meetings. Conversely, they fail to utilize this newsworthy means of focusing public attention on school policies and problems. Basil Walters, veteran news editor, has advised schoolmen: "Maybe if you really had debate on some of these problems . . . if you would invite in citizens to debate out the issues, it might be beneficial. It would be painful . . . but it is the only way in which to educate the American people in such a way that they can form an enlightened and intelligent public opinion." Newspapers are increasingly insistent on this point. The New Bedford, Massachusetts *Standard-Times,* for example, hammered away publicly at its board for 18 months before the board opened its doors.

The starting point of any program is the careful determination of the publics involved, channels of two-way communication with them, and agreement on objectives. The able school executive will be the first to recognize that he often must go against popular opinion to serve the best interest of the pupils. If the decision is for the welfare of the children, it will be the right decision over the long pull. But the public must be persuaded that it was the right decision. The able executive recognizes that performance is basic and does not confuse publicity with the whole of public relations. There are also practitioners in education who tend to get cart and horse mixed up. PR must serve education, and not the reverse. With some it tends to become an end in itself. *A program is a means.*

Sound programs begin with fact-finding and opinion research. As educators have repeatedly said: "The community should be so organized that citizen control of its public school policies is respected in principle and facilitated in practice." One of the surest ways to facilitate citizen control is through periodic surveys of community opinion. The Denver public schools have, since 1951, made such surveys at three-year intervals with profitable results. Through these polls, in the words of the Denver superintendent, Denver's administrators and teachers "obtain a sort of group concept of what the parents want and what the citizens of this community want —their concept of what good schools are." The results of these surveys, fully reported to staff and the community, serve as guides for Denver schools in their program and public relations planning. Such opinion research also serves to delineate the Denver schools' publics, their composition, and the channels of communication to them.

There are various publics in school relations that must be reached.

Internal	*External*
School board	Parents
Teachers	Taxpayer groups
Children	Service clubs
Staff employees	Patriotic groups
	Civic groups
	Industry
	School neighbors
	Churches
	Alumni
	Athletic boosters
	Labor unions

The children are perhaps the most influential of a school's publics. Much of the information and the attitudes held by the general public are transmitted from pupil to parent to public on the community grapevine. There is no surer route to a person's heart—or resentment—than through his child. When the program of a school system rests on a foundation of classroom accomplishment, it is like a house built upon a rock. Ill-founded criticism will not overwhelm it. The pupil's role as an intermediary is a strategic one. Public relations, *truly,* starts in the classroom.

The school executive should determine whether students are enthusiastic boosters. He should see that they are well informed about policies, strive for courses which satisfy their needs and challenge their abilities, provide individual attention for those who require it insofar as possible, and build the kind of atmosphere which engenders the pride of pupils and of parents in their schools. Proud, satisfied parents will ring the doorbells to win a school bond vote.[13]

It is important that pupil and parent get off on the right foot. This starts with kindergarten. Many schools have effective programs for introducing parent and child to the school. A typical one starts with preregistration in the spring before the child starts school. This includes enrollment by the principal so that he can get acquainted, a visit by the mother and her child to the room the child will enter in September, and a leisurely cup of coffee with the principal and other teachers who may be free that hour. This is followed in August by mailing the parents a Kindergarten Handbook which tells them what is expected of the budding pupil. *Informality, information,* and *consideration* are the keys to a pleasant introduction.

Schools dare not rely upon the child's often twisted reports to keep parents fully, accurately informed. Good parent relationships are built by frequent, frank communication between teacher and parent. Although teachers

---

13 For an excellent "how to" booklet on school bond campaigns, see *Workbook to Win Votes in School Campaigns* (Washington, D.C.: National Education Association, 1963).

and parents share the same goals, there are many blocks to communication. Communication means include report cards which report, not merely score; conferences; encouragement of parents to observe pupils in normal classroom situations; special class programs for parents; and home visits by the teachers to handle ticklish problems. P.T.A. meetings with a purpose—not just excuses for a social hour—are a tool of proven worth in school-parent communication.

Sound relationships with parents are best built on *at least* annual conferences of parents and teacher. In this connection a ticklish public relations program has developed concurrently with our schools' extensive testing programs—"To what information are parents entitled?" As Paul Woodring comments: [14] "Parents in several American communities have charged that the schools are withholding important information about their children. Some have taken legal action to require that the full record on each child be made available to his parents. Teachers and administrators are troubled and frightened by these demands because they have compiled a great deal of . . . information about each student and many school systems have no clear policy regarding what may be released to parents." The only prudent course is to develop carefully thought-out, clearly stated policies in this matter and then enforce them.

Another effective way to build school-parent understanding is to hold special night courses for parents. In recent years many high schools have instituted such courses to introduce parents to the new mathematical concepts and the new methods of math teaching. Such courses have met with an enthusiastic response in most cities. Parents are anxious to know the content of their sons' and daughters' courses and thus to be able to assist the students with their homework. Smart schoolmen capitalize on this parental interest.

Each member of the school staff, from principal to bus driver to janitor to school nurse, must be brought into the program. This can best be accomplished through a continuing in-service training program. Also, the qualities and attitudes of a person should be given due weight in staff recruitment. Finally, it should be remembered that the happy, satisfied teacher or employee is the one who generally makes the best public relations representative.

The residents of a given school district who foot the bill, provide the children, and shape the school's environment must be the ultimate target. This public is composed of many groups: parents, taxpayers, and citizens with positive ideas about "what our schools ought to be teaching." The public can be reached through the pupil, P.T.A., press, service clubs, church groups, and in countless other ways. Community influentials can be reached most effectively through consultation on school matters.

Changes in school policy, organization, and curricula and plans for new schools should be cleared with key public groups. The counsel of lay leaders

---

[14] In editorial, "The Parent's Right to Know," *Saturday Review*, Vol. 44, November 18, 1961.

should be sought as often as possible and practicable. Location of new schools directly involves city government, real estate developers, businessmen, bankers, and others. Cooperative planning can be coordinated through councils, committees, and commissions. It should be based on a continuous process of self-analysis. Broadly based planning makes available a wealth of good ideas. It also serves to clear the path for important changes. Public hearings on major issues can be a profitable, if at times uncomfortable, procedure.

For example, the Pasadena, California, school has set up a number of citizen-staff advisory committees to deal with particular problems or issues. One was created to deal with the system's multi-million-dollar building program. Another was organized to advise on how best to develop a vocational education program. These citizen-staff committees have also been used on the problems of equitable districting, released time for religious education, and programs for the retarded. In this way many fresh ideas are obtained, possible criticisms are eliminated beforehand, and two-way communication is firmly established with the community's influentials.

The Columbus, Ohio, school district took another approach to this objective of closer citizen-school ties when it instituted a series of successful neighborhood seminars. These seminars were an outgrowth of a series of Saturday morning conferences held the year before by the school board president and carefully chosen Columbus civic leaders. The neighborhood seminars, sponsored by a City-Wide Seminar Committee, were devoted to discussions of the Columbus schools' program and financial needs. Study guides were prepared and distributed ahead of time. These served as the basis of the discussions. When the series was announced the first time, some 4,000 Columbus citizens signed up; when the seminars were held, another 3,000 turned out. Columbus officials have found these neighborhood ideas highly productive.

Another example of this cooperative planning—one of many—is found in the constructive contributions of Detroit's Better Schools Association. Committees of this association delved deeply into Detroit's school problems. One committee found ways of cutting costs of building construction. Another found a better site than the board had chosen for a new school, and the board made the shift. Ways were found to cut some red tape and waste in school operation. The association put great stress on getting the facts about the public schools and publicizing those facts. Constructive groups are to be encouraged. Those with an axe to grind must be either converted or repelled.

COMMUNICATIONS

The need for keeping the school community informed was underscored years ago by J. Flint Waller. He found, after study of the pressures on schools, "the most harmful demands and pressures are due to the promoters being uninformed or misinformed." A community fortified by full information on its schools will enable school officials to beat back attacks on "fads and frills" or "unAmericanism." An informed community will enable the schools to stand off selfish drives to hitch the schools to political machines. An informed community enables a school head to withstand the anger of an irate parent.

The objectives of educational publicity have been listed by Benjamin Fine, for many years education editor of *The New York Times*, as follows: [15] (1) to build goodwill for the schools; (2) to gain public support for sufficient funds; (3) to acquaint the public with new educational trends; (4) to add to the reputation of the schools through full reporting of accomplishments; and (5) to build sound working relationships with the press.

Yet press coverage of schools still emphasizes athletics and student activities—by a wide margin. A few years ago the school news content of a representative sample of Michigan newspapers (daily and weekly) was measured and analyzed for one year. Authors of the study concluded that school news is one of the least well-written portions of the newspaper, and that the absence of "significant news" is a more acute problem. In the opinion of the director of the study, these figures "speak eloquently on the failure of some vital school problems to receive sufficient treatment in the Michigan press." [16]

In another study, two researchers studied 19 well-known newspapers for one month and clipped all education news except sports. Each of these newspapers had a full-time education writer, but the researchers concluded that the quality of stories was good but, by and large, the news was not substantive. They found that these newspapers concentrated on "student extracurricular activities, teacher appointments and activities, school finance and buildings, scholarships and honors, awards, the school bus, PTA notes, and a variety of news about colleges." [17] They noted that little was said about educational speeches, what teachers think, their preparation for teaching, and their stands on educational issues. In these authors' view, only about five per cent of the clippings exhibited imaginative, informed reporting. A journalism educator, commenting on the Dapper-Carter study, asserts: [18] "If you depend on your local newspaper for information on education, chances are that you have virtually no information or perspective on the major national issues in education and only the most fragmentary view of the local school picture."

The press is slowly revising its news values to include more news of posi-

---

[15] In his book, *Educational Publicity* (New York: Harper & Row, Publishers, rev. ed., 1951). Book deals only with publicity aspects of education PR.

[16] See William H. Roe, ed., *Schools Are News,* Michigan Communications Study (East Lansing: Michigan State University, 1957).

[17] Gloria Dapper and Barbara Carter, "Is Education News?", *Saturday Review,* Vol. 45, March 17, 1962, pp. 103-6.

[18] Professor George Gerbner, "Teachers and Schools in the Mass Media," *Phi Delta Kappan,* Vol. 44, February, 1963.

tive educational developments. The trend was started some years ago by the news magazines. It needs to be speeded. The local newspaper is the primary means of giving the entire public a knowledge of what the schools are trying to do and what they contend with in doing it. This requires continuous reporting. If this job is to be done, the schools must take the initiative. This requires a planned informational program directed by a trained practitioner.

Increased coverage of the hard news of education is being encouraged by reader demand and by the National School Bell Awards program, which provides recognition for distinguished service in the interpretation of education to the public. The sponsors are: American Association of School Administrators; Council of Chief State School Officers; National Association of State Teachers Associations; the NEA, and other educational bodies. The National School Public Relations Association is the coordinator of this program. Awards are given at the national, state, and local levels.

News—disseminated through the school paper, community papers, over radio and TV, through personal contacts, and in public meetings—forms the hard core of the informational program. The media coverage of education must be strengthened and supplemented. One method of doing this is to get a readable annual report into the hands of parents and community leaders. The Kalamazoo, Michigan, schools have found it effective to publish an annual report as a supplement to the local daily paper. Reasons given were (1) reasonable cost; (2) broad distribution; (3) low cost of extra copies; (4) newspaper personnel assistance in preparation, layout, and so forth; (5) can be published during American Education Week to increase focus on this annual event.

Many schools use American Education Week to stage open houses and to gain the community's attention. Education-Business Days represent another effective adaptation of a PR tool by educators. Filmstrips and motion pictures, which need not be expensive, are another effective tool. One administrator, an amateur photographer, took a series of pictures of the school day starting with the bus pickup and showing every school activity. The slides were grouped according to grade levels and extracurricular activities. No planned script was used for narration, and this informality and lack of education jargon strengthened the presentation. Such slides can be used in P.T.A.'s and before local civic and service groups with good results.

Motion pictures on a variety of subjects of interest to parents—or, for that matter, any citizen interested in his schools—are readily available. State education associations, state departments of education, and many colleges and universities maintain film libraries which are well-stocked with films explaining all aspects of education. Many of these come from the National Education Association, which produces films specifically for the general public to help them understand the goals and problems of education.

An imaginative way of reaching the public by using its channels of communication is a daily radio program initiated by Dean Lindley J. Stiles, of the University of Wisconsin School of Education. For several years Dean

Stiles had a daily 15-minute program in which he mixed relaxed comments about education with music. The program was first carried on a radio station appealing primarily to devotees of rock 'n roll, jazz, and folk music. Asked about this program, subsequently carried on a large number of stations, Stiles said: "Being identified with rock 'n roll doesn't bother me. We're trying to entice people to think about educational problems, and I think it is important to reach high school and college-age people." His fan mail tells him he is on the right track.

The informational task cannot be assigned to any specific medium. The prime importance of personal contact between school personnel and public must be kept foremost. A survey of California educators showed that they regard personal contacts as "the most important channel in keeping the general public informed about the schools." Those interviewed rated the daily newspaper and reports carried home by children next in importance.[19] Further, it is essential that the relationship between the publicity objective and the base objective of wholesome two-way relationships of school and community be kept clearly in mind. The program should be developed so that there is direct contact with every home in the community.

The two-way communications task between school and patron is sufficiently important and demanding to deserve the full-time efforts of a trained practitioner. But many school districts insist they cannot afford this. Effective programs can be developed by part-time specialists if they get the cooperation of administrators and teachers. One such program is that directed by Mrs. Mary Ericsson of Pittsburg, California. An able teacher, she was given two days a week to work on public relations. "How could she, in two days a week, handle all the public relations and publicity requirements of nine schools?" she asked herself. Her imaginative solution was to make her fellow teachers partners in her project. With only one group meeting of a 10-member faculty public relations committee, this is what Mrs. Ericsson and her fellow teachers accomplished in one school year:

1. Radio series of six weekly broadcasts with teachers as speakers.
2. Teachers appeared before local civic and service organizations to tell the school's story under the auspices of a Teachers Speakers Bureau.
3. Development of a visual school story, using teacher-taken slides and motion pictures.
4. Arranging classroom work in a traveling display case for exhibition in downtown banks and department store windows.
5. A series of articles written for local newspapers by teachers and carrying their by-lines.
6. A teachers' talent show to raise funds for a music camp.

The informational task must be indigenous and must be modified by each school's environment, needs, problems, and personnel available to do the job. *It takes public relations-mindedness and planning more than it does money.*

---

19 Roy E. Carter, Jr., *op. cit.*

Additional Reading

Clifford Brownell, Leo Gans, and Tufie Maroon, *Public Relations in Education.* New York: McGraw-Hill, Inc., 1955.

Grace Graham, *The Public School in the American Community.* New York: Harper & Row, Publishers, 1963. The school in its societal setting.

J. E. Grinnell and Raymond J. Young, *The School and the Community.* New York: The Ronald Press Company, 1955.

Stewart Harral, *Tested Public Relations for Schools.* Norman, Okla.: University of Oklahoma Press, 1952.

James Hymes, *Effective Home-School Relations.* Englewood Cliffs, N.J.: Prentice-Hall, Inc., 1953.

James J. Jones and Irving W. Stout, *School Public Relations: Issues and Cases.* New York: G. P. Putnam's Sons, 1960.

Leslie W. Kindred, *How to Tell the School Story.* Englewood Cliffs, N.J.: Prentice-Hall, Inc., 1960.

————, *School Public Relations.* Englewood Cliffs, N.J.: Prentice-Hall, Inc., 1957.

Gordon McCloskey, *Education and Public Understanding.* New York: Harper & Row, Publishers, 1959.

Arthur B. Moehlman and James A. van Zwoll, *School Public Relations.* New York: Appleton-Century-Crofts, Inc., 1957.

Ward Reeder, *Introduction to Public School Relations.* New York: The Macmillan Company, rev. ed., 1953.

Edward M. Tuttle, *School Board Leadership in America.* Danville, Ill.: Interstate, 1963.

CASE PROBLEM

You are director of public relations for University City's school system. You have a secretary and a small budget.

The city's voters will be asked to approve a bond issue of $3,420,000 at a city election two months hence. This will provide two additional grade schools and an addition to one junior high school. It is estimated that University City will have to provide for an *additional* 1,000 pupils each year for the next 10 years. The city has doubled in population and tripled in area since 1940. This bond issue will cost the taxpayers 69 cents per $1,000 assessed valuation. The alternatives to providing additional schools are half-day sessions or oversized classes and more bus transportation. University City voters approved a similar bond issue four years ago by a vote of 3 to 1.

Plan an informational campaign to win voters' interest and support for this bond issue. The P T A Council has promised to provide needed manpower. The superintendent and principals will provide organizational leadership.

Chapter Twenty-Four

HIGHER

EDUCATION

The importance of an informed public opinion about higher education is now quite widely accepted among educators.—David D. Henry.

Institutions of higher learning were among the first to set about winning public favor on a systematic basis. A few college programs date back to the last century. In the early 1900's, several major universities organized news and publicity bureaus. Big spurts of development came in the postwar periods after World War I and World War II. Colleges were among the first to recognize the new-found power of publicity demonstrated by the Creel Committee in World War I. Adaptation of public information techniques was spurred by the expansion of higher education and the fund-raising drives required to finance it in the 1920's.

The years after World War II brought the biggest boom in collegiate problems and programs. The years 1945-1950 brought the "GI bulge" when colleges were forced to handle doubled enrollments with inadequate staffs, inadequate facilities, and tight budgets. Next came the Korean War and another defense mobilization. This was followed by a period of declining enrollments coupled with spiraling costs. Then, in the mid-1960's, came a new wave of mounting student enrollments which is straining college faculties and facilities to their outermost limits. This is no temporary bulge. Today's large numbers of college students and the research explosion are markedly changing the nature and course of the nation's colleges and universities. This exploding growth brought with it many complex problems.

These problems, on the positive side, did much to reinvigorate and freshen educational thinking. They brought to the campus an increased awareness of the value of good public relationships. Collegiate public relations moved far and fast in this period. Now once more the nation's colleges are confronted with mounting numbers of students to be taught with too few teachers and too few facilities to accommodate them if quality standards are to be maintained. In the immediate years ahead teachers must be *recruited,* buildings must be *financed,* and students must be *selected.* These impose a heavy burden on the collegiate practitioner.

The development of the professional association in this field is indicative. Organized in 1917 as the American Association of College News Bureaus, in 1930 it became the American College Publicity Association. In May, 1946, it evolved into the American College Public Relations Association. It is on public relations and fund raising, rather than on publicity, that its emphasis is placed today. This association in 1963-1964 had a membership of nearly 2,700, as contrasted with a membership of 451 in 1939-1940. These figures graphically reflect the growth in this field. The association is a strong force in the gradual development of public relations for higher education. An increasing percentage of its members are college fund raisers or development officers. There is a resultant shift in emphasis. The association's change in name and in emphasis over the years is symbolic.

More and more, the selection of college presidents is taking into account the candidates' abilities in public relations. More institutions are moving the function to the policy-making level. More institutions are converting old-line publicity bureaus into effective public relations agencies. More college presidents are thinking and talking public relations with their trustees, with their faculties, with their alumni, and with their students. These are fairly widespread trends.

Indicative of this increased emphasis and the broadened concept is this counsel offered future university presidents by Herman B. Wells shortly before his retirement as president of Indiana University: [1]

> Find a public relations counsellor in whom you have confidence for your close associate who has the ability and courage to tell you when you are wrong—and that's difficult. . . . The faculty and students are the most effective public relations representatives of a university. When they believe in their institution, they will tell the world of their enthusiasm. Elaborately contrived public relations departments which do not command faculty respect are in the long run self-defeating. A university cannot be "sold" by the Madison Avenue techniques used to sell cosmetics or automobiles.

And a conference of educators on improving the effectiveness of college faculties agreed upon this as one of ten factors which can contribute to faculty morale and better college teaching: "Maintenance of a free flow of information, ideas, and suggestions within the institution and between the institution and outside agencies." Yet it is only fair to caution that there is still too much emphasis on publicity. And much of the publicity smacks of

---

[1] In *Transactions and Proceedings of the National Association of State Universities in the United States of America* (Washington, D.C.: The Association, 1962), pp. 59 and 64.

press-agentry. Higher education still has too many press agents who put the spotlight on the college sideshows of beauty queens, athletic heroes, and contrived gags. A picture of a pretty coed throwing books and legs in the air to celebrate the end of exams does little to tell what higher education is all about. Many institutions still have their "public relations offices" in some remote temporary instead of in the administrative suite.

Acceptance of solid principles and practice comes slowly to educators reared in another generation. Many collegiate practitioners, prodded by books, professional journals, and their association discussions, are spending themselves on the barricades of faculty and administrative resistance. Scope and skill of performance, not the place on the organization chart, will decide the ultimate role.

The practitioner must expect some internal opposition. Faculty members of the old school tend to regard the function as sheer press-agentry. They consider it a waste of money that would be better spent on salaries. One professor has classified the faculty into three unequal parts: "(1) an "Anti-Public Relations Faction," which is small but very influential; (2) the "Neutrals," who comprise the overwhelming majority; (3) the "Pro-Public Relations Faction," which is the smallest group of all." [2]

The professor's cooperation is essential in an effective program. Yet, many faculty members remain aloof, others are merely indifferent, and a few are plainly hostile to the idea of a well-organized, intensive public relations program. To some faculty men, public relations smacks of that dirty word *propaganda*. The coldness of others stems from a suspicion of the press held by many in higher education. Sometimes it is the result of overzealousness on the part of the collegiate practitioner. As one university PR director admits: "Publicity people occasionally overextend themselves, even against the conservative background of a university. Inadvertently, a few unsteady practitioners assault the basic rights of the professor without the professor knowing it." An example of such an assault is the occasional misguided effort to "centralize" or "coordinate" all faculty expressions through the central PR office.

The best way to win the faculty's cooperation is through patient internal education and through the provision of help when the professor needs it. Emanuel Goldberg suggests ways in which the public relations department can serve the professor: [3] "It can serve as a buffer between a potentially articulate and socially useful scholar and the raw press; that is, it can at least prepare a release in a manner satisfactory to the professor's wishes even though there is never a guarantee that newspapers or broadcasting media will cast it in the same form, or even use it. Whenever a faculty member takes the trouble to document and deliver a speech . . . the news bureau can reach a larger and more general public. Books, articles, travel, papers, institutes,

---

[2] A. S. Balinky, "Public Relations and the Faculty," *Pride*, Vol. 1, March, 1957, p. 16.
[3] In "The Professor and the Press," *College and University Journal*, Vol. 2, Summer, 1963, pp. 57 and 59.

research, pet projects, civic and governmental service—all these are grist. They can be turned nicely to the professor's, the University's, and the community's advantage." In these and other ways, the practitioner must strive, ceaselessly, to clear away faculty and administrator misconceptions of the function.

One of the strongest misconceptions is the idea that to have a strong program is to pander to public opinion and thus undercut a university's true purpose. Robert Hutchins reflected on this:

> The most dangerous aspect of public relations work is its reflex action: we find that the public does not like something about the University; our temptation is to change this so that the public will like us. Our duty is to change public opinion so that the public will like what the University does, and, if this cannot be immediately accomplished, to hold out against the public until it can be. Public relations work in a university is a phase of its efforts in adult education.

Even practitioners have doubts about the educational impact in those universities which go all out for public relations, as one, Clay Schoenfeld, told his fellow practitioners.[4]

> I have the uneasy feeling that so-called "public relations" practices are muzzling and muffing our colleges. We have set out with great zeal to make friends and influence the public, and in so doing we have not only persuaded our professors to be more discreet; we have drugged these same professors into absolute silence. . . . This may be sound public relations for a department store or a barbershop but it is errant nonsense for a university.

These conflicting views of the function in higher education lay bare two serious and not uncommon errors in collegiate public relations. On one hand there are some administrations so imbued with the necessity of winning public support that they try to stifle whatever appears controversial. Then there are administrations so determined to protect academic prerogatives that they shut off the wells of public support that higher education urgently needs. Both represent unsound, unwise extremes.

Over all, it can now be said that the public relations function is widely accepted on the college campus and is daily demonstrating its worth to administrators, professors, and students. President David D. Henry of the University of Illinois correctly observes: [5] "The importance of an informed public opinion about the individual institution and higher education in general is now quite widely accepted among educators. The hostility toward the lay adviser has disappeared; the resentment of the journalistic interpretation of science is nearly gone; the isolation of the academic community is no longer celebrated as a major virtue."

---

4 In a speech, "Public Relations—Selective or Sentimental?" printed in *College Public Relations Quarterly,* Vol. 7, October, 1955, p. 9.

5 In *What Priority for Education?* (Champaign-Urbana, Ill.: University of Illinois Press, 1961), pp. 76-77.

FREEDOM, FUNDS, AND
FRESHMEN

Higher education faces three continuing problems. Its academic freedom is frequently in question, if not in danger. Its financial support is precarious and insufficient. The competition for qualified students is spirited. In the decades ahead, the student problem will not be one of recruiting numbers but in determining who should go to college. This is an even tougher problem. Couple these with the widespread lack of understanding of higher education, and there results a need for effective public relations. The tremendous task of intelligently interpreting higher education to the people who must defend its freedom and provide its funds is an unending task. Colleges and universities need more salesmen and more effective salesmanship. J. Kenneth Little, a former president of the N.E.A.'s Department of Higher Education, stated this need.[6]

> . . . Despite the fact that our educational system, both private and public, bears eloquent testimony of the high regard with which schooling is held, there are alarming signs that the average American citizen is both complacent and ignorant about the purposes, scope, adequacy, and needs of higher education. . . . Erudite faculty committees have issued profound documents upon the purposes, functions, policies and programs of higher education. But few people other than educators will read these reports. More people do not know that the reports exist.
>
> What is the significance of the fact that individuals, foundations, and corporations now give their monies to the support of research, educational experimentation, and fellowships, instead of to buildings, endowments, and operating expense? Why do foundations which appeal to the general public for funds for the study of poliomyelitis, cancer, or heart disease receive a more generous response than appeals for funds in support of higher education? . . .
>
> There is the need for clear, forceful, and dramatic interpretation of higher education—an interpretation which will focus upon the problems and issues of higher education as a whole, rather than upon the needs of single institutions, or types of institutions. . . . There is a job to do for our country. In this task, public relations experts must help supply educational statesmanship and social vision, as well as imaginative technique and ingenious device.

The need is clear. Repeatedly the public demonstrates great faith in the values and aspirations represented in higher education. Just as often it demonstrates a lack of understanding of the funds, faculties, and facilities required to meet the demands on today's colleges and multiversities. For example, one survey found that the American Dream for a large sector of the population includes "at least a chance for a college education." The survey concluded: [7] "This proportion is sufficiently high to create meaningful and

---

6 In "Higher Education Needs Interpretation," *College Public Relations Quarterly,* Vol. 1, April, 1950, pp. 5-9.

7 "A Third Report . . . The Public's Picture of Higher Education in the State of Michigan: Information, Evaluation, and Enrollment Plans." A multilithed report of a state-wide survey by the Survey Research Center, University of Michigan, issued in 1960. P. 7.

challenging pressures on the ability of higher education to handle the number of applicants, but it is also so high that a sizeable number of families must be disappointed in their aspirations." Such disappointments bring a backlash of resentment against the colleges.

The public relations task here is formidable; the progress, slow. In 1949, in an exhaustive survey of attitudes toward higher education, the *Fortune Survey* found unbounded faith in collegiate institutions but little real understanding of their function. *Fortune's* pollsters found great interest in, but little information on, education. They found great faith in education's ability to enable a person to earn more money, but little concern for its objective of enabling a person to live a fruitful, enjoyable life. The *Fortune Survey* concluded that "the subject of higher education is very little understood by the American people generally."

In a survey made eleven years later, the University of Michigan Survey Research Center found the same unbounded faith in education but a comparable lack of public understanding of it. This survey, using criteria it established, found that "only one adult in ten can be regarded as well informed" about higher education. The researchers added, "Information about colleges and universities is apparently somewhat haphazardly received, depending largely on individual interest and chance exposures in newspaper reading. . . ." [8] Ponder the public relations problems inherent in this survey finding: [9] "Current levels of tax support for higher education will not permit the education in public college of all of the children for whom parents expressed . . . college aspirations. Since current public opinion is not strongly in favor of increased taxes to support higher education, it is clear that when the children in question reach college age, the voters will either have to support the necessary public expenditures, revise their expectations . . . or provide substantially more direct financial support for the education than they are currently planning to provide."

More recent public opinion polls only serve to emphasize that people, generally, lack an adequate understanding of education—its purposes, its methods, and its importance to our way of life. This lack of informed support is a problem of great seriousness. In a century hinged to the struggle between democracy and communism, to see which can outlast the other, education takes on a fateful significance.

NEED FOR FREEDOM

No student, no teacher can be worth his salt unless he lives and works in an environment of freedom. Free inquiry as the fundamental of scholarship has long been recognized, generally observed. The teacher must have

---

[8] *Ibid.,* p. 17.

[9] Wilbur J. Cohen, "College Aspirations and the Future Demand for Higher Education," *Higher Education,* Vol. 19, October-November, 1962, p. 10.

freedom to teach, not merely for his own sake or for the sake of his students, but for the future of America and what America can mean to mankind. Yet, the freedom of the student to learn and of the teacher to teach comes under frequent attack. It is sometimes abridged, frontally or indirectly. Protecting and defending intellectual freedom is a continuing task.

The defense becomes doubly difficult in periods of internal tensions fed by threats of external aggressions when fear and hysteria break loose. In an emotionally tense social climate, all ideas that diverge from the *status quo* become "dangerous" and open to suspicion—and pressure. In the years following World War II there were numerous legislative committee investigations, requirements of loyalty oaths for teachers, and similar incursions on academic freedom.

This is typical: In New Mexico the American Legion sharply criticized faculty members of the University of New Mexico for opposing the disclaimer affidavit required of students who received loans under the National Defense Education Act. This reproach triggered a series of controversies which brought demands for a legislative probe as well as pressure to fire certain faculty members. Wisely, the university's president, Mr. Tom Popejoy, boldly used these attacks as a springboard for a vigorous defense of academic freedom. Periodically the political extremes, the Far Right and the Far Left, assault academic freedom. These limitations on free inquiry take a variety of forms. "Their net effect," as the *New York Times* points out, "is a widening tendency toward passive acceptance of the status quo, conformity, and a narrowing area of tolerance in which students, faculty, and administrators feel free to speak, act, and think independently." The consequences pose a grave threat to education. Such attacks must be repulsed. A former president of the University of Kentucky once said that the most important activity a president has to perform is to keep the university free.

The college or university that is fearlessly seeking the truth out of the conflict of ideas cannot escape pressure. It must have the backing of an informed public which cherishes free inquiry to reckon with such pressures. Education cannot, like the ostrich, safely hide its head in the sands of the past. Such a position is both undignified and vulnerable. It is the public relations function to persuade the people that, as Bernard de Voto said, "On this campus all books, all expressions, all opinions are free." An institution of learning cannot dispense with controversial ideas and live.

The task here is to demonstrate the vital necessity of freedom for the student to learn and for the scholar to search for the truth without restriction. Too often, college men tend to make academic freedom appear as something of a special license for the professor. The emphasis needs to be placed more on the by-products of the denial of academic freedom. Citizens need to be reminded forcefully that, as academic freedom has disappeared in other countries, so also has the freedom of all citizens. Freedom is indivisible.

College practitioners man the front lines in its defense. It is no easy task. Defending a loyal American professor's refusal to sign a noncommunist oath as a matter of principle is no easy task. Yet it is a task which has confronted more than one college public relations official. The state can abolish the freedom of learning only if the people are uninformed and inert. Loyalty oath controversies, painful though they are, do provide an opportunity to dramatize these fundamentals.

For many institutions, these political pressures beat most violently around the problem of racial integration of college student bodies. One practitioner, John A. Griffin of Florida State University, points out: [10]

> Whether or not we have so far admitted it, colleges and universities have heavy responsibilities in race relations, both on the campus and in the communities. . . . Thus for urban institutions and for many nonurban colleges and universities, North and South, race relations is increasingly a fact of life. This means that the colleges and universities, like the armed services, need staff persons who are specialists in race relations. . . . The problems that need attention range all the way from accreditation to football. . . . Public relations and development people need to give thoughtful attention to their responsibilities of sensitizing their institutions in regard to their responsibilities and their opportunities in race relations.

NEED FOR FUNDS

No institution of higher education is self-supporting. It is almost trite to talk about the "financial crisis" facing collegiate institutions. Yet the years ahead pose problems of truly critical proportions. The facts are simple, their impact staggering. Today's full-time college enrollment of more than four million students is expected to double within ten years and to remain permanently at the higher level. This is no temporary "GI bulge" pouring in the college gates.

The college-age population will increase to 14.2 million in 1970 and to between 16 and 17 million in 1980. It is estimated that by 1970 we shall have 7,000,000 students in our colleges and universities—3,000,000 more than there were in 1963. This doubling of college enrollments places a heavy financial burden on these colleges and universities. In part, these increased costs will be met by rising tuition fees. The issues here are many.

Teacher shortages are acute. Many professors are leaving teaching for better-paying jobs. If present teacher-student ratios are to be maintained, colleges must recruit some 500,000 *additional teachers* over the next decade. That they will be able to find this number of competent scholars is highly improbable. A study of the teacher supply and demand by NEA published in 1963 concluded: [11] "The total number of persons with high-level skills and

---

10 In a speech, "Higher Education and Race Relations," given before American College Public Relations Association convention, June 25, 1963.

11 Research Division, National Education Association, *Teacher Supply and Demand in Universities, Colleges, and Junior Colleges, 1961-62 and 1962-63* (Washington, D.C.: NEA, 1963), p. 9.

comprehensive preparation does not equal the present demand. Business, industry, and government enjoy a favorable position. Universities and colleges find themselves more embarrassed day by day. . . . Right now the total resources of the institutions of higher education are not equal to the total task which only they can perform. If they continue to be priced out of the market—as is now the case on many campuses—the tragic result is clear. . . . In short, this means second-rate education for a larger and larger number of our youth."

To take care of these rising enrollments and research needs, our institutions of higher education must build more classrooms, more laboratories, more libraries, and more dormitories. According to one estimate, the nation's educational plant must be expanded at the rate of $12.5 billion dollars over the next decade. In these 10 years, the nation must build as many schools, college classrooms, and buildings as it did in the previous 150 years. A staggering fact.

The extent and enormous complexity of the problems presented by this explosive growth on the nation's campuses is illustrated in the extreme by the University of California's size, scope, and costs. Its president offered this summary: [12] "The University of California—as a statewide public entity—had operating expenditures last year of nearly half a billion dollars, with almost another $100 million for construction; a total employment of over 40,000 people . . . ; operations in more than 100 locations . . . ; nearly 10,000 courses in the catalogs; some form of contact with nearly every industry, nearly every level of government, nearly every person in its region. . . . Soon it will also have 100,000 students—30,000 of them at the graduate level. . . ." California epitomizes the complexity of the modern American multiversity. Also, it dramatizes the collegiate practitioner's enormous task.

This new crisis is compounded of three trends converging on the campus: (1) the explosive increase in enrollments and in scientific research; (2) the mounting burden of educational costs; (3) the drying up of traditional sources of support. The United States Office of Education estimates that colleges and universities will have to spend an average of 2.2 billion dollars a year over the next ten years to handle this influx of students. This represents a need of close to 1 billion dollars per year in *new money* over the next decade. Where will this money come from? There are only three major sources: (1) tuition fees, (2) the federal government, and (3) gifts and bequests.

A veteran fund-raiser, Robert F. Duncan, predicts: "Tuition fees will greatly increase, more federal money will become available, and both tax-assisted and independent schools, colleges, and universities will be forced to press on more vigorously than ever in the fields of annual giving, bequests, and capital campaigns." The latter means, inevitably, greater pressure on the public relations office.

Privately endowed and sectarian colleges are especially hard hit. Gifts and

---

[12] Clark Kerr, *The Use of the University* (Cambridge, Mass.: Harvard University Press, 1963). A publication of Kerr's Godkin lectures. This quote is from the introductory lecture, "The Multiversity."

incomes from endowments fail to keep pace with the inflationary costs of frogs, footballs, and faculty members. America needs the strong, independent college free of political control and influence. These colleges have already raised their tuitions to the limit—if not beyond. Some have been forced to shift investments from securities to riskier common stocks. Others have dipped into reserves to keep going. Private institutions are leaning more and more on gifts from corporations and annual alumni fund drives. The Council for Financial Aid to Education estimates that, based on the 1954-1961 rates of increase in voluntary support, the colleges should be receiving $2 billion in contributions by 1969-70. Alumni, nonalumni individuals, general welfare foundations, and business corporations are likely to provide more than 85 per cent of this support. The Council describes this 2 billion dollars as a "fair share" of the institutions' expenditures, which are expected to reach the level of 9 billion to 11 billion dollars by 1969-1970.[13]

A new development in the fund raising of private colleges is the united college fund. The idea, first tried out in the 1920's, emerged anew in 1944 as the United Negro College Fund. The idea was given new dimension in the 1950's by Frank H. Sparks, at the time president of Wabash College. At some difficulty he persuaded other private colleges in Indiana and a few corporations of the worth of the idea of a united fund for private colleges. The idea caught on. Nearby Ohio was quick to follow suit. Although Indiana gets credit for the idea, Ohio was the first state to start a united fund appeal on an incorporated, organized basis. The Ohio Foundation, started in 1951, had, by 1961, 29 colleges participating in the campaign for corporate gifts and sharing the proceeds on a ratio based on enrollments. Corporations giving to colleges promote the idea because it eliminates the sticky problem of deciding what colleges to support and what ones to turn down in a particular region. Within a decade, Sparks' idea had grown to multi-million-dollar dimensions. By 1960 there were 40 such funds operating on a regional or state basis.

State-supported colleges are finding the going tougher all the time as their costs go up. They are faced with strong competition for the taxpayer's dollars. More and more state tax monies are going into pensions and benefits for the aged and handicapped, for improving institutional care and mental health programs, to public schools, highways, and hard-pressed cities and counties. Consequently, state universities are putting more emphasis on voluntary support and are intensively promoting alumni giving. Private support is increasing markedly for all state universities. From 1950-1959 to 1960-1961, for example, voluntary support for state universities increased by 31 per cent, with the total rising from 88 million to 115 million dollars. This makes the competition for the donor's dollar all the keener and results in intensified PR programs in both sectors of the higher education establishment.

The solution cannot be found in higher tuition fees. There is a genuine

---

[13] In report, *Guide Lines to Voluntary Support of American Higher Education* (New York: the Council, 1963), pp. 4 and 5.

danger of pricing the nation out of the talent market. The *New York Times* reported in 1963 that average tuition fees in private colleges had doubled in the 12 years between 1948 and 1960. That paper estimated that tuition charges would triple by the end of this decade. The solution seems to lie in more campaigns for voluntary donations and in increased federal support to both public and private colleges. But, as Dr. Alvin C. Eurich, of the Fund for the Advancement of Education, warns, the competition for the federal and local tax dollar is such that we cannot expect anything like a sufficient flow of tax money to diminish the pressure on institutions to build more financial support. Developing mass public support for mass giving on a regular basis seems to be one of the hopeful trends in this situation. It certainly spells more emphasis on public relations.

WHAT FRESHMEN?

In years past, much of the college PR effort was on recruiting students. Often these campaigns to get students used the techniques of advertising more than those of information and interpretation. The emphasis in the past has been too much on getting students and too little on the social responsibility involved. The intense promotional publicity to get new students is responsible, in part at least, for the questionable notion that to "get ahead in the world" one must go to college. In the years ahead the emphasis will be on recruiting the best-qualified students and in raising scholarship support for those who cannot afford today's high college costs.

In student recruitment we have a paradox. On one hand, colleges are worried about their overcrowded classrooms. On the other, they are trying to get still more students to enter. But there is an explanation. College officials know that something like 250,000 gifted high school graduates do not go on to college each year. Half are prevented from doing so by lack of money. Educators want to encourage and finance the brilliant and talented students because they know that this nation needs more *educated manpower* than is available to meet America's expanding needs. Solution of this "freshman" problem will take statesmanship, not salesmanship.

THE PUBLICS

The pitch and emphasis to the different publics of a collegiate institution will vary according to the size, base of support, and philosophy of the institution.

STUDENTS. Foremost of the public relations agents are the students, first as students, later as alumni. Student attitudes and conduct are powerful factors in determining public attitudes. Students come from the farms and the mining camps, from the metropolitan city and the village, from all parts of the nation. These students become "authoritative" interpreters of their college in their hometowns. If they have pride in and enthusiasm for their college, it will be reflected. If they have an unhappy educational experience, that, too, will be reflected—and for years to come.

Examples of student conduct winning goodwill and gifts for colleges are legion. The reverse side of the coin is that thoughtless pranks and misconduct have brought serious damage to more than one institution. Who can estimate the damage caused by blazing headlines such as: "Eight More Men Taken to Court as Police Rush U. Morals Probe," "Coeds Dormitory Raided by Masked College Youths," "Coed Says She Choked Newborn Babe in Room," "U. Frat Men Fined for Tree Damage," "College Man Dies in Fraternity Initiation," ad infinitum.

Imaginative public relations can convert a student prank into an asset. One Homecoming Eve, some thoughtless pranksters unbolted and carried away the University of Wisconsin's famed "sifting and winnowing plaque." This symbol of the university's policy of academic freedom had long stood as a shield against those who would censor free thought. When it appeared that the historic bronze plaque was lost forever, the University organized a "Freedom Plaque Fund" to raise funds to replace it and to establish a "Freedom Scholarship." The key idea was to extend pride of ownership in the symbol to as many people as possible. Start of the drive brought the plaque out of hiding. The drive was halted, but the University went ahead with an impressive rededication ceremony of what today is known as "the freedom plaque." One newsman wrote in his lead: "An idea was engraved on the heart of the University of Wisconsin Friday afternoon as firmly as a plaque was bolted to Bascom Hall."

A university must develop an enthusiastic, responsible body of students as goodwill ambassadors. With the fast turnover of the student body, this is a difficult task. The surest way to develop the student's appreciation of his responsibility is to bring him into active participation in the program. Personable, well-groomed, clean-cut college students are the most effective public symbol a college can have. Students can be brought into the program through the organization of campus host and guide groups, High School Day, Legislator Day, or Parents' Week-end; through tours by the college choir, glee clubs, or drama groups; and in many other ways. College administrators, faculty members, and student leaders must guide the student in this responsibility.

There is another important aspect. A student may be in school from one to four years, but he is an alumnus for his life. Too many institutions wait until a student is an alumnus before they start to woo him. One college practitioner points out: "Public relations between the university and alumni are usually the most emphasized. Those with the students are the most neglected." The student who has good teachers, who is given wise counsel and helpful individual attention, generally becomes a loyal alumnus. An educational program revealing the sources of educational support could do much in developing a sense of responsibility in future alumni.

One good way to do this is to start a drive for continuing gifts by the senior class each year. Another aspect of the student as a supporting public is through free-flowing channels between the administrator and the student. Too often, with bigness, these break down. Student-administrator relationships need improvement on many campuses. For the large university, a President's Council of student leaders, meeting informally in the president's home, is a recommended device. It is essential that president, dean, teacher, and secretary keep in mind the fact that students are an important and articulate group.

FACULTY AND STAFF. The college or university president and the janitor—each plays an important role. People think in terms of people, the personal symbol, the concrete. The personalities of people identified in the public mind with an institution will largely determine the kind of confidence and support the institutions have. The personal symbol is particularly important for a college, whose leaders and teachers are constantly in the public spotlight, free to speak out as they see fit.

College presidents and professors are a prolific source of news. Developing the staff of an institution into an effective team is the starting point for the program. The college or university president, by reason of his position and prestige, must be the leader. The president personifies the institution. A strong personality can bring prestige, stature, and public confidence. A president whose mental radar is sensitive to public relations can contribute much to developing this awareness.

The faculty member can contribute most by inspired teaching, by counseling his students, by research accomplishments, and by lending his talents to public service. Faculty members, especially those of the younger generation, are increasingly aware of their responsibilities. Members of the university's housekeeping staff, the secretaries, the telephone operators, the policemen, must be imbued with the spirit of friendly service. The important thing is that these staff members be kept adequately informed of the university's policies, programs, and problems. This requires a continuing internal information program. The college staff must be gently, but *persistently,* reminded of its public relations responsibilities.

Members of the governing board constitute an important internal public that functions as the official intermediary between key publics and the college. A strategic group, generally recruited from opinion leadership, they must be convinced of the need of giving consideration to public relations aspects of its policy making. Consistent but subtle pressure is required to prompt the board to give full and sympathetic consideration to public opinion. This key group must be kept adequately informed of the university's aims and problems so that they may interpret them correctly. Informing them is primarily a task of the president.

COMMUNITY. Next, in planning a program, come the important external publics to be reached and influenced. "Town-gown" relationships provide the environment. Colleges and universities are lagging well behind industry in recognizing the importance of good community relations. There is a real need to do more to win and keep the support of local citizens. This can be won by giving the citizens a voice and sympathetic hearing, through consultation, in college matters which directly affect the community. There are a number of natural irritations which may develop if town-gown relations are neglected —for example, the tax-exempt status of educational institutions may come to stand out as partiality. Municipalities are increasingly hard pressed to find adequate revenues to pay for their expanding services. Many institutions have wisely taken steps to dramatize their recognition of this problem. One state university, for example, arranged to buy a new fire truck for its community and to employ a third of the firemen.

Another problem is faced by metropolitan institutions that must expand in already built-up areas. This growth means just one thing to the taxpayer: removal of property from the tax rolls and, hence, more taxes. Such moves should not be suddenly thrust upon a surprised community. The moves, of course, are of great benefit to the community. The college must properly explain them to its neighbors.

Traffic congestion created by university facilities or activities has caused harsh irritations in some college towns. There are many other examples. On the other hand, there are many positive advantages which the college can and does offer the community. Townspeople need to be reminded of these, lest they take them for granted. If an institution cannot have the enthusiastic support of its friends at home, it is difficult to expect it away from home.

PARENTS. Parents of students are a ready-made nucleus of support. They have a vital stake in the institution. They can be welded into an effective group of allies. More collegiate institutions are in the process of developing stronger relationships with parents. Providing a good home away from home and giving sons and daughters kindly, personalized attention win parental support. But this potential goodwill needs to be activated and reinforced. Parents' Week-end, frequent letters from president to parent, and Dad's clubs bring parents closer to the school.

ALUMNI. Maintaining the interest of the alumni has long been given emphasis—with varying degrees of success. Too often the alumni interest centers almost exclusively on the fortunes of the football team. The problem seems to be to get the alumnus as interested in education as he is in football. Practically every college has a going alumni association. Often its sole concern is in keeping alive the flames of loyalty. Sometimes the alumni influence can be—and is—mobilized to override sound educational policy. Sometimes alumni associations tend to become vested interests and ends in themselves. The alumni association must be kept harnessed to its basic objective—support of Alma Mater through organized effort. Emerson Reck has pointed this out: [14]

---

14 W. Emerson Reck, *Public Relations: A Program for Colleges and Universities* (New York: Harper & Row, Publishers, 1946), p. 182.

The alumni form the most important off-campus public of most colleges and, universities, and there is no limit to the good they can do for their institutions provided (1) the experiences of their undergraduate years can be recalled with appreciation and pleasure; (2) they are kept fully informed regarding the objectives, policies, progress and problems of their *alma maters;* (3) they are given an opportunity to perform challenging tasks for their institutions.

The critical problems faced by higher education make it essential that alumni groups and universities forge a stronger bond between themselves. The bond needs to be intellectual as well as sentimental and social. Informed alumni can be a strong base of support. Uninformed alumni can represent a disturbing interference in the conduct of the college. Those irresistible drives to fire the coach have led many faculties and administrators to fear alumni influence. There is a real need to do a better job of keeping alumni informed of more than merely his classmates' doings and the football statistics. Alumni magazines reach six million persons annually. Many of these contain little intellectual meat with the traditional chroniclings.

The PR objective, vis-à-vis alumni, should be one of getting more than dollars. Colleges should strive to gain loyalty, interest, and counsel from their alumni. Win those, and the dollars will follow. Charles P. McCurdy, a former president of the American Alumni Council, has said: "I do not believe that we can continue to beseech our alumni or anybody else to contribute for *things.* We will have to begin asking them to contribute for *principles.*"

OTHER PUBLICS. Other publics which must represent focal points of planning and execution of the college PR program are many. These may include prospective students, parents of prospective students, present and prospective donors, opinion leaders, the various philanthropic foundations, sister educational institutions, legislators and state officials for the state-supported school, the armed forces, and various agencies of the federal government—particularly those with research programs.

Institutions of higher learning, public, and private—the capstone of the unique American educational system—face many difficult but not insoluble problems in the foreseeable future. These problems can be fundamental: such as definite decisions concerning the true function and purpose of the college and university. They can be specific: such as developing a sound relationship between the main function of education and the extracurricular activity, athletics. The evils of proselyting, commercialism, gambling, and overemphasis, which cloud intercollegiate athletics from time to time, represent a tough but typical problem for the practitioner.

For years ahead, institutions of higher learning must grapple with a host of thorny problems. Funds must be raised to pay professors and to build buildings. Emotional attacks on teachers and doctrines must be beaten back. There will be the squeeze of doing more and more research and public service—particularly, adult education. American education and science must match the accomplishments of our potential enemies. An increasing number of applicants will be denied admission to colleges, especially the private ones.

Their parents must be dealt with. This adds up to a need for all the confidence and support that can be mustered through effective public relations.

Additional Reading

William B. Benton, "The University of Chicago's Public Relations," *College and University Journal,* Vol. 1, Spring, 1962. A hitherto unpublished study made of Chicago's PR needs in 1936.

Harold E. Gibson, *Public Relations in Colleges for Women.* Jacksonville, Ill.: Mid-West Publishing Co., 1948.

Seymour Harris, "Higher Education; Resources and Finance," *College and University Journal,* Vol. 1, Summer, 1962.

Richard B. Hovey, "The Inarticulate Professor," *Saturday Review,* Vol. 42, April 18, 1959.

Douglas M. Knight, ed., *The Federal Government and Higher Education.* Englewood Cliffs, N.J.: Prentice-Hall, Inc., 1960.

Robert E. Nelson, "Alumni?", *College and University Journal,* Vol. 1, Fall, 1962.

Delbert C. Miller, "Town and Gown: The Power Structure of a University Town," *College and University Journal,* Vol. 2, Summer, 1963.

W. Emerson Reck, ed., *College Publicity Manual.* New York: Harper & Row, Publishers, 1948.

Clarence A. Schoenfeld, *The University and Its Publics.* New York: Harper & Row, Publishers, 1954.

CASE PROBLEM

A large, widely known university has a president and several faculty members who are outstanding authorities on international relations. A wealthy alumnus, anonymous except to the trustees, offers to give two million dollars to endow a school of international relations if the university will raise the additional two million required. The trustees approve the idea and direct that a fund-raising drive be started and that building plans be prepared.

Shortly after the fund-raising drive gets under way, the House of Representatives Un-American Activities Committee issues a report which labels four members of the faculty—including one in international relations—as communist sympathizers and possibly former members of the party. The report produces widespread repercussions and has an immediate adverse effect on the fund-raising effort.

As public relations adviser to the university president, what action would you recommend to clear up the situation?

Chapter Twenty-Five

THE

ARMED

FORCES

No organization so directly concerned with the public interest can hope to escape the effects of popular opinion, nor can personnel . . . do their best work without adequate knowledge of where they fit in.—General Omar Bradley.

For their common defense, the people of the United States support a large and expensive military establishment. The armed forces make a heavy drain on the nation's wealth,. manpower, and natural resources. Support of this costly military machine will require sacrifices on the part of the American people for the foreseeable future. People must be convinced of the need for paying taxes and having sons drafted. They must have confidence in the spenders and the commanders. *It is mandatory, therefore, that the armed forces create public understanding of their mission.*

No organization faces a stiffer, continuing public relations assignment. In gaining support, the armed forces must fight uphill against the basic dislike for military force inherent in our culture. The enormity of this task was clearly seen by the first Secretary of Defense, James Forrestal, who said: "I know of no task that is more complex, except possibly the task of government itself, than that of engendering in a democracy an appreciation of the role of the armed forces."

To cope with this problem, the military has developed a large public relations organization. Its scope is reflected in these figures. It is estimated that the armed forces use more than 3,000 practitioners, military and civilian. In 1961 the total information budget was $4,000,000 for personnel, supplies, travel, and publications. These are estimates. They do not include the time and expense which other officers, especially commanders, put into public relations. There are many shifting and "additional duty" assignments which make a head count difficult; additional clerical personnel are not usually included. The pressure to camouflage government practice operates here, too, to prevent preciseness.

These figures do show the degree to which military leaders have accepted the necessity of *winning public support* and *building an informed fighting force*. The following contrast is significant. During the Civil War, following the Battle of the Wilderness, General George Meade had a newspaper correspondent ridden out of camp astride a horse with a sign reading "Libeller of the Press" hung about the reporter's neck. Almost ninety years later, General Dwight D. Eisenhower wrote: "I believe that the proper attitude of the commander toward representatives of the press was to regard them as quasi staff officers; to recognize their mission in the war and to assist them in carrying it out."

Today's top military men provide a leadership fully responsive to public opinion. Consequently, they are keenly aware of the place and purpose of public relations. This trend represents a sharp break from the insulation which largely prevailed until World War II. The attitude at the top is gradually permeating the whole establishment. Between the top leadership and younger officers there remains some suspicion and apathy. But this encrustation is gradually crumbling under the impact of public opinion and emphasis from the top. Such an effect was accelerated in the regime of John F. Kennedy as Commander in Chief. The Cold War further accentuated the need for an adroit understanding of public opinion.

In the military the term *IO*, Information Officer, is used. Essentially the same meaning is conveyed to the military and the press, although the military uses *PIO*, Public Information Officer, to indicate those officers specifically dealing with the media. "Troop Information Officer" is used to indicate those charged with communicating to the internal audience of the services—officers, troops, and civilian employees. In large staffs, the IO is likely to have both a PIO and a TIO serving under him. The purpose and programs vary slightly among the services.[1] In response to congressional criticism, the term *public relations* was abandoned—in formal documents, if not in informal talk —several years ago. The military concept has progressed beyond publicity to include troop, community, and public relations in the full sense of those terms. In 1964 the Army changed the term for troop information to *command information*.

---

[1] Troop information and education were split by the Army in 1956. Education was assigned to the personnel function (G-1). Congressional relations and public relations were separated—organizationally—earlier in all the services. The Marine Corps public information organization does not include the internal relations function, which is viewed as a command function. The entire Navy Department thus conducts internal information partly in the Office of Information and partly in the Bureau of Naval Personnel. Additionally, all services use materials prepared by the Armed Forces Information and Education Directorate of the Department of Defense. Under Secretary McNamara, the Department of Defense exercises more control and coordination than under any previous secretaries over all service PR programs.

FROM THREE PIO'S TO
THREE THOUSAND

Growth of the function in the armed forces has a long, up-and-down history. In the Revolutionary War, little was done, once the war started, to mobilize public support for the fighting forces. Revolutionary political leaders put great stress on gaining support for independence but made no efforts on behalf of the Continental Army. Philip Davidson found that United States propaganda activity declined during the war.[2] Basically the Founding Fathers feared a strong standing army. The military was equally slow to recognize the importance of molding a favorable public opinion. In the Civil War, for example, reporters continually complained of their lack of standing and mistreatment by the military. " 'West Pointers' were especially unfriendly to the press." [3] One reporter wrote his editor: "Until it is clearly settled that an accredited journalist, in the legitimate exercise of his calling, has just as much right in the Army as the Commander himself, he will be considered by a large majority of Regular Army officers as an unauthorized hanger-on and treated accordingly." [4] Today's newsman is accepted by the armed forces.

The United States Marine Corps led the way in the early years. The initial impetus was to outbid other services for recruits. This branch is justly famed for its heroic exploits and its skilled practice of public relations. The Corps established the first military PR office when it set up the Chicago Publicity Bureau in 1907. This office provided releases, pictorial material, and other publicity matter to newspapers throughout the Midwest. Today this is commonplace; then it was unusual.

This success of the Chicago office led to the establishment of a Marine Corps Recruiting Publicity Bureau in New York City in 1911. Later moved to Philadelphia, this office, under various titles, has since furnished the nation's media with every conceivable kind of promotional material to attract recruits. In 1924 the publicity function was moved into the top administration of the Corps. That year Major General John A. Lejeune appointed an officer in charge of "all publicity in connection with recruiting." A year later the scope of this officer's duties was broadened and he was given the title "Marine Corps Publicity Officer."

The Corps pioneered in building today's concept of public relations. In 1920 a Marine Corps sergeant, Percy A. Webb, a pioneer, said: "We must not forget that it is the cumulative effect of what the Marines do in the battle zones coupled with what is said or printed about them, radio programs,

---

[2] For a discussion of the decline in propaganda, see his *Propaganda and the American Revolution*, pp. 345-48.

[3] Sylvanus Cadwallader, *Three Years With Grant* (New York: Alfred A. Knopf, Inc., 1955), p. 11.

[4] Louis M. Starr, *Bohemian Brigade* (New York: Alfred A. Knopf, Inc., 1954), p. 119.

motion pictures . . . and every report about them, good or bad, which help to formulate public opinion." In 1925 Major General Lejeune phrased today's concept when he said: "The future success of the Marine Corps depends on two factors: First, an efficient performance of all the duties to which its officers and men may be assigned; second, promptly bringing this efficiency to the attention of the proper officials of the government and the American people."

A Marine Corps officer was among the first to recognize the distinction between publicity and public relations. In 1927 Capt. Jonas H. Platt wrote: "At its worst publicity is the cunning art of putting one's best foot forward —and lying about the foot. At its best publicity is the science of so governing one's public relations that the average citizen will have no reason to think of one with anything but the deepest respect. Why not jettison the word publicity once and for all? Public relations is a better term. . . ." [5]

Historically, the Army initiated reports to Congress as early as 1777. It did not formally report directly to the people until the outbreak of the Spanish-American War. Then, an unnamed correspondent persuaded the War Department to publish information for the press daily by posting it on a bulletin board outside the office of the Secretary of War. This was the casual beginning of today's extensive information program.

In 1904, the Adjutant General of the Army made the first formal press release to newspaper correspondents. This practice constituted the Army's "public relations" program until the eve of World War I. In June, 1916, Secretary of War Newton D. Baker was busy getting ready for what looked like war. News interest in the War Department had perked up. To get inquiring reporters off his neck, Baker called in a promising young major, Douglas MacArthur, and appointed him Press Release Officer of the War Department. MacArthur had an instinctive feel for news. He knew the Army and War Department and, by consensus of Washington correspondents, he "made an excellent public relations officer." He later went on to France with the A.E.F. and demonstrated publicity showmanship in building the spirit and legend of the Rainbow Division. In his later career in World War II, and, particularly, in directing the occupation of Japan, he displayed a shrewd sense of public relations.

The demands of the press led to the creation of a press section in the A.E.F. Headquarters in France in 1917. Near the end of the war, in October, 1918, public relations was formally recognized as an Army staff function. It was given definite status on the General Staff level with the creation of the Public Relations Branch in G-2, Military Intelligence. With the peace of the 1920's, the Army's interest in public relations as such withered. The military crawled back into its shell.

Public interest and support of the armed forces languished. The armed

5 The foregoing information on the Marine Corps is taken from Robert Lindsay's *This High Name: Public Relations and U. S. Marine Corps* (Madison: University of Wisconsin Press). Recommended reading.

forces' interest in public support was rather indifferent until the mid-1930's. Then the gathering Nazi war clouds in Europe brought the nation's military weakness into public focus. In 1935 General MacArthur, then Army Chief of Staff, brought in Major Alexander Surles, on duty at the War College, as head of the Public Relations Branch. Surles' staff totaled three: another major, a captain, and himself. Major Surles and his two aides took on, with skill and enthusiasm, the "dual job of getting before the public the War Department's anxiety over the shape of things to come in Europe and of helping newspapermen to pry stories out of the War Department."

In January, 1941, General Surles was asked by the War Department to draft a plan for setting up a "man-size bureau of public relations." A month later, Major General Robert C. Richardson III, one of the Army's top commanders and organizers, was ordered to Washington to organize the War Department Bureau of Public Relations. Richardson served in this post until August, 1941, when, his mission accomplished with great efficiency, he was ordered to take command of an Army Corps. Surles replaced him and was Director of the War Department BPR through World War II. In the words of one Washington editor, Surles "came through with laurels and the affectionate respect of the newspapermen with whom he had to deal." The WDBPR directed the Army's far-flung public relations operations during the war.[6]

Concurrently, the Navy Department was moving to expand and strengthen its public relations organization. It moved slowly. The youngster of the armed forces, the Army Air Force, headed by General H. H. Arnold and less bound by tradition, moved rapidly to capitalize on the glamor and color of this new weapon of war. General Arnold had started blazing the trail for air force public relations as far back as 1925, when he was chief of the information division, office of the Chief of Air Service, in the War Department. His successful career reflected a shrewd grasp of public relations. The Army Air Force, as war broke, quickly recruited a large number of skilled public relations and advertising men. The Army Air Force public information shop was consolidated with the War Department Bureau of Public Relations in September, 1942. The Air Force did not operate independently until it became a separate force in 1947.

Even though the armed services went into World War II ill equipped for public relations, they acquitted themselves well. The work was largely a matter of publicity, censorship, and assistance to war correspondents. Naturally, mistakes were made. Senior commanders, with brilliant exceptions at the top, were not public relations-minded. They had matured in an era when the services were relatively unconcerned about public opinion. The result was that many commanders gave little support or personal attention to the efforts of their PIO staffs. In a few cases they opposed such efforts.

Another factor that initially bred some headaches was the fact that public

---

6 Information based on Colonel Sidney A. Knutson's thesis, "History of Public Relations Program of the U.S. Army" (University of Wisconsin, 1953).

information staffs were recruited overnight. Many were experienced newsmen or practitioners in civilian life. Others had had little training and held the fuzziest of PR concepts. Some of the amateur PIO's brought about bruised public relationships. Given the size of the task and the rapidity of recruitment, it was amazing, actually, that there were not more square pegs put into round PIO holes.

A third factor was that the PIO staffs were put under the secrecy-minded G-2 and A-2 intelligence staffs who often sought to suppress too much on the grounds of military security. Intelligence officers had a broad, rubbery definition of military security. Some PIO's confused information endangering military security with that endangering the reputation of fellow officers who made mistakes. Despite mistakes and handicaps, public relations personnel made significant contributions to soldier morale, home-front morale, and war production. They assisted news agencies in making World War II the best-reported in history.

The incompatibility of the public information and intelligence functions was ultimately recognized. Consequently, the functions were separated and public relations recognized as a staff function in its own right. *Air Training,* an Air Force publication, recorded the evolution of an information officer:

> Before World War II AF public relations was buried in the intelligence staff section. We say buried because one duty of an intelligence man is to keep his and everyone else's mouth shut, while good public relations prescribes that the public has a right to know everything that wouldn't help our enemies more than it helps us. Early in the war, with demand for armed forces news at its peak, the job was divorced from intelligence and called PRO. In 1947, the title was changed to public information officer (PIO) to more accurately reflect the job, which was not to shape public opinion as much as to present all releasable facts about the Air Force. Under both these titles the job was directed at the civilian public. . . . In 1954 a new name was chosen, Office of Information Services (OIS) which includes public information (press and community relations), internal information for troops, and two other related functions—the preparation of base histories, and the reception of visitors.

Military public relations has experienced a sounder, more orderly development since World War II. A basic lesson was driven home by the overnight dismantling of the military machine. In response to public opinion, the armed forces were quickly stripped down after the war's end. The public, understandably, assumed victory in war meant peace. Those charged with providing national security saw the necessity for rebuilding the machine.

As a result there began a drive for recruits and Congressional appropriations. The campaigns for appropriations and manpower brought renewed emphasis on public relations. This need continued and stimulated development of staffs and programs in all services. Interservice rivalry for talented recruits and Congressional support has been one of the sharpest spurs in advancing public relations in the armed forces. It is also the source of some glaring PR mistakes and bitter public fights. The Air Force, once it gained independent status, took the lead in publicizing and proselytizing but all services vie spiritedly for the public's support. The Secretary of Defense, operating through the Assistant Secretary for Public Affairs, tries to mute service disputes in the public arena but is not always successful. The organization extends from this Assistant Secretary to junior officers at Army posts, Air Force and Marine bases, and aboard Navy ships.

IT STARTS AT THE TOP

Direction and impetus for the military's large staff and extensive program is centered in the Department of Defense. The President, as Commander in Chief, inevitably plays an important role in setting the tone and themes of defense information. The Secretary of Defense "regards public information as a *prime reponsibility* of the Office of the Secretary of Defense and of each of the military departments." From 1949 until 1954, the program was directed from the Office of Public Information in the Defense Department. The O.P.I. was abolished July 30, 1954.

James Forrestal, first Secretary of Defense, set up the O.P.I. in March, 1949, to unify and coordinate the programs of all services. One of his aims was to eliminate the feuding which had been rampant in the scramble for funds and manpower. His successor, Louis A. Johnson, moved to implement the Forrestal order. Through his Assistant to the Secretary, he set up eight divisions in O.P.I. and stripped the service staffs in the Pentagon. The Army was left with about 16 PIO officers and civilians, and the other two services retained about 30 officials in the top echelon. It was a sharp cut for each service. Johnson envisioned O.P.I. as the public relations office for the whole military establishment in Washington. He ruled O.P.I. would be "the sole agency of the Establishment at the seat of government for dissemination of public information."

Thus far the new setup has not proved wholly effective. Centralization is passively resisted by information men in the services who want their point of view publicized and by reporters who prefer to go directly to expert sources of information. However logical centralized control of military information may appear to the President and his Secretary of Defense, the service secretaries will insist, properly, on their need for a public relations staff. Likewise, military reporters will insist, properly, on dealing with the service experts, not with spokesmen one or two steps removed. Nor is it wholly against the public interest to have service differences aired in public.

With the expansion of the armed forces for the Korean War, the PR setup in each service was steadily built up again. The O.P.I.—with all its elaborate organization—operated mainly as a referral agency for persons seeking information. Its primary tasks were to communicate top defense policies, to counsel the Secretary and his staff, and to mediate conflicts with the press over security regulations—a recurring headache. As of May, 1963, there were 507 persons assigned to public relations duty in the Pentagon. These included:

149 in the office of the Secretary of Defense; 119 in the Army; 116 in the Air Force; 99 in the Navy, and 24 in the Marine Corps.

Secretary of Defense Robert McNamara, operating through the Assistant Secretary for Public Affairs, has been more successful than his predecessors in tightening his control over the service PR staffs. In 1964, after a public airing of the rivalries of the Army and Air Force over military air support control, the Secretary cut the number of civilian and military personnel assigned to PR duties, moved the service book-magazine and organization liaison sections to DOD, and eliminated the separate military service desks in DOD.

The current functions of the Assistant Secretary of Defense (Public Affairs) are stated in the July 10, 1961, directive enumerating his responsibilities: [7]

> The assistant Secretary of Defense (Public Affairs) is the principal staff assistant to the Secretary of Defense for public information and community relations. He is responsible within the Department of Defense for an integrated . . . public affairs program which will:
>
> 1. Provide the American people with maximum information about the Department of Defense consistent with national security.
> 2. Initiate and support activities contributing to good relations between the Department of Defense and all segments of the public at home and abroad. These activities will be carried out in overseas areas collaboration with the Department of State and the United States Information Agency.
> 3. Plan for Department of Defense censorship activities during a declared National Emergency.

The conduct of military public relations in the Kennedy and Johnson administrations shared most of the same criticisms applied to governmental PR in other years. The furor over Arthur Sylvester's use of "news management" as a weapon in the Cold War has been discussed. The Berlin call-up of 1961 and the Cuba Crisis of 1962 created opportunities for a test of PR finesse in the military establishment.

This period of revamping of military strategy to meet changing defense needs, especially for the Air Force and Navy, brought a return to fierce budget battles for new weapons and men, which had been so much a part of the Eisenhower administration.[8] In their battles for what they consider their rightful share of the multi-billion-dollar defense budget, all four services utilize the help of military manufacturers and their "alumni associations." Woll notes: [9] "For example, Lockheed Aircraft, prime contractor for the Polaris submarine missile, has used its public relations and advertising departments to help publicize the importance of the Navy, while Douglas Aircraft has boosted the Army or the Air Force for which it is building missiles. Defense

---

[7] Department of Defense Directive No. 5122.5, July 10, 1961.

[8] For a partial glimpse, see William S. Fairfield, "PR for the Services in Uniform and in Mufti," *The Reporter,* Vol. 18, May 15, 1958.

[9] In his *American Bureaucracy* (New York: W. W. Norton & Company, Inc., 1963), pp. 134-35.

contractors are often willing to boost any service that uses their products. . . ."
In such a situation, the service public relations organizations get close scrutiny.

THE SERVICE SETUPS

Experience gained in World War II and in the Korean War, unification
of the services, and creation of a centralized coordinating agency in the Department of Defense have served to modify the organization of the function
in the services. These organizations remain rather fluid and are periodically
revamped. More changes are likely to occur from time to time. Even so, it
might be helpful to outline briefly the pattern of the service PR programs.

AIR FORCES. The United States Air Force program originates in the
Office of Information in the Office of the Secretary of the Air Force. This is
abbreviated: SAF-OI. It is headed by a director who is a major general. Four
primary divisions handle most of the work. These are entitled "Public Information," "Internal Information," "Community Relations," and "Plans and
Programs." Also reporting to the Director are the offices of Bands and Music,
Reserve Forces Liaison, and Security Preview; special assistants for information who are assigned directly to most offices of the Air Staff; and field extension offices in New York, Chicago, and Los Angeles. SAF-OI plans, policies,
and programs are implemented in the field by information staffs at major air
commands, numbered air forces, and bases.

The division organization of the top echelon is generally duplicated at all
command levels down to air bases. In addition, a historical division appears
below the SAF-OI levels. History on an Air Force-wide basis is handled by a
separate organization of the Air University at Maxwell AFB, Alabama. The
Air Force keeps the information function at a special staff level and avoids
having it regarded as an "additional duty," except in small, detached units.
Air Force policy concerning information has been expressed by Air Force
Chief of Staff General Curtis E. LeMay as follows:

> The American citizenry has the right to know all the information about the Air
> Force that is consistent with national security. The Air Force must help the
> American people, including Air Force members, to know the national evaluation
> of the nature of the aggressive threats to our country and the rest of the Free
> World.

Air Force commanders use the information program to keep their personnel informed and motivated for maximum production and service, and to
fulfill the obligation to keep the public informed of Air Force activities.
Strong emphasis is placed upon the internal information program as a
management tool. This is done to instill in each member the sense of personal dedication to country and duty necessary for him to be efficient in his
job at all times.

ARMY. The Army centers its program of public and troop information in the Office of the Chief of Information. The mission of this office is to discharge "Army staff responsibility for all matters pertaining to public and troop information, and for Department of the Army Information plans and programs in support of Army basic plans and programs." In plainer language, this means that the Chief of Information advises the entire Army leadership in the Pentagon, military and civilian, on the conduct of public and troop information activities. In this role, the Army operates under policy guidance from the Secretary of Defense.

ARMY'S ORGANIZATION OF FUNCTION

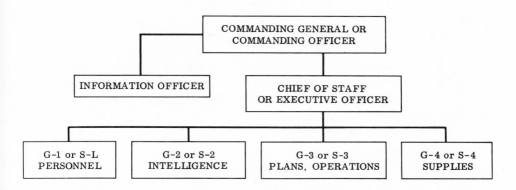

The over-all objective of Army information is "to insure understanding of the importance of the Army's role in a sound national military program, and to win support for the Army as part of the Armed Forces of the United States." The Army office includes division of public information, command information, civil liaison, and policy, plans, and programs.

The Army organization is similar in its principal field commands—the Continental Army, Army Materiel, and Army Combat Developments Commands. Under the Information Officer at CONARC are branches for plans and programs, public affairs, and internal information. The public affairs branch breaks down into sections for community relations, special projects, press, and audio-visual. Smaller offices organized along the same lines are located in the headquarters of the six continental armies. Much smaller information staffs are used at posts, camps, and stations, with divisions in the field.

Army regulations provide that information officers will be appointed to the staff of each battalion and of all commanders down to and including the battalion or unit of an equivalent size. Those specifically provided for in tables of organization have the status of special staff officers when information is their primary duty. The Army states that *"direct access* to the commander at all times is essential to the information officer for him to perform properly his duties." Within the military organization, this rapid entry matches problems with decision authority.

Besides the long-range Army objectives come specific, short-range ones, illustrated by the subjects for emphasis set in 1963: "United States Army—Essential for Freedom"; "Ready for Any Mission—in War or Peace"; "For Rapid Response—One Army"; "The Soldier—Key to Landpower"; "Modern Materiel for a Modern Army"; and "A Progressive Army." All Army information actions are related to these themes.

NAVY. At the apex of the Navy organization is the Office of Information in the Department of the Navy. The Navy Chief of Information reports directly to the Secretary of the Navy, and has additional duty as Chief Public Relations Advisor to the Chief of Naval Operations. The Navy's public information program is designed to keep the public—domestic and foreign—informed of the activities of the Navy, the importance of seapower, the role of the Navy as an instrument of national security, and the Navy's contribution to the defense of the Free World; to stimulate public information in naval activities through liaison with civilian organizations; to assure that the public is informed of the accomplishments of naval personnel and commands; and to contribute to the foreign relations of the United States by gaining understanding and respect of the people of foreign countries for our government, our objectives, and the people of the United States.

NAVY'S INFORMATION ORGANIZATION

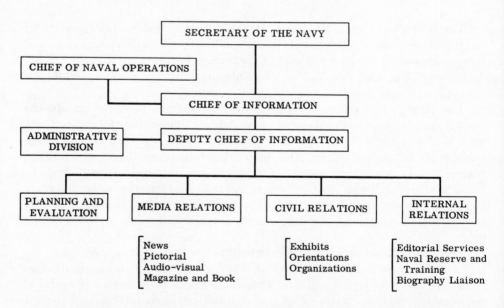

In Washington, each Navy bureau or office (the Bureau of Naval Weapons, for example) has a PI officer or a civilian information specialist. The size of the staff varies according to need and includes civilians, naval officers, and enlisted men. Ashore, the Commandant of each naval district or river command has a public information office, and the Commandant is reponsible for all Navy public information within his area of responsibility.

All commanders and commanding officers are required to designate an officer to handle public information as a collateral assignment if the command does not have a full-time public information officer. Afloat, fleet commanders have public information officers assigned to their staffs, while aboard ship a qualified officer handles information as a collateral duty.

All services operate centralized news centers. The Navy established a Naval Fleet Home Town News Center in 1945 at Great Lakes, Ill. The Army set up a similar center at Kansas City in 1951, and the Air Force established one at Oklahoma City in 1961. These centers take the news in the rough from ships at sea and units overseas. They edit or rewrite news releases, prepare pictures and mats, duplicate recorded radio and TV tapes, and so forth, and distribute these to the hometown media of soldiers, airmen, sailors, and Marines. One writer in a critical essay estimated the output of two of the news centers at 15,000 releases a day.[10]

In 1946 the Army set up an information school at Carlisle Barracks, Pennsylvania, with courses for officers and enlisted personnel. With unification it became the Armed Forces Information School. It was moved to Fort Slocum, New York, in 1951 and until 1954 served all the Armed Forces. In 1954 it became the Army Information School again and subsequently trained few men of the other services. The Navy has had a separate school at Great Lakes. But both the Navy and the Air Force have sent some students to the Army school. In 1964 the Secretary of Defense directed that all service training in public relations again be conducted within a single military school but excepted graduate-level schooling from the requirement. Accordingly, the Army has been designated the executive agent for the Department of Defense Information School.

All services have sent officers to universities for graduate education in journalism and public relations to prepare these men for military public relations assignments. The Army led the way, and since it started its graduate program for career officers in 1946, more than 100 officers have been professionally trained for public relations. Outstanding among these officers are Maj. Gen. Chester V. Clifton, Jr., long-time Army deputy chief of public information and later military aide to Presidents Kennedy and Johnson, and Maj. Gen. George V. Underwood, Jr., who served both as deputy chief and as chief of Army information. Underwood was the first specially trained officer to reach the top slot in his service. This recognition by the armed forces of the importance of professional public relations training has been a boon to PR practice generally.

---

10 William Stucky, "How to Collect Military Information," *Harper's Magazine,* Vol. 210, February, 1955, pp. 55-61. Critical of PI output.

PUBLICS OF THE
ARMED FORCES

INTERNAL. The armed forces fully realize that the officers and enlisted men and women are their most important goodwill ambassadors. The best—or worst—representative of the Army, Air Force, Navy, or Marines is the soldier, airman, or sailor. This is reflected in assignment of troop information to the information staffs. Secretary of War Patterson once said: "What he knows, what he thinks and what he feels about the Army will be reflected in the attitude of the public. The soldier comes from the people and he goes back to the people, not only by his eventual return to civilian life but by his visits, his letters, his very presence on the street. You cannot have an informed public until you have an informed Army."

Typical of the advice related to the Army are excerpts from *Officers' Call* entitled "Your Soldiers":

> In many respects the commander himself is the best projector of the Army image and motives, both to his soldiers and to the public which supports them. Direct command participation is particularly important at the platoon and company level. There, on a day-to-day basis, the meaning, purpose, and requirements of the Army are being interpreted and displayed for soldiers and their friends at home. At the higher echelons information is a staff aid to the commander for bringing together and projecting all sides of complex Army operations. . . .
>
> Every soldier must be imbued with the truth that he personally is the basic Army image, the basic Army weapon, and the basic Army unit. To the extent that the individual functions as a good soldier—to that extent will the Army image be good.
>
> In both troop and public information the Army theme is always, within the dictates of intelligence security, to present itself factually, frankly, and in good time.

Thus, military leaders recognize that it takes more than information programs to make a good soldier. It takes *action*. It takes good leadership and good treatment. American soldiers and sailors are the best fed, best clothed, and best cared-for military men in the world. The Army has made great strides since World War II to improve the status of the soldier and to clothe him with dignity. As Omar Bradley once said: "We cannot induce men to become soldiers if in the process they are divested of their dignity and human rights."

Military leaders recognize, further, that the soldier is the most important link between the public and the military. Crude, carousing soldiers, sailors, airmen, and Marines playing tough in nightclubs at home or abroad can do much to offset the inspiring leadership of a Taylor or a LeMay. In 1963 American troops were in effect "on trial" in some 90 foreign lands. Commanders are bearing down hard to make their men behave while off duty. Before troops leave the United States, they are briefed on their new stations, customs of the country, and reminders of their role as representatives of America. Training in how to get along with foreign people continues overseas.

RESERVISTS. Reserve personnel and the National Guard units offer an excellent bridge between the armed forces and the public. Reserves are primarily civilians but still possess a strong, continuing interest in the armed forces. This reserve membership reaches down into every city and hamlet of the nation. These reservists offer a ready-made transmission belt to carry information to the public and back again. In the immediate postwar years of 1945-1950, the armed forces failed to use this PR opportunity. During this period, reservists were ill-informed, confused, and largely ignored in the postwar military establishment. Reservist relations were also irritated by the contradictory and confusing recall policies followed after the outbreak of the Korean War. The 1961 callup in the Berlin Crisis also produced some confusion, irritation, and controversy.

One officer who studied this problem from the PR standpoint concluded: "Successful development of mutual trust and confidence between the United States Army and the Organized Reserve Corps can be expected to accomplish even more than improving the military strength of the United States. Such development of trust and confidence can be expected to affect the Army's relations with the citizens of the United States as well." The same, of course, holds true for the Navy, Air Force, and Marines.

All the military departments direct special attention to their reserve personnel. Since 1959, the Army has made a special effort to recognize the importance of the reservists, both Army Reserve and Army National Guard, to the effectiveness of its forces. The contribution of all components of the Army family, part-time, full-time, military, and civilian, has been highlighted as essential. The Army has placed this "One Army" concept as one of its major annual information themes since 1959. It has yet to put the idea across effectively. The Berlin call-up of 1961 re-emphasized the need for such special information effort for reserve personnel, and the Army has fully recognized it with an expanded program designed for this audience alone.[11]

One important source of information for those with special interest in the military is the military service association—the "alumni" organizations. The Navy League, Air Force Association, Association of the United States Army, Marine Corps Reserve Officers Association, American Legion, Veterans of Foreign Wars, and Military Orders of World Wars are the largest organizations with close military ties. Their annual conventions become top news stories and are often the forum from which important defense stories emanate. Each of these groups maintains local chapters and conducts public relations activities of varied sorts. These groups are often called upon by the military when support in Congress is needed.[12]

---

11 For a case study, see Lt. Col. Joseph F. H. Cutrona, "Information Program for Released Reservists Produces Good Will," *Public Relations Journal*, Vol. 19, July, 1963.

12 For an account of one civilian supporting arm, see Armin Rappaport, *The Navy League of the U.S.* (Detroit: Wayne State University Press, 1962).

CONGRESS. The Congress of the United States, which grants funds for the armed forces and determines their respective roles, is the smallest but most vital public of all. Public support, or its lack, eventually comes to focus in Congress. Actual relationships with the Congress are the responsibility of small, compact legislative liaison units in the top echelons. Their pitch and their problems are ultimately reflected in the information units. Every PIO must keep this key group constantly in mind. Public relations and legislative liaison are parts of the same whole. The effort to win congressional support is intense and unremitting. *Each public relations program and each policy guiding that program must be weighed in terms of the ultimate reaction in Congress and in the Executive Branch of government, seats of civilian control.*

EMPLOYEES. From World War II on, the armed forces have employed thousands of civilians, from topflight specialists to maintenance workers. In the process the military has learned the problems and procedures that go with good employee relations. Military leaders have learned the difference in dealing with a civilian free to choose his employment and with a soldier drafted to serve wherever he is assigned. Civilian employees form another important link with the general public, particularly at the post and base level. They must be included in the program's publics.

INDUSTRY. America's industrial machine provides the sinews for the national security. The relations of the armed forces and American industry are close and complex. As the military machine becomes increasingly a mechanized machine, these relations grow in importance and in complexity. The armed forces recognize this and have special industrial relations sections in all top headquarters. The officials of the military and of industry have many problems and projects in common. They find themselves, with increasing frequency, working together in a common interest. Just as the armed forces form an important public for industry, so does industry constitute an important public of the armed forces. The close, complex relationships of the two give rise to many public relations problems—and to many public relations opportunities.

To bridge the gap between defense policy makers and industrial leaders the Defense Department initiated some years ago the Joint Civilian Orientation Conference. The JCOC plan originated with Secretary Forrestal and was followed through by his successors. Periodically, some 70 to 80 civilian leaders have been invited to participate in an orientation program as guests of the Secretary. The purpose of the week-long program has been to acquaint opinion leaders with the circumstances and problems of the department and the place of national defense in world affairs. These leaders get close-up looks at installations and the latest weapons. The exchange of information and ideas is encouraged all the way through. The JCOC program was ultimately broadened to include leaders from all walks of life.

COMMUNITY RELATIONS. This phase of military PR is getting increased emphasis. There has been a complete about-face from the days when the Army post was an isolated island in an unconcerned community. The key to this policy of being *a part of* instead of *apart from* the community was laid down by the Doolittle Board shortly after World War II. It recommended: "Close contact and association with civilians should be encouraged and maintained since a citizens' army is a result of combined interest, effort, and contribution of both military and public. A mutual exchange of information will enhance the military organization. . . . A maximum of military personnel living in civilian communities rather than on Army posts will accomplish this." Military forces, more and more, are "living off the post."

All information offices now include a community relations section. The Army program is typical. It is outlined in Army Regulation 360-55, issued on January 23, 1957, the first such regulation. A checklist for a military community relations program is found in Chapter 15. In advising top Army leaders in 1963, the Army Chief of Staff, Gen. Earle G. Wheeler, said:

> The community relations program is intended to promote abiding cordial relationships between the Army and the citizens of cities, towns, and villages adjacent to military installations. Army men and women in uniform and our Army civilian employees who take an enthusiastic and active part in community affairs enhance the prestige, influence, and public understanding of the Army as a whole. Command interest, attention, and supervision are essential to a successful community relations program.

The Air Force and Navy put similar stress on community relations. Navy shore-based commands conduct intensive community relations programs, and many of the Navy's ship visits to domestic and foreign ports are used to generate public understanding of the mission of the Navy. Military bands and exhibits are a familiar sight, and the Army's "Golden Knights" parachute team, the Navy's "Blue Angels," and the Air Force's "Thunderbirds" flying teams have thrilled spectators throughout the country.

But military community relations problems involve far more than being a good citizen in local communities. There are some real sticklers. Some were posed by the difficult problem of maintaining adequate world-wide facilities for all military forces. When, early in the Johnson Administration, Secretary McNamara announced a list of installations to be closed within the states, the announcement generated both favorable and unfavorable comment. The move was praised as a long needed economy in all places unaffected by the closures. Some congressmen want economy in someone else's district. In some communities, such closings become a direct political issue; for example, Raritan Arsenal in New Jersey was an object of contention in the 1962 gubernatorial campaign. Although some of the large military reservations are on lands of small commercial value, the large number of small installations that all military services have maintained near or in major metropolitan areas have been the focus of criticism.

The Presidio of San Francisco would make a fine residential project adjacent to Golden Gate Bridge; Fort Sam Houston is now surrounded by the burgeoning suburbs of San Antonio. Some industrial-type facilities remain which might be needed for future emergencies—yet they represent sites for industrial complexes that are unavailable elsewhere.[13] Within the national capital alone, the Naval Gun Factory, Bolling Air Force Base, and the Anacostia Naval Air Station remain as monuments to the history of the earlier military era—at greater cost than some think is warranted. The real estate holdings of the American military forces—valued at $35.4 billion, located at 7,000 installations on 30.6 million acres—make DOD a landlord having all the difficulties attached to that role.

With the Kennedy administration instructions to the Secretary of Defense to take actions to secure equal opportunity for all their personnel, the military services moved into an area of special sensitivity. This action, directed at the Negro segregation problem, caused political controversy when the President's committee, headed by Gerhard A. Gesell, in the summer of 1963 pointed the finger at off-post discrimination against military personnel as a major inequity. Discrimination within the services had been largely eliminated shortly after World War II. The national conscience was impaled on the twin prongs of desire to insure fair treatment for all service personnel and the traditional fear of any incursion of military authority into the civil domain.

The services faced the PR quandary of "damned if they do and damned if they don't." They did—and continue to—receive embittered salvos with each step taken, both from segregationists and from those concerned about a possible loss of military subordination to civil authority. Secretary McNamara has borne the brunt of the attack within the military establishment, but he struck a promising public relations theme when he commented that there was no intent to reform society, that what he was trying to do was to look after military morale and efficiency.

This will be an area for PR people to continue to watch with both professional and civic interest.

The Air Force has a unique and especially tough problem in those cities near which it bases jet planes. Aircraft noise has been "the basis of mounting opposition to aviation activities in general and to jet operation in particular." [14] The Air Force first encountered this problem when it hurriedly moved jet fighter squadrons into Truax Field, Madison, Wisconsin, with the outbreak of the Korean War. The emergency compelled the Air Force to reclaim this base, which had been converted into a municipal airport after World War II. The abrupt reactivation of the base and the jet noise combined to build fires of community resentment. Strong political pressure built up against the Air Force. A patient, painstaking program of *fact-finding, planning,* and *community relations* ultimately turned the tide. An *informed public understood.*

PRESS. Relationships with the mass media constitute an important and sometimes difficult phase of military public relations. Clashes come on press

---

[13] A discussion of one base sought by commercial developers is reported in "The Second Battle of San Jacinto," by Clifton Brock, *The Reporter,* May 23, 1962.

[14] For problems in community relations brought by the jet age, see *Air Force,* Vol. 40, April, 1957, pp. 57-82; also see "Flow of Information," same issue, pp. 108-34.

insistence on the public's right to know and the military's obligation to prevent release of secret information which would be of value to the nation's enemies. Much improvement has been made in this relationship, but this basic conflict is not likely ever to be fully resolved. The armed forces, *policy-wise,* now fully accept the right of the public to all information not censored for reasons of military security. The Office of the Secretary of Defense maintains a Security Review Office to determine whether information is classified or not. This puts in its hands a weapon that unwise or autocratic officers can abuse. Some do abuse it.

An example of an outdated military gag attitude is offered in the case of Major General Samuel Anderson's actions while in command of the Carswell Air Force Base, home of the Eighth Air Force. Because General Anderson objected to the *Fort Worth Press'* treatment of a B-36 crash near Albuquerque, New Mexico, he ordered the *Press* reporters barred from the base and issued orders that the *Press* was to get no information from the base. No question of military security or the publication of classified news was involved. The General's anger and action were based on what he termed "sensationalism." It took a flying trip from Washington by the Air Force PR director to straighten out the General and get the ban lifted. General Anderson had given the military another black eye with press and public alike.[15]

Here are some others. A few years ago an Assistant Secretary of Defense for Public Relations refused to release to the W.C.T.U. a list of military bases at which liquor was sold to servicemen. The Eleventh Naval District headquartered in San Diego once invoked, without warning or explanation, wartime censorship on news of Navy plane crashes and issued a "gag" to the Coast Guard in that district. This reversal of the Coast Guard's peacetime practice of promptly making public the nature of its search and rescue missions was cancelled by the Naval District commandant after strong protest from the press. There was still another black eye for the military. In Oakland, California, an Army officer ordered M.P.'s to keep reporters and photographers away from the wedding of an Army captain and a Japanese girl. Reporters were threatened with guns, and one photographer was thrown into the guard house for an hour for trying to take a picture at the church.

Clashes between news photographers and military authorities at scenes of disaster on and off military reservations are all too frequent. Sometimes this represents an effort by military police to prevent the photographing of secret equipment; sometimes the abrasive actions are less justified. In October, 1063, the Department of Defense, prodded by Congressman Moss' committee, made a new effort to modify military policies on this score. The new directive bars military police from using force against reporters or photographers at the scene of a plane crash or other accidents. The rule enforces a principle basic to a democratic society—that the military has no right to exercise authority

---

15 For this story, see Delbert Willis, "The Press vs. the General," *Nieman Reports,* Vol. 5, July, 1951.

over civilians in civilian areas. All three services were advised to call on civilian law enforcement officers if and when necessary.[16]

Considerable progress has been made in military PR in recent years as the number of trained IO's increase. Industries at work on weapons and materiel have been given more leeway. The Marine Corps fully and candidly reported the details of "the death march" at Parris Island. If sympathetically administered, there can be no quarrel with the military policy that *"a minimum of information will be withheld from the public consistent with security."* But relations with the press often involve more subtle problems than direct clashes of opposing interests. A military officer making a scholarly study of the Pentagon press corps' performance found that the accuracy and completeness of reporting on defense matters are a function of the reporter's energy and trustworthiness, news deadlines, and the accessibility and responsiveness of official sources. If primary official sources are uncommunicative, the reporter relies on lesser sources, usually at a loss to the public, the Defense Department, and the press.[17]

Censorship is abhorrent to the American press and public alike. But both the press and the public recognize its necessity in time of war. No American ever wants, knowingly, to be the cause of death and destruction among his defenders. Even so, wartime censorship is a difficult task at best. Press censorship preserves the security of American and allied combat forces by *temporarily* delaying or withholding from public dissemination any information that might aid or comfort the enemy until such time as this information will be of no value to any enemy.

Military men need to accept fully the democratic principle of the public's right to know compatible with genuine security requirements. One editor, J. Russell Wiggins, says: "Wise censorship, by democratic definition, ought to be a censorship that yields the most security with the least interference with the news. The military cannot have all the security it wishes without denying to the people the information they must have to maintain their understanding of and support for an effective defense. The people cannot have all the information they would like to have without endangering security." [18]

Additional Reading

William Brinkley, *Don't Go Near the Water*. New York: Random House, 1956. (A novel satirizing Navy PIO's in World War II.)

Robert Lindsay, "Perspectives on Public Relations," *Marine Corps Gazette,* Vol. 40, January, 1956.

Gene M. Lyons, "PR and the Pentagon," *The New Leader,* Vol. 43, October 17, 1960.

---

16 Department of Defense Directive No. 5410.14, October, 1963.

17 Information based on Colonel George V. Underwood's thesis, "The Washington Military Correspondents" (University of Wisconsin Library, 1960).

18 See "Wise Censorship Must Be a Compromise," *Quill,* Vol. 38, October, 1950.

A Dartmouth professor discusses the dilemma raised in the minds of many by Pentagon PR.

Capt. R. B. Morrisey, "Pub Info—A Command Function," *Marine Corps Gazette,* Vol. 41, February, 1957.

Barney Oldfield, *Never a Shot in Anger.* New York: Duell, Sloan, and Pearce, 1956. (Reminiscences of an Air Force PIO who retired in 1963.)

Jack Raymond, *Power at the Pentagon.* New York: Harper & Row, 1964. Thoughtful overview by *New York Times* military reporter.

John M. Swomley, Jr., *Press Agents of the Pentagon.* Washington: National Council Against Conscription, July, 1953.

U. S. House of Representatives, Subcommittee on Government Operations, Eighty-Eighth Congress, *Government Information Plans and Policies.* Part I—*News Media Panel Discussion;* Part II—*Office of Emergency Planning;* Part III—*Information Procedures in the Department of Defense;* Part IV—*Vietnam News Coverage* (Washington, D.C.: The Committee, U.S. Government Printing Office, 1963).

CASE PROBLEM

You are Public Information Officer on the special staff of the Commanding General of Fort Leonard Wood, Missouri, a 71,000-acre Army camp. It was designated as a permanent post 18 months ago. Several millions of dollars have been spent in this period building new officers' quarters, renovating old barracks and mess halls, and so forth. On the strength of Wood's designation as a permanent post, businessmen in the nearby communities of Rolla, Lebanon, and St. Robert have also spent a considerable sum in building new buildings, expanding stocks, and the like. At capacity, Fort Leonard Wood has a payroll of 40 million dollars a year.

Owing to congressional cutbacks of Army appropriations and changes in the Army's mission, the Secretary of Army and Army Chief of Staff reluctantly agree to shut down the post at the end of this year. This decision is communicated to your Commanding General with the direction to announce and explain the decision to post employees and the people of the neighboring communities. He directs you to draft an Information Plan to accomplish this order. Submit a plan for his approval.

Chapter Twenty-Six

PUBLIC

RELATIONS

AROUND

THE

WORLD

A NEW FRONTIER
BECKONS

Public relations around a fast-shrinking world—both within and across national boundaries—is the bright new frontier beckoning young people with the aptitudes, ability, and sense of adventure. International practice will accelerate to meet the needs born of a hotly competitive world market and of a spirited economic and political struggle between East and West in a world linked by rapid international telecommunication and transportation. In a day of satellite-relayed world-wide radio and television, supersonic jetliners that make intercontinental trips a matter of a few hours and world travel commonplace, international public relations is bound to grow at a fast pace.

These advances in telecommunications and transportation have brought people into the closest contact in the history of civilization. Never before have ideas and information had the rapid and far-reaching impact they have today. The same ecological factors which compelled the development of public relations in the United States are operating to bring it about on a global scale—only faster. Public relations to a great extent was originated and developed first in the United States. Today it is being adapted to the needs of business firms, nonprofit institutions, and nations of the world at a breathtaking rate. Our business firms and the U.S.I.A. are leading the way in spreading PR practice to what once were far corners of the world.

American firms are extending their operations around the world in increasing magnitude and rapidity.

At the start of this decade, 2,500 American companies had a more than 30-billion-dollar investment in foreign countries. In ever-increasing numbers, United States companies are operating abroad through subsidiaries, branches, and distributors. For them, as Arthur Reef points out, "Certain conditions and circumstances make a good public relations program even more essential for American firms operating overseas than for business inside the U.S." [1] Abroad they have to buck the onus of absentee ownership, avert the threat of exappropriation, and combat the hatreds bred by Soviet and Red Chinese propaganda. All this is dramatically illustrated in the operations and PR program of International Telephone and Telegraph Corp. (ITT), which has extensive operations in the United States and Canada and sells to customers in 115 nations of the world. [2]

These world-wide programs require the employment of nationals in the countries where affiliates and subsidiaries are located, and this, in turn, speeds extension of the practice. United States firms need and, in most cases, retain counsel in countries abroad. Each nation has its own culture, its particular pride and prejudices, its special way of doing things. To communicate effectively with audiences abroad, the communicator must know the culture, the language, and the value systems of the people who comprise the audiences.

Growth of international trade has induced a number of United States counseling agencies to extend their operations around the globe. This is done by either establishing a branch office abroad or establishing an affiliation with a local firm in one or more nations. Hill & Knowlton has extended its operations around the world for three kinds of clients—United States firms doing business overseas, foreign companies competing in the United States market, and foreign governments. The Government of Japan is an active client in the latter category. Bert Goss, H. & K.'s president, says, "The practice of modern PR extends anywhere in the world where there are publics to inform—and clients who want to attract their attention." [3] The other giant, Carl Byoir & Associates, does not use affiliate firms, although it once did. It has its own offices abroad because, as Board Chairman Gerry Swinehart expresses it, "Our kind of work can only be done by Byoir men. So in Paris— and Europe is one of the really big PR growth areas—we decided to follow our star, to be advocates." [4] Infoplan, first wholly owned world-wide public relations organization, was established in 1962 by Interpublic, Inc. It has offices in the United States, Canada, United Kingdom, West Germany, France, Italy, Brazil, Mexico, and Japan. [5] There are many patterns in this evolving world-

---

[1] In an article, "International Public Relations," *Exporters' Digest,* Vol. 30, No. 12. Also see Reef's "International Public Relations—a Challenge," *Public Relations Practice,* September, 1961.

[2] Robert B. McIntyre, "Global ITT Operation Calls for Global PR," *Editor & Publisher,* Vol. 96, August 31, 1963, pp. 16, 36, and 38.

[3] Robert B. McIntyre, "European Press Many Things to H & K Executives," *Editor & Publisher,* Vol. 96, March 23, 1963, p. 20.

[4] Prentice-Hall, Inc., *Executive Report,* "Inside Public Relations," *op. cit.,* p. 9.

[5] Anonymous, "Interpublic Sets Up World-Wide PR Firm," *Editor & Publisher,* Vol. 95, December 8, 1962, p. 36.

wide operation of PR agencies. European agencies also are building networks of affiliation, mainly within the frontiers of the Common Market. Advertising agencies follow the same patterns.

The main thrust for the quickening pace of public relations in the Western World has been provided by the European Common Market, today a booming market of affluent consumers. In 1957 six countries—France, Germany, Italy, the Netherlands, Belgium, and Luxemburg—formed the European Economic Community, generally called the Common Market, to provide for the free circulation of goods, capital, and manpower by progressive stages. The six established a common tariff for the outside world. The Common Market is one of the great events of our century, a landmark in the widening field of international public relations. Given these accelerating technological advances in telecommunication and transportation, coupled with the stepped-up economic and political struggles, it is little wonder that *Public Relations Journal* well describes public relations around the world as being in a state of "thriving infancy."

THE COMMON MARKET

The creation and success of the European Common Market both demonstrate the value of public relations and provide a strong stimulus for extension of the practice in member nations and beyond. By precept and by example Common Market agencies place great stress on PR. The public information program of the trail-blazing Coal and Steel Community did much to win European support for the Common Market, which came into being in 1958. Nearly 200 persons are employed in the information departments of the several agencies federated under the umbrella term *Common Market*. Embraced in this short-hand term are the European Coal and Steel Community, founded in 1952, the European Atomic Energy Community (Euratom), and the European Economic Community (Common Market). Each of the three communities, as well as the European Parliament, has its own small group of PR specialists. However, the three community executives have pooled their technical information services into one common service, which is divided into different divisions, each dealing wth a medium or a public.

Most of these 200 information officers are stationed in Brussels and Luxemburg, where the Communities have their provisional seat, and occasionally in Strasbourg, where the European Parliament meets in plenary session. In the four capitals of the other member nations—Bonn, The Hague, Paris, and Rome—the Executives have small information offices. Information offices are also maintained in London, Washington, and Geneva. As one information officer observes: "The Community has not generally planned public relations policy and the actual attitude towards information is either dictated by events or arrived at pragmatically on a non-policy level." [6]

Nonetheless, public relations thinking and practice play key roles in all Common Market agencies. As would be expected, "the outward-looking information services are more systematical" than is the public opinion research phase of the work. The unplanned evolution of the total information program reflects the loose federation of these several agencies and the pragmatic democratic approach. These practitioners face difficult tasks in communicating highly technical economic and scientific information to a world of many cultures and many languages. In persuading the people of Europe to adopt and support the Common Market, and in making it a successful enterprise, its public relations practitioners have paved the way for specialists of the future.

GREAT BRITAIN

Public relations practice in Canada and Great Britain is quite comparable to that of the United States in terms of skill, management acceptance, and stage of maturity. PR developments in these sister Anglo-Saxon nations have proceeded in parallel courses. The free flow of commerce, executive personnel, and students between the United States and Canada have served to develop this specialty along identical lines in these two nations. In comparing British PR with that of the United States, London's *Financial Times* asserts that "by contrast, the position of public relations is a good deal less secure, and the industry is certainly one of those about which very little is known or understood." In the British Government the function is fully accepted and practiced with mature sophistication. "Public Relations Officer" (PRO) is the most widely accepted title for public relations practitioners, but a number of other titles are also used.

The advance of mature public relations is being spearheaded by the British Institute of Public Relations, organized in 1948—the same year that PRSA was founded. This Institute sets high standards for its membership and requires applicants to pass two examinations before gaining full membership. A candidate for the Intermediate Examination must be at least 20 years of age and have an adequate education. For the Final Examination, a candidate must be at least 21 years of age, have passed both papers of the Intermediate Examination, and have spent at least three years in public relations practice. To enable candidates to prepare for these examinations, the Institute, in

---

[6] Much of this information comes from a special report prepared for the authors by a former student, Miss Clara C. Meyers, a member of the Spokesman Group staff. Opinions expressed are ours.

cooperation with the Regent Street Polytechnic, conducts evening classes. There is a waiting list for these courses. Because of England's traditionally conservative concept of a classic education, universities do not teach public relations. The British Institute of Public Relations has more than 1,500 members, maintains a strong central office, and publishes a quarterly, *Public Relations*. As in the United States, Britain's counseling firms have organized their own group, The Society of Independent Public Relations Consultants. It accepts only Institute members, and the two groups work together closely.

Use of public relations in government dates from 1912, paralleling its growth in our federal government. In 1912, after passage of the National Insurance Act, Lloyd George organized a corps of lecturers to explain the new legislation to employers and workers in all parts of the country. The outbreak of war with Germany in 1914 led to a rapid expansion of official information work in Britain and overseas. After 1918, its war-born organizations were abolished, but some of their functions were transferred to other departments—mainly to the Foreign Office. The Air Ministry has had a Press Officer from its inception in 1919, and in the same year the Ministry of Health set up an Information Department. An important stage in British Government PR's development was the creation of the Empire Marketing Board in 1926 to promote agricultural production and marketing throughout the Commonwealth. This work was directed by the late Sir Stephen Tallents, one of PR's pioneers. He often told his countrymen: "No civilized country can today afford either to neglect the projection of its national personality or to resign its projection to others." [7] World War II brought another period of expansion to PR in Britain's government.

Reflecting British political traditions, the function is highly centralized in Britain's government. At the apex of the structure is the Central Office of Information, created April 1, 1946, in a postwar reorganization of public relations. The COI provides the PRO's of the various ministries with all the production, technical, and distribution facilities they need. It has no officers of its own overseas, but supplies material to Information Officers stationed abroad by the Foreign Office, the Commonwealth Relations Office, and the Colonial Office. The British Information Services overseas are made up of three organizations: (1) the Information Services of the Overseas Departments; (2) the British Council; and (3) the External Services of the British Broadcasting Corporation.[8] Centralization of such services as TV production, film production, news release production and dissemination, and exhibits in the COI frees the PRO's to concentrate on matters of counseling and policy making. This system deserves more study by U.S. governmental leaders than it has had.

Broadly speaking, the function is not so mature and secure in commerce

---

[7] In *The Projection of England* (London: Published by Olen Press for Film Centre Ltd., 1955), p. 11.

[8] C.O.I., *An Outline of the Functions and Organizations of the Central Office of Information* (London: The COI, London SE 1), pp. 3-5.

and industry as in government, where virtually every agency has a PRO. An Institute official holds, "I think it is safe to say that public relations is now recognized as being an important function of management in this country." Yet much of the emphasis in commerce is on publicity getting, because, in the view of the *Financial Times,* "too many firms try to measure it (PR) by counting the Press cuttings that result from the P.R. programmes, and putting pressure on the P.R.O. when competitors' names appear in the Press." Another observer estimates that 80 per cent of self-styled practitioners make their living by obtaining free publicity in the Press—daily and weekly newspapers and the industrial, trade, and technical journals." [9] But the direction is toward maturity and away from publicity getting. Increasingly British businessmen recognize the importance of PR. The turn-around of the staid Stock Exchange is typical. This venerable institution opened a visitors' gallery in 1953, employed guides to explain its operations in 1958, made a film to explain its role to school children and lay groups in 1959, and in 1960 set up a full-fledged PR department.[10] American firms operating in England are exerting a strong influence on this trend toward maturity, but the intense competition of Common Market firms in markets long dominated by the British is providing the big push toward adoption of the full-range of PR services.

WEST GERMANY

Public Relations, both as a management concept and as a specialized skill, was virtually unknown in West Germany some 15 years ago. Today there is wide appreciation of its importance in industry and government. Public relations' rapid growth in West Germany reflects her booming industrial economy built upon the rubble of World War II and her adoption of democratic government. There was no satisfactory equivalent in the German language, so the English term *public relations* has been incorporated into the German language. (This is also true of the Scandinavian languages.) Much of the impetus for PR's growth is born of the need for aggressive marketing programs to sell the consumer goods pouring out of Germany's productive industrial plant in affluent Germany and in world markets. The shift from the indifference to public opinion that marked the cartel-minded businessman to today's hard-sell marketing tactics is reflected in the spectacular growth of advertising. Early in the 1960's, advertising reached the billion-dollar a year level in West Germany—a 300 per cent increase in one decade. Public relations has had a comparable if not so spectacular a growth. The new emphasis on public relations and advertising has brought several United States advertising and public relations agencies to West Germany.

9 Blake Ozias, "London Notes on Public Relations," *Public Relations Journal,* Vol. 13, February, 1957.

10 See John Brooks, "Thaw on Threadneedle Street," *The New Yorker,* Vol. 36, December 31, 1960, pp. 31-39, for the full story.

At the start of 1963 it was estimated that there were 1,000 public relations counselors in the Federal Republic of Germany. That same year the German Public Relations Society (Deutsche Public Relations-Gesellschaft) had 125 members. Admission requires several years' experience at the management level and that "the principles established by it for the profession are observed." Almost half these members are directors of departments in industry, not quite a fourth are consultants or employed by trade associations, and the others are employed in government. The president of the Federal Republic, the Federal Diet, the Federal Government, almost all Federal ministries, all Land governments, a number of Land ministries, several cities, and the government broadcasting corporation employ a large number of public officers. As is usually true of the mushrooming period in PR, "Unfortunately, there are many people who abuse the term 'public relations' to take advantage of the rapid development of this field in Germany." [11]

Typical of the origin and growth of the function in German industry is the department in the giant Bayer Farbenfabriken firm which is best described as the DuPont company of Germany. This chemical giant markets more than 13,000 products around the world. Bayer's PR department was set up in 1951 on the eve of its establishment as an independent firm in the decartelization of I. G. Farben. It employs a large staff of specialists in a "Department of Social Sciences," which is divided into these sections: Stockholder Information, Commercial Policy, Marketing, Motivation Research and Statistics, Community Relations, and Press Relations. The PR department gives only technical advice to the employee relations department on employee communications.

The German government has placed strong emphasis on public relations—as distinct from its former reliance on Goebbels-style propaganda—since its reorganization. It employs a large staff to win approval of its policies at home and abroad. This effort is directed by the German Press and Information Agency, headed by a civil servant who has title, "State Secretary." Its director, Hans Gunther Von Hase, sees his job as being "to explain the press to the government and the government to the press," which reflects the heavy emphasis on publicity that characterizes German public relations today.[12] This agency also directs an extensive overseas information program through its Deutsche Welle radio broadcasts and the corps of able press officers in its consulates and embassies around the world. In addition, for several years it has employed two United States firms to represent German interests in this country.

In Germany, staff practitioners are much concerned about participation in management's decision making both in industry and government. A German practitioner observes: "Those in West Germany who edit house organs, ana-

---

[11] Dr. Albert Oeckl, "Too Much or Too Little Public Relations Work?", *Frankfurter Allegmeine Zeitung,* December 27, 1962.

[12] Gerry Van der Heuvel, "Free World's Image Makers: They Report & They Censor," *Editor & Publisher,* Vol. 95, November 24, 1962, pp. 11 and 58.

lyze the world's economic and political news for an industrial boss or the governor of a state, work to improve management relations, or prepare an industrial film . . . are nearly all known to be 'specialists' of great skill. But there are few men in public relations who actually help to shape the vital decisions of large corporations. . . ." [13]

A gain for public relations came in 1961, when the University of Heidelberg introduced the first course at the university level. Several years prior to this, the Aachen Institute of Technology had been offering a course. A few other nonuniversity institutes teach it.

FRANCE

Public relations in France is developing at a slower pace than in other Western European countries. Practitioners must fight their way uphill against strong cultural, business, and journalistic traditions. Historically the French climate has been hostile to both the concept and practice, although it was a Frenchman, Jean-Jacques Rousseau, who eloquently voiced the concept of public opinion nearly three centuries ago. Barriers to the advance of public relations here include: (1) an inherently hostile cultural climate; (2) the traditional "it's none of the public's business" attitude of French industrialists; (3) the historic interlocking structure of French newspaper publishing and French advertising space sales; (4) strong opposition from the French advertising agencies; (5) the traditional aloofness of the government in its dealings with the press.

In the early 1950's, several major industrial firms established departments as the reconstruction period came to a close. As is often the case, the international oil companies led the way. In 1952 ten pioneer practitioners from these firms organized a club, "La Maison de Verre,"—The Glass House—under the leadership of Etienne Bloch. They took their cue, as Frenchmen would, from the words of a French philosopher, Auguste Comte, who wrote, more than a hundred years ago: *"A business enterprise must be open, like a glass house, for all to see. It is the duty of businessmen, who are entrusted with a legitimate power, to enlighten public opinion on their activities and trends."* Not all French businessmen yet accept this view.

Recalling the origins of this club, Claude Chapeau has written: "This first appearance was made 'on tiptoe.' " As the number of practitioners increased, the club was reorganized as the French Public Relations Association. This Association Française des Relations Publiques has established a Code of Ethics and sponsors a two-year course in the College Libre des Sciences Sociales in Paris. In addition there is a Union which functions as a professional corporate group to advance the interests of the small number of French public relations agencies.

---

13 Hanns Dietrich Ahrens, "Western Germany—Public Relations in the Making," *PR*, Vol. 4, October, 1959.

The French Government took official cognizance of the emerging practice in June, 1955, when the Minister of Commerce recommended creation of public relations offices within the organization of the chambers of commerce, which in France are public bodies, unlike those in the United States. In 1957 the Deputy Minister for Civil Service and Administrative Reform issued a memorandum creating civic service positions for "offices of orientation, reception and information." His memorandum read, in part: [the creation] "of such offices comes within the framework of a better organization of public relations, the importance of which asserts itself more and more in all productivity research." In 1960 the French minister of Posts, Tele-Communication (PNT), issued an administrative edict to all regional directors of the department instructing them to appoint part-time public relations men from their local staffs. This large department, which provides the postal and communication services for France, has some 130 men working in public relations, the largest PR staff in France. The basic government attitude in dealing with the press is still generally one of aloofness, however.

Two practitioners, after a study of the state of French public relations, conclude: [14] "There is wide variation—not only in the scope but also in the quality of French public relations programs. The most outstanding programs are found in large organizations. Medium-sized business firms generally do not indulge in public relations activities, except in such specialized fields as fashions and perfumes where public relations are almost exclusively linked to product promotion." But they see hopeful signs that French management's attitude will change as practitioners prove their worth and as younger men, trained in management techniques, take over top managerial roles. The schools of business administration, now functioning within the framework of France's universities, are giving increased emphasis to PR's importance.

ITALY

As in many other Western European nations, public relations was little known in Italy at the end of World War II. The birth of democratic government and the rise of a booming industrial economy in Northern Italy have provided the impetus for PR's growth. An increasing number of Italian manufacturers and businessmen realize that public relations techniques are an indispensable means for creating favorable relations with employees, customers, and the public. Similarly, the Italian government is using public relations in winning support for its leaders and their policies. The government is the main employer. Reflecting the North-South cleavage in Italy, there are two associations, one headquartered in Rome, one in Milan. The former one,

---

14 Loet Velmans and Frances Newton, "Special Report: The State of French Public Relations," *Public Relations Journal*, Vol. 18, September, 1962. Their article and Claude Chapeau's report, "Public Relations in France," presented to the First World Congress in 1958, were the main sources for this section.

Associazione Italiana Per Le Relazioni Pubbliche, is the second largest in Europe. Founded in 1954, it has more than 500 members. Not all these are practitioners. It has promoted the teaching of PR in specialized institutes. The first university-level course was introduced at the University of Torino in 1961. This textbook was published in an Italian edition in 1960 and has gone through two printings. Several universities and advanced institutes now offer PR courses. A monthly review, *Relazioni Pubbliche,* has promoted under-standing of the fundamentals of sound practice.[15]

Italian industrialists, once remote and aloof from the public, increasingly take the public into account in their employee, community, and marketing policies. In something of an understatement, the president of Shell Italiana says: "All of us will agree that public relations originates in, and draws its justification from, the profound evolution that we have seen pervade the structure of our society in the last few years." Here, too, the international oil companies have set the pace.

ELSEWHERE IN EUROPE

Norway has set the pace in the Scandinavian countries. It has an active professional association, Den Norske Public Relations Klubb, and several strong counseling firms; major industries utilize public relations in their management and marketing. Increasingly, Norway's transportation, shipping, porcelain, and paper industries are employing specialists in their employee and marketing programs. PR has been used quite successfully to promote Designs of Scandinavia. One practitioner reports: "A lack of understanding of public relations on the part of business management which was dominant only a few years ago has now given place to a more progressive view." Norway's government also utilizes public relations specialists.[16]

The Norwegian association, founded in October, 1949, has sponsored seminars and courses in technical institutes. No university yet offers a course. As in most countries, the United States is looked to for instruction and inno-vation. The only book in Norwegian in this field is one by Nils M. Apeland, a successful counselor, describing PR practice in the United States. A contest to promote improvement in annual reports, modeled after that sponsored by *Financial World,* was started in 1954, and today corporations vie for the Farmand award.

Business' acceptance of PR in Sweden dates from the early 1950's. Earlier, however, some United States companies with plants in Sweden had estab-lished PR departments, and this ultimately brought imitation. One practi-tioner reports: "Swedish public relations, however, differs in many respects

---

15 Frank Gervasi, "Public Relations in Italy," *Public Relations Journal,* Vol. 14, February, 1958.

16 Nils M. Apeland, "Public Relations in Norway," *Public Relations Journal,* Vol. 14, July, 1958.

from public relations in the USA. The man in the street, for example, is still more or less unaware of its significance. The educated man confuses it with advertising, and there is as yet no adequate translation of these Anglo-Saxon words." The first professional meeting was held in Sweden in 1948 under the auspices of the Swedish Advertising Association. This undoubtedly added to the confusion of these fields in the minds of Sweden's businessmen. Since then several counseling firms have been established and the number of practitioners is steadily increasing. A PR book, *Public Relations—The Company's New Function,* by Nils Tengberg, was published in Stockholm in 1960. It presents "practical viewpoints and experiences from the PR field."

Public relations has developed much more slowly in Denmark and Finland, although both these nations are expert in designing and marketing consumer goods of smart contemporary design. Finland has a public relations association; Denmark does not. In Belgium before 1952, the idea of public relations was generally unknown. Late that year a small number of practitioners formed the Centre Belgique des Relations Publiques, and by 1958 they were strong enough to successfully sponsor the first World Congress of Public Relations. Having the Common Market headquarters in Brussels has given a strong thrust to PR's development there. Businessmen's awareness of public relations also was advanced by wide dissemination of a report on "Public Relations in Belgium," published by the Committee for Free Enterprise in 1953. This committee advocated intensified programs to head off state ownership, a stimulus to PR's growth in many countries.[17]

The Holland association, Nederlands Genoopschap Voor Public Relations, was organized in 1954 and now has nearly 100 members. In cooperation with the Belgian Center, it sponsors a bimonthly PR journal published in the Dutch, French, and Flemish languages. Reflecting its lively international commerce, Switzerland has an active PR association with nearly 300 members. Fewer than 100 of these are full-time practitioners. It publishes *PR Revue* in the three native languages, and another periodical, *Public Relations Practice,* is published in English for international circulation. Several Swiss institutes and the University of St. Gall offer courses in public relations. Here, as in most of Europe, practitioners have difficulty in getting journalists to see publicity as news rather than advertising to be paid for at space rates. In Switzerland there are few public relations agencies. Most business firms use internal staffs. The number of firms is growing, but "in 95 per cent of the cases they handle publicity or do public relations work only as a sideline to advertising."[18]

Held back by Spain's totalitarian regime and backward economy, public relations has had comparatively little development in Spain. Nonetheless,

17 Committee of Free Enterprise, *Public Relations in Belgium* (Brussels: the Committee, 1954). Also see Pierre Janssen, "Public Relations in Belgium," *Public Relations Journal,* Vol. 14, May, 1958.

18 Charles R. Metzler, "Public Relations in Switzerland," *Public Relations Journal,* Vol. 14, January, 1958.

PR firms have been established and awareness of PR is spreading among Spain's businessmen and government officials. There are two large, well-organized agencies, one in Barcelona and one in Madrid, and some 30 individual counselors in Spain. The Associación Técnica Española de Relaciones Públicas has 200 members but still has to develop vitality and direction. The news media view practitioners with reserve and suspicion. Spain is utilizing PR to promote its rising tourist trade. This textbook, published in Spanish in 1961, has had a good sale in Spain and in Latin America.

Ireland's small number of practitioners have an association to promote PR's acceptance there.

INDIA

If public relations is in a fluid state of defining itself in Western countries, it is even more so in India. As of today, the concept of public relations as a management function is little understood or valued. This is understandable in the light of its newness in India and in the context of India's economic and political life. There the *raison d'être* of many businesses is determined at the federal and state government levels. Mostly, public relations in India means press and government relations. There are many organizations—private, semi-government and wholly government-owned—which employ public relations officers. In the majority of cases, these function as contact men with the press and other related institutions. Advertising agencies, too, have "public relations executives" on their staffs, but these persons are used mainly in the preparation of news releases, house organs, annual reports, and public relations advertising.[19]

Spearheading the growth of public relations in India are a few independent public relations practitioners who have set up counseling firms in recent years. In the light of the prevailing social, economic, and political climate in India, their task is understandably difficult. Nonetheless, such firms are charting a slow but steady rate of growth. Progressive institutions—mainly the international oil companies and a few top Indian business firms—have realized the value of public relations and are utilizing the services of this small group of sophisticated practitioners. Today in India, public relations thinking and practice are restricted to the upper echelons of commerce and industry and focus mainly on the relationships with federal and state governments. It can be reasonably predicted that the growth and development of public relations will keep pace with industrialization in India.

India's first university-level course in PR was taught in the University of Calcutta School of Journalism in 1959. In 1961 a noncredit course was introduced in a Bombay technical institute. American and English texts are used.

---

19 These observations are based on information supplied by a former student, P. S. Akerkar, who today owns a large agency, Consilium International, in Bombay.

JAPAN

Paralleling Japan's great industrial growth and its extension of democratic government since World War II has been a rapid growth in public relations. Before World War II the philosophy and practice of public relations were little known in the Orient. As of 1963, there were more than 1,000 public relations counselors offering their services in the Tokyo, Osaka, and Nagoya complexes.[20] Other observers think this estimate high. Japan's industrial prosperity, the increased power of public opinion, its extensive communications facilities, and its high degree of literacy provide fertile soil for PR's growth in this teeming nation of nearly 100 million people. Japan must build world markets for its accelerating production; public relations is being utilized primarily for this purpose. Because of Japan's growth as a market for American goods, more and more American firms are employing the services of Japanese counselors. Likewise, many United States public relations agencies are establishing offices or affiliates in Japan. A rising level of United States-Japan trade will spur this development. Advertising is experiencing a like boom in Japan. Its Dentsu Agency is the fifth largest agency in the world. Also, its government must guide citizens in the ways of democracy.

Public relations agencies in Japan have a wide range in fees (from $278 to $1,500 a month) and offer a wide range of services. One observer reports: "Japanese public relations firms set up tours, conferences, and receptions for their clients. They also publish and distribute an assortment of newsletters, brochures and booklets in Japanese and English. They keep in touch with their clients' customers and within the restricting bounds of their professional know-how. . . . One of the related activities . . . publishing and newsletters. Hitachi, an electrical manufacturer, for example, has a monthly news report for business executives." [21]

Most industrial firms have public relations departments, although it was Henry Rockwell's observation that "public relations in Japan is far behind the United States in reaching the executive level." In fact, many companies have two departments, one to handle corporate affairs and project "the corporate image," the other to promote the sale of goods by publicity. The latter is a responsibility of the advertising and public relations departments. Basically, Japanese industrialists are now in "the advertising stage." Rockwell reports "constant confusion and bickering between the two departments resulting from this arrangement." There is also a sharp cleavage between public relations and advertising agencies there, as here. With one exception, adver-

---

[20] Henry T. Rockwell, "Report from the Land of the Rising Public Relations Business," *Public Relations Journal*, Vol. 19, March, 1963.

[21] *Ibid*. (Also see "Standard of Japan in Deal with D-A-Y," *Editor & Publisher*, Vol. 95, May 26, 1962, pp. 22 and 26; and "Japanese Discover PR and Promotion," *ibid.*, Vol. 93, September 10, 1960, p. 32.)

tising and public relations counseling are not offered by the same agency. Integration of the function in management is in process. It will take years.

PR DOWN UNDER

Public relations has developed more extensively in the Western-oriented Pacific nations of Australia and New Zealand, although not on the scale of Japan. The Public Relations Institute of Australia had a membership of 300 in 1964, although its president admitted, "PR hasn't achieved the recognition in my country it has in the United States." It is estimated that there are 100 counseling firms in this large nation. The Sydney telephone directory listed just two such firms in 1950 and 75 a decade later. The Institute publishes a monthly *PR News*. As of 1963, there were no public relations courses in Australia's universities, although journalism, advertising, and business administration are taught in some. The University of Sydney introduced public relations as part of the curriculum for its Graduate Summer School of Industrial Management a few years ago.

The emphasis in Australia has been on press-agentry—as it was in the United States decades ago. Most of Australia's practitioners have little background in the broader aspects of public relations, at least in the view of one observer. An Australian practitioner says, "Most of the PR here is reasonably good press-agentry, but little more." [22] Consequently, in the words of the Institute's secretary, "Newspapers are still inclined to be suspicious of public relations practitioners, but this is being overcome. . . ." *Public Relations Review* reported a few years ago that "some Australian newspapers have barred commercial public relations personnel from their offices, and the New Zealand press looks with a suspicious eye at nongovernment practitioners in the field." Newspapers in Australia accredit the advertising agencies, and their attitude is indicated by the fact that accreditation agreement includes a stipulation that the agency will not seek free publicity.

In New Zealand there are fewer than 100 full-time practitioners. Most of these hold membership in the Public Relations Institute of New Zealand, organized in 1953. The function is fully recognized in national and local government, but little acknowledged in business. There are only a few counseling firms in the nation's 14 urban centers. New Zealand has no public relations publication, and none of its universities offers a course. New Zealand and Australian practitioners rely heavily on the PR books and journals from the United States and Great Britain for guidance.

Knowledge and practice of public relations are slowly spreading through the Pacific Area, but not at the spectacular rate of growth recorded in Japan or Australia. Awareness of public relations is fostered in this area by the Pan

---

[22] Contained in a report prepared for the authors by a former student, Philip C. Minter, now a Sydney practitioner.

Pacific Public Relations Group and by Roy J. Leffingwell's *Public Relations Review,* published in Honolulu.[23] The Pan Pacific Public Relations Group was organized July 1, 1958, and has since held biennial conferences in Hong Kong, Tokyo, and Honolulu. It limits its membership to one firm from each of these countries: Canada, Taiwan, Thailand, India, Philippine Islands, Japan, Hong Kong, Australia, New Zealand, and the United States, the latter represented by Leffingwell.

LATIN AMERICA

Generally speaking, public relations is in its embryonic stage in Latin America, but a period of growth appears in the offing. Several active professional associations, introduction of courses in many universities, and the public relations programs of international companies are contributing to awareness of PR's importance. Taking the lead in promoting recognition of this field is the Inter-American Federation of PR Associations, which sponsors annually an Inter-American Conference on Public Relations. This conference, which first met in Mexico City in 1960, provides a forum for the exchange of ideas among Latin American specialists. There are several national associations federated with this over-all body. Development of specialized courses at the university level has been encouraged by the International Center for Journalism Education for Latin America (CIESPAL) in Quito, Ecuador. Each year CIESPAL gives a seminar for some 40 journalists and teachers, and public relations is included in the curriculum.

The main thrust in building awareness of public relations in these countries comes from Latin contacts with United States business firms and with various United States agencies in promoting the Alliance for Progress. Public relations has had its strongest growth in Mexico, reflecting that nation's advanced stage of industrialization in comparison with other Hispanic nations. The Mexican association (Asociasión Mexicana de Professionales en Relaciones Publicas), organized in 1952, has carried on a vigorous program, largely under the direction of Federico Sanchez Fogarty, an international figure in this field. Mexican public relations had its beginnings in the mid-1930's with the advent of commercial air transportation. Wilbur L. Morrison of Pan American Airways is credited with pioneering PR in Mexico. The first agency was opened in 1944 by Senor Sanchez Fogarty. The second one started a year later.[24]

Characteristic of PR's early stages, there is considerable confusion between publicity and public relations and between advertising and public relations in the minds of Latin business and government leaders. To make matters worse, in Spanish *publicidad* means "advertising"; Spanish for "publicity" is

---

23 This is a multilithed monthly newsletter "designed to keep practitioners informed of world-wide public relations activities," published by Leffingwell Associates.

24 Ramirez de Aguilar, "Breves Apuntes para la Historia de las Relaciones Publicas en Mexico," *Voces R P,* Vol. 3, March 25, 1961.

información; "public relations" is *relaciones públicas.* Howard Stephenson found, in his visit to Peru, that "there is widespread misconception in Peru as to just what public relations is all about." [25] In Hispanic America, public relations must earn its place working uphill against a lack of tradition of social responsibility by those in power, an underdeveloped economy, lack of a strong middle class, and widespread illiteracy. The possibilities are there; the faint beginnings can be seen.

INTERNATIONAL
ASSOCIATION ORGANIZED

A developing *esprit* and exchange of information among the world's practitioners have been furthered by organization of the International Public Relations Association. This Association had its origins in 1949, when a group of Netherlands industries invited some 20 public relations men from Western Europe and the United States to discuss informally their mutual interests in Holland.

Out of three days of spirited shop talk came a provisional committee to study the feasibility of an international association. This committee was organized in 1950 with Odd Medbøe of Norway as chairman and Tim Traverse-Healy of England as secretary. The organizing group found widespread support for the proposed association, but getting international agreement took time. IPRA was finally organized at a meeting in London in 1955, with Tom Fife Clark of Great Britain as its first president.

IPRA's early years were spent in selecting a limited number of members from the various countries and in organizing its committees. This is an association of individual members, not a superstructure over the national public relations associations which now circle the world. In 1961, meeting at the II World Congress of Public Relations, IPRA adopted a Code of Conduct to set the standards for public relations at the international level. This code was written out of nearly five years' conferences and correspondence in IPRA. This association meets annually. By 1964, it had 254 members from 27 different countries.

The international association provided the impetus for organizing the World Congress of Public Relations, which has stimulated and facilitated exchange of ideas and provided a meeting place for practitioners from all countries. The first Congress, held in Brussels in 1958, attracted 237 delegates from 23 countries, including Russia.[26] The second Congress was held in Venice, Italy, in 1961 and had 700 delegates from 41 nations participating in its deliberations. Russia did not send delegates to Venice. The third World

---

[25] "Peru Has Growing Pains in Public Relations," *Public Relations Journal,* Vol. 16, November, 1960.

[26] Kenneth W. Haagensen, "The First World Congress of Public Relations," *Public Relations Journal,* Vol. 14, October, 1958.

Congress was held in Montreal, Canada, in 1964. The friendships, shop talk, and printed proceedings of these world-wide conclaves have done much to promote a sense of professionalism and international communication among practitioners.

Additional Reading

British Institute of Public Relations, *A Guide to the Practice of Public Relations.* London: Newman Neame, Ltd., 1958.

Pierre Bruneau, *Magiciens de la publicité.* Paris: Gallimard, 1956.

Burton M. Halpern, "Public Relations in Israel," *Public Relations Journal,* Vol. 15, May, 1959.

Bruno Heini, *Public Relations Die Vertrauenswerbung der Privatunternechmung.* Winterthur: P. G. Keller, 1960.

Hans Edgar Jahn, *Vertrauen Verantwortung Mitarbeit.* (A Study of Public Relations Work in Germany.) Oberlahnstein/Rhein: Fritz Nohr & Sohne, 1953.

Olle Kellerman, "Public Relations in Scandinavia," *Gazette,* Vol. 9, No. 2, 1963.

David L. Lewis, "International Networks: PR's New Golden Age," *PR,* October, 1957.

Eric Lindstrom, *PR Fallet, tjugoen exempel pa public relations i praktiken.* Stockholm: Forum, 1959. (The Question of Public Relations. Twenty-one Examples.)

R. A. Paget-Cooke, "Public Relations Examinations in Great Britain," *Public Relations Journal,* Vol. 15, April, 1959.

Arthur Reef, "International PR for American Companies Abroad," *PR,* Vol. 5, January, 1960.

Relations publiques et publicité. Paris: Hachette, 1962.

Bengt Sjosteen, "Public Relations in Sweden . . . ," *Public Relations Journal,* Vol. 14, November, 1958.

World Congress of Public Relations, *Proceedings.* Brussels: Belgian Centre de Relations Publiques, 1959.

CASE PROBLEM

You are a citizen of the United States and have been in the public relations department of Moon Motors, Inc., for five years. As a reward for stellar performance in the home office, you were promoted to public relations director of the French division of Moon Motors, Inc. You took over this post in Paris six months ago. Your firm has found that the French version of the Moon is not competing successfully against the French automobiles in France's industrial resurgence. It decides to consolidate all European production in its new automated Netherland plant. This requires dropping 3,100 French workers. This is done by divisional management in consultation with the director of employee relations. A terse notice is issued. A storm of protest breaks. The French Minister of Industry heatedly declares: "In the future, new foreign investment programs, particularly from United States firms, must be examined with greatest care." Unions join in demonstrations of protest. French newspapers carry angry editorials. There is much damning of absentee ownership. This violent reaction catches your management flatfooted. Now—

a. What steps do you recommend that management take to end the protests and repair the damage done its reputation in France?

b. What program can you suggest as a means of meeting a similar problem in the future without creating such bitter reaction on the part of the local citizenry, if you are consulted ahead of time?

Chapter Twenty-Seven

PERSONAL

EQUIPMENT

Of all the frustrations of public relations management, there is none more frustrating than the search for able, qualified personnel.—
An Employer.

Some people are better cooks than others. So it is with public relations. Some have a better natural feel for it than others. Some are better trained. Others are backed by years of useful experience. Some make it on the basis of winning personalities. It would be difficult, if not impossible, to write a set of qualifications which would produce a good practitioner every time. The recipe would not stand up in every case. Different employers emphasize different qualities.

Basically the practitioner must have (1) a personality and character that command respect and inspire confidence; (2) skill in communication—particularly, an ability to write; (3) a sure grasp of public opinion—its process and its analysis; (4) knowledge of the field in which he works—be it business, social welfare, education, or whatever; (5) ideas and imagination.

The demand for these talents will endure and grow. Their scarcity will bring a premium to those possessing them. It is estimated that the number of practitioners will double in the next decade. Even now the number of applicants qualified by *personality, ability,* and *preparation* does not equal the demand. Public relations is young. It has the vitality, enthusiasm, and exciting interest of youth. It also shows some of the awkwardness and overconfidence of adolescence.

The risks—and the rewards—are somewhat higher in public relations than in the older fields of journalism. There is challenge and real opportunity in getting in on the ground floor of a young calling—a vocation on its way to becoming a profession. As one practitioner put it: "It is far more exhilarating to enter a field when it is new, when all the inevitable discoveries have not been made, when there is pioneering to be done."

One employer, in lamenting the lack of qualified personnel in this field, described the ideal applicant.[1]

> A man who is pleasant spoken, obviously intelligent, with a spark of humor, a sense of proportion, with a sound background of experience; a man who dresses well but not ostentatiously, a man whom you find yourself respecting (it isn't necessary to like him; public relations is not a popularity contest); a man who you believe not only has ideas but will stand up for them and put them over to people in your organization who must be sold if they are to be implemented.

Qualification is seldom a case of education alone. Two persons can take the same course in history. They won't react the same way to what the teacher or textbook says. Nor will they have the same views on history when it is all over. They will still be two totally different persons with somewhat differing thoughts.

Along with education there must be the natural inclination of a personality toward one kind of work or another. That means having traits that will help the individual succeed. It takes more than a desire "to work with people." It takes ability to deal with ideas and imagination to create new ones. It means being able to derive a personal satisfaction from a certain type of work.

The direction of programs demands more from a person than the beginner can hope to deliver at the outset. Practitioners have to deal constantly with seasoned people. They have to understand how organizations function at the policy level and how the work of various departments links together. They have to be able to organize—to get people to work together. They must know how to meet people of diverse interests, speak their languages, and win their goodwill and respect. They must know staff work.

Most important of all, perhaps, the practitioner who would succeed must know the field he serves. If he is effectively to interpret business, education, social work, conservation, recreation, or medicine, he must have a ready grasp of his subject matter. Further, he must be able to deal with his colleagues on an equal basis. Lack of this substantive knowledge has been termed the practitioner's "deadliest pitfall."

Robert E. Curtin, Jr. believes that the biggest cause of failure in public relations results from *"failure to learn the business."* "Not failure to learn public relations technique, but failure to understand, in a mature and sophisticated way, the business of the client or employer, whether small merchant, large industrialist, welfare agency or college." [2]

It has been emphasized repeatedly in this book that *the first and indispensable step in public relations is to earn the confidence of management.*

---

[1] Anonymous, "So You Want to Be in Public Relations?", *Public Relations Journal,* Vol. 12, July, 1956.

[2] Robert E. Curtin, Jr., "Deadliest Pitfall," *Public Relations Journal,* Vol. 12, September, 1956.

This can be done only by practitioners with the maturity and knowledge that enable them to comprehend management's problems. Unless the staff specialist can discuss intelligently the substantive problems confronting his organization, he is not likely to get a hearing. Wisely, many employers make it a practice to give prospective PR staffers work experience in other phases of the organization before putting them into the public relations department.

We have emphasized that, increasingly, the practitioner will be expected to provide management with a sensitive interpretation of the society in which it will prosper or perish. This requires an ability to understand and assess current political, economic, and social trends and to be able to predict, with some certainty, where these trends will lead. Such an assessment requires more than periodic public opinion polls. It requires a person with a broad education who keeps it up to date; also, it requires a person with a compassionate sensitivity to the welfare of others. Today's managers are swamped with pressing problems involving personnel, production, procurement, finance, marketing, and politics. Most of them live apart and aloof from the workaday world. Consequently, they find it difficult to keep abreast of what is going on in the public opinion market place. This they expect, or should expect, their staff counselors to do for them.

All this is a lot to ask of a young person. For that reason the function of director, officer, or counselor is not often assigned to the new college graduate. Tomorrow's practitioner will have coupled a college education with seasoning experience in the mass media or in internships in departments or counseling firms.

In past years newspapers and advertising departments or agencies have been the primary sources of practitioners. A lesser number came in through the sales or personnel doors. Some graduated from industrial editing. The majority of today's counselors and staff directors were formerly newspapermen, writers, advertising men, and publicists. The migration and conversion were logical. The practice was still in an experimental stage. It was desirable to put the experimenting into the hands of men and women who knew from experience how to ferret out and present facts, who knew to get along with all sorts of people, and who were sensitive to public likes and dislikes. No one could meet these specifications as well as the people already working with public opinion through the mass media, advertising, and selling.

Douglas Lyke found in his study of Chicago-area practitioners that today's typical PR director is 46 years old, went to college majoring in business or journalism, had engaged in newspaper work, has a special ability for handling people, expresses his thoughts clearly and simply, whether speaking or writing, knows business administration, and spends a substantial part of his time representing his organization before various publics, and that his assistants have had more college education than he had.[3]

---

[3] In *Public Relations as a Management Function in Chicago Area Companies* (New York: Public Relations Society of America, 1954). The survey shows the background of typical practitioners of that vintage.

In their study, Moore and Seifert found Columbus practitioners well-educated as a group, and that most had prior experience in the communications media. Fifty-four of those surveyed had bachelor's degrees, 23 of these in journalism. Four also had a master's degree in journalism. Only two had had no college education. Of the degrees earned outside journalism, four were in commerce, three in English, and two in education, with several others scattered over a wide variety of disciplines. These practitioners came from such varied work backgrounds as college coach, manager of a cooperative utility, and the ministry. Fifty-five per cent, however, had work experience in communications before taking their present jobs.[4]

Dominance of prior media experience in the preparation of today's practitioner is further reflected in the "Function and Manpower Survey" made by the Public Relations Society. The PRSA research committee found that the majority of practitioners surveyed had done some sort of newspaper work on a full-time basis in the past. These were the answers to the question, "What other positions have you held on a full-time basis in the past?"[5]

	Per Cent of Total Respondents
Newspaper work	53
Public relations	43
Advertising	27
Sales and merchandising	16
Magazine work	10
Teaching and educational work	10
Radio, movies, and TV work	6
Business and trade associations	5
Military service	5
Others	26

As public relations matures and expands in scope, it is increasingly realized that skilled practice takes more than a few years' newspaper experience. Tomorrow's specialist must be broadly trained in the social sciences and equipped to use the tools of these sciences if he is to be a *communicator,* not just a disseminator. Increasingly, the practitioner will use the knowledge of social psychology, industrial sociology, and opinion measurement to facilitate an inflow of representative opinions to managers. Contemporary practice requires the talents of a *trained specialist,* not a publicist.

News-media experience is useful and not to be underrated. But it is not the whole of preparation needed. As a successful practitioner wrote his former teacher: "The ability to communicate is only an admission ticket. The ability to generate ideas, to formulate policies, and to advance the welfare of the enterprise with which we are associated is the key to our progress, once that admission ticket is punched."

---

4 William C. Moore, "A Critical Analysis of Public Relations Practitioners in a Midwestern Metropolitan Area," unpublished master's thesis, Ohio State University, 1962, pp. 18-20.

5 *Report of the National Research Committee of the Public Relations Society of America* (New York: the Society, 1956).

This is reflected in the changing pattern of recruitment. One researcher has listed three reasons for this changing pattern: (1) increased visibility of public relations as an occupational alternative; (2) increased gap between earlier-acquired vocational skills and those necessary today; (3) increased stability and definiteness of the field, which has led to more planned entries and fewer people happening into public relations. An employment agency executive who specializes in job placement of practitioners observes two trends in the hiring of personnel: (1) Employers are concerned not only with the skills and knowledge of the applicant, but with personality; (2) The trend toward specialization, because the field is now too broad for any one person to master all facets.[6]

More and more it is possible for the college graduate with a liberal arts-journalism education to go directly into public relations work. Practitioners responding to a PRSA questionnaire a few years ago reflected a greatly increased willingness to hire college graduates without experience. In all, 44 per cent expected to hire one or more persons in the five years following the study. For all respondents combined, the five-year projection indicated that one out of every three persons to be hired would be the college graduate without experience.[7] Practitioner Don Campbell gives a realistic answer to the question frequently asked by the young person interested in PR: "Do you have to have newspaper experience to succeed in public relations?" His answer: "Public relations directors who have been newspapermen think such experience is very important, while public relations directors who have not been newspapermen feel that such experience is not at all essential."

Most practitioners regard journalism courses as useful. This was borne out in a survey directed by Professor Stewart Harral. In querying a sample of 400 practitioners, he found that 86 per cent of them regard journalism courses as useful in some degree. The professionals replied as follows on this question: nearly 56 per cent described journalism courses as "extremely useful"; nearly 30 per cent, as "of some use"; and only 2.2 per cent said such courses were of "no use." Others in the sample did not respond on this question.[8]

The ideal preparation, in our view, is a good liberal arts education with or without a journalism major, a few years' work experience, preferably in the media, and then a master's-degree program which includes courses in communications, public opinion, public relations, and the substantive field in which the student plans to work. Few students can plan their programs and

---

6 Edwin B. Stern, "Getting a Job in PR," *PR*, Vol. 2, January, 1957.

7 *Staffing for Public Relations*, A Report of the National Education Committee, Public Relations Society of America (New York: the Society, 1959), p. 6.

8 Survey completed and distributed in 1963 by Education Committee of Public Relations Society of America. Mimeographed. The value of journalism education and media experience in the preparation of today's practitioner was further evidenced in a later survey of more than 2,000 practitioners by Ohio State University's School of Journalism. For results, see: Daniel E. Costello and Walter W. Seifert, "National Survey Finds Practitioners Favoring Increased Study." *Public Relations Journal*, Vol. 20, May, 1964, pp. 20-21.

lives this methodically. Lack of money, marriage and children, and job opportunities tend to upset such planning.

Two developments have resulted from the increased demand for more broadly and carefully trained practitioners: (1) an increasing number of courses and majors in colleges and universities to provide an educational foundation for a career; (2) an increasing number of apprenticeships and in-service training programs. The number has been steadily growing. Apprenticeships include other than mass-media experience.

> Interviewer or analyst in attitude research; leg man on news, publication, and speech-writing research.
>
> Editor or assistant editor of house publication.
>
> Handyman or writer in PR department, counseling firm, advertising department, or agency.
>
> Assistant in trade association, writer on trade publications, assistant in personnel or recreation departments.
>
> Assistant in radio or TV station production, motion-picture production shop, or other jobs which develop skill in media and techniques.

An increasing number of large corporations are developing *planned* in-service training programs which go a step beyond providing apprentice jobs. J. Stanford Smith of General Electric has counseled fellow employers that "The only way all of us can make major progress in developing men of leadership is for all of us to be willing to make the investment of going to the colleges and recruiting men and then helping them get the necessary experience and training on the job." GE recruits men direct from college for its advertising and public relations training courses. These developments will bring about a gradual change in the background on the new practitioner. What are the criteria most likely to be used in measuring applicants for tomorrow's jobs?

THE MAKEUP OF
THE MAN

Considering the kind of work required, the employer or client can be expected to measure applicants by six yardsticks:

1. Personality	4. Education or experience
2. Character	5. Administrative ability
3. Intelligence	6. Income requirements

PERSONALITY. The practitioner needs, above all else, to have the ability to persuade without offense. No two people are alike in personality, although everyone tends to fall into a type. The basic type is not so important. It is not necessary to be either an extrovert or an introvert. The important thing is that the individual be able to handle himself or herself in such a way that other people are attracted rather than repulsed. It boils down to being *likable*.

People tend to believe what they like to believe. When a person is subjected to opposing people or viewpoints, he tends to believe the ones he likes best. Being likable helps make it possible for the practitioner to stand between opposing groups and work to bring about an understanding without being coerced or scuttled by either group in the process. The practitioner spends much of his time being "the man in the middle."

Most people know whether they are liked by someone else. They don't always know why. Some of the attributes of a likable personality are clear-cut. For example, it helps a person to be cheerful and not to take himself too seriously. A spark of humor breaks many a cloud of crisis. A *genuine* desire to be helpful to others carries many practitioners far.

The employer or client who evaluates an applicant wants a person whose personality and words persuade others. Most probably, he judges the letter of application or the interview by whether or not he is favorably impressed. The practitioner needs to be a combination of diplomat, strategist, and leader. There must be a flair for words and for showmanship. These are common denominators.

CHARACTER. The practitioner is a front-man. That is, he or she represents the organization a little more directly with the public and a little more importantly than most other employees or associates. The practitioner is seen by the press, by highly placed people in public life, and by the community. Not only is he seen, but he is heard. His words are read by those outsiders and many others. The organization will be judged again and again by its PR people. The character of the organization will appear to many to be of the same caliber as its PR spokesman. That calls for statesmanship in communication rather than mouthpiecemanship. It calls for all the old-fashioned virtues of a respectable character. The practitioner, inside the organization and out, must earn respect for integrity, ethics, behavior, and decency. These qualities breed confidence. The practitioner must have this to serve effectively as an intermediary.

These components of character are not acquired through any course of study, nor are they affixed as a part of a college diploma. They result or fail to result from a combination of environment, training, and a self-imposed restraint.

Not to be overlooked, however, is the help in achieving character that is provided by formal education. Even today, when millions receive college degrees annually, the public still attaches a certain stamp of approval on the graduate. The value of that stamp exists unless the individual proves it is unwarranted. The four-year exposure to arts and sciences provides guidance in appreciating some of those intangible values other than the necessities to keep fed, sheltered, and clothed. There is a strong recommendation in this. There is, however, no guarantee.

INTELLIGENCE. A new vocation or profession is always on trial in its first few generations. It is on trial with people thinking about entering it as a life's work. It is on trial with those who employ its services. It is on trial with those who are influenced by its work. For that reason it needs the best brains it can attract. Beyond the need for native intelligence, the practitioner must have a special way of applying that intelligence to problems in communication. He must possess an unceasing interest in what people think and why they think that way. He must be curious about human behavior. He must be interested in the motives behind human behavior.

Without inquisitive intelligence, the practitioner is handicapped. It is vital that the curiosity and the interest be genuine. *They cannot be feigned for any length of time with any degree of success.* It must really be of importance to the PR man to understand why certain people tremble when it thunders, go to a movie every Wednesday night, join the Ku Klux Klan, read comic books, have hysterics, love cats, go to fortune tellers, steal from each other, lie about the size of a fish, or refuse to believe the truth.

The special kind of intelligence the practitioner needs enables him not only to understand people better, but also, in understanding, to improve their information and thus influence their opinions. Underscored in native intelligence, of course, is *common sense*.

EDUCATION AND EXPERIENCE. Employers naturally look for paragons—those who have had a complete education and a broad variety of experiences pertinent to the field. J. Stanford Smith outlined the qualities that GE looks for.[9]

1. Well above average intelligence backed up by well above average grades.
2. A sound general education. We are inclined to be skeptical of vocational training courses.
3. An extracurricular record that shows drive, an interest in the human equation, and ability to gain voluntary cooperation.
4. A working knowledge of business economics.
5. A sophisticated appreciation of current politics.
6. A knowledge of our company and our industry.
7. Communication skills—both mass and man-to-man.

One survey of employers' preferences in educational background of men and women they would hire came up with a ranking of college subjects.

1. Journalism
2. Economics
3. Social sciences
4. Business administration
5. Psychology
6. Writing courses
7. Public speaking
8. History
9. Public relations
10. Political science
11. Literature
12. Physical sciences

These respondents divided evenly on the value of a graduate degree as part of a practitioner's preparation. They were in agreement on the importance of extracurricular activities and ranked them in this order: 1. school publications; 2. campus activities (athletics, student government, fraternities, etc.); 3. employment in college (selling especially); 4. advertising work on school publications; 5. part-time PR work; 6. public speaking. Employers stress these qualifications in dealing with college placement services.

---

9 In "Developing Men for Leadership," *PR*, Vol. 3, January, 1958.

Corporation public relations trainee: degree in social sciences with courses in public relations, English, economics, industrial relations, sales and merchandising; minor courses in personnel, government, and public speaking.

PR assistant for Connecticut welfare agency: college graduate, preferably with courses in journalism and public relations and demonstrated ability to write.

Large corporation publicity representative: journalism graduate with experience, with strong emphasis on industrial and business rather than consumer publications. Technical or engineering training or association most helpful. Sales experience also vital.

Chemical company product publicity section: formal training in journalism or liberal arts and a healthy amount of social sciences in their college training. Prefer someone with two or three years' writing experience with a newspaper or magazine.

Counseling firm trainee: recent journalism graduate with emphasis on public relations; some writing experience, preferably college daily or stringing for newspaper or wire service; one with good personality who meets people easily and who likes to meet people.

A representative sample of PRSA's membership was queried in its manpower survey on "What skills or talents do you look for in a young person?" [10]

	Per Cent of Total Respondents
Writing ability	70
Some skill gained in public relations work	42
Speaking ability	30
Creative ability	28
General intelligence	28
Good general background	27
Sound judgment	25
Organizational ability	11

The Public Relations Society of America, in its most recent *Vocational Guide,* sums up the qualifications needed: [11]

Probably the "ideal" . . . public relations man or woman is the highly articulate and imaginative individual with more than a little salesmanship in his or her makeup. . . . Many public relations executives stress *judgment* as the most important single qualification. . . . Skill in practical action, based on reflective analysis, is an important part of the equipment. . . . In addition, he should have *imagination, verbalizing skills, extroverted traits, sensitivity to other people, organizing and planning skill,* and *managerial ability.*

ADMINISTRATIVE ABILITY. Much of what has been mentioned above adds up to leadership. In one sense, practitioners minister to the leadership of employers and their publics. In another sense, practitioners must execute programs conceived and administer the affairs of a department or counseling firm. Without attempting to define leadership *per se,* it is well to be aware of the pitfalls of executive leadership. According to Burleigh Gardner, there are twelve human traits commonly causing failure of executives.

---

10 PRSA Survey of the National Research Committee, *op. cit.*

11 Public Relations Society of America, *Let's Consider Public Relations* (New York: the Society, 1963). An occupational guide booklet.

1. Inability to see the forest—too detail-minded
2. Failure to carry responsibilities
3. Unconscious desire to be something else
4. Unconscious desire to be someone else
5. Yen for express trains—can't wait to get ahead
6. Inability to make room for other people—to work with others
7. Resistance to authority
8. Arrogance with subordinates
9. Prejudices which interfere with judgment
10. Overemphasis on work—and no time for play
11. Gravitation toward self-destruction—the fear of success
12. Mental ailments

Practitioners are expected by employers and clients to lead in the sphere for which they are responsible. This does not mean that they are expected to lead militantly or belligerently. It does mean that they must be able to organize all the people and equipment that go into a special event or program, to co-ordinate the efforts of those involved, deliver the best possible result, and keep an eye on the budget.

WORD TO THE LADIES. Public relations offers almost as much career opportunity to women as to men. Men hold no monopoly in the powers of persuasion. The function has that in common with advertising and journalism. In some areas, such as social welfare and the fashion industry, women often get the nod over men for jobs. Public relations, because it is a relatively new field, has fewer built-in prejudices against women than do some older ones.

One of the most demanding PR jobs in the nation is that for the New York Port Authority, which operates the airports, piers, and terminals that serve that great metropolis—a job that has been capably handled for years by Mrs. Lee K. Jaffe. Anna Rosenberg has long ranked among the foremost counselors in this field. Dorothy Ducas, now a consultant, supplied much of the public relations imagination and drive that made the March of Dimes the spectacular fund-raising success it was. Jane Buck contributed much to the success of the Carl Byoir agency in serving that firm more than 30 years. Today's top circus press agent is a woman—Mae Lyons. Prior to this job, she was a Broadway press agent. Mabel Flanley and Sally Woodward have long operated a successful agency. Also in counseling there have been many successful husband-and-wife teams, such as Edward and Doris (Fleischman) Bernays, Robert and Marg (Sammons) Newcomb, and Clem and Leone Baxter Whitaker.

A CHECKLIST

Robert McDevitt, a former newsman and long-time practitioner, has constructed a checklist for those pondering careers in this field. This checklist was built on a survey of PR executives, employment and personnel specialists, PR educators, and others in a position to gauge the field's requirements. It is offered as a guide to the college student trying to measure a PR career for size.

PR CAREER CHECKLIST

Although employer standards and judgments vary, a survey of 165 PR employers brings out the following main personal qualities and qualifications of applicants as desirable. How do you stand? What can you do to improve your chances?

- Have you prepared yourself education-wise?

☐ College degree

1 _____ Journalism
2 _____ Economics
3 _____ Social Services
4 _____ Business Administration
5 _____ Psychology
6 _____ Writing Courses
7 _____ Public Relations Courses

☐ Extracurricular Participant

1 _____ School publication
editorial experience
2 _____ Campus activities (athletic,
student government, etc.)
3 _____ Selling

- Can you claim and demonstrate these Qualities and Qualifications?

1 _____ Ability to think
2 _____ Judgment
3 _____ Ability to write
4 _____ Pleasant personality

1 _____ Newspaper writing
experience
2 _____ Sales experience
3 _____ Industrial relations
4 _____ Public opinion, attitude
measurement work
5 _____ Ad agency experience

- Are you preparing for advancement in these "coming fields" of PR?

1 _____ Management
2 _____ Public relations counseling firms
3 _____ Employe communications
4 _____ Community relations
5 _____ PR to aid sales

- _____ Have you prepared and widely placed your résumé in line with a carefully planned letter-interview-use of friends campaign?

- _____ Are you willing to get experience, either by newspaper work or unrelated assignments in your target company or organization—or in other allied fields?

- _____ Will you go forth smilingly when told: "Go get experience . . . or go get a newspaper job"? Unsmilingly will you follow this advice, keeping the adviser advised of your progress?

- _____ Have you chosen your target employers? What do *they* want from you? Can you deliver?

- _____ If you're making a living, have you started your own One Man Employment Guidance Agency?

Additional Reading

Edward L. Bernays, *Your Future in Public Relations.* New York: Richards Rosen Press, 1961. A career guide book.

James D. Gamble, "Newspaper Experience Ranked Too High?" *Public Relations Journal,* Vol. 8, April, 1952. (See June, 1952, issue for rebuttals.)

Robert McDevitt, "PR Help Wanted," *Public Relations Journal,* Vol. 10, July, 1954.

Hale Nelson, "Training for Public Relations," *Public Relations Journal,* Vol. 12, September, 1956.

Adrian A. Paradis, *For Immediate Release.* New York: David McKay Co., Inc., 1955. A vocational guidance manual.

Bernard Rubin, "The Practitional and the Professional," *Public Relations Journal,* Vol. 18, September, 1962.

Edwin B. Stern, "How the PR Job Market Looks Today," *PR,* Vol. 4, April, 1959.

Chapter Twenty-Eight

TOWARD

A

PROFESSION

Neither ambition, social snobbery, nor self-assertion will serve to create a profession or define its area of autonomy; these will in the long run be determined by the function fulfilled.
—Willard Hurst.

The past two decades have seen a phenomenal growth in public relations. This rapid growth since World War II has now leveled off, although it continues at a slower rate. This period has brought visible beginnings of professionalism. Public relations, as an organized calling, has come a long way since the days of Theodore Vail, Ivy Lee, and George Creel. It still has considerable distance to go before it matures into a profession comparable with those now established as such by *definition* and by *public acceptance.*

Events of the post-Depression period awakened widespread interest and increased acceptance of the public relations concept. World War II brought new opportunities, new demonstrations of utility, and new techniques and channels of communication. The tensions and problems of the uneasy postwar years accentuated and extended these developments. National prosperity underwrote the expansion of old programs and the birth of new ones. Expanding world trade extended the practice abroad. After a generation of somewhat dizzy mushrooming, public relations is in the process of settling down.

Contemporary practice has been highlighted by these developments:

1. Steady growth in number of programs in industries, institutions, social agencies, government bureaus, and trade associations. Already established programs have tended to mature and to move beyond straight publicity.
2. An accelerated growth in the number of independent counseling firms, especially in the communication hubs of New York, Washington, Chicago, and Los Angeles.
3. A tremendous spurt in the number of books, articles, and journals

devoted to the practice, its philosophy, problems, and techniques. The literature
is already voluminous, though somewhat repetitive.

4. Organization of new associations for practitioners and a redirection of those
already established.

5. An increase in the number of college courses and students, coupled with growth
in breadth and depth of the courses. Increased support for collegiate preparation from practitioners.

Reflecting on these and like developments, Pimlott has observed: "As is
illustrated by the literature, the growth of the associations, and the state of
university training, the public relations group has made dramatic progress
during and since the war, but its evolution is still in a fluid phase. It is coher-
ing but still inchoate. It is uncertain of itself. It is immature. Its place in
management is ill-defined. . . . Hence the vitality, sometimes naïve enthusiasm,
even missionary spirit, which are among the most agreeable expressions of its
youthfulness." [1]

In the years since Pimlott made his study, the function has gained wider
acceptance, become more secure within organizations, and strengthened its
competence. The practice is steadily moving toward maturity as it shifts its
emphasis to counseling and communication. Today few debate the function's
essentiality in a society in desperate need of clarifying communication and
skillful mediation of its many conflicts. Today the questions focus on the *ethics*
and *competence* of practitioners.

OUT OF THE SHADOWS

Public relations has come to occupy an important role in society, and, consequently, it is coming under closer public scrutiny. This is proper. Irwin Ross
argues, rightly, in his *Image Merchants:* [2] "We would all gain, in sum, if the
PR man were edged out of the shadows and subjected to the glare of attention
normally reserved for his clients. These days he is important enough to warrant
continual scrutiny."

Public concern about the practitioner and his impact on society has been
aroused by a number of spectacular cases that made the nation's front pages
in recent years. Each of these is laden with issues of concern to the public and
the practitioner alike.

1. THE TRUCKERS VERSUS THE RAILROADS AND CARL BYOIR. A bitter no-holds-
barred public relations battle between the trucking industry and the railroads
culminated in a lengthy legal battle that established the practitioner's right
to plead a client's case in the court of public opinion however unethical such

---

1 J. A. R. Pimlott, *Public Relations and American Democracy* (Princeton, N.J.: Princeton
University Press, 1951), p. 21.

2 This book, published by Doubleday & Co. in 1959, profiled the major PR agencies and
offered illuminating insights on a PR man's life and role in society. The quote is from
page 271.

pleading might be. In what *Fortune* termed "The Railroad-Truckers Brawl," [3] both parties used dubious and dishonest means to sway public opinion. The railroads had hired Carl Byoir & Associates, one of the nation's largest PR agencies, in August, 1949. Four other PR agencies seeking the account recommended plans similar to those proposed by the Byoir firm. The Pennsylvania Motor Truck Association engaged Allied Public Relations Associates, another New York agency, to present the truckers' case. The propaganda battle was on.

The legal battle opened in 1953, when 41 interstate long-haul trucking firms and their trade association, the Pennsylvania Motor Truck Association, brought suit against 35 Eastern railroads, the Eastern Railroad Presidents Conference, and Carl Byoir & Associates. The truckers charged the defendants with conspiring to drive them out of business in violation of the Sherman antitrust law. The suit had been triggered when a disgruntled Byoir employee took the railroad account files over to the truckers. Once court action was joined, the railroads filed a counterclaim asserting that the truckers were engaged in an identical conspiracy and asking for $120,000,000 in damages. It was a case of the pot calling the kettle black.

Although Byoir's firm was not accused of engineering the conspiracy to restrain trade, the truckers' suit cited it as a participant in the planning and the major instrument in execution of the alleged conspiracy. This was the first time a public relations counselor had been singled out as a conspirator to restrain trade in a *civil* suit. Previously Carl Byoir had been found guilty and fined on a *criminal* charge of conspiring to restrain trade. In 1946 the A & P was convicted of conspiracy to violate the Antitrust Act and was fined $175,000. Byoir, long-time A & P counselor, was fined $5,000. The Pennsylvania truckers charged that a conspiracy dated from 1949 and reached its climax in 1952, when Pennsylvania Governor John Fine vetoed a bill favoring the truckers. The plaintiffs sought treble damages in the amount of $250,000,000.

The trial was heard by Judge Thomas J. Clary without a jury in the United States District Court for Eastern Pennsylvania. In the year-long trial, more than 6,000 pages of testimony were taken and 968 exhibits were introduced. One hundred twenty-two lawyers were engaged in the legal contest. In October, 1957, Judge Clary handed down a 45,000-word opinion finding for the truckers. He awarded them nominal damages of six cents and special damages to be determined later.[4] In July, 1958, Judge Clary assessed special damages totaling $052,000, directing the railroads to pay 80 per cent of this sum, and Byoir's firm, the remainder. These damages were to compensate the

---

[3] *Fortune*, Vol. 47, June 1953. Also see Robert Bendiner, "The 'Engineering of Consent'— A Case Study," *The Reporter*, Vol. 13, August 11, 1955.

[4] For the decision, see "Noerr Motor Freight, Inc. *et al.* v. Eastern Railroad Presidents Conference, *et al.*, *Federal Supplement*, Vol. 155, Dec. 23, 1957, pp. 768-841. For thoughtful discussion of this case, see: "Pressure Politics in Pennsylvania: The Truckers vs. The Railroads," by Andrew Hacker in *The Uses of Power*, ed. Alan F. Westin (Harcourt, Brace, and World, 1962).

truckers for the losses sustained as a result of the conspiracy and Byoir's public relations campaign.

The Byoir firm and the railroads appealed. The United States Court of Appeals upheld Judge Clary in a 2-to-1 decision handed down in 1959. The dissenter was Chief Judge Wallace Biggs, who saw Judge Clary's decision as a threat to the right of free speech and free petition. In dissent, he wrote: [5] "If the interpretation of the court below and this court be correct the reach of the First Amendment which guarantees freedom of petition will be unduly limited and to an extent at least destroyed." Judge Biggs noted, however: "The methods employed by the public relations agencies of both the Railroads and the Truckers left much to be desired in respect to moral consciousness. Sources of propaganda were concealed by both sides by the use of the so-called 'third-party' technique."

Encouraged by Biggs' dissent, Byoir and the Railroads carried their case to the United States Supreme Court. They contended that a campaign aimed at influencing public opinion—no matter how untruthful—could not constitute a violation of the Antitrust Law. Moreover, they held that Judge Clary's enjoinment of them from further public relations activity stood as an infringement of their rights of free speech. The United States Supreme Court agreed and reversed the decision of the lower court in a unanimous opinion handed down February 20, 1961. Justice Hugo Black wrote the opinion, which said, in part: [6]

> In doing so, we have restored what appears to be the true nature of the case—a "no-holds-barred fight" between two industries both of which are seeking control of a profitable source of income. Inherent in such fights, which are commonplace in the halls of legislative bodies, is the possibility, and in many instances even the probability, that one group or the other will get hurt by the arguments that are made. In this particular instance, each group appears to have utilized all the political powers it could muster in an attempt to bring about the passage of laws that would help it or injure the other. But the contest itself appears to have been conducted along lines normally accepted in our political system, except to the extent that each group has deliberately deceived the public and public officials. And that deception, reprehensible as it is, can be of no consequence so far as the Sherman Act is concerned. . . ."

The Court's unanimous opinion "was a rather resounding affirmation of a legal right which has almost never been involved in litigation, the right of petition." A noted authority on Constitutional law further notes "that the right of people to associate together in order to make their activities effective" was closely allied in this case.[7] The legal right of a counselor to plead a cause in public is now clearly defined. The ethical problems posed by the malpractice of both PR agencies remain for solution.

2. THE S.E.C. INVESTIGATION. A biting indictment of the malpractices of a

---

[5] In 273 F. 2d 218 (1959).

[6] 81 *Supreme Court Reporter*, 523, February 20, 1961.

[7] David Fellman, *The Constitutional Right of Association* (Chicago: University of Chicago Press, 1963), pp. 10-12.

handful of PR practitioners was made in 1963 by the United States Securities and Exchange Commission. This event also provoked much public discussion and private soul-searching on the matter of public relations ethics and the press' responsibility. In a voluminous report, climaxing several years' investigation of the securities market, the S.E.C. indicted financial publicists for using false or misleading information to manipulate the stock market and for trading in the stocks of their clients.[8] Financial editors were found guilty of violating their responsibilities to readers in similar ways. For example, a business editor of *Time* was found to be profiting from his selection and play of business news. He was dismissed by *Time*.

The S.E.C. report said, "Corporate publicity examined ran the gamut from straightforward reporting of corporate affairs to what can only be described as deliberate attempts to falsify a company's financial position and prospects." In citing cases of practitioners greatly profiting from stock trading, the S.E.C. said that these examples "are set forth not to imply manipulative or any other improper intent, but only to demonstrate the conflicts of interest in such situations." [9]

Reporter Peter Bart places most of the responsibility for correcting "this sorry picture" on the press. He says, "PR men are not going to build an effective self-regulatory code nor are advertisers likely to exercise self-restraint in tampering with the news pages." Bart writes: [10]

> If we are to have better reporting, newspapers must assign their top talent, not their castaways, to the business . . . pages. They must pay them as well as they do their top writers. . . . On the negative side, newspaper and magazine editors must deal sternly with reporters who do favors for friends and help plant dishonest stories. They must also bar junkets for reporters and for financial editors. And they must find a way to keep the PR men out of the newsroom. . . .

It must be strongly emphasized that these abuses exposed by the S.E.C. involved only a few journalists and a few financial publicists.

3. THE FULBRIGHT HEARINGS. Widespread public discussion about the propriety of United States public relations firms representing foreign governments and the need to label foreign propaganda ensued in the wake of extensive hearings held by the United States Senate Committee on Foreign Relations in 1963. This committee, headed by Senator J. W. Fulbright, conducted an extensive investigation over a two-year period into the "activities of nondiplomatic representatives of foreign principals in the United States." [11] The

---

8 Securities and Exchange Commission, *The Report of Special Study of the Securities Markets,* Parts I and III (Washington, D.C.: Government Printing Office, 1963). A summary appeared in *The New York Times,* April 4, 1963.

9 For examples, see "SEC Runs Up Red Flag on Stock-Selling Publicity," *Editor & Publisher,* Vol. 96, April 13, 1963, pp. 13 and 62.

10 In "How to Read the Financial Pages Without Going Broke," *Harper's Magazine,* Vol. 227, August, 1963.

11 *Activities of Nondiplomatic Representatives of Foreign Principals in the United States.* Hearings Before the Committee on Foreign Relations, 88th Congress, 1963. Parts 1 through 13. Available from U.S. Government Printing Office. These hearings provide illuminating reading.

probe was triggered by the work of lobbyists representing foreign sugar interests. This probe raised anew an old and thorny question for practitioners and the public alike. This question had been debated in the mid-1930's by congressional committees investigating the services rendered Nazi Germany by the Carl Byoir and Ivy Lee-T. J. Ross public relations firms. This led to the passage of a Foreign Agents Registration Act in 1938. This law was not intended to muzzle spokesmen for foreign countries but to make them identify themselves so that officials and the public would not be misled by what they said or did. As of 1963, about 500 such agents were registered. Many of these are practitioners.

The right of a public relations firm to represent a foreign principal was not challenged in this investigation. In Senator Fulbright's view, two serious problems were raised by the findings: [12] (1) Identification of material emanating from foreign governments so that the reader or viewer may know the source of such information. He recognized that disclosure of the source of materials fed from foreign principals through their United States agents must be handled by editors and cannot be legislated. (2) The payment of money or other valuable consideration to newsmen for publication of material from foreign sources. In the latter category are listed press junkets, entertainment, and the presentation of gifts or money.

Fulbright's committee revealed that the 1938 law was being skirted, if not openly violated, and that many practitioners resorted to unscrupulous tactics. One of the flagrant violators was Hearst Columnist Igor Cassini, indicted in 1963 for failure to register as an agent of Rafael Trujillo, despicable dictator of the Dominican Republic. Cassini, who wrote under the name "Cholly Knickerbocker," also operated a public relations firm, the Martial Company, although he never took part in professional activities. His firm had $800,000 in billings in 1962.[13] Cassini pleaded "no contest" in 1964 and was fined $10,000 and placed on probation for six months. The Senate Committee exposed many unhealthy practices on the part of both practitioner and press.

The malpractices brought out in these and similar instances need to be kept in perspective. These infractions are those of a minority, "the tenth-tenth of public relations." L. L. L. Golden observes:[14] "Of course there are charlatans in public relations, as there are in every sphere of human activity. But there are probably no more frauds in public relations than in any other line of work. Most public relations agencies and individuals adhere to ethical standards."

Golden then makes the point that many practitioners fail to see: "One of the great problems in the new business of public relations is the refusal of many practitioners to face the fact that they are special pleaders. But if they

---

[12] Philip N. Schuyler, "U.S. Seeks Ways to Tell People Who Pays for News," *Editor & Publisher*, Vol. 96, August 24, 1963, pp. 9 and 52.

[13] See Peter Maas, "Boswell of the Jet Set," *Saturday Evening Post*, Vol. 236, January 19, 1963.

[14] In "When Washington Investigates," *Saturday Review*, Vol. 45, December 8, 1962, p. 70.

themselves recognize the role, and others with whom they deal are not given a false impression, part of the problem is solved." *The practitioner is an advocate,* not an objective seeker of the whole truth. Veteran John W. Hill sees this: [15] "Public relations can't cover up mistakes—and shouldn't. However, no one's going to put the worst face on anything. We're primarily advocates and we draw on a deep reservoir of experience in advocating our clients' causes."

This underlines what we conceive to be the social justification of the PR function in a free society: *to ethically, effectively plead the cause of a client or organization in the forum of public debate.* It is a basic democratic right that every idea, individual, or institution shall have a full and fair hearing in the public forum. *To obtain such a hearing today, the individual, idea, or institution needs the expertise of a skilled advocate.* It is our democratic philosophy that the merit of any idea or institution is determined by its ability to get accepted in the public opinion market place.

PR'S IMPACT ON SOCIETY

Of much more importance than these infrequent headline-making incidents is the fundamental question of PR's impact on society. The proponent of public relations can document many values of its work to society. The critic of public relations can cite, with equal validity, many harmful effects. These do not damn the function nor vitiate its essentiality; they stand as a challenge to those who would make this a constructive calling. Two large minuses can be written against public relations practice: (1) Public relations has corroded our channels of communication with cynicism; (2) Public relations has cluttered our channels of communication with the debris of pseudo-events and phony phrases that confuse rather than clarify the public dialogue.

The large plusses in public relations' favor are: (1) By stressing the need for public approval, practitioners improve the conduct of organizations they serve; (2) Practitioners serve the public interest in making all points of view articulate in the public forum; (3) Practitioners serve our segmented, scattered society by using their talents of communication and mediation to replace misinformation with information, and discord with rapport.

Robert Heilbroner recognizes public relations as a social force and charges it with a major part "in the general debasement of communications from which we suffer." He wrote: [16]

No one can quarrel with the essential function that public relations fills as a purveyor of genuine ideas and information. No one denies that many public

---

15 Prentice-Hall, *Executive Report*, Special Release, "Inside Public Relations," p. 16.
16 "Public Relations: The Invisible Sell," *Harper's Magazine*, Vol. 214, June, 1957, pp. 23-31.

relations men, working for corporations as well as for colleges or causes, honestly communicate things which are worth communicating. Nor can anyone absolve public relations for loading the communications channels with noise. We read the news and suspect that behind it lies the "news release." We encounter the reputation and ascribe it to publicity. Worst of all, we no longer credit good behavior with good motives, but cheapen it to the level of "good public relations."

This is true. Today when a large corporation announces a scholarship program for deserving youths or makes a big gift to the hospital drive, we cynically shrug it off as "smart public relations." Typical is this reaction of a *Milwaukee Journal* editorial writer in commenting on an oil company giving away cardboard bluebird houses: "Perhaps some crafty public relations man is behind the scheme." The award of a plaque or citation is a standard gimmick in public relations. This has reached the point where it is difficult to distinguish the award for achievement from the award for publicity purposes. Eric Sevareid notes wryly: [17]

> For some time now, Gresham's Law has been operating with wild abandon—bad honorary degrees, scrolls, plaques, medals, and gilt-painted zinc trophies have been driving out the good ones, exactly as "celebrity" has been driving out the precious word, "fame," and as the serried rows of Publicity Saints have been taking over the field from Great Men.

Practitioners also stand indicted, with some validity, for loading our channels of communication with noise and clogging them with the clutter of pseudo-events. In his book, *The Image,* Historian Daniel Boorstin introduces a useful term, *pseudo-events,* and argues that these serve to blur, rather than clarify, public issues. Boorstin writes: [18]

> The disproportion between what an informed citizen needs to know and what he can know is ever greater. The disproportion grows with the increase of the officials' power of concealment and contrivance. The news gatherers' need to select, invent, and plan correspondingly increases. Thus inevitably our whole system of public information produces always more "packaged" news, more pseudo-events.

Though Boorstin primarily blames newsmen for this, public relations practitioners are the major producers of pseudo-events. They regard this as staging newsworthy events to gain the public's attention for a client or a cause. An event planned to promote a cause in the public interest and in keeping with the character of the sponsor has a legitimate place in public relations. This no one will deny. It is the phony event to promote a dubious product or cause that comes under fire. Precious news space or time given to Miss Universe cannot be used in explaining the complex situation in Southeast Asia.

---

[17] In his weekly column for June 10, 1963. Quoted from *Wisconsin State Journal* of that date.

[18] The quotation is from page 17. This is a provocative if somewhat petty and peevish book but one worth reading. (New York: Atheneum publishers, 1962.)

These harmful effects on our channels of public communication come at a time when complex and crucial issues face our nation as it must make drastic adjustments to the changed economic structure of Western Europe, to the changed power structure of the world, and to racial strife and unrest. This whole process cannot proceed much faster than the development of public understanding. *Ethical public relations contributes to clarification of public issues, not to their distortion or obfuscation.*

Even after the practitioners representing competing parties have served their roles as *advocates* by providing the public with a persuasive presentation of each party's position, there remains a nagging doubt whether the public is adequately informed as a result. One of the epochal public relations battles of modern time was that waged between the advocates of the nation's steel companies and the United Steelworkers' Union in 1959 and 1960. Both sides spent millions of dollars presenting their case before and during the long 1959-1960 steel strike but with little noticeable result. A special committee of the National Council of Churches of Christ which made an exhaustive study of the implications of this dispute said, "Both sides in this dispute indulged in one of the most spectacular utilizations of mass communications media to be employed in an industrial conflict. This involved advertisement, radio, and television programs, and direct mailings."

This Council of Churches committee raises a basic question: [19]

> The methodology for influencing public opinion is full of ethical issues and it is to be noted that during the steel dispute no way was available whereby the public could obtain an objective evaluation of the claims which were being pushed so energetically by both sides.

A like question is raised by a similar conclusion in a study of the press' treatment of scientific findings linking cigaret smoking to lung cancer, a study made by editors of *The Columbia Journalism Review:* "Coverage has been sufficiently fragmented, uneven, and affected by publicity efforts on both sides to cause confusion." [20]

Presenting all sides of an issue and providing an objective, balanced appraisal of the merits of conflicting views is a responsibility of the news media, not the practitioner. This the Council of Churches Committee recognized: "When the media of mass communications are used by great power groups to try to win the American public to accept their point of view there is an open necessity for some objective evaluation of the disputed facts. We feel that the newspapers and magazines did not serve the public adequately in this regard and that the radio and television networks did little better. . . ." The editors of the *Columbia Journalism Review* made the same point: "An important place for clarifying confusing news—the editorial page—has been little

---

19 "In Search of Maturity in Industrial Relations," The Report of a Special Committee of the National Council of the Churches of Christ in the U.S.A., 1960. See Part IV.

20 "Smoking and News Coverage of a Decade of Controversy," in Vol. II, Summer, 1963, issue, p. 12.

used. . . . Here journalism has failed to assume the kind of initiative that it has shown in many other issues of public health."

But, as Heilbroner admits, there is a shinier side to the public relations coin. Much constructive good can be accurately ascribed to the ethical practice of public relations on behalf of our nation, on behalf of our colleges and community chests, on behalf of our corporations and conservation, on behalf of mental health and professional associations. Such opportunities have been stressed throughout this book. Public relations' benefits are written in sound economic enterprises providing profits for investors, jobs for employees, and goods for consumers; in the billions raised to build buildings, endow professorships, and provide scholarships in our nation's colleges; in the campaigns for eradication of disease, in the elimination of racial and religious discrimination, and in broader understanding of our national and international problems. *The potential good inherent in ethical, effective public relations is as limitless as the potential for enduring world peace which must be won in the minds of men.*

A SEARCH FOR STANDARDS

As public relations has gained stability, and as public debate about its social role has mounted, the search by practitioners for ethical standards has been intensified. There has been a great sensitivity to "public relations for public relations" in this period. This introspection has brought some pious platitudes and some self-serving rationalization. It has also brought some honest soul-searching and honest effort to enforce ethical standards within the craft. There are three main aspects to this introspection.

One aspect is the serious effort being made by practitioners jointly to surround performance of the function with the status and methods of a profession—in short, *to qualify functionally*. The second aspect is concern for the behavior of individual practitioners—the effort *to qualify morally*. The third aspect is the calibre and kind of training required for recruits and the need for more basic communications research. This represents an effort *to qualify through knowledge and expertness*. These aspects tend to fuse with each other in the history of the function in the period of its most rapid growth.

Stirring of a professional conscience has been reflected in a spate of writings on the need for responsibility, maturity, and training in this mushrooming business. Years ago, Edward L. Bernays voiced this plea: "Because our complex civilization demands professional counsel on public relations in order that there may be a better integration between the component parts of our society, we propose that courses on public relations in our universities be extended, that public relations men and women organize a professional group with high standards of social responsibility, and that the state provide legal safeguards so that all who practice . . . have the qualifications of character and learning which society demands."

Unfortunately, much of the craft's discussion of ethics and standards is akin to whistling one's way through a graveyard. Counselor David Finn says bluntly: [21] "Unfortunately, it is a subject not being discussed openly and straightforwardly in business circles, which in itself is not a good sign. Rationalizations, self-righteousness, and platitudes do not get rid of discerning challenges—nor do untalked-about skeletons in the closet make for well-adjusted consciences."

It ought to be kept in mind that "no abstract logic has created the concept of the professions." Rather, as a noted legal historian has pointed out, "practice and experience in making society function have led to the definition of some occupations as professional, and have from time to time determined which ways of earning a living should fit the professional category." [22] Many callings have striven for the status of profession. Few have won it. Much of this effort is self-serving; some of it is public-spirited.

In one sociologist's opinion, this ceaseless striving for status and prestige is characteristic of the new middle class in America—the group to which most practitioners belong. He thinks this new class, no longer having status and security in property, is caught up in a vicious circle of prestige-seeking. Americans have a strong urge toward building new professions. Whatever the motivation, the strong drive toward professionalism in this field will serve the calling and society well in the long run.

Charles Dollard, while president of the Carnegie Corporation, observed: "While this pressure toward professionalism might in one sense be labeled selfish, the results are beneficent for society as a whole. Professionalizing any activity tends to institutionalize the best ways of doing the job, and to create standards of quality which serve the public interest. This extension of the professional idea has by and large brought us safer bridges, better houses, higher standards in business, banking, and other fields."

To measure the advance of contemporary practice toward this much-sought goal, there must be yardsticks. Lawrence Appley, among others, has listed the hallmarks of a profession. In his opinion a profession requires (1) extensive and intensive preparation for the rendering of a highly specialized service; (2) specific and well-established principles and philosophies; (3) certain inherent skills and capabilities which give it the elements of an art; (4) application of established techniques and methods required of a science; (5) a strong motive of public service; (6) establishment and maintenance of research, formal instruction, internships, and concentrated practice; (7) objective evaluation of results and progress; (8) exchange of experience through professional associations.[23]

Even though practitioners continue to be "beset with all sorts of complexes

---

21 In "Struggle for Ethics in Public Relations," *Harvard Business Review*, Vol. 37, January/February 1959, p. 50.

22 Willard Hurst, "The Professions of American Life," *Public Relations Journal*, Vol. 13, August, 1957.

23 "The Obligations of a New Profession," *ibid.*, Vol. 4, December, 1948.

and doubts as to their own worthiness," movement in these professional directions is apparent. Many stabilizing influences are at work. Much solid progress has been recorded.

In 1949, *Fortune* asserted: "Public relations is still not a profession because too many of its practitioners do not yet possess either the *knowledge* or *capacity* or *ethics* of a professional." [24] In 1955, the same magazine said: "There is no question but what in the quarter-century ahead, public relations as a management function will grow still bigger. Top management clearly has decided on that course." [25] The next year, veteran practitioner Paul Garrett noted "a growing recognition on the part of management that every policy decision and every operating move has a public relations aspect that must be considered." In 1959 Irwin Ross saw public relations as one of the fastest-growing service trades in the United States. Prentice-Hall's *Executive Report* in 1963 concluded that public relations was "the fastest-growing business service in the United States."

The trend toward professionalism can be seen in these assets: (1) a strong national society supplemented by several strong specialized associations; (2) a Code of Ethics clearly spelled out; (3) a National Judicial Council created to enforce its standards upon PRSA members and the beginnings of such enforcement in the early 1960's; (4) tighter eligibility standards for membership in PRSA and a program of voluntary self-accreditation started in 1964; (5) training, education, and research in many universities and colleges, a small part of which is supported by PRSA; (6) a large and growing body of technical books, papers, and journals; (7) organizational status for the practitioner; (8) increasing contributions to the public service by practitioners.

The 1960's saw most of the foundation stones for a professional structure being put into place. When this foundation is complete, an enduring profession can be built upon something more substantial than self-pleading. Professional recognition cannot be a simple case of practitioners lifting themselves by telling one another that they are professionals. Public opinion determines what is a profession. This practitioners ought to know better than most. *The task of the practitioner is to earn the status.* Many are doing that.

TOWARD A CODE
OF ETHICS

As self-consciousness and a sense of cohesiveness have developed there has been increasing concern for social responsibility. Most practitioners are demonstrating an earnest effort to qualify morally. These exertions are reflected in a number of codes of professional standards for public relations practice. The principal code is that of the Public Relations Society of America. PRSA's first

---

24 "Business Is Still in Trouble," *Fortune*, Vol. 39, May, 1949.
25 "Management's Self-Conscious Spokesmen," *Fortune*, Vol. 52, November, 1955.

Code of Professional Standards was adopted in 1954. It was revised in 1959 and its enforcement machinery strengthened "to promote and maintain high standards of public service and conduct among its members." The Code was further strengthened in 1963. The first penalty for violation of these standards was meted out in 1962, when a member was censured for attempting to take away the account of another practitioner. Two more members were censured in 1963. Another was suspended in 1964.

Such codes will lack effective means of enforcement until and unless there is legal certification of practitioners. We believe that there must be controlled access, through licensing, to the title of "public relations counselor." This is the only way that the frauds and flacks can be separated from legitimate practitioners. This should be done to protect society as well as to advance the cause of professonalism. Codes of ethics are not the whole answer.

Practical men know that adoption of a code of ethics does not automatically bring morality to a calling, but such codes do reflect a concern among the leaders for raising the ethical level. They provide yardsticks of measurement. And, like a New Englander's conscience, a code can make a practitioner "durned uneasy." A distinguished Canadian counselor, Leonard L. Knott, says: [26] "Unfortunately, these codes have little real value unless they are accepted in turn by the employers of PR people and applied to the conduct of the business itself."

The skill, ethics, and PR concepts used by the wide variety of practitioners vary greatly. In appraising the ethics, it is well to remember that there is no watertight bulkhead between the practitioners and the society in which they operate. Moreover, they are generally found at the foci of power. And power is not always gained and held by playing according to the rules. When a university scholar can assert that "graft, crime, corruption, 'the fix' are embedded in the very fabric of our highly competitive society," there is no reason to presume that all practitioners will be immune. When the four horsemen of calumny—"fear, ignorance, bigotry, and smear"—gallop madly about, it is natural to find a few of those skilled in communication and propaganda riding with them. Practitioners will be found to be representative of the institutions and causes they serve.

PROFESSIONAL
ORGANIZATIONS

The growth of strong professional associations reflects the serious efforts being made by many practitioners to surround the function with status and to advance its competence. Although these associations include only a minority of those in public relations, they exert considerable influence through their

---

[26] In his book, *Plain Talk About Public Relations* (Toronto: McClelland and Stewart, 1961), p. 23.

publications, conferences, seminars, awards programs, and central office activities. The largest of these associations is the Public Relations Society of America, which as of 1964 had nearly 5,000 members. The Society is an amalgam of three older associations organized to win public recognition for this emerging specialty.

The PRSA was formed February 4, 1948, by the merger of the National Association of Public Relations Counsel and the American Council on Public Relations. The former group was first organized in 1936 as the National Association of Accredited Publicity Directors. This organization changed its name in 1944 to reflect the shift in emphasis to public relations. Its membership was composed largely of New York City counselors. The words *national* and *accredited* were used in a very loose sense by this pioneering group. The American Council on Public Relations was started in San Francisco in 1939 as an association for West Coast practitioners. Its chief architect and promoter was Rex F. Harlow.

The goal of forward-looking practitioners and educators for one strong national association serving all fields of practice was finally realized July 1, 1961, when the American Public Relations Association was merged into PRSA as the culmination of several years' negotiations. The American Public Relations Association, headquartered in Washington, D. C. and dominated by trade association practitioners, was organized in 1944 after some seven years' effort among Washington practitioners. At the time of the merger in 1961, PRSA had 3,359 members and APRA, 826; 100 practitioners held membership in both organizations. The majority of APRA's members remained in PRSA the ensuing year.

The APRA made two contributions to advancement of this craft—its Silver Anvil Awards program to recognize successful programs and its *Quarterly Review of Public Relations*. This publication passed to the ownership of its founding editor, Howard P. Hudson, at the time of the merger and was purchased by Public Relations Aids, Inc., in 1963. Started in 1955, it is a publication of substance. PRSA has continued the Silver Anvil Awards program, which is the PR field's version of Hollywood's Oscar Awards program. The PRSA does much to foster the exchange of ideas, to promote a sense of professionalism, and to remind practitioners of the need for more ethical behavior.

The counselors in the Public Relations Society organized a Counselors' Section in 1960 as a means of dealing more specifically and more effectively with the problems of special concern to public relations agencies. This Section has made a study of counseling fees, issued a booklet defining the role of the counselor, and in 1963 gained PRSA's approval of a voluntary plan of self-accreditation based on character, experience, and examination. The Counselors' Section had nearly 570 members in 1964. PRSA members who were engaged in association work followed suit when they won PRSA's approval for a "Business and Professional Association Section" in 1963. As PRSA continues to expand in size and scope, these Sections may well set the pattern for other specialized interest groups. Practitioners for nonprofit agencies sometimes complain about the dominance of corporate practitioners in the management of PRSA's affairs.

The challenge to the enlarged, more affluent PRSA was put in these terms by Richard L. Tobin at the time of the merger: [27]

> What is impressive about the new PR association is not its large and unified membership . . . or its richer treasury (and staff) but the patent public opportunity now available in a trade or profession shot through with unethical tradition and shady practice. PR is a relatively fresh field. It is growing more rapidly than any other in the area of communication. . . . But the rapid growth always brings the problem of proper assimilation, especially at the ethical level. And it is in the field of ethics and enforcement procedures to be handled through the new society that opportunity to serve the public appears to be the greatest. Simply becoming a big, prosperous, but bland PR association won't be good enough. . . .

Several specialized national organizations also have served as spurs for solidarity and professional growth. The broad membership embraced in these vertical groups also indicates the growth in this field. It reflects a sense of common interests and an emerging *esprit de corps* of professionalism.

Title	Date Organized
Agricultural Relations Council	1953
American College Public Relations Assn.	1917
Chemical Public Relations Assn.	1952
Financial Public Relations Assn.	1916
Government Public Relations Assn.	1949
Library Public Relations Council	1939
National Public Relations Council of Health and Welfare Services	1922
National School Public Relations Assn.	1935
Railroad Public Relations Assn.	1952
Religious Public Relations Council	1929

PROFESSIONAL
LITERATURE

Related, somewhat, to these associational developments has been the growth in number of journals devoted exclusively to this field, increased space in established periodicals, and a long list of books devoted to this new calling. PRSA's *Public Relations Journal* emphasizes professionalism, presents case studies, articulates philosophy, and provides a forum for debate on practice and ethics. The *Public Relations Quarterly* is comparable in content, but its articles are often of more depth. *Public Relations News* was started July 17, 1944, by the late Glenn Griswold and Denny Griswold as a commercial venture. She continues to publish this four-page newsletter. A competitor, *The PR Reporter,* started in 1958 by Charles H. Prout, is now published at

---

[27] "PR's Golden Chance to Clean House," in *Saturday Review*, Vol. 44, March 11, 1961, pp. 79-80.

Meriden, N. H., by Robert Barbour. Critical scrutiny of the field was strengthened by the introduction of a monthly Communications Issue in *Saturday Review*. These specialized publications publicize and promote the maturing practice of public relations.

The first comprehensive bibliography of book and periodical literature in this field was published in 1957 under the auspices of PRSA. It listed more than 3,500 entries culled from a possible 5,000 published since the turn of the century.[28] Other publications contribute to the expanding knowledge of public opinion, communications, and public relations:

Advertising Age	*Journal of Applied Psychology*
American City	*Journal of Broadcasting*
A-V Communications Review	*Journal of Social Psychology*
Broadcasting	*Journal of Marketing*
Channels	*Journalism Quarterly*
College and University Journal	*Nieman Reports*
Columbia Journalism Review	*PR in Canada*
Editor & Publisher	*Printers' Ink*
Fortune	*Public Opinion Quarterly*
Harvard Business Review	*Quill*
Human Relations	*Saturday Review*
It Starts in the Classroom	*Trends in School Public Relations*

PROFESSIONAL EDUCATION

University-level instruction in public relations dates from 1920. Concurrent with the beginning of the Publicity Boom of the 1920's, that year Jos. F. Wright introduced a publicity course at the University of Illinois. Wright admits that the course was created to bring prestige to his new calling, not in response to student demand. Two years later, in 1922, Frank R. Elliott introduced a publicity course at Indiana University. Both Wright and Elliott organized the first publicity programs for their institutions and taught these courses on a part-time basis. Teaching such courses gave these pioneers faculty status, something they needed in order to earn support among faculty men who looked askance at "propagandists."

The first public relations course by this title was that offered in 1923 by Edward L. Bernays, pioneer practitioner who had just written his *Crystallizing Public Opinion*. Bernays taught the one-semester-credit course in the Department of Journalism of New York University's School of Commerce, Accounts, and Finance for only two years. It was not reinstituted until 1939, when Professor Alfred McClung Lee began teaching it. Typical of the growing demand for skilled publicists to build support was that found in the new fields

---

28 Compiled by Scott M. Cutlip, *A Public Relations Bibliography* (Madison: The University of Wisconsin Press, 1957).

of social work and philanthropic fund raising. Evart and Mary Swain Routzahn, pioneers of social work public relations, first offered a course in social work publicity in the New York School of Social Work in 1923.

Across the continent, the University of Oregon first offered a course in publicity in 1927-1928 taught by George Godfrey, that university's first public relations officer. Godfrey used as a text *Principles of Publicity,* co-authored by Glenn C. Quiett and Ralph D. Casey, one of the best publicity books to appear in that decade. The University of Minnesota made its first offering in 1929 with a course in "Press Relations." In this same period, Professor Byron Christian was pioneering with a course at the University of Washington. In these early years, newspapermen were bitterly critical of giving academic recognition to what they sneeringly derided as "press-agentry." Some still are. For this and other reasons, only a handful of universities added public relations courses to their curricula in the two decades between the two World Wars. By 1945 only 21 institutions were offering PR courses.

The years since World War II have brought phenomenal growth in number and depth of public relations courses. In 1946 Professor Lee surveyed 59 major educational institutions and found that at least 30 offered 47 courses under public relations titles. Twenty-three of these were being taught in schools or departments of journalism.[29] American journalism schools, which date from the early 1900's, have dominated in the development of public relations education. Many practitioners are dubious about this. In just one decade after Lee's survey, the Public Relations Society of America made the most thorough survey of PR teaching yet made, and found that the number of colleges offering the subject had tripled in ten years.[30] Today more than 200 universities and colleges offer one or more courses in public relations.

In PRSA's 1956 survey, 136 colleges and universities reported that they recognized public relations training varying from integrated principles in other courses to a full curriculum in a school of public relations. The survey reported that 1 university had a school of public relations, 2 had departments, 11 offered a major, and 19 institutions taught two or more courses as electives. It found journalism schools "predominant in the teaching of PR." Nelson wrote, evaluating this survey: [31]

> The *extent* of public relations education gives us only one dimension of the whole picture. *What is taught* is a more significant measurement. . . . One very reassuring finding is the practically universal agreement that all public relations career education should be founded on at least two years of liberal arts. . . . What happens in the junior and senior year varies greatly. The Journalism-oriented PR teaching will bear down heavily on written communications. In the liberal arts-oriented school there is greater emphasis on the social sciences.

---

[29] "Trends in Public Relations Training," *Public Opinion Quarterly,* Vol. 11, Spring, 1947.

[30] *Public Relations Education in American Colleges and Universities* (New York: Public Relations Society of America, August, 1956).

[31] Hale Nelson, "Training for Public Relations," *Public Relations Journal,* Vol. 12, September, 1956.

The rapid development of public relations education in these postwar years is typified by the Boston University School of Public Relations and Communication. It was opened in 1947 as the School of Public Relations, embracing public relations, journalism (which had been a separate school), radio, speech, motion pictures, and visual aids. A research division was added in 1963. The name and concept were later broadened to include communications. A former dean, Melvin Brodshaug, sums up the Boston philosophy in these words: "The only way to prepare for public relations is through a systematically designed curriculum. Only when this principle is universally accepted can we claim that public relations is a profession. Special advanced education is one criterion of a profession." Similar emphasis was given by the University of Maryland when it established a Department of Journalism and Public Relations in 1949. The American University followed suit in 1961, when it set up a Department of Journalism and Public Relations.[32] The Boston pattern was not widely copied and in 1964 Boston University changed the name to the School of Public Communication. Dropping public relations from the school's title brought lament from practitioners but won the plaudits of educators. Because skill in communications and knowledge of public opinion constitute the backbone of the practice, it is logical that most PR courses would be centered in schools of journalism and communications.

On the surface it would appear that the value of public relations instruction has been widely recognized, yet many of America's front-rank institutions still do not teach it. Although we have had more than 40 years of public relations teaching, the pattern of education in this field remains fluid, experimental, somewhat fragmentary, and still controversial. There continues to be debate by both professional educators and practitioners whether or how to teach public relations. However different their approaches, *public relations teachers are agreed on the need for a specialized program.* They recognize, as do an increasing number of practitioners, that university education and research must play a major role if there is to be progress toward professional status.

The dominance of journalism-centered training squared with the demands of the profession, at least in mid-century. A 1951 PRSA education survey— this one directed by Counselor Bruce Watson—found that "when asked about their preference in hiring a college graduate, the respondents rated the school of journalism above a public relations school or college, or a liberal arts college." However, many practitioners, including Mr. Watson, are critical of this journalism emphasis for future practitioners. Professor Stewart Harral's 1963 survey and the 1964 Ohio State University study confirmed that a majority of practitioners still support journalism-centered public relations education.

In the good journalism school today, only about one-fourth of the student's study is devoted to journalism subjects. An even smaller fraction is given to

---

[32] See "The University's Role in Public Relations Education," *Journalism Quarterly,* Vol. 34, Winter, 1957. For a different view, see Howard Stephenson, "Can Public Relations Be Taught in Schools?", *Public Relations Journal,* Vol. 13, March, 1957.

technique courses. Journalism sequences include not only the technique courses, but also public opinion psychology, public opinion research methods, media analysis, communications media, and public relations. Built around these courses are studies in American history, economics, labor, business management, psychology, sociology, anthropology, and political science. Today's journalism graduate possesses a strong liberal arts education oriented to communications in American society. Sequences in journalism can serve those training for all fields, whereas courses in schools of commerce or education must, of necessity, be oriented to those specialized fields. Journalism educators today define journalism broadly as encompassing all media of communication.

Public relations instruction, as it comes to be supported by scholarly research, will grow in scope and in service to this emerging profession. Such training is likely to center on a core of communication skills and public opinion anatomy and analysis. Around this core a serviceable pattern of courses in the social sciences and humanities will be developed to meet the needs. The demand for college training is still not strong. It will grow, however, just as it has in comparable fields.

RESEARCH REQUIRED

To earn the title, the practitioner must accept the obligation to work for the advancement of knowledge in the profession. Theodore Roosevelt said: "Every man owes some part of his time to the building up of the industry or profession of which he is a part." *A profession must be built upon a specialized body of knowledge and be devoted to the public interest above the private interest.* Using this yardstick, we should examine this calling's claims to professional status. First, this question: How much specialized knowledge have practitioners contributed to the art of human relations and communication? Are not the scientific methods and procedures borrowed from the social sciences of psychology, sociology, economics, history, and journalism? Can practitioners be hitch-hikers and still lay claim to the title of professional?

THE PRSA CODE

DECLARATION OF PRINCIPLES

Members of the Public Relations Society of America acknowledge and publicly declare that the public relations profession in serving the legitimate interests of clients or employers is dedicated fundamentally to the goals of better mutual understanding and cooperation among the diverse individuals, groups, institutions and elements of our modern society.

In the performance of this mission, we pledge ourselves:

1. To conduct ourselves both privately and professionally in accord with the public welfare.
2. To be guided in all our activities by the generally accepted standards of truth, accuracy, fair dealing, and good taste.

3. To support efforts designed to increase the proficiency of the profession by encouraging the continuous development of sound training and resourceful education in the practice of public relations.
4. To adhere faithfully to provisions of the duly adopted Code of Professional Standards for the Practice of Public Relations, a copy of which is in the possession of every member.

CODE
OF
PROFESSIONAL STANDARDS
FOR THE PRACTICE OF
PUBLIC RELATIONS

This Code of Professional Standards for the Practice of Public Relations is adopted by the Public Relations Society of America to promote and maintain high standards of public service and conduct among its members in order that membership in the Society may be deemed a badge of ethical conduct; that Public Relations justly may be regarded as a profession; that the public may have increasing confidence in its integrity; and that the practice of Public Relations may best serve the public interest.

1. A member has a general duty of fair dealing towards his clients or employers, past and present, his fellow members and the general public.
2. A member shall conduct his professional life in accord with the public welfare.
3. A member has the affirmative duty of adhering to generally accepted standards of accuracy, truth and good taste.
4. A member shall not represent conflicting or competing interests without the express consent of those concerned, given after a full disclosure of the facts; nor shall he place himself in a position where his interest is or may be in conflict with his duty to his client, employer, another member or the public, without a full disclosure of such interests to all concerned.
5. A member shall safeguard the confidences of both present and former clients or employers and shall not accept retainers or employment which may involve the disclosure or use of these confidences to the disadvantage or prejudice of such clients or employers.
6. A member shall not engage in any practice which tends to corrupt the integrity of channels of public communication.
7. A member shall not intentionally disseminate false or misleading information and is obligated to use ordinary care to avoid dissemination of false or misleading information.
8. A member shall be prepared to identify to the public the source of any communication for which he is responsible, including the name of the client or employer on whose behalf the communication is made.
9. A member shall not make use of any individual or organization purporting to serve or represent some announced cause, or purporting to be independent or unbiased, but actually serving an undisclosed special or private interest of a member or his client or his employer.
10. A member shall not intentionally injure the professional reputation or practice of another member. However, if a member has evidence that another member has been guilty of unethical, illegal or unfair practices, including practices in violation of this Code, he should present the information to the

proper authorities of the Society for action in accordance with the procedure set forth in Article XIII of the Bylaws.

11. A member shall not employ methods tending to be derogatory of another member's client or employer or of the products, business or services of such client or employer.
12. In performing services for a client or employer a member shall not accept fees, commissions or any other valuable consideration in connection with those services from anyone other than his client or employer without the express consent of his client or employer, given after a full disclosure of the facts.
13. A member shall not propose to a prospective client or employer that his fee or other compensation be contingent on the achievement of certain results; nor shall he enter into any fee agreement to the same effect.
14. A member shall not encroach upon the professional employment of another member. Where there are two engagements, both must be assured that there is no conflict between them.
15. A member shall, as soon as possible, sever his relations with any organization when he knows or should know that his continued employment would require him to conduct himself contrary to the principles of this Code.
16. A member called as a witness in a proceeding for the enforcement of this Code shall be bound to appear unless, for sufficient reason, he shall be excused by the panel hearing the same.
17. A member shall co-operate with fellow members in upholding and enforcing this Code.

One of the sure signs of advancement in public relations toward the professional horizon is the increasing demand for research and increasing critical self-examination of old theories. Awareness is growing of the need for re-examination and redirection. Factual foundations will serve to dispel the idea of the PR worker as a sort of witch doctor. In today's world the public relations problems of industry, for example, are every bit as tough and complicated as those of engineering, production, or distribution. Practitioners must approach them as methodically and as thoroughly prepared with facts as engineers, production men, and marketers. Such an approach can come only through extensive research. *Practitioners should strive for certainty in their work.*

"Research," as a term and a concept, has been enveloped in something of an aura. What purports to be research has been used to sell cigarettes and hair oil as well as to probe the inner mysteries of the physical and human world. Owing mainly to the striking accomplishments in the scientific field, people have an almost child-like faith in research. This has led to exploitation and distortion.

Research is not a matter of putting a quarter in the slot, pulling a lever, and then picking up the answers in a tray below. Research takes time and sweat, as well as money. Research in any field is the laborious building of one little brick on another until the structure is finished. It takes lots of bricklayers to build a building. If enough people work at it, the building gets built. *Research, simply put, is the act of searching for information—accurate, reliable, useful information—and organizing this information so that sound conclusions can be drawn.* Research is as much an attitude as it is a method. Research requires an itch and a scratch. The itch is the curiosity to know; the scratch, the will to satisfy the itch.

Public relations research centers on methodical study of human behavior and communications—at all times and under all conditions an extremely complex and difficult field of study. Research in public relations leads swiftly into the related fields of psychology, anthropology, sociology, psychiatry, and communications, including semantics. Knowledge and methods from these fields are being applied with increasing frequency in the areas of opinion research, consumer research, and media analysis.

There are two dangers to be avoided in going all out for research. *First,* all too often research becomes an objective in itself, an end instead of a means. This is sometimes true in the academic world. *Second,* research will provide no magic, pat answers to all the problems that perplex practitioners. Research is no dictionary. Much of today's opinion and communications research is faulty, some of it is phony, and some of it is pebble-picking. But research, as a method and as an attitude, does offer public relations rich rewards in achieving an understanding of the attitudes and opinions of those with whom practitioners seek communion and in evaluating communications with them. This becomes important when it is understood that *communication requires more than dissemination of information. It also requires active integration and acceptance on the part of the receiver.*

TOWARD NEW HORIZONS

At mid-century a practitioner could be described this way: [33]

> The public relations counsel is a specialist in verbal symbols. He has been well trained by his home environment and school career in the art of phrase-making. He is prosperous, on the whole, but nevertheless tends to be somewhat more nonconformist, in a political and economic sense, than do his clients. He has been mobile in an upward direction economically, and has often experienced geographic and social mobility as well. He has thus been sensitized to the outlook of people from many social strata. . . . The job of the public relations man is to keep open a two-way channel of communication so that no "misunderstandings" can arise to disturb the true harmony of interests between the publics and management. . . . His is an ideology of defense.

Despite the considerable progress recorded in this generation, public relations still stands short of public acceptance as a true profession. The field lacks maturity, effective self-regulation, full-fledged devotion to the public interest, a generally approved course of training, and a research pro-

---

33 Leila A. Sussman, "The Personnel and Ideology of Public Relations," *Public Opinion Quarterly,* Vol. 12, Winter 1948-49. Also see Irwin Ross' chapter, "The PR Life," in his *Image Merchants* (New York: Doubleday & Company, Inc., 1959).

gram of its own. Public relations continues to be plagued with press agents parading as counselors. Then there are those who are more interested in manipulating the opinions of others than in understanding them. There is still evidence that the function is not fully and widely understood. The field still has those who cannot qualify *functionally, morally,* or *through knowledge and expertness.* Many do. *More are needed.*

A start has been made toward deserving the professional status which practitioners seek. But it is only a start. If public relations practitioners demonstrate a sense of social responsibility and build a specialized body of knowledge that they can properly claim as their own, they will surround the function with the status and prestige its exponents desire. Practitioners know, better than most, that the way to gain public confidence is to deserve it. This they tell their employers. The practitioner cannot be content to let professional organizations adopt codes of ethics and express his views.

A newspaper publisher once remarked: "Morality is a highly personal matter; it is not to be found in the majority vote of the board of directors of a trade association, or in public expressions of association executives. . . ." Counselor Earl Newsom echoed this when he told his fellow practitioners: "I suggest that sober self-examination at this point requires that we come to an understanding of ourselves and what it is we really want to accomplish. This is not a problem that can be resolved by our Society or by any committees thereof. It is purely a personal matter. Each of us lives but once, and each of us wants to spend his life constructively. . . . I am as certain as can be that if each one of us establishes the highest of standards for his own conduct, we shall eventually earn the status of profession." [34]

In the light of the progress made in recent years, the future looks promising. The public relations calling has become an important link in the free communications network upon which this nation depends for its culture, cohesion, and solidarity. *This profession has an important role to play in a nation that begs unity, a communion of purpose, and understanding and support among its people—in short, a sense of community.* In the sustaining of unity and the achievement of it where it does not now exist, the role of public relations is potentially a vital one. If practitioners as a group measure up, they will have to practice positive public relations. They will have to stand for things. Community will not be achieved in singing hymns of hate.

Today's practitioners and the recruits now in training will largely determine the course this calling will take. Public relations can move on to accept John Dewey's challenge of ". . . a responsive art of communication" that will "take possession of the physical machinery of transmission and circulation and breathe life into it."

It can accomplish these things in the best interests of all. Or it can ac-

---

[34] In "Business Does Not Function by Divine Right," *Public Relations Journal*, Vol. 19, January, 1963. In same issue, see Scott M. Cutlip's article, "A Re-Examination of Public Relations' Platitudes."

complish these things for a greedy minority at the expense of the whole public. Public relations as a technique is a power device. It can be used for good or evil. It can steadily advance toward a mature, responsible profession that contributes to the unity, progress, and public welfare. Or it can decline into what Philosophy Professor William Earnest Hocking has described as a "conscienceless publicity racket" which brings the premiums of advancement to those who have "learned to surround their doings with a cackle of ignorant noise." *Those skilled in its techniques will have to decide which way it will go.*

Additional Reading

Anonymous, "Public Relations Today," *Business Week.* A Special Report. July 2, 1960.

Anonymous, "SEC Reports on Public Relations' Impact on Securities Markets and Public Investors," *Public Relations Journal,* Vol. 19, June, 1963.

W. Howard Chase, "Nothing Just Happens, Somebody Makes It Happen," *ibid.,* Vol. 18, November, 1962.

Scott M. Cutlip, "History of Public Relations Education in the U.S.," *Journalism Quarterly,* Vol. 38, Summer, 1961.

Stephen E. Fitzgerald, "Public Relations: A Profession in Search of Professionals," *Public Opinion Quarterly,* Vol. 10, Summer, 1946.

————, "How Do You Know?", *Nieman Reports,* Vol. 16, January, 1962.

Edward J. Robinson, "Research in Public Relations," *Public Relations Journal,* Vol. 17, January, 1961.

Raymond Simon, "Scholarly Research in Public Relations," *Public Relations Journal,* Vol. 17, May, 1961.

Hal D. Steward, "Ethics of Public Relations: It's What You Do That Counts," *PR,* Vol. 3, April, 1958.

Albert J. Sullivan, "The Value Systems of Public Relations," *Public Relations Quarterly,* Vol. 8, April, July, Oct., 1963. In Three Parts.

James A. Wechsler, "A Study in Suppression. Propaganda in the Press," *The Progressive,* Vol. 27, August, 1963.

INDEX